The Great Men who made Iran

Illustrations on previous page

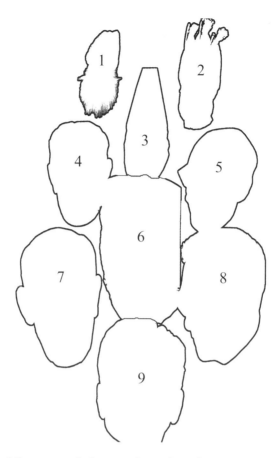

1 : Abbas Mirza, a period engraving taken from *La Perse* by Louis Dubreux, Firmin-Didot, Paris, 1841
2 : Nader Shah, *ibidem*.
3 : Amir Kabir, a period portrait (the only existing one) by Mirza Ebrahim-Khan, *Amir Kabir et Iran*, Kharazami, Tehran, 1967, p.779.
4 : Mohammad Ali Foroughi, when he first rose to the post of Prime Minister.
5 : Ahmad Ghavam, on July 20th 1952, in Tehran.
6 : Reza Shah, when he was back from Khuzestan – a portrait by Hossein Kazemi – the original painting belongs to Mehrdad Pahlbod.
7 : Mohammad Mossadegh, on July 22nd 1952, in The Hague.
8 : General Fazlollah Zahedi, a portrait by Mehdi Sadjadi – the original one is in the family villa 'Les Roses' in Montreux, Switzerland.
9 : One of the last photos of Mohammad Reza Pahlavi during his exile in Mexico. Part of Mehrdad Pahlbod's collection.

IRAN

THE CLASH OF AMBITIONS

WORKS BY HOUCHANG NAHAVANDI

Iran, deux rêves brisés, Albin Michel, 1981

*

Le dossier noir de l'intégrisme islamique,
Nouvelles Editions Debresse, 1985

*

Le voile déchiré de l'islamisme, Première Ligne, 1994.

*

Shah Abbas, empereur de Perse, Perrin – avec Yves Bomati – ouvrage couronné par l'Académie française en 1999

*

Révolution iranienne, vérité et mensonges, L'Âge d'Homme, 2000

*

Carnets secrets, Chute et mort du Shah, Editions Osmondes, 2004
(Second edition, 2005)
Persian edition, Los Angeles, 2004
English edition: *The Last Shah of Iran*, Aquilion, 2005
Published in Polish (Dialog, Varsaw)

*

Iran, le choc des ambitions, Aquilion, 2006

HOUCHANG NAHAVANDI

IRAN

THE CLASH OF AMBITIONS

Aquilion

Aquilion Ltd.
The Nova Building
Herschel street
Slough, Berkshire
SL1 1XS   United Kingdom

First published in French by Aquilion, 2006:
Iran, le choc des ambitions (ISBN 2 9517415-3-7)
English translation Copyright © Martine Jackson

This edition, revised an enlarged, published by Aquilion Ltd 2006

Copyright © Houchang Nahavandi 2006

ISBN-10: 1-904997-04-X
ISBN-13: 978-1-904997-04-7
10 9 8 7 6 5 4 3 2 1
Set in Times New Roman

Printed and bound in Spain by Itxaropena

The right of Houchang Nahavandi to be identified as the author, and Martine Jackson to be identified as the translator of this work has been asserted by them in accordance with the Copyright, Designs and Patents Act, 1988.

All rights reserved. No part of this publication may be reproduced, stored in a retrieval system, or transmitted, in any form or any means, elecronics, mechanical, photocopying, recording or otherwise, without the prior permission of the publishers.

This book is sold subject to the condition that it shall not, by way of trade or otherwise, be lent, re-sold, hired out or otherwise circulated without the publisher's consent in any form of binding or cover other than in which it is published without a similar condition including this condition being imposed on the subsequent purchaser.

In memory of my father whose strict patriotism, uncompromising integrity and family sense have always been my guiding light.

Contents

Acknowledgment and Sources ... 11

PROLOGUE ... 17

PART ONE – *Resurrection and crises*
I. I, Reza ... 43
II. The Second World War – *An old philosopher saves Iran* ... 99
III. The Tudeh – *Seventy years at the service of the Soviet Union* ... 129
IV. The Azerbaijan crisis – *The man who defeated Stalin* ... 157
V. The oil crisis – *The man who chased the British away* ... 189
VI. Iran's twist of fate – *An Exceptional General* ... 225
VII. The Savak – *A great misunderstanding* ... 275

PART TWO – *The flight of Icarus*
VIII. The authoritarian monarchy – *The White Revolution* ... 299
IX. A certain idea of Iran ... 335
X. A policy of power and national independence
  'Absolutely intolerable ambitions' ... 385

PART THREE – *The islamic revolution*
XI. 'A kind of social-democratic saint' – *'A miracle in Paris'* ... 415
XII. Iran and the West – *Ambiguous relations* ... 453
XIII. Moscow and Tehran – *The Soviet Union's double game bear fruit* ... 483
XIV. The imperial power hesitates – *'It's another Louis XVI'* ... 499
XV. Panic and death throes – *The Shah 'hears' the voice of the revolution* ... 537
XVI. The fall of the monarchy and the triumph of the revolution
  The handing over of keys ... 565

EPILOGUE – *The suffering and tragedy of a lone man* ... 609

ANNEXE – A CHRONOLOGY OF THE PRIME MINISTERS ... 643

NOTES ... 651

INDEX ... 721

Acknowledgment and Sources

Two of my friends, Amir A. Heydari and Mehrdad Pahlbod, greatly influenced me to write this book.

Merhdad Pahlbod, my colleague in three successive governments, a man who has always been of sound advice, a fervent patriot whose memoirs one would like to read one day.

Amir A. Heydari, a friend and comrade since we were in the Firouzcouhi primary school in Tehran. He has kept memories of his native land and loved it for over half a century, even though he has been away from it.

*

M.R.M., a lifelong friend, has followed the drafting of this book and supported me in this task since the very beginning.

*

For several days, I was able to consult the archives of my friend Ardeshir Zahedi whose name is so often mentioned in several chapters of this book. His particularly rich collection represents an important source for the knowledge and study of Iran's diplomatic and political history since the beginning of the 20th century.

The access to documents from the archives of the Centre Européen d'Information (CEI), directed by Pierre Faillant de Villemarest – archives incorporated today in those of the French National Defence – proved to be very useful.

*

My friends professor Hadi Hedayati, former minister of education, Rector Parviz Amouzegar and Dean Yves Bomati gave me useful advice during the two years spent writing this book.

*

Many compatriots and friends contributed with great enthusiasm to the documentation of this book by sending me manuscripts or unpublished notes, old press cuttings, publications that were nowhere to be found, or by giving me their testimonies.

Each time, I took it upon myself to cite their names in the appendix, except for those who are in Iran and whose safety could be compromised.

*

I am most deeply grateful to all of you. I cannot, of course, forget about William Wolf, my publisher, who has become a friend, and who is so enthusiastic, sometimes so patient, and most of all, passionate about his work.

H. N.
Brussels, February 15th 2006

An army general can be killed, but you can't kill ambition in a man's heart.

CONFUCIUS

PROLOGUE

Prologue

Nader, the one who was later called 'the last Asian conqueror', and whom Napoleon admired for his art of strategy, was assassinated following a conspiracy woven by his entourage during the night of June 19th/20th 1747.

The man, who came from nowhere – a bandit in his youth – was ambitious and strong-willed. He first managed to rebuild the totally broken up Persian Empire by crushing the Russian and Ottoman invaders as well as the Afghan hordes who had even succeeded in grabbing the throne – all this in a few years' time. Then, like in amazing dream, he had conquered the Indian subcontinent and brought back fabulous treasures. A Sunnit, he had also tried to reconcile the Shiites and the Sunnits, but in vain.

His health had deteriorated in these twenty years of almost incessant military campaigns, and the acts of cruelty committed during the last months of his reign had something to do with his assassination. He was fifty-nine years old when he died.

Nader's empire did not outlive him. It was more of a military dictatorship than an organized state. Iran fell back into a state of confusion, anarchy and conflicts between the various clans. The imperial dream of Iran and its vague desire of territorial expansion disappeared with Nader for ever.

Thanks to the good Karim Khan Zand, a great part of the centre of the country, the whole South and the West knew a period of peace and prosperity for a few years .Even though he was only the chieftain of a little tribe from Luristan, his determination to reconcile parties and his well thought-out actions helped to impose his authority on a major part of the country. He chose Shiraz as the capital city, made it look more attractive – just like Shah Abbas had done for Esfahan before. Karim Khan did not even proclaim himself Shah, and satisfied himself with the title of "Vakil-Ol-Roâyâ, the representative of the subjects of the realm".

The Qajar tribe already dominated a great part of the North of the country after his death. They ended up imposing their authority on the whole of Iran thanks to a very cruel castrated prince who was an invincible and cunning strategist. His name was Agha Mohammad Khan [1] – he was sometimes compared to Louis XI.

Agha Mohammad was crowned Shah-an-Shah in 1794. He was the founder of the Qajar dynasty that reigned over the country until 1925.

He reunified Iran, rebuilt the army, imposed his iron will on the feudal lords and vassal princes, reoccupied Georgia and the north of the Caucasus.

The Russian offensive had now become a constant threat in the North of the empire. Agha Mohammad moved the capital city to Tehran, then a modest village near the ancient Rayy [2], so that the danger coming from the North could be controlled.

His reign as 'Emperor' only lasted four years. He was assassinated in nearly the same fashion as Nader.

In 1797, crown prince Khan Baba Khan, his nephew, had himself crowned under the name of Fath Ali Shah [3].

The long decline of Iran started under his reign. The country could not gain access either to modernity, or to the industrial revolution that was about to transform some of the other great powers.

Besides, Fath Ali Shah did not even have the will to do so.

Iran was still a great power with its immense territory, its geographical position and potential resources. His presence, however, was needed in the North as well as in the South.

The Russian raids in the Caucasus, a failed landing on the Iranian shores of the Caspian Sea, the insubordination of a few vassals that were manipulated by the Russians in Georgia, in the north of Azerbaijan and in Armenia drove Fath Ali to react strongly, which his country could not afford anymore.

He then sought alliance with France. The latter cherished the idea of having an ally against Russia, and of setting aside for itself, if possible, a stopover on the road to India which Napoleon was after. Three French military missions then arrived in Tehran, one after the other. The Shah was hoping to get modern weapons and military instructors. Some plans were outlined despite the distance, and they were difficult to bring into operation. However, the Tilsit agreement between emperors Napoleon and Alexander 1st brought these plans to an end. France abandoned Iran.

Yet Fath Ali did not give up his plan to take the war to the Russian border. He amassed a sixty-thousand-man army and entrusted his son Abbas Mirza [4] to be in command. The war lasted ten years. The Iranian army was defeated after many hard-fought battles, despite the Iranians' bravery that was admired even by its opponents, and a young prince who excelled in the art of command. In the Treaty of Golestan ratified in 1813, Iran lost Georgia and some of the Caucasus.

Abbas Mirza was aware of the reasons for his country's defeat, and he then chose to launch the first set of reforms and modernization in Iran.

Young Iranians were sent to Europe – to Austria, France, Prussia, England in particular – to study modern science, warfare techniques, fortification methods… Moreover, foreign instructors, mostly from Austria, were hired.

Abbas Mirza had the first printing house set up in Iran*, he considered the publishing of a newspaper and ordered a few translations of basic technical books.

In order to counter Russian ambitions, the Shah appointed him Governor of Azerbaijan. It then became a tradition among the Qajars for all the following princes afterwards. The provinces became a good place to experiment with the modernization and control of administrative structures.

At the beginning of the 1820's, a so-called Sayyid Mohammad Mojahed, a fanatical and violently anti-Russian religious leader, launched a violent popular campaign to retrieve the provinces that had been lost in the Treaty of Golestan. He declared a state of Holy War.

Prince Abbas Mirza begged his father not to yield, and the Shah put up a resistance, arguing that the army had been weakened since the defeat, and that the country was in a terrible state after ten years of war. He was overcome however, and declared a state of war.

The prince obeyed his father despite his deteriorating health condition – he had been suffering from a bone disease since the age of five which was soon to kill him. He led the campaign with a weak army. Iran was quickly defeated.

---

* In fact, the first printing house in the country had been created under the reign of Shah Abbas the Great (1587 – 1629), but it was dismantled after his death and then moved to Istanbul to be set up there.

Prologue

In 1828, Iran lost the north of Azerbaijan and what was left of Armenia still under Iranian rule, in the treaty of Turkmanchay. Iran was to pay a colossal war indemnity, and the Russian army continued to occupy several towns and strongholds to the south of the Aras river, then declared the official border between the two countries for as long as the indemnity had not been settled. Fath Ali, who was an extravagant sovereign when it came to the building of his palaces and the expenses of his harem, refused to pay. So prince Abbas Mirza was compelled to make drastic sacrifices to deduct the funds from the income he had from his provinces so that the Russians would accept to evacuate them. He even had to sell the silverware from his residence, his tableware and carpets – several other princes in his entourage did the same.

The Russians, nonetheless, did not hesitate to loot the royal residences and to also take the fabulous treasure from the mausoleum of Sheikh Safi (died 1334) in Ardabil. Many of its pieces can be seen today at the Hermitage museum in St Petersburg.

Sayyid Mohammad disappeared after the defeat. Trace of him was found in Moscow a few months later, where he had been lavishly welcomed and housed by the Russians. He had, indeed, been their 'agent provocateur'. His descendants benefited from a pension until the October Revolution. The imperialistic powers had just inaugurated the use of a formidable weapon: the use of religious fanatics to weaken a state and a nation.

Fath Ali's long reign, which started in 1797, ended in 1834. He has left a very negative image of himself in the history of Iran. The world was in movement, Iran was going through a decline, it was being dismembered. He was nevertheless at the head of a literary revival movement, and encouraged a few of the great poets of his time. He personally liked to write verse. A few passages, here and there, in his collection of poems entitled *Divan*, are worthy of attention and interest. He is the only king to have been a poet in the history of Iran since the beginning of the 16th century.

In 1833, the reforming prince, Abbas Mirza, disappeared at the age of thirty-six after having spent over ten years in command of his army to defend his country. As far as history is concerned, he was the first leader who wanted to take up the challenge of modernization, and to undertake reforms.

Fath Ali gave the crown to his heir's son, Mohammad, out of a guilty conscience and a feeling of gratitude. The latter succeeded him as from 1834 onwards.

*   *

*

The new Iranian ambition: modernization, did not disappear with Abbas Mirza's death.

Mohammad Shah was a weak character, even a superstitious one, who first chose one of his father's advisers as Great Chancellor: Mirza Abolghasem Gha'em-Magham-é-Farahani. A very cultured man of letters, a sponsor and a visionary, he tried to carry on with the reforms of the late prince, which annoyed many people.

A plot against the Chancellor was fomented under the aegis of the Shah's private tutor, Hadji Mirza Aghassi, a rather ridiculous dervish. He was accused of impiety – Had he not welcomed foreign dignitaries to his residence? -, of being an enemy of the Crown – had he not cut people off from the civil list? – and even of being a traitor – he had sent Iranians abroad where they had nothing to learn, and where they became perverted.

Mohammad was influenced and yielded to the pressure, he had his chancellor assassinated on June 26th 1835. Dervish Aghassi replaced him. It was another ill-fated day and a new failure in the ambition to modernize.

Iran was tempted to send troops to restore order in the Herat provinces, in the western part of today's Afghanistan, where there were disturbances and rebellions. The British threat of an invasion of the South, of heavy gunfire on the harbours of the Persian Gulf was a deterrent.

Mohammad was sick – he suffered from terrible gout – and he was not capable of governing the country. His private tutor and chancellor's buffoonery could not solve the problems. The princes were plotting, and so were the foreigners, Russian and British.

When the Shah died in September 1848, his crown prince, Naser Ol Din, who then ruled over Azerbaijan, did not even have the financial means to go to Tehran. His coffers were as empty as those of the State.

One of the men in his entourage, Mirza Taqi Khan, who had the position of Vice-Governor, took control. He was a disciple, a man from Gha'em-Magham's entourage, the assassinated chancellor. He had previously succeeded in negotiating the difficult boundaries between Iran and the Ottoman Empire; he had accompanied a young Qajar prince on his official mission to Russia. This is when he had become aware of the deep causes of the Iranian crisis. He was also helped by his reading, his contacts with Westerners and his diplomatic trips. He had watched Abbas Mirza's reforms and shared his view on modernization. He took control of the situation.

While Madhe Olya, the Queen Mother, was actually trying

to be the regent, and keep the throne for her son, Mirza Taqi Khan borrowed the necessary sums from some of the local businessmen who demanded his own signature rather than the "Government's stamp" before lending them to him. An escort that was worthy of the new Shah was formed.

Thus Mirza Taqi Khan brought young Naser Ol Din to Tehran where he was crowned.

The Shah appointed him Amir Nezaam, commander-in-chief of the armed forces, and then Amir Kabir, great chancellor.

Mirza Taqi Khan stayed in power for less than four years, but he left a mark in History for ever. He has only been referred to as 'Amir Kabir' since then. His was an unusual fate which ended like a Greek tragedy [5].

*   *

*

Mirza Bozorg Khan, the father of the assassinated chancellor, had a cook, and he was his son. However, as was often the case with the aristocratic families of the time, he was allowed to study with the 'master's' children, with the same tutors. Thus, he benefited from the best possible education in one of the most powerful families in the country. 'I envy Karbalaee Ghorban*, and I fear for his son. The boy will make huge progress. He will leave unforgettable marks in History' Gha'em-Magham wrote about him in a letter to one of his friends and relatives.

He started working for the State at the age of fifteen or sixteen, when he was already fully-developed. In fact, he

---

* Amir Kabir's father's name.

worked for the Gha'em-Maghams, father and son, who were successively Abbas Mirza's ministers and the future Mohammad Shah's ones. By dint of work, honesty and loyalty, he went up the ranks and even took Naser Ol Din to Tehran where he became the 'Great Chancellor' of the young king who had not yet turned twenty.

What this 'iron' chancellor did from September 1848 to December 1851 to redress the balance in Iran so as to make it a modern state, following the example of the great powers of the time, is clearly unimaginable.

His first months in power were spent restoring order in the country. There was an open rebellion against the Crown in Khorasan and in Baluchestan. Amir Kabir managed to crush it with only a small army.

Austrian and Italian instructors were hired to train the new Iranian army, basing themselves on the latest European models, despite an opposition from the British and the Russians. The chancellor founded weapon manufactures and regulated the organisation of military forces:

'It is not in our interest to let the Iranians have powerful armed forces…We will have to position considerable troops in the region to be able to face Iran's potential stray impulses' wrote Great Britain's minister to Lord Palmerston [6].

According to the same diplomatic source, Iran had managed to create an army of 137,247 men, Supply Corps included, by the end of Amir Kabir's first year in power. The rank system had been decided on, all the officers, non-commissioned officers and soldiers were paid a salary on a regular basis. This was unheard of at the time. A Royal Guard of 400 men was created to ensure the protection and the service of the Sovereign.

He then decided to set up a navy in the Persian Gulf. The

Minister of Great Britain was asked to see if his country would sell four ships to Iran, two of which would be equipped with 25 canons each. The latter prevaricated but in his report to London, he deemed it necessary to warn the authorities against Iran's potential ambition [7]. Lord Palmerston's reply war clear: 'I order you to let Amir Kabir know that her Majesty's Government cannot accept his proposal to acquire those war ships.'[8]

Amir Kabir made similar attempts on the French side, and especially on the American one. He was murdered before any decision was made. Iran had to wait until the 1920's and the 1930's to finally have a small navy that the British actually hastened to completely destroy in August 1941.

Amir Kabir's first tasks were to establish people's safety as well as that of their goods, and restore order in the whole country. He also set up an army worthy of its name.

Amir Kabir managed to do all this in less than a year, but he needed funds. As soon as he came to power, he entrusted a group of experts called 'Mostofis' with the reorganisation of public finance, the slashing of public expenditure – he reduced the number of people on the civil list, cut down the expenses of the Court, including those of the King and of the Queen Mother. He pitilessly put an end to all kinds of abuses: regiments that only existed on paper, salaries that were, in theory, paid to a certain number of civil servants but who never actually saw the light of them because they would 'disappear' on the way.

Duties and taxes started coming in. After a few months, the State could finally honour its commitments and secure the financing of reforms.

The latter are numerous: compulsory vaccination against the smallpox, the inauguration of the first public hospital in the country in Tehran, the creation of a Post Office etc...

He created an intelligence service called 'Khofieh-nevisses'to keep corrupt civil servants under close surveillance which quickly expanded its network to foreign embassies.

Amir Kabir founded the first newspaper in the country called *Vaqaye Etefaqieh*, set up a public translation service institution, one of Gha'em-Magham's initiatives which was abandoned after his death. Many books were ordered : the first ones – a book on international law, another on Napoleon in two volumes, a history of France – were published when the 'Great Chancellor' was still alive. He gave the order to buy a selection of about two thousand books in France and in Austria so as to create a reference collection.

He made deep reforms in all kinds of fields: civil courts were created, which greatly lessened the competence and influence of the clergy; an implacable fight to end the corruption in the administration of the State started, and harsh sanctions were taken against it; urbanization plans were made.

Amir Kabir set up a real national economic policy; he protected domestic production thanks to appropriate custom duties, planned the construction of a railroad system.... Although they were rivals, the Russians and the British decided to become allied to protest against the plan, the reorganisation of the Customs service, and the restrictions on their exports to Iran. The 'Great Chancellor' cared nothing about it and refused to listen to them. Moreover, he declared that he was exasperated by the manoeuvring of the diplomats of both countries and made it be felt. He got closer to Austria, Prussia – powers that did not have a real 'stake' in Iranian affairs- and established diplomatic links with the United States; two treaties were actually signed with the latter. One of the constant moves in Iran's foreign policy then became the desire to find a 'third alliance'.

Amir Kabir decreed that the relationship between the State and religious minorities (Jews, Christians, Zoroastrians...) was to change. Their disputes were no longer the competence of religious courts which applied the 'shari'a', and became that of civil courts. The special tax they had to pay – the status of 'Dhimmitude' – was abolished. They could legally have their schools which were protected. They were considered to be Iranians like any others. Nothing more, nothing less.

It was not as easy with the followers of a new religion called Babism, later changed into Baha'ism*, a form of rebellion against the strong hold of the mullahs on social life. It, however, seriously jeopardized the unity and security of the nation since the Baha'is organized armed rebellions and attacked the police. The State repression was harsh, and went on after Amir Kabir's death, especially after the assassination attempt on the Shah that the Baha'is were considered responsible for.

Amir Kabir's major reform was probably the creation of the first Iranian university of a Western type, which he judged to be the pivot for all the structural changes that the breakthrough of the nation required. It was his greatest ambition.

Iranian architects, chosen among those Abbas Mirza had sent to Europe, are selected for the building of this 'Dar ol-Fonun'.

---

* The religion of the disciples of Baha' Ullah (Tehran 1817 – Old Acre 1892); Baha'ism is widely spread today in many countries. There are neither worship nor rites, and it is an attempt at synthesizing other religions. It has a really globalizing approach. The Muslim religious authorities, whatever their leanings, have always considered it to be a 'cursed sect', a form of apostasy.

One of its primary missions was to participate in the training of military high-ranking officers. A 'special correspondent' was sent to Austria to hire professors. Young emperor Franz Joseph greeted him in person, and saw to it that everything ran smoothly. Seven Austrians, among whom was Doctor Polak [9], but also two Italians, one French and a Dutch were hired and went to Iran.

There were seven departments at Dar ol-Fonun – among which were civil engineering, sciences, medicine, foreign languages (French, English and Russian), and, of course, "military arts" and "fortification techniques". Each foreign professor had an Iranian translator. The quick progress made by Iranian students who were learning foreign languages soon made the presence of translators useless. Almost all the lectures were given in French. The first year counted one hundred and five students, who all had scholarships.

Dar ol-Fonun was inaugurated on December 30th 1851 by the Shah. Amir Kabir was not there anymore, he was in exile, and was to be assassinated eleven days later.

*   *

*

Amir Kabir's reforms started well before the Meiji era in Japan, and would probably have had the same results, of course, with Iranian specificities. They displeased too many people though, the Court, more particularly the Queen Mother whose moral standards were not very conventional, and who resented the moral order established by the incorruptible chancellor, but there were also the corrupt civil servants, the clergy who was under constant check, the Baha'is, and especially the country's two powerful neighbours, Russia and the British Empire. The latter tolerated a weak Iran which was deprived of everything, backward, a sort of buffer state but not really a powerful one, or a strong nation, an ambitious one.

A conspiracy is formed to dismiss Amir Kabir, and is getting ahead. Its initiators are to be found in the entourage of the Queen Mother and in a character who was openly corrupted by the British Embassy, called Mirza Agha Khan Nuri. Amir Kabir had married Naser Ol Din's only real sister, princess Ezat ol Dowleh. The couple was very close, despite the age difference. Did the chancellor believe that being the Shah's brother-in-law was a protection? He was wrong.

The pressure on the young king was too strong. The plotters first succeeded in having Amir Kabir dismissed from his position of Great Chancellor, a position that Mirza Agha Khan coveted. The latter benefited from the Queen Mother's support, and especially from that of the British which he quickly got.

The Shah sent his mentor letter after letter to swear that he would protect him and remain loyal to him for the rest of his life.

Although he kept his title of commander-in-chief of the armed forces for a few days, he was put under house arrest before being exiled in Kashan, south of Tehran. The Court wanted to stop his wife from going there with him. She courageously refused. She could feel the threat on her husband's life, and believed her presence would be a form of protection for him. The couple settled in a palace in Bagh-e Fin, whose origin goes back to the Sassanid period, and which was redesigned by Shah Abbas the Great himself in the 17th century.

The Shah sometimes regretted this exile, even felt guilty about his ingratitude, and continued to send reassuring letters to his brother-in-law. The plotters feared he would come back in favour, knowing that if this were the case, Amir Kabir's vengeance would be terrible. They wanted his death from then on, so they decided to brandish the threat of his vengeance in front of the King, adding that he would present a danger for the throne if he were to stay alive. Naser Ol Din ended up yielding under their pressure. He signed a document authorizing ' Mirza Taqi Khan's deliverance'. The Queen Mother and her accomplice, Mirza Agha Khan, sent the execution team to Kashan on the spot. There is no document proving that the two embassies gave any signs of encouragement for the murder, particularly the Russian one which apparently feared him. However, it is possible that they had been made aware of it.

The Shah changed his mind a few hours after signing the document but he was told that it was too late, the executioners had already left. He looked as if he was about to send a counter-order, but never did it.

The exiles in Kashan were terribly anxious. Princess Ezat ol Dowleh was probably right in believing that if she stayed near her husband, no one would make an attempt on his life. She tasted the dishes that were presented to him before he touched them, and accompanied him in his walks.

Mirza Taqi Khan wanted to take a bath on January 10th 1852, which he had not had the opportunity to do for about a fortnight – a severe hardship for an Iranian. His wife tried to dissuade him from it, she wanted to go there with him and stay outside the door. 'It would be improper' her husband said, before adding 'I will come back quickly'. He, and his escort, walked towards the baths which were only about a dozen yards from the palace. He went into the changing room of the magnificent marble hammam, which dated back to the Safavid era. The executioners had been waiting for him for hours. As soon as he was alone, the chief executioner rushed into the changing room, pretending to have a royal message for him. The chancellor was alone. The messenger looked lugubrious and said : 'My Lord, it is the King's will that you should die, but out of respect for your rank, He allows you to choose the way you want to be executed'. He then showed him Naser Ol Din's document. 'Which form of execution would you prefer? We can't spend all night. Everything must be over in an hour's time.' The chief executioner added. 'Very well, be my wrists slashed then', the chancellor said, strangely calm. The royal emissary waved and two executioners entered the room. Amir Kabir dismissed them, and added: 'I do not want to die by the hand of these servants. Bring me my dagger!' They obeyed him, and he slashed his wrists without any hesitation [10].

Amir Kabir dipped his hand in his blood before he fainted, and impregnated the marble wall with it [11]. The Princess's worries and precautions were justified [12]. Their exile had lasted forty days.

With Amir Kabir's assassination, a whole, ambitious policy of national restoration and of modernisation of the state is shattered. A reviewer wrote that it was 'The major crime in history'. All of the reformer's great plans are abandoned, except Dar ol-Fonun's, which lasted a few years. Naser Ol Din continued to show an interest in it.

One had to wait until the 20's of the following century, till 1922 , to see a man from Mazandaran make Abbas Mirza's and Amir Kabir's ambitions his own.

Iran did not adapt to changing circumstances as far as its modernisation and industrialisation were concerned, but Amir Kabir became a legend. Hundreds of streets, squares, schools, public monuments bear his name in Iran, and even the Islamic Republic will not dare change anything. Naser Ol Din quickly regretted having let the murder be committed. His reign was stained forever.

Prologue

*   *

*

Iran was to be confronted with problems in its Herat province (in the western part of today's Afghanistan) once more in the following years. One year after the Great Chancellor's murder, in January 1853, Tehran signed a treaty with London in which it abandoned any claims on the suzerainty of Afghanistan.

Rebellions broke out in several Afghan provinces and Naser Ol Din took advantage of the situation to send his troops to retake Herat. Russia, which was right in the middle of the Crimean War, discreetly encouraged him to deal the British a blow. Prince Morad Mirza, Hessam ol-Saltaneh, one of Abbas Mirza's sons, the King's uncle, was in command of the Iranian forces, and laid siege to Herat which surrendered after seven months, on October 25th 1856. London could not tolerate the Iranian onset .On November 1st, the Governor General of India declared war on Iran. On December 4th, the British fleet arrived at Kharg island and occupied it, then seized the important harbour of Bushehr before going back at sea in the direction of the far end of the Persian Gulf, to go up the Karoun river. Iran had no navy – London's manoeuvring to prevent Amir Kabir from setting up one had just proved useful –, and could not react. Hessam ol-Saltaneh, whom the Iranians called the 'Conqueror of Herat', 'The last great man of the dynasty' [13] from then on, received the order to evacuate Afghanistan.

The Treaty of Paris was signed on March 4th 1857 – the French acting as mediators –, and ended the war. Iran gave up its claims to Afghanistan and recognized its independence.

In 1881, Iran lost Tadzhikistan, most of its Turkoman territories and its possessions in Central Asia. Those regions were then annexed to the Russian Empire since Tehran could not protect them without armed forces.

In the meantime, Britain imposed its domination on the Bahrain Islands, and on a big part of Belushestan, which was then annexed to the Indian Empire. Iran was thus limited to its current borders.

*   *

*

Naser Ol Din's reign lasted forty-eight years. It was a long period of political, economic and social immobilization in a world of constant changes. He went on three expensive trips abroad in 1873, 1878 and 1889 to find, according to his entourage, 'ideas for reforms', which he never found.

Iran was, however, affected by new ideas. Baha'ism transformed into a religion dividing up the country more than anything else. Many groups were becoming active under the influence of Seyed Jamal ed Din Assad Abadi, a dignitary and religious reformer [14], one of the forerunners of Free Masonry in Iran [15]. His long stay in Tehran caused a stir. He was exiled, travelled abroad, and had polemical exchanges in the Parisian press with Ernest Renan on Islam and modernity.

No publications were allowed except for Amir Kabir's, which came out fairly regularly. On the other hand, three newspapers created by Iranians abroad were available in the country,and were even widely distributed : *Akhtar*, founded in Istanbul in 1875; *Ghanoon*, founded in London by Mirza

Malkhom Khan, an ambassador who had fallen into disfavour; and *Habl el Matin*, founded in Calcutta in 1893.

Iran had another aspiration at the time, for want of a providential figure: democracy.

Naser Ol Din was assassinated by a disciple of Assad Abadi during a pilgrimage in May 1896 – probably with the latter's support, who did not prove to be very lucky: he died of poisoning shortly afterwards in Istanbul, most likely on the Sultan's order.

Mozaffar Ol Din, the Shah's son and Crown Prince, who was already declining, succeeded him.

*   *

*

There were demonstrations and serious unrest in Tehran in August 1896, following a general discontent of the population caused by the abuses of the Royal Authorities, their inability to govern, but also by the rising prices of staple foods, and the growing insecurity in urban and rural areas. Many members of the clergy expressed this popular discontent; under the supervision of the Masonic lodges, the nascent westernized intelligentsia gave this movement its liberal and social dimension. King Mozaffar Ol Din was unwell and could feel his end was near. He was a peace-loving person who believed in conciliation, so he yielded, and officialized a Constitution that was widely inspired from the one of the Belgian Kingdom. Iran then stopped being a monarchy by divine right: its sovereignty belonged to the nation, and was exercised through its representatives. It 'entrusted' the Shah with the throne, but could therefore also take it away from him.

The deep crisis in the Iranian society, caused by a hundred-year-old decline, humiliations and its leaders' incompetence, continued nevertheless. The country was not governed, its economy was in a disastrous state. The successive Cabinets in Tehran had no power. The capital city itself was nearly in the hands of armed gangs.

'Nothing was going right' in Iran.

Mozaffar Ol Din died shortly after granting the Constitution. His son, Mohammad Ali Shah, mounted a coup against the Parliament, but was forced to flee when the provinces revolted to defend the Constitution, and he was eventually deposed, after a two-year reign.

The spectre of a world war and the German threats on a balance of power in Europe led France, Great Britain and Russia to get closer to one another. Paris intervened between London and St Petersburg to settle one of their everlasting bones of contention: Iran. With the French as mediators, a treaty was signed in St Petersburg on August 31st 1907, which divided Iran up into zones of influence between the Russian and British Empires. The armed forces of both countries then entered Iran, leaving the central government – which was no longer a government- with only a buffer zone. The czarist forces carried out summary executions of patriots in certain towns. The hangings without trials were particularly gruesome in Tabriz and Rasht.

This state of affairs lasted until World War I. Even though Iran was a neutral country, it was the theatre of bloody conflicts between the belligerents.

The Russian revolution raised a few hopes. After the peace treaty in Brest-Litovsk (March 3rd 1918), the Soviets gave up on all the advantages and concessions the Czars had gained in Iran since 1813, without, of course, returning the regions they had annexed by force. Iran thus became the first country to recognize the new Russian regime, which was not able yet – but only for a short while – to interfere with Iranian affairs.

Great Britain, the only dominant power in the region, did not waste any time to impose a real protectorate on Iran. It wanted to take advantage of the void left after the collapse of Imperial Russia, but also to create a zone of stability on the borders of a new, unpredictable state, Bolshevik Russia.

Then, a treaty was signed in 1919. A few Iranian politicians, Hassan Vosough, Vosough ol-Dowleh, the Qajar Princes Sarem od-Dowleh and Nosrat od-Dowleh, lent themselves to the operation. It quickly became known that they had been 'bought': a few years later, Reza Shah and his Prime Minister, Mohammad Ali Foroughi made them publicly return the amount of money they had been given by Great Britain.

The head of the Vosough od-Dowleh government later said that he could not see any other solution to restore order in the country and prevent its dismantling.

The opposition to the treaty was characterized by an upsurge of patriotism, a unanimous national movement. Even the frail Ahmad Shah pretended to be against it.

That was the time when London contemplated the possibility of a coup. The idea was to favour the implementation of a strong authority that could restore the State, prevent the dismantling of the country, and hold back the Bolshevik raids in the North.
A journalist and talented polemicist called Sayyid Zia Ol-Din Tabataba'i was approached, and became the leader of the movement. However, a 'strike force' was necessary for such an operation. The Iranian army had only one, the Cossack division

that had been founded after an agreement passed between Naser Ol Din and Russia. This force was highly disciplined, and counted about 2,500 men. It was led by officers of the Imperial Russian army. It was not the same anymore after the October Revolution, since most of its officers had left it to join the White Russian army so that they could fight the triumphant Bolshevism in their country. It deserved to exist though, with its group of experienced officers who had sometimes been trained in Russia itself, and who were united around a self-educated leader. The latter was feared but also admired by his colleagues, and was devoured with ambition for his country. His name was Reza Khan, he held the rank of 'Mir Pandj', that is, brigadier general.

Tehran was then a capital deprived of everything. It was plunged into darkness as soon as the sun set, dozens of people, even hundreds of them, died of hunger and diseases every day, and the poor had no other solution but to throw the corpses into the streets so that they would be picked up by the municipal services. There was a general state of insecurity. The King barricaded himself in his palaces. The foreign interference was such that the British legation had taken the liberty to publicly forbid the inhabitants of a village situated to the north of the capital city, called Gholhak, to sell or simply let their gardens without its prior authorisation. It had even covered the streets with notices to that effect. The reason was that it was the place of the summer residence of the British, and that they wanted to be in good company [16]

The factions kept fighting with one another, the politicians were quarrelling, the people suffering and often dying of starvation or illness.

In the provinces, the situation was even worse, and the influence of the central State was hardly symbolic, even non-existent, since there were open rebellions in many regions.

Prologue

* *

*

General Ironside , the leader of a British task force, was sent to hold back the Bolshevik offensive in the South, to start the 'Coup' operation, and get in touch with the leaders of the Cossack division : general Reza Khan surrounded by Morteza Khan (Yazdan Panah), Ahmad Agha Khan (Amir Ahmadi), Reza Gholi Khan (Amir Koshravi), Fazlollah Khan (Zahedi), and some others. Reza Khan was extremely sensitive and ultra-nationalistic, and contacts with him were not easy. The British knew him to be a hardliner, and so did he.

Two officers of the small Iranian gendarmerie under Swedish command joined Reza Khan's team: colonel Kazem Khan (Sayah) and sergeant major Massoud Khan (Keyhan). They were of the intellectual type. Colonel Kazem Khan is the one who established contact between Sayyid Zia and the troops.

Thus, the various units of the Cossack division met up in Agha Baha, 150 kilometers north-west of Tehran before moving towards the capital.

Prime Minister Sepahdar Azam had apparently been informed, but he did not react. He did not have the means to do so anyway, and neither did the Shah.

General Reza Khan's troops entered the capital on February 21st 1921. He had been dreaming of a position, an opportunity to get Iran out of trouble. He suffered as a patriot, and this was no secret. As soon as he met Sayyid Zia Ol-Din Tabataba'i, he understood that the brilliant polemicist would not be a challenge for his strength and determination.

On February 22nd, after having met some resistance from a few police stations, his troops controlled the capital, and positioned themselves around the Palace. Sayyid Zia, who was already arrogant at the time, presented himself to the Shah. He was appointed Prime Minister and formed a Cabinet which did not even include the general.

Reza Khan did not need the position.

His real problem came from Britain. The Iran they wanted was not the one he was trying to build.

PART ONE

RESURRECTION AND CRISES

Chapter 1

I, REZA

On February 23rd 1921, at dawn, the capital city dwellers discovered a proclamation on public buildings, in the mosques and the bazaar:

'I, myself, order :

All the inhabitants of Tehran must obey the following regulations and personally contribute to them. Whoever infringes them shall be severely chastised.

Every inhabitant must obey military orders...'

Then, there were several points on the newly established martial law, the curfew after 8 p.m., the suspension of the publication of newspapers until new orders were given, the closing down of government offices, except for the ones in charge of ensuring the distribution of food. Each time, the statement was followed by a sentence which was always the same: 'Any offender shall be brought before a military tribunal, and punished.'

The same threat appeared in point eight: 'Those who do not obey the above-mentioned orders will be brought before a military tribunal, and will be subject to the worst possible punishments.'

The proclamation was signed 'Reza, Commander-in-Chief of her Majesty's armed forces.'

Military tribunals did not really exist then.

Reza was only the general of a division. He was only appointed Commander-in-Chief of the armed forces three days later – there were hardly any armed forces at the time, except for his own Cossack division – and only received the title of Sardar Sepah, Commander-in-Chief, on February 27th. He had, however, made his entrance into History.

Iran now had the strong figure nearly everyone had been waiting for; the one who would get it out of trouble, restore hope and ambition in the Iranian people.

*   *

*

Reza was born in Alasht, in the region of Savad Kouh in the Mazandaran province on the Caspian Sea(1), a land of freedom that was protected from invasions by the high summits of Mount Elbrouz, a favoured refuge, a sort of 'Iranian Vercors', for patriots, when there were Arab and Mongolian attacks. It was an area which had stayed off the beaten tracks, like its neighbour, Guilan.

It is a land that was honoured by many poets, Ferdowsi in particular :

Remember Mazandaran well, our native country.
May its fields and villages always be prosperous,

I, Reza

its gardens in constant bloom,
Its mountain slopes carpeted with hyacinths
and tulips.
The air is pure, the scenery magnificent; the weather
neither hot nor cold, like an eternal spring...

Alasht is one of the villages of this lush area. Reza was a member of a small tribe, or a very big family: the Pahlavans, hardy individuals who lived cloistered on their lands, and whose sons often served their country in the armed forces. They were like small feudal lords, but poor ones.

Reza's father, Abbas Ali Khan, was a major in the Qajar army. His mother, Noush Afarin, was 'Georgian' according to the rumour, but in fact, came from a family that had lived in Georgia when it was Iranian in the middle of the century. Then left when Iran lost Georgia* in 1828, and settled down in a safe place in Mazandaran.

The Iran of 1878 was poor. Abbas Ali Khan actually acted as clan chief, but his little mud dwelling was extremely basic: the only room with any heating had a sort of brazier under the table they shared.

Reza was only a few months old when his father died on November 26th 1878. Noush Afarin, the "foreigner", the 'Georgian', was badly accepted by her in-laws. She took her baby and left the poor village of Alasht to go to the capital city, where some of her relatives still lived, to ensure her son a better future. He was all she had. She joined a caravan of muleteers in the winter, in freezing weather, and walked through passes and passages on barely practicable paths, in the snow, to reach the capital. The baby nearly died of cold on the way. They stopped

---

* See prologue.

in a little village about 10,000 feet above sea level, and found shelter in a mausoleum called Emamzadeh Hachem, where Reza was looked after, and miraculously saved. They finally reached Tehran.

Two of Noush Afarin's brothers were serving in the Qajar army. She went to live with one of them called Hakim Ali Khan, a doctor and captain under Kamran Mirza's orders. The latter was the governor of Tehran, and Shah Naser Ol Din's son. They lived in poverty, but not in destitution, a meagre existence. Reza grew up and did not even go to school. His family could not afford it.

Noush Afarin died in 1885 when Reza was barely seven years old. One of his other uncles then took care of him. He was a military man too, who became a colonel at the end of his career. His name was Abol Qasem Khan Irvanlu. He was the one who influenced his nephew – a great strapping lad, who was strong, proud and sensitive, apparently always ready for a scrap and to take up arms. He enlisted at the age of fifteen, started to learn how to read and write. There are many examples left of his writing when he was a king: a rather primitive calligraphy, spelling errors...Reza was not, and never became a cultured man. He had many other qualities, though. They helped him to be very vigilant during the training and instruction of his crown prince – even too much so, according to some people.

He had no family backing or a name that could be of help for his promotion. He did come from a very respectable family, but they were poor, had no title or connections. His future could only be limited in the Iran of the time. Yet, he was ambitious, and wanted to go far in life with his strength, tenacity, and courage.

He was affected to the "Cossack" division of the army that was under Russian officers' command, and then promoted 'Nayeb', that is, lieutenant. He was called Reza Khan Savad Kuhi, after the name of the small region of Savadkuh he originated from. He was put in charge of a machine gunners' unit. The type of weapon they were using was a 'Maxim', and he was soon nicknamed 'Reza Maxim'.

All the testimonies concur: from then on, Reza could hardly bear to be under the orders of foreigners, and did not appreciate the fact that the language used for giving orders was Russian, not Persian. He suffered because the Iranian army was in a deplorable state, and the only organized unit was that Cossack division. The soldiers were not paid; they scraped a living by working here and there, or by pilfering. The officers – his uncles on his mother's side were officers – led a meagre existence by being at the disposal of princes, of the rich and powerful. The Shah was hardly obeyed in his kingdom, for want of an army. The country was already going down the drain. Reza suffered from it.

*   *

*

He first got married in 1903, and in 1912, had a daughter called Fatemeh, later to be called Hamdam ol Saltaneh. His wife died shortly after giving birth.

Reza Khan had already made a name for himself in the army in 1915. He had taken part in many operations and had been wounded several times. He had a reputation for being a hardliner; a perfectly honest man; someone uncompromising when it came to discipline, who was endowed with natural authority, a sense of command, while being both loved and feared.

He had to get married. Aged thirty-seven, a colonel in the Cossack division, he had to think about his future, and marry someone whose social position would increase his prestige. It was not easy when one had neither title nor wealth, a widower who already had a daughter.

Reza put his contacts to work, borrowed money to pay for a middle-class wedding and asked for the hand of a general's daughter. He was called Teimour Khan and was also a descendant of Iranians from the Caucasus who had fled Russian occupation, like Reza's family on his mother's side.

Teimour Khan had three daughters and one son. Nimtaj Khanoum, one of his daughters, was twenty-four years old and was not yet married. Being still at home, she was considered to be an 'old maid' at the time. She was said not to be very pretty and hard-tempered.

The marriage was agreed upon after the usual negotiations. Nimtaj Khanoum was soon called, or so to speak conferred the title of, Tal Ol Molouk.

Four children were born in this marriage. The first one was a girl, called Shams, then, there were twins on October 26th 1919 – Mohammad Reza and Ashraf. The official version was that the boy, the future crown prince to be king, was born first.

Finally, a fourth child was born in 1921: Ali Reza, who died in a plane crash in 1954, on October 26th, the day of his brother's birthday.

I, Reza

* *

*

After the collapse of the Czarist empire, most of the Russian officers left, especially to join the White Russian army that was fighting against Bolshevism. However, the Cossack division kept its traditions, its purely Russian-type discipline that was hard, sometimes even inhuman. A man from the ranks, a born leader imposed himself at its command: Reza Khan Mir-Pandj, brigadier general Reza Khan [2].

* *

*

Reza Khan, a self proclaimed commander-in-chief who did not have an official title yet, had a first worry: restore order and tranquillity in a capital city that was under the control of armed gangs, brigands and gangsters, and whose inhabitants had to lie low in their homes before nightfall, shut themselves in. The few rich and mighty who wanted to get about in a city that was nearly plunged into darkness had to have body guards and lantern bearers.

Of course, the situation was even worse in the provinces.

He decided to consolidate the squads of gendarmes, and the Cossack division took control of the police forces, and of the capital.

Members of the police force were deployed in town, and order was restored. The capital city dwellers were eventually able to move about. A few criminals were arrested and severely punished.

Sayyid Zia had been appointed Prime Minister and he introduced his government on February 25th. Reza Khan was not a member of the Cabinet.

The Prime Minister orders the arrest of eighty personalities, many of whom were princes and former dignitaries.

On the 26th, a decree issued by the Council of Ministers declared the treaty of the semi-protectorate signed with Great Britain null and void.

On the 27th, following the negotiations started months before, Iran recognized the new regime in Moscow, born with the October Revolution. A treaty of friendship and good neighbourly terms was signed with the Soviet Union.

These measures ensured a certain popularity to the 'new regime'. Reza, now Commander-in-Chief, a symbol of order and a man whose reputation was to be irreproachable, reaped the political benefit from it.

Sayyid Zia's off-hand attitude with the Shah gave rise to tensions between the two men at the top of power.

Sayyid Zia was already finding it difficult to bear Reza's growing popularity and plotted against him. He offered the Shah a position in his Cabinet for Reza, but suggested relieving him of his command to somewhat comply with the law.

Ahmad Shah cunningly pretended to accept the offer.

On April 22nd, the Head of the Executive power reshuffled his Cabinet and introduced the new one: the Commander-in-Chief was now the Minister of War. The Shah did not relieve him of his title of Commander of the armed forces however.

The crisis between the two men had now become public knowledge. Reza could see its advantages. The whole of the political establishment was against the arrogant Sayyid Zia, an intelligent but rather incompetent man. The public could not see anything coming, apart from a certain return to order in the capital. The distribution of food was badly organized, and there was unrest in the provinces.

The Commander-in-Chief did not hide his national ambitions anymore. The Shah asked him if he could have his support, provided Sayyid Zia was to be dismissed, which would annoy London. Sayyid Zia was summoned to the Palace and he was officially notified of his dismissal in the presence of the Commander-in-Chief.

Reza was standing slightly back from the Shah. The dismissed Prime Minister reacted rather unpleasantly. The Commander-in-Chief had everything ready. He called for a car that was ready to take him away, for a few officers as well, and told them: 'Drive this gentleman to Khanegheyn', a town on the border of Iran and Iraq. Sayyid Zia was under duress, he got into the car and was escorted by a security vehicle. He left, went to Europe and then settled down in Palestine under British mandate. He only went back to his country in 1942.

Reza Khan's career had been given a boost by this new coup on May 25th 1921.

Ahmad Ghavam, Ghavam Saltaneh, the governor of Khorasan, had been dismissed and arrested on Sayyid Zia's order. He was present in Sharoud on that very day – half way between the capital and Meshed, the administrative centre of his province – and was in the custody of many gendarmes to be transferred to Tehran. That is where 'the prisoner' received a telegram informing him of his appointment as Head of the Government.

Reza Khan, the Commander-in-Chief, was to be his Minister of War, as in all the following Cabinets, in the corrupt and chaotic "democracy" of a country that had sunk into havoc and anarchy.

The one who was beginning to be considered the strong figure of Iran at home and abroad then set himself a priority: re-establish order everywhere, stop the dismantling of the country, and this, with totally inadequate forces, but with an iron will. Deep reforms were to follow. He was already thinking of them and progressively surrounded himself with a few honest intellectuals.

*   *

*

Towards the end of March 1921, on the occasion of the Iranian New Year, the authorities made it publicly known that Iran had nine hospital and forty-one clinics, where twelve physicians and four qualified nurses worked.

That same year, there were 440 primary schools with 43,000 pupils, and 46 secondary schools with 9,300 pupils in the whole of the country. One may add here that there were 91 students in higher education.

The members of the press had certain doubts about those figures, they found them to be exaggerated. They nevertheless reveal the level of sanitary and educational services in a country whose population was considered to be of about 12 million people since there were no registry and census offices.

*   *

*

The communists in the North of the country, led by

someone called Ehsanollah Khan, and the men of a visionary, truly patriotic figure called Mirza Kuchik Khan (who were manipulating one another), were in a state of open insurrection against the central power :

A thousand men and a few artillery cannons were entrusted to colonel Fazlollah Zahedi who was helped by a rescue column under colonel Shahbakhti'orders. Together, they managed to crush the rebellion in stages.

Ehsanollah Khan and a few of his men who had survived, fled in the direction of Baku. Mirza Kuchik and a German died of cold in the Talesh mountains. His corpse was retrieved on December 5th 1921.

Zahedi entered Rasht, the administrative centre of the Guilan province on order of the Commander-in-Chief. He declared a general amnesty for all the insurgents. Most of the taxes and duties owed for the seven previous years and that had not been paid because of the troubles were cancelled. A decree was issued to forbid land owners to claim their rent from tenant farmers and sharecroppers during the same period.

People's wounds had to be tended but the rug had to be pulled from under the extremists' feet as well.

Zahedi's policy was one of reassurance; he wanted to prevent old scores from being settled. It was not as if the place was owned.

The insurgent had been in control of many towns and villages in the Kurdish areas, Mazandaran and Fars, for years. They ignored the central power and people lived in fear of them.

General Ahmad Agha Khan, Amir Ahmadi, crushed the rebellion in Mazandaran with a small army. Then, colonel Zahedi helped the task force sent to stop Simitghou, a kind of highwayman who operated between the Kurdistan and

Azerbaijan, and he was overcome without any trouble.

Colonel Mohammad Taqi Khan Pessian, a cultured and patriotic man, indeed, led his gendarmes from Khorasan to the capital city. He had in mind the repetition of the scenario of the 'Coup'. Reza Khan was taking the necessary steps to face up to him, but Ghavam used his networks in the local tribes, and the insurgent colonel was attacked and put to death. He, at least, was to be remembered as a victim, if not a martyr.

Shortly afterwards, the whole area of Luristan, in the West, was under the threat of insurrection from a few tribes. Amir Ahmadi was the one supposed to bring back peace there. He quickly carried out his business, and the area was safe again. Amir Ahmadi was criticized for his cruelty.
In August 1922, the tribes of the coastal areas of the Persian Gulf started showing signs of unrest. The army restored order pretty swiftly.

In fact, these rebellions were due to the reestablishment of authority of the State in the capital city. The regional potentates each had a certain autonomy *de facto*. They submitted people to their laws, plundered them, generally abused of their authority, and sometimes sent presents to the Court to save appearances and buy their impunity. When they realized that order prevailed again in Tehran, they panicked and rose up to intimidate those in power.

They had no idea who Reza Khan was, what he wanted or what his ambition was. His small army was mobile. It had found a leader who surrounded himself with general and field officers who knew how to give orders. They overcame the rioters.

The country was nearly pacified barely eighteen months after the Coup of February 1921. Order was re-established, the centrifugal forces had been defeated. People could finally start to live safely again, and move about without the fear of brigands. The safety in towns and villages gradually rekindled a thriving economy. The wounds were being healed and people could breathe again.

Public opinion was, in a vast majority, grateful to Reza Khan, the Commander-in-Chief. He was hugely popular. Many politicians got closer to him, some out of worry for national interest, others for less noble reasons, however, another fraction of the political class that was backed by the Embassy of Great Britain openly plotted against him. The 'lost love' between London and Reza Khan progressively turned into hatred. His rise to power was going to put an end to London's interference in Iran's domestic affairs.

* *

*

During the two years after the Coup, Reza Khan's efforts were mainly geared towards the foundation of a real army. At the same time, he brilliantly succeeded in re-establishing people's safety and that of their properties.

Decisions were made one after the other to that effect, and his were not supposed to be simply impressive, they were followed to the letter.

The Cossack division was dissolved on November 17th 1921. Its forces and those of the gendarmerie were united, and thus, the 'Iranian army' was created.

Reza Khan announced the setting-up of a 'general staff of the armed forces.'

On January 4th 1922, the use of foreign terms in the army was forbidden: battalion, brigade and division were replaced by Persian terms. The creation of five military zones was announced, each one with a division.

On that same day, the creation of a special training school for the members of the officer corps, the future Military Academy of Tehran, was made public. It started recruiting its first students and went into operation.

Brigadier General Amanollah Djahanbani – a Qajar prince who held a qualification from the most prestigious military academy in Imperial Russia – was appointed First Head of the General Staff of the Armed Forces.

With the agreement of the Parliament, the government borrowed a million dollars from the United States to equip the new Iranian army.

On January 9th, the new army was given a 'uniform garment', and each of its components had its own insignia.

On March 1st, an old-age pension system for officers and non-commissioned officers was set up, an official payscale for salaries and wages was approved of by the Council of Ministers and promulgated.

On June 8th, the Parliament authorized the Ministry of War to send sixty youths to France to be trained in the profession of soldiering .The future members of the Iranian officer corps were thus to be French trained.

On June 26th, a health service was created for the armed forces. Saïd Malek, a medicine general trained in France, was appointed at its head.

On August 11th, a special military order called 'Zolfaghar' after the name of the sword carried by Imam Ali, was founded.

On September 16th, the armed forces had a military police.
On October 21st, five officers who had become renowned for their military operations of pacification were appointed members of the Zolfaghar order: the first three were Fazlollah Zahedi, who had become Brigadier General in the meantime, General Djahanbani and Second Lieutenant Gholam Ali Bayandor, the Commander of an artillery unit and the future Commander-in- Chief of the navy who was killed during the Allied Forces' attack in 1941.

On June 3rd 1923, forty-six young Iranians left for France to be trained in military schools. The Head of the General Staff of the Armed Forces went with them to start a Franco-Iranian cooperation. Others groups followed.
That is how, for over a quarter of a century, the officers who were trained in Saint-Cyr, at the artillery school of Fontainebleau, the medical school of Lyon... constituted the essential part of the officer corps of the imperial army. Some even went into politics like General Razmara. The French also took part in the creation of the Military Academy of Tehran, a breeding-ground for the future officers of the armed forces. The Iranian army remained strongly marked by this French tradition until the arrival of American advisers during the last decade of this quarter of century. The latter, however, never had commanding positions, but helped with the use of weapons bought in the United States.
This is what Reza wanted for both reasons of national

interest and political balance. There was actually a new Iranian army from then on.

On June 1st 1924, an air force was officially added to it. Its officers were to be trained in France, and the planes, bought in Germany.

*   *

*

Shah Ahmad went to Europe three times to have a rest during the three years that followed the Coup. He did not come back from his third trip.

*   *

*

Political games and chaos went on in Tehran, and a strong feeling of disgust pervaded public opinion while Commander-in-Chief Reza Khan was firmly established in his position at the Ministry of War and at the head of the armed forces. He was setting up and organizing a force that would ensure domestic safety, territorial integrity and a minimum defence against foreign threats.

Ahmad Ghavam had replaced Sayyid Zia on May 25th 1921. In September, he was forced to resign, and formed a new Cabinet on the 30th, which he reshuffled eight days later. On January 22nd 1922, he was ousted out of office. Hassan Pirnia, Moshir Ol Dowleh takes his position.

The new Prime Minister is one of the most respected and most popular men in the country.

Foreign embassies continued their interferences – particularly the British. There were parliamentary intrigues, a mess in public finance, and the economy was in the doldrums.

Moshir Ol Dowleh got exasperated by these intrigues and resigned on June 16th.

June 17th 1922 marked Ghavam's return. He held out for eight months, enough time to start reforming the State finances, decide on the creation of a higher school of agriculture, and have a law on the civil service voted in. He was forced to leave his position on February 6th.

On February 14th 1923, the Shah appointed Hassan Mostofi, Mostofi Ol Mamalek, another icon of Iranian politics. He had time to have a law on the obligation of the State to use national products as a priority voted in, to create the Treasury, implement the first regulations concerning the obligatory registration of real estate transactions, and the creation of a land register.

He found it difficult as well to put up with political feuds, the fights between factions in Parliament and in the streets. He resigned on June 14th.

Moshir Ol Dowleh came back to power on the same day. It was time for the government to take out a five-million-dollar loan from the United States to meet the expenses of the army, found the Institut Pasteur of Tehran – with a French man appointed at its head – and start the reorganisation of the Customs. Supported by the Prime Minister, the Commander-in-Chief planned the creation of Red Lion and Sun, the Iranian- type Red Cross.

The same reasons had the same effects: the irreproachable and popular Pirnia managed to last a bare five months. He resigned on October 24th, unable to bear the ongoing confusion and the parliamentary intrigues.

There was only one element of stability in the country, the

Army; only one man seemed to be able to tidy up national affairs: Reza Khan, Sardar Sepah, the Commander-in-Chief.

Ahmad Shah was eager to go to Europe to 'be taken care of and have a break,' according to an official declaration made by the Court. He put Reza Khan in charge of forming the government.

On October 28th 1923, the latter introduced his seven Ministers, but kept the Home Office and the Ministry of War.
He appointed an erudite who was already famous for having held several ministerial positions before: Mohammad Ali Foroughi. Qajar Prince Soleiman Mirza Eskandari, the future president of the Iranian communist party, got the Education Department.

The road to power was laid out for him.

*   *

*

The Commander-in-Chief was now a famous man who was fawned upon by a majority of people, and respected and feared by many. He could afford to marry someone with even more prestige than the daughter of a general of the old Qajar army.

He asked prestigious and wealthy prince Madjd Ol Dowleh, the Chief of one of the important branches of the Qajars, for his granddaughter's hand, and got it. The very young girl's opinion was not even a question [3].
He had a son by her called Gholam Reza, born in 1923, during their relatively short marriage.

He then married another Qajar princess called Esmat Dowlatshahi. It appears that this marriage was out of love. Several children were born out of that union; they are all dead now. The first one, Abdol Reza, was born on October 1st 1924, then came Princes Ahmad Reza and Mahmoud Reza, Princess Fatemeh and Prince Hamid Reza.

The latter died in prison during the Islamic Republic. Esmat Dowlatshahi stayed in Iran after the fall of the monarchy, and her life ended in near misery.

Tal Ol Molouk remained the first spouse who, it is said, was always feared by her omnipotent husband. She became Queen – 'Malakeh'– after Reza's coronation, before becoming Queen Mother after her son Mohammad Reza's accession to the throne. She died in America on March 10th 1982. Due to her old age and a severe illness, she apparently never realized what had happened in Iran; she did not know about her son's fall and his death.

*   *

*

Reza Khan's troubles were not about to end once he had become Prime Minister .The Iranian political life of the time was particularly chaotic; intrigues were more and more common, and so were plots of all kinds.

The situation had to be dealt with. Reza was not the type of man to shirk from his obligations. He wanted to be in power and did not hide his ambition to create a unified Iran, a strong and centralized State, his wish to fight corruption in politics and elsewhere, to end foreign interference and conspiracy.

Much of public opinion was behind him. People were

weary of intrigues, disorder, and longed for a recovery, a national restoration, not to say a nationalistic one, and were suffering from their past humiliations.

He had a small army at his disposal. It was still badly equipped, but had become operational after almost a century, and, at its head, there were officers whom he had won to his side, they were his close guards.

He was surrounded with a group of intellectuals who had often been trained abroad, in France, Switzerland or notably Germany. They were thirsty for reforms and were looking for the right man who could implement them.

*   *

*

Some of them formed a think tank called Andjomane Iran Djavan, the Young Iran Association. They were 'dreaming' of tomorrow's Iran, making plans and laying down reforms.

Soon after he had taken over the Cabinet, the Commander-in-Chief and Prime Minister summoned the members of the association [4]. They came to his private residence. They were kept waiting in the garden. They saw him arriving: 'He was really impressive.' He sat down and asked them to take a seat on the chairs around him.

'You, who were trained in Europe, what have you got to say? What's the meaning of the association you've just created?

We want progress for Iran, we suffer from the underdevelopment of our country, from our humiliation. We have ambitions for the progress and greatness of Iran. It's all written down in our program.

What program?'

He was handed it. He read it slowly and silently, out of respect.

'This is very, very good. I can see that you are real patriots, you long for progress in this country and nourish great ambitions for Iran. Spread the news and your ideas around. I will do what you have your hearts set on. I assure you, no, I give you my word, that I will make your ambitions for Iran come true. All your ambitions are mine as well. I shall implement your program. Leave this text with me. We will get back together in a few years' time, you'll see.'

Rector Ali Akbar Siassi wrote: 'We were won over, dazzled, astounded,' and he was not a fan of the Pahlavis... 'It was too good to be true, we thought. Yet, in less than twenty years, he managed to carry out everything that was in our program' he concluded.

*   *

*

Ahmad Shah's departure and Reza Khan's arrival in power caused new tensions.

A strong trend in favour of the abolition of the monarchy and the proclamation of a republic was causing unrest in the country. Of course, all eyes turned to look at Reza Khan. He did not intervene. There was an increasing number of political meetings and of mass gatherings in favour of the republic.

The Shah had neither the strength nor the will to resist. He was even said to be unwell. His brother, however, Crown Prince Mohammad Hassan Mirza, quickly became the pivot of the action led against the Prime Minister's political ambition. The latter still continued to be perfectly courteous with the Prince and respected, at least it seems so, his function and prerogatives.

A plot against Reza Khan's life was unfolded whilst the republicans and anti-republicans were fighting in the streets, flooding the Parliament with messages and delegations. The Crown Prince seemed to be its main instigator. Ahmad Ghavam, Ghavam Saltaneh was accused of having financed it.

An ex-convict known as Youssef Armani (the Armenian) was arrested. He was supposed to have been paid to commit the murder. The latter accused Mohammad Hassan Mirza in particular. The press got hold of the story.

The Commander-in-Chief responded swiftly. The newpapers were ordered not to mention the Prince's name and Ghavam was requested to head for Europe. He stayed there for ten years before coming back for a brief period of time, and then left again. The case was, in fact, hushed up, but there were sequels.

Now Reza knew that he was fighting to the death.

The movement for the republic was reaching the provinces and openly affecting the Parliament. It was like a tidal wave: a majority of Iranians mixed up the country's decadence, the unrest, on-going corruption and the Qajars. Frail Ahmad Shah's attitude, his costly trips and indifference for the affairs of the State were not really in his favour, neither were the Crown Prince's manoeuvring and intrigues.

The people, in its majority, had already chosen between a man who was determined, honest; a nationalist with an iron will to proceed to reforms, and a king who was, indeed, not really unpleasant but weak, and more preoccupied with his trips abroad, his 'harem', than with the affairs of the State.

Reza Khan's attitude was very subtle when he was faced with the demonstrations for the republic and his opponents' reactions – fairly modest ones in comparison .It was irreproachable, legally speaking.

In an official announcement made on April 4th 1924, he asked the people to abstain from requesting a republic; instead, he wanted them to lift all the obstacles to the reforms, to progress, and to think of the consolidation of national unity. He finally asked all the 'homeland lovers' to unite themselves behind him so that they could work together.

Three days later, on April 7th 1924, he gave his resignation from all his civilian and military functions to the Chamber in a short letter, using an incisive tone, saying he was 'tired of all the plotting, all the intrigues against his person and against the interest of the State carried out by foreign agents.'

On the same day, he declared he wanted to leave the capital to go to Roudehen , a few miles away from Tehran. It was a political move meant to rally his supporters and accelerate his accession to the supreme power, according to what some of his opponents said and wrote later on.

Whatever...His decision sounded serious to his immediate entourage [5]. He had many suitcases packed, summoned his notary, Sheikh Mehdi Nadjmabadi, so as to empower colonel Karim Bouzardjomehri to manage his affairs. He then went to Kerbela on a short pilgrimage, he said, before deciding on his place of residence in another foreign country. Was he thinking about Turkey?

Ahmad Shah said he accepted his Prime Minister's resignation in a dispatch sent from France, and put Mostofi Ol Mamalek – a man of consensus, who was popular and respected by all – in charge of forming a new government. The latter abstained from it.

The rumour of the departure spread in the capital after the resignation. The provinces were soon informed.

Three personalities who rallied all the tendencies in public opinion, former Prime Ministers Moshir Ol Dowleh and Mostofi Ol Mamalek – the very person asked by the Shah to form the Cabinet – and Motamen Ol Molk, the President of the Chamber, paid a visit to the Commander-in-Chief. The meeting lasted a long time. By and by, many other members of Parliament gathered in Reza Khan's residence to dissuade him from leaving.

Being his usual democrat and legalist, the President of the Chamber suggested referring to the representatives. National representation was to arbitrate.

Reza left for Roudehen.

The Shah, by way of various telegrams, named Moshir Ol Dowleh Minister of War, appointed a new commander of the armed forces, and kept the head of his general staff – all this while the resigning Prime Minister was far away from the capital. A few politicians and journalists in the entourage of the Crown Prince, a religious dignitary and Sayyid Hassan Modaress, were plotting against Reza Khan.

Thousands of people demonstrated in front of the Parliament in his favour. His supporters organized meetings in most cities, stormed the telegraph offices, sent messages to the Parliament, and requested his return to the affairs of the State. They benefited from the protection of military leaders everywhere. The latter used the same technique and addressed the Parliament.

Popular and military pressure was very strong. A group of representatives led by Mostofi Ol Mamalek, the Prime

Minister appointed by the Shah, and by Moshir Ol Dowleh, his Minister of War who had been contacted, went to Roudehen and brought back the Commander-in-Chief to Tehran.

He won the Chamber's confidence again by an overwhelming margin. The destabilization operation had failed. Reza Khan reshuffled his Cabinet, and to show his bad mood, asked his new, very temporary Foreign Secretary, Mohammad Mossadegh – a popular representative of the capital city – to introduce him to Crown Prince Mohammad Hassan Mirza who acted as regent.

The Russian, American, French, Turkish, Belgian and German embassies congratulated Reza Khan after his return, but London remained silent.

*   *

*

From then on, a new element had to be considered: the clergy.

Mustafa Kemal Ataturk had just proclaimed a secular republic in Turkey which Reza Khan already showed an interest in, and whose action and decisions he followed, was a source of worry for the Shiite hierarchy. A possible contagiousness was feared.

The religious dignitaries visited the Commander-in-Chief more and more often [6] while the movement for the implementation of a republic was developing in Iran. Reza, who was most probably interested but did not want to show it, let it progress in the meantime. Almost the whole clergy supported Reza Khan and encouraged him to take the throne so as to avoid having a republican regime. Modaress was an exception. He was close to the Crown Prince and, no doubt, received considerable sums from the Khuzistan Khazaal potentate* that was under London's protection to destabilize the Commander-in-Chief's course of action [7]. The great chiefs, 'Sources of Imitation', of Qom and Najaf came to meet him or sent him delegates: the population wished for, and requested the fall of the Qajars – so be it; they also wanted Reza to be proclaimed Shah in Shah, while respecting constitutional procedure. These changes of dynasties did not really go against the country's traditions**!

Reza Khan let himself be discreetly persuaded.

It was at that precise moment that he took a patronymic name, that of Pahlavi, the one of the language spoken by Iranians before the Arab invasion and the advent of Islam, a symbol.

The movement for the fall of the Qajars was intensified. Commander-in-Chief Reza Khan was to be the next Shah.

In the meantime, he continued to play the faithful one to the reigning Shah, and sent him many telegrams to ask for his return. The latter knew he was not popular, that his House had done its time, and that he could not measure up with his omnipotent and ambitious Prime Minister.

The Crown Prince was plotting, spending money and uniting his supporters, to no avail. The die was already cast.

---

* See further on.
* From the Medes on to the last of the Pahlavis, Mohammad Reza, 446 shahs reigned on all or part of the Iranian territory (Shoja Ol Din Shafa, *Partow-Iran*, March 1997. Before Islam, from the time of the foundation of the empire in 556 BC until the Arab invasion and the assassination of the last emperor in 652, only three dynasties reigned over Iran: the Achaemenids (556 BC to 331 BC), the Arsacids (249 BC to 224 AD), the Sassanids (224 AD to 652 AD).After two centuries of Arab occupation, many dynasties, sometimes of foreign origin but Iranianized, reigned over the territory. The Qajars reigned since 1796, succeeding the Zands and the Afshars.

On February 14th 1925, during a solemn session presided by Hossein Pirnia, Motamen Ol Molk, the Chamber conferred the title of 'Supreme Chief of the Armed Forces' so far reserved for the Shah, to "generalissimo" Reza Khan, the Commander-in-Chief of the armed forces. It was a first step towards the throne. The popular representative of Tehran, Mohammad Mossadegh, gave his warm support to this nomination [8].

*   *

*

What happened in Tehran, the fact that most of the country was safe again, all this did not put an end to the plotting against Reza Khan, on the contrary.

In Belushistan, a province in the south-east on the border of India, a local chief rebelled, and even went so far as to mint money in his name – the sign of a will of independence. The army, helped by loyalist tribes, quelled the rebellion.

On May 31st 1924, British Petroleum agents were said to be distributing money to the Bakhtiaris to stir them up against the central power. A certain number of oil wells were in their region.
On July 8th, the presence of an English officer was reported in the Kurdish region. He was distributing weapons to the men of a chief called Sayyid Taha. Tehran protested.

The worst was to come from Khuzistan.
The local potentate, Sheikh Khazaal, an official protégé of the British, created a coordination committee with several of the Bakhtiari chiefs. He wrote to Ahmad Shah asking him for his support and even for his coming to the region so as to

become the symbol of his movement. The Shah encouraged him, but did not move. Mounted soldiers and armed men from the Bakhtiaris especially, but also from the Ghasghais and from some other tribes of the Fars area, flocked to Mohamareh (today's Khoramshahr), where the seat of the Sheikh was. It was said that 30,000 people were ready to take action against the central power.

Reza Khan decided to go and liquidate the upsurge. 'Otherwise, I will be buried under the ruins of Susa' he proclaimed before heading south.

London's reaction was sharp. A note of protest was given to the Foreign Secretary. The note was dated November 14th, three days after Reza Khan's departure, and reminded the Iranian government that the Sheikh and his subjects had been under the protection of her Majesty's Government since November 1914, and that any raid in his land would face a brisk reaction.

Mohammad Ali Foroughi, the Prime Minister in the interim, received the note, and forwarded it to the Commander-in-Chief who was in Esfahan and said: 'Reject the embassy's arguments, I do not have to listen to that kind of remark.'

Four columns of the army, backed by an "air force" for the first time, in fact three aeroplanes, were converging towards the region under the control of the insurgents. The latter were first defeated in Zeydoun on November 1st.

On the 17th, the army crushed the rebels although it was really inferior in numbers. That time, Reza was the one in direct command. The problem was solved from the military point of view.

On the 19th, the Sheikh sent a telegram to Reza Khan: 'regret the past', 'ask for your pardon'. 'I will accept your regrets under the condition that you surrender', replied the latter.

On December 2nd, the Sheikh, who did not want to surrender, was still hoping for an intervention from the Shah and relied on the protection of Britain. So, he sent his son with a letter for Reza Khan, asking for his pardon again. It is true that he was nearly surrounded, but he wanted to gain time.

Reza, to end the story, decided to grab hold of him, dead or alive. Young Brigadier General Fazlollah Zahedi was put in charge of the operation. The latter succeeded in organising a real commando operation with a few well trained men; he kidnapped and arrested the Sheikh without a blood shed. He was later called Khazaal's victor.

On the 4th, Khazaal was received by Reza Khan in Naseriyeh – Ahwaz today – the administrative centre of the province. He threw himself to his feet, and asked for his pardon which was granted to him. He was sent to Tehran where he lived for years, was even granted an audience by Reza Shah, and died in peace.

The Commander-in-Chief made a triumphant entrance in the capital on January 1st 1925, after a short pilgrimage to Kerbela.

From then on, the movement for the fall of the Qajars was irreversible. On October 28th, a collective of political parties, patriots' associations, members of the Bar, representatives of the three big religious communities – the Jewish, Christian and Zoroastrian ones – and the whole of the clergy demanded their fall.

On October 31st 1925, the Chamber nearly unanimously deposed the reigning dynasty. Only Mohammad Mossadegh opposed this decision openly, but in an indirect manner*. Three other representatives who actually had a brilliant career afterwards expressed reservations.

Reza Khan Pahlavi was appointed President of the provisional government and received the title of His Serene Highness, Valahazrate Aghdasse.

In accordance with the Constitution, a constituent assembly was summoned to decide on the institutional future of the country.
Crown Prince Mohammad Hassan Mirza took the road to exile.

On December 6th 1925, the Constituent Assembly met. On the 12th, it 'handed the crown over to His Majesty Reza Pahlavi.'
He immediately went to the Parliament and swore allegiance to the Constitution.

On the 16th, he welcomed the constituent bodies and the ambassadors or ministers from the fifteen countries represented in Tehran at the Golestan Palace. As fate would have it, the British envoy, the most senior member of the diplomatic corps, was the one to present him with their best wishes and congratulations.

On the 19th, he put Mohammad Ali Foroughi in charge of forming the first government of his reign. Sixteen years later, he became his last Prime Minister.

On January 28th 1926, in application of article 30 of the

---

* See chapter V: The oil crisis – The man who chased the British away.

Constitution, Prince Mohammad Reza, the eldest son of the new Shah, was officially proclaimed Heir to the Throne.

The solemn coronation ceremony only took place four months later.

*   *

*

The true and constant course of action Reza undertook for the economic development, social progress, and the restoration of national values indeed started after the fall of the Qajars and his victory over Khazaal. The main obstacles in his path seemed to have been gotten rid of.

After bringing peace back to his country and ensuring its territorial integrity, Reza focused on diverse policies: the development of the economy, the reforming of structures, modernisation, a strengthening of national cohesion.

*   *

*

Hélène Carrère d'Encausse wrote: 'Reza Shah had given his country an ideology, the one of a particularly independent and strong nation which revived the tradition of greatness of past centuries.' [9]

The coronation that was celebrated in the room of the same name at the Golestan Palace on April 25th 1926 already reflected the desire of returning to their roots: several crowns from previous dynasties were brought in, following a solemn process, as well as the sword of Nader, the great conqueror, and those of Shah Esmail, who founded the Safavid dynasty, of Shah Abbas the Great, with other weapons and symbols from past sovereigns. The new Shah wanted to place himself in a national and dynastic continuity.

Already before his coronation, when he was still His Most Serene Highness, he had founded the Association for the Conservation of the National Heritage – Andjomane Assar Melli – on Mohammad Ali Foroughi's suggestion. He had accepted to be its Honorary President.

The first decision made by the Association was to celebrate the thousandth anniversary of the birth of Ferdowsi, the father of Persian nationalism, and to build a grandiose mausoleum in his honour in Toos. Funds were allocated to that effect.

In a governmental decision, the Iranian calendar was modernized, the Persian names for the twelve months of the year, which had fallen into disuse for centuries, were used again instead of the Arab or Turkish ones.

On May 1st, shortly after the vote in Parliament of the new criminal and commercial codes, and a complete revision of the judicial system based on the secularization of courts, the 'capitulations', jurisdiction privileges granted to foreign nationals since the 19th century, were abolished [11]. It was a spectacular step towards the country's political independence.

From September 1926 onwards, and each year, fifty to one hundred young Iranians who were selected after a highly competitive examination and without taking their backgrounds into consideration, were sent to Europe, mainly France, to go into higher education. They progressively constituted the backbone of the new institutions in the country. For decades, the Iranian elite were Francophone, and France was used as a reference model not only for the army, but also for the administration, universities, and all the new laws.

On May 4th 1925, the first wholly Iranian bank was inaugurated. It was responsible for managing the army pension funds, among other things. It was called Sepah Bank.

On November 2nd 1926, it was the turn of Bank Rahni, inspired by the French Crédit Foncier, and destined to finance the building of accommodation.

On September 8th 1928, the National Bank of Iran was inaugurated. On May 12th 1930, the National Bank became responsible for issuing banknotes. The British, whose privilege it was, received 200,000 pounds in compensation.

Iran now had its own national currency, and banking structures that were adapted to its needs. Moreover, they were under the control of its own authorities.

From then on, new laws on foreign trade, on the control of exchange rates, the prohibition of the export of precious metals were voted in, and enforced. Iran was provided with a fundamental law which created the 'rial', its new national currency.

Other banks, among which those for agricultural development – Bank Kechavavzi – were created.

On March 1st 1932, the new Mint – Zarrabkhanehe Shahinshahi – started its activity. Iran minted its own metal coins from then on.

*   *

*

The real passion for development and for equipment often appears to be the most spectacular aspect of the period, probably mistakenly so. The judicial reforms, new civil, criminal, commercial, procedural codes and those for the implementation of modern notarial structures ending the privileges of the clergy, as well as the creation of a modern and national credit system, were undoubtedly, if not more so, of a great importance.

The equipment and the material development of a country that barely had anything were, of course, more easily perceptible.

The symbolic masterpiece of this equipment was to be the Transiranian. On February 9th 1926, the Parliament voted a law authorizing the levying of a 2-rial tax on 3 kilos of sugar, and of two more on each kilo of tea to finance its construction, without resorting to foreign credits. Only one representative, Mohammad Mossadegh, certainly not the least important one, violently opposed the project. He was blamed for it later on. He considered the project to be 'an act of treason against the nation,' [12] something that went against economic rules – 'Think about the interest the sums invested in that ruinous project could draw'- and that was dangerous for the independence of the country. He also opposed the north-south route (from the Persian Gulf to the Caspian Sea) and preferred the east-west one, 'the road to paradise' – a reference to Imam Reza's mausoleum, located to the east of Tehran.

The law was passed, and the execution of the project started.

On August 26th 1938, in Sefid Cheshmeh, a town located 400 kilometers away from the capital city, the junction of the northern and southern sections of the Transiranian was inaugurated in the presence of the Shah and of the Crown Prince.

The Shah said: 'The eighty-year-old Iranian dream has just come true'. It was the work of a lifetime. Iran was thus entering an era of modernity, according to him. 224 tunnels were added to the 90 railway stations already in operation (59 to the south and 31 to the north of Tehran), and so were many bridges, among which the one of Veresk that is 110 meters above sea level; the longest one over the Karun River was 1,100 meters long. The railway network covered 1,394 kilometers and cost the equivalent of 17.5 million pounds sterling, a very important sum at the time. It was all paid for by the Iranians, without resorting to foreign credits. The Khuzistan and Luristan regions that had often known turmoil in the past, were crossed by the railway tracks, as well as Mazandaran, in the North, also crossed by the Transiranian.

There were celebrations all over the country on that occasion. Many foreign governments sent warm messages to Tehran to pay their tribute to the achievement.

On October 30th 1938, the construction of the second Transiranian (from east to west) that links Tabriz, the administrative centre of Azerbaijan, to Meshed, the one of Khorazan, was under way. A little later, on December 4th, it was the turn of the tracks that were to link Tehran to Esfahan and Yazd. The work moved forward quickly but was interrupted by the war, to be resumed afterwards. On the eve of the Islamic Revolution, Tehran was linked not only to Tabriz to the west, but also to the towns on the border of the USSR and Turkey. On the other side, once the Tehran-Esfahan line was built, the former capital city of the empire was also linked to Yazd, Kerman, and then to Bandarabbas, on the Strait of Hormuz.

Thousands of kilometres of roads that were suitable for motor vehicles were built. They linked nearly all the towns in the country in between themselves and to the capital.

Town planning held an important place in the development programs.

Tehran, a city with narrow and dusty streets was completely redesigned and altered. A brother in arms of the Shah, colonel, then general Karim Bouzardjomehri, was the great main contractor of this urban transformation during a whole decade. He was a real 'Baron Haussmann-style' Iranian, who sometimes made the same errors. The whole work is of an impressive nature however. In sixteen years, the population of the capital went from 200,000 to over 530,000 on the eve of WWII.

All the Iranian cities underwent modernisation and town planning schemes.

* *

*

Industrialization was another political issue at the time, and the objective was clearly displayed: self-sufficiency in the food-processing industry – eight sugar refineries were built –, in textiles – Esfahan, Yazd and Rasht became some of the important centres in that field – and in general consumption products.

Exports were encouraged and imports were protected, thanks to a law implementing a monopoly in foreign trade. The latter became balanced, the army, administrations and all the sectors that benefited from public support were strictly requested to consume products made in Iran. It was a really rigorous Colbert-style policy that gave the necessary boost to the national economy.

On the eve of WWII, Iran was a self-sufficient country, economically speaking, and in many other fields. It gave rise to national pride and was one of the very cunning propaganda themes of the regime.

The construction contract for the first steelworks in the country was signed with German companies. The work started in Karaj, 40 kilometers west of the capital, and was nearly finished on the eve of the war. Despite Iranian protest, the ships transporting machinery and equipment were impounded and confiscated by the British as soon as the hostilities broke out. Iran had to wait for decades to be able to fulfil its ambition. It had been part of all the governmental programmes since the revolution of 1906, even though the USA opposed it as well as the main western powers and the World Bank.

*   *

*

These ambitious plans had to be financed without any foreign debt. Reza's Iran did not want to resort to foreign credit to finance its development, even less so to a budget deficit, since the balance of public finance was one of the principles which the Shah was very attached to, as a good family man with sound and simple ideas. To cover equipment expenses, there was thus only one solution: the oil that the British exploited.

The first big confrontation with London on that subject was becoming unavoidable.

On June 27th 1932, Hassan Taghizadeh, the Finance Minister, officially notified the President of the Anglo-Persian Oil Company (APOC) that the imperial government would refuse to receive the royalties paid by the company from then on; they were deemed to be 'insufficient' and 'not in proportion' to the needs of Iran.

The British reply was not a long time coming: the President of the APOC retorted that these royalties were calculated on the basis of 16% of the 'net profit' of the company, in accordance with the treaty signed by Qajar King Mozaffar Ol Din and William Knox d'Arcy in 1901, for a period of sixty years.

The agreement had been drafted in French, the only foreign language spoken by the Court, and did not indicate what the precise calculation base for the taxable income the 16% were to be paid from should be. D'Arcy had paid the Shah 20,000 pounds sterling. The latter had an urgent need for the money to take a pleasure-trip to Europe. Afterwards, the weak Tehran governments had accepted the fact that the calculation base was limited to a minimum: to the net operating profit – and that, without any control.

A big campaign against the company spread in Iran. On August 8th, London vividly protested against it.

On October 29th, Reza did something spectacular: he went to the southern Iranian oil terminal of Abadan and, in front of an audience of many civilian and military personalities and press photographers, he had a tap opened. The 'black gold' started pouring into the sea. The Shah stayed there and watched in silence. No-one dared intervene. It lasted for an end-less time, thirty minutes, apparently. The Sovereign then declared: 'Since this oil is of no profit to us, it might as well be wasted for everybody.' The message was clear.

On that same day, the first nine 'real' warships ordered by Tehran in Italy, with their officers who had been trained in the very country, arrived in the harbour of Bushehr, in the Persian Gulf. After centuries, Iran had, at last, acquired a navy. Colonel Gholam Ali Bayandor was promoted Admiral after adequate training in Italy, and became the Commander-in-Chief of the Imperial Navy.

On November 5th, the Shah inaugurated a new harbour on the Gulf, in Shahpur, a town which had completely sprung from the desert in a few years' time. The birth of a national navy was solemnly celebrated.

It meant hours of euphoria for Iranians. One of their old dreams had just come true. It was also a way of displaying their strength and the time for a trial with London.

On November 27th, the government officially proclaimed the abolition of the 'd'Arcy concession'. The Finance Minister notified the President of the APOC that since the concession had been granted before the constitutional revolution and without the slightest popular and parliamentary authorization, it could only be considered as 'null and void' from then on. Minister Taghizadeh also insisted on the 'lack of remuneration' for Iran, without any possibility for the beneficiary to control its fairness.

London refused to make any compromises, and stood on a purely legal ground: the contract was drafted up in due form.

On November 30th, the Foreign Office Secretary, Sir John Simon, forcefully protested to his counterpart Mohammad Ali Foroughi, who firmly replied to him.

The same day, the Parliament solemnly abolished the 'd'Arcy concession.'

On December 3rd and 10th, there were exchanges of biting notes and words between both governments. London threatened to take the case to the International Court of Justice in The Hague whose competence Iran had just recognized in a convention on June 14th 1931. Tehran replied that it was a domestic affair and insisted on the incompetence of the Court in that field.

On December 16th, Great Britain took the case to the League of Nations. Mohammad Ali Foroughi had to work very hard at countering the diplomatic action of the first world power from then on.

A gunboat policy accompanied the diplomatic pressure London was exerting on Iran. Some of His British Majesty's war ships were deployed in the Persian Gulf, some of His army units were on manoeuvres in Iraq which, as a matter of fact, was a British protectorate.

Tehran's response was the movements of its small, recent navy. The Khuzistan division was in a state of maximum alert on February 2nd 1933, followed by the division based East, on the border of the two Belushistans, the Iranian and the English ones, on the 12th.

The same scenario was repeated two decades later after the nationalisation of oil.

The Council of the League of Nations granted the two parties a four-month delay to find a solution to their disagreement by using direct negotiations.

Edvard Beneš, the Czech Foreign Minister, played the part of mediator and peacemaker.

Negotiations started in Tehran and in Geneva. They resulted in an agreement. On the Iranian side, Minister Hassan Taghizadeh presided over the delegation, helped by Foroughi, the Minister of Foreign Affairs, and Ali Akbar Davar, the Minister of Justice, together with a learned assembly of experts. The Iran of the 30's had men who were able to face up to the most experienced British experts.

On May 14th, an agreement in 26 points was reached, and was approved by the Parliament on the 28th. The agreement was more favourable to Iran in many ways: Iran was to receive 20% of the profits instead of the previous 16%, and had the right to use an auditor based in London to control accounts. Iran's share was thus increased by 25%. The exploitation area was limited to 100,000 square kilometres instead of 280,000. The British were losing the monopoly in transports and distribution inside the country. On the other hand, the new agreement extended the period of exploitation from 1961, which had been previously decided on, to 1993. This was held against Reza Shah and his Minister Taghizadeh during the nationalisation campaign of the 1950's.

The immediate effects of the agreement were, on the one hand, a strong increase in Iran's revenue which permitted to speed up the development plans and, on the other hand, a certain quietening down in bilateral relations. London's distrust of the Pahlavis did not disappear however.

*   *

*

The relations between Reza Shah's Iran and the Soviet Union knew different stages.

There is no doubt that "generalissimo" Reza Khan's coming to power and his anti-British attitude could not displease Moscow. Iran was becoming a zone of stability on the southern borders of the USSR, a buffer country between the latter and the British Empire, and, at the same time, an interesting economic partner. Therefore, Moscow sacrificed its protégés*, as it used to, on the altar of its strategic and imperial interests. The bilateral relations with Iran were excellent until the beginning of the 30's. Moscow was pleased to see the Shah's exceptional firmness towards Khazaal. According to certain authors, the Soviet secret services did not hesitate, even a few times, to warn Reza of certain plots against him and his policy, in which London's agents were involved [13]. Reza's daily appointment book showed a non-standard frequency of audiences granted to the Kremlin's envoys during all that period [14].

As far as state to state relations were concerned, there were more and more cooperation agreements during that period:

Two cooperation agreements on telegraphic and postal exchanges were signed on January 25th and February 3rd 1925.

---

*See chapter III: The Tudeh – Seventy years in the service of the Soviet Union.

A treaty specifying how rivers and streams on the borders of the country could be used, and demarcating the fishing zones in the Caspian Sea, was finalized on February 20th 1926.

A cooperation agreement on the security of common borders was made on October 1st 1927. The one on the fisheries of the Caspian Sea and on the bilateral cooperation of customs services happened on the 23rd of the same month.

On December 28th, the layout of the borders between the two countries was finalized.

Etc...

Nevertheless, a story which has remained obscure until today cast a shadow on the relations between the two countries: Teymourtach, the all-mighty Minister of the Imperial Court, made a stay in Moscow, where he was welcomed with exceptional consideration.

Did the Soviet secret services try to – and succeed in – manipulating the man by blackmailing him because of an affair he had had with one of their female spies? The Minister's weakness in that respect was known and the Soviet services excelled in that matter. Had he made Moscow political or diplomatic promises? Had he been made aware of a secret understanding between London and Moscow – a known fact later on – so that the latter did not support Tehran in its oil confrontation with the British, and did he abstain from informing the Shah? Why? Was he threatened that certain disclosures would be made?

The 'Teymourtach affair' is still an object of speculations for Iranian authors, and has remained a mystery. The Minister was in disgrace after his return from Moscow; he was kept away from the negotiations with London, then he was dismissed, put in jail, where he died. It is alleged that someone actually put an end to his life there. His family was driven away from the capital, which was not customary for the regime.

In 1934-1935, the expulsion from the USSR of a certain number of Iranians, among whom many agents were noticed, and the case of Dr Erani*'s Iranian Communist Party contributed to the cooling-down of bilateral relations. The economic, technical cooperation and the commercial exchanges between the two countries did not stop, however.

From 1939 onwards and from the start of WWII, Reza Shah somewhat reconsidered his distrust of Moscow. He wanted to balance out the excellence of the relations Iran had with the member countries of the Axis, especially with Germany**.

* *

*

It is under Reza Shah's reign that Iranian diplomacy was most innovative in its relations with Kemal Ataturk's Turkey.

On June 2nd 1934, Reza left Tehran by road to pay a state visit to Turkey. His Foreign Affairs Minister, Bagher Kazemi, and the great master of imperial protocol, Hossein Samii, who was actualy one of the most famous poets of his time, as well as a delegation of forty civilian and military personalities went with him. On the way there, he stopped for a long time in Tabriz, and inaugurated an exhibition of agricultural, industrial and traditional products from the province. He received a lot of visits.

On the 12th, he crossed the border.

On the 17th, he was in Ankara where Mustafa Kemal and Turkey gave him a warm and grandiose welcome. Both heads of states had long discussions. Reza attended military manoeuvres, the demonstration of the Turkish air force; he visited monuments, museums, institutions created by the new secular republic. And, a very unusual gesture, he went to put a wreath

---

* See chapter III: The Tudeh – Seventy years at the service of the Soviet Union.
** See chapter II: The Second World War. – An old philosopher saves Iran.

on the grave of Ataturk's mother. It was a homage to a woman, to women in general.

His voyage lasted a month and was to be the only visit abroad Reza made before he was exiled. The understanding between both men was complete, it was a real fusion. It confirms the admiration the Shah of Iran felt for the founder of secular Turkey.

Reza came back from Turkey with images in his head, ideas for what he wanted his country to be. His action for national unity in Iran, secularism, the development of state education became stronger from then on.

* *

*

For Iranians, Iran had always been called Iran, since the beginnings of History, since Cyrus the Great. It was the revival of Iranian nationalism that Ferdowsi had celebrated, sung and glorified. It was also in the name of Iran that Abbas the Great had imposed the national emblem, the lion and the sun, as a symbol of their superiority over the crescent of the Sultan of Constantinople. It was for Iran that Nader had led his army to the conquest of the Indies. Yet, that country was called Persia abroad, and Iranian diplomacy had tolerated it before accepting it: the Shah of Persia, the Persian Legation... For Iranians, it was a kind of usage they considered to be humiliating.

On December 27th 1934, the country resumed usage of his lifelong name in a solemn decision. Persia existed no longer. The Iran that was revived encompassed all the people of different faith who lived in it. The news caused a real storm in the chanceries. For Iranian people, it was a return to their roots.

On May 20th 1935, an imperial ordinance created the Iranian Academy, the reflection of the one Richelieu gave France. It was to defend the Persian language and culture, adapt the language to modern times. Mohammad Ali Foroughi had briefly become Prime Minister again. He was the main instigator of the idea and became its first President. Another man from the entourage of the Sovereign, the great poet Hossein Samii, replaced him; then there was yet another poet, Hassan Vosough, Vosough ol Dowleh, the disparaged Prime Minister of the 1919 treaty that Reza did not really like, but who was respected in the literary world...

The Iranian Academy accomplished enormous feats in order to adapt and modernize the language [15], even if it went downhill after the war.

On January 8th 1936, a special law forbade women to wear the veil. It was often roughly enforced and imposed, which sometimes provoked violent reactions among the members of the clergy, and gave rise to protest movements in Qom and Meshed. The police forces quelled them unceremoniously. The fact that the veil was forbidden brought about the completion of the break between the Shah and the mullahs, as the military service, the implementation of a registry system and of patronymic names, together with the secularization of judicial institutions had done.

On January 9th, Queen Tal Ol Molouk and Princesses Shams and Ashraf appeared in a public ceemony without a veil, and dressed according to 'European' fashion, in fact normally. Apparently, the Queen had felt somewhat reluctant to do so, but had yielded under her husband's brutal order [16].

The Shah's decision in the matter had been taken during his stay in Turkey. It was a real revolution which left its marks for decades. Even if a great easing of restrictions was seen after the Shah's departure in 1941, one had to wait until 1979 to see the 'hedjab' imposed on Iranian women by the Islamists.

* *

*

The privileged partnership with Turkey resulted in a treaty that gave a final lay-out to the borders: it was a treaty of friendship and mutual security, and another one of economic cooperation.

On Tehran's initiative, Turkey, Iran and Iraq signed a non-aggression treaty in Geneva on October 10th 1935, they 'committed themselves to finding a peaceful solution to any possible dispute that could arise between them.'

The way was paved for the signature of a solemn document and the big diplomatic ceremony of the reign, after numerous ministerial trips and Faisal I of Iraq's visit to Tehran.

On July 8th 1937, the Foreign Ministers of Iran, Turkey and Iraq signed a pact of non-aggression, of acknowledgement of their mutual borders, and of military and political cooperation.

The ceremony took place in Saad Abad, the Shah's summer palace, hence the name given to the treaty by historians.

Further events revealed the limits of these commitments. Yet, this 'Saad Abad pact' that had been orchestrated and concluded by Iranian diplomacy, proved to be a considerable success for Iran on an international level.

* *

*

The true symbols of Reza's reign are probably a monument and a happening, like about four decades later, Cyrus's celebration in honour of Mohammad Reza Pahlavi's: the inauguration of Ferdowsi's* mausoleum – Ferdowsi was the real father of Iranian nationalism – and the celebration of the thousandth anniversary of his birth.

On October 12th 1934, Reza inaugurated the mausoleum and delivered a beautiful speech in homage of the nation's Poet in front of a learned assembly of iranologues and orientalists from all over the world.

The foreign participants were all pleasantly surprised, if not amazed, by the deep transformation Iran had undergone [17].

Many academic ceremonies were also organized abroad to celebrate the event. The ones in Paris, epecially a solemn session at the Sorbonne in the presence of the President of the Republic, took on a particular glamour: the poet Paul Fort composed a really beautiful ode in honour of the author of the *Book of Kings* and a member of the French Academy, Abel Bonnard, made a lyrical speech in front of his counterparts, "Les Immortels" [18].

It was an excellent public relations operation for Iran.

*   *

*

The other major work under his reign was the new foundation of the University. Amir Kabir had founded the first modern university in the country**, Dar ol-Fonun. On the eve of Reza's reign, it had virtually disappeared.

Starting at the beginning of the 20th century, a few small centres of higher education had been created: the most impor-

---

* Ferdowsi (934-1020), the author of the *Book of Kings*, standardized the Persian language after the Arab invasion.
** See Prologue.

tant one was the National Institute of Political Science, founded by the historian and statesman Hassan Pirnia, Moshir Ol Dowleh [19], with the help of his brother Hossein Pirnia (Motamen ol Molk) and of Mohammad Ali Foroughi. After a selective entry, there were less than 20 students when it was first opened.

On March 9th 1921, a National Law Institute opened; it was run by a French man. The teaching was partly made in Molière's language.

In 1922, a National Institute of Pharmacology was created, under the authority of the director of the Medical School of the Dar ol-Fonun – a dying institution at the time – then, it was the turn of a National Institute of Agronomics.

In 1926, the Ministry of Education founded the first National Institute of Trade in the country.

Another great national ambition also had to be realized, a lifelong dream that Amir Kabir's assassination had broken: the creation of a big University.

The old Medical School was reorganized, modernized, and given a professional staff worthy of its name, and finally turned into a Faculty of Medecine in 1928.

That same year, the "École Normale Supérieure" – a prestigious grande école for teachers and researchers -, the Faculty of Arts and the one of Science are created.

The foundation of a faculty of vocational education preceded the vote of a law organizing the University of Tehran which counted eight faculties at the beginning. During the first three years of its existence, the Minister of Education assumed their rectorship. Then another law was passed, and the University became independent. It was managed by its Council which was composed of elected deans and representatives of the lecturers and professors of each faculty.

In 1934, the State bought a 300,000 square meter plot of land for the University campus. A French man, André Godard, was in charge of designing its main plan. The major faculties – medical, law, and dentistry – were built in no time, and then inaugurated. Other sites followed, but were only finished after the war.

While the law on the purchasing of the land and on the credits needed for the building of the faculties was being discussed in Parliament, several representatives vividly criticized the Minister of Education, Ali Asghar Hekmat, for his ambitious views. Why such a big plot of land? They wanted to know.

As the Shah was laying the first stone of the first faculty, a medical one, he asked his Minister what he thought of the size of the land. The latter started giving complicated explanations to justify his decision. Reza's reply was clear: 'You'll see, soon you won't have enough space on this campus, and you will need millions of square meters for a university that is worthy of our capital city." This quickly turned out to be true.

The University of Tehran soon had several hospitals that were turned into university hospitals (CHU), and on the eve of the revolution, there were three big campuses in the capital, save for a few buildings all over town, like its really beautiful Theological Institute, its huge university hospitals – three thousand beds in all –, its thirty-four Research Institutes, etc... In Tehran only, there were several other universities.

In 1922, there were 22 students in higher education in Iran. In 1934, the year the University was officially founded and organized, there were 866. On the eve of the Second World War, their numbers reached 3,000, and during the Islamic Revolution [20], over 200,000.

Thus, the work started under Amir Kabir's reign – building a modern university for the country – was effected when Reza was in power, thanks to his willpower.

*　　　*

*

There was another great priority during his reign – the base of the regime – : it was to create, or rather recreate, a genuine army for Iran, to ensure its integrity, external security – a real instrument of its power.

As soon as there was the Coup of February 1921, "generalissimo" Reza Khan's task was to reorganize the modest forces the country had. It proved to be his main strength, the instrument of his ascent, of his influence, of his rise to power.

In June 1925, as Reza Khan had not acceded to the throne yet, a law establishing a national military service was passed in Parliament. It was a social revolution which encountered a vivid reaction from the members of the Clergy, who deemed the project to be contrary to the precepts of Islam. Their reaction was sometimes harshly quelled. Reza created the structures of a modern army, its ranks, military decorations, and founded military academies to train young people for the army. Then, with the help of French advisors and basing himself on the model of Saint-Cyr, he founded the Military Academy of Tehran. In 1931, it was the turn of the Military Aviation Technical College, to train and get the pilots and air force officers ready for action. The first officers were actually mainly trained in France.

In 1935, the Shah founded a National War Institute, the future Institute of Advanced Studies of National Defence, to train military officers. He set up an air force and opened two aeroplane manufacturing plants – the Shahbaz and Shahin ones – first supposed to assemble spare parts imported from France and Germany, and then, from the mid-1940's onwards, to actually manufacture most aeroplanes on the site.

Iran had almost never been a naval power since the defeat of Salamine (480 BC) where the admiral of the fleet was a woman, most probably a unique example in history.

One had to wait nearly two thousand years to see a Safavid, Abbas II (1642-1666) give the country a navy. There were a few warships in the Caspian Sea then.

Nader, the great conqueror (1736-1747), had launched the construction of a real war fleet in the Persian Gulf. His work remained unfinished to be abandoned later, after his murder.

Amir Kabir persevered in resuming the project. One of the reasons why London was in favour of his destitution, not to say his murder, was the fact that the great reformer insisted on realizing this project, because he deemed it necessary for Iran, and he was right, but the British found it 'absolutely unacceptable.'

Reza re-appropriated the project despite a British opposition. On the eve of the war, Iran had about twenty war ships, among which two destroyers, in the Persian Gulf. They had all been built in Italy, where the officers of the Imperial Navy had been trained. The Iranian war ships were the first targets of the British during the invasion of Iran. Most of them were sunk, their officers killed, in particular their commander-in-chief, Admiral Bayandor.

Years later, under Mohammad Reza Pahlavi's reign, Iran finally managed to have a powerful navy, which permitted to exert a real influence over the Persian Gulf and the Indian Ocean, in short, to become a real naval power. It was also the sign of an unbearable ambition for many.

*   *

*

Another spectacular aspect of that reign was no doubt, and stayed, the revival of arts, culture, architecture, and literature.

The national restoration and State sponsorship played an important part in this revival. Reza cared very much about it and saw to it personally. He was not a man of much culture, but he was endowed with a rare view of the world.
The creation of the Company for the conservation of the national heritage is an example, and so are Ferdowsi's thousandth anniversary and the building of a mausoleum in his honour which quickly became, and has remained, a centre of pilgrimage and popular fervour.

As soon as 1930, the Sovereign had a law passed regulating and protecting archaeological excavations. He was encouraged by his entourage of nationalistic intellectuals. Thus, an end was put to the plundering of Iran's historical heritage in favour of foreign museums and collections.
The National Service of Archaeology was created under the direction of a French man, André Godard. André Godard designed the Archaeological Museum of Tehran, and Reza supervised its construction with loving care. The National Library was designed by the same architect and built not too far from the museum.
The impressive musem of Astane Ghodose was created. It was adjacent to mausoleum of Reza – the eighth Shiite Imam –, and gathered several scattered collections of religious art.
The list of cultural initiatives during his reign is endless: there were the first national conservatoire, the Symphonic Orchestra of Tehran, public libraries in almost all the major cities, and a movement for the translation of the fundamental books of the cultural heritage of humanity. The man who had probably never read anything in his life, apart a few collections of poetry, kept repeating: 'Translate, translate, translate.'

Despite modest financial means, and so many other priorities, Iran started making a serious effort to safeguard and restore its historical monuments, like in Esfahan, Persepolis, Shiraz, Meshed, Ardabil and Hamadan, for instance.

Unfortunately, a few beautiful buildings of the Qajar era were sacrificed because of these town planning schemes, especially in Tehran.

The State carried out a gigantic construction and building work like in the days of Shah Abbas the Great (1587-1629). Russian architects who had fled Bolshevism, then French and sometimes German ones, got down to it, together with two or three Iranians from the Qajar era, before young Iranians who had been trained in Europe and later in the brand new School of Fine Arts took over.

Reza liked architectural beauty and harmony, and it somewhat influenced his son, though the latter was more obsessed with grandiose buildings than with beautiful ones. The Sepah Square, in the centre of the historical area in Tehran – which was unfortunately disfigured later on – the Ministry of Foreign Affairs, of Justice, of the Interior; the Officers' Club of Tehran, all the public buildings built in the provinces; schools, hospitals, hotels…constitute the references of a revival area, of a certain style, a rare taste and a spirit of harmony.

Reza went down in History as another Abbas the Great, as far as all this is concerned.

Some eminent writers and poets of the Iranian 20th century also partly or fully owe their work to that era: Ali Dashti, Mohammad Hedjazi, Saïd Nafissi, Sadegh Hedayat, the great poet Bahar, without forgetting Mohammad Ali Foroughi who actually has other famous titles.

*   *

*

The two or three years preceding the outbreak of the Second World War marked a period of exceptional development and spectacular achievements for Iran: a progress in the elimination of illiteracy; sanitary and hospital equipments; the generalisation of vaccinations that existed at the time; electricity brought to the capital city and to almost all urban centres; automatic telephones...

*   *

*

The whole policy of national restoration and of economic development could not be carried out without a certain rigidity. A certain discipline prevailed, like at the time of Abbas the Great, or Amir Kabir, who was only a Chancellor of the empire. The police and the army were present and sometimes acted roughly. The huge majority of people benefited from a retrieved safety, prosperity, an economic development, and new equipments. Reza did not tolerate corruption, even from his relatives and friends, and occasionally had excessive reactions.

A formal democracy and the separation of power were respected. The Parliament would discuss, often amend, and pass laws. But there is no doubt that its representatives were short-listed by the government. It was ascertained that they actually represented their constituencies, and were links between the central power and the people.

Freedom of speech was limited as far as politics were concerned. The communist party was forbidden and its activities repressed: its members were either imprisoned or exiled, but never executed.

The government was not heavy-handed, except for the execution of the leaders of armed rebellions during the pacification of the country. These were a few isolated cases, but still too numerous, however they confirm the rules.

He acted respectfully, even humbly, with the great statesmen of the Qajar era, while many of them showed open reserve towards him. The Court was open for them. Some played tricktrack (Reza's favourite game) with the Sovereign, during the two hours before dinner, when it was possible to see him and have one or two cups of tea with him.

*   *

*

Reza's personal life was very austere. There are no rumours of love affairs with women, or of evenings when he had too much to drink or to eat. An omnipotent King, he always led the life of a soldier, dressed modestly, imposed sanctions when there were abuses. His only occupations and preoccupations were his country, before anything else, relentless work, and his family.

Unfortunately, during the last years of his reign, he had acquired a few big agricultural estates in his native province of Mazandaran, south of the Caspian Sea. The conditions in which he purchased them were often unfair, even if the more or less forced transfers of properties were accompanied with measures of equipment, housing, land draining, and elimination of illiteracy which quickly resulted in an improvement in the level of life of simple farmers. The province had changed, but these acquisitions were often reproached to him afterwards, and as soon as 1942, some of these estates were returned to their former owners with payments for excessive and critical compensation.

The civil list should have been enough for the Shah and his family, and if there had been no distraction of the kind, his reign would have nearly been flawless.

*   *

*

'What was Iran [before Reza]? Nothing. What did Reza Shah want? Everything. What did he do during his reign? Many things. Few kings before him were that able... He was not only the founder of a political State, but also of an economic one.' [21]

His work was at the origin of a huge step forward for Iran. His dream was shattered. Serious crises followed the revival, but the country knew another fresh start later.

And, more than sixty years after his death, Reza has become a legend for Iranians.

Chapter II

THE SECOND WORLD WAR
An old philosopher saves Iran

The Second World War started on September 1st 1939, when the troops of Nazi Germany invaded Poland. It was to change the destiny of Iran.

The very next day, Tehran declared the neutrality of Iran in the conflict and asked all the foreign nationals, especially those of the belligerent countries, not to manifest feelings that could infringe on this neutrality. On September 12th, the Shah himself insisted on the policy, and reiterated his words on October 26th, when he inaugurated the new legislature.

According to the Constitution, the established Cabinet resigned. Ahmad Matin-Daftari, the previous Minister of Justice, was appointed Prime Minister. On November 12th, his nomination was approved by the Chamber. The new Head of the Executive was thought of as being pro-German. His appointment was considered to be a political gesture in favour of the powers of the Axis. Was the Shah inclined towards them?

This is what he was reproached. Did he think that Germany would win, and that he had to put his country in the winning camp? This is what was written so as to discredit him. In the light of the documents which are available today, we know that it was not the case.

Iran could not stay away from a conflict which was soon to become a worldwide one. The country had become 'a strategic area, if not a tactical one, and one of foremost importance.' [1] He made sure that its neutrality would be scrupulously respected.

On November 24th 1939, the Shah welcomed the plenipotentiary Minister of Great Britain who was taking his leave. He told him about his preference for a victory of the Allies. He said to London's [2] envoy: 'Iran is not powerful enough to be able to take part in that conflict. It is not weak enough either to have its rights trampled on. Its neutrality policy is necessary for its national interest. It is also in the belligerents' interest since it guarantees peace in the region.'

Tehran also saw to it that the impression British propaganda had given of its pro-German policy should be corrected: two agreements of exchanges of economic cooperation and development were signed on March 12th and 25th 1940 with the Soviet Union, and they were rapidly approved by the Parliament on April 4th.

The Minister of the Interior made sure that the activities of the nationals from the Axis countries would be strictly checked in Iran. To reassure Great Britain on Iran's vigilance, about sixty of them were asked to leave the country because their presence was not essential to the execution of economic plans, or ordered not to go to the oil areas that London considered to be sensitive. The police even arrested a German businessman who was accused of spying.

On June 26th 1940, Matin-Daftari, the Prime Minister who

was renowned for being pro-German, was dismissed and replaced by the allegedly pro-British Ali Mansour. It was an obvious move to reassure London.

*   *

*

The economic development of the country went on at a higher pace during this vigilant period of neutrality, and this despite the problems the conflict caused: new railroad tracks, the Nowshahr harbour on the Caspian Sea, new factories were inaugurated; one saw the extension of the University of Tehran, the speeding up of the program to fight illiteracy, the starting up of the national radio...

*   *

*

The German army invasion of the USSR on June 22nd 1941 completely changed the deal. With good reason, Iran now feared the union of two imperialisms which had systematically threatened it for over a century.

London and Moscow immediately started exerting a very strong diplomatic and media-staged pressure against Iran which was accused of being in connivance with the Axis powers. The importance of Iran's stance considerably changed things: 'It was highly desirable to establish a highly effective communication route with Russia across Persia.'[3] The relations Iran had with the Axis powers – considered to be privileged ones at the time- were going to be used as a pretext to take over the control of that 'communication route' and reach a few other political and economic targets as well.

*   *

*

Iran had become closer to Italy and Germany for a few years. In doing so, the Iranian diplomatic corps only followed an old tradition which consisted in bringing closer third order powers so as to counterbalance the hegemonic influences of Russia and of the British Empire.

France was the chosen country young Iranians were sent to, to go into higher education. French officers were also the ones who were asked to modernize the Military Academy of Tehran which took its inspiration from Saint-Cyr; some eminent French academics were asked to help with the foundation of the University of Tehran, the first and biggest one in the country, where they are still vividly remembered. Eminent specialists came from France as well, to create the Iranian Archaeological Service, the Museum of Tehran, the National Library...

When Iran decided to set up a navy in the thirties – an old patriotic dream London had always been opposed to, and the execution of which it had succeeded in stopping – Italy was its privileged partner. Italy trained the officers of the Imperial Navy and built its first ships. Yet, the Shah had a poor view of Mussolini whom he considered to be a 'braggart.' [4]

The Shah had been attracted by Germany's power and sense of discipline since 1933, and yet he had no liking for the national-socialist ideology.

Thus, on the eve of the Second World War, Germany held the first place in the country's foreign trade and economy. Berlin was providing Iran with railroad and air equipment as well factories and machinery. It equipped the Imperial Army and, at the end of barter agreements which were particularly favourable to Iranians, bought most of Iran's non-oil exports. They had virtually no outlets in the western world that was suffering from the Great Depression. Over five thousand German engineers, businessmen, instructors and technicians worked in Iran. The only air link between Tehran and Europe was run by the Germans.

Despite the official policy of neutrality and the reinforced surveillance of German nationals, and later, of Italian ones, Iranian public opinion was widely in favour of the Axis powers, more so out of atavistic feelings – a distrust and hatred of the British and the Russians – than out of ideological reasons which left people indifferent.

*   *

*

Both powers exerted pressure to end the presence of the nationals from the Axis countries in Iran, and obtain transit facilities. This pressure became stronger and stronger from June 1941 onwards, when the conflict extended to the Soviet Union. London and Moscow organized intense radio propaganda against the Shah and his 'pro-German' policy. Right then, a military invasion and even a dividing-up of Iran into zones of influence [5] were envisaged, like in 1907, when the French acted as mediators.

On June 26th, July 29th and August 16th 1941, the plenipotentiaries of both powers presented more and more threatening notes to the Iranian authorities – they were almost ultimatums. The British air force violated the Iranian air space on several occasions. The air defence retaliated with warning shots. Tehran then protested and sent very curt notes to London.

During all those weeks, the international press openly contemplated the possibility, and then the eventuality and preparations for a combined attack on Iran. The Iranian Diplomatic Representatives in Iraq, Japan, Lebanon, Turkey, and Great Britain... gave explanations to their departments. The Shah must have known about these reports. The ones from Cairo were even more alarming. [6]

The Shah reacted at different levels: the Allies were reassured, the surveillance and control of Germans were reinforced; however, their deportation was not envisaged; precautionary measures were taken to ensure the functioning of institutions and the food supply for the population in case of crisis. The army also reinforced its border garrisons, especially in the North, where they were faced with the Soviets. All leave was suppressed and a state of alert was discreetly triggered.

Did the Sovereign rely too much on the power of deterrent of the Iranian army? as certain declarations implied. [7] In any case, he gave the impression that he wanted to use it to deter the Allies from invading Iran. He delivered a virile speech on August 20th during the consecration of the new promotion of the Military Academy of Tehran. The new officers were immediately sent to their new units.

What is more likely is that time had to be saved to see how things would turn out. At the end of the summer of 1941, the German advance in Russia was spectacular and Iranian public opinion would not have understood the concessions made to the Allies; moreover, the Shah's entourage apparently believed in their defeat.

Tehran then tried to get the United States of America involved in the crisis – the first call for help to Americans. In his reply, Cordell Hull, the Secretary of State, contented himself with encouraging Iran to cooperate with the Allies as much as they could, and to refuse any help to the Axis countries.

It was a situation of deadlock and lack of understanding.

The invasion of Iran was unavoidable. Churchill wrote later on: 'It is not without worrying that I will enter into this war against Persia.' Yet, he believed the Iranian army to be 'weak and decrepit.' [9]

*   *

*

Thus, on August 25th 1941, at five in the morning, the Soviet troops in the North and the British ones in the South and South-West invaded the Iranian territory.

At the same time in Tehran, Great Britain's Minister and the ambassador of the Soviet Union knocked on the door of the private residence of Prime Minister Ali Mansour, in a rather undiplomatic fashion. They woke him up and handed him a note specifying that 'both states were under the obligation to take unilateral and military measures against Iran that would not infringe on the sovereignty of the country in any way, but which would prevent any subversive action on behalf of the Germans.' [10]

The Prime Minister had received the two diplomats in his dressing gown. As soon as they had left, he got dressed and set off for the palace of Saad Abad, north of the capital, the summer residence of the imperial family. The Sovereign, an early riser, greeted them without delay and had the two plenipotentiaries immediately summoned. Djavad Ameri, acting as Minister of Foreign Affairs, came with them and was their interpreter. The conversation was held in French.

The Shah asked them: 'What do you want? If you want war, there is no point in talking any more. If you want the Germans to leave, I had actually assured you of their departure.'

The Minister of Great Britain answered: 'Time for diplomacy is over, Sir. It's now time to take up arms. The military leaders are henceforth in charge.' [11] The conversation continued on that line. The British diplomat promised he would give London an immediate account. Then, they both left.

In the afternoon, the German minister was granted an audience. He simply read a text to the Sovereign which said that his government supported Iran's neutrality policy. [12]

The Cabinet was summoned in the evening. Crown Prince Mohammad Reza was also present. It is during that meeting that it was decided to appeal to the United States again for help to cease the hostilities. The message contained a brief account of the bombing and the invasion of the country. The Shah signed the text in Persian. It was translated into French by Nasrollah Entezam on his order. The message President Roosevelt received shortly afterwards was therefore in French. [13]

The Chamber was also summoned in great haste and listened to a report written by the Prime Minister on the day's events. Then, the representatives parted without having a debate on the issue.

*   *

*

Iran bravely resisted the invasion of the world's two greatest armies, trapped, as it was, in a pincer movement like Poland in 1939. Many cities were bombed, including the capital. The air defence retaliated. The small Iranian navy, a favourite target of the British, was wiped out in a few hours, and most of its officers were killed in combat, notably their commander-in-chief, Admiral Bayandor. When the news was given to the Shah, it brought tears to his eyes – the only time this ever happened in those days -: 'But what are they going to leave us with?'

The British advance was stopped in the West by the division based in Kermanshah. The artillery battle raged for a few hours around Ahwaz, the administrative centre of Khuzistan, an oil province in the South... However, the outcome of 'a conflict between overwhelming forces' and a weak country that had barely emerged from nearly two centuries of decline and humiliation, could only be certain. On August 27th 1941, Tehran asked for 'a cease-fire'. The government notified the Germans and the Italians that they had to close down their legations and repatriate their nationals. A radical change of policy was necessary. Ali Mansour presented his resignation to the Shah who accepted it at once.

After consulting with the outgoing members of his Cabinet and the Crown Prince in particular, he asked for Mohammad Ali Foroughi's help. The latter was seventy-five years old. He had already been his Prime Minister and was going to be his last, a really experienced statesman, a great diplomat who was known in international circles, and more particularly a writer, researcher and philosopher respected by all.

The two men had not been on good terms for over five years. Foroughi lived in a state of interior exile which was made worse by his declining health.

He had been a representative, presided over the Chamber; he became Foreign Affairs Minister, Minister of Finance and later Minister of War. He thus knew the political circles, the administration and the army extremely well.

107

Yet, he did not belong to a clan, kept away from intrigues, and led a modest life. He often happened to do his shopping himself for want of servants in the last few years of his life. His integrity, absence of bias, erudition and age, made a sort of icon, even saint out of him.

He was the right man for the job.

As Minister of Foreign Affairs, he had managed the Iranian delegation at the general assemblies of the League of Nations three times and had been appointed President of the latter in 1928. Foreign countries knew him and respected him. That also made him the man of the time.

*   *

*

Foroughi spent nearly all his time in bed as he had a heart condition. The Shah knew it. He had been his Prime Minister from December 16th 1925 until June 6th 1926, and then from December 17th 1933 to December 3rd 1935.

However, for Iranians, Foroughi was also, and foremost, an erudite, the wise man par excellence: the first president of the Iranian Academy, founder and first president of the prestigious Association for the Safeguard of the National Heritage, editor of the classics in Persian – Ferdowsi, Khayyam, Saadi and Hafiz*, among others, to whom he had consecrated part of his life .

---

*Ferdowsi or Fidousi, the greatest Persian poet who was born near Toos in around 935 and died in1020.It took him thirty-five years to write a 60,000 – verse poem, the *Shah Nameh*, the legendary history of the kings of Iran from the very beginning. The poem fixed the Persian language, like *The Divine Comedy* fixed the Italian one. Ferdowsi is considered like the symbol of the cultural revival of Iran after the Arab invasion, and the father of Iranian nationalism.

He was a philosopher and his history of western philosophy still is authoritative today. He had also translated Montaigne's and René Descartes' work into Persian. His translation of the *Discours de la Méthode* is so precise and so beautiful that the reader who is not initiated could wonder which one is the original version and which one the translation.

*   *

*

Reza could have paid a high price for asking Foroughi for help. He had kept him out of power for a few years and even felt a certain suspicion towards him. But the Sovereign had a rare quality: he knew men and could sacrifice his own feelings for the interests of the nation.

Thirty-seven years later, his son could have done with someone like Foroughi, Iran was left in a state of anarchy and revolution.

Khayyam, poet and mathematician (1040 – 1122).He tried to classify equations of various degrees according to the number of terms they contained, studied cubical equations and found a geometrical solution for some of them. He is also the one who made the Iranian solar calendar, the so-called malekshahi. His poetical work is extremely popular and essentially constituted of quatrains with a heavy touch of agnosticism. He celebrated wine, beauty and denounced intolerance and stupidity in them.

Saadi (1213-1292), was the author of the *Golestan* and the *Boustan*, and of many poems which reveal his attraction to Sufism and the indulgent morals of a disillusioned man. It is through his work that the Western World was initiated to Persian poetry, the *Golestan* having been translated into French as soon as 1634.

Hafiz (1320-1389) was the author of the ghazals, the poetical genre of which he perfected. He celebrated wine, beauty and tolerance. He is perhaps the most popular poet among Iranians.

Mohammad Ali Foroughi devoted long introductions to the publication of each of the poets' works. Even today, these texts are not only a reference for researchers, but also masterpieces of Persian prose.

The Shah asked him to come and see him on the evening of August 28th. The Head of Protocol called him on the phone. Foroughi said he was honoured by 'His Majesty's delicate attention' – he could somehow guess the reason for his summoning – but added, being sincere: 'You know that I am unwell. It is getting late [it was 7 p.m.] and I do not have a car. Could we not postpone the audience until tomorrow or till the King comes into town?' – the Court was in Saad Abad, in the higher areas of the capital city.

The Head of Protocol did not specify the reason for the meeting, reminded him that these were emergency circumstances and added that a car would be sent to fetch him. The Sovereign then asked Entezam to escort Foroughi in person.

The philosopher finally arrived at the summer palace at about 9 p.m. and was granted an audience. The conversation was long. When he left the Shah's office, he greeted Crown Prince Mohammad Reza and told the people who were present: 'In difficult times like these, I could only resume my service,' and he left. It became known a few moments later, that after he had accepted his nomination, he had agreed with the Shah to keep all the Ministers for the moment, except the one of Foreign Affairs: Ali Soheili, an experienced diplomat who was in the Department of the Interior, swapped his portfolio with Djavad Ameri.

The new Prime Minister immediately devoted himself to three objectives of strict priority:

– Reach a state of bona fide armistice and then obtain guarantees for the safeguard of Iran's independence and integrity.

– Save the monarchy he thought would be a guarantee and symbol of this independence and integrity, and the form of government that would be best adapted to the history and traditions of the country.

– Re-establish a less formal political and parliamentary regime than under

Reza's authoritarian reign; put Iran again on the way to a western-style democracy that would be in keeping with the spirit of the 1906 Constitution. [15]

He managed to reach his three objectives.

*   *

*

On the 29th, a strange incident broke the tension at the top of the government and, for the first and only time during the last days of his reign, Reza lost control of his actions, he who had always remained imperturbable and kept his self-control: the Minister of War, air vice-marshal Ahmad Nakhdjavan, without referring to the commander-in-chief of the armed forces, the Shah, or to the Prime Minister, gave the order of demobilization to all the conscripts. In a few hours' time, the Iranian army did not have any more soldiers. At the time, there was such an atmosphere of defeat that many soldiers left without even handing back their personal weapons to the people in charge. It was a state of rout.

The Shah stripped the Minister and another officer accused of connivance of their ranks during a stormy meeting. He even asked someone to fetch his arm to shoot 'the traitors' on the spot! People helped him calm down. The government had thus lost a trump card, the king was exposed.

Thirty-seven years later, towards the end of Mohammad Reza Pahlavi's reign, another similar decision that was inspired by the Americans and initiated by two disloyal officers provoked the quasi-dismantling of the Iranian army, thus paving the way for the triumph of the revolution.

What motivated the general who was the Minister of War? After Reza's departure in exile, he was 'rehabilitated' by his son but never had a commanding position again? He is not known to have offered any explanation.

It is still a mystery.

*   *

*

Two days later, general Amir Ahmadi, the sovereign's brother-in-arms, a prestigious officer kept aside in an honorary position, was summoned to the Ministry of War and appointed Military Governor of the capital. The new minister had no army. He got a few hundred officers and non-commissioned officers back. They were people he could trust. He gave them weapons and had them march down the streets of the capital to reassure the population and deter possible trouble-makers. Three hundred men were positioned around the national palaces, especially around the Parliament.

There was a certain return to peace. Public services were working properly.

'The cease-fire' required by the outgoing Cabinet had taken effect despite a few incidents. Foroughi and his Minister of Foreign Affairs could get down to their hard task.

*   *

*

On August 30th, the three governments succeeded in settling the problems raised by the presence of Russian and British troops in the country. Three distinct zones were created, like in 1907, but with Tehran's consent.

The allied troops had to stay mainly in the North (the Soviets), and the South-West (the British). Their presence in the capital was to be only symbolic. Iran accepted to cooperate with the Allies. By way of compensation, Iran received, like in the past, the royalties from the exploitation of oil in Khuzistan by the British, and of the fisheries on the Caspian Sea managed by the Russians. The administration of the country remained entirely in the hands of the Iranian government, as well as the maintenance of law and order, which were the responsibility of the national gendarmerie and police. The army was not dismantled. Several garrisons were even kept in the zones where the allied troops were present. The two powers promised to withdraw their troops as soon as the military situation allowed for it.

Two days later, the President of the United States congratulated the Shah in a warm message for the arrangement they had come to, and stressed his interest and support for the safeguard of the independence and integrity of Iran. His gesture was highly appreciated in Tehran.

*　　　　　*

*

As soon as the cease-fire was effective, another problem arose, a very serious one this time. The two powers suggested, then asked for, and finally demanded Reza's abdication, not to say the end of the monarchy.

The British hated Reza Pahlavi, his nationalism and ambitions for Iran, and had not really forgotten about his conflict with the Anglo-Iranian Oil Company (AIOC). The Soviets did not care for him very much, and could not forgive him his anti-communist policy, even though the relations between the two countries had been decent under his reign and the commercial exchanges had quickly developed. People thought that the republican regime would be more easily influenced, more easily manipulated.

An intense radio campaign was launched by London, Moscow and Dehli, more particularly, and heavy diplomatic pressure was exerted to get the Sovereign to leave, not to say have the monarchy abolished. The 'symbolic' Russian detachments were getting closer to Tehran. The threat of Reza Pahlavi's arrest and deportation was real. He was made to understand that he had to go.

At the beginning, Foroughi pretended not to hear, and replied to the ambassadors of the allied countries that they were not to interfere in the domestic matters of Iran. He knew, however, that his resistance only had a symbolic meaning, and so did Reza Pahlavi. He would have liked to save the throne, at least, for Mohammad Reza, the Crown Prince. He wanted to put him in his Prime Minister's care, being tactful as only Iranians can be. He then took an unprecedented step, considering the practices and protocol of the time.

*   *

*

On September 15th, an unwell Foroughi was confined to bed. Ali Soheili, his Minister of Foreign Affairs, told him on the phone about a joint visit of the two ambassadors of the allied countries. They demanded the Shah's abdication and his departure from the capital within the next twenty-four hours, otherwise the allied troops would 'occupy' the capital and solve the problem by using force.

Reza Pahlavi did not ignore the pressure either.

Early in the afternoon, during the siesta, someone knocked on the door of the modest private residence of the Prime Minister, on avenue Sepah in Tehran. Nobody was announced. His son, Mohsen Foroughi, was there. [16] He went to open the door. It was the Shah in person, in uniform. Only one security car escorted his.

The Shah went in. Mohsen took him to the residence sitting-room, and then went to tell his father who quickly got dressed. When he met up with the Shah, he had even forgotten to put his braces on, they were dangling down! The two men sat down facing each other. Mohsen brought in two cups of tea and served the Shah and his father. Reza Pahlavi asked him to leave them alone and to let nobody in. The meeting lasted two hours. The Shah left his Prime Minister shortly after 4 p.m. What did they talk about? Nobody will ever know.

Mohammad Ali Foroughi and his son walked the Shah back to his car. As he returned inside the house, the Prime Minister said to his son: 'His Majesty lit a cigarette. When he realized how bad my cough was, he immediately put it out and apologized.'

When Mohsen Foroughi went back to the sitting-room, he, indeed, found a cigarette in the ashtray that had barely been lit!

It can easily be guessed that the Shah had come to settle the problem of his abdication and put his son in the old 'wise' man's care.

The next day, the Prime Minister set off for the Palace to draft the letter of abdication. Both men were very moved, as can be understood. '[Foroughi] had to make three attempts. When the Shah was finally satisfied, he wrote it up in the beautiful calligraphy of a well-read old Persian'. [18] The Shah signed it: '...I feel weary, the time has come for a younger force to pursue a task which requires so much vigour...'

Mohammad Reza, the Crown Prince, was invited to come.

The atmosphere was tense. The Shah told his son: 'I have made the necessary arrangements with the Prime Minister.' Then turning towards the latter, he added: 'I entrust my son to you , and put both of you in the care of the Almighty.'

He held his son close in his arms. He was moved. He had tears in his eyes. He turned around so that they could not be seen and walked down to the garden where his car was waiting for him. He took the one-way road to exile, and never saw his son again.

*   *

*

Reza Pahlavi's fate was sorted out; however, there was still another problem, a trickier one, this time.

As soon as Reza Pahlavi had left, the Prime Minister called Ali Soheili, his Minister of Foreign Affairs. He informed him of the event and requested him to convey the news to the British and Soviet envoys. It was done on the spot.

Ali Soheili related later: 'Soon after, I had the visit of both ambassadors': 'You are undoubtedly going to make the Crown Prince take the oath*. We have come to let you know that both our governments will not recognize him.' 'I told them that both powers had committed themselves not to interfere in Iranian domestic affairs.' The British Minister replied: 'This is of no relevance. We have come to tell you that we will not accept his accession to the throne.'

In the meantime, the Prime Minister had gone back to his

---

* The Crown Prince had to take the oath of allegiance to the Constitution in Parliament to be actually recognized as the Shah.

temporary office on the third floor of the palace of the Ministry of Foreign Affairs. Soheili knew it. He begged the two diplomats to talk straight to Foroughi, the only master on board.

Foroughi greeted them. The two diplomats made their point again. The British envoy was vehement. The old 'wise' man answered immediately and in a curt voice: 'We attach no value to the position your governments hold. Our decision is made. The Crown Prince will go to Parliament tomorrow.' The British diplomat replied: 'You know our position. It's up to you to draw the right conclusions.' Both diplomats took their leave of him.

Foroughi eventually went to see the one who was not Crown Prince any more, and not Shah yet. Mohammad Reza Pahlavi had already been kept informed by some of the personalities of the Court. He was sad and worried. He immediately said to Foroughi: 'I know what you have come to tell me. They will not recognize my reign. If you believe that I should give up my throne in the interest of the nation, I am ready to do it. Do what they want.' Foroughi was very upset and retorted: 'The decision has been made. You shall go to Parliament tomorrow. The Russian and English representatives will be notified of it.' Then he withdrew to show him he knew what he had to do and did not expect any objections on behalf of the Prince. [19]

It was later known that both powers had contemplated a regency. This they had first suggested to Mohammad Saed, an old, prestigious diplomat who was ambassador in Moscow at the time, and then to Foroughi himself, even suggesting that he should take the presidency of the republic. The latter had flatly refused. [20]

The British had also considered the return to the throne of the Qajar pretender, Hamid Mirza. The latter had been trained in France and later, in the United Kingdom. He could not speak Persian! The idea was quickly abandoned. [21]

*

On September 16th 1941, the Chamber was summoned by its President, Haj Mohtachem ol Saltaneh Esfandiari. All the exits in the building were closed. General Amir Ahmadi had many non-commissioned officers positioned around the Baharestan, the seat of Parliament, to be able to deal with any possible incident;

In the morning, the Prime Minister came to read Reza Pahlavi's letter of abdication. The latter was already far away from the capital. The representatives took note of it. Iran did not have a king any more. During a few hours, an old, frail erudite who was unwell, had to assume its destiny alone.

Foroughi went back to the Palace. The Prime Minister was informed of the advance of the allied troops in the direction of Tehran. The days were numbered.

The Prime Minister took advantage of a quiet, warm afternoon towards the end of summer, and of siesta time, to drive Mohammad Reza Pahlavi to Parliament in a discreet car. They were both in 'civilian' clothes, not wearing the required ceremonial uniform. The uniforms were in suitcases in the only escort car behind them.

The car entered Parliament through a hidden door. Both men and a chamberlain got dressed in front of an officer in a different room each. Prince Mohammad Reza was helped by an officer.

At the same time, President Esfandiari summoned the representatives back to a plenary session. The latter had all been elected thanks to the Shah, at least with his approval, and never missed an opportunity to flatter him, and sometimes with a certain hypocrisy. Yet, for some time, a few of them had started criticising him, sometimes harshly. Some were dreaming of a liberal republic which would give them all the powers. They were surprised to see Prince Mohammad Reza appear in ceremonial dress. He was wearing the insignia of Grand Master of the Imperial Orders, and his father's sword with a gold and silver pommel.

The Prince walked up to the rostrum of the Chamber, with the President of the Chamber and the Prime Minister around him, supported by them, so to speak. He took the oath on the Koran, and on the Constitution to respect the latter, and defend the independence and integrity of the country. Then he briefly addressed the Chamber to confirm his oath in a beautiful and heartrending speech written by Foroughi. The surprise effect, thus symbolized, was such that his accession to the throne was greeted by thunderous applause.

Over fifteen years before, during Reza Pahlavi's coronation, his Prime Minister, Mohammad Ali Foroughi had addressed him in a memorable speech, reminding him of his duties for the nation in really beautiful words. Both texts would deserve to appear in the selected passages of Persian prose which is not short of masterpieces. [22]

The Crown Prince made his entrance in Parliament at 3.15 p.m. Shah Mohammad Reza Pahlavi came out at 3.30 p.m. The news spread all over town, and the crowd had already started gathering on the Baharestan square, in front of Parliament, and in the neighbouring streets. The young Shah had arrived on the sly. He returned to the Palace, escorted by a huge crowd. The people were protecting him.

A few units of the Soviet and British troops were entering the capital city at about the same time. Were they coming to arrest Reza and stop his son's accession to the throne? [23]

An old philosopher who was endowed with an exceptional grasp of what the State needed had fooled the British and the Soviets.

The first of Foroughi's great objectives had been reached: the monarchy had been saved.

Thirty-seven years later, on November 7th 1978, the intrigues fomented by a small coterie forced a Mohammad Reza Pahlavi who had become sick and exhausted to repeat five times in a message to the nation that he had not respected the Constitution and thus, broken his promise. He regretted these words until he died. They meant the end of the monarchy. [24]

Later, Mohammad Reza Pahlavi wrote the following about Foroughi: 'I was happy to be able to lean on an educated and powerful Prime Minister who could hold his ground with the Allies.' [25]

*   *

*

Reza Pahlavi temporarily settled down in Esfahan after his departure from Tehran. He and most of his family and relatives left for Yazd on September 22nd, then for Kerman, before arriving in Bandar-Abbas on the Persian Gulf. There, he went on board a small English steamer which was very uncomfortable and tiny called the Bandara, to sail for a destination which was kept secret from him. As he was leaving Iran, one of his ears was inflamed and he had a temperature of 40°. His wish – on Foroughi's advice, it seems – was to go and settle down in South America. Before leaving his native soil, he picked up a handful of dirt which he kept until he died.

The Bandara moored in Bombay a few days later where it broke down. Reza was not given permission to land. The English

Governor, Sir Clermont Skrine, informed of the place chosen for his exile: Mauritius. Reza was indignant. He had three telegrams of protest drafted and then he signed them. He was not allowed to send them. He was held prisoner, like Napoleon after the Hundred Days. They changed boats, embarked on another one, the Burma, which was as uncomfortable as the first one, and reached Mauritius on October 19th. The Governor was tactful enough, at least, to have an Iranian flag hoisted outside the residence where the exile was under house arrest.

The stay on Mauritius lasted six months. Then, on Tehran's intervention, the whole group was given permission to migrate to South Africa. On March 30th 1942, they landed in Durban. Reza was a sick man who was weakened, worn out, almost silent. Everybody settled down in hotels at first, then left for Johannesburg where a big, decrepit villa was rented, not without difficulty. Reza hardly ever left it, and quickly declined. His end came on July 26th 1944.

The Court in Tehran declared a rather discreet period of mourning. His remains were transferred to Cairo and temporarily buried there. His ashes only came back in the spring of 1950, to be moved again during the revolution.

*   *

*

As soon as Reza had left and his frail heir had ascended to the throne, the Tehran government tackled a task which Foroughi and Ali Soheili, his Minister of Foreign Affairs, successfully carried out. The question was to sign a treaty with the Allies that would settle the tripartite relations, and solemnly guarantee the future of the country and the safeguard of its integrity.

The Prime Minister was concerned that the role of the Parliament should be strengthened, so he asked for a small mission of parliamentary follow-up to be associated to it. [26] He thus relied on parliamentary representation, brandishing the threat of a refusal to ratify the treaty in order to resist the powers which had, at first, demanded a sort of military occupation that would be accepted by Iran, and not a partnership.[27]

The negotiations were tough and lasted eleven weeks: exhausting weeks for a man that was worn out by illness and helpless in front of two superpowers. The balance of power was too unequal indeed. Yet, an agreement was reached.

The treaty indicated a certain number of obligations [28]. Iran was to officially side with the Allies, and formally recognize the right for the powers fighting the Axis countries to have their troops cross its territory – 'the fact that they were stationing there could not be considered like a military occupation'. Moreover, Iran accepted to give them all the help they needed;

The Allies recognized the sovereignty, political independence and territorial integrity of Iran. They promised they would ensure its defence against any possible aggression and especially 'commit themselves to leaving the territory at the latest six months after the suspension of hostilities which was to be made official by an armistice between the Allies and Germany and its partners; or they were to leave when peace was declared, if it happened before the end of the six months.' Four years later, this hard-won commitment, thanks to Foroughi's cleverness and tenacity, proved to be of major importance for Iran.

The Allies finally agreed to make big efforts – which, of course, they never made – to safeguard the economic life of the country, despite the hardships and difficulties of war.

Thus, thanks to the efforts made by the government and

more particularly by its head, Iran, an invaded and occupied country, was becoming an Ally, a recognized partner.

The last thing was to get the adherence, and especially the support of the United States. Foroughi got it in the form of an official message from President F.D. Roosevelt, on February 6th 1942. The United States were committing themselves to defending the independence and the integrity of Iran. This guarantee also revealed itself to be important in the years to come.

The Parliament was reticent and public opinion was rather hostile, because of his anti-British and anti-Russian feelings.

Nevertheless, the government got the treaty unanimously ratified.

Foroughi immediately got very unpopular. The radio stations of the Axis countries, especially the ones from Berlin, launched an obnoxious propaganda against him, calling him a Jew – which was not true – a free mason – which was true – and a traitor in favour of the Russians at certain times, of the English at others, and eventually of the Americans! He escaped an assassination attempt on January 25th 1942. Once they were reassured, the representatives started plotting against the government... these are the delights of parliamentary life!

The Soviets, as far as they were concerned, did not make it any easier for the government. Hundreds of officers and soldiers who were held prisoners were only very sparingly released. Conflicts broke out between the command of the Red Army and the local Iranian authorities...

The British's attitude was hardly any better. They were raising the tribes of the South against the central power so as to weaken it. The army and a few units that had barely been brought together in haste had to intervene everywhere to restore a minimum of law and order.

On the other hand, the Russian soldiers were subjected to an iron-fisted discipline and behaved impeccably, contrarily to what people feared, whereas a few unpleasant quarrels broke out with the soldiers of the British Empire.

Foroughi was tired. He reshuffled his Cabinet twice before forming a new one, once the new legislature had been inaugurated. He thought his task was over. He knew his days were numbered and wanted to devote them to improving his knowledge of the Arabic language and of a few Sufi philosophers. So, he presented his resignation to the Shah on March 7th 1942. The Chamber suggested to the government to appoint Ali Soheili, the Minister of Foreign Affair. The latter formed a new government.

On March 10th, Foroughi was appointed Minister of the Imperial Court, a then honorific title. The nomination was but a solemn homage to the saviour of the country, who had regained a certain popularity with the evolution of the war and more particularly the Americans' entry into war. Public opinion realized that he had guessed things correctly and that they had been ungrateful.

Life in the country was only a series of domestic problems, insecurity in the provinces which was often fostered by the Allies, destitution, constant increase in prices and political intrigues. The young Shah who was inexperienced and lacking in means struggled as he could to deal with the situation. He was present on all fronts to reassure the population and solve minor problems.

That period affected him for ever.

There was one transient government after another. Ali Soheili only lasted six months. Ahmad Ghavam succeeded him for a period of seven months. Soheili was back in power for three months. Mohammad Saed who had been ambassador in Moscow when the allied troops entered Iran, then Minister of Foreign Affairs, lasted a little longer: nine months; then it was Morteza Gholi Bayat's turn, four months, Ebrahim Hakimi, two; Mohsen Sadre, a little longer, five. Hakimi came back for three months. In the end, the crisis in Azerbaijan, the non-respect of the treaty signed by the Soviets and the danger of an implosion of the country brought the members of Parliament back to reason. Ahmad Ghavam was called back. He stayed and saved the country.

*   *

*

In foreign affairs, all these heads of the executive power who were often men with strong personalities, all honest and attached to the independence and integrity of the country, faced up to the Soviet and British interferences with determination. The former were brutal and the latter, subtle.

When national interest was at stake, the Shah supported them and ignored his personal feelings, especially in cases such as Ghavam's.

A few events marked these years of uncertainty on the level of international relations.

From March 1942 onwards, Iran had to welcome forty thousand Polish refugees who had been deported by the Soviets before being released. Many of them stayed in the country and integrated the national way of life. Others went on their road to exile.

A few American contingents settled down in Iran. Despite the sometimes offhand attitude of certain young GI's which was not well appreciated, the Iranians felt their presence reassuring. It is a known fact that they had no particular designs on Iran.

Iran broke its diplomatic relations with Japan in April 1942. The Japanese nationals were expelled and returned to their country via the Russian territory.

On June 10th 1942, Iran recognized General De Gaulle's free France, and sent an ambassador to the man of June 18th.

The British arrested and deported many personalities who were suspected of being hostile to the Allies, despite the protest of the Iranian government.

Arrests and deportations started as soon as 1942. The first one on this long list was General Fazlollah Zahedi, the commander of the Esfahan garrison.

On September 16th 1943, Iran declared war on Germany.
On December 2nd of the same year, the three great men, Roosevelt, Churchill and Stalin, gathered in Tehran. In a solemn declaration, they confirmed their attachment to the independence and integrity of the country. It was a diplomatic victory for Iran. However, the Shah was rather badly treated, if not humiliated by these 'guests' Iran had not invited. He never forgot it.

*   *

*

These events took place in a country which had been bled white and laid to waste. Foroughi had been gone a long time. The condition of his health had worsened, so the Shah suggested sending him abroad to be treated. Washington's 'consent' had been asked for so that he could be appointed ambassador to the United States. He was officially nominated on October 17th 1942. He could not go there however, he died on November 29th. The capital city paid him solemn homage. The young Shah who owed him his crown was present. [29]

*   *

*

There was a spectacular revival of the Tudeh, the Iranian communist party, as soon as the allied troops entered Iran. It played a deciding part during the years after the event and was supported, financed and supervised by the Soviet Union.

Chapter III

THE TUDEH

Seventy years at the service of the Soviet Union

As soon as the British and Soviet troops had settled down, the Iranian communist party rose from the ashes by taking advantage of the atmosphere of freedom, not to say of a certain anarchy, that prevailed in the country, but also, and foremost, thanks to the help and protection of the Red Army. Strangely enough, the British also helped, at least financially speaking, as we will see later on. The party took the name of Tudeh this time, meaning 'the masses'. It did not stop playing a part in the Iranian political life which could be important in different ways, especially during the Islamic revolution, and this, until the collapse of the Soviet Empire.

* *

*

Nearly all western historians and especially the Americans, date the constitution of the Iranian communist Party back to September and October 1941.

In reality, the first core of the party was created as soon as 1917. It was, in a way, an expression of the Party for justice which had just taken over control of the Russian Azerbaijan on behalf of the new masters in Moscow.

Some authors are still discussing to find out who the real founders of this movement were. [1] The crosschecking of documents, reports and studies which are available today, make it possible to advance that a group of about 150 people had joined the Iranian section of the Party for Justice. Their leader was a certain Avetis Mikaelian, who was born in 1889 in Maragheh (Iran) and known under the name of Soltan-Zadeh. He left his native town at the age of twelve, did his secondary studies in Armenia – which was Russian at the time – and later studied at the Business Institute of Moscow. He joined the Bolshevik party in 1913 and then played an important part during the Russian revolution, in the apparatus of the communist International and within the Soviet State. After being arrested on Stalin's order on January 20th 1938, he was executed on January 8th 1941. All the survivors of this first core, over a hundred of them, were thus eliminated during the Stalinist purges of the thirties. [2]

*   *

*

After many meetings and dealings, the Iranian communist Party was officially created in 1919. A first preparatory meeting had been held in May 1917 in Baku, in premises in the Sabountchi area. A certain Assadolah Ghaffar Zadeh was sent to Rasht, in the north of Iran, to create the first party networks. He was assassinated in the middle of the street soon after his arrival. [3] The constitutive congress of the party was held in Anzali (later known as Bandar Pahlavi, an Iranian harbour on the Caspian Sea) in July 1920, and appointed Heydar Amu-Oghli at its head. The latter was already well-known in Iran. He became the first leader of Iranian communism in history.

Heydar Khan Afshar, also called Amu-Oghli, came from

an Iranian family originating from the town of Orumieh (Rezaieh) in the north-west of Iran, but who had been living in Russian Azerbaijan for two generations. [4]

He was trained as an electrical engineer in Russia, and was hired by the Iranian authorities to run the electrical plants of Meshed and then Tehran at the beginning of the century. He was involved right away in the events which led to the proclamation of a constitutional monarchy in 1906.

A member of the Russian social-democratic party, he trained militants and instructed young Persian revolutionaries in the use of arms and how to make explosives. As he was involved in several political acts which were harmful to State security, he was forced to leave Iran in 1909. He was reported to be in Russia, and later in Western Europe where he led an active life among the exiles of various oriental countries, and again in Russia during the events of 1917. He reappeared in Iran later on where he took part in the political upheavals which shook the country during the last months of the First World War.

Iran was going through a very serious crisis at the time.* Despite a state of neutrality which had been officially proclaimed, the country had been laid to waste by the British, Russian and Ottoman troops during the war. Owing to the temporary exclusion of Russia which was set aflame by the revolution and the civil war, the British tried to impose a real protectorate on Iran by bribing a few shady politicians who ended up conceding London a treaty along those lines in 1919.

---

* See chapter I: I, Reza.

Movements of rebellion were getting organized in several regions, notably in the Caspian province of Guilan where Mirza Koutchik, a young religious patriot who was somewhat of a visionary, took the lead of the insurgents. This was done in an atmosphere of unanimous national resistance against British pretensions and pressures – even the frail Ahmad Shah Qajar abstained from approving the treaty.

It was in this atmosphere of confusion and using the flight to Iran of the survivors of General Denikin's White Army as an excuse that the red troops under the command of political commissar Raskolnikov landed in Anzali on May 18th 1920. This is how the 'constitutive congress' of the communist party was held under the protection of the invaders who asserted their intention to support the local insurgents.

Heydar Amu-Oghli took advantage of Mirza Koutchik's naivety and of his hatred for the British. He tried right away to create a Soviet republic in the North of the country with the help of a team of real professionals in the revolutionary field. Mirza Koutchik was appointed at its head before being quickly got rid of. He went underground again to fight against the central power and the 'Reds.'

The communists formed a new government which was nicknamed 'revolutionary'. Several of its members were of foreign origin or from Caucasia; among the latter was a certain Sayed Djafar Djavadof, a commissioner in the Department of the Interior, who was to be found again under the name of Pichevari just after the Second World War*. The running of the different Boards of the armed forces, of the 'Cheka', the military police, the 'unrest-propaganda', was simply put in the hands of the Russians.

---

* See chapter IV: The Azerbaijan crisis – The man who defeated Stalin.

In September 1920, Heydar Amu-Oghli presided over the Iranian delegation at the impressive Conference of the Peoples from the Orient which the new regime in Moscow had organized in Baku with over 1,800 participants.

He played an important part in it, together with other Bolshevik leaders such as Zinoviev, Radek or Kirov [5].

Once back in Iran, he tried to make up with Mirza Koutchik and his followers so as to calm the unrest in the local population against the new separatist regime of Guilan and its expropriation and collectivization measures. He fell into an ambush on his way back from a meeting with the latter on October 29th 1921, and was killed. He was forty-one years old at the time.

In the meantime, the situation had radically changed. Spurred on by general Reza Khan, the Iranian army had pulled itself together and was restructured. The British had lost hope of imposing their protectorate, and looked favourably upon Iran's recovery because the country could form a barrier against the Soviet invasion that threatened their Empire, particularly in the East Indies. The Tehran government had been concerned about solving the bilateral problems with the new masters of Russia for a few months and had just recognized the new regime in Moscow. A treaty of friendship and neighbourly terms had been negotiated and signed on February 26th 1921, thus eliminating the aftermath of a serious hundred-year-old dispute between the two countries and guaranteeing the safety of the southern borders of the USSR.

Moscow found no interest in fostering a separatist rebellion in the North of the country any more, and could now abandon its protégés, as it later did in 1946, with its puppet republics of Azerbaijan and Kurdistan, and in the eighties, with the Tudeh.

Consequently, it is highly plausible that Heydar Amu-

Oghli was assassinated, or that nothing was done to stop it. The Iranian army restored law and order in the Guilan province in a few days, and nearly without shedding any blood or exerting particular repression. At the time, its leader was young brigadier general named Fazlollah Zahedi. He was often found at the heart of things in the country later on.

The communist insurrection had just known the same fate as the one of the Spartacists in Berlin, the ephemeral communist republic of Bela Khun in Hungary and the first Chinese revolution; they were all contemporary.

The communist party was thus a political group that had been imported from abroad, right from the start. Its action was destined to only serve the interest of the Soviet Empire and of international communism. As soon as Moscow was able to ensure its own strategic objectives – when political realism took over ideological considerations – it abandoned its protégés to their fate, and they fell into disarray, for want of roots and popular support.

* *

*

No particular measures of repression against the local communist were to follow the dismantling of the separatist regime of the Guilan province and Heydar Amu-Oghli's death. Some of them left Iran for the Soviet Union where they were decimated during Stalinist purges. [7] Others stayed, settled down or led a discreet political life. Sayed Djafar Djavadof (later called Pichevari) was, for instance, the editorial writer of the newspaper called *Haghighat*, printed in Tehran, [8] before being arrested on other grounds. During a decade, from 1921 to 1931, Mikaelian, nicknamed Soltan-Zadeh, continued to bear the title of spokesman for the Iranian communist Party in Moscow, although it did not exist in the country any more, and he represented it at the Comintern and in 'sister parties.'

In 1928, a law was passed by the Iranian Parliament. It prohibited all 'activities with a collectivist ideology' according to a constitutional clause prohibiting activities that go against Islam and public order.

Among the few communists who were arrested after 1925, mainly for their spying activities for the benefit of the USSR, was Djavadof-Pichevari.

1937 was the year when a relatively important network of communists – mostly intellectuals from the urban middle-class, or from illustrious families, notably Qajar princes – was discovered. Fifty-three people were brought before courts, thus the name 'group of the 53' that was given to them. [9]

Its main leader was a physicist who had been trained in Germany, called Taqi Erani, who was a part-time lecturer at the University of Tehran. The group had a monthly journal published – not a clandestine one – called *Donya*, and there were no legal proceedings against it, thanks to its scientific and cultural aspect.

The network seems to have had a purely intellectual activity that was originally independent from Moscow. It is during the summer of 1935 that Erani happened to go on a scientific trip to Europe via Moscow to get in touch with the authorities of the Comintern – probably to have his organisation officially approved. Nassrollah Kamran Aslani, a delegate from the Comintern, was then sent to Iran in secret. This is when it was decided to turn the group into an Iranian communist Party, the second one of the name. A steering committee of three members was formed while they were waiting for the secret congress to be called together: there were Taqi Erani, the general-secretary, Abdolssamad Kambakhsh, an air force officer and Qajar Prince, and Mohammad Bahrami, a physician who came from an important middle-class family, in charge of finance. All the leaders of the Tudeh who had their memoirs published later on name Kambakhsh Qajar as the main representative of the Soviet apparatus in the party. [11]

The network was discovered by the police and thus the plan remained pending. The preliminary investigation for the trial of the '53' was long, the procedural rules were scrupulously respected. [12] There were many denunciations. Later, during the trial, Erani behaved impeccably. He accused Kambakhsh in particular of weakness and complicity with the police. [13] He was the future founder and then general-secretary of the Tudeh. Iradj Eskandari is very precise on the subject: 'He [Kambakhsh] had reported all the names, how the whole thing had started, who was doing what, where we had been, how we were organized... All the details... As if he had written a book...' [14]

The trial took place a year after the members of the network had been arrested. All the accused were given the right to choose their lawyers. Some of the latter contented themselves with a brief defense, others asked the Court to be lenient on account of the youth and lack of experience of their clients. Two top Tehran barristers, Mr Aghayan, who was also a member of the Chamber, and Mr Ahmad Kasrani, one of the most famous Iranian historians of the last century, pleaded with such authority that even the accused were surprised; they went way beyond legal arguments. This shows that the trial was neither formal nor set up. Taqi Erani, according to what those who knew him say, was a genuine Marxist, he was honest and even patriotic, if not nationalistic. He played his part and displayed great courage in his speech for the defense.

Many of the accused benefited from extenuating circumstances. Taqi Erani was sentenced to ten years in jail. He died on February 5th 1939. The communist propaganda pretended for a long time that he was assassinated in prison on the Shah's order. In a publication of the party which came out after the Islamic revolution, it is suggested that he had typhus and died for want of sufficient care [15]. Other leaders of the Tudeh and members of the 'group of the 53' have since confirmed this assumption. Dr Nosratollah Djahanshahlu Afshar confirmed this theory without accusing the authorities of neglecting to take care of him [16]. He was a student in his last year of medical studies when he was arrested and imprisoned with Erani. He was the future vice-Prime Minister of the separatist communist government of Azerbaijan. Anwar Khameï, another one of Erani's companions of misfortune, even suggested that the prison authorities, with Kambakhsh's complicity [17], had transferred him into a cell where a man who was sick with typhus had stayed. He even talked about Erani's transfer into a hospital [18], which would completely exonerate the authorities, but it did not prove to be true. As for Iradj Eskandari, he did not even mention Erani's death in his political memoirs.

When the trial was over and *Donya* magazine banned, the activities of Iranian communists virtually remained at a standstill until the allied troops entered Iran in 1941.

*   *

*

The new Iranian communist party was constituted in September 1941, shortly after the allied troops had invaded Iran. It was named Tudeh, 'the masses', as a precautionary measure, so that the law of 1928 could not be cited against it.

The majority of the '53', with a few survivors of the other small communist groups of the years 1921-1941, formed the core of the new group. There were also a few intellectuals from the middle-class and upper middle-class.

Prince Soleiman Mirza Eskandari, an old politician and ex-Minister of Reza Shah, was elected provisional president of the party. His role seems to have been representational and more particularly destined to be used as a front for public opinion. The party was, in fact, taken over by Marxists who had a strict Soviet allegiance and were managed by the USSR embassy. Iradj Eskandari's memoirs, among many other documents, leave no doubt about it.

At the same time, the Tudeh created a trade union confederation, called Shoraye Mottahedeh Markazi that was run by Reza Rousta. The latter was thought to be one of the men the Soviet embassy listened to most.

The Tudeh was well established in the provinces in the north of Iran that were under the control of the Soviet army, and also in Esfahan, the centre of the textile industry, in Khuzistan, the centre of the oil industry, and, of course, in the capital city.

The Anglo-Iranian Company, the franchise holder of the exploitation of Iranian oilfields and of the Abadan refinery, as well as the British embassy, helped the party financially and assisted it. Édouard Sablier [19] wrote: 'The AIOC will thus give [the party] important allowances and employ well-known militants in its installations.' In his memoirs, Iradj Eskandari gives stupefying, sometimes even comical details, on that collaboration which, on the face of it, was unnatural, and orchestrated by an Iranian employee of the British Secret Services, Mostafa Fateh [20]. The Soviet embassy provided the paper for the abundant press of the party; the one of Great Britain covered the other expenses by even offering fictitious jobs to a few journalists. Anwar Khameï relates that the latter sometimes even sent international papers to the members of the 'group of the 53' who were in prison [21]. Later, collaborators from the British embassy even published articles that were not signed in the party press [22].

The British were thus infiltrating the political instrument of their potential rival on the Iranian scene, hoping that it could prove to be useful against the national Iranian government. This is what they did later on concerning Mossadegh, the nationalist leader, and this is also how they countered certain aspects of Mohammad Reza Pahlavi's policies.

The communist leaders, for whom the end justifies the means, might have wanted to secure certain guarantees from the other foreign power that was present in the country. Some people paid attention to the help from a colonialist power that the party disparaged. The Soviet embassy used Reza Rousta [23] as a main intermediary to force them to be quiet. Everybody obeyed.

In the general elections of the summer of 1943, the Tudeh got eight seats out of thirty-six in Parliament, seven of which in the areas under the control of the Red Army, and one in Esfahan. On the other hand, the Parliament unanimously refused to validate Djavadof-Pichevari's mandate as a representative which the Red Army had helped him to win. It invoked his past as a separatist and especially as a spy.

During the years from 1941 to 1944, the party was protected by the Red Army and firmly run by the Soviet embassy, but it benefited, of course, from a few British allowances. It was extremely well established in a large part of the country. It was obviously careful not to hinder the activities of the allied forces and the war effort against the Axis powers.

As the war was coming to an end, and the victory of the Allies becoming inevitable, Moscow went back to its traditional policies of invasions and occupation that had been constant since Peter the Great, and resumed by Lenin [24].

Their immediate objective was to obtain the exploitation of the oilfields in the North of Iran. On September 26th 1944, a Soviet delegation presided by Serguei Kaftaradze, the Deputy Minister of Foreign Affairs, arrived in Tehran. Using heavy pressure, they formulated a demand in the form of a threatening note, which came to the following: they wanted the concession of the research and exploitation of the oilfields in the five provinces in the North of the country. In fact, Moscow was demanding a zone of economic influence where the communists were already very well established under the protection of the Red Army.

The Prime Minister at the time, Mohammad Saed, resisted and refused, being discreetly but courageously supported by the young Shah. The Tudeh organized violent spontaneous demonstrations to 'demand' an immediate acceptance of the Soviet diktat.

Counterdemonstrations were feared in Tehran so the Soviet troops defended the demonstrators by sending tanks and trucks brimming with armed soldiers. Iradj Eskandari was then a representative in Parliament and one of the main party leaders, consequently one of the main decision-makers concerning the demonstration. He wrote forty years later that the demonstrations were meant, in fact, to provoke the fall of the Saed Cabinet, that the 'intervention of Soviet troops was an error that was exploited by Imperialism and reactionary movements. It had distorted the main objective.' [25]

This was when a bill was passed unanimously, less the dissenting votes of eight communists, on Mohammad

Mossadegh's initiative. It forbade the government to make 'any negotiations concerning oilfields as long as foreign troops remained present on national soil.'

In the short term, the Tudeh and its custodians had just suffered a total failure. Moscow tried to reach its objectives in a different manner. In the end, the craving for oil was to cause its fall on the Iranian scene*. The Azerbaijan crisis had broken out. As regards this new Soviet defeat, it forced the Tudeh to choose a new strategy. All the more so, since over 250 important members of the party and one of its most prominent leaders, Khalil Maleki, left it together; several of them got closer to the National Front that Mossadegh was about to create, others moved away from political life**.

*   *

*

In an Iran weakened by the war and its aftermath, governed by ephemeral cabinets though they were often presided by men of quality and experience, the Tudeh, which was greatly reduced and saw its trade union organisation completely dismantled, chose a strategy of inflicting chaos so as to hasten the end of the regime, the decline of the country and take over the power in a coup of a more 'conventional' style – at least, this is what its leaders believed.

A Komiteyeterror , or litteraly speaking, 'terror committee', was founded within the party with the authorisation, it seems,

---

* See chapter IV: The Azerbaijan crisis.
** This event was called 'ensheab'or scission, and was a severe blow from the inside for the Tudeh. Khalil Maleki explained the ideological stance of the group in a book called *Confrontation*. After they had got closer to the National Front, several members of that group, still led by Maleki, created a small more or less underground socialist party which disappeared with the passing of time.

of its official management so as to supervise the operations [26], though some of its members tried to hush it up afterwards.

The first of its actions was the assassination of the journalist and writer Mohammad Massoud who was killed by two party members, among whom an officer, Captain Khosrow Ruzbeh [27].

Massoud was not a party opponent but one of the Imperial Court. The Tudeh propaganda was cleverly orchestrated and immediately held the entourage of Princess Ashraf responsible for the assassination attempt: this was a usual disinformation process whose objective was to discredit the monarchy in the eyes of public opinion. Princess Ashraf was the Shah's twin sister and the writer's favourite target.

Then there was the assassination of the representative and anti-communist journalist Ahmad Dehghan by a party member called Hassan Djaffari [28]. This time, the idea was to terrify the opponents of the party and of the Soviet Union.

Hassan Djaffari was arrested and given the death penalty during a resounding trial where he claimed responsibility for his actions. The party was subtle enough to have a certain Lieutenant Ghobadi put into the police force by its own network. He was the leader of the group that was to take Djaffari to the execution spot. Ghobadi had ensured the assassin that a commando would come to free him at the last minute [29], which explains the calm and look of expectation for 'something' to happen that were noticed by the press during the execution [30]. The Tudeh propaganda put it down to his courage.

Then spectacular acts of sabotage happened inside the Babre destroyer and at the military airport of Ghale Morghi, near the capital. The Tudeh also proceeded with the elimination of one of its own leaders, Hessam Lankarani, who was later accused of being in contact with the police [31] by his general-secretary.

The assassination attempt which was probably the main objective and was to be the final outcome of these acts of violence was the one carried out against the Shah on February 4th 1949, within the University of Tehran, where the Sovereign had gone to take part in an academic ceremony.

Two days before, the Tudeh was to commemorate the anniversary of Taqi Erani's death – the word 'martyrdom' was still used. The ceremony had been postponed by two days without any explanation to allow for the party activists – one may think – to get together in arms without drawing attention, and to intervene en masse to take control of the capital. The Shah, however, escaped by some miracle from the five bullets shot at him by Nasser Fakhr Araï, a well-known and active member of the Tudeh. His mission, for several months, had been to follow him – he had an accreditation card as a press photographer – and to assassinate him [32]. Professor Manutshehr Eghbal, a physician by trade, Minister of the Interior, the future Rector of the University, then Prime Minister, was present on the scene. He took the Sovereign in his arms, carried him to his car and drove him to the military hospital where the bullets were extracted by doctors on duty. The operation was supervised and finished by the famous surgeon, professor Yahya Adle, who had been called in emergency. Mohammad Reza Pahlavi stayed in hospital for twenty-four hours before going back to the Palace [33].

In the ensuing state of panic, the Shah's close protection was almost non-existent, and in any case, not very professional. The criminal was shot down. No precise identification of the origin of the mortal blow was possible because of the number of bullets shot at him. Rector Siassi did not care much for the chief of police, General Mohammad Ali Saffari, a man of full integrity and loyalty. In his memoirs, he accuses him of being the perpetrator of the shot that was fatal for the criminal so as to make any further inquiry impossible! What a fanciful assumption! It is true that the learned academic continued to consider General Haj Ali Razmara, the head of general staff at the time, responsible after all the documents were published – among which the narrations and memoirs of the very leaders of the Tudeh. He might have wanted to give credence to the theory of a certain connivance between the two of them.

The communist leaders went underground [34] in the moments that followed the failure of the Shah's assassination attempt. It was immediately broadcast on the national radio channel so as to reassure people.

In the last few years, after the Islamic revolution and the collapse of communism, nearly all the leaders of the party have recognized its responsibility in this infamy while trying to exonerate themselves and accusing one another [35].

Shortly after the attempt, the government had a law passed that 'outlawed' the party. Most of its leaders left Iran for the Soviet Union. Some were arrested and later managed to find incredible ways of fleeing to the same place.

The Tudeh was led to change its tactics yet another time.

*   *

*

The Tudeh continued to have a public activity though it was officially forbidden and pretended to have gone underground. The government did not have the means to fight it, and maybe not even the desire to do so, so as not to hurt the Soviet leaders' feelings. A famous morning newspaper called *Bessouye-Ayandeh* was presented in such a way that it really looked like *Rahbar*, the party's banned paper, and reflected its positions.

The party benefited from vast and luxurious premises, its members met in public and organized street demonstrations under the cover of the Association for the Defence of Peace ("L'Appel de Stockholm" or Stockholm Appeal), the Association of Iranian Women, the Cultural Iran-Soviet Association, etc...

The authorities did not react.

In these times of trouble and uncertainty, a new problem shook Iran: the movement for the nationalisation of all the oil resources that was launched and symbolized by Mohammad Mossadegh*, the great eloquent speaker.

Public opinion was nearly unanimous. The Shah unreservedly supported the man who was soon to be his head of government, despite British pressure and a certain mutual incompatibility which was to get worse later on between them. The historian Arthur Conte [36] wrote: 'For London, the worst thing was that, in that situation, Mohammad Reza Pahlavi, the King of Kings, exceptionally agreed with a minister that he hated.'

The only opposition then came from the Tudeh which created an Association for the abrogation of the agreements passed with the Anglo-Iranian Oil Company, condemned the nationalisation of oil resources and continued to claim the right granted to the Soviets to exploit the oil concessions in the North of the country. One of the main leaders of the party [37] admitted later on, like all the others, that it was a suicidal attitude and wrote: 'We think that this will lead to a strengthening of democracy and freedom in Iran. It will lessen the influence of the British company on the country.'

---

* See chapter V: The oil crisis – The man who chased the British away.

All its leaders admitted later on that the party attitude was particularly negative and unclear* during that whole period of strong unrest. The party was the main reason for a reversal of public opinion in 1953 and for Mossadegh's fall**. It paid a high price for it. A long period of political wilderness, clandestinity, exile and personal tragedy then started for its members. It was to last from 1953 until 1978.

* *

*

As soon as the Mossadegh era was over, the authorities ruthlessly fought the party, dismantled its networks, chased its active militants by enforcing a law on national security that had been promulgated by the latter, and by creating the Savak***.

In the autumn of 1953, the military organisation of the party was discovered and rapidly dismantled. The Iranian special services arrested a certain Captain Abolhassan Abbassi, apparently quite by chance, and managed to identify and expose about six hundred officers who were members of the military organisation of the party. They were all prosecuted. Twenty-seven of them were executed. Yet, the list of the non-commissioned officers who belonged to the organisation could never be found.

Public opinion in Iran and abroad was amazed to see the extent to which the Iranian armed forces had been penetrated by the Soviets. Some of the officers arrested even held key positions in the Imperial guard. Was it a question of staging a military coup, which Stalin already seemed to have considered in 1927, in order to overthrow Reza Shah, whereas he had a

---

* See chapter V: The oil crisis – The man who chased the British away.
** *Ibidem.*
*** See chapter VII: The Savak – A great misunderstanding.

lot less elements? It is not impossible [38]. Moscow managed to have a lasting influence in several countries of the Third World later on, thanks to coups organised by 'progressive' officers.

As for Captain Abbassi, it became known after the Islamic revolution that he was with Ruzbeh, one of the two assassins of the journalist and writer Mohammad Massoud, and probably the one who carried out the fatal blow [39].

Soon after he was arrested, and because of his 'cooperation', Captain Abbassi benefited from a preferential measure and was released. The Iranian 2nd Bureau organized his departure for the United States, ensuring him he would remain incognito and be safe; then he was lost track of [40].

Three general-secretaries ran the exiled party apparatus from 1953 to 1978:
– Abdolssamad Kambakhsh, a Qajar Prince, the man of the Soviet apparatus in the party, until 1961.
– Reza Radmanesh, born into a famous influential family from the North of Iran, former university professor, until January 1971.
– Iradj Eskandari, another Qajar Prince, a nephew of the one who had been symbolically chosen as chairman of the party in 1941, a professional lawyer, till January 23rd 1979.

During that period and until 1974, the activity inside the party was most limited, whereas, outside, there were ridiculous quarrels over people's ambitions which opposed party members – three thousand, according to a serious estimate [41] – many of whom were interned in Soviet camps or relegated to the far away regions of central Asia [42]. Many of them died there.

Moscow maintained excellent relations with Iran whose rising power and determination were certain, and the 500 [43] to 1,000 [44] Iranians there who were still affiliated to the party at the beginning of the seventies, kept a very discreet attitude towards the government. The main opposition came from small ultra-left groups, who mainly acted as terrorists.

The activity of the Tudeh was progressively strengthened from 1974 onwards, at the same time some serious problems arose in the country.

During the decisive year of 1978, the members of the Tudeh played an important part in the revolutionary process, the outcome of which was the fall of the monarchy and Ruhollah Khomeini's seizure of power.

*   *

*

The Tudeh reappeared on the Iranian political scene in 1978 without meeting any resistance from the authorities which were most anxious not to go against the liberalisation policy suggested by the Carter administration. *Navid*, the party newspaper, was circulated freely in Tehran. The former members of the party had sometimes become senior civil servants of the Imperial administration, and now made a point of being seen. Like in the two years that followed the attempt against the Shah in 1949, the Tudeh created or took part in creating organisations which were used as relays or covers for its activity: The National Association of Writers, National Association of Academics. The dialogue, not to say cooperation, between the communists and the extremists identifying with Islam – those who were later called 'fundamentalists', and then 'Islamic fundamentalists' – as well as elements from the National Front declaring themselves supporters of former Prime Minister Mossadegh' ideas, and more particularly the Marxist ultra-left groups, openly became clear and was of a deciding influence later on.

It is also from September 1978 onwards that the extent of the infiltration of communist networks in the oil and banking sectors, and more particularly in the national television – as the Shah bitterly remarked -was discovered. As for the television, its obliging management, or complicity, let them take over most of the control levers – these were usual tactics followed in infiltration measures and also often used elsewhere.

At the time, a certain reservation seemed to be shown by party members regarding such a public and active cooperation with the religious extremists. Even though he approved of the current movement, Iradj Eskandari allegedly did not hesitate to denounce – in private, one must say – 'Khomeini's obscurantism, and that of the mullahs around him' [46]. The same Eskandari, who was the general-secretary of the Tudeh at that time, failed to mention Khomeini's name in an official declaration in support of the revolutionary process [47]. The Soviet Union assessed the advantages it could draw from the events, and once more disregarded the ideological considerations. The Tudeh followed Moscow's line to the letter.

On January 23rd 1979, a few days after the Shah had left Iran and Moscow had become certain that the process started by Washington would work out*, there was a spectacular reversal in the Tudeh's strategy. Once again, it is likely to have been imposed by Moscow.

The central committee of the party declared in a press release that 'comrade Iradj Eskandari had been relieved from his post of general-secretary on January 16th**, and comrade Dr Nourreddine Kianouri had been appointed to take over.'
By having these changes operated, the Soviets believed

---
* See chapter XII: Iran and the West – Ambiguous relations.
** The date of Mohammad Reza Shah Pahlavi's departure.

that they could manipulate and infiltrate the fundamentalist clergy more easily and that they could make the American plan fall through: the USA wanted to create an 'Islamic belt' in the South of the USSR, even encourage a certain religious unrest within the Soviet Empire.

Kianouri, the new general-secretary, was the man who was to symbolize these new tactics and see them through. He came from a well-known family of religious people. Sheikh Fazlollah Nouri, his grand-father, was a famous ultra-reactionary prelate whom Khomeini openly admired. The revolutionaries had him executed after a failed coup against the Constitution in 1909.

As soon as he was appointed, Kianouri did not stop flaunting servile admiration in front of Khomeini and the Islamic revolution: 'We believe that the Iranian revolution is one of the greatest revolutions in modern times whose innovations deserve to be studied by researchers and sociologists... Indeed, this revolution has a religious aspect, but it is not its main characteristic, for it is above all anti-imperialist*, popular and democratic.' 48

The role the party played was thus determining for the Islamic revolution. Édouard Sablier even wrote: 'the Tudeh is the one who will wreck the monarchical regime.' 49

Ayatollah Khomeini's triumph corresponded with the take-over of Islamic courts by the members of the party who had come out of their dormant condition, and by those who were coming back from exile. They also took control of broadcasting companies and of several widely-distributed newspapers which were expropriated and became state-owned.

---

* Years later, Kianouri's predecessor, Iradj Eskandari, admitted the American origin, thus the 'imperialist' origin in his eyes, of the Khomeini operation. *Mémoires politiques*, *op.cit.*,1988, volume II, p.204.

Some of them grew a beard wore the turban and converted to genuine false hodjatoleslam or ayatollahs*.

At the same time, the ultra-left extremist groups such as the people's Mujaheddins – today considered to be dissidents – professed a 'Marxist-Islamic' ideology which was very close to that of the Cambodian Pol Pot. They took care of the dirty work for the new regime: executions, assassinations, looting, supervision and surveillance of prisons. There was a remarkable division of labour within the 'progressive left.' [50]

Two and a half years later, when the orthodox wing of the regime got rid of its ultra-left – now useless – allies in a terrible blood-shed, the Tudeh also severely condemned its leftist comrades, and took part in their elimination without any hesitation. Their attitude could be compared to that of the communists towards the anarchists and Trotskyists during the Spanish civil war.

Together with Kianouri, the Tudeh began a permanent and enthusiastic collaborationist policy with the Islamic regime. It even became the only official party authorized outside the Islamic Revolution Party, the official governmental group, from 1981 till 1983. It did not spare any effort to support and consolidate the totalitarianism of a religious nature that had been set up in Iran. According to a French personality who was very close to the leading circles in Tehran [51], the Tudeh was used as a driving belt by the authorities of the Islamic regime, for information of a strategic, military or political nature that came from Moscow, especially the one concerning the Iraqi invasion of September 1980.

The party unreservedly condemned its former ultra-left allies and approved of their elimination [52]; it nonetheless called

---

* Titles given to the members of the Shiite clergy.

for the 'union of all the popular forces for the victory of the great anti-dictatorial, anti-imperialist and popular revolution in Iran.'[53] Besides, its leader insisted on 'the convergence of interests in Iran between the communists and the Muslims [that were] part of a global development that unites Marxists and popular religious forces.'[54]

*   *

*

There was a big surprise in February 1983, despite the perfect integration of Iranian communists into the Islamic regime and the determining role they played in it: the Islamic prosecutor of the capital ordered the 'suspension' of the party. Some of its well-known leaders, notably general-secretary Kianouri and his wife, Maryam Firouz, also called 'the red princess' – she came from an influential side of the Qajar dynasty –, were arrested and imprisoned. Given the presence of very many members of the party in the special services of the regime and in the public prosecutor's department, it is hard to imagine that its leaders had not been warned, that the scenario had not been negotiated in some sort of a way, or that the order to let them catch them had not come from a higher level, from the Soviets. 'The easiness with which Mr Kianouri and his friends were arrested – they were nabbed in bed at the milkman's hour'[55] surprised more than one observer. They saw their doubts and questions somewhat confirmed by the events of the aftermath.

The Islamic regime was involved in an endless war with Iraq that started in 1980 and ended in 1988. It was isolated on the diplomatic level, accused, not without reason, of being involved in international terrorism, with a Western world that worried about its progressive 'Sovietization'*. So it needed to give credence to the theory of a change of direction and a return to an 'authentic nonalignment' – one of the most common slogans during the revolution.

Moscow was going to keep most of its influence while dropping some of its discredited and now useless pawns. Once again, like in so many other countries, Moscow's imperial strategy prevailed over its ideological preoccupations.

When the measure was made public, an intense propaganda action was immediately triggered in the West, more particularly in France. The famous Parisian papers ran as a headline: 'A decisive turning point for Iran' [56], 'The great quarrel that opposes Iran and the USSR' [57], 'A political failure for the Kremlin' [58]... In spite of all the facts that prove this hasty and naïve interpretation wrong, even a 'break between Tehran and Moscow' [59] was evoked later on.

Nevertheless, the Tudeh reasserted its support for the regime which was apparently persecuting its leaders shortly afterwards: 'Even after the arrest of our leaders, our policy of support for the Islamic revolution has not changed.' [60]

The affair was kept silent for months, once the effect of its announcement had been achieved. Numerous important revelations were made on the central role played by the Iranian regime in international terrorism, and particularly on the extreme or ultra-left revolutionary subversion which was ransacking many countries. The resumption of the propaganda – or disinformation – operation concerning the anti-communist attitude of the Tehran government now became useful again. A 'major lawsuit' against the Tudeh was announced right away.

---

* See chapters III and XIII.

The campaign was generously relayed by some of the media, especially the European ones.

On January 21st 1984, 'the heavy prison sentence' given to 86 leaders of the Tudeh by a 'revolutionary tribunal of the armed forces' was announced. Some media talked of the 'intensification of the anti-communist campaign in Iran.' Some of the newspapers even dedicated some of their editorials to the subject.
Yet:
– Only completely unknown names appeared on the list of the people convicted on January 21st, and there were none of the party leaders.Provided these people actually existed, did they even belong to the list of 50,000 members designed by some of the party's trustworthy researchers [62]?
– 'The revolutionary tribunal of the armed forces' was, in fact, constituted of one judge only, Mohammad Nik, also called ayatollah Reycharri, who was well known to Western anti-terrorism services, but for other reasons: his involvement in certain networks in the West and especially in the Levant.
— In the meantime, an ideological lobbyist group, the Hodjatieh was 'dissolved'. It had originally been responsible for the 'suspension' of the Tudeh and had provided the indictment file for it. The Minister of the Interior, Nategh Nouri, even declared himself in favour of a 'death sentence' for the party [63]

On April 30th 1983, Mr Kianouri and some other incarcerated leaders appeared on T.V. The general-secretary praised the Islamic revolution once more, 'firmly admitting' [64] and declared 'having betrayed Imam [Khomeini]'s party line and deserving the harshest punishment.' [65] Shortly afterwards, the Tudeh leaders were transferred to villas to the North of the Iranian capital. Only one of them, Ehsan Tabari, a talented writer and number two of the hierarchy, even continued for a certain time to write for the Tehran newspapers which were all state-owned.

They were quickly forgotten. Sometimes, the death of one or of the other would be announced.
This is how the last stage of the existence and activity of one of the oldest communist parties in the world ended, 'a genuine tragic farce.' 66

*   *

*

The reaction of the Soviet press to this process was extremely discreet and limited to the official apparatus of the CPSU.
As for the Soviet government, it paid homage to the Tehran leaders, resuming the theory often set forth by communist ideologists according to which the Islamic revolution was only a first step of the revolution*: 'The clergy' Moscow declared officially, 'made a good job of the immediate tasks of the national struggle.' 67
In that episode, the Soviet government had, like in so many other times, and not only in Iran, privileged the interest and imperial objectives of the USSR. They simply regarded the ideological discourse as a means to an end.
The 'suspension' of the Tudeh and the disinformation organized in the West to substantiate the idea of an anti-communist tendency of the regime that stemmed from the Islamic revolution thus contributed to making the sovietizing of Iran easier, without arousing too much emotion.

---
* See chapters III and XIII.

That episode resembles the Soviet approach to some other regimes subjected to Moscow's rule which nevertheless harshly reprimanded communist parties.

When Leonid Brezhnev referred to the Soviet policy in the Arab-Muslim world, he declared in front of several Eastern leaders, among whom Mr Gomulka and Mr Ulbricht: 'Nasser has his head in the clouds, at least concerning questions of ideology, but he is a decent chap and he has proved that he can be counted on ... If we want to make some progress, we, indeed, have to accept certain sacrifices... One of these sacrifices is the fact that Nasser is persecuting Egyptian communists; he, nevertheless, has the right temperament to put himself at the head of the Arab liberation movement, which, for us, is priceless at the moment. This is exactly where the application of Leninist principles reveals itself to be fruitful: one is to join forces with certain movements of different tendencies, if it can, at one time or another, be useful to the revolution. Once the Arab masses have become aware of their true interests, we won't need a Nasser any more.' [68]

*   *

*

Since the collapse of the Soviet Empire, a few rare survivors of the Iranian communist movement, and sometimes of the Gulag, have still claimed to be faithful to 'scientific socialism', and, in their exile, they have founded small groups that are inspired by this ideology. Several of them have completely dropped any political activity. Others belong to the leading spheres of the Islamic republic. Others yet, are using the old tactics of infiltration and try to exercise an intellectual magisterium in certain circles of the Iranian diaspora.

Chapter IV

THE AZERBAIJAN CRISIS
The man who defeated Stalin

Germany surrendered in May 1945, and Japan, in August. On September 2nd, the Japanese Empire's act of surrender was signed in Tokyo harbour. That is when the six months period started, at the end of which the Americans, British and Soviets were to have left the country.

Iranian diplomats immediately began to take the necessary steps to define and organize the conditions of the evacuation.

On October 21st, Anoushivaran Sepahbodi, the Minister of Foreign Affairs, declared to Parliament that following exchanges of notes with London and Moscow, and assurance the Iranian ambassadors accredited to the two capitals received, the allied forces would have ended this evacuation on March 2nd 1946, at the latest.

The American forces were not mentioned in his declaration. They had already started preparing for their departure. Besides, neither the government, nor public opinion, wished to see them leave before the other two. Their presence was seen more as a guarantee than anything else.

The evacuation of British troops started on October 29th. Despite the solemn commitments, the tripartite treaty and the declaration at the Tehran conference, the Soviets did not move.

Iran was going to be one of the first scenes of the East-West confrontation of the 'cold war', after having been subjected to the world war and its aftermath. What historians later called the 'Iranian crisis' then started.

* *

*

Iran was coming out of the war bled white, and this is but a euphemism.

As soon as the allied troops had entered the country and demobilization time had been decided on, this, without the authorization of the commander-in-chief of the armed forces – the Shah – and without consulting with the general staff, most of the army's weapons were impounded before being shipped to the Soviet Union. This was done in the name of 'British aid', for an amount of 10 million pounds Sterling [1]. London apparently wanted to use this booty to offer urgent assistance to the USSR.

All the goods that belonged to Iran were confiscated in Great Britain and in the Soviet Union, for a total of 33.5 million pounds.

The Iranian railroads were submitted to similar financial losses which, according to the British, amounted to 8,951,332 pounds. When the allied troops entered the country, Iran had 80 locomotives. The British provided another 270 to increase the turnround of the Transiranian. The ones which could still be used were sent back to Great Britain as soon as the hostilities ended. The British demanded that the others, the ones left on the spot – wrecks more than anything else – should be paid for. This is what was done. Thus, in spite of the commitments made, no compensation was given to the Iranian 'ally' for the use of the Transiranian, the main rail link with the USSR. It was actually left in such a pitiful state that over a decade was needed to restore it.

The Iranian railroads had 1,993 carriages. The Allies provided another 7,792 for their own use, not without demanding that they should be paid by Iran. There were 3,500 technicians and workers who were assigned to the Allies' military activities by the Iranian railroads. They were completely remunerated by Iran, despite the commitments made.

Thus, the damage was assessed to be of 64,153,166 pounds Sterling, at the very least.

All of the public companies were exploited for the benefit of the Allies during the war. There was no compensation! As for the Soviets, they were engaged in a thorough looting of the zone they were stationed in.

There is no need to even talk about collateral damage. During the whole time, diplomats and the Iranian authorities would protest about one case after another, gather documents, work on files. The Ministry of Foreign Affairs had prepared a 'white paper' in two big volumes on the subject. [2] It was not even deemed worthy to be published since the country had other, more serious problems to deal with, and, more particularly, needed the support of the USA and Great Britain when faced with Moscow. It was better to avoid a dispute on the subject.

The American attitude was more decent on the whole. All the services and goods provided by the Iranians were properly paid. Nevertheless, the 11 million dollars in Iranian assets in the United States, everything the country owned there, were demanded and received in payment of the goods, equipments and buildings left in Iran.

On April 17th 1947, a global assessment of the Iranian war debt was carried out and published: it reached 955 million dollars, a colossal amount at the time [3].

As Iran was to face one of the most severe crises in its history, it found itself destitute and exhausted. The figures did not mean much any more. In any case, the Anglo-American allies never completely settled their debts. However, they obviously supported Iran in the adversity of its confrontation with the USSR. Yet, the attitude of Great Britain, as we will see, was often on the verge of double-dealing, and this, in the tradition of its relations with Iran since the beginning of the 19th century.

*   *

*

While the Americans and British were causing no problems evacuating the country, the Red Army not only stayed – a violation of its commitments – but they also multiplied incidents in their zone.

On November 5th 1945, the distribution by the Soviets to the members of the Tudeh of two trucks carrying light weapons in the town of Adjabchir in Azerbaijan was reported. During the night of November 5th-6th, over five hundred armed men blocked the way on the Tehran-Tabriz road. On the 15th, there was unrest in Maraghe, a town in the province of the same name. The local gendarmerie intervened and thirteen suspects were arrested. The next day, the Red Army besieged the prison and released them. On the 20th, the town of Sarabe was handed over to the rioters by the Red Army. They slaughtered gendarmes and systematically looted the place.

On the 21st, The Red Army gave seven trucks full of weapons to the Kurds subjected to the Tudeh's rule in the small town of Mahabad.

On November 25th, the communists took control of several towns in the province; the Red Army disarmed the tiny garrisons of the gendarmerie and handed their weapons over to the insurgents.

On the 24th, the United States protested to Moscow against these interferences. On the 27th, Washington and London together, sent Moscow harsh words against the violation of its commitments, and they called for the respect of the signed treaties. It was in vain.

There were large-scale popular demonstrations in the whole country to support the central government, including in the zone that was now occupied by the Red Army. Reza Pahlavi's name and portrait became again the symbols of national resistance. The Shah multiplied his visits in the capital as well as in the provinces. He was cheered by the crowds everywhere he went.

A small detachment of the gendarmerie that had been sent by the town of Saghez to Mahabad was stopped by the Red Army.

On the 26th, the Chamber unanimously demanded, except for eight representatives from the Tudeh, the evacuation of the Soviet forces, and protested against Moscow's interferences.

On November 29th, the garrison in Tabriz, the main

administrative centre of the Azerbaijan province, was attacked by a group of rebels. The Red Army stood aside. The attack was repelled by the army.

On December 1st, the Soviet Union Embassy declared in a note handed over to the Iranian government that the USSR was in no way involved in the current events.

On December 2nd, the Chamber solemnly condemned the events. The rebellion was officially called 'an armed uprising against the independence and territorial integrity of the country.'

A small task force was sent from Tehran so as to reinforce the Tabriz garrison – two army and one gendarmerie units, half a dozen tanks from the thirties. They were stopped in their tracks by the Red Army 100 kilometres west of the capital, at the place called Charif-Abad.

On December 4th, the town of Marand fell under the control of the communists after a bloody riot. The local policemen were slaughtered, and many houses and businesses looted.

Morteza Gholi Bayat, a former Prime Minister who was famous for his 'spirit of conciliation' and his 'great patience', as the Tehran press wrote, was appointed Governor of Azerbaijan and managed to land in Tabriz.

On December 6th, he asked the population for calm, and 'all the political groups' to an honest debate.

The government had now lost control over the whole Azerbaijan province and a small part of Kurdistan. The Governor was surrounded, the Tabriz garrison stopped by the Red Army.

*   *

*

The Tudeh, the communist party, wound itself up in both of these provinces and then integrated into the two newly formed political groups: the Azerbaijan Democratic Party and the Kurdistan Democratic Party. One of the Tudeh leaders pretended years later that the decision was made without the party's assent, and that he had been notified during a meeting of his central committee. It was allegedly during that meeting that it was decided to send a letter of protest to the secretariat of the CPSU, but not one of the fifteen members present apparently dared sign the letter, and thus it was never sent. [4]

While the events were unfolding and a certain national unanimity manifested itself all over the country around a sovereign who showed good will, and exuded energy but remained, however inexperienced. The capital was nothing but political intrigues, clan struggles and personal rivalries. The Soviet and British embassies played a transparent part in all this. The Tudeh was protected by the presence of Soviet troops and fuelled permanent unrest.

A few politicians were the only pillars of stability and especially, of a certain continuity of the State. They rallied round the Shah and protected him.

The Cabinet of the time was presided over by Ebrahim Hakimi. Following the affairs that occurred from November 1st 1945 to January 21st 1946, it decided to take the case to the United Nations. The Tudeh, the political factions and the Soviets provoked a general outcry against the head of government. He held out, and the case was put on the agenda of the Security Council with the support of the Americans and the British. In London and Washington, ambassadors

Hassan Taghizadeh and Hossein Ala distinguished themselves in difficult procedures and manoeuvres – a genuine David against Goliath type of fight to defend the cause of their country.

The fact that the case was taken to the recently created United Nations was a success for Tehran which was faced with a violently opposed Moscow.

*   *

*

Then things started moving really fast.

On December 12th, armed men protected by Soviet soldiers took control of Tabriz. Eighty people who called themselves members of Azerbaijan Parliament then chose a Prime Minister, Djafar Pichevari, an old hobbyhorse who had come back from the Soviet stables. The latter chose ten ministers. The autonomous government of Azerbaijan was put in place. The same scenario unfolded, on a smaller scale, in Mahabad, under the supervision of the Ghazi brothers.

Governor Bayat was sent back to Tehran. Brigadier general Derakhchani, the Tabriz garrison commander, received the order from his hierarchy to destroy all his weapons and ammunition, organise the departure of his officers and non-commissioned officers for the capital, and demobilize the conscripts. Any armed confrontation with the Soviet forces was inconceivable.

The resistance in the small garrison of Rezaieh, the main town in western Azerbaijan, led to a massacre which is not unlike the one of Katyn that was perpetrated by the Red Army in 1943.

In Tabriz, General Derakhchani disobeyed orders and took over the power of the police and the gendarmerie. He then declared that the order had been given to lay down arms and evacuate the barracks, folowing a decision taken during 'a meeting of the senior officers of the garrison.' 5

In February 1979, it was also the invocation of a decision made during a meeting of senior officers that had no legal existence, and under American pressure, that made the Iranian army let the revolutionaries take control of the country.

During a press conference, Derakhchani justified his decision, thanked the 'leftist press' for supporting him, qualified the government of having shown 'no good judgement', and of being 'idiotic.' 6 When a reporter said to him: 'You are accused of yielding in front of 200 professional armed rioters who had come from the other side of the border [Causasia]', the General answered: 'No, this was an authentic movement...'

Back in Tehran, Derakhchani was arrested and brought before a military tribunal. He was given the death penalty for disobeying orders and for treason. The Shah commuted the sentence to fifteen years in jail. Derakhchani benefited from a reduction of sentence and was thus released early. He was even polemical in the press to justify himself. In 1976, He was involved in a spy network for the benefit of the Soviet Union and got caught in flagrante delicto. He was brought before a court again. This time, the Islamic revolution saved him. One may think that he was a Soviet agent.

*   *

*

With the proclamation of Azerbaijan's separatism, Iran got involved in a crisis that was set up by the USSR, a scenario for a civil war, a division of the country, like in Korea, Vietnam or Greece at about the same time.

Notwithstanding the Tudeh, a few elements in Tehran gave their support to the separatist attempt. The most surprising one is that of the Iran party, which identified with Mossadegh, the nationalist leader, and which soon got involved in a popular front type operation with the Tudeh: the Iran party qualified the Azerbaijan events in its paper of a 'movement for the creation of a national government, an insurrection against the enemies of the people, an insurrection against all those who want to smother and pull apart the people, and those who govern.' [7]

*   *

*

On January 9th 1946, a big religious ceremony was organised by the government in Tehran, to pay homage to the soldiers, non-commissioned officers and officers who had been murdered by the rebels or who had died fighting them. Great numbers of people came and gave a symbolic support to the upholders of national unity.

On the 10th, an Arab armed group, under the orders of Sheikh Abdollah Djasseb, Sheikh Khazaal' son, crossed the border over to Iraq which was then under the military control of Great Britain, and actually a British protectorate. They attacked the Khoramshahr harbour on the Shatt al Arab, occupied the customs house, and committed a few acts of violence. The police forces reacted immediately. The invaders fled, crossed the border again and remained unpunished on the other side.

The British intrigues started in the South of the country.

On January 13th, the Parliament passed a law to provide pensions for the families of the officers and soldiers who had died in Azerbaijan, this despite a strong opposition from the Tudeh representatives and from a few bedfellows.

On the 21st, violent fighting took place in the town of Zanjan between guerrilla fighters led by the Zolfaghari brothers, an old local aristocratic family, and the separatist forces. Armed resistance did not stop increasing in Azerbaijan after that.

On the same January 21st, the Hakimi government fell.
On the 27th, Ahmad Ghavam was contacted by Parliament to become Prime Minister. The same day, he was asked to form a government by the Shah, with the mission to 'solve the crisis' and 'restore order in the country.'

* *

*

'In that critical situation, the prowess of Prime Minister Ahmad Ghavam, a veteran of the Iranian political world, was put to the test.' [8]

Édouard Sablier wrote: 'When he became Prime Minister for the third time, Ahmad Ghavam was sixty-four years old, he was a veteran in Iranian politics. For the first time, in 1921, he had succeeded in having foreign troops evacuated, in stabilizing finances, in establishing a balance between the Russian and English influences. This time, the situation was even more dramatic: the opponent was not the frail Bolshevik Russia any more, but the powerful Soviet Union which had just gained a victory over Germany, and appeared like one of the two giants who fought over the world.' [9] This time, Ghavam had to face Stalin who made the world tremble.

Ahmad Ghavam came from a family of senior civil servants of the Qajar dynasty. He was Hassan Vosough ol Dowleh's younger brother, a famous poet, but also the Prime Minister who signed a treaty for a quasi-protectorate with Great Britain, and who never got over it, politically speaking. Ahmad Ghavam was a man who was haughty, cultured, elegant, self-important, and who believed in his mission for Iran. He had General Reza Khan as Minister of War, and knowing that he inspired fear and restraint in the latter, he left the country shortly before he ascended to the throne and went to spend many years in Paris. It seems that both men did not really care much for each other, but that they respected each other.

Even before he formed a government, Ghavam tried to clear the way to find a political solution to the crisis with the Soviet Union. He ordered the Iranian representative to the United Nations to carry on with the complaint filed with the Security Council. At the Security Council, on January 29th 1946, ambassador Hassan Taghizadeh was, once more, to face Andreï Vichinsky, the notorious prosecutor from the Moscow trials who represented the USSR at the U.N. On the 30th, the Council unanimously suggested to the two parties to start direct negotiations so as to reach a solution. Despite the insistence of the Moscow representative, the Council did not get rid of the file. Iran had scored a goal.

On February 4th, ambassador Taghizadeh welcomed Andreï Vichinsky to his embassy in London. The American and British ambassadors to the United Nations attended the meeting. Ali Soheili, the old diplomat who had negotiated the tripartite treaty before becoming Prime Minister, gave Taghizadeh the help of his great experience.

On the same day, Moscow declared that the Soviet government was ready to welcome an Iranian delegation. The Red Army did not move from the North of Iran. Azerbaijan and a small part of Kurdistan knew a state of rebellion, and Tehran, apart from a positive point of law that was made against Moscow, had virtually no trump card in hand.

*   *

*

The situation on the field was confused... The town of Meianeh, where the population lacked enthusiasm for the separatists, was left in the hands of the looters on February 1st. Many dwellings were set on fire and opponents killed.

On February 9th, the Zolfaghari brothers called the whole population of the province to an uprising against the separatist power. Many people went underground.

On the 11th, in Mian Do Ab, a Kurdish town, the population rose up against the separatists and chased them out. The national Iranian flag was hoisted on the subprefecture.

Demonstrations in favour of the central power were organised all over the country.

On February 14th, Ahmad Ghavam eventually presented his ministers to Parliament and the representatives gave their consent.

*   *

*

On February 18th, he left for Moscow at the head of a delegation. Iran did not even have an aeroplane to transport its delegation. A Russian, non-pressurized twin-engined aircraft was used. It landed in Moscow on the 19th, after a stop-over in Baku. On the 20th, there was a first work session at the Kremlin with Molotov, the Soviet Minister of Foreign Affairs.

On February 21st, Stalin and Ghavam had a tête-à-tête which lasted two hours. The two delegations met separately.

On March 2nd, the Soviet forces evacuated the towns of Semnan and Sharud, in the Khorasan province, in the northeast of the country. It was a first sign of good will, or maybe the beginning of the execution of the commitments made. On the 4th, it was the turn of Meshed, the main administrative town in the province, to be evacuated.

On March 5th, Stalin, with much pomp, gave a dinner at the Kremlin in Ghavam's honour. There was a diplomatic incident: Ghavam noticed that his whole delegation had not been invited, and refused to go. The Soviet protocol did not dare inform Stalin; they begged the Iranian Prime Minister to come, but he stood his ground, of course. The Little Father of the people was finally informed. The Iranians were offered official excuses. The dinner took place much later but the Russians saved face and the atmosphere was decent. According to various testimonies in the press, Ghavam had a haughty attitude with Stalin.

On March 6th, the United States summoned Moscow to respect its commitments and to evacuate its forces.

The Tudeh intensified unrest in Tehran and in several other cities so as to put pressure on the government. Pro- and anti-communists were fighting in the streets of the capital. On that very day of March 6th, the great Iranian historian Ahmad Kasrani and his secretary were assassinated in broad daylight by two members of the group called the Fedayeen of Islam, an Iranian branch of the Muslim Brothers. Small groups which were later called Islamists got their names in the papers in Iran for the first time.

On March 10th, Ghavam and his delegation came back from Moscow. Two procedures seemed to be taking place at the same time.

The trip to Moscow apparently did not end up with an agreement. The Prime Minister declared to an Iranian newspaper on March 15th: 'The Soviet government did not want to accept my insistent request to evacuate its armed forces. As far as I am concerned, I could not tolerate some of its requests. Since the Red Army has not evacuated the country and Azerbaijan continues to claim its autonomy and self-determination, the Iranian delegation went home without obtaining the expected results.' [10] Consequently, Iran increased its pressure on the United Nations on Ghavam's instructions.

On March 26th and 27th, there were stormy sessions at the Security Council. The United States gave their full support to the Iranian cause.

On the other hand, a secret arrangement procedure seemed to have been made. On March 25th, Joseph Stalin himself declared that the Soviet Union would respect its commitments and 'progressively' evacuate its armed forces. The same day, the troops that were stationed around the capital organized their departure, and before long, were quickly on the move.

Sadtchicov was appointed as new ambassador to Tehran.

He was invested with full powers to negotiate and reach an agreement.

On April 4th 1946, a declaration in three points that had

been signed by Ghavam and Sadtchicov was published in Tehran:

– The evacuation of Soviet troops was to end on May 4th.

– A mixed Iranian and Soviet company was to be created to exploit the oil fields in the North of the country. The law allowing for its creation was to be submitted to Parliament within seven months, as soon as the legislative elections had taken place.

– The Azerbaijan problem was a domestic affair for Iran. The Iranian government was to commit itself to finding a peaceful solution in a spirit of benevolence and conciliation.

Iran had been given some respite.
Moscow believed it had won the game.
The diplomatic game was to go on.

*   *

*

Ghavam started endless negotiations with the separatists, to no avail. Each time he was under strong pressure, he pleaded that he had to refer to the Sovereign, then came back to say he had failed in reaching his agreement.

The Tabriz and Mahabad authorities reinforced their military cooperation. A central command was set up, supervised by Red Army officers who were presented as 'advisers'. Moscow armed the separatists. A certain Gholam Yahya, a Soviet citizen and KGB officer, was appointed general and promoted to commander-in-chief of that united army.

While Ghavam was playing the card of a solution

that would be favourable to Moscow to all appearances, a potential armed confrontation was discreetly being prepared in Tehran.

The Soviet Union thought it had got the concession of the oil in the North of the country which was subject to further ratification by the Parliament. On August 3rd 1946, Ghavam had three communist ministers become members of his government so as to reassure them even more. Besides, Allahyar Saleh of the Iran party was entrusted with the Justice portfolio; he was then one of the communists' road companions.

Moscow had good reasons to be satisfied: there were two strongly armed separatist regimes in the North-West, three communist ministers in the government, and a very powerful Tudeh in a part of the country. A scenario which can be compared to the one of Czechoslovakia later on was being set up.

But Ghavam was not Beneš.

*   *

*

Ghavam showed indifference to this game which seemed strange, and worrying to the population. He no doubt acted with the Shah's agreement, who was covering up for him and even sent his twin sister, Princess Ashraf, to Moscow on a courtesy visit in July. Ghavam even attended a sumptuous dinner party given by the Tudeh in his honour, to the indignation of some. In fact, he arrived there late and acted offhandedly with the communist leaders – his usual method.

He said to Abolhassan Ebtehaj, the Governor of the National Bank, a reliable man who was worrying about the presence of communists in the Cabinet: 'I will chase them out. They won't have any power. It's a negligible problem.' [11] His elder brother, Vosough ol Dowleh, sent a young diplomat called Amir Khosrow Afshar to tell him about his concern. Ghavam smiled, asked his diplomatic adviser to reassure his brother, and then expressed his contempt for those who doubted in his political savoir-faire. [12]

*   *

*

Ghavam's problems did not only come from the Soviet side. He had to lead a battle on another front: there was unrest in the South that was organized by tribes whose chiefs traditionally had ties with the British. A plan for an uprising was discovered in the Bakhtiari tribe that lived in the centre of the country. On September 8th 1946, there were many arrests in the region and a state of siege was declared in Esfahan. The plot was unravelled. The unrest gathered momentum. On September 20th, Nasser Ghashghai, the chief of the eponymous tribe, sent a telegram to the Prime Minister in which he demanded internal autonomy for the Fars province in the South of the country, ministers in the Cabinet, and a local assembly. He gave the government forty-eight hours to comply with his request. Gendarmerie stations were attacked in the tribal region as far as the surrounding areas of Shiraz and Esfahan.

Ghavam refused. General Fazlollah Zahedi was appointed at the head of the army in the South, and invested with civilian and military powers. Reinforcements were sent to the region, which actually depleted the troops on the demarcation line with the separatists in the North-West.

General Zahedi defeated the rebel forces around Bushehr, on the Persian Gulf. However, a few small towns like Genaveh, Rig and Deylam, fell and the population started fleeing towards the big urban centres.

A conciliatory mission was sent to Shiraz, but it failed. The Prime Minister sent an ultimatum to the rebels: a negotiation was possible if they laid down arms and if there was a return to calm, otherwise the army would be given the order to crush the rebellion.

On September 29th, General Zahedi managed to temporarily save the important garrison of Kazeroon, halfway between Shiraz and the Persian Gulf. But on the 30th, the town of Bushehr fell, and the Kazeroon garrison could not hold out against the tribes' counteroffensive on October 2nd; it fought until the end, but the town fell.

In fact, Iran did not have the necessary military forces to re-establish order. Yet, a column of soldiers and a few old tanks were sent to Shiraz as reinforcements. The population was reassured and gave them a warm welcome.

On October 12th, the Cabinet reasserted the fact that General Zahedi had been granted full powers. They added that he had been sent to negotiate with the tribes, and this, within the limits of the Constitution, under the condition that their chiefs accepted to disarm and evacuate the towns they had conquered.

The whole of the general staff threatened these chiefs with the worst possible punishments if the situation did not get back to normal. The Shah and the Prime Minister spoke the same words. The small Iranian army and its few, nearly vintage aircrafts proved to be mobile and effective.

The situation progressively went back to calm.

It was a strange flash in the pan, a real stab in the back which can be explained by different factors.

In Tehran, the press and the political circles held British conspirators responsible. The London networks were, indeed, still linked to the chiefs of the local tribes who thus wanted to find a certain support against the central power. It cannot be ruled out that in such circumstances, London might have wanted to favour this rebellion, either out of dislike for Ghavam, and subsidiarily for the Shah, or to ensure a zone of influence in the South – something that had been tempting the British for a while.

The tribal chiefs, as far as they were concerned, seemed to have wanted to retrieve part of, or the whole of, the feudal prerogatives that an iron-handed Reza Shah had made them lose.

The attempt failed. The Shah forgave the episode, but never forgot it. Neither did the chiefs. A new confrontation was to take place during the sixties over the agrarian reform. This time, the tribal chiefs definitely lost the game and paid a high price for their attitude, their 'successive acts of treason', according to the government.

The Prime Minister's cleverness bore fruit when faced with the rebellion in the South. Two generals of the imperial army distinguished themselves there as well: Zahedi, a clever tactician and strong leader, and general Razmara, trained in Saint-Cyr, who had recently been promoted head of the general staff and who showed a great know-how with a weak and badly equipped army. They were both to play an important part in the following years.

*   *

*

At the end of spring and during the summer months the government had to face another big unrest that was organized by a Tudeh at the height of its power and given winner of the legislative elections in the autumn. [13]

On May 1st, Labour Day, the party organized a general strike which even affected a part of the bazaar and of the university. The secondary schools of the capital were forced to close and their pupils were sent to swell the ranks of the demonstrators. The next day, the Tudeh apparatus [14] estimated the number of demonstrators to be 80,000, and that of the spectators who had come 'to encourage them and bring their support,' 150,000. These figures are obviously unlikely to be correct in a city where the population did not exceed 600,000 at the time. According to what was written in the Tudeh press, there had been 80,000 demonstrators in Abadan, the centre of the oil industry; 40,000 in Esfahan and 20,000 in Yazd. There were 6 casualties and many injured in the bloody fights that opposed the supporters and opponents of the Tudeh in Kermanshah.

Then, the Tudeh organized general strikes in several cities of the country as a form of support for the separatists of Azerbaijan. In some cities, even the factories were occupied.

Ghavam held out and pretended to remain indifferent. However, he asked the Soviets to calm things down. The latter thought they had all the trump cards and urged the communists to be more moderate.

On June 30th, and to everybody's surprise, the Prime Minister launched his own political group, the Democratic Party of Iran. [15] The display of the Tudeh's strength had scared people. The Prime Minister's party benefited from his political aura and from his influence. It very quickly gathered most of the people of the same political obedience in the country. For a few months, it even benefited from the discreet support of the Court and from the favours of the clergy. A workers' union was also created under the direction of Khosrow Hedayat, a brilliant engineer of the Iranian railroads, who was to lead a remarkable political and diplomatic career in the decades to come.

Thus, in a few weeks, a genuine, organized, political force was set up. It could face the powerful machine of the Tudeh and its 'United Council of Unions.'

Ghavam's party considerably changed the Iranian political scene with its young members and its independence from foreign countries. It was to become a powerful instrument in the Prime Minister's hands for the new steps he was to take.

*   *

*

When the North of Iran was evacuated, the situation in the South virtually normal again, his political party well on its way due to circumstances, Ghavam began a new phase of his strategy which may seem surprisingly coherent today.

On October 20th, he dismissed the three communist ministers and their road companion from the Iran Party. Their presence in the government had lasted just over two months.

The negotiations with the separatists in Azerbaijan and Kurdistan were stopped. Now, Pichevari and his ministers multiplied their belligerent declarations in Tabriz.

The forces in Tabriz and Mahabad were heavily armed and supervised by the Soviets, a civil war like the Greek one now seemed inevitable. But Ghavam continued to reassure Moscow and to remind it of the commitments made: the Russians were to have the oil from the North.

The Iranian army started deploying its forces and made a slow advance on Tabriz. The protests from the separatist authorities and the violent demonstrations of the Tudeh left the government indifferent.

In such difficult times, two important events changed the face of things, on the political and on the diplomatic levels.
First, on November 5th, ayatollah Sayed Abolhassan Esfahani, the Supreme Leader of the world Shiite community, died in Najaf, Iraq.

Millions of people paid their tribute and took part in mourning ceremonies all over the country. On the 7th, the Shah, the Prime Minister, the army leaders were at the head of the funeral procession in Tehran. There is such a unanimous feeling in the nation that the Tudeh demonstrations were to seem pathetic later on. The Iranians showed that they were behind their leaders. The street did not belong to the communists any more.
Then, President Harry Truman addressed a firm message from Washington to Marshal Stalin to deter him from any military intervention in the Iranian conflict. It was a question of letting Iranians deal with their own business, he said. The Soviets still had their eyes on the oil fields in the North, and were relying on the overarmed forces of Azerbaijan and the communist unrest. Ghavam went on reassuring them and Stalin was still fooled.

On November 13th, the city of Zanjan was evacuated by the communist militia under popular pressure, and the Iranian army arrived in a city that had already been freed.

On the 25th, it is officially declared in Tehran that the imperial armed forces were to continue their advance on Tabriz so as to restore order there, and to make general elections possible. They were to be held across the whole country.

On November 28th, then on December 1st, the Prime Minister sent messages to the leaders of Tabriz to warn them that any resistance to the army columns would be considered as an act of rebellion.

On December 6th, Shah Mohammad Reza Pahlavi, the constitutional Commander-in-Chief of the Armed Forces, went to Zanjan, and took personal control of the operations. It was a symbolic act, and thanks to it, public opinion was to hold him in high esteem.

On December 9th, Ahmad Ghavam once more addressed the Tabriz leaders: any resistance to the police forces would be severely chastised, no infringement of the integrity of the national territory would be tolerated.

This time, the Soviets panicked. The Soviet ambassador to Moscow tried to contact the Prime Minister who was also in charge of the Ministry of Foreign Affairs.

Ghavam was told he was tired and left to find some rest on his estate in Lahijan, on the Caspian Sea. He could not be contacted by phone either, since there were none in town!

The Shah was on the front line, and his other ministers were incompetent. The Soviet embassy vainly harassed politicians in the capital. No-one could do anything with the head of government absent. He had left to find some rest in the North but would not be long coming back. Ambassador Sadtchicov was cordially invited to be patient.

*   *

*

The two communist regimes of the North-West were only to hold out for a few hours. When the Azerbaijan population heard that the national army was soon to arrive, they rose up, overthrew the communist government and welcomed the liberation forces cheerfully. A religious man who was locally notorious at the time, called Sayed Kazem Shariat-Madari, was the leader of the popular movement. He became famous nation-wide. He was heard of again during the 1978-1979 revolution.

Most of the leaders of the two separatist regimes fled to the Soviet Union, some were arrested, and sometimes judged and executed, like the three Ghazi brothers from Mahabad. But most of them were progressively released.

Although the repression was severe, it was fortunately not to be compared with the acts of violence, looting and massacres perpetrated by the separatists.

*   *

*

Pichevari crossed the border again with about a hundred people from his entourage. The Red Army protected a fleeing caravan of forty cars, over a hundred lorries with various goods, thirty-five jeeps, and seven buses; the one that was to follow the fugitive.*

The separatist forces left a large quantity of weapons and ammunition. They were shown to the international press on December 16th: there were 50,000 rifles, 5,000 submachine-guns and machine-guns, several hundred artillery cannons, and a few tanks.

Between December 12th, when Tabriz was liberated, the 15th, when it was Mahabad's turn, and the 17th, the whole territory which had been under the separatists' control was liberated.

---

* On August 3rd 1947, Pichevari's death 'in a car crash' was announced. It was soon public knowledge that he had been executed on Stalin's orders because the latter never forgave him for his rout.
His wife came from an excellent old family. She stayed in the Soviet Union and got by in miserable conditions. Years later, during one of the Shah's visits to Moscow, she managed to draw a member of the Iranian delegation's attention, general and doctor Ayadi. She asked for the Shah's intervention to organize her return home, which the Shah discreetly did. A military aeroplane brought Pichevari's widow back to Iran even before the Shah had left the USSR. It was the only way to guarantee her repatriation. The separatist leader's wife was protected by the government of her country and discreetly died there years later, in dignity.
As for Pichevari's only son, called Dariush (or Kaveh, according to other sources), he was put in his uncle's care, a captain and doctor of the Red Army. He lived on, studied, got married in Baku and had two children. He ended up fleeing the USSR and finding refuge in West Germany during the sixties, just before the Wall was built. (information taken from a book that was published in Baku recently : *The Peak and the Decline of the Democratic Party of Azerbaijan*, *Kayhan*, June 7th-13th 2005. Djamil Hassanli translated it into Persian and published the interesting pages).

On the 12th, Ghavam reappeared in Tehran where he welcomed the Russian and American ambassadors. The Azerbaijan affair was nearly solved, and his diplomatic holiday had just come to an end.

* * *

*

Ghavam did not stop making reforms from the moment he started running the country, despite the huge difficulties he had to face.

Thus, in less than two years, he created the Ministry of Labour and Social Affairs, had the first Labour Code voted in Parliament, and set up a system of social insurance for the workers of industrial companies, which was to be a first for the region.

On April 9th 1946, he had a decree voted on that would increase the share farmers had in tenant farming or in sharecropping contracts with their landowners.

On May 28th, another decree triggered the division and sale of the State's arable land for the benefit of the farmers; then, on June 3rd, the first agricultural cooperatives appeared.

These three measures formed the beginning of a true agrarian reform which was only to become successful in the sixties.

It is also thanks to Ghavam's political vision that there were the creation of the Organisation of the plan, and the beginning of the first septennial development plan: there was to be a programming over several years of public investments, and guidance measures for private investments. It was in the same spirit that the Bank of Industrial and Mining Development was founded on June 4th 1946.

In spite of all the budget restrictions and special expenses, the first measures for the recovery of the national economy were enforced: the purchase of a big electrical plant for the capital on August 18th 1946; the creation of a special fund for the renovation of national roads and their tarring – they had fallen into a pitiful state, and had virtually not been maintained during the war years. There were also the beginnings of the construction of four hundred social dwellings in Tehran on August 29th. On November 18th, the contract for the drinking water pipework was signed by the town and a British company – a project which should have started in 1940. On December 10th, the State launched a project for the extension of the telephone network of the capital, and expected ten thousand new lines to be opened...

Ghavam was thus the initiator of the economic momentum in the post-war Iran, and this, by taking innovating measures which were often ahead of their time.

*   *

*

On May 26th 1947, the United States settled all of the expenses caused by the presence of its troops in Iran during the war.

*   *

*

Once the Azerbaijan problem had been solved, the future of the oil agreement had to be decided on.

The new elections took place and Ghavam's Democratic Party of Iran won a landslide victory. Four sympathisers of the Tudeh represented the all-powerful communist party, which, for want of a protector, had no more electors.

Ghavam handed his resignation to the King on August 27th 1947, in agreement with the Constitution. On the 30th, the Parliament considered his new position again, and immediately charged him with forming the new government. He presented his ministers on September 11th. 93 out of 120 members of Parliament approved of his decision.

On October 22nd, he presented the Iranian-Soviet oil agreement to the Chamber.

Before that, he granted an interview to a journalist from *Le Monde*, his friend and almost accomplice, Édouard Sablier. The conversation was held in French, a language the Prime Minister mastered perfectly well, he said: 'A promise is a promise: the agreement in principle that we signed, remains an obligation. I refuse to have the reputation of a man who does not keep his word, so I will submit the project in question to Parliament. However, the circumstances have changed. The representatives who were elected by universal suffrage benefit from a complete freedom of thought and appreciation. We would not impose a decision that went against their wishes. If we did, we would risk seeing the principle of the agreement rejected by Parliament. I consider this possibility to be undesirable, it would create a misunderstanding with our Soviet neighbours.' Édouard Sablier then asked: 'Must I understand that there are chances for the Russian-Iranian treaty to be rejected by the Majlis [Parliament]?'

The Prime Minister replied: 'This is not what I am saying, but the two contracting parties must take the new conditions into account...' The word had been uttered. Ghavam asked Édouard Sablier, a journalist who had become a protagonist in a subtle game, in "a Persian trick," he wrote later on, to communicate the whole text of the interview to the local press, with the details the Parisian newspaper did not find relevant to give.

The word had been given to Moscow and to the representatives. All the members of Parliament, except two out of the four close to the communists, refused to ratify the agreement. [16]

Moscow's failure was complete.
The Soviet radio and press launched an intense campaign against Iran, and more particularly, against Ghavam, who had become the enemy to kill.
On November 5th, the rejection of the agreement was officially notified to Moscow. On the 21st, Moscow replied in a particularly virulent note. On December 2nd, another threatening note was sent to Tehran. Ghavam had all the notes made public to rally opinion, contrary to diplomatic use. It was to be his last political gesture.

Stalin had been fooled and he was furious. Moscow and the communists never forgave Ghavam. André Fontaine later wrote that he had succeeded 'in fooling Stalin better than anyone may boast to have done... And the USSR was beaten hollow.' [17]

Ghavam was then to know what had happened to Bismarck with Wilhelm II, to Clemenceau after the First World War, and to De Gaulle after the Second: ingratitude.
When the danger was over, everyone wanted to resume political games and free themselves from the yoke of a remarkable man.

Mohammad Reza Pahlavi had never liked him, but the union of the two men had been unwavering in times of crisis.

'[He] did not ignore what he owed Ghavam; he owed him as much as he did to Foroughi who had saved the throne and the dynasty. It is embarrassing for a young sovereign, however, to be dependent on Prime Ministers when he could be their son, especially when these old, well-experienced politicians manage to solve problems which seemed to be insolvable, and only leave the Shah a chance to give his blessing.' [18]

When alluding to the Azerbaijan crisis, Chapour Bakhtiar, the Shah's last Prime Minister who hated Ghavam, called him an 'ageing horse, a sly speculator who is not very honest and has no democratic convictions.' [19] He was, nevertheless, also led to admit that 'the affair had been dealt with on a political and diplomatic level by Ghavam, to whom Mohammad Reza Shah was always unfair because he did not want his name to be associated with the liberation of Azerbaijan, for the simple reason that he wanted to capitalize on that historic episode.' [20]

This is what the imperial family's attitude to Ghavam was like. It took the Shah's last brother alive over sixty years to finally pay Ghavam homage and admit to the part he had played in History, which History had already acknowledged: Prince Gholam Reza Pahlavi recognized 'the personal animosity [of his brother] which had been observed by the chroniclers of the time towards this haughty, cultured, deeply patriotic, but very difficult to deal with, and authoritarian character.' He also recognized his 'stroke of genius', and his 'dimension of a great Statesman'... 'Ahmad Ghavam had more private means than the leaders of Czechoslovakia, Poland and of the other European countries, and probably more will-power to fight communism.' [21]

Ahmad Ghavam was not a man who would cling onto power.

He went to Parliament, where his party held a vast

majority, and made a report of a great sobriety on his action and achievement. He then asked for a vote of confidence but only got 16 votes in his favour, out of 112!

On the same day, December 10th 1947, he went to see the Shah to hand in his resignation.

He was to suffer from ingratitude and hatred until the day he died.

Chapter V

THE OIL CRISIS
The man who chased the British away

The collapse of the two separatist regimes the Soviets had set up in the North-West of the country, and the rejection of the bestowing on the latter of the concession of the exploitation of oil fields in the North, did not only start a long crisis with Moscow, but it also started a long process of confrontations and negotiations which, step by step, crisis after crisis, led to the 1978-1979 revolution, the fall of the monarchy and the establishment of an Islamic republic in Iran.

When Parliament rejected the oil agreement with the Soviet Union, it passed a bill on October 22nd 1947, according to which:

– all discussions or negotiations passed concerning possible oil concessions for the Soviet government were declared void;

– the Iranian government was not, in any case whatsoever, to give oil concessions to foreign powers, be it for oil prospecting, extracting or refining;

– the government was to start negotiations with the Anglo-Iranian Oil Company so as to reach fair conditions concerning the sharing of profit and the exploitation of oil resources in the South of the country;

– in case new oilfields were discovered in the next three years, the government should be ready to negotiate the sale of the extracted oil with the USSR.

That bill was part of the traditional approach of the Iranian diplomacy to ensure a certain balance between the interests of the great powers. Moscow was being notified that the Iranian attitude was not anti-Soviet, but solely a national one, and that London would also be requested to radically changed its political attitude with Iran, and finally, that new perspectives would be offered to the Soviet Union.
It was a cunning approach.
The initiator of this new stipulation was a very popular representative of the capital, Mohammad Mossadegh, and it was not long before the latter made his entry in the history of Iran, and even in that of the Third World.

*   *

*

The oil production had been rising since the end of the war: 19 million tons in 1946, 21 million in 1947. It reached 25 million in 1948. It allowed Iran to start its first reconstruction and development projects, those launched by Ahmad Ghavam which had been completely halted for half a decade. The former Prime Minister had created an 'Organisation of the plan', and the first septennial plan had just been launched. The country had an urgent need to increase its resources.

At this point, Washington was little implicated in Iranian affairs. Iran wanted to show it was determined to balance its firmness with Moscow, and started putting pressure on London to negotiate a new oil agreement.

On the economic level, it was necessary to finance the development programme on the one hand, and, on the other hand, to satisfy a strong, delayed demand – the consumption needs of a people submitted to privations during the war. The new resources could only come from the oil, the main source of wealth in the country at that time.

Public opinion, which was traditionally anti-British, unreservedly supported a firm and demanding policy with London. His Britannic Majesty's government had been the main shareholder of the Anglo-Iranian company since the eve of WWI, and a real diplomatic face-à-face started between the two countries.
London then made a serious mistake, which it was to cost them dearly. Tehran demanded oil agreements that would be similar, or fairly close, to those which govern the exploitation of oil fields in Saudi Arabia by American companies. Public opinion would then be satisfied. It would not only involve the application of the 50/50 principle, instead of the 20% Iran was getting at the time, but also an increase in social investments, a right of control of the operating accounts and a progressive Iranianising of executives.
London virtually refused any honourable compromise, and did not want to give anything up. Anti-British demonstrations gathered momentum in Iran. One man soon became their symbol, the great public speaker Mossadegh. Historian Arthur Conte [1] later wrote he was: 'a very strange old man with silver hair, a large nose and heavy jowls who was immensely rich. He only knew passion in his life. He was an emotional character.'

Ephemeral cabinets followed one another in Tehran, voted in and out by a Chamber which was subject to conspiracy, in a chaotic democratic system. The country plunged into a situation of disorder and nearly violent confrontations between factions. It was deemed desirable in many circles to resort to a man who had the qualities of a disciplinarian, who could master the situation and come to a decent agreement with the British. This is how, in June 1949, Parliament designated General Haj Ali Razmara to be the man to lead the government. He was the head of the general staff of the armed forces. The Sovereign appointed him Prime Minister, even if he was somewhat apprehensive concerning his ambitions. There were stormy sessions, but the appointment of the General Prime Minister was eventually approved of by both Chambers, and he was invested in his function.

He had been trained in Saint-Cyr, was short but very cultured [2], and according to all his supporters, opponents and enemies, he was an exceptional character. He was the author of a geography treatise of Iran in eight volumes. Even if there was no doubt about his integrity, many thought of him as an apprentice-dictator, or a republican at heart. Like General Zahedi, his main rival in the army, he is considered to be a political genius. He hardly hid his ambitions for reforms, his admiration for Ahmad Ghavam, whom he served as head of general staff. He wanted to govern and, one is led to believe, only leave the Shah a symbolic role, which the latter liked less and less.

Though the Razmara government had benefited from a vast vote of confidence in both Chambers, it was paralysed by violent parliamentary opposition and street demonstrations orchestrated by mainly Mossadegh's supporters. As the General Prime Minister had made a close move towards the USSR, the Tudeh kept relatively quiet.

The cabinet was reshuffled a few times in several months, a few spectacular projects were launched, and it seemed that an agreement would soon be reached with London on the 50/50 basis, concerning the exploitation of oil. The British flaunted their friendship at the Prime Minister, which was a handicap; some people even saw in it a perfidious manoeuvre to discredit him with public opinion – a well-known tradition of the London cabinet. The Razmara government was paralysed despite its leader's obvious good-will and hard work – up to twenty hours a day.

Mohammad Mossadegh then launched his "magic" slogan for the nationalization of oil which was immediately unanimously accepted in the country. Razmara and his last Minister of Finance, Forouhar, tried to show how difficult it would be by using technical arguments. Nobody listened to them. Only the communists, who were strongly marginalized, violently opposed the nationalization of oil, and continued to push for the bestowing of an oil concession to the Soviet Union so as to compensate for the advantages the British had got.

As for the clergy, it was divided: a religious man called ayatollah Kashani, who used violent language and who was said to be secretly manipulated by London since he had lived in many countries under British mandate, joined the movement for nationalization before betraying it. In his entourage, there was a junior mullah called Ruhollah Khomeini. Kashani was immediately introduced by the western press as the spokesman of the 'hard', 'radical', even 'nationalist' tendency of the clergy. Another influential and powerful ayatollah, Sayed Mohammad Behbahani, the son of one of the founding fathers of the liberal Constitution of 1906, showed more reserve. He was immediately nicknamed a 'conservative', sometimes 'close to the Palace', even 'pro-west'. The supreme authorities of Shiism, be it in Qom or in Najaf, kept out of things.

On March 7th 1951, General Razmara was assassinated by a terrorist and fanatic of Fedayane Islam (the Iranian section of the Muslim Brothers). Kashani immediately blessed the murder.

The Razmara era was over. In the eyes of Iranian historians, the man, his policy and real intentions remain enigmatic.

In less than two months, two Prime Ministers were appointed: Khalil Fahimi, who dispatched current affairs for three days, and then, Hossein Ala, who formed a new government, was approved of by the Chambers, but did not do anything else either but dispatch current affairs.

On March 19th 1951, Parliament unanimously voted in the nationalization of oil. The Shah ratified the law the next day, by publicly giving it his enthusiastic and genuine support.

It was a festive day for Iran.

Hossein Ala offered his resignation.

On April 28th, the Chamber designated Mossadegh, the promoter of the nationalization but also leader of the opposition until then, at a majority of only one vote. The Shah appointed him right away and asked him to form the new government.

The festivities continued.

A new political phase which was followed by numerous events and had heavy consequences was about to start.

*   *

*

When Mohammad Mossadegh ascended to power, he was in his seventies, since, according to his official biographical details, he was born on May 20th, 1882. [3] His mother was a Qajar Princess. His father, Mirza Hedayat, had been the Lord High Treasurer of a king from that dynasty, and was responsible for the province of Khorasan in the North-East of Iran when he died. Mohammad, who was fourteen at the time, inherited his father's responsibility and the title of Mossadegh ol-Saltaneh, thus the family name he chose later on: Mossadegh.[4]

He followed classical studies, married a Qajar Princess, a daughter of King Naser Ol Din. She was called Zia-Ashraf, and got the title of Zia-ol-Saltaneh. The couple had six children in the following years, five of whom survived: two sons and three daughters. Both sons were sent to Europe to study. The eldest, Ahmad, qualified at the Ponts et Chaussées, and led a brilliant career in the Iranian railroads. He was their Managing Director for several years. The second, Gholam Hossein, a doctor, became a famous gynaecologist, a University Professor. As for the three girls, two got married to cousins, and the third, who was unwell, was sent to a specialised home in Switzerland.

It was a family from the upper aristocracy. They were cultured, wealthy and had a perfect reputation.

At the age of twenty, Mohammad Mossadegh was initiated at Adamiyat (mankind), a Masonic lodge. The man kept very strong secular convictions, if not anticlerical ones, like many Iranian free masons of the period.

At the age of twenty-five, in 1906, he was elected representative for Esfahan. Since he was not old enough to be eligible – thirty – he could not participate in the work of this first constituent-legislative Assembly in Iranian history, and left for Europe to continue his studies: he went to the École libre des sciences politiques in Paris (Free School of Political Science), to the universities of Liege (Belgium) and Neufchâtel (Switzerland) where he got his PhD in law, thus becoming the first Iranian to have the honour. At the beginning of 1914, he defended his PhD thesis on inheritance law in Islam. His criticism earned him biting reproaches from certain mullahs.

Back in Iran at the end of 1914, he was appointed Professor at the High School of Political Science, which had been founded a few years before on the French model. He started a political career at the same time, due to his family position and his university background which was exceptional for the times: Under-Secretary of State in the Finance Department, and general Paymaster of Iran, Minister of Justice, Governor of the Fars province, the main administrative town of which is Shiraz, Minister of Finance, of Foreign Affairs, Governor of Azerbaijan. Cabinets did not last long then, thus, these responsibilities were short-lived.

When he was a member of Parliament for Tehran, in 1924, and the Chamber voted the downfall of the Qajars, he delivered a speech there which has remained famous in the parliamentary history of the country:

'You want to pronounce the downfall of a dynasty, that of the Qajars, so as to place the Sardar-Sepah [Commander-in-Chief] Reza Khan at the head of the country, and proclaim him King. I am not opposed to the fall of a dynasty which caused its own downfall because of its errors and weaknesses, neither am I opposed to Reza Khan himself, but either Reza Khan, once King, will abide by our Constitution – and you know that, according to this very Constitution, the King reigns but does not rule, so that the country will be deprived of Reza Khan's authority – or he will rule as a dictatorial sovereign, and the Constitution will be violated.' [5] He said, to give the gist of it.

His reasoning followed a rigorous sense of logic, which the Parliament did not come to terms with. That is, perhaps, where a certain resentment or distrust between the Pahlavis and Mossadegh originated [6]. Yet, Mossadegh was reelected member of Parliament for Tehran. He was even to be offered the Ministry of Foreign Affairs, and, it seems, the position of Prime Minister by the new Shah [7] during an audience. He kept seeing the Sovereign [8] in private audiences for a few years, and participated in some official ceremonies. Then, he was progressively manoeuvred out of power, managed his fortune, travelled inside the country and even went abroad, at least once.

A few years later, in June 1940, he was apparently denounced to the authorities and arrested; he spent six days in jail in Tehran and was then deported to Birjan, in the Khorasan province. He spent six months there before being released and put under house arrest in his residence of Ahmad-Abad, not far from the capital city. He owed this favour to a direct personal intervention of Crown prince Mohammad Reza Pahlavi, who had been approached by doctor Gholam Hossein Mossadegh. He referred to him when addressing the Chamber on May 25th 1950: '... The crown prince went to see his father to ask for my release. The Shah asked him to wait a little. Twenty days later, the order was given to transfer me from Birjand to Ahmad-Abad. Recently, during an audience, I told His Majesty that I would never forget his kindness, and that I would be his faithful servant for the rest of my life. I do not know of any person with better intentions than His Majesty. The Shahanshah loves his country... I do not think that there is anyone who cares so much for this country...We, who love the Shah, must do our utmost to increase his popularity.' [9]

Even before Reza Shah's abdication, the Foroughi Cabinet had put an end to his house arrest and he could thus return to his summer residence in the Baghe Ferdows area, north of the Iranian capital.

Basking in the glory of the persecutions he had been the victim of, he was elected member of Parliament for Tehran in 1943, coming out first, thanks to the number of votes in his favour. A cunning, powerful orator, he played his part of a great actor of political life. Knowing how to provoke and use his own emotions and those of others, he made you feel welcome, was extremely courteous, and knew how to talk to young people, but he could also be very vindictive, even rude.

Mossadegh became the popular symbol of the resistance to the economic grip held by Britain on Iran, and to any foreign political interference.

Once appointed Premier, he held all the trump cards. He was the idol of not only the nationalist bourgeoisie but also of an entire people, with the exception of the highly marginalized communists.

His relationship with Mohammad Reza Pahlavi was excellent, as it was with Empress Soraya. He showed her the delicate consideration of an old Persian aristocrat, and she called him "old lion" from then on. The Shah did not like the English, and knew the hatred felt by British politicians for his father. He had not forgotten the pressure exerted by London or their interference to evict him from the throne in 1941. As a constitutional monarch who must respect a certain reserve, he appreciated it when someone dared speak their minds openly. However, and all the testimonies concur on this particular point, he did not like Mossadegh, did not trust him and, perhaps, did not like the fact that the statue of the great man could cast a dominating shadow over him. It had already been the case with Ahmad Ghavam, the other political giant. Yet, their respective patriotism, their sense of national interest brought them closer. 'The worst thing for London is that, under these circumstances, the King of Kings, Mohammad Reza Pahlavi is exceptionally in agreement with his minister, whom he hates.' [10] Both men often had long tête-à-têtes: two hours on September 17th 1951, one and a half hours on the 18th, two hours on the 23rd, and two hours again on the 25th of the same month. On November 23rd, their conversation lasted six hours [11]... Public opinion, in its vast majority, rejoiced over the good terms they were on; unfortunately, it was not to last long!

*   *

*

Designated on April 28th 1951, and immediately appointed at the head of the executive power, Mossadegh presented his ministers to the Sovereign on May 2nd, to the Chamber on the 3rd, and to the Senate on the 5th. Several of his ministers came from his own political group, the National Front, which was a disparate gathering of personalities and groups: Bagher Kazemi, in Foreign Affairs, Karim Sanjabi in Education, Youssef Moshar in Telecommunications, Amir Teymour Kalali in Labour, Amir Alaï in Justice. Some of the others were independent, but had a definite political reputation. At the Ministry of the Interior, there was General Fazlollah Zahedi, who was known, among other things, for his anti-British feelings and his independent mind. Mossadegh and his political friends had had good relations with this atypical general for years. He had assured that the legislative elections would take place, and had provided the right protection for them when he was at the head of the national Police forces. It had made the presence of representatives of the National Front in the Chamber possible. [12]

All the ministers of that government had a solid reputation for their integrity, as was the case for all the ministers and people close to Mossadegh until the end. His ministers and team's integrity are part of the Mossadegh legend which was to last.

*   *

*

Mossadegh's political programme was succinct: he wanted the full implementation of the nationalization of the oil industry, and the reform of the electoral code. As for the first item, he demanded and immediately had a law passed allowing for the 'ousting' of the AIOC.

During the debates on this programme at the Chamber, a member of Parliament who was close to the extreme left, called Ashtiani-Zadeh, reproached him sharply for the presence of several free masons among the ministers, and of a 'cossack' at the Interior.

On May 9th, both Chambers nevertheless approved of the appointments in a massive vote of confidence, and the government was invested in its functions. The new Prime Minister occupied the offices of the presidency for a few days, and then used the Parliament, saying he was under threat, and 'was looking for safety in the house of the nation.' It did not last long. Mossadegh transferred his office to his private residence, avenue Kakh, not far from the palace.

His adventure was to begin.

*　　　　　*

*

The British were 'ousted' from the management of the oil sector in several rapid steps. A house search at the residence of the local president of the AIOC resulted in the confiscation of extremely compromising documents for the British, for they clearly revealed a flagrant interference in the political life of the country. The governmental propaganda made clever use of this discovery. Public opinion rejoiced.

The British engineers and employees were asked to leave the country. Even if their departure was organized in a dignified and courteous way, greatly reported on in the press, and shown on the news, it stirred unanimous enthusiasm among Iranians. The 'old lion' now appeared as a victor of the British; he was the man who had chased them out of Iran.

The London propaganda which was relayed by a few 'friends' inside the country had given credence to the idea that the Iranians would not be able to operate the oil installations. It was just the opposite which happened. The oil fields were exploited, the two refineries in the country in Abadan and Kermanshah were in operation, and the distribution of oil inside the country was ensured, even if Iran could not really export its oil. A first agreement was signed with Afghanistan on September 13th 1951, but it was to be only symbolic. People in Tehran believed, or at least pretended to, that the West could not do without the Iranian oil. This was to be the fatal error made by Mossadegh's oil advisors.

When faced with the 'ousting' and departure of the British engineers and technicians who called it an illegal expropriation, London sent a war fleet to the Persian Gulf. There was a general mobilisation in Iran. Mohammad Reza Pahlavi, the constitutional Commander-in-Chief of the Armed Forces solemnly proclaimed that he would go 'to the front line' to take effective command of his troops, so as to 'defend his country until he had shed his last drop of blood.' People cried with emotion in their homes, and public opinion was inflamed. Iran had not yielded to the threat and London called its gunboats back. The Iranians crowed over their victory. They were not wrong to do so.

The affair was now being developed on three levels: on the judicial, diplomatic and economic levels.

*   *

*

Great Britain took the case to the International Court of Justice in The Hague. Despite Tehran's opposition, the Court accepted to put the case on its agenda and ordered protective measures to be taken on July 6th 1951. It was a setback for the Iranians, even though no basic verdict had been pronounced. From July 8th onwards, important demonstrations took place all over Iran in protest against the Court's position. Parliament solemnly took sides in their favour. On July 12th, the Iranian government notified the British ambassador that it refused to accept the decision rendered by the court in The Hague.

London decided to take the matter to the Security Council of the United Nations which accepted to put it on its agenda on October 1st.

Two days later, Mossadegh decided to go to the United Nations in person to plead Iran's cause. The oil crisis was now 'on the headlines' of world news. Even though there was an intense mobilization in London, the cause of Iran met with great sympathy in international opinion; the theatrical attitude of the 'old lion' who managed to appear like a victim of British imperialism made him become a hero of the Third World and a cause for the liberation of oppressed people.

Mossadegh addressed the Security Council in New York on October 15th. [13] He delivered a formal speech in French, in a 'trembling' and pathetic voice at first, insisting on the British interferences in Iran, the hardships his people were to endure, the unfairness of the fate reserved to Third World countries. Allahyar Saleh, one of his main companions, pleaded the merits of the case in a long, dull but solidly prepared speech to demonstrate the incompetence of the Council. He spoke in perfect English for two hours.

China, the USSR, Yugoslavia, and the Republic of Ecuador gave their full support to Iran. The United States adopted a discreet attitude, and France tried to find an equitable solution. It played a decisive role in the matter.

Sir Gladwyn Jebb, the British representative, made a reply which was not very convincing. On France's suggestion, the Council abstained from giving a ruling on the case while it waited for the court in The Hague to pronounce itself on the merits of the case. It was not even put on the agenda.

It was a setback for London and a resounding victory for Iran, for Mossadegh.

On October 20th, the day after this success, Mohammad Reza Pahlavi sent a telegram to Mossadegh. 'I was particularly happy to hear the news of the Iranian success at the Security Council. I congratulate you on your victory in this important case. It is with enthusiasm that I would like to tell you how satisfied I am with your efforts and your contribution to this case. I would be glad to hear about your health.' [15] It was not a very formal text – the formal 'we' was replaced by a very friendly 'I'– in an almost filial tone. Later on, the propaganda of the imperial regime tried to cover this up. On the 21st, Mossadegh replied to the Sovereign in an exceptionally courteous and deferential message [16]. He wrote: 'These successes were only possible thanks to Your Majesty, to the advice you lavished on us, to your supervision.'

These words were referred to for years to make the role of the Shah stand out. In fact, both men had agreed on the course of events in the interest of the nation.

Basking in his glory, Mossadegh went from New York to Washington where he had long meetings with the American leaders, and most particularly, with President Truman. They all wished for a quick solution to the crisis with London, fearing that Moscow might take advantage of it, but they were not really unfavourable to the Iranian cause. This is when an intervention of the World Bank emerged to solve the problem in a non-bilateral setting, which would save he face of both parties, and humour Iranians, something one can understand and even approve of.

On November 20th, Mossadegh stopped in Cairo on his way back home. Egypt was then ruled by Nahas Pasha and also played a hard game against London to free itself from the British trusteeship, abrogate the 1936 treaty, and have the military bases which were supposed to be protecting the Suez Canal, evacuated. There again, the British refused to make any significant concessions whereas they were facing a people who were unanimously opposed to them.

The Egypt of Nahas Pasha and Mossadegh's Iran had certain interests in common, and a real solidarity. Cairo gave the 'old lion' a triumphant, popular and official welcome. On November 22nd, the two Prime Ministers signed a common declaration, which was a prestigious success for both of them.

On the 23rd, Mossadegh went back to Tehran. A frenzied welcome awaited him. Had he not just won another battle against the British? The Shah received him on the 24th. The apparent good terms between them were still deceptive. Both Chambers listened to the report made by the government and approved it.

Only the communists from the Tudeh, who could sense a reconciliation with the West, stirred unrest. It was quelled by the police.

The state of euphoria continued on the whole, but Iran could not manage to dispose of its oil. The first load of oil that was exported – 900 tons – was impounded by the British authorities in Aden on June 18th 1952. Since Iran could not really export its oil, its economy suffered more and more.

The Iranian-British dispute was taken to the court in The Hague again. An eminent Belgian legal expert, Professor Henri Rollin, was chosen by Tehran to be its lawyer and prepare the Iranian case.

On May 28th, Mossadegh left for The Hague at the head of an important delegation to plead Iran's cause himself. It was a good media-staged event. Very many Iranians, especially the young, came from all over Europe to give him a warm welcome in Holland. He spoke to the Court in French, pleaded the incompetence of the U.N. jurisdiction and granted the press many interviews. On June 24th 1952, he was back in Tehran. Henri Rollin stayed in The Hague to follow the case.

*   *

*

The weeks that followed his return were very agitated. The legislative elections, come-back of an internal opposition which was particularly active, permanent unrest, exaggerated promises made by the communists, and especially the quick deterioration of the economic situation were the reasons for this agitation. His ministers and close team, upright and often competent men, tried to face it using all possible means: a national loan was proposed and rapidly subscribed to, the gold and currency reserves of the Central Bank were drawn on, drastic budget economy measures were taken, exports were encouraged and imports restrained. The Governor of the issuing Bank, Professor Mohammad Nassiri, showed genuine dexterity on monetary issues, which allowed the government to pay its civil servants and face the most urgent expenses. But the 'economy without oil' was in a deadlock. Inflation, unemployment and even a certain shortage of money could be felt.

Disillusionment was soon to come.

Mossadegh had succeeded in the negative aspect of his undertakings, the British had been forced out of their own game. It was already a political and psychological victory, a historical revenge in the eyes of almost all Iranians. Yet, he had not been able to size up his powerful opponents. Even in the Americans' eyes, who had first looked favourably on the action of a great nationalist public speaker, not to say a Populist one, the growing instability of the domestic situation of the country was becoming worrying.

Neither Mossadegh nor his immediate entourage had a realistic view of what would happen after a virtually improvised nationalization, and especially after the enforcement of the ousting law. The Iranians were able to extract and refine oil, but, because of the hostility of the British and of the big oil companies, they could not export it.

'I thought that the English would yield after one or two months,' Mossadegh said to a group of representatives at the beginning of the second year of his government, when difficulties were accumulating. 'I did not really think that this affair would drag on for so long. I had no plan. Let's get together to solve the problems.' When his acting Minister of Foreign Affairs came to deplore the bad effect these words had had on public opinion and on the diplomatic action of Iran – they had been taken up by all the press and blown out of all proportion by opponents – he replied quite frankly: 'I told them the truth.' [17]

The main oil advisor of the Prime Minister, Kazem Hassibi, an ex-student from the École Polytechnique, wanted him to believe that once the tap of Iranian oil was closed, the West would go down on their knees. It was a serious mistake.

The Iranian oil was quickly replaced on the market by the one from Iraq, Kuwait, and from Saudi Arabia.

When, after many comings and goings, Averell Harriman and Richard Stocks, the American and British envoys, and more particularly the mission from the World Bank, made proposals to him that respected the principle of nationalization, and suggested the implementation of a multinational sale and marketing organisation that Iran would have absolute control over, all of Mossadegh's advisors suggested reaching an agreement and accepting the proposal, at least as a basis for further negotiation.

After the victory in front of the Security Council, Iran was in a position of strength. Yet, the 'old lion' followed Kazem Hassibi's negative suggestion and stuck to his refusal since, as he said: 'public opinion would accuse him of weakness towards the English.'[18]

This is how the crisis developed, with the coffers empty, with an economy that was losing momentum, a growing opposition of a part of the population and a disagreement between the two powers at the head of the State. The Sovereign did not say it publicly, but he did not hide his wish for the country to quickly come out of the crisis any more, or his fear that the situation could be exploited by the communists and the Soviet Union.

*   *

*

General legislative and mid-term senatorial elections had just been held in the country in the spring and in the summer. The government had organized and supervised them, so it had no doubt about their integrity. However, the opponents were denouncing the interference of the government.

On July 5th 1952, the Chamber voted in its president, ayatollah Sayed Hassan Emami, a moderate religious man of consensus who was also a professor of civil law at the University of Tehran.

According to the Constitution, the government was to hand in its resignation to the Sovereign, which the Prime Minister immediately did.

On the 6th, in accordance with the rules of etiquette, the Shah saw the recently formed committees of both Chambers of Parliament to ask them to present a new Prime Minister. He declared: 'No matter what the next government, it will have to continue with the nationalization procedure of our oil and implement the corresponding laws with much tenacity.'

The representatives suggested Mossadegh's nomination to a small majority. At the Senate, only fourteen senators voted in his favour, out of the thirty-six present. As was the custom, the representatives' votes played a prominent part. The Head of State consequently renewed the mandate of the resigning Head of Government on the 10th.

On the 13th, Mossadegh went to a session of the Chamber that was not opened to the public and demanded that full powers, and thus the right to legislate by decrees, be granted to him so that he could face the crisis. He also expressed the desire to take the portfolio of Minister of War, that is to say the effective command of the armed forces when the King is their constitutional Commander-in-Chief. The disagreement between the Sovereign and the Prime Minister thus broke out in broad daylight.

The Chamber refused, deeming that the process was not

in accordance with constitutional habits. The Prime Minister it had designated was demanding full powers, even before the Cabinet had been formed and invested.

On the 16th, Mohammad Mossadegh was granted an audience by the Shah. Their conversation was friendly and courteous, according to the press of the time. It lasted three hours. The Prime Minister that had been considered by the Chamber informed the Sovereign that he did not accept his nomination and renounced his position.
According to various sources, the Shah would have wished for a moderate personality of the National Front to be designated, someone like Allahyar Saleh or the vice-president of the Chamber, Abdollah Moazzami, who was also a Professor of private international law at the University of Tehran. The Chamber did not follow him. On July 17th, Ahmad Ghavam, the liberator of Azerbaijan, had a very small majority of the votes in inclination of his designation. It was an unexpected and unpleasant choice for Mohammad Reza Pahlavi who nevertheless accepted the representatives' decision, and reluctantly asked Ghavam to form the new government.

*   *

*

Ahmad Ghavam had stayed away from politic since he had left the government*, and had spent a long time in France. His relations with Mohammad Reza Pahlavi remained cold, even almost non-existant.
In the spring of 1950, a written altercation had publicly opposed the two characters. On March 17th, Ghavam had

---

* See chapter IV: The Azerbaijan crisis – The man who defeated Stalin.

criticized the constitutional reform in a letter with harsh tones, but which was naturally deferential and haughty. This reform had been made on the Sovereign's initiative. It reinforced the powers of the executive and granted the Head of State the right to ask for a second reading of the laws voted in Parliament, but also for the right to dissolve the Chambers under certain very restrictive conditions. The letter had been given to the press which would publish it and generously comment on it.

On April 8th, Ebrahim Hakimi, a Court Minister, had replied to Ghavam in a missive that had also been made public, but which was, unfortunately, improper. Without any evidence, the Prime Minister was accused of embezzlement, even of weakness in front of the Soviets, and of sabotage during the liberation of Azerbaijan!

The effect on public opinion had been disastrous, so much so as 'on His imperial Majesty's order', and as a form of ultimate courteousness, the title of Djenab-é-ashraf (Most Serene) that had been granted to Ahmad Ghavam after the liberation of the provinces of the North-West, had just been taken away from him.

When that letter was published, Ahamd Ghavam had just had an operation and was in a hospital on the French Riviera. He only found out about it later on. Cut to the quick, and spurred on by the positive impact of his first letter and on the negative one the Court's answer had on public opinion, and especially on the 'story of the title', the Iranians did not actually care much for ingratitude, Ghavam addressed a very harsh second letter to the Shah, reminding him, among other things, of his manuscript letter of thanks on the day after the liberation of Azerbaijan*, which he was to 'keep forever as a sign of honour.' [19]

---

* As far as we know, the text of the manuscript letter has never been published.

Designated on the 17th, Ghavam was charged with forming the government [20] on the 18th. The Shah himself gave him his title back!

His nomination provoked violent demonstrations that were mainly organized by the communists. Moscow and its supporters had an old score to settle with the new Prime Minister. Mossadegh's own supporters and ayatollah Kashani's networks joined them. The latter gave a fatwa, a religious order, to assassinate the Prime Minister.

As soon as he was nominated, Ghavam addressed the population. He spoke about the urgency of a 'break' with the previous government's policy in order to respect the principle of the nationalization of oil. He insisted on the restoration of safety for people and their possessions, of an economic recovery, and more particularly, on the separation of the church and politics, which was really unexpected. Like his predecessor, Ahmad Ghavam was a free mason who was in favour of an independent policy concerning denominational options.

On July 19th, and especially on the 20th and 21st of July 1952, there were riots in Tehran and in a few big cities. At the beginning, the police and the armed forces intervened to restore order. Then, on the Shah's order – he was the Commander-in-Chief and constitutional leader – they refused to intervene. Ghavam gave up, and those in power were defeated. The episode was to have serious consequences. The old statesman the representatives had designated was not popular, it is true, but he was very prestigious among the elite and in business circles. Even if he had been away from the country in the past few years, he had maintained his influential networks. He was respected, if not feared, and considered to be able to solve a crisis which was causing the division and ruin of the country.

By abandoning him, Mohammad Reza Pahlavi was to make a political error which did not allow for a possible reconciliation with Mossadegh. The old public speaker would never forgive the Shah for his ambiguous position.

In the evening of the 21st, Ghavam went to the Palace and offered his resignation to the Shah who immediately accepted it. It had been previously announced on the radio.

On July 22nd, Parliament stepped back and designated Mossadegh who was immediately charged with forming the government. He was not yet to run the Ministry of War, which had been renamed Ministry of National Defence in the meantime, so as to reassure the Sovereign. It was given to General Vossough, a close relative of the Prime Minister. He was also a relative of his predecessor who had been deposed after a short time in power.

Ahmad Ghavam was to be exposed to the prosecution and punishment of the communists and of Kashani's henchmen. A group of rioters set his house on fire and wanted to lynch him. Several foreign embassies offered him asylum. 'I'd rather be lynched by my fellow countrymen than find refuge in a foreign embassy,' he answered to an American envoy who had come to offer him the protection of the American embassy and even a special aeroplane to get him out of the country. [21]

The new Cabinet was under ayatollah Kashani and the Tudeh's pressure. It had two laws passed successively allowing for the confiscation of Ahmad Ghavam's possessions – they were not based on any legal ground, however – and instigating legal proceedings against him. Some of Kashani and of the Tudeh's henchmen looked for him all over the capital to assassinate him. He changed hide-outs several times. Mossadegh might have felt bad about the two laws he had just had passed, and discreetly put him under the protection of the police. Then, he slowed down the implementation of the law allowing for the confiscation of his possessions. It was only to be abrogated under General Zahedi's government.

*   *

*

On the very day Mossadegh was designate to become Prime Minister, on the 22nd, the International Court of Justice in The Hague declared itself incompetent to rule on the London-Tehran dispute. The nationalization of the Anglo-Iranian Oil Company was deemed to be a 'domestic matter for Iran'.

It was a great victory for Iran. Yet, the enthusiasm which had followed the victory in front of the Security Council of the United Nations was well in the past. There was a general disillusionment. The crisis had deeply scarred the country and people were getting more and more pessimistic.

The Sovereign nevertheless decided to address a message to the nation to mark his satisfaction and his joy. He reiterated it on August 5th, on the forty-seventh anniversary of the constitutional revolution of 1906, hoping that this political and juridical victory might help solve the oil crisis.

A few weeks later, *Time*, the famous New York magazine, elected Mossadegh, 'man of the year'. He had succeeded in 'defeating an empire by shedding contrived tears': this is what was written at the time.

These two happenings are at the height of Mossadegh's diplomatic career.

*   *

*

The new phase of Mossadegh's government had its painful beginnings, and continued in a situation of increasing domestic and exterior tension. Meanwhile, the relations between the Shah and the Prime Minister were deteriorating. At first, they continued to meet up. The audiences were exceptionally long: three hours on August 1st (1952), two hours on the 30th, three hours again on September 14th, a long time on October 5th and 7th – one does not know how long they lasted; then a long time on the 16th, and again some time on November 8th. A new habit progressively fell into place: Bagher Kazemi, who, at first, was Minister of Foreign Affairs, and then of Finance, and Vice-Prime Minister, started replacing Mossadegh when seeing the King.

As far as the oil crisis is concerned, all the propositions made to come out of it were judged unacceptable by the 'old lion'. Iran could not sell its oil any more. There seemed to be no way out.

Mossadegh tried to rush ahead. He resorted to ever more violent repressive measures when faced with a rising opposition. There was constant fighting in the streets of the capital and of the major cities, and there was fighting inside the Chamber. It was rather grim. The communists were the only ones to take advantage of it.

On October 16th, the diplomatic relations with London which had already been limited to the level of chargé d'affaires, were broken. Great Britain's chargé d'affaires in

Tehran was virtually expelled, though in a courteous manner. Mossadegh, not without good reason, believed that the British embassy was trying to oust him from power.

Though the tensions between the head of the executive and the Shah had now become public knowledge, the latter multiplied his trips to the provinces and often appeared in public in Tehran, whether officially or spontaneously. He was warmly welcomed everywhere. The point was to show how popular he was, and that he actually 'existed'.

Mossadegh enacted a law by decree on national security which was not very democratic; he dissolved the Supreme Court, had the judicial branch purged and many newspapers banned. The situation of unrest was not brought under control, on the contrary, and the democratic image of the 'old lion' was seriously tarnished.

The country had become like an aimlessly drifting boat. There was, indeed, no-one at the helm.
The full powers the Prime Minister had secured for himself were used to enact a few laws by decree which soon became void. Mossadegh's entourage was divided. Ayatollah Kashani who had himself elected president of the Chamber hardly ever went there. He turned against Mossadegh in his usual violent way. Some of his companions, Mozaffar Baghaï, Hossein Makki, Heaeri Zadeh, joined the opposition. Two of the most respected ones, Bagher Kazemi and Allahyar Saleh, had themselves appointed ambassadors: the first one in Paris, the second one in Washington. Hossein Fatemi, a journalist and talented polemicist who had been appointed Minister of Foreign Affairs, led an open campaign against the monarchy and often absented himself from the country, leaving Abdolhossein Meftah, his deputy, in charge.

The ones from his entourage who were left were divided. There were even weird ideas going round so as to create a certain diversion and keep public opinion busy: on June 27th 1953, Gholam Hossein Sadighi, Minister of the Interior, vice-Prime Minister acting as head of the government – Bagher Kazemi was not a member of the Cabinet any more – summoned an ultra-secret council to conduct a military offensive against Iraq, declaring that that country had become the basis for all the plotting against Iran. Meftah, who acted as Minister of Foreign Affairs, opposed the idea, claiming that such an operation was absurd and was doomed to fail (the chief of general staff said nothing, however). He added that there was the danger of a Soviet military intervention if, as was written in a cooperation treaty between both countries that was ratified in 1921, foreign forces managed to enter the national territory after a counter-offensive, which could not be ruled out because of the Iraq-Britain military alliance. Gholam Hossein Sadighi could not care less and said: 'There must be a diversion, public opinion must be kept busy.' It was Mossadegh's in extremis refusal which stopped this crazy and ridiculous operation. 22

*   *

*

Rushing ahead, the Prime Minister and his entourage urged the Shah and Empress Soraya to leave the country after Princess Ashraf, the Shah's twin sister, and some other members of the family had accepted to go away. Mohammad Reza Pahlavi accepted to go as well, either because he was weak or cunning. Passports were discreetly made for the imperial couple and their entourage. They were signed by Minister Fatemi himself. The National Bank prepared a tidy sum in foreign currencies and had it handed to the Prime Minister so that he could give it to them.

The date for their departure was secretly set. They were to travel by road towards Iraq.

On February 28th 1953, the Prime Minister went to the Palace in the early morning to wish the imperial couple a good trip.

The secret was soon to be uncovered. The shops in the bazaar were closed as a sign of protest. Sports clubs mobilized to stop the plan. The association of officers and non-commissioned officers asked its members to get together and demonstrate. Some of the most prestigious army officers joined them. Ayatollah Behbahani, who was a powerful religious leader, walked ahead of his followers to the Palace. Ghavam, a patriot with no grudge to bear, operated his networks from his hide-out.

Between 10 and 11 in the morning, dozens of thousands of people surrounded the imperial palace, shouting slogans in the Shah's favour, but also against Mossadegh. The crowd refused to let the Shah go, it wanted him to stay.

Empress Soraya wrote: 'The old lion is ashen-faced. He is sweating. I feel pity for him. I take his hand and whisper into his ear: take the door at the end of the alleyway... Mossadegh has retreated and Mohammad Reza [Pahlavi] has a megaphone brought to him to thank the crowds of people standing in front of the gates...' [24] He promised to stay and then came out of his residence under wild applause. Mossadegh was forced to ask for the protection of the imperial guard to leave the palace and get to his residence which was only 200 meters away. The crowd meant to assault him, and the police intervened.

'Mohammad Reza felt a new hope rise in him. He was not the only one, many Persians were still loyal to him...' [25]

The fear of communism, dead-end in the oil negotiations,

worsening of the economic situation and general unrest made the Shah appear like the person to turn to. He became aware of the fact that he could have his own popularity which would be independent from his support to Mossadegh's nationalist movement. However, since he was confined to his constitutional role, he could not take direct action. A credible alternative to the 'old lion' had to be found, a plan of action was needed.

*   *

*

General Eisenhower, a republican, was elected president of the United States in November 1952. John Foster Dulles became his Secretary of State. In Washington, the resistance to the growing appetite of the Soviet Union on a world scale now became predominant in American diplomacy.

In London, Winston Churchill was back in power. Mossadegh now had uncompromising partners, who, because of the intensification of the cold war, hardened their positions towards Iran, where the Tudeh was progressively becoming more influential and threatening.

Some people in Mossadegh's entourage advocated a rapprochement with the extreme left; they were influential lawyers like Ali Shayegan and Karim Sandjabi, the advisor on oil matters Kazem Hassibi, even the Minister of Foreign Affairs Hossein Fatemi, who did not really hide his republican leaning and his aversion for the Pahlavis. Others like the President of the Chamber, Abdollah Moazzami, who had just replaced the resigning ayatollah Kashani, the new ambassadors to Washington and Paris, Allahyar Saleh and Bagher Kazemi, the number two in Iranian diplomacy, Abdolhossein Meftah, the governor of the National Bank,

Mohammad Nassiri... were all suspicious of the communist influence, and urged their old leader to adopt a conciliatory attitude.

Mossadegh hesitated – or was not interested in immediate business any more – he was only thinking about his place in History. The man was anti-communist and sometimes had the Tudeh held back, but also used it as a bogeyman to lead the Westerners to accept his requirements which were not very clear to start with. It was a dangerous game.

Sadtchicov, the old diplomat who had been at the head of the Soviet diplomatic mission in Tehran since the end of the war, said his farewells, and Anatoli Lavrentiev, who was said to be from the secret services and a 'specialist' in the brutal changes of regimes – Was this a war of nerves? – replaced him. He presented his letters of introduction to the Shah. Moscow was ready to pick the 'ripe fruit', as Stalin had previously said about Iran.

*   *

*

The unrest spread all over the country.

On March 1st, thousands of people converged towards the Prime Minister's residence, wanting to storm it. The police forces sealed the area off and shot at the demonstrators. There were one casualty and twenty-nine people wounded.

On the 2nd, people demonstrated against Mossadegh outside the Parliament. There was another confrontation with the police. There was one casualty again, and a few people were wounded.

The government had many arrests ordered, and a list of a hundred and seventy other people wanted was issued.

On the 3rd, there were new demonstrations and bloody confrontations between people who were pro- and anti-Mossadegh. Many people were wounded.

The government which had had General Zahedi, Mossadegh's former Minister of the Interior, arrested, had him released on March 17th. The latter found refuge inside the Parliament, where he was supposed to be safe.

The New Year celebrations that were held at the beginning of spring brought a lull.

On April 7th 1953, and on the 9th, there were still demonstrations and counter-demonstrations and the streets of the capital bathed in blood. There were many victims. The government had people arrested.

There were yet other street fights in Tehran on April 14th. One person died, and many were injured.

On April 15th, demonstrators who claimed to be supporters of the Prime Minister, but who, in fact were Tudeh members, set shops on fire in Shiraz, as well as a cultural centre and even a few dwellings. The police made use of their arms again. One person was killed and many were wounded.

On the 17th, the government declared a state of siege in Shiraz. The governor of the town, chief of police and commander of the local garrison were relieved from their duties.

On the same day, there were bloody demonstrations in Dezful, a major town in the Khuzistan province. There were four casualties with many people wounded, and martial law was proclaimed.

The same thing happened in Kermanshah, a big Kurdish city in the West. Another city was under siege.

On April 20th, the Tehran chief of police was kidnapped in the street. From April 22nd to May 2nd, many government opponents were accused of the crime and arrested. On the 26th, the chief of police's corpse was found in the mountains north of the capital city.

On May 14th, and 17th, workers from several factories in the capital went on strike to protest against the failure to pay their wages. Many strikers were arrested.

On May 10th and 19th, and on June 6th, the representatives who were for and against the government had a fight during a public session of the Chamber.

On May 5th, the Tudeh demonstrated in Mahabad, a Kurdish town – one does not really know why. A child was killed, and many people were injured.

On June 27th, 40,000 workers from the brick factories of the capital demonstrated in the streets to demand a pay rise. The police intervened.

On July 10th, Mossadegh addressed a message to the nation, declaring his intention to organize a referendum so that the people could arbitrate between him and the representatives. Yet, the Chamber had been elected under his government and he benefited from a comfortable majority there. After Kashani's resignation, his friend Abdollah Moazzami had been elected its president. Being a level-headed man, he had done everything he could to reconcile the Shah and the Prime Minister.

As far as the Constitution was concerned, he could have asked the sovereign to dissolve the Chamber. He did not wish to do so. The procedure for a referendum did not exist in elementary law. The 'old lion' was thus putting himself in a delicate situation, playing into his opponents' hands and weakening his position at the same time.

To make it easier for him, fifty representatives of the National Front parliamentary group resigned on July 14th, to be joined, two days later, by the members of a small transitional group, the Kechvar, and a few representatives who were not registered. There was no official legislative power since the Chamber formed its pivot.

On July 21st, Mossadegh's followers organized important demonstrations in support of the Prime Minister in Tehran and in several provincial towns.

The same day, Mossadegh announced the organisation of his referendum to dissolve a Chamber of representatives that had practically dissolved itself already. The non-resigning representatives protested vehemently and appealed to the Supreme Court. Ayatollah Kashani gave them his support.

On August 1st, a bomb exploded in the prelate's home during a public meeting. One person died and many were injured. There were fights nearly everywhere in the streets of Tehran and in many provincial towns.

On August 2nd, Abdollah Moazzami, the president of the Chamber, resigned from his position and from his mandate as a representative.

On the 3rd, there was the referendum in Tehran. There was only one ballot box for those who wanted to vote against the dissolution. It was separated from the others and left well in sight. A big group of Mossadegh's followers stood around it. A donkey was solemnly brought in to inaugurate the vote! The operation had turned into a farce.

On the 10th, it was time for the provinces to vote. There was such a confusion that the vote was nearly always suspended.

Nevertheless, the Prime Minister declared in a message on the radio on the 14th that, following the referendum, 'the seventeenth legislature' was dissolved.

The imperial couple had left the capital three days before and were in the North of the country, on the Caspian Sea.

On the 15th, the Prime Minister asked for the dissolution of the Chamber in a letter to the Head of State, according to the results of the referendum. The Shah made a blunt refusal for lack of respect of constitutional dispositions. He was right, judicially speaking, but it was to be a political trial of strength.

The crisis of the regime had just started.

*   *

*

For months, both in the political circles of the capital and abroad – particularly in Washington and London – a solution to the crisis had been sought: it had progressively turned into a political chaos and a constitutional deadlock.

The Shah had found shelter in a way, and a procedure was to start which was desired by much of public opinion, and backed by the United States and Great Britain.

A man was to be its symbol: General Fazlollah Zahedi.

Chapitre VI

IRAN'S TWIST OF FATE
An Exceptional General

During the first months, even the first year of the Mossadegh government, almost all Iranians supported his movement with pride and were ready to make sacrifices to see the nationalization of oil succeed, Iran assuming the management and export of its resources, and the latter being used for national development.

Mossadegh was a finicky patriot, an outstanding public speaker who was emotional and passionate. The people were behind him, and so was the Shah, who was sincere about it, although he did not like him.

He did have opponents, but his ascendancy was such that they barely dared express their ideas. The communists were against him, but it was known that they were under the orders of a foreign power and served the latter's interests.

All along during this first stage, the British never stopped plotting against him [1], trying to find and supporting men who could overthrow him or, at least, take over from him. It was all in vain.

225

The Americans and their ambassador to Tehran, Doctor Grady, had shown a certain friendliness since the early days of the nationalization movement – this, out of an anticolonialist tradition, but also out of interest. Weren't the American oil companies the rivals of British Petroleum, the mother company of the AIOC, although they were all bound together inside an informal cartel which was all powerful and called 'the Seven Sisters'- there were actually eight of them?

*   *

*

The 'old lion's' failure to achieve the first important stage of the nationalization programme, the growing disillusionment of a large part of the population, economic difficulties, the change of Administration in Washington and the rise of the communist peril gave a new boost to the movement in favour of a change.

Ghavam's failure put him out of the game.

The British supported Sayyid Zia Ol-Din Tabataba'i, the man of the coup d'État of 1921*, whom they fully trusted. He was known for being a competent and fine political tactician, although he had spent many years abroad in the last three decades, particularly in Palestine, which was under Britain's mandate, and had only been a representative for two years. The Shah was contacted by the British ambassador, but had certain doubts over the issue. He distrusted the men from London. Besides, it was hard to imagine a man who was reputed to be pro-English replace the national hero in the fight against British imperialism without causing indignation and rebellion.

Ali Soheili's name was mentioned. He was a former Prime

---

* See prologue.

An Exceptional General

Minister from the forties, a proud diplomat indeed, but not the right man in a time of crisis [2].

The Shah preferred a moderate from Mossadegh's entourage, Allahyar Saleh or Abdollah Moazzami. Neither of them would accept the position without Mossadegh's assent, so it was an impossible solution.

Even after Ghavam's fall, Washington still preferred an arrangement with the 'old lion' to any other possibility. The latter's intransigence, the Soviet-communist danger, London's pressure and the coming to power of General Eisenhower were to progressively change America's political leanings.

*   *

*

A man was to impose himself in the country in the converging trends in public opinion, as the main spokesman and the genuine, credible leader of the opposition, the symbol of an alternative solution: General (retired) and elected senator Fazlollah Zahedi [3], Mossadegh's former Minister of the Interior, the one the British government had considered to be its most dangerous enemy in Iran [4], and whom the ambassador to Tehran continued to distrust [5], saying he was 'absolutely not worthy of trust.'

As for the Americans, they hardly knew the man. He did not really seek contact with accredited foreign diplomats in the Iranian capital. The American ambassador to Tehran had only met him once when he was Mossadegh's much appreciated Minister of the Interior [6], before he actually got to power.

After he had left the government a few months before

and had returned to the Senate where he was co-opted, the general continued to more or less support the government*. However, the situation evolved rapidly and the outlook got bleaker. He was solicited by many politicians, including those from the National Front**, and had trials and tribulations with the government***.

On October 15th 1952, he addressed the Senate for a long time when he was feeling a little unwell. He recalled his long convergence with the Head of Government, their meetings, the role he played to ensure and guarantee the freedom of legislative elections which enabled members of the National Front to sit in Parliament, and led to the nomination of Mossadegh at the head of the executive branch. He talked about his months spent in the Cabinet, of his support for the government, once he had left it.

Then he recalled his past, his arrest by the British, his deportation, the three years he spent in English jails. He said how sad he was to observe the failure of the government in reform plans, the stagnation of the oil crisis, the division in public opinion, the dictatorial measures used to choke the opposition. 'Is it my fault?' He spent a long time denying the accusations in some of the press and the content of a government press release against him. 'It is neither a sin, nor a crime to want to serve one's country as Prime Minister. Yet, I want you to know that I am not the man of a coup d'État.' He demanded the creation of a parliamentary committee to investigate into the accusations (of a coup) made against him. 'Wake up, Mister Prime Minister,' [7] he concluded.

---

* See later.
** Idem.
*** Idem.

An Exceptional General

The next day, the same themes were developed in a long press release from the general. It was also sent to numerous political and religious personalities in separate letters.

The domestic opposition had finally found its leader in a short time. The man was known for his anti-British past and had suffered from it in his own blood and flesh. He had been Mossadegh's minister and held excellent relations with some members of the latter's entourage, as well as with the clergy. His integrity was known to all. He dared suggest and alternative solution. His founding speech and the excessive reactions of the government were to establish him as the main, even the only, alternative.

*   *

*

Fazlollah Zahedi was born in 1893 in Hamadan, the former capital of the Medes located in the Western part of Iran. His father, whose title was Bassir-Divan, was a big land owner in the region. Fazlollah had a private tutor and also followed the teaching of the traditional schools of his town. His good knowledge of Persian literature, his taste for poetry – he is alleged to have sometimes even written verses – a calligraphy (a form of art Iranians appreciate a lot) that was notably above average, date back to that period.

His family advised him to take up a military career when he was still a teenager, after his father's death. His taste for being in command, at that time already, his sense of discipline, his fine figure of a man and his love of hunting, and thus of the use of weapons, which he felt all his life, predestined him for it.

He joined a small unit of the army at the end of the Qajar period. His military training was assumed by a few officers of the imperial Russian Army who had served in that army, and then found refuge in Iran after the Bolshevik revolution. Thus he learned Russian, a language he was to master perfectly well, while also learning his mother tongue and spoken Turkish, which many Iranians of the region were more or less fluent in.

He joined the so-called Cossack division, the only organized unit in the Iranian army of the time, and thus was in the troop which occupied Tehran in 1921, under General Reza Khan'orders, the future emperor, during a 'coup d'État' carried out by Sayyid Zia Ol-Din Tabataba'i*.

The future emperor liked his culture, innate authority and sense of politics. The fortunes of the Pahlavis and Zahedis were now to be linked. At the age of twenty-five, Fazlollah Zahedi was to be the youngest brigadier general of the new Iranian army, the one founded by Commander-in-Chief Reza Khan. He then received his father's title and became General Fazlollah-Khan Bassir-Divan, before he actually took the patronymic of Zahedi, which comes from a remote ancestor called Sheikh Zahed. [8]

He distinguished himself in several delicate operations. When he was under Reza's orders, he crushed the separatist rebellion in the Khuzistan province that had been strongly and ostensibly backed by the British. He managed to catch its leader, the fantastically wealthy and powerfully armed Sheikh Kazaal, without shedding a drop of blood. The press nicknamed him the 'liberator of Khuzistan.' He brought peace back to the province of Guilan, in the North, where unrest was caused by communist gangs that were manipulated by the brand-new Soviet government, and by a fanatical and

---

* See prologue.

illuminate patriot called Mirza Kuchik Khan. Thanks to his savoir-faire, he succeeded in establishing the authority of the central power there, virtually without any clashes. He was appointed Governor of the province.

In Rasht, the main administrative town in Guilan, he supported a local cultural association to create the first public library in the country, founded a theatre, a music academy. He had concerts organised, launched town planning ventures, and modernized the main harbour in the province. These achievements were not always to the mullahs' liking. Reza, who had just ascended to the throne partly thanks to the religious hierarchy, called him back to Tehran to calm them down. However, the reputation of a general involved in politics, of a peacemaker and builder was already established.

He held the position of chief of the National Police Forces for a brief period of time, but was moved aside after a disagreement with the Sovereign. He was even placed under close arrest for a few days before being released. He had fallen into disfavour however. He took advantage from that period to launch a car-import business. One has to live!

Once back in favour, he was appointed manager of the new officer's club whose stately building had just been completed – the Shah wanted it to be first-rate. He founded a library there, among other things, and entrusted erudite Zabih Behrouz with its management. It was soon to be turned into a real research centre on Iranian history and culture, a centre for nationalist intellectuals.

The Shah advised him to take up French: 'You will need it.' He said to him. Was he thinking of entrusting him with a political or diplomatic mission? The general applied himself to it. Those who knew him years later said and wrote that he spoke French reasonably well.

Foroughi appointed him chief of the national gendarmerie. He then happened to become the commander of the Esfahan garrison, shortly after the allied troops had entered Iran, and was later promoted to the rank of major general.

When he was at the head of the garrison in that town, he quickly came up against the interferences and plotting of the British Consulate General, but he could not care less. He did not tolerate the disorder and imposed his authority. The consul general multiplied reports against him, accusing him of preparing a plot against the Allies with the help of the Germans – 'a pro-German coup d'État'. It is true that, as a patriot, the general did not hide his nationalist feelings, but he was disciplined, and followed the policy of the government of his country which had become the ally of the British and the Soviets. The event which caused a clash between the British and Zahedi was the latter's decision to ban the massive buying – in fact, the confiscation – of the cereals harvested in the region by the British forces, so as to prevent a shortage of bread and famine in Esfahan and in the region. During the autumn of 1942, Bullard, Great Britain's ambassador, multiplied alarming reports on Zahedi. London decided on his arrest and deportation. Thus, over a thousand overarmed soldiers and armoured vehicles besieged the general's residence in December 1942, at the dawn of a grey day, and arrested him. He was taken to a close airport and deported to Palestine where he was held in secrecy for thirty-two months. The personal intervention of the Shah, the vivid protests of the government were to no avail. Other Iranians were also to be arrested, but in a less brutal way. General Zahedi had become a national celebrity on his release. [9]

* *

*

Ahlad Ghavam bestowed him with full powers to pacify the South* during the Azerbaijan crisis and the tribal rebellion in Fars. He did extremely well. He was then named as the Inspector General of the army, before becoming

Chief of the National Police Forces. His reforms when exercising this function, and especially his role to guarantee the freedom of the general legislative elections earned him a certain popularity. His relations with the National Front were excellent. He had regular lunches and dinners with the eminent members of the Front. [10]

General Razmara, who had become the head of government, replaced him at the head of the police forces. A civilian and former minister was appointed there. Zahedi was elected to the Senate. A few months later, after the assassination of the ambitious general-Prime Minister, he was appointed Minister of the Interior in Ala's Cabinet. When Mossadegh came to power, the main members of the National Front advised him to take over from the general at the Ministry of the Interior [11]. He accepted without any hesitation (May 2nd 1951). The relations between the two men were excellent for a few months.

On July 15th, when Averell Harriman arrived in Tehran as a special envoy from the president of the United States, the Tudeh displayed its strength in front of the Parliament and the demonstrators, who were sometimes armed, tried to storm it. The police intervened on order of General Hassan Baghaï, the Chief of the National Police. There were victims. The Prime Minister, who had chosen the general in person, and suggested his appointment to the Ministry of the Interior – probably to spare the left – had his dismissal announced on the national radio, and then publicly declared his intention to take him to court.

---

* See chapter IV: The Azerbaijan crisis – The man who defeated Stalin.

The Minister of the Interior sent a written protest to his direct chief: it was Mossadegh himself who had suggested general Baghaï's name; he was to warn the minister, the hierarchical chief of the person in charge of the National Police Forces, beforehand that he had decided to dismiss him, and not let him discover the information in the news. Moreover, the police had only done its duty by protecting the Parliament.

On the 16th, the Council of Ministers tackled the subject. Both men confronted each other courteously but firmly. The Prime Minister is alleged to have said to the general: 'You are responsible too, you know.' [12] The latter waited for the departure of the American envoy then offered his resignation on August 2nd. It was immediately accepted. He went back to the Senate where his seat had not yet been taken.

Between that very August 16th 1951 and October 15th 1952, the date of his 'founding speech', Zahedi went from a selective form of support to a more or less discreetly critical position in power. From October 1952 on, he became the undisputed leader of the opposition. The government chose him as their main target. As for foreign countries, Washington and even London, which were still distrustful – and this is but a euphemism – found an interest in him. He could not be ignored any more.

During that delicate period, his son Ardeshir, a young engineer in agronomics who had been trained in a famous American university, became his main companion, his emissary, and his only interpreter as well, when foreign speakers did not know any French, a language that was still much used in diplomatic conversations since the general could not use his Russian.

*   *

*

IRAN'S TWIST OF FATE
An Exceptional General

Ardeshir was born in 1928, and was the first of Fazlollah Zahedi's two children. He also had a girl called Homa, who was born in 1932. She was to lead a social and political career, though a rather discreet one.

When the Prime Minister was a young and successful soldier, his first wife was Hossein Pirnia (Motamen ol Molk)'s daughter, one of the founding fathers of the 1906 Constitution (which was in force until the Islamic revolution), a statesman who was unanimously respected, the president of the Parliament during five successive legislatures, a man twice designated as head of the government, a sort of national icon. Many years later, the two spouses had separated on a mutual agreement, but grand-father Pirnia, who had taken a particular liking for Ardeshir, had well looked after him and given him much advice.

The general's second wife was the daughter of the Ettehadiehs, a good middle-class family. The marriage did not last long and the couple had no children together.

At the time when the general appeared on the national and then international scene, he had a well-established reputation: even his most determined opponents did not contest his integrity, even if they often accused him of being a 'reveller' (ahl-eh-bazm). He was a proficient rider, a good shot, liked classical music, and was keen on history. When the British put him in solitary confinement after having abducted him, he only asked them for one thing: history books, and more particularly the monumental *History of Old Iran*, his bedside book, it seems [13], written by Hassan Pirnia, his father-in-law's brother. He actually knew classic Persian poetry rather well. He often peppered his speeches and letters with quotations from poems.

He was also a seducer and is alleged to have had quite a few affairs. Empress Soraya remembered her first encounter with the general: 'Zahedi is looking at me and sees right through me. He has the eyes of an eagle and, at the same time, the eyes of a man who knows he is attractive to women. Zahedi has the reputation of being a Don Juan and many are the ones he has seduced. He is the warrior who stands at ease...

Zahedi is more of a warrior than a womanizer however. He is an energetic man who can only find fulfilment in action.' [14] Many were his critics or enemies, but he also had devoted friends who were completely loyal to him. He was very loyal to them as well. His gratefulness to those who did him favours and his loyalty as a friend are even recognised by his critics. Yet, some of the latter took advantage of it to the detriment of Zahedi's image.

*   *

*

The man who was undoubtedly the closest to the general was his son Ardeshir who resembles his father in many ways, and not only physically.

He went back to Iran in 1950, once he had completed his studies, and was hired by the 'Administration of the Point IV program', an agency that was created by the United States in many countries as a direct application of the 'Point IV' of the Truman doctrine to manage technical, social and humanitarian aid to developing countries. He soon became the Iranian executive assistant to the managing director. It was a useful relation in the times of crisis mainly caused by his father, that Iran was to live through. Two years later, when the relations between Mossadegh and Zahedi went wrong, the government asked for his resignation and got it. He was even arrested and ill-treated in prison – he still suffering from the after-effects – and went underground once he was released.

He was to play an important role, even a determining

one, on his father's side during the events which brought about Mossadegh's fall, but also, and more particularly, in the political and diplomatic life of his country for a quarter of a century. On Mossadegh's fall, he was given the honorific title of 'civilian aide-de-camp of His Imperial Majesty' and also ran an aid program for Iranians students abroad. He was to be the favoured intermediary between his father and Mohammad Reza Pahlavi, as well as with politicians and the clergy.

In 1959, he became the Iranian Ambassador to the United States, and in 1963, to Saint James's Court. In the meantime he married for love princess Shahnaz, the daughter of the Shah and princess Fawzieh of Egypt. She was his first wife. Their marriage was to last only seven years. He became Minister of Foreign Affairs in 1966, then Ambassador to Washington again in 1973, until Chapour Bakhtiar was appointed at the head of the government.

He was to be a very active minister once at the head of Iranian diplomacy. He established personal relations with some of the world's greatest figures, left his mark on the major political leanings in Iranian foreign politics, and carried out thorough reforms in his department. He had many friends but also many foes, among whom Prime Minister Hoveyda and, more particularly, the Savak. His legendary outspokenness and the brutality of some of his decisions were to create him enmities. His nationalism, which his opponents called excessive, if not outdated, was to irritate people in some of the capital cities, especially in London. The five years he spent at the head of Iranian diplomacy are undoubtedly the most brilliant and active he had ever known.

During his second term as ambassador to Washington, Ardeshir Zahedi became a personality known to the press and to American political circles, a real star, thanks to his friendliness, courteousness, his sumptuous parties and his very much appreciated presents. He used this image with great talent to promote the objectives of Iranian diplomacy. Some were also to criticize him for his munificence, and even accused him of interfering in American politics!

Many were the ones who thought he could be the man to turn to during the difficult months of the year 1978. The Shah and the Shahbanoo Farah then played a determining role in the conduct of domestic affairs, and seemed to have ruled this option out. They were scared of the character's radical methods and of his open desire to get rid of 'a few rotten elements'.

He nevertheless continued to take good care of the Shah after the fall of the monarchy, and to organize his successive stays in Egypt, Morocco and then in Mexico, while always giving him the support of his international relations.

The relations between the general and his son were exceptional, even fusional. The father deeply trusted his son, even if he happened to admonish him. The son respected and admired his father [15], he still admires him. His father has remained a reference, a model for him to follow. They worked in tandem for years.

*   *

*

Fazlollah Zahedi was a man under threat from October 15th 1952 onwards. Then, the Senate being dissolved, he was deprived of his diplomatic immunity and was arrested by the police on accusation of conspiracy against the government. He spent two months in jail. Once released, he immediately found refuge inside Parliament's impregnable walls. There, he entertained a lot and even sought advice to form his cabinet. The U.S. ambassador to Tehran envisaged his coming to power for the first time, although 'he was not an ideal successor to replace Mossadegh.' He added: 'I do not know his entourage and will continue to follow events.' [16]

The struggle between Mossadegh and his former Minister of the Interior then started taking exceptional proportions. The representatives of the National Front offered their resignation so as to paralyze Parliament. Mossadegh decided to dissolve the Chamber in a referendum*. The general left Parliament which was not deemed to be a safe place any more, and went underground. It was the President of the Chamber, Abdollah Moazzami who, though he was an eminent member of the National Front and a close friend of the Prime Minister, drove him in his official car with the official pennant – thus in full immunity – to his first hide-out. [17]

A considerable bounty was offered by the government for his arrest, thus Zahedi often changed hide-outs; a complete network of friends who were often in the military or in the reserve, ensured his protection. 'Disguised as dervishes, water carriers, watermelon sellers, they carried guns and hand grenades hidden under their kaftans,' [18] Empress Soraya wrote, yet the picturesque details are not likely to be true.

It was also written that, during that period, he had found refuge at an American diplomat's home. It is not an established fact. [19] Kermit Roosevelt, the head of the CIA's Middle East division, published a book called *Countercoup* on Mossadegh's fall, many years after Zahedi's death, in which he particularly wanted to put himself forward – he even recalls a long tête-à-tête conversation in German with the general while he was underground. Now, the general did not know a word of German, which Roosevelt was unaware of. The latter believed that since

---

* See chapter V: The oil crisis – The man who chased the British away.

the general had been arrested for being pro-German, he had to speak German!

While general Zahedi was leading his own course of action, passing himself off as the only possible alternative to the Mossadegh government, the contacts between the Palace and American circles became more and more frequent. Many envoys arrived in Iran to consider the 'old lion's' fall – the latter was told about it but did not react. [20]

Despite a certain hesitation, Mohammad Reza Pahlavi resigned himself to a direct intervention in the crisis and to call on General Zahedi. Their first – and not the only one – encounter during these days of extreme tension was, it seems, on August 2nd 1953. [21] Yet, Ardeshir Zahedi was sometimes used as an emissary between them, and no document proves that there were one or several encounters between the general and American or British envoys during that period which was actually rather short. The fact that Zahedi had gone underground forced him to be extremely cautious, and the American and British envoys were under close surveillance.

* *

*

On August 13th 1953, once the Shah was sure of the backing of the United States and, ultimately, of that of Great Britain, he signed an ordinance to relieve Mossadegh from his duties as Prime Minister. On the same day, the decree for the nomination of 'His Excellency Fazlollah Zahedi' at the head of the government was signed. The general had been retired for years. He had been a senator, and then Minister of the Interior, notably under Mossadegh. It was thus meant to show that a 'civilian' was in charge of forming the cabinet.

IRAN'S TWIST OF FATE
An Exceptional General

The Sovereign had the constitutional, formal right to appoint and dismiss ministers, including the Prime Minister. However, the rule was that he did so when Parliament proposed it, or after a vote of no confidence. In such a case, there was a gap in the Constitution. The Senate had ceased to be. The Chamber had first dissolved itself with the collective resignation of all the supporters of the 'old lion'; then, it had been officially dissolved in a referendum which the government had organized, which was disputed and disputable. Mossadegh had made a major error by provoking this process, he said so himself. The Shah could not have taken such an initiative with an active Parliament. He was to constantly declare that he had acted as the guarantor of national unity so as to prevent a disintegration of the State. A judgment on this last statement can only be subjective; yet, the standpoint is juridically and politically justifiable. A few months later, the subject was to be debated on during the 'old lion's' trial for days in a row, but nobody was on the same wavelength.

The imperial ordinances were signed and Colonel Nematollah Nassiri, the commander of the imperial guard, was put in charge of handing General Zahedi his ordinance, which he did after he had managed to locate him at Mostafa Moghaddam's place, and notified Prime Minister Mossadegh.

The notification of the ordinance to Mossadegh took place in strange, even incredible circumstances. The colonel was escorted by three trucks full of Guards and one (two or three, according to other versions) light armoured vehicle. He called on the Prime Minister's residence shortly before midnight and knocked on the door. Colonel Momtaz, who was the latter's Guards' Commander, opened the door and asked for the purpose of his visit at such an unusual hour. His colleague from the imperial guard answered: 'I have to hand his Excellence the Prime Minister a letter from His Imperial Majesty.' Momtaz

241

showed him in the residence and, as security measures required, asked him to hand him his gun. Nassiri complied. Momtaz went to wake up Mossadegh. The latter had been informed that a small detachment of the imperial guard had been sent to his residence (one will never know who told him), but he had apparently not said anything about it to the Guards' Commander. He told the latter: 'Take the envelope and bring it to me. I will give you a receipt for Colonel Nassiri.' Both officers did as they were told. Mossadegh opened the envelope, his hands slightly trembling, but he quickly pulled himself together and, surprisingly cold-bloodedly, using particularly polite expressions in an emphatic way, acknowledged receipt of 'His Imperial Majesty's letter' and handed the paper back to Colonel Momtaz who was not aware of the contents of the letter addressed to the Head of Government. In a voice void of emotions, he added for Momtaz: 'Arrest Colonel Nassiri and have all the soldiers who are with him disarmed.' Then, he pretended to be going back to sleep. [22] The colonel executed the head of government's orders without the slightest resistance from Nassiri who was disarmed, or from his men, who were sent to the barracks of the military police.

What was to be later called 'the military coup' had failed. It was a question of a letter handed over in ridiculous conditions!

*   *

*

The Shah and Empress Soraya were in Kelardasht near the Caspian Sea. When informed of the failure of Colonel Nassiri's mission [23], they immediately took a 'four-seat crate' to Ramsar, a near-by seaside resort. They were only carrying a small suitcase and were accompanied by a military pilot, Commander Khatam, and by a civil servant from the Court. In Ramsar, they got on the Shah's twin-engined aircraft, a Beechcraft, and flew to Baghdad which they reached a few hours later.

For fear of incidents or assassination attempts, Mohammad Reza Pahlavi refused to disclose his identity to the air control tower in Baghdad: 'Passenger aeroplane... Engine failure... Require permission to land...' he declared to the airport authorities. The plane was kept waiting at the end of the runway. There was a large deployment of police forces at the airport. The fugitives feared arrest on Tehran's orders. They quickly discovered that young King Faisal II of Iraq's aeroplane was to arrive any minute from Amman. The Shah scribbled a few words in English on a piece of paper and asked a police officer who had come to find out about the situation to hand it to Faisal as soon as he had landed. The four Iranians were allowed to leave their plane and were taken to a room away from the main building where it was stifling hot; the building was guarded by the Iraqi police. After waiting a long time, the Iraqi Minister of Foreign Affairs, who was sent by his Sovereign, came to fetch the imperial couple and settle them down in an Iraqi royal pavilion. The encounter with King Faisal took place later. A reception was hastily organized in honour of the Shah and of his wife who were to leave two days later for Rome. When they got off their airliner, they were welcomed by a crowd of reporters, by Hossein Sadegh, an Iranian civil servant from the FAO, and by Iranian businessmen, among whom was Morad Erieh, an eminent figure of the Jewish community. The Iranian ambassador, Nezam Khadjenouri was not there although he was the former Head of Protocol of the Court. He even had Mohammad Reza Pahlavi's personal car sealed off when it was parked in an embassy car park.

The couple were put up at the Excelsior Hotel.

* *

*

The news of the Shah's departure was now common knowledge in Tehran. The official spokespeople emphasized 'the failure of a coup attempt' by Colonel Nassiri and the imperial guard. The dismissal of the Prime Minister and the appointment of his successor were kept secret. There was an attempt to mobilize public opinion.

According to American diplomatic documents [24], Washington's envoys considered their attempt to provoke Mossadegh's fall to be a failure. Ambassador Henderson asked for an audience with the Prime Minister and was received. Their meeting lasted a long time.

Mossadegh's opponents were led by 'Retired Major General Fazlollah Zahedi', as the latter was named in a press release from the administrator of martial law in Tehran who offered a reward for his capture. They now acted autonomously as regards the Court, the official command of the army, and naturally, Washington's official or discreet envoys.
Mossadegh hesitated on what to do.
The news of the dismissal had not been made public yet and the administration of martial law and the police started arresting many of General Zahedi's supporters. He was now designated as the enemy to kill.

In the night of August 16th, Mossadegh summoned the general manager of the State radio station, Ali Asghar Bachir-Farahmand, a man he fully trusted. The latter was to give an account of his memories after the fall of the monarchy: 'I was summoned to the residence of the Prime Minister in the night of August 16th'. "I have just been relieved from my duties", he said to me. "Do what you have to do so that I can record my last message to the nation." I followed orders. The message was recorded so that it could be broadcasted the next day, the 17th. In his message, he said that he had just been relieved from his duties and asked the nation "to take their fate into their own hands" [25].' Was he thinking about the rebellion of the people that was provoked by Ahmad Ghavam's fall and his comeback to power hardly a year before, or was it a moving farewell message? Nobody knows.

Upon these facts, Hossein Fatemi, who, strangely enough, had come in his pyjamas and nightgown, Djahanguir Hagh-Chenass, the Minister of Transports, and Ahmad Zirak-Zadeh, the Under-Secretary of State in the Industry Department, all made their entrance. Mossadegh said to them: 'I have just been dismissed; my farewell message has been recorded and will be broadcasted in the morning.' Fatemi protested vehemently: 'You are the Prime Minister by law. No-one has the right to relieve you from your duties.' The others were in complete agreement with him. Four other personalities from the National Front were summoned, among whom a legal expert, Ali Shayegan, the former dean of the Law Faculty. The final decision was reached: Mossadegh was to stay. Another message from the government, and not from the 'old lion', was broadcasted on the 17th on the radio: 'An attempted coup has fallen through. Its organizers and conspirators have just been arrested...' [26]

In an article that was published later, Ebrahim Alami, the Minister of Labour and close adviser of the Prime Minister who had been "relieved from his duties", confirmed the reported facts, and led it to be believed that the Cabinet had never been made aware of these 'official events', the imperial ordinances [27].

While the confrontations had now reached the streets, Mossadegh consulted people to find a 'constitutional solution' to the crisis: the communists, as well as some of his own supporters – notably Hossein Fatemi, Ali Shayegan and Ahmad Razavi, the vice-president of the dissolved Chamber – were in favour of leaving the Constitution aside, and immediately proclaiming a Republic, even a formal alliance with the communist left [28] to take the power.

Mossadegh refused the proclamation of a Republic. He wanted to stay within the constitutional framework and opted for the implementation of a regency council. The Shah's eldest sister, Princess Shams was considered– the 'old lion' had always shown respect and friendship for her – then one of the Shah's brothers, Gholam Reza, whose mother was a Qajar; both options, however, were excluded. Eventually, Ali Akbar Dehkhoda, an authority on moral issues who was uncontested and apolitical, a famous man of letters, the Iranian Littré, accepted the offer.

The events that were to follow did not leave any time for that kind of consideration.

*   *

*

The news of the Shah's departure, which was first broadcasted by foreign media, soon became official. General Zahedi's entourage managed to have the ordinance about his nomination published in some of Tehran's newspapers. On his son Ardeshir's initiative, facsimiles of the ordinance were circulated in the capital. [30] The government could not deny the truth of a dismissal that they would rather have hidden to public opinion, or the nomination of General Zahedi, whose son even succeeded in organizing a meeting with three foreign reporters in Velenjak, in the mountains north of the capital, to keep them informed. [31]

There were violent demonstrations in Tehran on the initiative of the National Front and of the communists. The first one gathered forty thousand people, according to its organizers. The tone of the speech made by the Minister of Foreign Affairs was particularly offensive for the Shah and his family. The words he used were blunt, if not obscene. Ali Shayegan was hardly more moderate in what he said. Both demanded the proclamation of a republican regime. The Tudeh managed to display its strength with over a hundred thousand people. A "United Front" was asked for, with weapons for the people, and popular militia. The statues of the Shah and of his father were taken down, and the streets that bore their names were given other names. Red flags were hoisted on many public buildings. Slogans in favour of a "popular" republic appeared. The hunt for the true or supposed followers of the Shah and of General Zahedi was declared open and some old scores were settled, which was inevitable. In some northern towns, local Soviets had their names publicly announced, and were given official positions in town halls.

The 'old lion' was nearly isolated in his residence that had been turned into a bunker, and, according to all testimonies, lived in a state of despondency. He decided to organize a referendum so as to have the creation of a regency council approved. Gholam Hossein Sadighi, the Minister of the Interior, was summoned early in the morning on August 19th to give the necessary orders for its preparation. The latter objected to the 'old lion' that a Cabinet decision would be required to start the process. Mossadegh accepted and then changed his mind: 'Send your instructions without the formal approval of the Cabinet.

This is a matter of emergency.' Sadighi complied with the order and went back to his office. [32] Rumours of demonstrations against Mossadegh came to his ears from different parts of the capital. He called General Modabber, the Chief of the Police Forces, who said he knew nothing about them.

A few minutes passed. General Riahi, the Chief of General Staff, called the minister, conveyed the 'order of the Prime Minister' to appoint a new Chief of the Police Forces, General Chahandeh. Sadighi wrote: 'I have asked the Head of Staff to prepare the necessary document and to bring it to me so I can sign it.'

There was more and more news coming from the capital. Everywhere, Mossadegh's opponents gathered in great numbers. The police forces reacted feebly or fraternized with the demonstrators. A hostile crowd gathered in front of the Ministry of Justice and some demonstrators tried to storm the Ministry of the Post Office and Telecommunications. They were held back, but the policemen applauded them. The minister called Colonel Ashrafi, the administrator of martial law to inquire about the situation. The Colonel's answer was worrying: he did not trust his troops any more because they either fraternized with the demonstrators or hardly reacted, standing there at ease.

Minister Sadighi received a telephone call from the Prime Minister at eleven o'clock. It was another counter-order: 'Appoint General Daftari [Mossadegh's nephew] at the head of the Police. I have given the order that he should also be nominated administrator of the martial law.' 'I was surprised and scared of these orders and counter-orders.' Sadighi added, who did not know at the time that Daftari had just sworn allegiance to General Zahedi, and that he was trying hard enough to ensure the transition from the offices of the administration of the martial law.

Soon after 11, the Minister of the Interior received more and more alarming reports: the mayor of the capital told him that demonstrators were storming the city hall. Sadighi learnt that the technical centre of the telegraph and of the telephone had been taken over by demonstrators. Panic-stricken, he called Mossadegh who replied: 'Have the national radio protected. If the demonstrators occupy it, the unrest will spread all over the country.' From noon onwards, the Ministry of the Interior was also surrounded by the crowd. The minister called for his car, his chauffeur and his bodyguard to be ready to leave. He was told that it was impossible to leave the Ministry, so he made his way to the adjacent building. He took the direction of the Prime Minister's residence, avenue Kakh, in an unmarked municipal car he had hastily requested, accompanied by his bodyguard.

Their car was stopped by soldiers near the residence. The minister made himself known to the soldiers and 'a young lieutenant who was most courteous' made him get out of his car – 'all traffic around the house has just been banned' he said to him – and requested him to continue his way on foot, which he did. As he was walking, he noticed that there were many soldiers and tanks positioned there to defend the 'old lion's' residence which he reached shortly afterwards.

He noticed the presence of several personalities near Mossadegh: Minister Hossein Fatemi, Ahmad Razavi, Ali Shayegan, and Ahmad Zirak-Zadeh. They were all worrying about the possible take-over of the radio. A set was turned on: one could hear the noise of the crowd, of collisions, then the imperial anthem. It was the signal for the end. They went into the neighbouring room, Mossadegh's: 'He was crying his heart out.'

From 3 p.m. on, the crowd started converging towards Mossadegh's residence, and then it was stormed. The guards responded bluntly. Both sides were shooting at each other. Mossadegh called the Chief of General Staff who, very moved, told him that the city was occupied by demonstrators, that General Fouladvand was going to deliver him a message, and that it was in the nation's interest to accept its content. It was clear then that the offices of the General Staff were occupied.

At 4.40 p.m., General Fouladvand arrived. He presented his respects to Mossadegh and asked him to make the guards stop fighting: 'It is necessary to avoid a division of the army,' he said to him. Mossadegh replied: 'I want to be killed here.' The general stood up and saluted, 'Sir, think of the lives of all those who are around you, of your neighbours', he said to him. Mossadegh nodded. Ahmad Razavi suggested making a public release declaring the residence 'defenceless'. A text was drafted. The people present signed it. It could not be made public, of course, and was not, but a white flag, in fact one of the 'old lion's' old sheets, was hoisted on the building. The guards stopped resisting the attack.

The last group of faithful followers left the house by using an adjacent wall. Mossadegh was hoisted on a ladder, another empty house was crossed, the party entered a third house that 'belonged to a businessman called Haristchi'. The small group was given a warm welcome. Tea and cakes were served. They were made to feel at home. Two rooms were reserved for them. Mossadegh laid down on a mattress in one of them, all dressed in his pyjama-clothes. He cried when he saw the demonstrators from a distance, setting his house on fire. He said: 'It does not really matter, but I am ashamed for my wife who does not even have her own house tonight to pray in.' Late in the night, the resigning President of the dissolved Chamber arrived at the house. The neighbourhood was calm again. Mossadegh was embarrassed; he did not want to cause the owner of the house and his family problems.

This is how the night was spent.

At 5 in the morning, the small group separated. The city was calm.

Together with Gholam Hossein Sadighi and his Minister of Telecommunications, Seyfollah Moazzami, Mossadegh went by car to the latter's house which he shared with his mother. The radio had just given a press release from the new administrator of the martial law, General Dadsehtan, in which Mossadegh was given twenty-four hours to present himself to the authorities. The latter said: 'I'm going to present myself to them.' He was advised to wait until the end of the extension that had been given. He accepted to do so. The master of the house called his brother-in-law Djafar Sharif-Emami*. He asked him to come and begged him to go and see General Zahedi to settle the details of the "surrender", which the latter did not do, or could not do. [33]

In fact, the authorities knew where Mossadegh was hiding from the early hours of his flight, and the house was under close surveillance. [34] The idea was to wait until things had calmed down and go about it in a decent manner.

*   *

*

Tehran was in turmoil during these comings and goings on August 19th. Dozens of thousands of people had gone to the streets to demand the return of the Shah and the end of Mossadegh's government. They had been warned by various networks, particularly those of the two powerful religious leaders of the capital, ayatollahs Kashani, who had been Mossadegh's friend until recently, and Behbahani, as well as by sports clubs, the powerful association of officers and

---

* The future Prime Minister.

non-commissioned officers from the reserve, and dissident parties of the National Front, in particular Mozzafar Baghaï's Zahmatkehchan.

The bazaar chiefs had called Boroujerdi, the great ayatollah of Qom, to ask him what they should do. The Shiites' supreme leader had given them permission to demonstrate. This was probably when everything went wrong.

Zahedi's small circle of friends had thoroughly coordinated the movement. Thirteen months before, a similar movement in Mossadegh's favour had manoeuvred Ahmad Ghavam out of power and ransacked his home. One could not really talk about a coup d'État in either case.

Fazlollah Zahedi, who was only a retired major general, had no troops at this disposal during these five days of August 1953. There was not one organized unit that mobilized against the government. The street actually caused his fall, his confusing constitutional situation had already weakened him.

*   *

*

On that very August 19th, when Mossadegh was led away from his residence, General Zahedi got on a tank to go to the radio station. He was accompanied by many vehicles that were hooting their horns and by a crowd brandishing Iranian flags and portraits of the Shah. The radio station was already under the control of his followers. Once there, he announced he was 'the Prime Minister of Iran by law', and that he was in full control of the situation.

Mossadegh's government had lasted two years, three months and twenty days.

Some of the men of the Esfahan garrison who had been informed by Ardeshir Zahedi [34], and the Kermanshah brigade

IRAN'S TWIST OF FATE
An Exceptional General

that was under the command of Colonel Teymour Bakhtiar, were ready to move towards Tehran if Mossadegh's faithful supporters and the Tudeh managed to keep the power and crush the people's rebellion. They did not have to intervene, and a civil war was avoided.

On August 20th and 21st, the United States Ambassador to Tehran gave an account of the reversal of the situation [35] in two long dispatches. He was obviously very surprised.

On that very August 19th, the General and Prime Minister had put on his military uniform out of his own will, and started making his first nominations: General Nader Batmanghehlitch was appointed at the head of General Staff; the Chief of Police who had been designated by Mossadegh, General Daftari, saw his position confirmed; the administrator of the martial law in the capital was replaced. All the political prisoners were released. Some of Mossadegh's team's main men or his relatives and friends took their places in jail. This was to be a very temporary measure in almost all cases. The Prime Minister sent a message to the Shah asking him to come back to his country.

Mohammad Reza Pahlavi, who was in Rome, sent two thank-you telegrams to ayatollah Behbahani and to the great ayatollah Boroujerdi. The first's answer was very formal. The second's, more succinct: 'Safety and religion will be safeguarded with your return to Iran.' [36] Iranians addressed the Shah using the third person plural, or the second person singular. The great ayatollah had chosen the latter form.

*   *

*

On August 21st, *Le Monde*, which duly accredited the theory of a CIA coup d'État, later on published on the spot: 'On August 19th at dawn, Dr Mossadegh was in control of the

253

situation after the failure of the military coup d'État that had occurred three days before in Iran. The same day at noon, his regime was collapsing.

Royalist demonstrations were started by some young people and gathered momentum until the arrival of military detachments quickly summoned by General Zahedi. This is how a street fight was turned into a revolution.

To everybody's surprise, neither the police nor the army reacted to defend Dr Mossadegh. The crowd, which had remained undecided for a while, rapidly took the side of the strongest, i.e., the royalists. This tremendous reversal was due to the Tudeh's withdrawal: not one leftist extremist went to the street to defend Mossadegh's regime...

In fact, and already for a long time, the nationalist ideal Dr Mossadegh had supported had been emptied of its content: the only thing that was left from the terminology was the fight against imperialism, i.e. the slogan *par excellence* of the ultra-left party.' [37]

In fact, the Tudeh's excesses for months, more particularly after the Shah's departure, had made the silent majority come out of its passive state. Yet, it was rather more in favour of that 'nationalist ideal.' The clergy's influence was a determining element in the mobilization of the masses. General Zahedi was a remarkable strategist and organiser.

The CIA had been aware of Colonel Nassiri's [38] farcical attempt and was backing it. It did not play any role in the popular uprising of the 19th. It later tried to claim the "merit" for the whole happening for itself. The ultra-left obviously took a part in it when it abandoned the 'old lion'. The American central agency could only be the ideal scapegoat. Analysts have much evolved since then. When the expiry date for the confidentiality of the CIA documents arrived a few years ago, it was declared that the archives on that event had disappeared in a fire and would thus not be available for consultation any more. The doubts many people had then vanished. Kermit Roosevelt should not be taken seriously any longer; he had greatly contributed to the development of that version of the facts in his book [39].

As for the Sovieto-communist attitude, it could be understood that the Tudeh was surprised by the popular uprising of the 19th since it obviously took its inspiration from the Soviet intelligence services and from the Soviet embassy. From then on, its infiltration in the army which was soon to be discovered, allowed it to carry out subtle manoeuvres to control the situation. The decision-making process must have been slow, and Moscow was caught unawares. Mossadegh also acted as a patriot by not authorising the distribution of weapons to the 'people' and the creation of 'anti-imperialist militias.'

The Sovieto-communists, who were the prisoners of a few 'revolutionary' models, were thus deprived of a victory. Iran was saved from the communist hold as suggested Anwar Khameï, one of their theorists, when he chose 'The great opportunity that was lost' for a title in the third volume of his memoirs dedicated to that episode. [41]

*   *

*

Mossadegh and his Minister of the Interior, Gholam Hossein Sadighi, were at Seyfollah Moazzami's during the long hours that followed the fall of his government. Those in power knew about it and kept the place under close surveillance. Ahmad Matin-Daftari, Mossadegh's nephew and adviser, a former Prime Minister, worked as an intermediary to organize his "surrender".

After the release made by the administrator of the martial law that followed regulations to the letter and gave the 'old lion' twenty-four hours to present himself to the authorities, and once the negotiations were well advanced, it was the General Prime Minister himself who made a public declaration in which 'he begged His Excellency Dr Mossadegh to present himself to the authorities', assuring him that 'his safety and respect would be guaranteed.'

On August 21st, police vehicles went to fetch the former Prime Minister at Seyfollah Moazzami's. Mossadegh and both his ministers, Sadighi and Moazzami, were taken to the officer's club where General Zahedi had temporarily established his quarters. He had organized the protocole of the famous prisoner's [42] arrival himself. Before that, he had declared to all his entourage: 'Bear in mind that I will have anybody who shows disrespect to him shot!'*

When Mossadegh and his friends arrived at the club, General Batmanghehlitch, the Chief of General Staff, General Daftari, the Chief of the Police Forces (and the prisoner's nephew), and General Dadsehtan, the administrator of the martial law, were all waiting for him on the doorstep. Mossadegh shook their hands. All the military officers saluted him with respect.

---

* A few days before, when the general was in hiding and a reward was offered for his capture, Mossadegh, who had guessed how he could contact him, had requested Mr Seyf Afshar to go and tell him that he was ready to have him granted a diplomatic passport and given 'an envelope full of foreign currencies' so that he could go abroad and rest for a while with his son Ardeshir, who was wanted as well. Zahedi had replied: 'I am staying and I will fight. If Mossadegh succeeds, I know he's going to bump me off. If I succeed, I give him my word as a soldier that I will oust him from power and leave him at peace. I will go right to the end.' The reply was brought back to the 'old lion' who was really 'hurt'. A testimony reported by Mr Alamouti, *op.cit.*,pp.292-293.

The Chief of General Staff helped Mossadegh walk up the steps and they took the lift to the first floor to the general office. The others used the impressive staircase of the club.

The General Prime Minister was standing in the middle of his office, awaiting them. He was in uniform. There were several high-ranking officers behind him, notably old General Shahbakhti, one of Reza Shah's companions whom Mossadegh had had imprisoned. Mossadegh and Zahedi shook hands for a long time. 'I am your prisoner', Mossadegh said to his successor. 'You are my most respected guest', the general answered. They sat down. Tea is quickly served.

Mossadegh was led to the 'Royal suite' of the club. He had a telephone at his disposal. General Reza Zahedi, a cousin of the Prime Minister, was designated as the one in charge of his safety and comfort. Doctor and Colonel Moghaddam, a well-known surgeon, was responsible for looking after his health together with Doctor Gholam Hossein Mossadegh, his son. The Prime Minister allowed the doctor and colonel to ensure the exchange of letters between his 'guest' and his family.

The other two prisoners had the right to telephone their families to assure them of their good health and inform them on the location of their detention. Then, their phone lines were cut.

Mossadegh stayed at the officer's club for eight days. He was then transferred to the armoured division's officer's club, where he awaited the legal proceedings the new government wanted to institute against him.

*   *

*

On August 22nd in the afternoon, the Shah went back to

his country without Empress Soraya. The latter joined him two weeks later. The government reserved him an official and grandiose welcome; the civilian and military authorities, accredited ambassadors to Tehran and constituent bodies were all there. The Shah and his Prime Minister shook hands for a long time and congratulated each other. There was a very warm popular welcome at the exit of the airport and in the streets of the capital city. Mohammad Reza Pahlavi was cheered in all sincerity. He seemed to be delighted and moved, he who had been a sovereign on the run a day before. A major part of the population and of the armed forces, the religious hierarchy, the savoir-faire of a general and the backing of the West had just given him his throne back. The next morning, the General Prime Minister presented his government to the Shah without having previously consulted him for the list of ministers. He meant to govern. The sovereign, it seems, was somewhat annoyed. [43] Zahedi had already appointed many civilians and service-men in the hours before the Shah's arrival whereas he should have requested the formal approval of the Head of State beforehand.

Mohammad Reza Pahlavi was nevertheless grateful to the general and showed it. Using his prerogatives as constitutional commander-in-chief of the armed forces, he granted him 'his third star'. He was promoted lieutenant general and received the highest honour in the country, the 'Grand-Croix of the Taj Order with a sash.'

*   *

*

Mossadegh's trial was the reason for the first confrontation between the Shah and his Prime Minister.

One question haunted the new people in power: what were they to do with Mossadegh?

Despite the failure that characterized the last months of his government, his inability to solve the oil crisis, measures taken which were not really compatible with his democratic and liberal discourse, he was still regarded by most Iranians as the hero who had privatized their oil, chased the British away and avenged them of all the humiliations they had suffered from for decades. The General Prime Minister who once was his minister thought that a Mossadegh trial would, politically speaking, risk to become a 'scandal for the regime.' Zahedi would say to whoever listened to him: 'Weren't we his companions in the fight for nationalization, His Majesty included?' The military leaders, many of whom had been imprisoned or forced to retire early, put pressure for the opposite solution, they demanded a trial.

The Shah decided to summon a sort of advisory committee with the Prime Minister; Ali Heyat, the Minister of Justice, an old, prestigious and irreproachable magistrate who had been public prosecutor at the Supreme Court for years; Mohammad Sajadi, Secretary of State, and General Abdollah Hedayat who was to be appointed Minister of War a few days later, and then Chief of the General Staff – a very popular man in the military as its representative. The committee started its work late in the evening. The Prime Minister apologized for not being able to come; in fact, he shied away. He wanted to avoid a head-on confrontation, probably knowing that his point of view would not be accepted. He had his son Ardeshir replace him with the order to present his point of view, which the latter did, concluding that, according to his father, Mossadegh should be released and 'respectfully' put under house arrest and surveillance on his huge estate in Ahmad-Abad. He was to have all the comfort and services he might need there.

The animated discussion lasted until dawn. Empress Soraya called her husband several times asking him to come home as soon as possible. The Shah ended up making a decision in the sense wanted by the military by saying that the court case should be limited to the former Prime Minister's non-observation of the Constitution after his dismissal, and to the action taken during that period. Ardeshir addressed the Sovereign with the ardour of his youth: 'My Father will know how to draw the consequences of this decision. He is opposed to any harsh sanction against Mossadegh.' The Shah, who was offended, did not say a word.

The Prime Minister had just settled down in power. He could not provoke a crisis and plunge his country again into doubt. He yielded. 44

*   *

*

During the trial which occurred a few months after these events Mossadegh was pathetic one day, threatening, ironical, contemptuous, and sometimes insulting another, but never towards the Shah. He confined himself to a strictly political level, deeming that his dismissal went against the spirit of the Constitution, and systematically introducing himself as Prime Minister. The military prosecutor, General Hossein Azmoudeh, tried to limit himself to exclusively legal considerations: since the dismissal had been in accordance with the letter of the Constitution, everything that had been done or decided during the three days after it could only be a rebellion against the State. It was a never-ending situation where nobody was on the same wavelength, where people were courteous at times, sordid at others – even the special menu prepared for the famous prisoner was referred to – and where everyone acted their parts for public opinion, if not for future generations.

Mossadegh artfully succeeded in turning the courtroom of the military tribunal that was supposed to try him into a show for the international press. He passed himself off as a martyr and it worked.

Fourteen witnesses were called to the bar. They were ministers, Mossadegh's relatives and friends, as well as some of the protagonists of the aforementioned events. Many behaved in a less than honourable manner, even General Taqi Riahi, the co-defendant, Chief of General Staff, who did not stop putting forward his role as a subordinate and not as a decision maker. Three witnesses were exceptions: Ahmad Razavi, the Vice-President of the Chamber who bowed in front of Mossadegh, talked about him as of the 'historic leader of the nation.' The former dean of the law faculty of the University of Tehran, and former representative Ali Shayegan, supported the defendant's constitutional standpoint. Sociology Professor Gholam Hossein Sadighi, who was Minister of the Interior and Vice-President of the Cabinet, bowed ceremoniously in front of the defendant. He started by declaring: 'The official motto of Iran is God, our King, our Country. Mine is God, our Country, our King. I have not changed and will never change.' He took responsibility for all his decisions and his instructions as vice-president, and justified them. Mossadegh said in a loud voice: 'He is a master.' The prosecutor then went to see him in his cell to tell him that, despite the fact he disagreed, he wanted to congratulate him for his courage and his loyalty. He was to be released soon after that.

At the end of the trial, the military judges upheld all the charges against the defendant, which made him liable to capital punishment – there was, however, to be no execution since in imperial Iran, neither elderly people of over sixty, nor women could be executed. The sentence was three years in prison only, 'with regard to his old age, services rendered to the nation before his dismissal and His Majesty the Shah-in-Shah's mansuetude.' [45]

A few days before the end of the trial on first hearing, Youssef Moshar, a member of the National Front, former minister and still a close friend of Mossadegh's who kept on good relations with the new power, had a long meeting with the Shah. He explained the devastation caused by the court case, the services rendered by Mossadegh, the support the Sovereign had long given him. He asked Mohammad Reza Pahlavi to 'order' the adjournment of the 'old lion's' case and his transfer to Ahamd-Abad where he would be put under house arrest. The Shah answered: 'If Mossadegh accepts it' and added: 'Get in touch with his lawyer, Colonel Bozorgmehr.' This is what Youssef Moshar did. Bozorgmehr first consulted two eminent legal experts and then had a long talk with Mossadegh who did not say 'no', but who did not believe the Shah was sincere. A legal pretext was found for the adjournment of the case – the 'defendant's' illness – and a transfer to Ahmad-Abad for health reasons. Mossadegh continued to believe it was one of the Shah's tricks. The endless talks lasted until the end, and the verdict was returned. [46]

A serious mistake had just been made.

After three years spent in an apartment of the officer's club of the Tehran armoured division in Saltanat-Abad, a former palace of the Qajar kings, Mossadegh was put under house arrest on his big estate in Ahmad-Abad, 70 kilometres away from the capital city. There, he could receive his family, a few rare friends, and immerse himself in reading. Abolfath Atabaï, the 'Master of the Royal Hunt' of the imperial Court, an old man with outdated manners who had already been in service with the former king of the Qajar dynasty, and then with Reza Khan, would pay him regular visits and 'kiss his hands,' as he used to say to a few rare people who shared his secret. He would 'ask for news of his health on behalf of His Majesty.' It was a strange dialogue from afar between two characters who probably hated each other and had a certain esteem for each other at the same time.

When the agrarian reform was launched at the beginning of the sixties, the Shah asked the government to exempt Mossadegh's land from it as long as he was alive.

Towards the middle of the winter of 1967, Mossadegh's health condition got worse. He was already over eighty-five years old. His doctors decided to have him transported to a clinic of the capital city called Najmieh which belonged to a welfare foundation created by his mother in the past. There, he was followed by an areopage of specialists. He died on Sunday, March 7th. His family was advised to hold his funeral in the strictest privacy. About fifty friends and relatives came. His body was buried in the room which was used as a dining-room, on the ground floor of the small Ahmad-Abad residence. It is still there.

From 1968 and until the revolution, a small group of loyal friends would gather with the family to organize a ceremony for the anniversary of his death, on March 7th, and to remember him. On March 7th 1979, several hundred thousand people – a million according to the organisers – took part in the ceremony which took the turn of a deferred homage , but also of a form of hostility towards the new regime that was already a great source of disappointment.

The evocation of Mossadegh's memory was tolerated under the monarchy if it remained discreet, but it became forbidden and harshly punished afterwards. It only added to his legend.

*   *

*

The repression triggered after Mossadegh's fall especially affected the Tudeh members. Many of Mossadegh's supporters, among whom were a few ministers and close collaborators, were also arrested before being progressively, and often quickly, released. Several of them were given first-class political functions later on. Others were to become very successful in business.

Only Hossein Fatemi, the unpredictable and fiery Minister of Foreign Affairs was to be an exception. He was arrested much later and shot on November 10th 1954, despite General Zahedi and several other personalities' efforts to obtain his pardon. [47] The Shah evoked once more 'the pressure exerted by the military.' [48] Fatemi was especially reproached with having used violent and often offensive words with regard to Mohammad Reza Pahlavi and the imperial family. His execution was also a serious mistake made by the imperial regime. The Shah would have shown himself in the best possible light if he had pardoned him, as he was to often do later on, even concerning those who tried to kill him.

*   *

*

These events made another unexpected victim: Lavrentiev, the ambassador from the Soviet Union who tried to commit suicide.

The interim Minister of Foreign Affairs, Abdolhossein Meftah, wrote: 'On August 20th, as I arrived at my office at 8.30, my cabinet told me that I had had several calls from the Soviet embassy. I was very surprised and thought it was a joke. It was not a common habit for Soviet diplomats. Some checking was done. The phone calls did come from the USSR embassy. I was called again. I took the call, after verifying its origin. The man talking to me said that the previous evening, ambassador Lavrentiev had tried to commit suicide by swallowing poison and had been taken to the Soviet hospital in Tehran*. The director of the hospital was at his bed-side.

After careful thought, I called the Head of Protocol and told him: 'Ambassador Lavrentiev is apparently unwell. Call the embassy to ask for news of his health and send him my best regards and all my wishes for a quick recovery.' The Head of Protocol did as he was told. The embassy kept him waiting for a long time, then thanked him and added that Mr Lavrentiev suffered from a bad case of influenza. He was in hospital and was not allowed to receive any visitors at all.

At the end of the day, I had the embassy called again by the director of the second department [which the USSR depended on]. He was told that the ambassador had been transferred to the embassy residence in the country in Zargandeh, and that 'he was still not allowed to receive any visitors; he needed a long convalescence.' [49]

Meftah specifies that it was known later that Lavrentiev had taken Mossadegh's fall and the take-over of power by General Zahedi as a personal failure. He had summoned the Tudeh leaders who allegedly told him they intended to maintain the state of unrest until the following day and then try to take over the power. They had consequently been caught unawares... [50] Ambassador Lavrentiev was looked after. Once he had recovered, he spent a few more months in Tehran before going back to Moscow.

*   *

*

---

* There was one in the Iranian capital. The quality of its service was appreciated by patients.

On August 28th 1953, the Iranian government announced the future opening of negotiations so as to solve the oil crisis. The economic situation meant that exports should be quickly resumed. The results of an audit ordered by the government were published on October 5th, and showed a disastrous situation: the coffers were empty, the monetary reserves almost non-existent, the State was heavily indebted. The United States granted an emergency aid of 45 million dollars on September 6th. Another aid of 23.4 million dollars was announced by Ambassador Henderson, taken from the funds of Point IV. There was to be a first cheque for 4.7 million dollars to be given to the Minister of Finance on October 19th. Neither the Shah nor the General and Prime Minister wanted their country to be dependent on foreign aid. The resumption of the oil rent was a must.

The negotiations started on October 22nd with the arrival in Tehran of Herbert J. Hoover, President Eisenhower's special advisor, who was granted his first audiences with the Sovereign and his head of government. Hoover suggested that a group of companies that belonged to Iran's 'allied and friendly' countries took in charge the running of the exploitation and marketing of Iranian oil so as to prevent any direct conflict between states. This would mean that the Americans would be involved in the Iranian oil game.

Hoover's plan also suggested that the French and the Dutch should be involved in the final compromise so as to give it a 'western aspect'. The British welcomed the proposal without any enthusiasm. Sir William Fraser, the president of the AIOC, was even kept aside from the negotiations because he had shown his disapproval.

At the beginning of 1954, the American administration even authorised the five biggest American oil companies to unite and form a cartel so as to take part in the exploitation and marketing of Iranian oil – this, despite the antitrust legislation.

So, on March 9th 1954, the creation of an 'international consortium for the distribution of Iranian oil' was announced. The Anglo-Iranian Oil Company (AIOC, so BP), held 40% of the shares, five big American companies 40%, Royal Dutch Shell 14% and the Compagnie Française de Pétrole 6%.

The negotiations started in Tehran on April 14th 1954. Ali Amini, Ahamad Ghavam's former minister, then Mossadegh's, who had become General Zahedi's Minister of Finance, led the Iranian delegation.

The general agreement, a 64-page document, was concluded on August 5th and made simultaneously public on September 21st both in London and Tehran. It solemnly recognized the principle of nationalization, ensured a compensation for the British, and organized the technical, economic, commercial and legal conditions for the extraction, refining, transport and marketing of the Iranian oil in detail, as well as related activities. The agreement was concluded for twenty-five years.

The National Iranian Oil Company (NIOC) that had been founded by Mossadegh became the owner and seller of oil to the consortium of eight companies considered to be its 'agent'. Iran now earned 25% of the profits, whereas the AIOC only used to give it a fifth of them. The foreign companies that belonged to the 'consortium' gave the State 25% in taxes so that the country actually got 50% of the profit due to its oil. Moreover, the NIOC benefited from the oil products that were necessary for domestic use at cost price, which was an important benefit for the development of the Iranian economy. It also had an increasing share of the production at its disposal for its marketing on the world market. These arrangements would have greatly satisfied the Iranians three years before. They, however, remained below the proposals made by the World Bank to Mossadegh. The new power in Tehran was not in a position of strength in front of the West. Ali Amini, the Minister of Finance, presented the agreement as 'the triumph of good sense but not the ideal solution.' The Shah was going to try to do better than Mossadegh could have done for over two decades. His efforts had to do with the attitude of certain 'major interests' and governments which were under their influence when faced with the Islamic revolution. Iran's open ambitions were to cost it a high price from 1974, and Mohammad Reza Pahlavi was not in a position to oppose the situation.

Barely ten years after the end of he Second World War, the data of Iranian politics, and the international situation of the country were to be fundamentally altered.

*   *

*

On September 21st 1954, the government presented all the oil agreements to the Chamber. The oil crisis was nearing its final settlement. The agreements were definitely approved of on October 29th.

In the meantime, a vast Tudeh network was discovered within the military, as well as weapon caches and secret printing houses.* It was becoming obvious how close the country had come to falling into the Soviet fold and how it had escaped the danger.

The oil problem was solved, the oil manna was back, the powerful military organisation of the Tudeh which had even infiltrated the imperial Guard and the intelligence services all the way up to the higher ranks was crushed.**

---

* See chapter III: The Tudeh – Seventy years at the service of the Soviet Union.
** According to a document referred to by N.M.Askari in November 1954, *Shah, Mossadegh et le général Zahédi, op. cit.*, p.242, a top-secret

IRAN'S TWIST OF FATE
An Exceptional General

*   *

*

From 1941 to 1953, three great statesmen of exceptional calibre had dominated Iranian politics: Foroughi, Ghavam and Mossadegh.

Foroughi, the man who saved the country and the monarchy in 1941, had neither personal ambition nor influence networks. He already knew that he was suffering from an illness that would soon cause his death when he took the reins of power. He sacrificed his life for his country.

Ghavam, on the other hand, was a man of power and national ambition. He had his own vision of the future of the country. He was at the head of a political party. Stalin's victor who was compared to Richelieu and Bismarck, respected the institution of the monarchy and the king himself, but he wanted, demanded that the latter would reign but not rule. As long as the Azerbaijan crisis was not solved, the Shah continued to support him out of patriotism and national interest. Then the relations between the two men became so awful that the Shah abandoned him in 1952. He still preferred Mossadegh to Ghavam's haughty and paternalistic authoritarianism.

His relations with Mossadegh, whom he would only call 'the stubborn old man' after his fall, soon turned sour too, especially after the failure of the attempts to find a solution to

---

report of the (military?) intelligence services denounced the relationship Hossein Fardoust (a friend and fellow student of the Shah) had with Soviet espionage. Mohammad Reza Pahlavi allegedly reacted really badly to the report which incriminated a person from his entourage. A quarter of a century later, the report proved to be accurate. The consequences it entailed will be seen later.

the oil crisis and to the growing power of the communist party which, understandably so, worried Mohammad Reza Pahlavi.

The Iranian Constitution was greatly inspired from the one of the Belgian kingdom. Ghavam and Mossadegh meant to give a democratic interpretation of it, and confine the sovereign to a symbolic role, or almost so.

The same problems soon arose with General Zahedi, who was a nationalist, a man endowed with integrity who was totally devoted to the Shah, and who had greatly contributed to his re-ascension to the throne.

The General Prime Minister also intended to rule. Once the major problems had been solved, there were frictions – very discreet ones it is true, but in Iran everything was very secret at the top of power, it is as simple as that. The frictions were over ministerial appointments, over Mossadegh and Fatemi's fate – history proved Zahedi right –, then over the economic policy of the country. In that respect, the Prime Minister advocated the allocation of most of the oil revenues to the development of agriculture, the building of housing, the improvement of road and rail networks, to small projects that would be quickly efficient from a social and human point of view. The Americans were putting pressure on Iran to strengthen its military power in front of the Soviet threat, which was very real. Mohammad Reza Pahlavi did the same, but for other reasons: he wanted a performing army as an instrument of the policy of power that he meant to lead. His Prime Minister, an outstanding general who was pragmatic, and closer to the worries of the people, would have preferred to see Iran's arming mainly financed by American aid, like in many other countries of the western camp. He would even have preferred, it seems, an army that would have been more used for questions of domestic security rather than for a regional or international role.

IRAN'S TWIST OF FATE
An Exceptional General

These sources of disagreement were not to remain secret. The ambassador of the United States had open discussions with the Shah over them and informed his government on September 18th 1953, then on the 29th, on November 14th, etc...

The disagreement almost became public over Abolhassan Ebtehaj's nomination at the head of the organisation of the project. He was the man Americans wished to see there – a supporter who was convinced he should call in engineering consultants from across the Atlantic and who was certain that the great projects Mohammad Reza Pahlavi also liked should be carried out.

The General Prime Minister preferred to keep him at the head of the National Bank, where his sense of rigour was needed.

The Shah was to impose it. He was appointed during the Cabinet meeting on September 1st 1954.

More or less influential personalities opposed Zahedi on political viewpoints: Amir Assadollah Alam, a close friend of the sovereign and former minister, and Hossein Ala, a minister from the imperial court. The embassy of Great Britain also plotted against the Prime Minister. [51]

Mohammad Reza Pahlavi went on an extensive trip abroad from December 5th 1954 to March 12th 1955, and spent a long time in the United States. Everywhere, he was welcomed as the sovereign of a country with a great future ahead that was potentially powerful, on the way to becoming the centrepiece of the stability in the region. The first performances of the Tehran government, its success in the fight against communist networks, the already fast pace of the economic recovery of Iran impressed everyone. He was given an exceptional welcome everywhere.

On his return to Iran – did he have the feeling he was supported by his western allies, especially the Americans? – he seemed to have decided to get rid of his Prime Minister who was fully loyal to him but authoritarian and well decided to rule. The general's trips to the provinces were often warmly greeted. His popularity within the military, his prestige with the clergy appeared to worry the Shah's entourage at least, and maybe him too.

When he was back from his trip, just one day before a luncheon the Prime Minister was invited to, Mohammad Reza Pahlavi said to Empress Soraya: 'Zahedi is becoming a little too cumbersome. I have to get rid of him.' [52] The Empress narrated: 'How could he decide to cast out the man he owed everything to, his friend in all situations, his loyal Prime Minister?', 'General Zahedi, the national hero.' [53]

Soraya continued her narration: 'The general's arrival was announced. Mohammad Reza greeted him warmly, as if nothing was the matter.

Suddenly, in the middle of the meal, he threw in his face: 'General, I thank you for everything you have done for me and for Iran, but I think that the responsibilities of your position have become too heavy for you. You ought to take some time to rest.'

In fact, the empress concluded, the Shah dreaded General Zahedi's too great a popularity. [54]

Empress Soraya was, in fact, only the witness of the official and formal notification of a decision that the general had well been informed of a few days before by Amir Assadollah Alam. He had been made aware of the fact that Hossein Ala was to be his successor. He was offered a position of ambassador in a major European embassy but turned the offer down. He contemptuously rejected a big bonus as well. Yet he was penniless. [55]

IRAN'S TWIST OF FATE
An Exceptional General

A possible scenario was discussed and perfected: the general was to hand his resignation to the Shah – which he did on April 6th 1955 – , leave for Europe and that is when the resignation would be made public. Everyone in Tehran already knew though.

On the 7th, he presided over his last Cabinet meeting, took leave of his collaborators and left for the airport. He was accompanied by a huge crowd and, especially, by a lot of servicemen. The sovereign was offended by it, according to hear-say.

In the following days, there was another unusual happening: both Chambers paid him a stirring homage.

His government did not even last two years. His departure inaugurated a long period of authoritarian monarchy and governments of technocrats for Iran.

*   *

*

Once General Zahedi was away from Tehran, a slander campaign was launched against him. He was accused of having received 5 million dollars from the American government to thank him for overthrowing Mossadegh. The biographies and studies published since then have proved the accusation wrong. The famous cheque was indeed received in the presence of several personalities, among whom the governor of the National Bank, but it was immediately given to the Treasury. [56]

The financial difficulty he faced, the loan he had made in Switzerland for a house in Montreux, and even more so, the documents on his fortune [57] published by the Ministry of Foreign Affairs of the Islamic republic leave no doubt as to his probity, whatever the opinion one might have on his political doings.

*   *

*

General Zahedi accepted the title of travelling ambassador and head of the Iranian Mission at the European office of the United Nations in Geneva two years after he had left Iran, and after his son's wedding with Princess Shahnaz, one of the Shah's daughters.

His health condition was already deteriorating: the after-effects of war injuries, a stomach ulcer and cardiovascular problems.

He nevertheless attended his son's wedding and welcomed the Shah and Empress Soraya to his villa in Montreux on several occasions.

All those who met him during that period of time have mentioned his immense bitterness.

He died in Montreux on December 2nd 1963 at the age of seventy.

Chapter VII

THE SAVAK
A great misunderstanding

The transformation of extraordinary measures in dealing with domestic safety problems and surveillance, even of repression of the most virulent oppositions, into a highly structured and professional organisation forms one the revealing aspects of Iran's integration into a collective system of defence and security.

Now, the point was to fight against Soviet-satellite espionage and subversion, but also against their interior political ramifications, to protect the regime from its opponents and ensure its stability in front of possible threats.
This was the purpose of the transformation and, unfortunately, the justification or the explanation for the excesses or abuses, real or not, which resulted from it or which were attributed to it.

*   *

*

'The image Westeners had of the Shah's regime was too often distorted in the Savak's mirror [1]. The Savak was, according to various people, a sort of super Gestapo plus the KGB multiplied by ten – which is wrong... As showed its inefficiency to foresee events and then to deal with them.' [2]

These lines were written by Alexandre de Marenches who was probably the most famous head of the French Secret Services. He was known and even well-known. They sum up the assessment of the work of that 'hub' in a suitable manner. It was to become the main weakness of the imperial regime. [3] The operation assumed proportions which are hard to fathom during the years that preceded the Islamic revolution. It still is today the main source of attacks against that regime.

In 1974, *Newsweek* assessed the annual budget of the Savak to be of over 310 million dollars, to which one should add, as was specified, 'colossal sums' scattered over the budgets and credits allocated to the various ministries and State institutions. [4]

A few weeks before the triumph of the revolution, *Le Monde* assessed the number of Savak collaborators [5] to 4,000 permanent employees, 50,000 salaried informers, and a million voluntary workers.

Amnesty International's report in 1976 showed the estimate number of political prisoners of the Savak to be between 25,000 and 100,000. It was assumed that the Savak had 6,000 jails. [6]

Shortly before the revolution, the same organisation declared that in five years' time, from 1972 to 1977, there had been 400 executions in Iran, 260 of which for drug dealing. 'It leaves 28 per year for political deeds. It is far too many, but once more, this is far from the massacres the monarchy is reproached with', Édouard Sablier wrote in *Iran, la poudrière...* which is still one of the most interesting works on the Iranian revolution today. [7]

The figures quoted here and there of these 'Savak victims' vary a lot: in a letter to Kurt Waldheim, the general secretary of the United Nations, Abol Hassan Bani Sadr, the first president of the Islamic republic, stated: 'The Shah organised massacres in towns all over the country in the last years of his reign.'
He estimated the number of victims to be of 100,000 during the last fifteen years of the reign. [8]
Other figures, from sources which are as 'official', were quoted and are still going round. Ayatollah Khomeini once asserted that there were 350,000 political prisoners in the Shah's time, 100,000 of whom were assassinated. [9] The same Khomeini wrote to Pope John-Paul II that 'he (the Shah) roasted our young people in pots, grilled them in glowing embers.' [10]

When the Shah was in exile in Cuernavaca in Mexico [11], the embassy of the Islamic republic gave an official press release according to which 365,995 people had been murdered for political reasons during his reign. [12]

At the time when the Islamic constitution was to be made official, one of the main revolutionary leaders took refuge in '40,000 martyrs' [13] to justify the repression launched by the Islamic regime. A figure was eventually publicly announced in the Constitution of the regime: 60,000. [14]

A gruesome form of arithmetic, without any precise dates, where the number of victims of political repression, of the Savak, according to the accepted way of saying it, varied from 400 to 365,995 people, and which keeps on being repeated without any serious effort to verify its foundation.
All these were rumours, fantasies, often anonymous

narratives, sometimes fanciful facts such as the attribution to the Savak of an estate on the island of Kish, a holiday resort in the Persian Gulf. [15] As years went by, it was insinuated that it was impossible for these wrongdoings not to be either committed on the Shah's orders or, at least, covered up by him. It has even been suggested that an 'underground passage' linked the imperial palace (without specifying which one) to the 'torture chambers.' [16]

*   *

*

The American secret services, mostly the CIA, but also the Mossad and the French and British intelligence agencies had cooperation agreements with the Savak. The common fight against the terrorist networks of the time – the Palestinians', the ultra-left-wing ones, also called in a more official manner, the communists – made this cooperation not only useful but also indispensable. The Americans and especially the Israelis gave technical advice to the Iranians, especially at the beginning. It was all the more important since all these networks were directly or indirectly linked to the Soviet Union. This was the famous 'red thread' that was written about. [17]

If, indeed, there were abuses, I will give a precise assessment of them in the following pages. The Americans and Westerners in general had to be informed. When President Jimmy Carter pretended to discover certain facts, whether they were established or not, he really started taking steps to support, or justify his stand against the imperial regime and the Shah: 'Despite the rise in the standard of living due to the distribution of oil revenues, the Shah's perseverance in pursuing his own objectives created an opposition between the intelligentsia and other groups who wished to take part in Iranian politics. The Savak was renowned for its ruthless repression of the opposition and I had been informed that there were 2,500 political prisoners in Iran – a figure the Shah deemed high.' [18]

* *

*

How was the Savak created?
How did it evolve?
How did it function?
What it true about its actions and its abuses?

I will give precise answers to these questions and support them with relevant documents.

* *

*

Mossadegh's government was indeed faced with numerous clashing oppositions which were often violent and sometimes secret. A whole section of the clergy did not really like this secular man's attitude. He was deeply anti-clerical as the Iranian free masons of the beginning of the 20th century could be, and this section of the clergy plotted against the power. And there were those who were paid or manipulated by the British who had some interest in Iranian oil and had been ousted from Iran but were still powerful. They plotted openly. The Tudeh fostered permanent unrest and went one higher than them in Moscow's interest and on its order. Finally, since the consummated break between the Court and the Prime Minister, the opposition of some of the Shah's entourage to the nationalistic leader was not a secret any more, and influenced the attitude of many officers and representatives.

The Prime Minister was indeed very popular. Some of public opinion, especially the middle class, together with many academics and students supported him. Nevertheless, the fear of a communist takeover of the country became more and more obvious among the first group.

Mossadegh and his cabinet had to deal ruthlessly with some, and reassure others. They extensively used the dispositions of the martial law. Iran then lived in a state of siege regime, which allowed the power to make arrests without resorting to courts, to forbid gatherings, to ban publications, and even to restrict traffic. The fact of resorting to martial law was obviously harshly criticised by all opponents, even if its efficiency was limited because the government worried about appearing too repressive. Besides, neither Mossadegh nor his main advisers such as Bagher Kazemi, Allhyar Saleh, Gholam Hossein Sadighi, the president of the Chamber Abdollah Moazzami who was an eminent legal expert, Mahmoud Nariman or the governor of the National Bank, Mohammad Nassiri, a real master of the economic policy of the time, were authoritarian. They were all very legalistic liberals who were forced to use exceptional measures considering the circumstances.

Therefore, there was a possible solution that was found: give the police, and thus the authorities, almost unlimited powers so as to quell the subversion that could come from virtually anywhere. Since Mossadegh had been given full powers* after the events of July 1952, a law-decree on national security had thus been prepared and ratified by the head of the executive. The powers thus given to the police consequently became in accordance with the law, and the reign of martial

---

* See chapter V: The oil crisis – The man who chased the British away.

law could be suspended, even if one preferred to temporarily abstain from it.[19] The implementation of the devices supposed to substitute the text to the clauses of the martial law was indeed going to take a little time.

The law-decree was made up of nine articles. It gave the administrative authorities the right to banish without trial any person encouraging disorder, strikes, or disturbing 'public peace' for a period of three to twelve months. [20]

The sentence was to be worse if the trouble makers were civil servants, and they were to be deprived of their salary. [21]

Any crowd formation within public and administrative buildings or places was also sanctioned by banishment. Besides, a simple report written by a civil servant of an administrative executive was considered to be enough evidence to enforce the sanction even before the contrary could be proved by the alleged offender; from then on, the State civil servants could be considered like officials of the Criminal Investigation Department. [22]

It is true that the law-decree had a purely repressive aspect and did not include any clause concerning the gathering of information and counterespionage. What was dealt with at the time was what was deemed to be a priority, or urgency.

After the fall of Mossadegh's government, the administration of martial law was entrusted with a young brigadier general of French training – he had gone to Saint-Cyr – called Teymour Bakhtiar by the new people in power. He adopted the national security law. In 1957, a law created the Savak and replaced the previous text, thus the martial law was temporarily put off. The new organisation was also in charge of collecting and exploiting the information on state security. This is how the Savak was becoming an organisation that would not only be responsible for domestic security, with a few guarantees for the defendant on a legal point of view – which was not the case with Mossadegh's law-decree – but also for espionage and counterespionage. It was to make it become really efficient, while, at the same time, be at the origin of the excesses and abuses it was to be blamed for.

The Savak was organised in the climate of cold war and international tension that prevailed at the time, with the active help of CIA experts, Israeli intelligence services and many other secret services from countries of the western camp. Its civil servants were trained by those services or perfected their training there, especially at first. The activity of the Savak as regards information and the fight against terrorism was naturally coordinated with that of the secret services from allied countries.

When the Savak was officially created, it had actually already been in operation within the organisation headed by Teymour Bakhtiar which administered the martial law. The powers of that organisation were reinforced by the clauses of Mossadegh's law on national security. It was, at first, essentially constituted of servicemen, officers and non-commissioned officers. Later on, it hired mostly civilians, a majority of whom had gone into higher education and were qualified, even highly qualified. Some of them were to have a brilliant career in politics or in diplomacy. One was even to be unexpectedly given the position of rector of a famous university by Amir Abbas Hoveyda, who was Prime Minister at the time. The results were not very convincing.

*   *

*

General Teymour Bakhtiar was at the head of the Savak from the day it was officially created in 1957 until 1961. He was an intelligent man who was cultured and extremely curious from an intellectual point of view. Teymour Bakhtiar had had a brilliant military career and had become famous during the Azerbaijan campaign in 1946*. He was more easily promoted after that since he was Soraya's, the Shah's second wife's cousin.

When he was the administrator of martial law in Tehran after Mossadegh's fall, he succeeded in dismantling the network the communist party had created in the Iranian armed forces (over 700 officers and non-commissioned officers), which probably saved the country from a pro-Soviet coup d'État**. It earned him the esteem of western secret services, especially the Americans'.

He quickly got a dreadful reputation once he was appointed at the head of Savak. His immoderate love of money and women, the use of violence which he encouraged or covered, and especially his inordinate ambition were to provoke his disrepute and ruin.

When the regime started being in a difficult situation and when its relations with Washington worsened in 1960, he thought he could realise his ambitions; it is also possible that the Kennedy administration was thinking of using him as an instrument to replace the Shah – one day history will tell us***. His situation could be compared to that of General Oufkir towards Hassan II a few years later in Morocco. What happened next is known. He was dismissed as soon as he got back from a trip to the United States during which he had been

---

* See chapter IV: The Azerbaijan crisis – The man who defeated Stalin.
** See chapter V: The oil crisis – The man who chased the British away.
*** See chapters VII and XII.

received by President Kennedy, went to Switzerland, then settled down in Lebanon before going to different countries to organise a movement that would overthrow the Iranian monarchy.

He ended up finally settling down in Iraq, which was the hub for all the conspiracies against the Shah at the time. He even became the ally of the people he had formerly fought against: some of Mossadegh's supporters, and especially the Tudeh. He was to be shot in 1971, during a shooting party, probably by the agents of the services he, himself, had created.

The second head of the Savak was Major General Hassan Pakravan, who was the complete opposite of his predecessor. He was born in 1911 and came from a well-known family – his father had been governor of the province, ambassador, Minister of Foreign Affairs, and his mother, a talented author who wrote in French, had been the winner of the Femina prize for foreigners. General Pakravan had been trained at Saint-Cyr, like his predecessor, and also qualified from the artillery school of Fontainebleau. He had spent all his career in the 2nd Bureau, but had also taught at the Military Academy of Tehran where he had Crown Prince Mohammad Reza Pahlavi as a student*. He was considered to be a real specialist in intelligence work.

He was a mathematician, a philosopher, a man who was keen on history and who was highly cultured, a polyglot, someone of proverbial integrity. He reorganised the services and excluded all the corrupt or compromised elements. He actually changed the methods used, and thus, the image people had of the Savak.

His running of affairs was faultless despite the existing difficulties, a legacy which was hard to get rid of, and the turbulences of the time.

---

* See chapter IX: A certain idea of Iran.

Intelligence and preventive work were favoured under his authority rather than repression and ill-treatment was forbidden and heavily sanctioned. The integrity of the civil servants in the services was constantly controlled.

He was a man whose sole ambition was to serve his country and the Shah, and yet he was moved away from power after the assassination attempt against the Prime Minister, Hassan Ali Mansour, in which the latter died in February 1965. When he was appointed Minister of Information, he launched a real policy of liberalisation. A few negative judgments passed on the American attitude in Vietnam that were heard on the national radio allegedly shocked the United States Embassy people; the possibility given to a few nonconformist intellectuals to be on the air, even if it was done with caution, annoyed the conservative circles and the security apparatus. He was consequently kept away from power and appointed Ambassador to Pakistan, a strategic position for Iranian diplomacy, then Ambassador to Paris, a very prestigious post, before going back home later, when he had reached the age limit. He was actually seriously ill – he suffered from a heart condition.

A few weeks before the fall of the regime, Pakravan was appointed vice-minister of the imperial court as he was considered to be a moral authority. He accepted the position despite his bad health condition. He was arrested by the revolutionaries after they had taken over the power, and horribly tortured. He was then put to death shortly afterwards, despite the mansuetude he had shown towards ayatollah Khomeini and so many other opponents.

His successor at the head of the Savak, from 1965 to 1978, was General Nematollah Nassiri, the former colonel and commander of the imperial guard who had failed in notifying Mossadegh his dismissal in 1954 in a rather incredible manner.

It was when he was at the head of the organisation, especially from 1970 onwards, and because of the wave of terrorist violence which affected Iran as well as so many other countries at the time, that the Savak was accused of using expeditive methods and earned itself a reputation which was to be used to discredit the imperial regime. A former minister of the monarchy who knew him well [23] said that he was a 'man of limited ability'; he was not very cultured and knew nothing about world affairs. He had a reputation for being cruel and corrupt. His only quality was a blind loyalty to the Shah as they had been in the same class at the Military Academy. He became the most hated man in Iran because of his methods, the 'Shah's damned soul' [24] – which seems somewhat exaggerated.

When the Savak was under his authority, it progressively got into the habit of giving preference to futile information to the detriment of an analysis of domestic policies. It was discreetly put forward that one was not supposed to worry the Shah. Prime Minister Hoveyda favoured that option.

Nassiri's entourage accused the new head of the agency of demoralizing the Sovereign after he had been eliminated, and when serious problems were dealt with again.

When his services were dispensed with in 1978 within the framework of the liberalisation policy in use at the time, he was appointed ambassador to Pakistan and replaced by Lieutenant General Nasser Moghaddam, an upright and far-sighted professional, the chief of the 2nd Bureau of General Staff, who did not really have time to redress the situation and who was put to death after the revolution, like both his predecessors.

General Nassiri showed a courage during the last months of his life which came within an inch from madness or 'the inability to analyse', as Alexandre de Marenches wrote. [25] When he was summoned to Tehran by the Azhari

THE SAVAK − *A great misunderstanding*

government*, he went back to the capital 'so as not to disobey orders', he said, although his friends had informed him forty-eight hours earlier that he would be arrested as soon as he got off the plane.

A commando from his former service came to deliver him in the night of February 11th to 12th. He refused: 'It would not be decent of me'. He was unwavering in front of the Islamist judges, despite the atrocious tortures that were inflicted on him. He even remained very dignified when he was shown on television shortly before his execution, his face swollen and his voice inaudible.

*   *

*

The organization chart of the Savak remained practically unchanged between 1957 and 1978: there were ten or so main departments to which only a health service was added and also called 'department'.

All of these departments covered the technical and supply services, espionage activities abroad and counterespionage, and, of course, internal security, the most important branch with a direct or indirect relation to the population.

The head of the Savak traditionally bore the title of Permanent Secretary of the Prime Minister. The latter was thus legally and officially his superior in the hierarchy and regularly met with him. The Shah did the same once, even twice a week.

The Savak sent daily reports to the Shah and the Prime Minister. Some were on official paper and were signed, others were 'white papers' − a term used in the political jargon.

---

* See chapter XVI: The fall of the monarchy and the triumph of the revolution − The handing over of keys.

Both types of reports were supposed to be identical. Were they always, indeed?

It could also use prisons, the most famous of which being Evine Prison. A 'special force' of about 500 men – almost all ex commando paras who were well trained – was directly under the head of the Savak's orders. The men of this special force were the ones who were in charge of the fight against terrorism on the ground and of delicate missions abroad, especially in neighbouring countries. They made arrests and did house searches, but they apparently never participated in the interrogations. The last head of that unit was not a regular serviceman.

However, there were nearly always officers at the head of the administration of the Savak in the provinces who were either on temporary assignments or retired. They often kept their positions for many years so as to be well integrated into their areas. [26]

On the whole, the Savak held functions which corresponded to those of the RG (special branch), DST (internal state security department) and DGSE (international intelligence agency) in France.

What was its budget? The figure given on the State budget and which was voted every year reached 800 million rials, during the last year (March 21st 1977 – March 21st 1978), so about 12 million dollars at the time. Another source of revenue for its treasury came from the secret funds of the Cabinet chairmanship and from the Ministry of War. A global sum of 75 million dollars could be put forward for 1977, when the oil revenue of the country was of over 34 billion dollars.

All the buildings and estates that the organization used belonged to the State and were submitted to common law. It did not exploit any hotel complex, industrial company or airline company, like other countries did. Its holiday resort was located on the Caspian Sea. It was not a business and was solely for the use of its civil servants. It apparently controlled a travel agency in the capital, whose manager then started working for the Islamic republic and acquired a certain fame for his more or less unlawful weapon dealings.

The national Police force also had its own intelligence service called Agahi, which dealt more with the surveillance of criminal activities, drug dealing, and general offences.

The 2nd Bureau of the military was independent and represented abroad by its military attachés. The tradition was to despise the Savak and not to trust it.

A 'special bureau' called Daftar-eh-vigeh which was mainly staffed by servicemen was in charge of coordinating and supervising all the intelligence and security services in the country. The manager of that "office", General Fardoust, was a very powerful man who was a double or triple agent, or mainly worked for the Soviet KGB, as many others did in other countries in the world which were not communist, and not the lesser ones. He openly betrayed the Shah in the end and participated in the creation of the secret services of the Islamic republic.

In 1970, a 'committee' for anti-terrorist activity was created under the direction of a high-ranking civil servant from the Savak. Its members came from the latter and from the national police force. It was a consequence of the increase in terrorist violence in connection with far or ultra-left European groups, and of the multiplication of attacks and assassinations. The committee had its own premises and benefited from a certain autonomy in its actions.

The Savak, like all secret services, had 'honourable correspondents' in nearly all the embassies in Iran. As is the habit in the world of intelligence, these agents were working under cover. Only their Chief of Station was supposed to know who they were. They had the ranks of attaché, third, second or first secretary, adviser, even of 'minister and adviser' – as was the case – on the staff list of the diplomatic corps. In fact, they were known to the whole staff and often, even, to the Iranian community in the country in question.

The most fanciful figures were given for the number of voluntary or salaried Savak 'informers'. They went up to 1,000,000! A year after the revolution, a 391-page book was published in Tehran which revealed 8,000 names of Savak 'informers' [27]. They could sometimes not be verified at all. The list might have been unofficial but the regime that stemmed from the Islamic revolution has imposed silence on the matter since then. Many of its leaders, including at least one of the members of the Revolutionary Council [28], could appear on it.

The figure of 8,000 seems to be very far from the truth, and the one of one million, just truly and naturally a form of disinformation. The Savak must have gathered much information and had many informers. Many of the latter ended up being discovered in the circles in which they operated after a while. If the Savak had had a million or even several dozens of thousands informers, whether volunteers or not, it would have had a much greater influence. Its intelligence networks were, I believe, much more efficient in the leading circles, ministries, high-society evenings or dinner parties in town, than among the opponents to the regime. As Count de Marenches wrote: 'What proves it, is its inability to foresee events and then to deal with them...Even when its own survival was at stake, the main head of the Savak [Nassiri] was unable to make a correct analysis of the situation. If he had been efficient, the Shah would still be [1986] on his throne and Khomeini in exile. [29]

It is true that all along that period, the head of the Savak was trying to cover up the gravity of a situation he should have analysed and foreseen. During the spring of 1978, for example, after he had received an alarming report, the Shah put a secret commission which was headed by his own Cabinet chairman in charge of analysing and assessing the importance of the unrest in religious circles. During the commission's work sessions and despite the gravity of the information at hand, General Nassiri had denied the truth in a particularly virulent tone. He had asserted that these worries were the fruit of people's imagination and that, with the exception of a few elements bribed by foreign countries, ' the Iranian clergy remained faithful to His Majesty, and only the Tudeh could be held responsible for the unrest,' – that is, the Iranian communist party! [30] His attitude was unbelievable. The Savak hardly ignored the gravity of a pre-revolutionary situation. General Nassiri's entire career and attitude prove that he did not betray the Sovereign, contrary to some other people. He only wished not to 'worry' him – this is the explanation some of his supporters gave. He thought that, in case of a political explosion, his services would be able to master the situation and bring order back to the country. His lack of analysis was to prove to be very costly. One can thus only come round to Alexandre de Marenches' opinion.

*   *

*

This 'main weakness' of the imperial regime was often highlighted to discredit it during the months before the revolution, then during the hostage affair and each time the events of the time are mentioned. Where does the truth stand concerning it?

Official documents which come from the authorities of the Islamic republic, thus which are unlikely to clear the assessment of the previous regime, and from radical circles opposed to the Shah, make it possible to determine the truth on the subject in an irrefutable manner.

An official enquiry commission presided by the then pro-Khomeini representative Ahmad Bani-Ahmad was set up right after ayatollah Khomeini's and his supporters' power take-over to draw an assessment of political repression during the fifteen previous years.

No report has been made public.

On March 20th 1979, an official release was published in the Iranian press which was then under full control. It was entitled 'the date and the place where the victims of the Shah's regime are buried.' [31] The list included 234 names. Each name was followed by a place name and a burial date. If a major part of the people quoted are known and classified for being killed in street fights or executed in accordance with the sentences delivered in court, others are fully unknown, and nothing, a priori, proves they were the victims of political repression or, even, actually existed. There is even a first name given without the surname.

In all cases, there were at the most 234 people.

A study led under the direction of Mr Ervan Abrahamian, a professor at New York University [32] and a leftist American academic who is known for his opposition to the Shah's regime, came to a similar conclusion to the one of the previous report, on the basis of documents provided by opponents to the imperial regime. There was a total of 341 deaths: 177 people died in combat, 164 were executed, disappeared, committed suicide or died in prison. These figures cover all the opposition movements: Orthodox communists, various Marxist, Islamist

Marxists and Islamic tendencies. For most of them, the Mujaheddins, the figure to be remembered is 73. 36 of them died in combat, 15 were executed, 20 died in jail, 1 disappeared and one committed suicide.

A new figure: 341.
There is an official document available concerning the Mujaheddins: 'The collection of proclamations and political stands of the Iranian people's Mujaheddins' which dates back to March 18th 1979 [33] The document makes the surnames, first names, dates and circumstances for the 'martyrdom' of the dead who are claimed by the organization, public. The number of the latter would be 25 (73, according to Abrahamian's study), 7 of whom were executed (15), 2 'killed by opportunists', they were rehabilitated afterwards however, 3 who died in prison (20), 11 in combat (36), and 2 for no given reason.

Consequently, Abrahamian's study attributed more victims to that organization (nearly three times as many) than it actually claimed itself. Therefore, the importance of its conclusion should be understated.

Another movement is particularly active in the use of violence and in bomb attacks, the Mujaheddin Khalgh Organization (the People's Fedayeens). They tend to be from the ultra-left, Marxist-Leninist, Maoist, Trotskyist, and claim 155 victims for the same period, giving people's surnames, first names, professions and dates of their 'martyrdom'. 106 of them 'died in combat', and 36 were 'executed' [34]

Consequently, the presumed number of victims is of a maximum of about 250 people. Two hundred and fifty too many, indeed, but the figure has nothing to do with the completely fanciful figures quoted by some people or, of course, with that of 60,000 written in the Constitution of the Islamic republic.

It was a disinformation operation [35] which the imperial regime, haughty and condescending as it was for it believe to be in its right, did not really try to thwart.

The bad treatments inflicted onto prisoners also constituted another major grievance against the regime. At the time of the hostage-taking from the United States embassy in Tehran – an operation the Islamic republic presented like 'the greatest experience in the history of humanity' [36] – this campaign reached its peak.

When Mr Kurt Waldheim, the general secretary of the United Nations, went on a mission to Tehran to obtain the release of the hostages, droves of crippled people were presented to him as the victims of the 'Savak's tortures'. The international press and audio-visual media covered this presentation widely, and its impact on public opinion was considerable. A quarter of a century later, the same images are sometimes used to refer to the imperial regime.
Pierre Salinger revealed in his enquiry on the hostage-taking affair that 'none of the Iranians he met in Tehran could show him the slightest document already prepared on the subject.' [37]

The lawyer of the Tehran government even declared to the investigation committee from the United Nations: 'You are already being deceived. Do you remember the little boy who had no arm [he had been photographed in Mr Waldheim's arms who was crying with emotion]? It was alleged that the Savak had cut his arm off to make his father talk. You did believe he was a victim of the Savak. Well, in fact, he lost an arm in a car accident and his mother uses him to make money.' [38]

The investigation committee ended up by lending itself to the operation, and accepted to meet hundreds of people who were mutilated or crippled. They had been found in Tehran and in some other cities, and had received large sums of money for the occasion.

A few years later, Kurt Waldheim admitted himself that he had lent to that deception: 'The scene [of the child whose arm had allegedly been cut off by the Savak] made me shiver with horror. Yet, Ghotb-Zadeh, the Minister of Foreign Affairs who was by my side, had whispered into my ear: 'Don't be embarrassed. The child lost his arm in a car accident and not because of the Savak.' Since that time, my doubts concerning the reality of the suffering endured by the other victims had done nothing but get worse.' [39]

In fact, the part of disinformation in the whole campaign which was meant to give a diabolical image of the regime or destabilize it should not be forgotten. The above-mentioned cases, even if they were the most mediatized ones, can only be taken as examples among many others.

The cold war atmosphere, and terrorist attacks in many countries, especially in western ones, that were perpetrated by small groups of extremist activists who were all manipulated by the Soviet-satellite camp should not be glossed over. [40] Iran had to protect its security like all the other countries that were targets. The successes of Iranian counterespionage (all services together, but especially the Savak) were remarkable on the foreign level, according to the crosschecking of testimonies and documents available. The foreign subversion was under close surveillance, notably the 'Palestinian' camps which were allegedly the breeding ground for international terrorism at the time, and the Mossad often resorted to the help of the Iranian secret services.

It is nonetheless true that the Savak was powerless in front of the rise of the movement which was used as an instrument to get rid of the regime. It was powerless in its analysis as well as in the action it took.

Were its abuses 'unavoidable blunders' as the Shah said [41]? They were probably more than that. The 'Savak prisons' were not like the ones of certain countries which like to give lessons such as the ones we know today, and even less like the Nazi or Bolshevik gaols however. This is not an absolution but an observation. Massoud Radjavi, the historic leader of the people's Mujaheddins said later that: 'the Shah was merely a choir boy compared to the Imam [Khomeini].' [42] This is not an excuse as such either, even if for a lot of people the very fact of comparing both characters may seem improper for the first one, and perhaps, according to some other people, for the second one as well.

This aspect of the work of the secret services of the imperial regime remained a burden which it continued to bear until the end, which was to a great extent, unfair. It was also a great misunderstanding.

PART TWO

THE FLIGHT OF ICARUS

Chapter VIII

THE AUTHORITARIAN MONARCHY
The White Revolution

A new political era started in Iran when General Zahedi left : it was an authoritarian monarchy, a concentration of most of the essential powers of decision within the hands of the Shah. The parliamentary institutions operated in a formal way. A few political parties were mere on-lookers, but the general directions came from the Sovereign.

Mohammad Reza Pahlavi believed not without good reason that he had a popular mandate conferred upon him after the 'five days which changed the fate of Iran'*. He benefited from a nearly unconditional support from the West, and more particularly from the United States of America, and had a mystical awareness of his 'historical mission' to rebuild a prosperous and powerful nation. Thus, he tried to claim overall responsibility from then on, even assuming errors that others had committed, left himself exposed, and was often successful, but he ended up facing events alone a quarter of a century later which were overwhelming for the country and caused his downfall.

*   *

*

---

* See chapter VI: Iran's twist of fate – An Exceptional General.

Iran had an often chaotic parliamentary regime from 1941 to 1954. A few statesmen of exceptional calibre, even if they were very different, marked the period: Foroughi, Ghavam, Mossadegh and General Zahedi. They were all loyal to the Shah and the monarchy, even the 'old lion', but they meant to rule as powerful men, only leaving the Head of the State a symbolic role. Other heads of governments maintained order in the country more or less efficiently, in often difficult circumstances.

Mohammad Reza Pahlavi had adapted to it. Being a patriot, he let Foroughi guide him, and supported Ghavam when the country was in danger. He was enthusiastic during the first stage of the national movement led by Mossadegh when the British were chased away. Towards the end, when things started to go wrong, he could accept the fact that his return to the throne was due to the clergy, the military, the West, and to one man: General Zahedi, who managed to coordinate all these factors and face adversity with the support of a major part of public opinion.

From then on he was to obstinately follow a few guiding political principles:
– To lessen the power and influence of the clergy, and continue the secularization process of institutions that had been largely started by his father. However, the permanent dialogue with the leaders of the Shiite hierarchy which all the Shahs had maintained for ages was to be progressively limited. He did not, or could not find a credible interlocutor any more in 1978. He was weakened and did not dare to get on or put up with some people to confront others. There was to be no-one to take over like before. The high clergy had become an impregnable bastion for the monarchy. He was to let himself be dominated by a radical group that was manipulated by foreign countries and felt abandoned and humiliated.

THE AUTHORITARIAN MONARCHY – *The White Revolution*

– To only govern with technocrats. The role politicians traditionally played, with their experience in manoeuvres, dialogues and compromises, would not be of any use any more, now that parliament had a figurative presence. The people whose age enabled them to be active were to find golden retirement positions at the Senate, in major embassies or at the head of the administrative board of certain companies. Mohammad Reza Pahlavi was to face the storm of 1978 alone. He was so distrustful that he did not even appeal to the few real politicians who still belonged to the regime and who could have confronted the situation. He was ill and exhausted and let people impose unfortunate decisions on him which were to prove very costly for the country.

Contrarily to what was said, the country had succeeded in its development with the technocrats who were almost all honest, and nearly always competent. The Shah pampered them and gave them a great power of decision. The country was now used as a reference for other nations which needed a model to follow, but Iran lacked statesmen who were capable of dominating the revolutionary storm.

– All the command structures of the armed forces were to be progressively transformed so as to avoid and prevent a coup d'État. Towards the end, only their commander-in-chief was in charge of coordinating them. Mohammad Reza Pahlavi had suffered from the fact that people not only shouted 'Long live the King' but also 'Long live Zahedi' during traditional walkabouts or visits in the provinces after Mossadegh's fall. He had found it difficult to bear the pressure exerted by the military when such and such a decision was made after his return to the throne, even if it sometimes counterbalanced the influence of a Prime Minister he did not trust. This is why he did his utmost, and succeeded in making sure that his armed forces were remarkably well organised but that he would be the only one to command them; there was to be no intermediary.

The Minister of War was only in charge of the supply corps, and the head of general staff had a role of mere representation, if not of protocole, especially towards the end.

When the Shah left office, and then the country, the military had no leader any more and was defeated without a fight. It was more of a political defeat than anything else, a sort of incapacity to take over, and assume its responsibility for the unity of the nation.

– From 1954, the whole imperial diplomacy was carried out with a great sense for national interest mainly to safeguard the independence of the country in front of the Soviet ogre and its appetites. It was probably the most successful and least questionable, or disputed, aspect of the reign. It was time for a privileged alliance with the West, and more particularly with the United States.

The more prosperous and powerful Iran got, the more Mohammad Reza Pahlavi tried to free it from the constraints of that alliance, let it play its own role, and pass off as the arbitrator of the balance in the region. These positions and initiatives were to deeply annoy Iran's privileged allies and make them turn against it, lead them to support, if not stir up, a revolution which they thought could put an end to the country's ambitions.

Iran was punished: the West was to pay a high price for it. The world was to suffer from it, as was shown in future events.

The monarchy was authoritarian and technocratic. The armed forces were controlled and commanded by competent officers who had no ambition and no political vision of things. The country's foreign policy became more and more independent from the Western alliance:

'I had no other solution; an authoritarian State was a

must. Otherwise, anarchy would have prevailed like the one you see today, with its abuses, madness, and violence. Did I have a choice?' [1] Mohammad Reza Pahlavi wrote much later on to justify the policy initiated at the time a posteriori.

*   *

*

Hossein Ala, General Zahedi's successor, came from a well-known aristocratic family. He was a diplomat who was not very tall but who was very cultured, refined and polyglot. He also had a long experience in Iranian domestic policy. He had already been at the head of an interim government before Mossadegh had come to power.

He left for Paris on the day of his nomination and of the presentation of his ministers because he was unwell and had to have an operation. Abdollah Entezam, who was at the head of Foreign Affairs, covered for him between April 9th and June 13th 1955.

Hossein Ala continued to run the country until April 4th 1957 without style or blunders. The economic development of Iran knew a boost. Many projects were completed or started: new factories, roads, railways, universities, hospitals, agricultural centres, dams... Mohammad Reza Pahlavi initiated the sharing out of the lands of the Crown between the farmers. This was to be the beginning of the major agrarian reform of the sixties.

Iran deliberately opted for a pro-Western and especially pro-American policy on the diplomatic level. The Shah who later became an open admirer of General De Gaulle, was fascinated by America, its power, universities, industrial productivity and sense of organization. He did not, without good reason, consider that the American alliance was necessary in front of Soviet designs and communist subversion. A bilateral cooperation agreement was concluded with the United States. The CIA and then the Israeli Mossad actively participated in the creation and organization of the Iranian secret services.

Washington was concerned about organising a defence system that was based on the northern cover of the Middle East by linking NATO and SEATO. Most Arab countries were agitated by a Nasserist trend. When Washington noticed it, and saw their hesitation, it encouraged Turkey, which was already a member of NATO, and Pakistan, which belonged to SEATO, to strike an alliance on the military level.

On April 2nd 1954, a military alliance pact was signed by Ankara and Karachi. John Foster Dulles actively strove to make other countries from the region to join. Adnan Menderes, the Turkish Prime Minister, went to the capital cities of the Middle East to seek their agreement. Damas, Beirut and Amman refused. Nouri Saïd, the Prime Minister in Baghdad, actual leader of the country and the man Great Britain trusted, very quickly agreed: 'Arab countries are not strong enough for their alliance – as it happened, the Arab countries that were the Arab League – to discourage a potential aggressor. This is why Iraq must find support outside the Arab bloc to ensure its security.' He declared [2].

The Turkish-Iraqi alliance pact was ratified on February 24th 1955, despite Colonel Nasser's vivid opposition and the reticence shown by several Arab capitals. Great Britain joined on April 4th. Pakistan, which was already Turkey's ally because of another agreement, joined on July 1st.

Djelal Bayar, the President of Turkey, paid an official visit to Iran from September 19th on. He was given a most exceptional welcome in which the military played a great part. A military cooperation agreement was signed by the two countries.

Iran joined the so-called 'Baghdad' pact on October 23rd 1955. It then became part of a defensive military alliance organization which included two non-regional powers.

The Soviets had a vivid reaction but Iran was now resolutely pro-West. The memories of the Azerbaijan crisis were still sharp, and over two thousand kilometres of land and sea borders with the USSR justified this policy in the Iranian people' eyes.

The conclusion of the alliance which had its seat in Baghdad was not only criticized by the Soviets and certain neutralist Arab countries, but also by a major part of public opinion in Western Europe, more particularly in France. It was considered to be an instrument of Anglo-American influence in the area.

King Faisal II, his whole family and Nouri Saïd were brutally assassinated, and the republic was declared during the pro-Soviet military coup d'État in Baghdad on July 14th 1958. It made Iraq fall into the camp of non-aligned countries which were close to Moscow. The Shah appeared to be very worried and even thought of calling General Zahedi back to power to face the situation. There were messages exchanged. General Zahedi, whose health condition was deteriorating, reassured the Sovereign as to the loyalty of the military and the solidity of the regime. Iraq became, and was to remain the basis for all the radical oppositions to the Tehran regime until 1975.

On a diplomatic level, the new republic denounced the military cooperation pact which actually transferred its seat to Ankara, and was to be called CENTO from then on – Central Treaty Organization. No Arab country belonged to it any more.

Mohammad Reza Pahlavi never stopped strengthening his authority and his influence until the beginning of the sixties. Parliamentary business carried on as usual, but the government of assemblies came to an end. The latter became more concerned with satisfying a powerful sovereign – and his government – and supporting their policies, without simply becoming rubber-stamp assemblies.

The Tudeh was not to play any political role any more. It was adamantly fought and silenced. The dismantling of its powerful military organization saved the country an Iraqi-type coup d'État. The USSR was taught a lesson and progressively normalized its relations with Iran. It knew that it could not turn the country into one of its satellites any more.

Mossadegh'supporters were often silenced without really being chased. Several of them got involved in politics. The economic prosperity of the time gave many of them the opportunity to get rich, and they took advantage of it. Some were to make the country pay a high price for the accumulated resentment. They became the docile instruments of the revolutionaries in 1978, before being overcome and purged by them.

From the on, the Shah called on technocrats and administrators who were able to deal with the complex problems of a rapidly developing economy. The time for an authoritarian monarchy, an enlightened despotism, according to some, came with the unstoppable rise of the technocrats. The latter were often the genuine allies of a monarch and their political future was linked to his. However, the technical nature of their points of view and their obsessive fear of carrying out the example of western development were sometimes detrimental to a good management of State affairs.

It is in that context that the Organisation of the Plan which had been created by Ghavam and carried out with an iron fist by the really pro-American Abolhassan Ebtehaj played a determining role. The latter was in favour of resorting mainly to western consulting engineers, especially to Americans, to conceive and control everything, and liked spectacular projects which the Shah actually appreciated. He was imposed on the Zahedi Cabinet for a few years and was untouchable.

*　　　　*

*

135 million tons of oil were extracted from Iranian oilfields, and 125 were exported, between 1955 and 1959. In five years, Iran made twice as much money as it had made between 1911 and 1951 (i.e. 300 million pounds sterling).

Measures were taken as soon as oil started being exported again so as to see the unfinished projects of the first septennial plan through. These projects had been started by Ahmad Ghavam's government just after WWII, or later.

A second septennial plan was prepared, and then voted on in Parliament. It was implemented on March 23rd, 1956, when the Iranian New year begins.

The foreseen investments amounted to slightly more than a billion dollars and could be divided into several essential sectors: agriculture, communications, industries and mines, social reforms, education and health, and public services.

The Plan was to receive 60% of oil revenues the first four years, then from 75% to 80% during the three following years. The State was authorized to resort to middle and long term international credit for up to 245 million dollars so that it could round off the resources affected to development.

The remarkable development of the Iranian economy was to start. The previously envisaged sums were quickly exceeded.

* *

*

Hossein Ala had just escaped an assassination attempt perpetrated by a member of the Iranian section of the Muslim Brothers when he handed in his resignation to the Head of State on April 3rd 1957. He was then appointed Minister of the Imperial Court.

On the 4th, Manutshehr Eghbal, a professor of medicine and former rector of the University of Tehran, was put in charge of forming a new government.

On the 14th, the new Prime Minister and his team were approved of in Parliament.

Manutshehr Eghbal came from the provincial middle class and went to medical school in France. When he came back home, he quickly became a professor and was soon one of the most appreciated doctors in the capital [4]. It was thanks to Ahmad Ghavam whose personal doctor he was, that he went into politics. He held several ministerial positions, was Governor of Azerbaijan, dean of the medical school, rector of the University of Tehran, and had an exceptional work capacity. He would start working at 6 a.m. This haughty and rather distant character led an austere life. He had a solid reputation for being honest which even his worst enemies (he did have some) could never question. He was thoroughly loyal to the Sovereign. The Shah appreciated the fact that he would avoid any contact that was not official or with high-society, embassies or foreign personalities, especially Anglo-Americans.

Iran knew a real boost of its economic development under his government.

It visibly changed and was turned into a huge working site. Gigantic dams were built and put into use; 1,500 kilometres of new railway tracks were inaugurated and new ones were on the way. Thousands of kilometres of new roads, four new universities, three major harbours and two international airports saw the light of day. Dozens of hospitals, stadiums, cultural centres, etc... were built and operated.

There was a soar in the activities of the textile and food industry more particularly, but also in the petrochemical industry, in the treatment of metals, and in the exploitation of mines. A system of loans for private industries helped develop the entrepreneurial spirit and concurred to the creation of genuine industrial and banking groups which were to know a rapid development during the following years [5].

Iran started openly showing its ambitions and attracting foreign investments. A special law on investments was passed in Parliament. It led to the creation of several all-purpose banks with the participation of big international financial groups.

As far as foreign affairs are concerned, Iran consolidated its deep links with the Western world and its relations with Israel which had been recognized de facto since 1949 were developed. Many common projects got off the ground. There was a strong tension with the Soviet bloc for a long time, and the propaganda war was raging. Iranians even installed powerful loud-speakers on many of their border sites with the USSR to spread anti-communist propaganda. The Iranian resolution proved to be successful. Moscow took good notice of it, and the tension subsided. Cooperation agreements were signed, and technical and commercial exchanges were developed. It was a really great success for the Shah, his diplomatic corps and his government. The good relations with the Eastern bloc carried on and developed until the revolution.

That was the time when one of Iran's old national ambitions which had been part of every government's programme since 1906 came up again: the creation of a heavy industry, the building of blast furnaces and steelworks. Iran appealed to the World Bank and received a blank 'no'. A first agreement was signed with German industrialists, but it was vetoed by Americans and by the German government. There were further negotiations with the Germans, however. Much later, in October 1960, the Vice-Chancellor and Minister for the Economy of the FRG was received in Tehran with great consideration. He discussed the issue and reiterated his government's refusal, despite Iranian hopes. Under pressure because of the questions asked during a meeting at the Chamber of Commerce of the capital, he ended up admitting: ' If you have the heavy industry, the blast furnaces and steelworks, what should Belgium and Western Germany do? Die?' [6] This was not very diplomatic. On October 5th 1960, when an honorary doctorate was awarded by the University of Tehran, professor Erhardt also insisted on the necessity of an international division of work that would confine developing countries into the role of producers of raw materials and 'simple' manufactured products.

These words were not appreciated by either the government or public opinion. In some newspapers, there was even mention of an insult for Iran. Mohammad Reza Pahlavi hid his reaction as usual, but he learnt a lesson for the future and eventually had his revenge.

*   *

*

Two series of major happenings were to change the course of events in Iran at the beginning of the 1960's, and provoke a serious crisis which the government was to overcome, but whose consequences were not to ever disappear.

The legislative elections of the middle of 1960, the so-called 'summer elections' raised a wave of protest that was limited to political circles and to the middle-class of the capital.

The Americans never liked the Prime Minister [7]. Washington was also annoyed [8] when Abolhassan Ebtehaj – the man in charge of the Plan – was replaced by Khosrow Hedayat, an engineer trained in Belgium. Yet, the latter turned out to be an excellent administrator without maintaining a permanent state of tension like his predecessor.

The protest against the outcome of the legislative elections of the summer of 1960 gave rise to a more direct move from the Ambassador of the United States [9]. The American stand, which was widely echoed in the press across the Atlantic, increased the pressure on the government and weakened it.

What was more serious was the rise in inflation due to an excessive expansion of credit and to the weakness of the banking system.

Mohammad Reza Pahlavi stepped back and rather unceremoniously asked the one who had been at the head of the government for forty-one months to resign.

He then called in Djafar Sharif-Emami, the Minister for Industry and Mines, a man of trust from the nascent industrial middle class and who was already heavily criticized. The latter presented his ministers on August 31st 1960. The term of the legislature being over, he did not need Parliament's approval. The elected representatives were asked to give up on mandates which they had not yet started because the electoral process had not completely ended. Most of them accepted. It was then decided that there should be new elections in the winter.

The return to an economic stability and the control of the inflationist process proved to be more difficult than political manoeuvres. The government had to appeal to the International Monetary Fund and the latter imposed a traditional 'stabilization plan' on Iran: a brutal reduction of the volume of public spending, of investments and credit to the private sector. Moreover, the government was to renounce its vague desires in matters of basic industry.

The plan rapidly provoked an economic recession. There was a slackening of activity and a sharp increase in unemployment because many public and private projects were dropped and work sites were closed down. There was a bad social climate on top of the political malaise. The Prime Minister's personality, integrity and competence were openly criticized. He went to see the Ambassador of Great Britain to complain, to accuse the Shah and Eghbal, the incumbent Prime Minister [10]!

The disparate and divided elements of the secular opposition did not fail to take advantage of the crisis. The change in the American attitude towards the regime encouraged them to do so. However, the religious hierarchy remained neutral and silent.

Indeed, John F. Kennedy's electoral campaign, his liberal and encouraging speeches, the critical distrust some members of his entourage felt for Mohammad Reza Pahlavi and his alleged links with republican personalities, then the election of November 1960, and the fact he took office as president in January 1961, were to create a less favourable atmosphere for trust between the United States and the Iranian Sovereign. That situation actually prefigured the one of 1978 and the Iranian-American relations during the Carter administration.

THE AUTHORITARIAN MONARCHY – *The White Revolution*

The rumour of a coup d'État fomented by Washington so as to overthrow the Shah became more and more persistent. The American president's entourage, like Jimmy Carter's in 1977-1978, denounced the brutality of the Iranian secret service, the Savak, even if it was working in close collaboration with the CIA. The president of the United States actually received the very unpopular head of the Savak, General Teymour Bakhtiar, which was very unusual. The hypothesis of a coup d'État to overthrow the Shah was allegedly evoked by the two men – a method Kennedy was to follow some time later in Vietnam to set up a team that would be docile with Washington*.

As for Bakhtiar, he openly plotted against the Shah. Mohammad Reza Pahlavi was immediately informed of it, either thanks to someone close to the general who was with him at the time, or to some American elements who opposed the scenario, as William Shawcross suggests [11] – he actually got the date of the meeting wrong by three years.

The Shah was extremely worried by Washington's manoeuvres, unlike in 1978, when he paid less attention to American actions and paid a high price for it. He probably decided on recoil tactics in front of the United States at that time, without showing it.

An anti-American atmosphere prevailed among the members of the Cabinet in Tehran. Ahmad Aramech, the minister in charge of the Plan who was the Prime Minister's brother-in-law at the time even went so far as to deliver speeches in Parliament that were very hostile to American politics, something which would have been inconceivable just a few months before.

---

* The military putsch and assassination of President Ngô Dinh Diêm in 1963.

It was during that situation of intense tension that ambassador Averell Harriman, one of president Kennedy's special envoys, arrived in Tehran to 'demand' a 'radical change' of the Shah's policy, as was reported in the American press.

Mossadegh, the historical leader and founder of the National Front, disavowed the latter right away when it took advantage of the atmosphere to come back to the stage, pretend to reorganize itself and demonstrate in Tehran. Primary state school teachers who were under the influence of a 'club' that had links with the American cultural centre in the capital, and who were openly supported by the United States embassy, did the same to ask for a big rise in their salaries and better working conditions.

On May 11th 1961, a teacher died in strange circumstances, probably after an act of provocation during a meeting in front of Parliament. These 'warnings' taught the Sharif-Emami Cabinet a lesson and it immediately handed in its resignation to the king who accepted it.

Ali Amini, a former minister of the Ghavam, Mossadegh and Zahedi governments who had then become ambassador to Washington, was put in charge of forming a new government [12]. The Shah wrote later: 'The USA wanted him [Sharif-Emami] to go so that he would leave his position to their man. I can still remember my first encounter with John Kennedy and his wife at the White House. Jacqueline Kennedy referred to Ali Amini's magnificent sparkling eyes in front of me, and confided to me that she deeply hoped I would appoint him Prime Minister. The pressure increased with time and I ended up yielding.' [13]

The new Prime Minister had been trained in France and was an extremely rich aristocrat, the grand-son of a king of the Qajar dynasty through his mother, and of a chancellor of the empire through his father. He was especially known for his immoderate ambition. He was said to be competent in the field of public finance, and to be a liberal open to dialogue.

When he ascended to power, he declared: 'We have to undertake a real crusade against corruption. Be as vigilant as I am. We will chase the incompetents, traitors and parasites with the help of the people, and will lead our nation to prosperity.' [14] Meanwhile, he had the Sovereign dissolve Parliament and ruled by decrees.

Many political and military personalities who were sometimes close to the Shah were arrested following this declaration. Despite the efforts made by his Minister of Justice, a former general secretary of the Iranian communist Party, and by the prosecution, they could not be taken to court. It was enough, however, to give Ali Amini the reputation of being incorruptible in some American circles.

He left a certain freedom of action to those who claimed to follow in Mossadegh's political footsteps at first. When they criticized him, however, he had some of them arrested as well.

After proclaiming the country 'bankrupt', he got an emergency aid of 35 million dollars from the United States – a ridiculous sum compared to the country's gross national product, and drastically enforced the 'stabilization' programme imposed by the IMF. The economic slump and the social discontent were only made worse. The Prime Minister then asked for measures to put restrictions on the credits to the armed forces. The Shah refused to give his assent. Amini then offered his resignation. He almost flaunted that he was nearly certain it could not be accepted because of the unconditional support he had from the Kennedy brothers. Yet, the Sovereign accepted it on July 16th 1962, after having relieved General Bakhtiar from his duties – another man Washington relied on – and protecting his rear, in a way. The 'Amini experience' lasted fourteen months.

Mohammad Reza Pahlavi came out stronger of this first, real trial of strength with Washington, but he was also determined to extend his personal power. When Ali Amini had Parliament dissolved in the winter of 1960, under the previous government, he found himself alone in front of the king, politically speaking. He was not very popular, and thus could not rely on the support of the people. Washington had been tricked.

As for Mohammad Reza Pahlavi, he wanted to beat everybody to it: the Americans, his political opponents, progressive intellectuals, and the masses. It was a great ambition.

It led to remarkable achievements, and to the final failure of the revolution.

*   *

*

On July 16th 1962, when the Shah accepted Ali Amini's resignation, he unexpectedly put his friend Amir Assadollah Alam, maybe the only friend he ever had, in charge of forming the new government. Alam was the director of the Pahlavi Foundation at the time.

He came from a well-known family that lived south of Khorasan, and studied to become an agronomist. In the mid 1940's, when he was twenty-six years old, he happened to be the youngest minister in the constitutional history of Iran, thus since 1906, and was appointed Minister of Agriculture. He then had other ministerial positions. Alam was tall and slim. He always dressed with a certain sobriety, in a very English style and was fond of horses, tennis, good wine – yet he was sober – and women – in his 'diary' [15], he talks about his affairs in a manner which sometimes lacks elegance. He could read and write in fluent English and spoke French fairly well. Alam had a great political understanding and an exceptional sense of public relations. He benefited from the Shah's full trust. Thanks to the Shah's trust and his closeness to him, he was free to manoeuvre almost as he pleased. It was the same for Ardeshir Zahedi later on, when he was at the head of Iranian diplomacy or at the Iranian embassy in the United States.

The team the new Prime Minister chose included some of Mossadegh's former collaborators, converted communists, technocrats who had no political experience, and a few traditional politicians. He decided to tackle a serious economic, social and consequently also political situation: an economic slump, unemployment, political discontent, a cooling down of relations with Washington, the country's main ally and the guarantor of its security in front of the Soviet Union. The legacy of the two previous cabinets was not easy.

Constitutionally speaking, the situation was rather paradoxical. As soon as Ali Amini ascended to power, and without even presenting himself to Parliament, he had both Chambers dissolved and decided to rule by decrees, which he was reproached for afterwards.

Thus, Assadollah Alam had to continue to rule in the same way. The Eghbal government had had a law passed for an agrarian reform which was well prepared, logical, technocratic but also really complicated and difficult to implement. Ali

Amini and Hassan Arsanjani, his fiery Minister of Agriculture, had launched another project, a pragmatic one, but one which had no legal foundation since it had not been voted on in Parliament. The launching and the implementation of the project had shaken the old agrarian and real estate structures; it aroused great unrest in the country, especially after the minister's strong language and his abrupt manners.

Politically speaking, it was difficult to organize new elections. From a social point of view, the crisis in the farming community had to be appeased and the threat of the Cuban spectre moved aside. Fidel Castro had been in power since 1959. Washington feared a similar revolution in Iran and made no secret of it. From an economic point of view, the urban population was shattered because of the slump and unemployment. Public opinion confusedly expected or dreaded events. The situation the Alam government was in was uncomfortable.

It was in that precise context of a crisis, even of deadlock, that the White Revolution was to be launched.

*   *

*

On January 9th 1963, Mohammad Reza Pahlavi claimed his desire to start a radical change of the social and economic structures in the country in front of the national Congress of agricultural cooperatives in Tehran, 'based on participation, cooperation, and gradual democratisation so as to reach a type of society that would be fair, equitable and fraternal.' His intention was not to base this society 'on imported ideologies, but on the respect of the traditions and deep beliefs of the

Iranian people, and to strive to make national culture bloom.' [16] Later on, the Shah wrote that it was 'a mainly practical programme, which was designed to address our problems in the order of their importance and urgency, and in accordance with our mentality and traditions.' [17]

Three days later, on January 12th, the Sovereign was on his way to dinner with the 4,800 participants in the Congress who were almost all simple farmers from all parts of the country. He became very lyrical: 'My heart only beats for you; I can only succeed with your support, your unity. This country is yours, it is the country of all Iranians, and it does not belong to one class in particular, or to one individual.' [18]

The next day, the congress decided to call him a 'just', as an honour. On the 14th, the congressional committee was received by the Sovereign and submitted their proposal to him. He rejected it, saying: 'I have done, and only do my duty. I act in accordance with my beliefs, and not for titles. I would like all

Iranians to be prosperous and happy.' [19]

*   *

*

The most important principles of what was first called 'The Shah and the People's revolution' and then 'the White Revolution' were the following: the agrarian reform and the abolition of the big feudal-type estate, the nationalization of forests, pastureland and natural water resources, the equality of political rights for men and women, the creation of literacy corps, of hygiene, health and development corps so as to transform the traditional structures of villages*, the participation of workers in the profits made by industrial companies, the implementation of a popular elective justice for villages and of urban mediators who were to be elected by local inhabitants [20].

On January 27th 1963, the first six principles, including the two most important and controversial ones in some circles, i.e. the agrarian reform and the man-woman equality, were approved of in a referendum which was indeed well supervised, but where the enthusiasm of the peasantry and of women, thus of the great majority of the people, was real. There were 5,598,711 votes for and 4,115 votes against them.

The Sovereign and his government broke the legislative

---

* The point was to assign all the young 'specialists' – holders of university degrees in the appropriate sectors – and most of the pupils who had passed their 'baccalauréat' (final secondary school examination) to literacy campaigns, to the development of medical care, and to the equipment of villages and of the rural sector in general.

The results as regards the elimination of illiteracy were spectacular: from 1963 to 1978, the literacy corps included 28 classes of young men and 18 of young women who were volunteers, thus a total of 166,948 people who were to join the network of the National Education services in the rural sector after a period of appropriate training. Therefore, and despite an average population growth rate of 2.7% per year during that period, the percentage of illiterates dropped from 85.1% to less than 50%.

The hygiene corps, with its 24 classes, had the support of 2,874 physicians, 279 dentists, 443 pharmacists and 14,754 'paramedics' for the sanitary network in the country, and was at the origin of the creation of 685 small country clinics. The statistics of the time show that 34,210,617 free medical consultations were given, and there were 19,541,540 vaccinations. These figures should, of course, be added on to the activity of the 'conventional' network.

It was a unique example for developing countries.

deadlock for the State by resorting to the referendum procedure. Even if this type of consultation was not formally recognized in the 1906 Constitution, it referred to it since it specified that 'national sovereignty belongs to the Iranian people', which the Islamic revolution was to abolish. It also allowed to rule by ordinances, even if it meant a later ratification by Parliament, once it was elected and summoned.

The two main points of the White Revolution drastically changed the fundamental structures of society: for the agrarian reform, on the social, economic and political level; for the man-woman equality, on the cultural and psychological one.

Some tribal chiefs were not long to react: the ones of the Fars region, in the South of the country, were more particularly opposed to the agrarian reform, and organized an armed rebellion against the power. Even if the tribal guerrilla units had no political programme, they still remained efficient. Once, they even reached the suburbs of Shiraz, the main administrative centre of the province. The insurgents' aim was to reach an air base, destroy a few military aeroplanes, maybe enter the city and then negotiate when they were in a position of strength. The army was awaiting them thanks to precise information, and crushed them. It was the beginning of the end.

The tribal rebellion benefited from the help of Gama Abdel Nasser, the Egyptian Rais, who had a hostile attitude towards Iran and its pro-West policy. Light weapons and explosives as well as suitcases full of banknotes were shipped to the insurgents on small boats via the small harbours of the Persian Gulf. The Cairo radio channel, La Voix des Arabes, (the Arabs' voice) broadcasted intense propaganda in their favour. It took the government several months to quell the rebellion. The Southern army was commanded by General Bahram Ariana, the future head of general staff. It had the order to proceed in an extremely cautious way so as to spare civilians. Air operations were limited for the same reason. There were still a few rebels left until 1965. Then, the main leaders of armed gangs were arrested, their lands were confiscated without any compensation, and they were brought before military tribunals. Some of them were executed.

From a political point of view, the demonstrations which broke out in Qom in June 1963 had a different meaning, and were to reach the capital. They were led by a mullah of Indian origin who spoke with a dialectal accent and with the violence of a by-gone era. His name was Ruhollah Khomeini. He achieved a certain notoriety for a limited period of time*.

A fanaticized crowd which was relatively limited in numbers was joined by communist elements, as further arrests showed. It protested against the sharing of land, the use of referendum, which were both deemed anti-Islamic, and especially against the political emancipation of women, who were 'mentally disturbed' as Ruhollah Khomeini then said. Schools, banks, cultural centres, buildings which represented 'modernity' were stormed, looted and set on fire. These tactics were to be widely used in 1978. The police forces were overwhelmed at first.

Important sums of money were distributed so that the rioters would be better organized by henchmen from the local underworld. The main leader of the riots in the capital was an ex-convict with a long record called Tayeb Haj Rezaï. He was soon to be arrested, tried and executed.

The government seemed to be faltering for a few hours.

---

* See chapter XI: 'A kind of social-democratic saint' – 'A miracle in Paris'.

The Shah allegedly thought of yielding, but Alam, the Prime Minister, reacted with authority. He was assured of the support of a majority of public opinion, so he had the national gendarmerie intervene to stop the demonstrators who had come from Qom to join Tehran and the army in the capital city. Things quickly went back to normal, but there were victims. A law-decree was to swiftly provide their families with compensation. It was a personal idea of the Prime Minister, which was to earn him great esteem.

The interest the intelligence services and certain American circles [21] had in Ruhollah Khomeini apparently dated back to that time.

Khomeini had then declared it was 'a simple flick to overthrow the regime.' [22] He was wrong. The government was strong, and public opinion, in its vast majority, had not changed. The army had intervened. The foreign backing – Nasser's Egypt and elements from the Tudeh – did not measure up. Assadolah Alam had defeated the little Iranian-Indian mullah. The lesson was to be remembered. Fifteen years later, the preparation work was to be meticulous and the government weakened beforehand.

When the connivance between communist elements and the supporters of a reactionary form of Islam – which was to be called Islamic fundamentalism later on, or more simply Islamism – was made known publicly as well as the foreign support to the unrest, the propaganda of the imperial regime did not stop denouncing 'the cursed alliance of red and black.' [23] The 1978-79 events proved it right – for the sake of History only.

*   *

*

The Alam government faced the mostly economic problems as well as it could. The tribal insurrection had been a problem for the army only, and the unrest caused by Khomeini, a small parenthesis which was quickly closed. When Alam came to power, the coffers of the State were empty. Despite the drastic enforcement of the IMF regulations, the budget deficit was of over 350 million dollars, and the monetary reserves of only 140 million dollars [24]. It was necessary to find an urgent way not to be hemmed in by these regulations which were partly responsible for the political crisis. That was what the government did, and it tried to give a new boost to the economy: a few projects which had been abandoned or not completely carried out were taken up again. A major construction plan for housing facilities was launched. It was meant to quickly create jobs.

On September 19th, a law-decree planned the start of the Third national development plan for March 21st of the following year. It was a five-year plan, not a seven-year one, like the two previous ones. Safi Asfia, a brilliant ex-student from the École Polytechnique, an honest and respected man, was put in charge. He was to become one of the major actors of the development of the country for years.

The Shah was personally involved in the implementation of the agrarian reform. He travelled across the country to hand the landowners their new titles, and did his walkabouts, which he seemed to appreciate.

Owing to the opportunities granted to the landowners after they had been stripped of their land by the agrarian reform, the government loan bonds they had received as compensation were massively reinvested in the private sector: the industry, building trade, and services to consumers. The enterprising spirit which the IMF stabilization plan had succeeded in stifling using imposed restrictions, was revived, and contributed to a new recovery.

The machine turned itself on again slowly, the atmosphere got better with the legislative and senatorial elections which were indeed not organized in the same conditions of freedom as in Western countries, but in an often sincere and genuine mood of enthusiasm, thanks to the arrival on the scene of new actors: women, workers and peasants.

The Senate, with its relatively limited constitutional prerogatives, was to remain a Chamber of notables, and sometimes a place for a golden retirement. However, the Chamber saw the massive arrival of representatives who were workers and peasants, of academics who had sometimes been anti-establishment, of cooperative managers and especially of several women who had been elected representatives. The White Revolution had just changed the political scenery in an impressive manner, and released a new leading elite.

Assadolah Alam handed in his resignation to the Sovereign who immediately asked him to form a new government as soon as the new legislature had started its work.

The new Cabinet was presented on October 21st 1963, and was not much different from the previous one. Hassan Arsanjani, the rowdy Minister of Agriculture who had made many enemies, was appointed ambassador to Rome. General Esmaïl Riahi replaced him. He was an honest, respected and level-headed man who was considered to be one of the rare political figures of the command of the armed forces. He was asked to see the first phase of the agrarian reform through, and succeeded while keeping his composure and authority.

A few days later, on November 5th 1963, Manutshehr Eghbal, a former Prime Minister who had resumed his position as a doctor and associate professor in a CHU (university hospital) of the French capital city, was appointed at the head of the National Iranian Oil Company. He was a man who could be trusted, although he was not a specialist, and he presided over the prodigious development of the oil sector of the country for fifteen years.

*   *

*

In March 1964, when the Shah was rid of his new extremist opponents, he wished to give a permanent boost to the development process and called in a talented and very promising young man to be in power. His name was Hassan Ali Mansour; he was the son of the Prime Minister who had witnessed the allied troops' invasion of 1941.

The adversaries of the new head of government said he was too ambitious. His enemies accused him of being supported by the Americans who had obviously taken a moderate liking for Amir Assadollah Alam. The latter had certainly never proved unworthy of the trust placed in him and, following an American habit, since he was not an academic, he was appointed rector of the University of Shiraz which had just changed its name for Pahlavi. The Shah had become its honorary president and real protector. Soon after, he was nominated to the ministry of the imperial Court, but kept his position as rector. The Shah's interest – he considered the university to be his and took a close interest in it – and Alam's influence turned it into a centre of excellence which soon acquired an international reputation. Mohammad Reza Pahlavi was dreaming of turning his campus (which was partially completed before the revolution) into the Persepolis of the 20th century.

*   *

*

The new Prime Minister, Hassan Ali Mansour, was forty-one years old. He was a career diplomat who had then become Junior Minister to the Prime Minister, Minister of Labour and Minister of Trade in the Eghbal Cabinet before finally being the managing director of the National Insurance Company and of its banking and hotel branches for over two years. He had just been elected representative for the capital in the new Chamber. Before, he had founded a political group called the Progressive Circle, several members of which had also been elected to Parliament.

The Progressive Circle then became a political party called Iran-eh-novin (New Iran). It was highly acclaimed by the workers unions and the associations of peasant-landowners.

Hassan Ali Mansour was an excellent orator with a prodigious memory. He was intelligent, affable, and polyglot, but most of all, a real visionary with a strong will to reform society, develop the country, equip it with solid institutions and promote a new political deal. He deeply believed in virtue in politics, in the necessity for the members of government to be fully honest, and he discarded any deviation, or dishonourable behaviour. Were his idealism, his political vision – which did not fit in with the deplorable practices of our contemporary world in the East as well as in the West – and his ambitions that could be in a way, a reason for his fall?

Mansour called in several technocrats and young academics who were not well known to the general public as well as experienced diplomats and politicians to form his government. One of Mossadegh's former companions, his governor of the National Bank, Professor Mohammad Nassiri – who was not related at all to the man from the Savak – was appointed Senior Minister. The Minister of Finance was a close friend of the Prime Minister, Amir Abbas Hoveyda.

When the Cabinet was presented to the Chambers, the Shah paid deep homage to the previous Cabinet and Prime Minister.

'This government must adapt the political and administrative structures of the country to the requirements of the White Revolution. Ministers have a political duty on top of their functions. There is no time to lose.' [26]

The government more particularly tackled the economic and social development and reflation. The organization of the plan was restructured; a reflation plan was implemented, and new ministries – Equipment and Housing, Energy – were created, with the Ministry of Culture a few weeks later. They were to be the spearhead of the new administration.

Unemployment soon went down, the economy picked up and trust was back. Foreign investors massively reappeared, and so did the IMF. Its experts pretended to dread the recurrence of inflationist pressure and of an excess of investments. They warned against open ambitions which, according to them, the Iranian economy could not sustain.

The IMF imposed a few unpopular measures such as the doubling of prices of all oil products, and a heavy tax on trips abroad in order to curb the fast increase in domestic consumption, and avoid a budget deficit which would generate inflationist pressure. Hassan Ali Mansour and his Minister of Finance, Amir Abbas Hoveyda, had the necessary legislative and statutory provisions passed on November 23rd 1964, despite the Shah's reservations – he let them go on with things anyway – and Manutshehr Eghbal's opposition as

President of the National Iranian Oil Company, and four of the Cabinet members' objections.

It had a devastating effect on public opinion.

On January 10th 1965, the government was forced to step back, but it was too late.

In the meantime, a judicial cooperation agreement about the military advisors who worked in Iran was signed with the United States. It was similar to all the agreements made with all the allied countries on the same issues, but it caused unrest, especially in Qom. The political atmosphere was bad in spite of the quasi spectacular economic achievements made in a few months.

On January 21st 1965, Hassan Ali Mansour was on his way to the Chamber to propose a bill allowing the government to conclude a new oil agreement that would end the 50-50 of profits between the 'seven Western sisters' and Iran, when a young terrorist named Mohammad Bokharaï shot him three times at close range. Mohammad Bokharaï was a member of a sub-group of the Muslim Brothers, a corporative Islamist association. The Prime Minister died five days later.

The confusing circumstances of the assassination attempt, the way the Prime Minister was taken care of, the silence around the whole affair, and the immediate replacement of General Pakravan by General Nassiri at the head of the Savak which was in charge of solving the case [27], make the hypothesis of a certain manipulation plausible, even if it can't be contested [28] that the Islamists were directly responsible – a guilt they publicly claimed after the revolution. When he commented on the event in his Diary [29], Amir Assadolah Alam did not hide a certain antipathy the Court felt for the assassinated Prime Minister*.

The event and its consequences could, in a way, be

compared with the assassination in Kiev of Stolypin, the Russian Chancellor and reformer, in 1911. He could have avoided Czar Nicholas II and his country the Bolshevik revolution. His bold reforms bothered the revolutionaries who saw the rug pulled from under their feet, and also people taking advantage of the situation: some of the Czar's entourage. The secret police manipulated the revolutionary terrorists and made them quickly disappear; it is now a historical fact.

The enigma over Mansour's assassination will remain a controversy, as in John F. Kennedy's case. From a political point of view, his death made the country lose a politician who had character, a reformer who was honest and courageous and who could have been very useful in times of crises. He would not even have been sixty in 1978.

*   *

*

A few hours after Mansour's death had been announced, the Shah put Amir Abbas Hoveyda, his Minister of Finance and also his closest friend, in charge of forming the new government. Hoveyda kept all the ministers his predecessor had chosen. The latter's brother, Djavad, who had previously been Junior Minister, was given a portfolio as a sort of posthumous homage to the deceased, and General Pakravan, who had been

---

* As Minister of Hassan Ali Mansour and later in the first two Hoveyda Cabinets – all in all from March 1964 to September 1968 – , then as rector of the Pahlavi (Shiraz) university where I took over from Alam, and of the university of Tehran, so over a period of fifteen years, I had the opportunity to mention Hassan Ali Mansour's name during my audiences and on several other occasions. The Shah always showed affection and a certain emotion. As for Hassan Ali Mansour, I have absolutely no doubt as to his total devotion to the Shah.

fired from the Savak, was appointed Minister of Information.

Hoveyda was at first considered to be a temporary Prime Minister, but he remained at the head of the government until August 7th 1977 [30].

A former career diplomat who had then been director of the National Iranian Oil Company, he was a cultured man who was a social success. He was born in the Levant where his father had a consular post. He did his primary and secondary studies in Lebanon, and thus mastered Arabic and its subtleties perfectly well, which was a rare quality among Iranians who had always shown disdain for Mahomet's language, for historical and cultural reasons. His real first mother tongue was French; then, he had learnt English, which he was fairly fluent at; he had also had taken a few lessons of Russian. His mastering of Persian, of its literature, subtleties and of the history of Iran left to be desired. He was a poor orator.

He had got married once, to Hassan Ali Mansour's sister-in-law. The marriage was short-lived.

He remained in power for thirteen years and was gifted with a good sense for public relations and a great capacity for bribery thanks to the secret funds of the presidency. He is probably the best known Iranian politician in the West, with, perhaps, the exception of Mossadegh and Ghavam. A great number of the Iranian development projects were carried out under his government. He is also greatly responsible for the errors made.

Hoveyda was certainly not the man of a foreign power, especially not of the United States of America. Maybe this is why the Shah liked him, as he distrusted the people close to Washington, even if it was supposed to be his main ally.

Contrarily to Mansour who was an ideologist and a visionary, he was a politician who was more involved in everyday affairs, an excellent tactician, but a mediocre strategist.

He was very attentive to public opinion at first, but he progressively took a liking for power for the sake of power, and not for the sake of the nation. He created his own influence network thanks to the Iran-eh-novin party which he turned into a formidable political instrument. He even infiltrated the secret services, which the Shah did not care too much for, and used them especially to eliminate his political rivals – he sometimes succeeded – and more particularly to create a reassuring atmosphere around the Shah, with the help of the Savak – 'everything is fine, everything is going better, everything is going better and better.' Shahbanoo Farah admitted it: 'He [Hoveyda] adopted more of an attitude which consisted in erasing some of the problems so as to present a constantly reassuring assessment of the situation of the country to the King.'[31]

He always tried to flatter the Shah, the Shahbanoo, the imperial family and their entourage by using all possible means, and would close his eyes to many abuses which he despised but tolerated. He was personally honest, though, as even his enemies or his executioners said.

This intellectual with advanced ideas who was 'never accused of having dirty money on his hands, or even less so, blood on his hands'[32] had become a disillusioned, plotting, cynical and dreaded politician towards the end of his career, even the Shah feared him.

He widely contributed to the rise in popular discontent from 1973 onwards with his flattery and errors. He was appointed Minister to the imperial Court to replace Amir Assadollah Alam who was dying of cancer, and remained in his position for thirteen months. He was then arrested with the consent, if not the encouragement of the Shah and Shahbanoo, on November 8th 1978, to be used as a scapegoat. He was brutally assassinated on April 9th 1979.

Amir Abbas Hoveyda was the victim of two regimes, the one he served, which had him imprisoned in a less than glorious manner, and the one from the Islamic revolution, which had him assassinated without even giving a chance to resist.

*   *

*

Hoveyda's successor was Djamshid Amouzegar. He came from a well-known, traditional middle-class family. He was an engineer trained in the United States who became Minister of Labour, of Health, of the Interior, and of Finance for a long time. He had made a reputation for himself as Iran's delegate to the Organization of Petroleum-Exporting Countries (OPEC), and during the hostage-taking of several ministers by the terrorist Carlos.

He was the prototype of the technocrat promoted under Mohammad Reza Pahlavi's reign. This honest, hard-working man with a prodigious memory was not very sociable and only cared about sometimes insignificant details. He formed a Cabinet of technicians who were often apolitical and mostly honest. He remained almost inert when faced with the rise of domestic discontent and international conspiracies. He was considered to be well appreciated by Americans and especially by the bigwigs of the Democratic Party, whether this is right or wrong. However, his presence at the head of the State did not seem to deter Washington from supporting the destabilization of the Shah.

Shahbanoo Farah wrote later on, evoking a conversation she had with the Prime Minister then: 'I had the feeling, while listening to him, that he had lost faith, faith in the strength and concord the King and I represented for the country.' [33]

The infernal destruction process of Iran had already started. To oppose it, a man cast in a different mould would have been needed, or the armed forces.

Djamshid Amouzegar remained in power until the summer of 1978 and was the last minister of the White Revolution, or the first of the revolutionary process.

Chapter IX

A CERTAIN IDEA OF IRAN

Mohammad Reza Pahlavi was born, if we may remind you, on October 26th 1919 in Tehran [1].

From 1921, as his father had become an important figure, his mother brought him up as was fit.

In 1925, as soon as his father had been crowned, and according to the Constitution, he became crown prince of the empire. A particular regime was immediately put into place for the training of the future sovereign. His father was self-taught. He demanded an education and upbringing for his son that were worthy of a future Shah, unlike the one for a prince from the Qajar dynasty, whose dissolute habits he condemned, but like the one for a modern king who was to be cultured, disciplined and aware of his duties for his country and his people.

A special class was created inside the Palace where the Prince and some children of his age who had been selected among the families of high-ranking officers could follow elementary lessons of spelling, arithmetic, history, geography and civics. A special place was given to physical education. It was a rather heavy curriculum, six days a week and six hours a day, for Friday had to be respected as a day off. The young prince was supervised to make sure he did his homework in the evening. Formal orders were given to instructors so that strict discipline would be enforced, and that no exception should be made for Prince Mohammad Reza.

Then, following the tradition in Iranian dynasties, notably in the Qajar dynasty, an elderly personality who is respected by the family, here the only possible one considering the Shah's family, his uncle Tehshragh-Ali Khan, who had been given the title of Amir Akram by a sovereign of the previous dynasty, was appointed pishkar, steward and private tutor of the prince [2].

This regime quickly changed. After a year of 'special lessons', he was registered in a 'military primary school', Dabestaneh nehzam. The curriculum was really heavy and the discipline, strict. The pupils wore the uniform of cadets in the armed forces, and were forced to do fairly hard physical exercises and even military exercises despite their young ages. The young prince had, on top of that, to take private lessons in history, Persian literature, and calligraphy – an art Iranians highly valued, and which was a sign of distinction. Mohammad Reza always had a beautiful handwriting. One of his masters at the time was Abdol Azim Gharib, a famous grammarian and an authority in Persian literature.

Amir Akram was a very dignified old man and he was already very ill. When he died, the Shah found another pishkar, doctor Moadab Nafissi, who had been trained in France, and who was also to keep an eye on his health. Then, his father chose a French governess, Madam Arfa*.

The French governess, indeed, taught him French, but also the history of Europe and of the great powers, and then she told him about the lives and work of famous personalities.

---

* Died in Paris in 1959.

He also learnt how to ride – he became an excellent rider – and practised wrestling, a national Iranian sport which he did not care for too much, it seems.

As soon as he turned nine, young Mohammad Reza, who already looked starchy, had to spend two hours a day with his father and regularly share his frugal lunch.

What was he left with from his earliest childhood and from the six years he spent in primary school? Probably the often expressed lack of 'a childhood like that of others', a certain shyness, a reserve in his relations with his entourage, a really great capacity to conceal emotions and a great self-control, but also the little care he showed for the intellectual and political training of his own crown-prince.

At the age of twelve, Mohammad Reza Pahlavi had a good knowledge of Persian and of its grammar, of the country's great poets and writers; he knew the history of Iran that he was systematically immersed in. He was also fluent in French, and his accent was already irreproachable. He admired Louis XI, the good king Henri IV, who was able to reconcile his subjects, and especially Richelieu and his national diplomacy. He did not ignore anything either about the gigantic work of Louis XIV, of Louis XVI's tragedy, and of the Napoleonic campaigns. Perhaps he owed Madam Arfa his taste for the study of events from a close and distant past.

From an early age on, he thus acquired a double culture, Iranian and French. His father, a finicky nationalist, and an Iranian through and through, had no objection to it. He only mistrusted the English – and this is only a euphemism – and the Russians, but not really the French.

On the other hand, a religious education and the practise

of Islam seem to have had no place in his education. Even if his father was a believer and a Muslim, he did not practise his religion much, and 'even showed the opposite' [3], as his son said later on. Thus, as in many other Iranian middle-class families of the time, and despite a mother who was rather devoted to her faith, the young prince could choose to practise or not out of his own free will. Mohammad Reza Pahlavi said it himself: 'I became a believer at a very young age... Being a believer does not necessarily mean that one has to bow down and slap one's chest. One can believe and practise in a discreet, inner fashion. That is my case.' [4] His 'conversion' apparently dates back to the time he suffered from a serious case of typhoid that he had caught while he was at primary school and which nearly killed him [5], and to the dream he made then.

Was this lack of religious upbringing to play a part in the future sovereign's often ambiguous policy with the clergy during the 1978-1979 events?

*   *

*

In June 1931, Mohammad Reza passed his primary education certificate. After many consultations, the Court decided to send him to Switzerland, a neutral country, to continue his studies in a Francophone school. The Rosey school, near Rolle, between Geneva and Lausanne, was chosen.

The prince left his country in early September after an eight-week holiday on the Caspian Sea. Three other young boys accompanied him so that he would not feel too lonely: his younger brother, Ali Reza, Teymourtach, the son of the Court's Minister, and Hossein Fardoust, the son of an officer and a pupil from the same elementary military school where the future Shah had just finished his studies, and apparently his best playmate. That friend became a general and a security coordinator, thus an important character of the regime during the last years of the Shah's reign. He was to betray his sovereign and play an important role in the revolutionary process.

Two private tutors also went on the trip: doctor Moadab Nafissi, his new pishkar, a cultured and strict man who was to keep an eye on his health and discipline, and who had to keep Tehran regularly informed, and Mr Mostashar, who was to bring to perfection his knowledge of the Persian language and literature, the history of his country, and who was to pay attention to his mastery of calligraphy.

The Shah and Queen Taj Ol Molouk accompanied the little group to the harbour of Anzali (Pahlavi) where it was supposed to take the boat to Baku. As they were embarking, the sovereign said to both tutors: 'Make men out of them.'

*   *

*

Mohammad Reza was only twelve. His childhood had just come to an end. The short boat trip, and then the long train journey in a special carriage placed at their disposal by the Soviet state across Poland and Germany lasted three weeks. The Iranian Minister in Switzerland welcomed the group at the station in Geneva. Mohammad Reza Pahlavi said to one of his biographers [6] later on: 'You should have seen our joy when we discovered the scenery, the cities, all these marvels. It was the joy of four schoolboys who had never yet left their country.'

Mohammad Reza stayed with a Swiss family, the Merciers, during the 1931-1932 school year. He improved his school knowledge in a preparatory school in Chailly and familiarized himself with the Western lifestyle. He entered the Rosey in September 1932. Two years later, his four half-brothers also entered the famous school.

The school had been founded in 1880 by a Belgian, Mr Carnal, and was and still is today, the most famous private secondary school in Switzerland. When the young prince arrived, the founder's son, Henri Carnal was in charge, and he was helped by his wife, an American.

At the time, and because of Madam Carnal's activity, the Rosey used to accommodate twice as many American children as all the other nationalities put together. These American children came from rich American families or from those of diplomats who were stationed in Europe. However, there were also the sons of royal families or from the nobility [7]. The prince made friends with some of his schoolmates, as well as with a certain Ernest Peron, the son of the school's bursar who was to play a certain role in the Tehran society.

As a whole, he did not have a joyous life there because of the strict supervision of his tutors and of the Iranian Minister. Every Tuesday [8], he was to write a long letter to his father in which he kept informed on his marks, his daily life events, and on the atmosphere in the school. He was not always too pleased with Mr Mostashar's private lessons and Dr Moadab's advice, but he dealt with them. He wanted the accounts given to his father by both men to be laudatory, which seems to have been the case if one judges by the Shah's reactions and joy [9].

The prince was the perfect example of a good pupil who did not have any problems. He was given one of the nicest and biggest rooms in the boarding-school. He had an excellent appetite and grew up fast: at fifteen, he was over five foot seven. He only excelled in sports. All his life, he remained an accomplished sportsman. He was also a very good student in history and geography. Decades later, he was still able to talk at long length about the flow of rivers in Europe and in America, or about such and such a particularity of the climate in Africa, Asia or Latin America. His memories would dazzle his interlocutors who were all struck by his 'academic culture.' He was good at French, which remained his second language, and had a decent knowledge of English, which he improved later on. He remained very weak in mathematics and was subjected to private lessons in Persian and in calligraphy five times a week. He did not keep good memories of them, as he did not keep good memories of the 'two cups of hot chocolate and Swiss pastries which he had to take almost every Sunday afternoon in good tea-rooms with his tutors and nearly always with a few affected diplomats who thought they were doing him a favour.' [10] The teaching of Persian, of calligraphy and of the history of his country proved to be very useful to the sovereign later on however.

During the summer of 1936, he went briefly back to Iran to see his family. His father was very proud of his progress, and he was extremely happy about it.

In June 1937, he passed the test of the 'maturité fédérale', the equivalent of the French baccalaureate. He had to go back home for good and kept excellent memories of the Rosey. Later, his schoolmates and friends were to talk about him and say what an excellent sportsman, pleasant and receptive friend he was.

His carefree youth had just ended with these years spent in Switzerland when he was not even nineteen.

*   *

*

When he went back home in 1937, Iran was different from the country he had left six years before. It had really changed: there were good roads for motor vehicles, a transiranian railroad, factories popping up everywhere, a certain urbanization, the impressive worksite of the central campus of the University of Tehran... and stylish, spacious villas surrounded with trees and lawns which were given the pompous name of palaces for the Shah's family.

Like any other young Iranian, he had to do his military service. It was to be done at the Military Academy of Tehran, as for all the holders of secondary school and university degrees.

For a year, he was submitted to a strict regime, the one of all the officers of the time, with thirty other young men his age: up at 5.30 a.m., winter and summer, physical education and various exercises from 7 to 9 a.m., classes from 9 to 12, and again from 2 p.m. to 5, lunch at the canteen and other exercises or lessons in between, then more exercises or lessons, study hall from 5 to 7 p.m. There were forced marches that lasted several days and simulated night attacks. It was proper commando training, and that was what his implacable father wanted. It is probably from that period that his obsession with order and exactness, punctuality, and a certain rigidity in his attitude came, but also a truly professional knowledge of military art which he kept improving and which impressed many of his interlocutors.

At the end of the 1938 spring, he became second-lieutenant and came out first in his year. He said, later on [11]: 'I do not know if my good marks were due to my ability and merit, or to my position.'

From then on, the prince had little time off or time for

leisure in his private life. He had to follow his father everywhere he went, attend, without intervening, the Cabinet meetings and various other meetings presided by the Sovereign. He, moreover, had his own obligations: visits, inaugurations, and a few audiences, etc...

His private life was thus limited to very little. He is said to have had affairs; he fell in love with a young woman from an excellent family, the niece of one of his future Prime Ministers, whom he wished to marry. His father was opposed to it, and he complied with his decision without hesitating. The young woman he loved married very well afterwards, and still lives with her husband today.

*   *

*

While the crown prince was following the courses of the Military Academy in Tehran, the sovereign's entourage tried their best to find him a future wife. A group of trusted men who were supposed to know the royal families was put in charge [12].

The first person to be considered was a daughter of Ahmad Shah, the last Qajar king. It would have been in the tradition of most Iranian dynasties since ancient times. By having a princess from the deposed ruling family marry the Shah or his crown prince, the reconciliation of the two lineages and a kind of dynastic continuity were ensured.

The idea was swiftly moved aside and a constitutional amendment was voted in 1925 forbidding any person from the Qajar lineage to come back to the throne. The fact that the future heir of Persia could be born to a Qajar mother could thus be a problem.

All the marriageable princesses from the Court of Afghanistan, in Iraq or in the Maghreb were screened: a princess from the deposed but still prestigious imperial Ottoman family was considered. The alliance with a republican and secular Turkey and the existing friendship and mutual esteem between the Shah and Kemal Ataturk whom one did not want to annoy made the marriage impossible.

The illustrated documentaries in the international press over the marriage of the Egyptian heir, Faruk, as well as the suggestions from, it seems, the leaders of Turkish diplomacy gave rise to the 'Egyptian option.'

The late king of Egypt, Fuad I, had four daughters. He was a sovereign with a good reputation, and was thought to come from a prestigious lineage. His eldest, and prettiest, was called Fawzieh. She was then aged seventeen. She was considered as the right choice in Tehran. Faruk, the new king, was neither old enough to rule yet, nor had he acquired the bad reputation that was to be his later on, so the country was governed by Prince Mohammad Ali, the king's uncle, who acted as regent, with the help of the leader of the Wafd, Nahas Pasha, the future great nationalist leader, who was Prime Minister. With the treaty of 1936, Great Britain was in charge of the control of the Suez Canal and therefore officially supervised the diplomacy and defence of the country. That was the only thing the Shah disliked. He did not ignore that the union would displease the British, but he did not care less.

On July 20th 1937, order was given to the Iranian Minister in Cairo to discreetly sound out the Egyptian government as regards the plan made by the Court in Tehran, and to also send a set of as many photographs and documents on the princess as possible.

The Iranian diplomat made a few awkward moves which provoked a rather unfavourable reaction in Cairo. It did not seem proper for Cairo that the 'son of an upstart' should be worthy of an Egyptian royal princess who was the descendant of the great Mehemet Ali (1769-1849) whose adventurous life and political record however bear a strong resemblance with Reza Shah's adventures and ascension to power.

When Cairo hesitated, the Iranian Minister lost his job. A new diplomat was appointed and joined the Egyptian capital. The plan had gone around all the salons of Tehran and now the rumour was that the Egyptian option had been dropped, and thus that the future wife of the heir to the throne would be Iranian. On April 6th 1938, the order was given to the new Minister of Persia to take up the case once again. A month later, the royal family and the Egyptian Cabinet gave their assent. Cairo asked for a mission of high importance presided by the Prime Minister himself to go to Cairo to ask for the princess's hand. Tehran accepted.

At the end of 1938, Prime Minister Mahmoud Djam arrived in Cairo. He was accompanied by Dr Moadab Nafissi, the former tutor of the prince who had become his Cabinet chairman and Grand Chamberlain, his own Cabinet chairman as well as two professors, Rachid Yassami and Ghassem Ghani, who were both representatives but also men of letters and polyglots. The mission crossed Iraq, Syria and Lebanon by car and sailed from Beirut to Alexandria on the Italian liner, the Marco Polo*.

As both Parliaments had been previously consulted and had given their approval, the principle of the marriage had now become official and it was made public. In the meantime, the

---

* If we give these details from Ghassem Ghani's notes, it is because of the often fanciful versions that were published concerning that trip.

Shah had notified his decision and choice to Mohammad Reza, who complied with it. He obviously could not have ignored it, like everybody else. The legations of both countries were promoted to the rank of embassies to mark the event, despite the pressure exerted by London on the Egyptians. Great Britain had been the only country represented by an ambassador in Cairo up to then, and wanted to keep that privilege. Tehran's insistence was to prevail over London's opposition.

The engagement took place, but there was still an obstacle to overcome: the princess could only have Iranian nationality after her marriage and after a long 'trial-period', if one was to follow common law. For the future prince to be of 'Iranian origin', as was required in the Constitution, and so that no-one could contest it, a special law, which might make one smile, granted the 'quality of being Iranian' to Princess Fawzieh.

Now Mohammad Reza could go to Cairo with a big delegation. A first wedding ceremony was celebrated there on March 13th 1939. It was only 'half a marriage'. There were a few celebrations to mark the occasion. The Egyptians treated the prince and his followers in a somewhat disdainful manner, especially young King Faruk and his mother, Queen Nazli. The future king of Iran never forgot it.

The Egyptian Queen Mother, the newly-weds and their suites then boarded the royal Egyptian yatch, the Mehemet Ali, in Alexandria, crossed the Suez Canal, the Red Sea and the Persian Gulf before arriving a few days later on Iranian soil at the little harbour of Shahpur, which had nothing to do with sumptuous Alexandria. The prince was already made to feel the difference, and he was hurt forever.

A second wedding ceremony was celebrated in Tehran with other festivities which seemed to be 'very dull' [13]. The

Egyptian Queen Mother continued to look down on the Iranian royal family and the Court in Tehran which was indeed very provincial and modest.

Nazli had openly been leading a rather unconventional lifestyle since her husband Fuad's death, and although she did not usually practise Islam, she suddenly decided to do her ritual prayers and required the necessary arrangements from the steward of the palace where she resided. It had not been planned, but she was given satisfaction less than an hour later. She made a scandal, and called the Iranians less than pleasant names [14]. The marriage took place however, and the popular festivities did not lack in style. Reza Shah had succeeded in achieving a great alliance for his heir, which actually enhanced the prestige of his family. The cumbersome Queen Mother went to France to have a good time, and the newly-weds had a honeymoon on the Caspian Sea.

The couple apparently got on well. The Shah saw to it personally: he had lunch regularly with his son and daughter-in-law, received them two hours a day, kept them informed on the Iranian social life and politics [15]. The young spouses spoke French together, but Fawzieh started learning Persian and quickly made good progress.

A 'happy event' was announced. On October 26th 1940, a daughter called Shahnaz was born, she was to be the couple's only child*. A boy had been wished for, but the Court still rejoiced over it, and especially the Shah who offered his grand-daughter a stylish little villa. He went to see her regularly and kept a close eye on her health and upbringing.

---

* Princess Shahnaz was first married to Ardeshir Zahedi, the son of the general who succeeded Mossadegh; then she got married again, to Khosrow Djahanbani, who also came from an excellent family. Today, she shares her time with her husband between Switzerland and the United States. She had a daughter by her first marriage, called Mahnaz, who was born in 1958.

The events of August-September 1941, Reza Shah's forced departure and Mohammad Reza's ascension to the throne shattered the family's apparent quietude, even on a private level. The new Shah was free now, at least in his own private life. The Pahlavi clan started making Queen Fawzieh pay for the humiliations of her family, and there was a lot of base plotting at the Court. The Queen already had a good knowledge of Persian and fulfilled her tasks in a suitable manner, but the relations between her and her husband – they had never really loved each other – deteriorated. There were rumours all over the capital of their respective infidelities which were a source of amusement in the salons and kept people busy. However, they really saddened the Prime Ministers who had to govern a country where the aftermath of the war and the unwanted presence of foreign troops were heavy to deal with; they could not be bothered by that kind of worry.

Fawzieh definitively left Iran after a first and long return to Egypt in the mid forties, and asked for a divorce. She had the support, and especially the backing of her brother, King Faruk. Professor Ghanem Ghani was a member of the delegation that had gone to the Court and to the government of Egypt to ask for the princess's hand. He was appointed ambassador to Cairo and put in charge of the negotiations for the conditions of a decent divorce. They were long and hard, sometimes sordid, but a deal was reached after a year [16]. The divorce was made public on November 18th 1948. Princess Shahnaz was put in the Shah's care, and she was to pay regular visits to her mother. The two separated spouses did not see each other ever again. They had no feelings for each other. The ex-empress got married again a year later to an Egyptian colonel who was close to Nasser, which allowed her to avoid an obligatory exile for her family. She has been a widow for a few years and now shares her time between Switzerland and her native country.

From a political and a psychological point of view, this unfortunate episode was to mark Mohammad Reza Pahlavi's life in several ways: the relations with Egypt were to constantly remain cold afterwards, in Faruk's time and after his downfall, but for many other reasons as well. It was under Sadat's presidency that the country became Iran's privileged ally, and at the end, Mohammad Reza Pahlavi's true refuge.

Mohammad Reza Shah never forgot the disdain with which the Egyptian Court had treated him. He sometimes talked about it to some of his confidants*. It was to be one of the humiliations he and his country suffered from, and which he spoke of so often and wanted to avenge.

The desire of the Court in Tehran was now to be equal to the other royal houses, especially with the much disputed apotheosis of the Persepolis celebrations in 1971.

Mohammad Reza Pahlavi was now single again and eventually tried to find a spouse among his compatriots, and if possible, marry out of love.

*   *

*

---

* After Nasser's death (1970), and before the official restoration of the suspended diplomatic relations between the two countries, the author of this book, who was a rector in Tehran at the time, went on a long trip to Egypt as head of an academic mission. When he was back in Iran, the Shah asked him long questions on the situation in Egypt. The country was devastated and going through a crisis then, while Iran had become powerful and prosperous, and knew a real resplendence. 'You cannot imagine our suffering when we were in Egypt and saw them flaunt the luxury and refinement of their Court and Palaces at us. But this is all in the past now, and things are so different, fortunately.' he said.

Mohammad Reza Pahlavi openly led the life of an international 'playboy' during the three years that followed the divorce of the Shah of Iran and of the Egyptian princess. He loved his wife and women in general. He took advantage of his new freedom. His country was finally rid of the presence of foreign troops; the integrity of national territory was ensured and the State resources were on the increase. The Shah did not rule yet, the Prime Ministers were in charge in a rather chaotic parliamentary system.

Mohammad Reza Pahlavi travelled abroad a lot. He had fun. At home, his adventures either amused or irritated public opinion. Everything remained secret at the Court, and this was to be the rule until the end of the monarchy in 1979. There was no mystery however, and everybody knew everything, which was also the case until the end. During that period of time, the international press reported the adventures of the young king who came from the East with supporting photographs. He was handsome, cheerful, affable and sporty. Cinema stars often played an important part in his life, but politics, public opinion's expectations and the remonstrances of his entourage incited him to settle down. The politicians of the time – almost all from the time his father reigned, sometimes from the Qajar era – still dared talk to the Shah, even in a harsh manner, and never hesitated to do so. They were hoping for a sovereign with a more suitable lifestyle.

It was in that context, and among a few other acquaintances, that his elder sister, Princess Shams, introduced him to a young woman from an excellent background: Soraya Esfandiary Bakhtiari. Her father, Khalil, was Iranian and belonged to one of the clans of the Bakhtiari tribe that the previous Shah had fought and pacified. Several members of his clan held important positions in politics, in the business world and in the armed forces, as in the past. Her mother was born in Moscow and was Baltic and German. Her name was Eva. Khalil was still a student when he married Eva in Berlin in June 1926.

Once his studies were over, Khalil went back home with his young wife and settled down in Esfahan, the former and still prestigious capital of the empire. This was where Soraya was born on June 22nd 1932 [17]. In 1947, the family went back to Europe and settled down in Zurich. Khalil, who was a polyglot, represented several Iranian businessmen in Europe and also dealt in the import of carpets. Soraya entered the institute called Les Roseaux in Lausanne, and was later sent to London to learn English. That was when she was introduced to the Shah.

The testimonies then, those from later on and until today, as well as all the biographers all concur. Mohammad Reza Pahlavi fell in love with Soraya at first sight. Their marriage was delayed because Soraya had contracted typhoid; it took place on February 12th 1951.

The couple were happy. Public rumour and its tendency to accentuate the slightest gossip that came from the Court showed no sign of infidelity from one or the other. The Shah and the Empress travelled a lot inside and outside the country and often made the 'front page' of the international press, especially of magazines. The political turmoil inside Iran did not trouble their family life very much. Soraya supported her husband in the difficult times he was going through, in his confrontation with Mossadegh, the 'old lion', as she used to call him. She apparently did not like him, but respected him, admired him sometimes, and the great eloquent speaker treated her as carefully as he could, with consideration and courteousness, in the oriental fashion.

However, the couple's life was progressively affected by a drama: Soraya could not have any children. The best Iranian, German, Swiss, French, American and Russian specialists were consulted, but to no avail. Ali Reza's plane crash in November 1954 gave a political dimension to the drama. The Sovereign's other brothers of the Qajar mother could not ascend to the throne according to the Constitution, so Ali Patrick, Ali Reza's son was considered for a while. His mother was French, which also caused a problem according to fundamental law – one can remember how Princess Fawzieh's case had been solved; the idea was therefore dropped. The Shah had consequently no successor and it was believed in his family (with the exception of Princess Shams who had remained friends with Soraya and who was opposed to a separation) and in his political entourage that the dynasty should continue. Mohammad Reza loved Soraya too much to choose a second wife as certain advisors had suggested, and as the Civil Code still allowed. A theatrical and tragic break seemed preferable to him. He informed Soraya of his decision during the last weeks of 1957.

In January 1958, the Empress left for Europe. The divorce was made public on March 14th. Soraya was given the title of Imperial Princess.

Soraya was indeed Mohammad Reza Pahlavi's only great love, the only woman he was ever fully in love with, some people still say today. Could another solution have been found to this family, political and dynastic drama instead of a brutal divorce?

The Shah kept deep feelings of attachment for Soraya despite the violence of the break-up. Was it out of regret, affection or love? The couple allegedly spent a long time together in Paris in a prestigious hotel on Avenue Montaigne, at the end of the sixties.

The letters Mohammad Reza Pahlavi exchanged with her through a few safe emissaries during the last months of his tragic life while he was in Mexico, Panama or Cairo were of great help to him. They gave an emotional support to a man who was overcome by his illness and by the revolution *.

*   *

*

Mohammad Reza Pahlavi had married once for reasons of State, and another time out of love, but he had had to get a divorce because he needed an heir. Now, he saw himself forced to quickly choose a wife when he was over forty, had become powerful, and was the authoritarian sovereign of a country in deep progress.

He had a serious affair with Princess Maria Gabrielle, aged 18, the daughter of the last and short-lived King of Italy, Umberto, on February 22nd 1958, according to the international press and rumours in the Iranian capital.

Mohammad Reza and Maria Gabrielle met on several occasions. The Princess was offered sumptuous presents. The Shah gave the impression he was carried away. The Princess had to convert to Islam so that the wedding could take place. Pope John XXIII apparently opposed it. The main Shiite dignitaries in Tehran, as well as some other 'wisemen' who were consulted advised against the marriage too. General Zahedi who had defeated Mossadegh, become Prime Minister and then ambassador to the United Nations now lived in Switzerland. He also disapproved, even if he often accommodated Mohammad Reza and Maria Gabrielle in his residence. They all suggested

---

* After a few episodes which caused a lot of ink to flow in some of the press, Soraya, who had settled down in Paris, died there.

an Iranian spouse to the Shah. Their age difference also seemed to be an obstacle. The plan was finally abandoned. The relations between the Court in Tehran and the House of Savoy were not affected by it*.

It had become necessary for the Shah to redress the situation, to quell contradictory and sometimes evil rumours, and to get married again. The failed project of a coup d'État organized by the Savak with the backing of the Americans also called for a strengthening of the dynasty.

*   *

*

It was a visit to Paris which triggered the process that allowed Mohammad Reza Pahlavi to find his third spouse, according to the official version. He received many Iranian students at the Iranian embassy of Paris on rue Fortuny, in the XVIIth district, on May 29th 1959. It was one of the Shah's habits and traditions. A young woman who was taller than the others came towards the Sovereign from across the room to hand him a letter asking him for a grant. They had an ordinary conversation. The Shah took the letter, gave it to a civil servant and told the young woman that the case would be followed up. A few months later, Ardeshir Zahedi, the Shah's son-in-law, who was responsible in Tehran for matters concerning Iranian students abroad and who had received the letter, saw the young woman to settle the problem. He found her remarks amusing, if not impertinent. He soon after reported the story to the Shah

---

* Princess Maria Gabrielle de Savoie was to marry the French real estate developer Robert de Balkany soon after that. The Pope gave the necessary dispensation although the latter was a divorcee and the father of two children, and the marriage was celebrated in church. The princess's brother, Victor Emmanuel, was a regular visitor at the Court of Tehran until the revolution.

who remembered the request and the young lady in question. Did he express the desire to meet her, as is suggested in some authorised biographies of the future empress, or was it Ardeshir Zahedi's initiative? It does not really matter. The latter had received a phone call in which the young lady's uncle on her father's side had recommended her. He was an important civil servant at the WTO. She was sent an invitation to tea in the Zahedis' residence, where they were to meet 'by chance' when the Shah was paying a visit to his daughter.

On December 21st 1959, Mohammad Reza Pahlavi married the young woman called Farah Diba. She was twenty-one years old, the age of his own daughter, Princess Shahnaz [18].

Farah's father, Sohrab, a former student at Saint-Cyr, came from a very good family from Azerbaijan. He had become a captain in the imperial army, then had to leave it and worked at the Yugoslavia embassy in Tehran. Farah was not even ten when he died of a long illness. Her mother, Taji, also called Farideh, née Ghotbi, came from a good old middle-class family from the region of Lahijan on the Caspian Sea. When Sohrab Diba died, the mother and daughter went to live in Mohammad Ali Ghotbi's house, for social and financial reasons. He was an engineer and a public contractor. This uncle, Madam Diba's younger brother, was in fact the real foster father and teacher of the future Shahbanoo. Reza, the Ghotbis' son, grew up with her and she considered him 'almost like a brother'. He was the future director of the Iranian National Television and Radio, and played an important and much disputed role during the months that preceded the revolution of 1978-1979.

Farah Diba did her primary studies at the Jeanne-d'Arc French school which was run by missionaries, then at the French lycée of Tehran before she went to Paris. She registered at the École spéciale d'architecture on boulevard Raspail, and lived in the Dutch house of the Hall of Residence ('Cité universitaire'). She was known for being anti-establishment, but not for being subservient to a political party.

It was undoubtedly to free herself from her uncle's financial guardianship and so as not to be dependent on him – reasons which can easily be understood – that she asked for a grant after completing her first year of higher education. What came next is known. Her stay in Paris hardly lasted two years.

On October 31st 1960, the young empress who now had the title of 'Shahbanoo' gave birth to crown prince Reza. Three other children followed, two girls and a boy.

'This lively, spontaneous, intelligent young woman born into an ordinary family', as the Shah later on said when he compared her with Soraya 'the most reserved, fragile and romantic of queens... a sweet and loving wife' [19], was to be an active, dynamic and highly mediatized empress in Iran and abroad for twenty years. She was the honorary president of two universities and devoted her life more particularly to charity and solidarity work, to the protection of childhood and youth, and even more so to the safeguard and promotion of national culture. When faced with the combined attacks of Prime Minister Hoveyda and the Savak against universities, she defended them herself more than once, and even protected them while trying to retain their traditional exemption rights and autonomy with a certain success when they were to be limited or suppressed.

She often took trips to the provinces, especially during the last three years of the reign. She was far less stiff than her husband, and sometimes unexpectedly visited popular areas or centres of activity, even at night. Her excessive taste for luxury was often criticized by public opinion, but her availability and relative open-mindedness were appreciated.

Her private entourage – her friends, as she used to call them, and everybody in Tehran also said so – were not exempt from reproaches. Some duly lent themselves to criticism. Her husband did not care much for them – and this is a euphemism – but he only reacted privately, in a few unpleasant words or sentences. He used to let them do what they wanted, even sometimes take advantage. During the last months of the reign, their hatred and accumulated rancour came out and led to intrigues and connivances which much tarnished the image of the regime and the coherence and efficiency of his acts. The Shahbanoo was also to pay a high price for it, but less, of course, than the country and the Shah.

In 1966, a constituent assembly included, in fundamental law the principle of a regency council that would be presided by the 'Shahbanoo, the crown prince's mother', in case the king disappeared before the crown prince was twenty and had the legal age to rule, or in case of abdication or prolonged absence. This was done on the Shah's initiative and despite some reservations expressed by the religious hierarchy and by the very members of the political establishment [20]. It was not a system of regency with a devolution of all the sovereign's prerogatives to his wife since the queen could only 'take action' within the framework of the 'council', but it constituted a consecration of a woman's place in domestic politics and an indirect homage to Farah. Iran had had a few ruling empresses before the Islamization of the country in the 7th century. Afterwards, and on a few occasions, the queen mothers of under age crown princes who had ascended to the throne had been de facto regents, but the Shah's initiative and his constitutional successors were a real innovation.

From 1976 on, the Shah became aware of the illness that was gnawing away at him and knew death was near. He entrusted the Shahbanoo with an ever more important political role. She was virtually at the head of the State during the last months of the monarchy, and was at the origin of a few unfortunate decisions.

*   *

*

Mohammad Reza Pahlavi's attitude to women in general remained one of a great Oriental lord, at least in private; it was sometimes described as being: protective, attentive and of an exquisite courteousness.

He was personally responsible for the effective and official recognition of Iranian women, for the granting of family, political and social rights to them, which gave rise to the anger of a large part of the Shiite clergy. He saw to their promotion within Iranian society. Iran indeed had women who were ministers, senior civil servants, high-ranking officers, magistrates... way before many Western countries which were quick to teach lessons to the whole world. On the eve of the revolution, equality between men and women had become part of everyday life. It was exceptional progress in an Islamic country.

He did so out of duty for the State, because he cared about the future of the country and about its rank in the world, which were his constant obsessions. It is all to his honour.

His married life was not very happy, it seems. Can happiness in a couple have the same meaning when one is at the head of power and might, and obsessed with the greatness of a country? There is no easy answer, and the examples that could be quoted are contradictory.

His first marriage, which was for reasons of State, fell apart. 'This marriage was a mistake, my spouse never adapted to Iran.' [21]

The second one was undoubtedly out of love. Public rumour, which is so little indulgent, never accused him of being unfaithful to Soraya, whose love he would evoke until the last hours of his life [22]. This marriage for love had a cruel ending.

The first years of his marital life with Farah were apparently trouble-free, at least publicly. At the beginning of the seventies, 'Tehran was a city where rumours were stirring, and the imperial couple's tiff was the main subject of conversation. [23] The Shah was considered to have a rather serious affair with a blond-haired woman – he liked blondes – called Talâ or Gilda. Her family came from the upper middle-class of the same region as that of the Shahbanoo's mother. While some of that person's relatives openly disapproved of her, others, in particular her parents and especially her mother, apparently had a rather incriminating attitude. Some of the Shahbanoo's close friends showed a certain uneasiness at dinner parties in town. The 'affair' became a source of interest at embassy receptions. People gossiped and spread true and false information. The CIA even reported it to Washington [24].

Mohammad Reza Pahlavi was too important a character on the international scene at the time to have a domestic crisis. He was too attached to his image of a sovereign who had granted women their rights. He would not have ridiculed himself in front of Iranians and abroad by having an official mistress. It was not done, and was inconceivable for him. Their relationship stopped. The young woman and her family were firmly asked to be discreet. The rumour vanished.

In September 1972, and for the first time, Mohammad Reza Pahlavi accompanied the Shahbanoo to the Shiraz festival she patronized, though he did not really like it, disapproving of what he called its avant-garde and leftist atmosphere, and he usually never went to it. He made numerous gestures of affection and consideration for her in front of the cameras of the whole world. The press was ordered to publish many photos illustrating the image of love the imperial couple wanted to give.

The reasons of State had prevailed. Mohammad Reza Pahlavi totally depended on them. From then on, he only furtively met a few young foreign women, especially French ones, during his trips to the provinces or in extremely discreet circumstances in a house of the Pol-eh-Rumi area, North of Tehran. Gossip and rumours were thus avoided.

*   *

*

Mohammad Reza Pahlavi appeared to be a loving and caring father for his children, even despite his obligations, the trips he had to go on, and the ceremonies he had to attend.

The eldest of the children he had by Farah, crown prince Reza, is wrong when he reproaches him for not having given him enough attention or often requested his opinion [26]. He seems to be right, though, to note that he never did anything about his political education: 'We never got on to the big questions of the reign, or analysed events. He never told me what I should do if I were to reign one day,' [27] he said. As regards this aspect of the problem, the last Shah did the exact opposite of his father. Had he not suffered from the obligations imposed on him as far on as his early childhood, the highly supervised education of a prince, and his private lessons? It cannot be excluded. However, when he ascended to the throne at the age of twenty-two, he was already a cultured man, he knew the political staff and ignored nothing of the affairs of the State. It is true that had a few short training sessions in politics organized for his heir when he became aware how serious his illness was, during the last two or three years of his reign. It seems it was more out of a bad conscience, nothing more, and nothing more serious than that. Wasn't the political, cultural and historical training of the one who was to succeed him when time came as important as learning how to become a pilot, or the passion for horse riding and photography which he encouraged his son and heir to pursue? The latter's training and behaviour were affected by it later on.

*   *

*

The royal residences remained rather modest and sober, even at the peak of Iran's power and wealth; they were big, beautiful and spacious villas like the ones so often found in the West, nothing compared with the royal or national palaces elsewhere. Only the Golestan palace, its coronation hall which was inspired by the Galerie des Glaces in Versailles, it seems, its huge dining-room..., were impressive. The palace dated back to the Qajar era and, after beautiful restoration work, had been turned into a national museum and was only used for ceremonies now and then.

Two or three palaces in Niavaran, the winter residence of the imperial family, also dated back to the Qajar era, especially the one where the Shah's huge office was. The family's private residence was a nice, modern and functional construction which had been built in the 60's of the 20th century by architect Abdol Aziz Farmanfarmaian, who was himself a prince from the old dynasty. The residence was often said to be a 'Palace from the Arabian Nights' of an 'amazing luxury', during the last years of the reign. Many rich Western businessmen, Hollywood artists, not to mention princes from such and such a country, would have found it unworthy of them [28].

There was nothing extraordinary about the protection the sovereign benefited from, even compared with that of the leaders of Western democracies. His office in Niavaran virtually overlooked a very busy public garden. The pavements near his residence were not banned to the public, as was the case for those of the Élysée palace in François Mitterrand's time, or of so many other residential palaces of leaders today.

No visitor, whatever his function or rank, would be searched at the entrance. During public ceremonies – seasonal greetings at various times of the year, inaugurations, solemn sessions in universities, etc...– thousands of people who just held invitations cards could approach the Shah. He often drove in town alone, sitting behind the wheel and only followed by one security vehicle. As he could not really stand air-conditioning, he always left a window of his car half opened, which went against security measures. When he went to the provinces, he sometimes used a convertible car and hated to see his guards stand too much between him and his compatriots, to the risk of his life.

During the three or four last years of his reign, and especially during the months that preceded the revolution, some of the international press tried to present Mohammad Reza Pahlavi as an Oriental potentate who led both a prodigious and anxious life in 'huge fortified palaces that were protected day and night by Savak henchmen who were armed to the teeth, and by armoured-cars and tanks.'

Reality was totally different, and the Savak, in particular, had no responsibility in the sovereign's protection which was ensured by the imperial guard who did not care much for the secret services.

He would dress in an elegant fashion indeed, except for official ceremonies and in the presence of foreigners, but it was always simple. He would sometimes wear a suit that was several years old, or even a worn shirt.

The mistake of the Persepolis celebrations, the excessive purchases made by a few members of the imperial family from such and such a famous foreign designer – even if they were much less important than those of other people who were never criticized or rarely referred to – as well as certain extravagances from friends of the Court, unfortunately all contributed to the disinformation the Shah was the victim of.

From the mid 1970's, as soon as the destabilization operation of Iran had been launched, and especially during the 'operational phase', the fury assumed the proportion of a 'worldwide lie', to use Vladimir Volkoff's accepted way of calling it [29].

While he was in exile, the Shah wondered: 'why is there such hatred, such fury against me?'

*   *

*

The hatred and fury were not only in the media. One can remember the assassination attempt of February 4th 1959 that was organized by the Tudeh, the Iranian communist party.

On April 10th 1965, at 9.30 a.m., when, punctual as usual, the Shah got out of his car in front of the marble palace on avenue Kakh, in Tehran, to begin his usual day of work, a conscript who was doing his military service in the imperial guard and who was on guard duty, ran towards the Sovereign and opened fire at him with his submachine gun. A gardener tried to stop him. The terrorist shot at him and wounded him. A body guard aimed at the young soldier, shot at him but was killed by the latter. In the meantime, the Shah ran zigzagging along to his garden-level office, closed the door and hid behind his desk. He was not armed. The bullets were now going through the office door which the murderer had reached, although he was already slightly wounded, but still acting as a real, determined professional. He was shot by another guard on duty in front of that door, who was himself shot in turn*.

Count Alexandre de Marenches testifies that [31] 'a French admiral who was one of my friends was received by him [the Shah] so that he could show him a highly technical file. The same day, he had been the object of an assassination attempt from a soldier of the guard. The Emperor barely escaped death, but the audience was neither cancelled nor delayed**. The French general presented himself to the Palace while the broken pieces of glass and other things still littered the ground and were being swept away ***. The walls were spattered with traces of blood from the fight. The general was shown into the Shah's office who discussed the file in question, remaining imperturbable.

My friend, the mariner, told me that the Shah knew the file in all its intricate technical details. There was no allusion made during the audience to the recent events which could have plunged the Empire into mourning.'

The next day, on April 11th, the Shah had a drive in a

---

* The Shah himself narrated the event to a few people he was receiving (among whom the author of this book, who was Minister of Development and Housing at the time) on the very afternoon of the assassination attempt, and on the premises where it was committed.

** It was Admiral Cabanier, head of general staff of the French navy.

*** The audience was held at 11 a.m. In fact, the agenda for the morning was slightly delayed.

convertible sports car without an escort through a few streets of Tehran. He stopped at red lights, and started off again; the crowd cheered him and the motorists sounded their horns to greet him.

He accepted and was in charge of the guardianship of the children of his two assassinated body guards, Ali Babayan and Ayat Lashkari, and kept a close eye on their studies until the revolution.

This is how he was. Fate or God's will had saved him, but his self-control and sangfroid aroused admiration.

The investigation soon led to an ultra-left group, of a Trotskyist tendency, all members of which, intellectuals who had often been trained in Anglo-Saxon universities, had ties with East Germany and the communist intelligence services*.

A long trial followed the preliminary investigation. The court pronounced two death sentences, a life sentence, sentences of three to nine years of imprisonment, and two acquittals.

The sentences were upheld in appeal, and the appeal to the Cour de Cassation (Final Appeal Court) was rejected, but a strange thing happened at the Palace: the leader of the group, Parviz Nic-Khah, was taken there, handcuffed soon after midnight by lieutenant general Kamal, the head of the 2nd Bureau. They were shown into the Sovereign's office who gave the order to remove the handcuffs from the prisoner's hands, and begged the general to leave them. The interview

---

* The Sovereign's protection system was reconsidered after the attempt. The imperial couple's move to Niavaran where the office and residence of the Shah were within the same walls was definitively decided on and hurried. There was thus no street to cross several times a day. Conscripts were excluded from the close protection of the Sovereign...

lasted seventy-five minutes. Tea was served twice. When Nic-Khah left the imperial office, his eyes were red, like the ones of a man who had cried a lot.

A few days later, the Shah used his constitutional prerogative to commute Nic-Khah's sentence. All the other people convicted benefited from the measure and were pardoned and definitively released in January 1971. Nic-Khah became one the main managers of the national Radio and Television*.

On May 19th 1967, an ultra-left commando attacked the Shah's car in a Tehran suburb. He was not in it.

On June 3rd of the same year, during one of the Shah's state visits in West Germany, an Iranian student who belonged to the ultra-left tried to throw a remotely controlled device which was full of explosives at the Shah's car when it was crossing one of Berlin's thoroughfares. The attempt failed. Its instigator was arrested by the federal police and sentenced to eight months of imprisonment five months later [32].

*　　　*

*

The Shah's 'colossal fortune' was often referred to during the last months of his reign, and especially of his life, as an argument in the media lynching operation that he was the victim of. From 1970, Iran made important investments abroad. Their total sum was of over 20 billion dollars on the eve of

---

* The event being referred to in an audience in 1976, and without revealing the subject of his conversation with the leader of the group which had tried to kill him, Mohammad Reza Pahlavi suddenly said to us: 'De Gaulle should have pardoned Bastien-Thiry.'
As for Parviz Nic-Khah, he was arrested and executed after the revolution for having benefited from the Shah's mercy.

the revolution. The operation had several objectives: first, to ensure the country substantial revenues in foreign currency and protect it from the unavoidable exhaustion of oil resources and reserves; then, to allow it to acquire an advanced technology; and finally to give it an economic power in industrially developed countries, on the world scene and among big conglomerates.

Every single acquisition was presented as the work of the Shah. It is still the case over a quarter of a century later, especially in the French press.

The acquisitions of holdings, often accompanied by blocking minorities and seats on boards of administration or on boards of directors, in companies such as Eurodif, Mercedes (12.5%), Krupp (25%) or oil refineries in India and in South Africa – to only quote a few – were made by and for the Iranian State. The operation was coordinated by the presidence of the Cabinet council in Tehran, and followed by a small team in Luxemburg that was headed by former ministers.

There was an effort made to create an amalgam in public opinion and collective memory so as to disinform, even to make things appear diabolical. The legitimate expression of a national ambition was being turned into an operation of personal enrichment.

When big French or American companies make acquisitions in other countries, which happens so often in a world economy which is more and more globalized, it is, of course, never suggested that Jacques Chirac, François Mitterrand, George Bush or Bill Clinton are making them or made them.

All these investments, state properties or properties of national Iranian companies, today belong to, or should belong to the Islamic Republic of Iran, if they have not been liquidated; but this is never specified.

It is the same for the Pahlavi Foundation, whose management can obviously lend itself to criticism. It is a parapublic legal entity, the assets of which were transferred to the Islamic State, including one of the most famous New York skyscrapers. Comments are still being made on 'the Shah's' New York skyscraper, even a quarter of a century later.

As soon as there was the affair of the hostages of the United States embassy in Tehran in November 1980, an 'official' figure for the Shah's 'fortune' appeared: 22 billion dollars.

Where did it come from and how was it calculated?

Mr Behzad Nabavi gave an explanation. He was one of the main leaders of the revolution, a minister at the time he delivered the following speech, and the Iranian negotiator in the hostage affair where the official pretext was the recovery of the 'Shah's fortune'. Here is his explanation:

'One of us had told us he had read somewhere in a newspaper that the Shah owned a fortune worth 22 billion dollars. So we said it did not cost us anything to officially declare it and to ask for such a sum back. We had no document, no evidence. We have not been able to find anything on the Shah's fortune and real estate assets abroad,' [33] and the leader of the regime added: 'It was a revolutionary political movement without precedent. Its aim was to prevent any rapprochement with America... The Shah's extradition and the restitution of his fortune were only pretexts... One of our sacred objectives was to overthrow the provisional government [the Bazargan Cabinet].'

As for Mohammad Reza Pahlavi himself, he later declared to Barbara Walters who was interviewing him in New York, 'that he was not poor but probably not any richer than some Americans.' [35] He was probably not any richer than so many kings, queens, princes and princesses, without forgetting the politicians from Western countries who like to teach lessons.

*   *

*

Mohammad Reza Pahlavi ruled but did not govern his country from 1941 until the downfall of the Mossadegh government. Conforming to a liberal understanding of the Constitution, he asked for the previous agreement of the Chamber when he wanted to appoint a Prime Minister who had to deal with the different factions to form his cabinet. Governments were ephemeral. The intrigues and political schemes were often manipulated from abroad and were numerous and paralysing. The heads of the executive were all patriots. They were sometimes of a high calibre, like Mohammad Saed, and did what they could with little means and in difficult circumstances.

Three political figures, men of exception, real statesmen, marked the history of Iran in a permanent way during that period: Mohammad Ali Foroughi, who saved Iran and the monarchy in 1941*; Ahmad Ghavam, the liberator of Azerbaijan and the man who defeated Stalin**; and Mohammad Mossadegh, the popular and eloquent speaker who nationalized oil and chased the British out of the country***, which thus gave him an international dimension and a place in the emancipation process of the Third World.

The young Shah who was inexperienced and lost in front of the cataclysm the Second World War was for Iran, remained irreproachable with Foroughi, surpassed himself and worked hard without making a fuss. Foroughi protected him and guided him. He was grateful for it. He always expressed his gratefulness for him and proved it later on with his family.

---

* See chapter II: The Second World War – An old philosopher saves Iran.
** See chapter IV: The Azerbaijan crisis – The man who defeated Stalin.
*** See chapter V: The oil crisis – The man who chased the British away.

Anyway, the old philosopher was already seriously affected by the illness which was to kill him. He was devoid of ambition, had neither political party nor network of inlfluence, and was not seeking favours– he did not even use his official car and walked everywhere he could in a rather restless capital. The slightest conflict of interest, of ambition or vision between the young Shah and the wise old man were inconceivable and never occurred.

It was not the same with Ghavam, and then with Mossadegh.

Mohammad Reza Pahlavi did not care much for Ghavam, and this is a known fact. Ghavam treated him like a young king who had to be respected, but considered his role to be figurative. The head of the executive power was the one to rule. Ghavam was a man of power, ambition and vision; he had his political party, a well-established influence network, and his own options in foreign policy.

Despite these positions and oppositions, both men did their duties in an irreproachable manner in times of crisis. As long as the provinces of the North-West were not freed, as the Soviet troops stayed on Iranian soil, the Shah's support to his head of government remained complete, even though he was sometimes irritated. Once the danger was over though, the masks were dropped on both sides. The Shah did not show any gratitude to the old statesman, and when there was the oil crisis, and Parliament called in Ghavam to get the country out of its sticky situation, he did not back him, far from it, and Iran thus lost an opportunity to solve the conflict differently than by provoking the brutal downfall of the old eloquent speaker, even if it was politically and economically impossible to avoid, and it caused a real national fracture.

Later on, Mohammad Reza Pahlavi did his utmost to be recognized in history as the only one who freed Azerbaijan.

The History of the world is unfortunately full of such examples and attitudes. Historians have recognized the eminent role Ghavam played in the affair, without failing to also recognize the support the young Shah had given him.

The Shah's record with Mossadegh is rather similar: enthusiastic and unreserved support at first, conflict, opposition and hatred afterwards, until the final confrontation.

Mohammad Reza Pahlavi did his utmost for a quarter of a century to do better than the one he called 'the stubborn old man' who had only been partly successful. He was as aware of the unfair fate of Iran due to international economic interests, and had a fierce ambition to ensure the independence and the power of his country.

In fact, could he bear the fact he had to share a place he wanted all for himself in front of History?

* *

*

Mohammad Reza Pahlavi openly showed his political, economic, social and military ambitions for Iran, his will to have his revenge and to erase past humiliations during the last two decades of his reign, and more particularly after the White Revolution. He had become one of the key characters in international affairs, the symbol of a powerful and prosperous country.

He appeared to be a well-informed man, especially in international politics, macroeconomic and geostrategical problems. He was cultured and had a prodigious memory, but before all, he was disciplined and rigorous:

'He was a disciplined man, a tireless worker.

He would be up early in the morning, and after a few minutes of exercising, his morning wash and a frugal breakfast he had alone, he would then devote more than an hour and a half of his time to the reading of different reports and news, writing notes in pencil on them and sometimes underlining passages; then, he would discover the national and especially the international press.' [36]

Shortly before 10 a.m., he would go to his office. There was one audience after another until 1.30 p.m. He usually had two or three small cups of tea with sugar during the morning. Then, he would go back to his residence to have lunch with the Shahbanoo, in theory. If the latter was late – she was not as punctual as he was – he would not wait for her. His lunch would be light for the Shah ate soberly and hardly drank. After a short pause, he would resume work until at least 7. His work day thus lasted ten hours minimum, and could continue with the reading of files, reports, or a few exceptional audiences. This was the case six days out of seven. He would spend long minutes with his children in the evenings. Every week, there were one or two family dinners and then film sessions would follow.

The people who attended these fashionable gatherings had the impression that the Shah felt subjected to them more than he liked them. He suffered from their monotony, from the trivialities of the conversations. He, alas, liked flattery, but he fortunately did not care much for flatterers.

The man followed a rigorous discipline and was as regular as clockwork, which sometimes annoyed his entourage, and he was said to be fussy. He was always extremely punctual during official ceremonies at the palace or outside. It often caused the security services problems. Some criminal intents, especially the two attempts which could have cost him his life, could have been avoided if he had been less punctual.

Contrary to his last wife, he did not like 'festivities' and always went to bed before midnight. He sometimes gave the impression he was having fun, would tell a funny story from time to time, and the Savak was one of his favourite targets at the time. It was often thought that he was a rather sad man, who was only fired with enthusiasm when there were major projects, who only dreamt about Iran which was his passion before it became his disappointment. There was almost no place for imagination in his behaviour. This perception of his personality does not seem to be too far from reality.

Mohammad Reza Pahlavi was, in fact, the first technocrat of the Empire. He had three particular fields:
1) diplomacy: only one of his Ministers of Foreign Affairs in the last two decades, Ardeshir Zahedi, was personally able to leave a mark on Iranian diplomacy* and give it some direction of his own choosing; the others were more like secretaries of state in international relations, and were often very competent;
2) the oil and energy policy;
3) national defence.

Contrary to what was sometimes said, he would leave his Prime Minister and other ministers full scope in the running of affairs, and rarely intervened in important nominations, while nevertheless refusing to 'be informed by the radio.'

*   *

*

---

* A rapprochement with moderate Arab countries, especially Egypt, with which he initiated the restoration of the diplomatic relations that had been interrupted since Nasser's time, and a privileged partnership, a modernization and rejuvenation of the ministry; these were initiatives destined to black Africa.

He practised numerous sports: tennis, swimming, riding, water skiing or Alpine skiing. He liked to pilot planes and fast cars, and had a passion for prestigious racing cars for many years.

It was often advanced that his predominant character trait was his pride. It was less of a feeling of vanity than of a kind of pride relative to the appearances and necessities of the imperial power. This pride often allowed him to conceal another very real aspect of his temper, shyness. In private, especially in a very small committee, during his trips to the provinces or abroad more particularly, when the people around him were usually worthy of trust, he could be charming, engaging, and talk about personal memories. He sometimes really enjoyed flaunting his knowledge, 'causing a sensation'.

He was not cruel, and hated to see cruelty, even to hear about other people's physical suffering, and he knew how to hide his perfectly well. During his life as a monarch, he widely used his constitutional right to pardon, even pardoning those who had made an attempt on his life, as we saw previously. 'My father would chastise, my brother pardoned. I do not bear any judgment, it is just an observation.' His brother wrote later on, and not without good reason [38].

*   *

*

Mohammad Reza Pahlavi was a man who was informed on the international situation. He strove to be up to it in a role which he not only believed in, but which he had an inflamed idea of.

He regularly read the international press, diplomatic reports and news which he often found superficial, summaries of analyses carried out by the Iranian intelligence services – which were more efficient than what was written in matters of domestic intelligence than of foreign ones – information given to him by certain allied countries services or by his own sources and correspondents. It made him, thanks also to his prodigious memory, a man who was thoroughly aware of what was going on in the world. He knew details that were sometimes amazing about the men in power or who were powerful in the leading countries of the world, on their private lives, their strengths and weaknesses, and he used them in the interest of his national diplomacy. It was the same with some of the greatest names of the international press.

Dean Rusk, the American Secretary of State, 'often said that [Mohammad Reza Pahlavi] was the best informed man in the world, after the American president.' [39]

Alexandre de Marenches [40] wrote later on: 'He was one of these men with whom you could talk geopolitics, international strategies, without him having only party politics in mind, like so many other leaders.'

He lacked clear-sightedness as regards Western policies – especially American policies – concerning him in the last three or four years of his reign however, and did not see the danger that was coming from them for the stability of his country.

Was it excessive rationality of his reasoning, when he deemed it unthinkable that the West, with such adventurous policies, could destroy the oasis of peace and stability Iran was at the time, ending its prosperity and power, which were the peace and balance factors in the region? Many testimonies are to that effect*.

Was it an indirect effect of his illness which was driving him away from immediate contingencies and from reality? Serious scientific studies do not exclude this possibility**.

There had been enough alarming information, troubling facts, and warnings***.

Concerning the domestic situation, the Shah was indeed only kept half aware of what was going on. He mastered macroeconomic data, sector-based figures, rates and growth perspectives, the cultivated areas of the main agricultural products, the variations in rainfalls, and could quote production figures. It could all impress his Iranian and foreign visitors.

He had his eyes riveted on far away horizons, and was sometimes more preoccupied with the international situation than with domestic problems. He worried more about the sharing of world riches from time to time, and about the fate of developing countries than about his own compatriots' difficulties. 'That is what the government is for' he used to say. He let discontent increase, and foreign countries took advantage of this discontent, manipulated, organized and even financed it during the last years.

The one who was his head of government for thirteen years, Amir Abbas Hoveyda, a true intellectual, a man who was clear-sighted, personally honest, had progressively turned into a Great Master of the Conspiracy of Silence out of a power game. He had made Mohammad Reza Pahlavi believe that everything was fine, that the criticisms, remarks, hitches could only come from malicious people.

---

* See chapter XII: Iran and the West – Ambiguous relations.
** See Epilog.
*** See chapter XIV: The imperial power hesitates – 'It's another Louis XVI'.

The intelligence services, in fact the Savak, could not have had no information on certain domestic problems, but the information was filtered, probably because of general Nassiri, a man of limited ability, but not a traitor to the Shah. He only saw plotting and malice where there was a real problem to be analyzed and solved, and privileged repression to prevention.

The conjunction – objective as well as subjective – between both these elements is highly responsible for the events which led the regime to its end.

The structured, even sophisticated analyses and the reports on the domestic situation were numerous: there was the one from the general staff in the mid seventies, and those from the Study Group of Iranian problems, from 1974 until the last weeks of the regime, also one from the 2nd Bureau in the spring of 1978. The Shah learnt about the facts and was sometimes annoyed – his dreams were interrupted, his Prime Minister and his secret services said the opposite – but he did not sanction their authors. He was less intolerant than some would say, listened to criticisms, but he unfortunately did not heed them, or heeded them too late.

There were two men in his immediate entourage, friends who had totally different characters, who could tell him certain things with frankness, even brutality, in a tone that had little to do with the sophisticated one of official reports, and they did not spare him, they were: Amir Assadollah Alam, probably his only friend, and Ardeshir Zahedi, his ex-son-in-law, and Minister of Foreign Affairs for five years, whose resignation Hoveyda had provoked, and who had been appointed to Washington. The first, who was ill and kept away, died a year before the revolution; the second was naturally more often in Washington than in Tehran. The Savak and the Prime Minister did everything they could to thwart him.

These power games were also very detrimental.

*   *

*

Mohammad Reza Pahlavi was a highly cultured man thanks to the very solid education he had received in his childhood and at the Rosey, to his natural curiosity for history, geography, military arts and later on, for development problems – even if the practical value of theories left him sceptical. He had a prodigious memory which only started faltering during the last few years, and he had a great capacity for listening to people.

Professor Ghassem Ghani, a man of letters and a character in politics and in diplomacy in the years before and after the Second World War, narrates an interesting episode in his *Notes and Documents*. The Shah had been told that a certain number of men of letters, important writers and poets*, long-time friends, used to meet every Tuesday, from 3 p.m. until dinner time to have tea at one or the other's house, and talk freely about literary matters or the current development of research work. He asked Hossein Ala, who was a member of his entourage then, the future Minister to the Court and Prime Minister, to do what was necessary so that he could take part in these meetings.

The first time he went, he was with general Morteza Yazdan-Panah, a prestigious officer who was cultured enough, and said 'very humbly' that his wish was to 'listen and learn,'

---

* There were, among others, Nasrollah Taghavi, the former president of the Iranian Academy; the erudite Mohammad Ghazvini, Haj Mohtashem-Ol-Saltaneh Esfandiari, a famous politician who wrote his odd poem now and again; Ali Akbar Dehkhoda, the initiator of the Iranian encyclopedia which was to bear his name; Hossein Samii, a famous poet and marshal of the Court; professor Chafagh, a specialist in Persian history and literature, and Ghassem Ghani himself.

that he would be 'honoured' if the guests accepted to come to his home when it was his turn. Thus, for three years, from 1945 to 1948, when he was free, which was rather often, it seems, he attended these literary teas from 3 p.m. until sometimes 9 p.m. Ghassem Ghani wrote in his diaries that he had once taken advantage of the development of the conversation to ask if he could have a full presentation on Avicenna's life, work, and contribution to the arts. Another time, he seized the opportunity to have one of Hafiz's poems recited to him, and to have its subtleties explained to him, and yet another time, to have information on the life and career of a reforming chancellor of the 19th century...[41]

When the author of this book was rector of the University of Tehran, the Shah learnt that he was giving a series of lectures at the Law and Political Science Faculty on Marxism and on the economies of countries which labelled themselves Marxist. When alluding to it, he asked me precise questions on the specificities of Maoism – he had read *The Little Red Book* – on the steps of the agrarian reform in popular China, the evolution of the industrialization policy of that country... The audience which normally lasted thirty minutes lasted three times as long, and perturbed the agenda for the day. Mohammad Reza Pahlavi had listened very carefully and made pertinent remarks.

A few days later, some of the personalities received in an audience were entitled to long dissertations made by the Sovereign on the Chinese economy, and especially on 'Maoism' to their great surprise, and talked about it all over town. The source of the information was, of course, never cited.

These are examples among so many others.

His vast culture, and mastery of foreign languages, especially French, often struck his interlocutors.

'He was a man who spoke French like one would wish

everyone to speak it in France, he was impregnated with the French culture. He was not very tall, slim, moved quickly, and was gifted with a rare intelligence and a surprising memory.' Alexandre de Marenches wrote, before adding: 'If it was not for his physical appearance which was well known, one would have been incapable, even with an acute sense of hearing, to know that he was not a Frenchman who was aware of everything, who was cultured. He was fully bi-cultural.' [42]

General De Gaulle did not pay compliments very easily. He admired in this head of a 'State which is as old as the history of the world, his deep knowledge of all the realities of his country.' [43]

John F. Kennedy was not one of his friends – this is a euphemism since he even tried to overthrow him – but he still found himself obliged to admit that 'he was certainly the most intelligent, lucid and remarkable statesman of the Middle-East.' [44]

*   *

*

Such was the man, with his strengths and weaknesses.

What really strikes a historian, and what History will probably remember from the man and the king, was his ambition for Iran.

'I never have any doubts that Iran will reach the highest peaks.' [45]

'The dreams he had for himself and for his country had no limits,' wrote Mohamed H. Heykal, who was an Egyptian politician and journalist, but not one of his friends [46].

'To become a leader in tomorrow's world – that was his dream for Iran – you first need a certain population where you can find men of genius, men who have brains; you need advanced technology, and there can't be any illiterate people; there must be social justice, some involvement; there must be a movement to spur the country into action... Iran is Iran... I know that we have all of this, we show it everyday.' [47]

'We will not tolerate any hurdle on our path towards progress and prosperity.' [48]

The more time passed, and he felt he might not have enough of it towards the end, the harder he strove to reach his distant aims, to make Iran become a power that could not be overlooked, give it armed forces that could face any non-nuclear intervention from a foreign country [49], manage to have the same standard of living as Europeans (the Western ones) by 1990 [50], and become a reference for developing countries. Wasn't his country succeeding in 'the only effective economic take-off of the Third World'? [51] Wasn't it described as the country of 'blue mosques and of growth without inflation'? [52].

The wish to lay stress on 'appearances', to avenge himself of the humiliations caused during the past two centuries, were obvious in his approach. It had almost become the only drive in his existence. The major projects, the prestigious projects which flattered the pride and vanity of the nation and showed foreign countries the success of open ambitions often drew his attention. He was haunted by what was grandiose. He sometimes mistook it for greatness. Such a nature could be considered as admirable, but it could also lead to errors which aroused the most cutting criticisms in those who found it hard to bear Iran's success. It was indeed the case for the Persepolis festivities which were probably an error, if not a mistake, more so in the way they were held than in the celebrations themselves.

There was soon talk of megalomania, but isn't a megalomaniac first a man who 'says out loud what everybody is quietly thinking about themselves?', as was thought at the time? He was accused of having 'delusions of grandeur'. The more attacks there were, the more violent Mohammad Reza Pahlavi's declarations against criticisms which all came from the West were, maybe out of spite or out of a feeling of total injustice for his country or himself. He was then called 'arrogant'.

'The Shah kept repeating that he would make Iran become one of the five industrial powers in the world before the end of the century, a model for not only the Third World, but also for the West. He never stopped denouncing the latter's decadence, laziness and waste, and more particularly Great Britain's... Iran's ambitions would come true because Iranians could make extraordinary efforts. That was where the difference could be seen between us [he would say] and blasé societies.' [53]

It was the harsh talk of a man whose passionate demands, high and noble ambitions for his country (he believed that the universal nature of his ambitions would automatically legitimize them abroad) conflicted with his thirst for revenge on past humiliations and on the indignation aroused in him by the childish yet vindictive jealousy of certain Western elites. They had plans for him and for Iran which were recognized by all to be less noble!

The Shah was aware of it: 'Certain things have to be said for them [Westerners] to wake up. I know that when somebody in this part of the world says the same things I say, it irritates them, but it is not going to change the state of things. That is the truth.' [54]

Mohammad Reza Pahlavi ended up being progressively

less attentive to problems of supply, to 'details', to accumulating problems which were and could be easy to solve by the government, and there he was right. But he had his eyes riveted on distant horizons, he was obsessed by the desire to make Iran become a second Japan, to outdo Europeans and to go to the end of his dreams. He thought that the 'great civilization' was at the corner of the road, and saw the people in position of power act like sycophants who could not wait to meet him. However, the authoritarian and centralized system of the last two decades had not made it possible to put a Foroughi into orbit, or a Ghavam. Those who had the calibre could not act.

This was how domestic discontent became more intense. The countries with an interest which could not tolerate a powerful, independent Iran that was a model and a reference in the region, those who were offended by the Shah's haughty words, those who worried over the country's ambitions did what had to be done to make it collapse. Iran had to be destroyed, like Carthage!

Iran, or a certain idea of Iran had meant much more than women, money or even power. It had been the only passion in his life.

The day he felt betrayed, he was a broken man and could not react. He felt dejected before the end of his life [55].

*   *

*

'Mohammad Reza Pahlavi did indeed embody the two-and-a-half- thousand-year tradition of the Iranian monarchy with dignity. He had ambition for his country, and put it on the path to economic transformation and social progress. He led Iran to a leading position among Middle-Eastern states. He would not let Iran become a satellite of the United States...

When we think of the tragic destiny of the Shah of Iran, we French people, cannot help thinking of our Louis XVI, who was also a victim of the Revolution, and who perished under the guillotine just a few yards from here. There are so many connections to be made.

Like the Shah of Iran, Louis XVI had to deal with disinformation, vulgar slander, and various techniques used to manipulate the crowds...

Like the Shah, Louis XVI wanted to make his people happy. Unfortunately, good intentions are not enough in politics. Power must be kept when one has it, and the necessary means must be used to quell subversion...

During the last months of his life, the Shah discovered deposition, humiliations and betrayals. It was the same for Louis XVI who was imprisoned in the tower of the Temple. The Shah, of course, was not to have a bloody death like Louis XVI and Nicholas II, but his ordeal was as bad as the other two sovereigns'. [56]

Chapitre X

A POLICY OF POWER AND NATIONAL INDEPENDENCE
Absolutely intolerable ambitions

The two great Arab and Mongol invasions caused us so much harm that for a very long time Iranians believed that they had to suffer and follow – as is written in La Fontaine's fable – 'the policy of the reed.' We will need time to become an oak again.

Of course, there are people who have followed 'the policy of the oak' and who have completely lost their roots. The ideal solution is a combination of both; one has to be flexible when necessary, but not always, be an oak and a reed at the same time. I hope this will be one of the characteristics of tomorrow's Iranian [1].

This is what Mohammad Reza Pahlavi said two years before the revolution. It was a premonitory declaration. Can the main cause of the international conspiracy which was exploiting the actual domestic discontent and led to the revolution of 1978-1979 not be found in that 'policy of power' [2] followed by Iran?

In 1977, while the destabilization scheme was already well on its way within certain pressure groups and think tanks, even in the Western leading circles, more particularly in the United States, and while the imperial power's hesitation was to lay itself open to all the plotting that was soon to develop, this country still gave an impression of remarkable solidity.

Civil and social peace prevailed, even if some of the domestic problems were already taking worrying proportions. Iranian leaders, especially the most eminent of them, the Shah, were respected and sometimes even wooed without shame abroad.

Mohammad Reza Pahlavi was considered to be one of the most powerful men in the world. The Iranian army was probably one of the best trained and most efficient of what was called the 'free world'. Its diplomacy was active. Iranian tourists would travel to all the countries of the world by the hundreds of thousands every year. They did not need visas, except for communist countries. Their passports were enough, provided they were valid. Many hotels, shops and travel agencies used to hire staff that could welcome this huge clientele with a big purchasing power in its own language. It was a sign of obvious prosperity.

Iran was resplendent and many were those who truly believed in the perenniality of a situation which some dared compare with the great moments of its history, particularly during the apogee of the Safavids.

Many Iranians and the true foreign friends of the country cherished the hope that Iran would definitely have a place which was its own, from a historical point of view, and legitimately so, up there with the leaders, in the first rank of the concert of nations.

A POLICY OF POWER AND NATIONAL INDEPENDENCE
Absolutely intolerable ambitions

*   *

*

In the year 1977, the Iranian population was of 35.6 million people. The population growth rate had been lowered from 3.4% to 2.6% per year with the success of the family planning programme that was due to a progress in education, in the development of heath services and of means of communication. No coercive measure had been taken.

During the last fifteen years before the revolution, the gross domestic product was multiplied by 13.25 and exceeded the global volume of 70 billion dollars, without including oil revenues. In 1977, the per capita income reached 2,450 dollars, against 160 twenty-five years before. Some of the best institutes for economic forecasts, particularly in the United States, were foreseeing that Iran's economic level would be superior to that of Spain in 2000, and that the per capita income would exceed 20,000 dollars [3].

It should not be forgotten that during that period, and particularly since 1973-1974, many free or nearly free services with strongly lowered costs which were consequently not entered into the accounts, were offered to the population: primary and secondary school education, health services, public insurances...

Despite a low growth rate in the agricultural sector – 3.7% per year during that period – Iran produced 5.5 million tons of wheat, 1.25 million tons of barley, 1.1 million tons of rice, 500,000 tons of cotton, 4 million tons of beetroot, and 65,000 tons of tea on the eve of the revolution. These figures are certified and published by international organizations.

Fifteen years before, some agricultural products were exported, even though their production was less important in absolute quantities. Before the agrarian reform, the rural self-consumption rate was very high. Then, the economy of the countryside had progressively become monetarist and global consumption had known a quick increase because of the demographic growth and the improvement of the standard of living and purchasing power. The food-processing deficit of the country had obviously not disappeared. Yet, the resources in currency made it possible to easily cover the costs of imports, even if the harbours of the Persian Gulf and the major roads remained saturated, which was a problem.

The effort made to build dams and irrigation networks was spectacular. In 1978, thirteen big dams which had all been designed and completed for a quarter of a century were already in full use. They allowed for the irrigation of 800,000 hectares of land and produced 1,804 megawatts of electricity per hour. The construction and opening of the tunnel for the transfer of water from the Sefid-Rud in the North, in the Guilan province, to the region of Foumanat, had made a permanent and rational irrigation of the region possible. That region was the rice granary of the country. Five other dams were under construction, the biggest of which was on the river Karun in Kuzistan, an oil region of the South. It was to allow for the irrigation of 150,000 hectares of land and for the production of 1,000 megawatts per hour all by itself. Besides, it was planned to build three more auxiliary dams on that river before 1990, which was to triple the figure of 1,000 megawatts per hour.

If one is to remain in the same context of production of energy, the capacity of Iranian plants of all categories went from 850 megawatts per hour in 1963 to over 7,500 in 1977, without taking into account the 2,400 megawatts per hour the two nuclear plants under construction in Bushehr, on the

A POLICY OF POWER AND NATIONAL INDEPENDENCE
Absolutely intolerable ambitions

Persian Gulf, were to produce. 80% of the work was already completed. Two more of a capacity of 800 megawatts per hour each, were also under construction in Kuzistan, and 15% of the work was completed. The country could thus have known a complete energetic independence, with abundant resources and the possibility to export electricity to neighbouring countries. However disruptions in the distribution of electricity had been a problem in every day life since 1976, especially in the capital city. The Hoveyda Cabinet, during its last year of existence, and Amouzegar's had not been able to remedy the problem, and the clash between a glorious, indisputable view of things and day to day reality were cunningly exploited by an opposition that was becoming more and more virulent.

The volume of crude oil exports was of over 6.5 million barrels a day on the eve of the revolution. The capacity of the various Iranian refineries was of 40 million tons per year. The country also exported refined oil. A network of oil and gas pipelines covered all the national territory and thus ensured a good distribution of oil products as well as their export to the Soviet Union. Iran was the second exporting country of oil in the world with 270 million tons in 1977. It had the biggest oil port in the world on Kharg island.

*   *

*

As for the industry, the production of steel by the public sector had exceeded 6 million tons in 1977, and that of the private sector – the Shahryar group – 600,000. The production of cement had crossed the threshold of 10 million tons. 100,000 cars were made that same year, and the million of automobiles was to be reached before the end of the century, some of which were destined for export.

Etc.

In 1977, the number of industrial units with more than 50 workers was 80,000. The average rate of industrial growth had reached 14% per year during the five years preceding the revolution.

Since 1975, 'the country had officially entered the club of the twenty richest nations in the world. It had seen its resources increase by 2,600% over a period of three years, according to the IMF.'(4) Its currency reserves were more important than those of the Netherlands, Italy, Belgium and Spain together (in 1975). The National Iranian Oil Company which ranked twenty-eighth in the world in 1973, ranked third the following year, according to the American magazine called *Fortune*.

Everything led to believe that Iran was to become the new Japan, the one of Western Asia. It was envisaged then that Iran would become a member of the OECD, and the necessary procedures had been started.

In that same year of 1977, the volume of public Iranian investments abroad, more particularly in Western Europe, in the United States and in South Africa, exceeded 20 billion dollars in fields which went from oil, the petrochemical industry, banking, the steel industry, to the car or nuclear industry.

On the eve of the revolution, the country had an important road network – 30,000 kilometres of roads were asphalted – and the first motorways were open to traffic. The construction of the 'royal way', the Persian Gulf-Caspian Sea motorway, in memory of a legendary road link which dated back to Darius I, was to start in 1980.

All the major cities in the country had very well equipped airports, just like some average or small towns. The ones of Tehran, Abadan and Shiraz were 'international airports'. The national civil aviation company called Iranair was considered an international one, and linked Iran to the five continents.

A POLICY OF POWER AND NATIONAL INDEPENDENCE
Absolutely intolerable ambitions

Despite these facts and a railroad network of over 4,500 kilometres, the quick economic growth had led to problems in the circulation of goods, some of the harbours would become saturated, and the roads would jam. It was a bottleneck situation which fueled the discontent of the last few years. The planning had not been successful. The government was aware of it and swift recovery measures had been thought of and implemented.

*   *

*

During the last fifteen years, from 1963 to 1978, the rate of pupils in nursery schools had increased by 1,350%, by 560% in primary education, 263% in intermediate education (careers courses), 331% in secondary education, and 1,550% in vocational and technical education.

In 1978, Iran had over 10 million pupils from nursery school up to secondary school, and over 200,000 students in its twenty universities and 135 further education institutions. The main universities in the country had their own hospital network which was free for users. There were three thousand beds for the University of Tehran with its four medical schools, and one thousand for the Pahlavi University (Shiraz), etc... This quality network completed those of the National Health Ministry and of the charity organizations or of the health insurance for industrial workers.

There was sometimes a waiting list for non-urgent serious medical care, as in many other countries, but the care was free in all these sectors, which led clinics and private institutions to somewhat moderate their prices.

The University of Tehran with its 20,000 students and 1,600 full-time teachers was known throughout the world and even renowned. Its annual budget came to 150 million dollars in 1977. The one of Shiraz had the best hospital complex in the Near and Middle East called the university hospital of Namazi. It was a centre of attraction for many foreign patients and students who even came from the United States to pass their specialization degree.

The Sovereign wanted the Pahlavi (Shiraz) University campus to be the Persepolis of the 20th century. It was a bilingual campus which was linked to several famous American universities by conventions such as the one of Pennsylvania, Kent... The University of Hamadan (Avicenna University) was to be Franco-Persian, the one of Rasht was to be dedicated to the practise of Persian and German. The purpose was to form bilingual specialists who would be open to the exterior world without being exclusive.

The research work on Iranian literature and civilisation held an important place at the University of Tehran, the biggest and oldest university in the country since it was created in the middle of the 19th century. Many foreign students used to come to it from everywhere in the world, and there were cooperation and exchange agreements that linked it to some of the most prestigious European or American universities, as well as to those of Cairo and to the Weizmann Institute in Israel.

The Melli University in Tehran, as well as the one from Esfahan had reached recognition at an international level. Nearly all the important regions in the country had their universities: the Ferdowsi University in Meshed, the University of Kerman, the University of Belushistan in Zabedan, two universities in Azerbaijan, in Tabriz and Rezaieh, the Razi University in Kermanshah, a Kurdish region and another one which was to be in the same region in Sanandaj. Mazandaran had just had its university called 'Reza Shah', the name of a child from these parts.

There were also three major universities of technology in

A POLICY OF POWER AND NATIONAL INDEPENDENCE
Absolutely intolerable ambitions

Tehran and many further education institutions, schools of management and foreign languages, and a Conservatoire, etc...just like in so many other university cities or ordinary cities of the provinces.

Mohammad Reza Pahlavi truly respected the autonomy and exemptions universities benefited from, but he considered himself to be their actual protector and often participated in academic ceremonies with the Shahbanoo, while keeping informed on their activities. His father had done the same [5]. For both of them, the training of the elites was an absolute priority: 'To become a leader in tomorrow's world, you first need a certain population where you can find men of genius, men who have brains; you need advanced technology, and there can't be any illiterate people; there must be social justice, some involvement; there must be a movement to spur the country into action at last... Iran is Iran... I know that we have all of this anyway, we show it everyday.' [6]

*   *

*

The development and promotion of culture were another aspect of the evolution of Iran during the years that preceded the revolution, of its power policy, of its efforts to restore national prestige.

The safeguard, upkeep and restoration of historical monuments, of the national heritage that had been modestly started under the reign of Reza Shah because of financial restrictions were to be progressively developed as the country got richer.

Esfahan, the resplendent capital of the Safavids [7] and

Shiraz, the city of poets and roses with its superb gardens and monuments, came alive and glowed again. The Ministry of Culture that had been created by Hassan Ali Mansour's government strove to revive traditional Persian arts, from classical music to ceramics, illumination to calligraphy. It fostered creativity, and gave prizes and subsidies.

The Rudaki hall of the Tehran Opera offered programmes which were Iranian as well as international. They packed out the house. The hall was considered to be one of the best in Asia. The most prestigious conductors and performers of the world came there. Every season, at least about fifty tickets were kept for the teaching profession, for unions and associations, and were free. It was thus tried to make art become available to all.

Two symphonic orchestras, several chamber orchestras including the one of the national Radio-Television, had an international reputation and were regularly invited abroad. Traditional music had taken on a new lease of life. The three television channels, two of which covered the country, showed over 60% of programmes, films, series, serials and entertainment programmes which were made in the country and often of remarkable quality. The political role of the national television which was sometimes judged to be harmful, even subversive, was often criticized. The artistic and technical quality of its production and programmes was rarely questioned though.

The Iranian film industry had made 75 feature films in 1977, and 132 the previous year [8]. During the seventies, several Persian films were given international awards and rewards. The activity and freedom of the Iranian film industry were hindered by the revolution, but the latter hardly managed to interrupt the tradition.

A POLICY OF POWER AND NATIONAL INDEPENDENCE
Absolutely intolerable ambitions

Many theatre companies, permanent or amateur ones, would perform in the capital. Their repertoire half consisted of modern Iranian plays or plays that derived from popular culture. In the capital, the City Theatre, the 25 Shahrivar Theatre and the Karehgah were subsidized. They were of very high standard. One should not forget many other theatres, private and public, in the provinces or in Tehran, or the Drama companies of the Academy of Arts of the University of Tehran who were directed by the film-director and dramatist Bahram Beyzaï during the years that preceded the revolution. He would sometimes put on three shows simultaneously on the university stages.

The Company for the protection of the national heritage was founded at the beginning of the twenties. Its particular mission was to give homage to the great men of the nation. That was how the mausoleums of Saadi, Hafiz, of Nader the great conqueror, of the Kurdish poet Baba Taher, of Avicenna, and of Saeb, etc... were built. Several of these mausoleums have become real sanctuaries and places of popular pilgrimage, like the ones of Ferdowsi and Omar Khayyam which date back to the period of Reza Shah's reign. A vast programme was being implemented in cooperation with the municipalities to build monuments or erect statues of the famous figures who came from various cities, villages or districts or who had a particular connection with them. It was a popular scheme which received the support of many associations and the warm backing of the Shah.

During the three years that preceded the revolution, the capital city saw the inauguration of the Qajar era Art Museum, of the Museum of contemporary Art, of the National Carpet Museum, and of the Reza Abassi Museum which was more particularly dedicated to Safavid art. The National Museum of

Earthenware and Ceramics was housed in Ahmad Ghavam's renovated palace and was to be opened to the public in September 1978. The official ceremony could not take place because of the tragic events that month, and was to take place after the fall of the monarchy.

A museum was dedicated to the bronze art from Luristan and was inaugurated inside the fortress of the town of Khorram Abad, the main administrative centre of the province. There were already collections of popular art and traditions in that building. A museum of modern art – paintings and sculptures – was founded in the town of Kerman. The building and some of the collections were sponsored by a rich local family, the San'atis...

Etc...

These museums, monuments, like hundreds of others that were due to the efforts of previous years and decades, were visited every day by thousands of people across the country. They all illustrated a real revival of national culture, just like cultural centres, youth centres, and art festivals, etc...

Other less ambitious projects were being completed or planned. They were dropped and sometimes discarded by the revolutionaries.

As for publishing, 3,500 new titles appeared in book shops in 1977. The University Press of Tehran, the first publishing house in the country in sciences, had alone published over 300 titles during that same year of 1977. The Pahlavi (in Shiraz), Ferdowsi (in Meshed), Esfahan and Melli (in Tehran) universities also had their own publishing houses which produced about fifty books a year each. Several charities financed the publication of Persian classics, or translations of texts from world literature. The Pahlavi Foundation was at their head. It was a specialized, semi-public association dealing exclusively with books, films and tapes for children or teenagers. All these efforts, of course, were to be added to those of the private sector in publishing.

The full bloom and influence of Iranian culture during the last twenty-five years before the revolution, and more particularly during the last decade, made the period become a genuine 'golden age' in the history of the country. It was a beautiful image of its spectacular prosperity and also of its will-to-power because public sponsorship played a determining role in it.

*   *

*

The celebration of the year of Cyrus the Great in 1977, in honour of the two thousand and five centenary of the creation of the Iranian Empire (or Persian Empire as people usually call it in the West) proceeded from the same way of thinking and the same will: the gratefulness of the nation for its 'Founder', but also the desire to 'renew the links [of contemporary Iran] with its history...and its glorious heritage.' [9]

Even if the celebration was tarnished in the Iranian people's eyes and in the eye of some of international opinion because of the 'Field of Cloth of Gold' which the Shah originally did not want, but which he did not oppose the construction of, and especially because of a banquet – a detail, it is true – that was organized by one of the best caterers in Europe – it was an error, worse, a mistake – it still illustrated that will-to-power, that desire to show national forces and a talent for organizing things, which were the characteristics of the imperial regime and of Mohammad Reza Pahlavi's psychology.

That celebration was a gigantic effort to embellish cities

like Shiraz and Esfahan, to restore many historical monuments, and to build several palaces of international standing thanks to private funds.

It also permitted the achievement and inauguration of gigantic monuments and works of public interest that corresponded to the Sovereign's tastes with great pomp and ceremony, and a wish for media exposure:

– The central library of the University of Tehran, with 600,000 volumes, a large collection of Persian manuscripts, 3,000 magazines and periodicals available to all, was inaugurated on September 24th 1971;

– The public library of the capital city was inaugurated on November 7th;

– The sports complex of the University of Shiraz, designed by the architect Mohammad Reza Moghtader, was inaugurated on April 28th 1978.

– A new oil refinery and a gas pumping station were inaugurated on December 17th.

– The construction of three big dams in the Kurdish region and an irrigation network that completed the ones built on the river Arax – an Iranian-Soviet project – were finished in June.

– The Iranian railroad network was linked up with the Turkish one.

– The Golestan Palace was transformed into national museums open to the public. It had been built in the 19th century by the Qajar kings, and the Marble Palace, built by Reza Shah.

– 2,500 village schools were opened, all sponsored by the private funds of people who wanted to have the name of a deceased loved-one on a school in their region.

Hundreds of other examples could be given.

There were two projects inaugurated in the presence of

A POLICY OF POWER AND NATIONAL INDEPENDENCE
Absolutely intolerable ambitions

many foreign heads of state which aroused a lot of criticism, especially abroad:
– the Shahyad, the kings'memorial, a Triumphal Arch which is 60 metres high, the work of young architect Hossein Amanat. It marks the main entrance of the Iranian capital. Its basement houses an 8,000 square metre museum which is dedicated to the history of the Persian Empire. It is a monument which was entirely financed by large private industrial and banking groups, and not by the State.
– The large sports complex of Tehran, the work of architect Abdol Aziz Farmanfarmaian, which was inaugurated on October 18th. Its central stadium can accommodate 100,000 spectators, the car parks, 10,000 cars and 600 buses. There are an artificial lake covering 28 hectares, the Olympic village, a sports centre with 12,000 seats, and restaurants open to the public.

This complex was at that time, and still is today, one of the most impressive and modern in the world. The organisation of the 7th Olympic Games of Asia in 1974 proved a huge success. The international press wrote that Iranians had done better than the Japanese in the previous Games. National pride could only be flattered.

Some of the Western press did not hesitate to hasten to denounce the Shah's megalomania when the complex was inaugurated. One could read here and there: 'Why does Iran need such sports complexes which are for 'advanced countries', and envisage the organisation of Olympic Games for the eighties?'

While the celebrations were going on in Persepolis, there was a big international Congress on Iranology organized by the Pahlavi National Library in Shiraz. The project of the library renewed with an Iranian tradition of the 7th century. The imperial library of Ctesiphone, the capital of the Arsacids and Sassanids was committed to the flames by the Arab invaders on the order of caliph Omar in 635. The latter had proclaimed that the Muslims should read only one book, the Koran, and that all the other books were to disappear.

This project had been getting off the ground for a few years. There was an international competition and the jury was formed. The library was to be one of the biggest in the world, if one considers its vocation and the regrouping of several others already in existence. Mohammad Reza Pahlavi wished it would be of the same standard as the ones of the American Congress, British Museum, and of the French National Library. The financing was essentially taken care of by the Pahlavi Foundation. The library was also to be the main world centre for research work on the history, culture and civilisation of Iran. That was why the Congress was organized. Shoja Ol Din Shafa, the Shah's cultural advisor, was its architect.

The central building of the halls of residence in Shiraz, its amphitheatre, restaurant and meeting rooms, were the work of architect Mohammad Reza Moghtader and associates. They were used for plenary or small congressional meetings and as a dwelling place for participants.

As he was declaring the congress open, Mohammad Reza Pahlavi said that all the celebrations were 'meant to promote the great Iranian culture. Any political and military domination inevitably has to end. The cultural influence and its values are forever. During our age-old history, our best soldiers have been these men and women who have ensured the perenniality of our culture and who still pass it on, making it become more and more influential as the generations go by.' [10]

Four hundred scientists, three hundred of whom had come from forty-four foreign countries, took part in the congress.

A POLICY OF POWER AND NATIONAL INDEPENDENCE
Absolutely intolerable ambitions

A thousand studies and research work were presented. Soon after, the Pahlavi National Library published a list of them in a 240-page volume. It was agreed that all the contributions were to be progressively published in about a hundred 500-page volumes. It was an unrivalled and colossal contribution to the knowledge of the Iranian culture and civilisation. The henchmen of the revolution confiscated all of this precious scientific treasure during the storming and occupation of the library in February 1979. What have they done with it?

Nobody knows.

*   *

*

Since the fall of the Mossadegh government, Iranian diplomacy had become the 'exclusive area' of the Head of State, even if under General Zahedi the latter often had a word to say or was duly consulted.

The successive Prime Ministers were obviously consulted and kept well informed, but the final decision was in the hands of the Sovereign.

From 1964, the relations with the Soviet Union regularly improved. Moscow, being pragmatic and realistic, took into account the political stability of Iran and of its determination to maintain privileged relations with the West so as to preserve its independence and integrity. There were only advantages seen in adopting a non-confrontation policy, then a neighbourly-term policy and finally one of cooperation with Iran. Moscow became a great economic partner of Iran. During the last five years of the monarchy, the USSR was even one of its weapons suppliers. It was a return of Iran to a policy of equilibrium which was in accordance with its more and more open wish for 'national independence' in its diplomatic approach.

Several major schemes symbolized that cooperation: the construction in common of dams and of an irrigation network on the Araks river that flows along the border, of the transiranian oil and gas pipelines which were the longest in the world... and especially the construction of a steel complex not far from Esfahan. The Shah declared in 1976: 'There was a time when we begged Westerners to sell us a blast furnace and a lousy little steel factory. They scornfully refused. We bought a big complex from the Easterners. It works perfectly well. When they noticed it, they came to us to beg us to accept another one from them. It was too late however. We will not tolerate any obstacle on our march towards the progress and prosperity of Iran.' [11] This episode reminds one of the crisis between Egypt and the United States after Washington and the World Bank's refusal to finance the tall dam of Aswan which hastened the rapprochement between Colonel Nasser and Moscow. Mohammad Reza Pahlavi was much shrewder and more experienced in international politics though, and the cooperation was limited to economic matters.

The cooperation policy with the USSR went together with a rapprochement with the other socialist countries of the time. Romania, Poland, Hungary and Czechoslovakia thus took an active part in equipping Iran. The production plant of machine tools of Arak, in the centre of Iran, was set up by the Czechs, and the tractor manufacturing complex of Tabriz is yet another example of this cooperation.

That policy did not prevent a rapprochement with populist China. The Shahbanoo and Prime Minister Hoveyda went there together in 1975. President Hua Guofeng was to be the last head of state received in Iran in October 1978. The Shah wrote: 'I had the feeling that the Chinese were then the only ones to want a powerful Iran.' [12]

A POLICY OF POWER AND NATIONAL INDEPENDENCE
Absolutely intolerable ambitions

It was on the occasion of that visit, shortly before the arrival of the Chinese president in Iran, that an ultra-secret agreement was signed for a cooperation to support nationalist resistance movements in an Afghanistan that was almost entirely sovietized [13]. The agreement did not remain secret for the Western, and especially the American, intelligence services. Washington did not yet want to get involved, and was talking about some sort of help that would transit via Pakistan and favour Islamist groups, and which would soon be set up. The Iranian decision originated in a more realistic and long-term view of the situation, and was another reason for the resentment felt towards the national independence policy initiated and led by the Shah.

The same realistic policy of presence and power was carried out with the Third World.

Iran led a military intervention in the sultanate of Oman on the Sultan's request to hold back communist infiltration and guerrilla groups. 'The Iranian Command considered the Dhofar engagement to be an exercise... An examination of the facts showed that the Sultan had chosen a wise solution. His armed forces were not sufficient to end the war and really comb the area. It seemed sensible, even necessary to ask for help, but who was he to turn to?... Iran was a clear and logical choice.' [14] 'If the Sultan of Oman had been overthrown, there would have been a permanent threat on the energy supply for the free world. This is why we acted swiftly. What makes us strong is the guarantee of our safety and that of the Persian Gulf before anything else.' [15] the Shah declared in 1975, long after the operation had ended.

On that occasion, the elite forces of the imperial army displayed their great operational and logistic ability, the officers and non-commissioned officers, their combat strength and the excellence of their training and of their savoir-faire.

There had been rejoicing here and there; admiration and gratefulness had been expressed, but it had also made more than one person think.

In 1975, during a conference attended by the heads of states of the Muslim community in Algiers, and following a long and difficult negotiation, an agreement was made with Mr Saddam Hussein, who was Vice-President of the Iraqi Republic at the time, and already the real number one in his country. The agreement definitely put an end to the disputes inherited from the colonial era [16].

Iran accepted rather reluctantly the principle of self-determination to settle the future of the Bahrain islands in the region of the Persian Gulf. They had been separated and under British domination since the middle of the 19th century. It led to the independence of the archipelago. Following it, the three key islands of the strait of Ormuz – Abu Musa, Greater and Lesser Tunb – which Iran had lost control over at the same time, were taken back in a quick commando operation. The British and the Arab countries were put in front of a fait accompli and protested as a matter of form. Iran had just displayed its strength and determination and could thus guarantee the safety of the Persian Gulf and of its ships. However it was to be feared in the region from then on, and to pay a high price for it.

The same attitude of cooperation for development and rapprochement was followed with the non-aligned countries of the Third World.

Ardeshir Zahedi was a very active Minister of Foreign Affairs who was mediatized and sometimes the subject of controversy for nearly five years from 1966 on. His diplomatic approach was flamboyant and he 'gave a new lease of life to the Ministry of Foreign Affairs' [17]. He was the great architect

A POLICY OF POWER AND NATIONAL INDEPENDENCE
Absolutely intolerable ambitions

of this policy which continued to be influential during his long post as ambassador to Washington and until the downfall of the monarchy. It was followed by his successor, the distinguished and discreet Abbas Khalatbari who was assassinated by the revolutionaries.

Iran then started leading a policy of often financial support or sometimes of technical help for the development of many countries: India, Pakistan, Afghanistan before the Soviet domination, Egypt, Jordan and Senegal... It was another aspect of the active Iranian diplomacy which also annoyed certain countries.

'A good understanding with all countries – whether they are from the Western World, the socialist camp of the Third World' [18] had actually been reached. It would be hard to deny that since Shah Abbas's reign (1587-1629) Iran had ever had such a brilliant diplomacy with such positive results. With this diplomacy which was very similar to the national independence policy led by General De Gaulle, Iran aspired to play an important role in the world, one that was worthy of its past.

It had the financial means for such a policy during the last years before the revolution. It had the required elites and had also succeeded in having the military power it needed.

*   *

*

The respect a country arouses is also based on its military power. The one of Iran was to ensure and guarantee its security and defence.

On the eve of the revolution, the army counted 540,000 men, had 3,000 modern tanks, 800 of which were Chieftains that had been specially designed for the country. Its artillery battalions had the same fire power as NATO units.

The air force was among the four or five most efficient in the world. It had 78 F14 with Phoenix missiles that had a 90-mile range. They were equipped with radars of a 150-mile range and could fire six missiles at the same time to hit six different targets. It also had several hundred Phantoms, 54 troop carriers and a fleet of refueling aircrafts.

Iran already had three airborne brigades in 1977 and would have had five of them in 1982, so over a division.

The navy had four 8,000-ton cruisers, missile launchers, twelve destroyers, three submarines on order, the crew members of which had already been trained and were ready to receive them. It had its own troop transportation fleet, reconnaissance aeroplanes, a hovercraft flotilla, the first in the world, the efficiency of which was demonstrated during the storming of the islands of the Strait of Ormuz.

This naval strength was not only capable of cruising in the Persian Gulf and ensuring its safety, but it could also reach the limits of the Indian Ocean.

The Iranian military objective was to be able to efficiently oppose any non-nuclear attack and to protect the country from one. The option to have nuclear weapons had been studied and envisaged. It had been decided to discard it. 'Iran is obviously the only country capable of having such a deterrent in this part of the world. Our armed forces would indeed have been able to stop or to prevent local disruptions in this highly strategic zone. Only Iran had the necessary money and men, especially the men, without whom money means nothing.' [19]

A POLICY OF POWER AND NATIONAL INDEPENDENCE
Absolutely intolerable ambitions

The imperial army was indeed actually and entirely national and Iranian. It was led by only officers and non-commissioned officers whose expertise and training aroused admiration from all observers. It was acquiring an appropriate weapons industry and its target was to reach the same level as Israel. There had already been different sources of supply for about ten years at the time of the revolution, including from Eastern countries, so as to be less dependent on the Americans.

It has often been written, and it is sometimes still the case, that this 'third', 'fourth' or 'fifth' army in the world according to some, collapsed under the violent attacks of the revolution and was unable to defend the regime. This is totally wrong! It remained faithful to its High Command until the end, even when the latter abandoned it. The cases of insubordination can be counted on the fingers of one hand. It was the inability of the political power, the indecision shown by the ones at the head of the country and American pressure which reduced it to inaction. It was sacrificed.

The Iranian army had not been trained to maintain peace and order in the country, except for demonstrations in big cities, especially in Tehran, and the soldiers were told not to use their weapons. It hardly intervened against the revolutionaries. The few units that were able to carry out this kind of operation – the paratroopers or special forces – were actually not answerable to the army and were virtually kept out of things. It was the same for the police squads.

The army was the last bastion of Iran. The Shah was first made to say that he had 'heard the voice of the revolution' when he was exhausted and badly ailing in order to neutralize the army. The 'voice of the revolution' was still only a riot, hardly a rebellion. The Shah was kept away from the country afterwards.

The army was too dependent on the Shah and could not take action without him. It was made to obey. There came a day when there was no-one anymore to give orders.

A famous French author wrote, as he was relating the day of July 14th 1789: 'Two squadrons, with their rifles aimed at the enemy or their swords in hand would undoubtedly have stopped the thousand or thousand two hundred Parisian rioters who managed to see the end of eight towers and three-metre wide walls that were defended by canons... but the king did not want to shed the French people's blood.' [20] These lines could reflect what the situation in Iran was like at the beginning of 1978.

Although it had been decapitated, demoralized, humiliated and vastly decimated, the army, or what was left of it, showed how efficient it was when faced with the Iraqi invasion of 1980. Iraq was almost unanimously backed by the Western world, but the Iranian army managed to preserve the honour and integrity of its country.

The 'stockpiling of weapons' policy of Iran during the last years of the monarchy has often been criticized. The events of the last quarter of a century and of the last few years have shown that Mohammad Reza Pahlavi had guessed things correctly and had well anticipated the future, even if one does not take the Iraqi episode into consideration, and if he went too far concerning one decision or the other. A strong national army which was well equipped vouched for the independence of Iran, its integrity and the respect it inspired in other countries. The Iranian army never failed in its mission.

*   *

*

A POLICY OF POWER AND NATIONAL INDEPENDENCE
Absolutely intolerable ambitions

In 1977, Iran was succeeding in 'the only effective economic take-off of the Third World.' [21] The wish to show off, to take its revenge on the humiliations of the past two centuries was obvious in that move. The main projects, the prestigious projects which flatter the vanity and pride of the nation and show the whole world the success of open ambitions held all the attention of the leaders. They corresponded, took their inspiration from – according to some – the Shah's profound penchant for them, his tendency to like glory, even if he was rather modest in his private life and avoided anything ostentatious.

Mohammad Reza Pahlavi was haunted by the grandiose which he sometimes took for grandeur. Such a temperament, which was admirable in a way, sometimes led him to make errors and laid him open to the most cutting criticisms from those who could not really bear the undeniable success of Iran. The politician and journalist M.H. Heykal who was not one of his friends wrote: 'The dreams he made for himself and for his country knew no bounds.' [22] He added: 'I never doubt that Iran will reach the highest summits.' [23]

Iran and the Shah were quickly accused of 'intolerable ambitions' and of 'delusions of grandeur'. The more he heard this kind of judgment, the more Mohammad Reza Pahlavi found them unfair and especially insincere since they came from 'his Western friends', and he multiplied sometimes excessive replies. He was then accused of being 'arrogant'. The people who give lessons rarely appreciate to be taught some. William Shawcross wrote in his highly critical voluminous biography: 'The Shah continually repeated that he would make Iran become one of the five industrial powers of the world before the end of the century, a model not only for the Third World, but also for the West, whose decadence, laziness and waste he kept denouncing, and he insisted more particularly on Great Britain'... 'All this would happen because the Iranians were capable of making extraordinary efforts. That is where the difference can be seen between us [Iranians] and blasé societies.' [24]

He said to another interlocutor: 'The West is becoming completely degenerate. We have nothing to learn from these people. They want to export their degenerate ideas, what they call democracy, but this is something we cannot accept.' [25]

This way of expressing himself like a serious schoolteacher who gives admonitions that are full of reproaches reveals an undeniable vanity and exasperated his interlocutors as well as much of the international press.

Those who had given the impression they wanted to humiliate were now humiliated in turn. They were not to forgive him for it.

The Shah declared to a journalist: 'People from abroad are rejoicing over power cuts in Tehran. It is shocking to be so jealous of a country. Why must a French person be able to consume 87 kilos of meat per year, and an American 130 kilos, and when we want to improve the level of consumption in our country, we are accused of having immoderate ambitions? According to a German newspaper, no Third World country, including Iran, should be able to reach the standard of living of 'little Austria'. Isn't that a form of racism? It reflects a mentality which is neither honest nor sensible. I am telling them that we will meet again some time in the future. Nothing is to be an obstacle to the progress of Iran.' [26]

There was to be a repercussion after all these indisputable and uncontested successes, after the sincere declarations.

There was another side to the medal. There was to be a hard awakening.

A POLICY OF POWER AND NATIONAL INDEPENDENCE
Absolutely intolerable ambitions

*   *

*

Seeing the leading people in the world sincerely or in a hypocritical light playing the sycophants eager to meet him, the Shah ended up being less and less attentive to the problems that were piling up and which were of secondary importance to him. He had his eyes fixed on far away horizons and was obsessed with the idea of making Iran become 'a second Japan', of outdoing Western countries. He thought that the 'great civilization', the only one he deemed worthy of Iran, was around the corner. The government was there to deal with these details, they were only management details. There was an undeniable failing on his behalf. The intelligence services hid the reality of a deteriorating situation from him. It also contributed to plunging the country into a crisis.

He took it all upon himself, but the price he and Iran were to pay was high.

*   *

*

In 1977, Mohammad Reza Pahlavi wrote the following proud sentences while he was prefacing a book on Iran. They seem to be premonitory today: 'My country is the geographic key of all the Middle East... If ever – God protect us – Iran were to collapse, the whole of the Middle East and the Indian sub-continent would collapse at the same time...
(...)
There is no other nation on earth which has been so often submitted to invasions, devastations and periods of decadence. It is such a marvellous nation which still remains quick to rise from its ashes.

When one has quashed the Greek conqueror, triumphed over the Roman army, assimilated Arab power, survived the Mongols, contained the Ottoman Empire, and then the Afghan and Indian hordes, and, almost a unique case in contemporary annals, loosened the grip of the Red Army on a whole province which one had nearly lost, what can one fear the future might hold?

The best argument for the existence of my country is that it has been able to survive until now.

Continuity is the word which comes to one's mind when one studies the history of Iran, despite the wars and the suffering, the tears and the mourning. Each time, the Iranian people not only managed to keep its national character intact, but it also submitted its invaders to its culture and civilisation.

The 20th century plague finally had to be faced: the big international companies which pretended to be helping us and getting us out of our underdevelopment only took advantage of us in a shameful manner.

(...)

It has been a fascinating adventure. It was full of all kinds of events...' [27]

These lines contain the proud explanation for a whole policy, the premonition of possible obstacles and today's tragedy, and, perhaps, hope for the future.

PART THREE

THE ISLAMIC REVOLUTION

Chapter XI

'A KIND OF SOCIAL-DEMOCRATIC SAINT'
'A miracle in Paris'

' In 1977, the United States decided to end it all with the Shah. The Iranian is not only the leader of the OPEC rebellion, under whose side the Middle-Eastern oil producers fight and are united like never before, but he has managed to get his entry into Eurodif's capital. He will become a nuclear power in the five years to come. He must be overthrown. Of course, the GI's are not the ones who will swoop down on Tehran. As usual, an opponent to the existing regime will be backed, and his ascension to power will be organized in the dark.

The Americans went for Ayatollah Khomeini, a professor of theological law who had been exiled in Iraq since 1963...
It was necessary to make Khomeini look like a revolutionary to get him out of Iraq. He could not just show up from Baghdad. Since France and the United States were on the same boat, the Americans decided to send Khomeini to Paris for a three-month training period in respectability.' [1]

The analysis was made by Dominique Lorentz, from *Libération*, and appeared in his particularly detailed study entitled *Une guerre* ('A War').

An analyst who participated in the Pentagon's work [2] for a long time recently wrote: 'The Americans were preparing Khomeini for the overthrow of the Shah.'

'One day, I mentioned to the Shah the names of the people in the United States who were supposed to envisage his departure and his replacement... How does one make the Shah abdicate and who does one find to replace him?' This is what Count Alexandre de Marenches wrote in his memoirs, before adding: 'The Americans had made up their minds.' [3] This testimony is hard to challenge.

'The American authorities had planned on overthrowing the Shah as soon as 1974-1975, because of the oil problem... In Neauphle-le-Château, the CIA occupied the house next to the one where the character of ayatollah Khomeini was being built up, and where his sermons were drafted; his tapes were sent in diplomatic bags. This is not the most glorious page in French history. It is difficult to understand why President Giscard d'Estaing acted so benevolently with the fake ayatollah, and let him benefit from such means.' [4]

This is the judgment Maurice Druon bore on the operation, the moral and political authority of which may not be contested.

Was Rouhollah Khomeini this 'inspired man with a beard' [5] – to repeat an expression already used – who was put in charge of the task?

While the destabilization process of Iran was well advanced, and the Tehran government was making one blunder, mistake or error after another, Rouhollah Khomeini, who was getting better known, arrived in Paris on October 6th 1978, and went to live in Neauphle-le-Château, where his character was to be 'built up'

'A KIND OF SOCIAL-DEMOCRATIC SAINT'
A miracle in Paris

*　　　　*

*

The man who was being helped to settle down in Neauphle-le-Château was very likely to have been born at the turn of the 20th century, in 1900 apparently, since his father was killed during a scuffle in 1901, and he was one at the time, according to official biographies.

So, he was seventy-eight years old when he became famous and started his political career [6].

His first name is very common in Iran, especially in the countryside. It is not 'a first name that was especially chosen by the Jews when they wanted people to believe that they had been converted' [7], as was written. Iranians of Jewish or Baha'i origin also bear that name. Nothing shows that his ancestors were not Muslims.

His name comes from Khomein, a small town in the centre of Iran where the grandfather and father of the future ayatollah went to live during the last twenty-five years of the 19th century. They were Indian Muslims; the first was called Ahmad, and the second, Mostafa. Both of them, like many of their compatriots of the time would travel across Iran telling people's fortune and mainly living on charity.

His grandfather Ahmad's date of death is not known, but it is known that Mostafa married a peasant woman from the area and not an 'imam's' daughter, as one of his biographers wrote when the character was being 'built up' in Neauphle-le-Château [8].

Ruhollah was the last of the family's three sons. The

417

eldest, Agha Morteza, was a notary. He had some judicial problems after the Second World War, and took the title of ayatollah after the revolution. The second, Nurollah, also called Agha Nur, was an ordinary lawyer who died in 1976.

Mostafa knew how to read and write and entered the service of a local feudal lord called Heshmat-Ol-Dowleh as a scribe. The latter, as was the tradition then, saw to it that his estate spread out to the detriment of the small and middle landowners of the area whose lands he would buy when they had debts. The transactions were automatically registered by the scribe for there were no notaries then. Mostafa took advantage of the situation and amassed a considerable fortune. Without consultation, he took the title of 'sayed' which is given in Iran to any of the prophet Mahomet's descendants. He made a lot of enemies among the peasants however, who often felt they had been wronged.

There was a drama towards the end of the 19th century. A small local landowner called Bahram Khan gathered a few friends and decided to take the law in his own hands. An ambush was set up for Mostafa on the road from Khomein to Arak, a neighbouring town, and the newly-called sayed was assassinated.

'According to the Khomeini legend, Mostafa was assassinated by Reza Shah's henchmen'[9], and this theory was 'made official' by the Islamic regime. At the time, the future general and emperor was only a young man who was barely twenty and who naturally ignored even the existence of the mullah scribe from Khomein.

Ruhollah Khomeini's official biographies and all the ones that have been spread around the world for three decades conceal his Indian origin even if there is nothing degrading

'A KIND OF SOCIAL-DEMOCRATIC SAINT'
'A miracle in Paris'

about it*. There is no document to prove his ancestry. Many witnesses who know the family have certified that the title of sayed is not engraved on his grandfather Ahmad's tombstone. Ruhollah would thus only be a false descendant of the Prophet.

The Constitution of the Islamic republic stipulates that 'the guide of the revolution' must be Iranian, and the President of the Republic 'Iranian, and of Iranian origin'. This was how shelter was found for Ruhollah Khomeini concerning any possible questioning of his authority and legitimacy. Besides, as soon as he was in power, the latter suppressed the 'cursed' [10] 'lion and sun', which had been the national Iranian emblem for centuries [11] for a drawing of Indian origin, more precisely of Kashmiri origin.

Certain sources tried to rectify the first version of the story that was fully invented during the man's stay in France about Reza Shah's role in father Khomeini's disappearance soon after it came out. According to the Islamic Republic embassy in Paris, 'when he [Khomeini] was five years old, his father was executed for his opposition to the regime.' It was even said that his father was 'a hero of the people's fight against the feudal lords,' and even 'the leader of the Khomein community.' [13] These are purely imaginary allegations.

Bahram Khan, Mostafa's alleged assassin, was arrested, transferred to Tehran, tried and hanged on the public square in the presence of a few members of the victim's family.

When, eighty years later, Ruhollah Khomeini whose

---

* Agha Morteza Passandideh, the character's eldest brother however declared the following in an interview, in all simplicity: 'Our late grandfather Agha sayed Ahmad was a Kashmiri; he came from India and spent a long time with our family in Khomeyn' (*Ettela'ât*, January 15th 1979).

hatred was deeply rooted took the power, Hossein Bahrami, the grandson of Bahram Khan who had paid for his crime with his life, presided over the Khomein town council. He was arrested on the ayatollah's order – the ayatollah had become the 'guide of the revolution' – for being a 'corrupter on earth'. He was whipped to death on the public square. All the family belongings were confiscated and their residences were looted. The new regime propaganda actually attached great importance to both events.

Right after Mostafa's death, his orphans were taken care of by a few well-off families of the region, in particular by Sadre-Ol-Ashraf's family [14], and started studying in Koranic schools.

*   *

*

At the beginning of the twenties, when the 'registry office' system was set up in Iran and citizens had to choose a 'surname', most of Ahmad and Mostafa's descendants decided to be called Hendi (Indian) or Hendi-Zadeh (of Indian ancestry) because of their origins. Ruhollah chose the name of Khomeini. It was rather common at the time for children born to the same parents to choose different surnames. It was the case in some well-known families from these towns.

So, Ruhollah first studied in Khomein, then in Mahallat and in Arak, bigger neighbouring towns, and eventually in Qom, where his masters were some of the famous members of the clergy of the time, as Haj Agha Abdolkarim Haeri Yazdi and Mohammad Ali Shah-Abadi. His fellow students of the time remember him and talk about him as a brilliant,

'A KIND OF SOCIAL-DEMOCRATIC SAINT'
'*A miracle in Paris*'

intelligent and excessively ambitious student [15].

At the beginning of the forties, like many theology students, he went to pursue his studies in Najaf in Iraq, which was then the most important Shiite centre. Before he left, he married a young woman from a well-known family who had a good dowry. She was called Batul and was eleven years old. It was legal then. Contrary to most mullahs, he remained monogamous and led an austere family life. The couple had many children, seven, it seems, and four of them survived. There were two boys called Mostafa and Ahmad who were to get their names in the papers later on. The daughters married into middle-class families and led ordinary lives.

However, once he was in power, Khomeini made polygamy legal again when it had been abolished for years, and he set the minimum age for girls to get married at nine: 'Make sure your daughters do not see their first menstrual blood in your own home' [16], he said.

*   *

*

From the very beginning of the forties until the 1963 events, Ruhollah Khomeini and his family led discreet lives. The eldest brother, Agha Morteza Passandideh, practised as a notary, the second was first a lawyer in Arak, then in Tehran. Ruhollah was a preacher, after that, he also taught theology and Islamic case law. Each one of the three brothers had inherited a village from their father in the region of Khomein. The one of the future ayatollah was called Zurghan [17]. The three brothers decided to go into business as well. They turned their father's house into a garage [18], dealt in car spare parts

421

and created a small coach line linking Khomein to several neighbouring towns. It was labelled 'Hendi', Indian, as a reference to the family's country of origin*.

During those years, even if the opposite was said and written later on, Ruhollah Khomeini was neither a subversive element nor an agitator, and he did not lead any political activity. He wrote in an opuscule which was published in Qom: 'The monarchy is not called into question by the clergy. On the contrary, a great number of well-respected theologians have worked with the kings... Even if governments and kings have mistreated them, they have not been opposed to the basic principle of the monarchy. The support given by the modjtaheds [doctors of the law] to the kings is indeed recorded in history books.' [19] 'We are not saying, and have never said, that the sovereign must be a religious dignitary. The Shah must come from the military, but he must abide by the laws of the land [20].' He wrote the following in a telegram addressed to Shah Mohammad Reza Pahlavi in the autumn of 1962, shortly before the riots of 1963 that he was to be the flag-bearer of,: 'After giving my respects and addressing my prayers to Your Majesty, I would like to say that according to the press, women are going to be given the right to vote. It worries the clergy and other parts of the population. I humbly beg you to give orders so as to suppress this sort of thing from the government and the political parties' programmes; the Muslim community will be grateful to you.' [21]

---

* The house had progressively fallen into ruin and was restored in 1980. It is now called 'Khaneheh-Agha', mister's house, or Sayed's house. It is now a kind of popular attraction and is visited from time to time by foreign journalists. It is a bungalow with eleven rooms around a big courtyard where two trees vegetate. There is only one WC in the house. When the Hendi business was on-going, the courtyard was used as a car park; the rooms were used as dormitories for the drivers and as a storage place for spare parts.

'A KIND OF SOCIAL-DEMOCRATIC SAINT'
A miracle in Paris

During the last years of the war and during the campaign for the nationalization of oil, Ruhollah Khomeini was part of ayatollah Kashani's entourage, who was an ally and backer of Mossadegh, the nationalist leader at first, before he became his violent and fierce opponent later on. According to some authors who still criticize the monarchic regime, Khomeini allegedly was one of the main protagonists of the unrest organized by ayatollah Kashani's entourage against Mossadegh. 'We are going to give Mossadegh a slap in the face, as he gave a slap in the face of Islam.' [22]

The politicization of the man's discourse undeniably comes from that period of time. It was to earn him a certain fame among a few traditionalist students and in the circles that were opposed to the nationalist but secular movement that Mossadegh symbolized. He is not known to have been anti-monarchy though.

A rebellion against the agrarian reform and women's emancipation broke out in 1963. It had been orchestrated by the Cairo regime and its Soviet friends and protectors to weaken, if not overthrow the Iranian monarchy, mullah Ruhollah Khomeini, in his haughty tone and with his devouring ambition, was the only member of the clergy to openly rise up against the very popular reforms. His interests had been harmed –as his family owned villages – and he thus became the spokesman of the opponents within the clergy and the bazaris.

From that time, Khomeini started being given the title of hodjatoleslam*, the vicar of Islam, and the man appeared to be particularly vain and distrustful. He overestimated his ability and was fuelled by incredible hatred. He also appeared to be

---

* It is a rank below that of ayatollah in the Shiite hierarchy. It is an Iranian custom or habit which is barely a century old since the titles did not have an official existence.

obstinate and had no consideration whatsoever for the human consequences of the decisions he was to impose on people. He gave signs of 'passionate idealism, of an attitude on the verge of abnormality' [23].

Much later, when he was the master of Iran and the 'guide of the revolution', hiding behind the screen of Islam, his Islam, he did everything and nothing, ordered and covered up for abominable crimes. After a first failed attempt in 1963, he waited patiently to impose his tyrannical ravings on whole peoples before trying to export them. He was able to do this thanks to an international context which was to use him afterwards.

A well-known journalist called Oriana Fallaci refused all interviews that were not spontaneous. She dared ask him in the face if he was capable of having human feelings, had ever cried out of grief, and was sensitive at all [24]. He grumbled a few words, said he was tired and dismissed her from his room [25].

Khomeini did not hesitate to have a lot of blood shed in 1963, and he had no hesitation ordering the massacre of tens of thousands of people from 1978 onwards. He used to proclaim that: 'The more Iran will bleed, the more successful the revolution will be' [26]. He laid open claim to his actions. Maybe he only saw in his victims 'the incarnation of Evil'.

*　　　　*

*

The two most important principles of the 'White Revolution', i.e. the agrarian reform and the bestowing on women of political, social and domestic rights as well as their access to all kinds of jobs, were approved of in a referendum on June 23rd 1963.

'A KIND OF SOCIAL-DEMOCRATIC SAINT'
'*A miracle in Paris*'

The reaction was not long to come. An armed rebellion broke out in a large part of the South. It was organized by some tribal chiefs of the Fars region who had been particularly wronged by the agrarian reform. There were violent demonstrations in Qom and Tehran, especially against the equality of men and women. They were limited but of extreme brutality. A few bank branches, cinemas, schools and cultural centres were set on fire in Tehran. Henchmen were recruited in the slums of the capital and led by the ex-convict Tayeb Haj Rezaï to do the dirty work. They were well paid for it. The funds came mainly from Colonel Nasser's secret services. This was clearly established in documents that were published later, and Mohammad H. Heykal, the latter's Minister and confident, admitted it later on, although he was an admirer of Ruhollah Khomeini [28].

The 1963 riots lasted three days. The government's firm attitude put an end to them. Ruhollah Khomeini was arrested and transferred from Qom to Tehran. He was accused of provocation, of fomenting trouble, inciting murder, justifying crime and of connivance with foreign powers. He was to be brought before a court and risked capital punishment.

From 1978 already, the Neauphle-le-Château era, propaganda, or rather disinformation, made this episode become the starting point for a revolutionary and anti-imperialist career devoted to 'the sublime uprising of a fighting Islam' [29]. 'It was in Qom, in 1963, that ayatollah Khomeini delivered his founding speech on the Islamic revolution,' was the recent headline of a famous Parisian newspaper [30].

The entire 'theoretical' discourse on these bloody riots could be summed up in three points: an opposition to the agrarian reform, to the promotion of women and a fatwa (religious ordinance) given by Khomeini to condemn the referendum procedure which went 'against the interest of Islam'*. The fatwa however started with: 'Although I have conveyed my observations to His Majesty...'[31]. There was nothing revolutionary there.

'The sublime uprising of a fighting Islam' and 'the founding speech of the Islamic revolution' can in fact be summed up in a riot that was led by the criminal underworld and financed by foreign countries.

Certain people who had various interests that were not incidental at first, formed a coalition aiming at destabilizing, if not destroying, a power which they disliked. They wanted to have an influence on its agrarian and social policy – it was the motive of the big landowners and local feudal lords – or on its opposition to the revolutionary and expansionist aims – that was the objective which caused Colonel Nasser's determination, together with those who manipulated or supported him.

Ruhollah Khomeini lent himself to the operation out of hatred, ambition, fanaticism or 'passionate idealism'. He became its ephemeral flag-bearer before he disappeared from the scene to come back – or be used – years later.

*   *

*

Here comes another episode in Ruhollah Khomeini's life which is concealed in the biographies that were spread around the world after his stay in Neauphle-le-Château. Following various people's interventions, notably that of a mullah who had always been a supporter of the Iranian communist party,

---

* The Islamic Republic twice resorted to them.

'A KIND OF SOCIAL-DEMOCRATIC SAINT'
'A miracle in Paris'

the Tudeh, and who was called Sheikh Hossein Lankarani [32], five important religious dignitaries* gave him the rank of 'modjtahed', doctor in law, and thus, according to established custom, gave him the right to bear the title of ayatollah**. Such a title meant political shelter for him. He personally assured the authorities of his good conduct. He was released after certain personalities had intervened out of a desire for peace, in particular after General Pakravan, the head of the Savak's intervention, and that of Mozzafar Baghai, one of Mossadegh's former friend and an influential man***, and so he went back to Qom.

Barely a year later, after a new incitement to rioting, he was arrested and transferred to Tehran again where he was briefly put in prison before being put under house arrest in a luxurious governmental villa (one of the future 'youth palaces' of the Iranian capital), and eventually forced to exile [33]. He first settled down in Istanbul and then in Najaf, Iraq. It is only in 1978 that his name was mentioned again.

In Iraq, he lived in a small one-storied house in a rather modest and dusty street. He stayed and received his visitors on the ground floor of the house. Upstairs, there were several rooms for his family. The children of many of the local families played in the street [34] which was therefore often noisy.

Two incidents in ayatollah Khomeini's private life at least mark his long stay in Iraq.

The first was accounted for by Count de Marenches.

---

* Ayatollahs Sheikh Bahaoldin Mahallati, Sayed Kazem Shariat-Madari, Sayed Hadi Milani, Haj Agha Ahmad Khonsari and Sharoudi.
** Since the Islamic revolution, this centennial custom has not been respected and religious titles are born without respect for traditional criteria and according to the authorities' good will.
*** They were assassinated on his order after the revolution.

Although it is only an anecdote, it reveals the man's character: 'The ayatollah had a terrible temper. He was a medieval tyrant. One day, one of his children had had a fight with a child from the neighbourhood. He wanted the latter to be put to death for having dared to raise his hand on his kid. The Iraqis obviously refused to give him satisfaction' [35].

The second one took on a political dimension. The ayatollah's eldest son, Mostafa, died on October 21st 1976, and not in 1978, as was written later on, and this to turn his death into an act of political vengeance when it was caused by a heart attack due to his bulimia.

Ayatollah Khomeini was not yet the important figure he was to become months later. The authorities did not show any objection to a religious ceremony in the Ark Mosque in the capital. Mehdi Bazargan presided over it. The rumour that the Savak was responsible for his death was progressively spread. After the ayatollah arrived in France, the entire world press maintained that Mostafa had been assassinated on Mohammad Reza Pahlavi's order.

Yet, Édouard Sablier wrote: 'Khomeini never stated that it was an assassination' [36]. He had even declared to a journalist from *Le Monde* who had asked him questions on the subject that 'he could not confirm it' [37], and to the Egyptian journalist and politician Mohammad H. Heykal who asked him the same question that: 'there was nothing true about the whole story' [38].

A French journalist who had inquired into the subject came to the same conclusion: 'the scraps of testimonies obtained in Iraq from Khomeini's entourage lead one to think that Mostafa died of a heart attack. As he was feeling unwell, he had allegedly even written a will a few months before his death, but it is nowhere to be found today' [39].

'A KIND OF SOCIAL-DEMOCRATIC SAINT'
'A miracle in Paris'

Once he had become the master of Iran, the ayatollah nevertheless declared a yearly day of national mourning in honour of his 'martyr' son's death, and gave the name of 'The martyr Mostafa Khomeini' to avenue Cyrus in Tehran, where many Iranian Jews used to live.

The man's official biographies and all the written documents about him which are politically correct still continue to convey the lie.

* *

*

From the very beginning of the seventies, as the idea of the destabilization of the imperial regime was taking shape, as Iran's ambitions did not stop being a source of worry in many circles, in the West as well as in the East, several secret services started taking an interest in Ruhollah Khomeini.

The fact that he was an instrument of Colonel Nasser's Egypt during the 1963 riots is well established today.

Was he a Soviet 'agent'? Colonel Michel Goleniewski, the number 2 in the Soviet-Polish counter-espionage who defected to the West allegedly said to the CIA as soon as 1961 that 'ayatollah Khomeini was one of Moscow's five informers within the Shiite clergy' [40].

I find it hard to subscribe to this point of view after having interviewed dozens of people who met him, knew about him, and after reading his 'written work' and his declarations myself, and studying his comportment.

The man was too limited and disinterested in material things to have been an 'agent'. On the other hand, his limited intellectual level, his fanaticism and his hatred were probably why he was so easily manipulated. The Soviet secret services were masters in the art, and there are so many clues and serious crosschecks that one may think that was the case. He was manipulated by one camp for years, and by both towards the end.

At the beginning of the seventies, serious sources draw attention on the preparation in Iraq which was still under Soviet influence then, of a conspiracy to destabilize Iran by using certain religious circles: 'The East-West confrontation could take over from the one which occurred in 1965-1970 on both sides of Suez. There is more and more plotting going on...Eastern Germany has something to do with this plotting and acts as a relay between the USSR and Iraq. Moscow always uses satellites so as not to be caught in between and implicated. The case is to be followed up...' [41] Then came names and specific information which some people only pretended to have discovered ten years later. A long time after the triumph of the revolution, some American authors, if one wants to only cite them, were to confirm this analysis a posteriori [42].

'The Soviet espionage central agency tried to get in touch with ayatollah Khomeini, one of the Shah's opponents whose prodigious destiny no-one could guess at the time. The latter had found refuge in the holy city of Najaf.' This was written in *Le Monde* [43] in 1984, *Le Monde* which had so much contributed to 'building up' this 'prodigious destiny' a few years before... 'Aliev* put an officer from the IADP (Iranian Azerbaijan Democratic Party), General Panahian, in charge of establishing this contact through General Teymour Bakhtiar. The latter had been at the head of the Savak and

---

* Geïdar Aliev was then the head of the KGB in Soviet Azerbaijan before being appointed incumbent of the Politburo of the CPSU and later number 2 in the Soviet hierarchy under Gorbachev, before he finally became President of Azerbaijan after the collapse of the USSR. Aliev had long served in Iran and was a 'specialist' of the country.

'A KIND OF SOCIAL-DEMOCRATIC SAINT'
A miracle in Paris

had then become an opponent to the Shah. He had also sought refuge in Iraq. He knew the religious dignitary well. The mission was carried out, and it was the Tudeh party which first published Khomeini's inflammatory texts against the imperial regime in Leipzig' [44].

Once General Bakhtiar had disappeared, 'ayatollah Khomeini took over. The current Vice-President of the Iranian Parliament used to make frequent trips between Najaf and Leipzig at the time' [45].

In reality, Ruhollah Khomeini was deeply involved in an atmosphere of intrigues, manipulations and struggles between the secret services which he was unable to understand. Perhaps he was being used without realizing it.

*   *

*

The silence and oblivion concerning Khomeini since his exile were broken on January 8th 1978 in Tehran. Tapes that came from Iraq, or which had most probably been recorded in that country, and then been sent to Iran via East Germany, had been distributed in Tehran and in Qom for a few weeks. The exile openly criticized the imperial regime in them and even attacked the Shah himself. Leaflets with the same content were handed out in small numbers.

On that January 8th, a famous evening paper called *Ettela'ât* published a diatribe against the man under a pseudonym. He was presented as being of Indian origin – which was absolutely true –, accused of being or having been a homosexual – which could not be proved and was part of everyday private life which was usually considered to be protected in the Iran of the time –, of having married

431

a 'street dancer' – which was completely wrong –, of being uneducated, and of being an agent who was manipulated by foreign intelligence services, etc... It was written in the article that he was a bad poet, yet Ruhollah Khomeini had never pretended to be a poet. Like so many other Iranians, he would write in verse from time to time. His poetical work is frankly mediocre but it is vastly superior to his theological writings which were soon after to become the butt of the world press's jokes.

It was a mixture of true elements and of falsehoods.

The crosschecking of various testimonies has made it possible to establish [46] that the idea of such a 'retort' had been suggested to the Shah by the Minister of the Imperial Court who was Amir Abbas Hoveyda at the time, and that the latter's draft had been entrusted to a famous journalist. This journalist, because of the little importance given to the person in question, had written a slapdash 'paper' based on the rumours, and had given it back to him. The Shah had naturally not read it. Prime Minister Djamshid Amouzegar had not read it either. The 'paper' was given to Homayoun, the Minister of Information, who had trouble forcing it on the editorship of *Ettela'ât*, but who said he had not read it [47].

Was it provocation, casualness, or a mixture of both? The publication of the article can be considered as the starting point for the process of putting Khomeini in orbit, and for the events which the Shah himself was led to call the revolution before anybody else. They were to lead to the downfall of the Iranian monarchy. The Pandora's box of radical Islamism had just been opened.

*   *

*

'A KIND OF SOCIAL-DEMOCRATIC SAINT'
'A miracle in Paris'

During the last months of 1978, while the periods of unrest, lull, liberal measures, firm words and gesticulations in all directions followed one another in Iran, the international press made ayatollah Khomeini progressively become a renowned character. He had not yet become the emblematic leader of the protest movement. He did not yet have the required calibre or influence..

Sharif-Emami, the Prime Minister the Shah chose to replace Amouzegar, wished to take the ayatollah away from Iraq when he was only considered to be an extremist agitator. The importance of the conspiracy, its internal dimension or even its international aspect had not yet been sized up.

When Ruhollah Khomeini asked for his passport which had expired long ago to be validated, Tehran immediately gave its approval. He wanted to leave Iraq. Baghdad consulted Tehran. The relations between the two countries had been excellent since 1975 and the Algiers agreements. After receiving a favourable answer from the Iranian government, the Command Council of the revolution which was already presided by Saddam Hussein, and not by President El-Bakr who was seriously ill, granted the authorisation as well. As long as Tehran was not annoyed, Baghdad, where Khomeini and the unrest he caused were not really appreciated, only saw advantages in getting rid of the character [48].

From a strictly Iranian point of view, this keeping him out of the country was a mistake. After attempting to enter Kuwait – was it a diversion? –, Ruhollah Khomeini landed in Paris on October 6th 1978 with an American citizen of Iranian origin called Ibrahim Yazdi who was to be his real mentor. He was awaited there. Everything was ready for him.

'Khomeini [was to be] built up by an East-West combination, otherwise he would never have existed' [49].

433

*　　　*

*

The man had a valid Iranian passport and so he did not need a visa. He did not ask for political asylum. Twenty years later, Valéry Giscard d'Estaing gave the first [50] and then the second explanation [51], the wrong one.

No political asylum had either been asked for or granted. He was a very particular traveller.

Tehran vaguely hoped that people in Paris would have the decency to remind him of his duty of confidentiality at least. It was an illusion.

*　　　*

*

Everything was ready and perfectly well organized for the welcoming and moving in of the man in Neauphle-le-Château, a peaceful town in the Paris suburbs which was to become from then on the capital of the Iranian revolution. His 'hôtel particulier' or mansion*, was guarded like the Saint Graal by French elite troops' [52]; in fact, there were two security force squadrons.

Ayatollah Khomeini was nevertheless very distrustful and asked for Algerian agents and for some Palestinians to help them. There were 'agents from all the secret services in the world around him: the CIA, IS, KGB, and SDECE. The CIA agents even went so far as to rent the house next door to

---

* At the beginning of the 1980's, the empty building was destroyed in an explosion that the press of the time attributed to the 'Shah's supporters'. The French police did not seem to follow the case up.

'A KIND OF SOCIAL-DEMOCRATIC SAINT'
'A miracle in Paris'

that of the ayatollah' [53]. The supply and logistics were taken care of by Iranian opponents to the Shah who had 'contacts with the Palestinian and leftist movements which were largely sponsored by Colonel Qadhafi, the Libyan dictator' [54]. They were helped by 'enthusiasts, leftists of all kinds who had rushed there from all the Western universities and by different specialists ad hoc who had mingled in' [55]. This is what the head of the French secret services of the time, Alexandre de Marenches, wrote later on.

The President of the Tehran Bar, Hassan Nazih, who was on the premises at the time as the man's legal adviser and who praised him in the columns of *Le Monde*, admitted later on: 'Khomeini benefited from numerous advantages at the time, such as telephone lines, radio contacts, air transit facilities for the tapes with his inflamed calls for rebellion and the rest...' [57]

It was a real takeover by force that was prepared and organized by a sort of East-West collaboration originating in the French capital which aimed at overthrowing the legal and legitimate regime of a friendly allied country.

Pierre de Villemarest, a personality known in the Resistance and a former member of the French intelligence services, a historian as well, who was a member of the editorial staff of *Valeurs Actuelles*, was the first French journalist to meet Ruhollah Khomeini. He had briefly evoked his name before [58]. Twenty years later, he testified the following: 'Thanks to some friends from the CEI in the United States, I knew what day he was to arrive at Neauphle-le-Château, and some Iranian students who had briefed me about their milieu had managed to recommend me to one of Khomeini's confidents who, according to them, was playing a double game between the CIA and the ayatollah's direct entourage...

Pretending to be a [press] correspondent, I arrived in

Neauphle and asked to see the Iranian whose name had been given to me; he had been sent elsewhere. Ghotb-Zadeh [who was to be shot on Khomeini's order later on] was the one who received me and who, after an endless talk, introduced me to Khomeini and worked as my interpreter for two hours... Khomeini went to have a rest in another home, a small detached house located further down the road... Tea was served...I heard noises in a room next door which reminded me of the radio programmes or recordings during the clandestine years. I pretended I had an urgent need, but instead of walking towards the exit, I opened the door of that room. Two people started screaming! I still had time to see a complete radio installation. I stammered out a few words of excuse for making a mistake... I was led outside to the toilets. When I came back, a quick glance allowed me to see wires which led to rather powerful aerials. I had the impression they were broadcasting, to what? To whom?... I rushed back to Paris to see the right authorities at the Home Office, wondering how Khomeini had the right to broadcast anything abroad from France...All this still proved that everything was well thought of. I was asked to mind my own business' [59].

The crosschecking of these testimonies which come from sources that are too serious to be challenged, leaves no doubt as to the fact that everything had been given careful thought, and had been well prepared and meticulously organized in advance. So, as it happened, there was indeed an entente, even if only a tacit one, between the East and the West. The Tehran government was wrong about the moderating role of the French authorities of the time. Thus, the departure of ayatollah Khomeini from Najaf, which was wished for and well considered at first in Tehran, 'had a boomerang effect', as the United States ambassador to Tehran wrote later on [60].

'A KIND OF SOCIAL-DEMOCRATIC SAINT'
A miracle in Paris

'The West was officially setting up the regime of the Islamic republic' [61].

*   *

*

When he arrived in Paris for his 'respectability internship', ayatollah Khomeini was only a prelate of a certain importance, of course, but he was far from being one of the highest ranking members of the Shiite hierarchy. He only benefited from a limited fame in Iran and from virtually no fame at all in the world.

It was necessary then to give him a certain calibre, a biography as an 'emblematic leader', 'to build up' the man, as someone who was close to him at the time wrote later on, once he had become a dissident [62].

His Indian origin was concealed, whereas there was nothing degrading about it.

His father, a simple scribe at the service of a local feudal lord, was made into 'the leader of the Khomein community'. It was a lie.

This father who was killed in a fight and whose murderer had been tried and hanged at the beginning of the century, was to be 'assassinated' on Reza Shah's order, when the latter only ascended to the throne twenty-five years later! He had thus become the son of a 'martyr'. It was another lie.

It was said that his life had been 'an anti-imperialist assault course'. It was a lie. The truth is known.

His son was to be 'assassinated' in 1978 on Mohammad Reza Pahlavi Shah's order as an act of vengeance against the people's uprising 'he was leading'. Yet another lie. This 'martyr' of a son had died of a heart attack due to his bulimia months before.

Finally, people started calling him 'imam'. The idea apparently came from a well-known French journalist born in an Arab country. The title was misused and even blasphemous. 'The 12 imams, the Prophet and his daughter form the terrestrial manifestation of the metaphysical totality of the 14 'Impeccables'. It is here a unique whole with 14 aspects. Mahomet is its exoteric side, and the imams are the esoteric one. Fatima is the confluence of both sides' [63]. Such is the indisputable Shiite point of view. The person who, in Paris, had launched the title of imam probably ignored this 'detail'. 'The imam does not represent the same functions for the Sunnites and the Shiites. The word imam, or 'guide' is usually used for the person who directs ritual prayers. It is also, in this general meaning, a personality of authority in a religious discipline. For the Shiites, however, the imam refers to Ali and his descendants [the lineage of the twelve imams], who have superhuman qualities and reflect the perfect essence of the cosmic and metaphysical imam, the very representation of his divine manifestation' [64].

These considerations were not to be taken into account in the media campaign that was launched to 'build up' the man. Some time later, the false title was to be consecrated by the Constitution of the Islamic republic. Indeed, Ruhollah Khomeini never pretended himself that he was an imam, but he went further than that when he proclaimed that his mission was to 'add the finishing touches to the work the Prophet could not finish on earth' [65]. He even said that the institutions that came from the revolution 'are unique in the world history... even superior to those of the dawn of Islam' [66].

It was yet another lie and blasphemy.

*   *

*

'A KIND OF SOCIAL-DEMOCRATIC SAINT'
'A miracle in Paris'

As soon as ayatollah Khomeini had settled down in Neauphle-le-Château, the media in the whole world became the instruments of the propaganda of the Iranian revolution, with a special role played by the television, a few radio stations and certain French newspapers. For four months, the whole world had its eyes riveted on the man. According to a French source, a total of one hundred and thirty-two interviews and fifty public declarations that were carefully retranscribed were to be organized for him [67].

At the beginning, the journalists could meet up with the host of Neauphle-le-Château for long periods of time. 'Professionals' were to rapidly rationalize these meetings during which, despite the presence of interpreters, slip-ups were not excluded.

'For three months, he [Khomeini] prepared his ascension to power, lent himself to interviews but knew the questions in advance, and waited for Washington's green light,' Dominique Lorentz wrote in his thorough inquiry on the episode [68].

If the questions were obligatorily given in advance, the answers were also prepared in the same way. Nothing was left to chance. Ibrahim Yazdi, an American citizen who was the ayatollah's main advisor and acted as a real 'officer in charge' then, was to give the following testimony twenty years later in Tehran, in an 'authorized'* publication: 'The method we had thought of for interviews was the following one: we would ask the journalists to give us their questions and told them 'Since Mr Khomeini does not speak any foreign language, we will translate your questions, we will get Mr Khomeini's answers and then translate them to give them to you'. With such a method, everything was organized and was under control... Since the questions were usually the same, Mr Khomeini put

---
* Literal translation.

439

a committee in charge of preparing the answers to draft them and then shown to him so he could check them out. Then he said that he did not need to see the answers'...'So the journalist would come, sit down near the imam, ask the questions he had given us beforehand, but the only translated answers he would get were the ones that had been prepared' [69]. As for Ibrahim Yazdi, he deems that there were 'about four hundred' press interviews that were thus 'organized under control' (by whom? For whom?) during the '112 days at Neauphle-le-Château'.

Even the interviews were made up.
Ayatollah Khomeini was made to say: 'We are for a regime of total freedom. The future regime must be a regime of liberty' [70]. 'The people's rights, notably those of the religious minorities, are respected [71]... are unique in the history of the world...even superior to those at the dawn of Islam'. 'I give myself no other function but that of the spiritual leader of the nation' [72]. The future foreign policy of Iran was to be geared 'neither towards the West, nor towards the East' and the country would not have to take positions in the conflict between Israel and the Arab countries' [73]. 'The Islamic government is a democratic government, in the real sense of the term' [74]. ' We are going to dissolve the Savak and all the leftist organizations will be able to express their opinions freely' [75]. 'Culprits must be neither insulted nor slapped' [76]. Women, like men, have a right of participation in the political and social fields. Women, like men, have the right to elect and be elected when the government is to be formed' [77].
Etc...
Everything that public opinion wished to hear and should hear.

*   *

*

'A KIND OF SOCIAL-DEMOCRATIC SAINT'
'A miracle in Paris'

A whole section of the Western, especially French, intelligentsia hailed it as a divine surprise. Support committees were created. Jean-Paul Sartre, Simone de Beauvoir and especially Michel Foucault were their leaders. Saint-Germain-des-Prés had found a new cause to defend and to promote, and mobilized to support Ruhollah Khomeini.

Michel Foucault went to Iran twice – in September and in November 1978 – and wrote a series of eulogistic articles on Ruhollah Khomeini in the quality Western press, notably in *Le Monde*. He met him at least once in Neauphle-le-Château, and analysed his philosophical stands.

Simone de Beauvoir also went to Iran to support the Islamic revolution. Jean-Paul Sartre contented himself with Parisian stands.

Later on, when Madame de Beauvoir saw how events were turning out, she somewhat rectified her position. As for Michel Foucault, he hardly contented himself with vague regrets [78].

During that period of time, intellectual terrorism forbade all doubts, all questions on the matter.

André Fontaine commented on the event in *Le Monde* by entitling his famous article 'The return of the divine' [79]. By comparing Ruhollah Khomeini with John-Paul II, he evoked 'the need for an identity, the essential element of consubstantial dignity for man' that the man's triumph inspired in him, and dreamt that 'the representatives of revealed religions [might] meet to see what they could do for peace in the world, since the bright minds had failed'. The article was translated and created quite a stir in Iran.

Jacques Madaule, still in the same daily [80], saw in the Khomeini movement 'some clamour which came from the depths of time, that of a people who once more refuse servitude, and the chains brought about by foreign countries' and he concluded with: 'Who knows after all, if the Iranian people's passion does not open the doors of the future to the human being'.

Gabriel Matzneff lucidly remarks that 'the impetuous ayatollah Khomeini is particularly lucky to be a Muslim and not a Christian. If a Russian Orthodox bishop staying in Paris suddenly started pronouncing anathemas upon Mr Brezhnev and vehemently inviting his country to rise up against the Soviet regime, it would provoke a general outcry. The left would drag the obscurantist bearded popes through the mud, and our Minister of the Interior would immediately take the necessary measures to silence the inopportune prelate'. This being said, the philosopher and writer still thinks that ayatollah Khomeini's attitude 'in the religious order is undoubtedly necessary and productive' [81].

The socialist Party led by François Mitterrand proclaimed its 'resolute support' to the movement [82]. The SP organized a public demonstration in its support and its executive office saluted the victory of the Islamic revolution on February 14th 1979: 'a popular movement of an exceptional dimension in contemporary history' [83].

Nobody had bothered to go and see what was going on behind the scenes in Neauphle-le-Château, or to read what the man had actually written. They did not want to know.

When things went wrong and when the truth broke out, none of these good souls, with the exception of one or two, expressed any regret. They looked away. They forgot everything, but they did not learn anything.

*   *

*

'A KIND OF SOCIAL-DEMOCRATIC SAINT'
'A miracle in Paris'

There was a certain gullibility, illusion and hysteria even among a few Iranian intellectuals.
The National Front, which had long ago been founded by Mossadegh, and which held a traditionally secular discourse, proclaimed: 'Khomeini is coming. The man who has made the cry for freedom reach the sky, the man who has crushed dictatorship and injustice, the man who has won over imperialism, the greatest man of the century is coming!...
Khomeini is coming. The man who symbolizes the dreams and ideals of a people, of the whole world, is coming...
In the whole history of humanity, this is the first time that the sun is rising in the West and coming to the East' [84].
The leftist writers Gholam Hossein Saedi and Mostafa Rahimi, the poets Djalal Sarfaraz and Freidun Guilani, the woman of letters Simine Danechvar, to name only a few, published laudatory texts on the 'imam'.
The most impassioned of all the sycophants was probably the journalist Ali Asghar Haj Sayed Djavadi, who was also a 'militant' for human rights after having been chief editor of the unofficial famous evening newspaper of the Iranian capital, *Ettela'ât* for a long time.

He published a 'prayer' by Taha Hedjazi in his weekly, *Djonbech*, which immediately became the official 'project' of the revolution:

> *'Where the imam returns to*
> *No-one will lie any more*
> *No-one will lock their doors*
> *People will all become brothers and sisters*
> *They will share their sadness and their joy*
> *In a spirit of justice and sincerity*
> *There will be no more waiting lines*
> *For bread and meat*

For oil and petrol
For the cinema and for the bus
The imam must come back
So that the Good settles on the throne
And the Evil and treason and grief
Disappear for ever and ever.'

The same intellectual, as so many other admirers at the time, who is today forced to live in exile, started one of his editorials in *Kayhan* like this:
'Let's greet the dawn laden with blood and legends...
Oh you, History! Be our witness that after so many sacrifices and efforts on our dear Iranian soil, this dawn which is covered in blood, this splendid dawn shall come and settle on it'. And he talked about ayatollah Khomeini as of 'the unique symbol of the Martyr, of Faith and Humanity' [86].

This was how the 'media bubble' was launched. The press, the radio, the television in the whole world gave Khomeini the calibre of a historical figurehead. This publicity played a double part. In Tehran, the crowds discovered the importance ayatollah Khomeini had gathered in foreign countries and they displayed thousands of copies of his portrait. In the world, the sight of his popularity in the streets of the Iranian capital gave him more importance.

*   *

*

Ruhollah Khomeini was presented to world opinion as a 'brilliant philosopher and theologian' [87], 'an example for all, and even his worst enemies have never been able to contest it' [88]. The various opuscules he made especially dealt with

'A KIND OF SOCIAL-DEMOCRATIC SAINT'
'A miracle in Paris'

'the way to urinate and to defecate', 'purity and impurity', and 'women and their periods'. In the others, one could here and there find a few thoughts of a philosophical, religious or political order: 'It is proved that the Western physicians are totally ignorant' [89], 'The women from the Prophet of Islam's lineage have their menopause at the age of sixty. The others at over the age of fifty' [90].

As for cultural matters:
'Music engenders immorality, lechery, licentiousness and stifles courage, bravery and gentlemanly behaviours; it is forbidden in the Koranic law and must not be taught in schools... It is not allowed to play the drums during competitions. It is also forbidden to play military music during military ceremonies' [91].
'If you want independence for this country, eliminate music from the radio and television programmes. Suppress it!' [92], 'The radio and television must prohibit songs, music, anti-Islamic laws, praises to tyrants, mendacious words, and the programmes which spread doubt and shatter virtue' [93]...

And for political issues:
'All the governments in the world rest on the power of bayonets. We do not know of a monarchy or republic in today's world which is based on equity and reason; they only stay in power thanks to oppression'...

'The leaders of our country have been so much influenced by the West that they have set the official time in their country on that of Europe [Greenwich]. This is a nightmare.

'Jews – may God abase them – have manipulated the editions of the Koran which were published in their occupation zones. These Jews and their supporters' aims are to destroy

445

Islam and to establish a universal Jewish government... May God preserve us from it...' [95]. 'It is a shame to be under the orders of a section head who is Jewish' [96].

'Islam alone is to govern' [97].

'Those who want to set up democracy want to drag our country into corruption and perdition. They are worse than the Jews. They must be hanged. They are not men. They have the blood of animals. Be they damned' [97].

'All the laws in the world, except those of the Islamic republic, come from a handful of idiotic syphilitics. They are null and void. Islam does not recognize any other law but its own in the world' [99].

Dozens of other examples could be given [100].

Finally, here are a few examples from the culture of the 'great theologian and philosopher':

'Empedocles, a great philosopher who lived under the reign of King David whose philosophy he learnt'* [101].

'Pythagoras, a philosopher at the time of King Solomon whom he owes his knowledge and wisdom to'** [102].

'Socrates, a great theologian. He learnt philosophy from Pythagoras and devoted himself totally to theology and ethic. He discarded worldly pleasures, took refuge in a cave in the mountains where he fully dedicated himself to the only God. He tried to convince people of other gods than the real one. After what he had said, the people demanded from the Sultan that he should be put to death. The latter was forced into it and poisoned him' [103]. No comments!

---

* David, the founder of Jerusalem and King of Israel (from 1010 to 970 BC). Empedocles, a Greek philosopher, physician and legislator of the 5th century BC.

** Solomon, David's son and successor, reigned from 970 to 931 BC, and had the Temple built from 969 to 962 BC. Pythagoras, a Greek mathematician and philosopher, lived in the 6th century BC.

'A KIND OF SOCIAL-DEMOCRATIC SAINT'
A miracle in Paris

'Aristotle was the son of Nikomachos from Stagira, one of the greatest philosophers in the world. Avicenna said that nobody was ever able to contradict his theories. Yet, the French Descartes thought he had discovered flaws in them later on; specialists, however, can easily realize how childish and groundless Descartes's claims in philosophical and theological matters were. Woe betide us Muslims for being intimidated by the West, for taking our own level of knowledge lightly when the Westerners will not be able to reach it before a thousand years' [104].

Soon after the man's arrival in Neauphle-le-Château, rumours about his writings reached the American Administration. What was to follow is known*.

Translations appeared in Paris after the triumph of the revolution in Iran. It was laughed about in the salons and forgotten.

These men's writings are nevertheless considered to be infallible in Iran today. They cannot be questioned without risking serious trouble, including capital punishment**.

After the triumph of the revolution, Ruhollah Khomeini escaped people's control. As the absolute Master of Iran, he said what he thought and did everything in his power to ensure the establishment of 'God's first government on earth' [105].

Indeed, a few phrases were said which made people smile: he gave the order to the Iranian Air Force to destroy

---

* See Chapter XII: Iran and the West – Ambiguous relations.
** 'The most important of all sciences, the only authentic one, is the one of the Imam's knowledge [Khomeini], the others only deal with epiphenomena'. This is what the one who was at the time 'the highest scientific authority in the country' declared in 1984, Dr Abbas Sheybani, the rector of the University of Tehran, president of the Order of Physicians and former Minister, *Kayhan* (from London), September 11th 1984.

American satellites, and to the Ministry of Agriculture, to flood the American market with Iranian wheat so as to make the economy of the 'Great Satan' become totally dependent*.

Other words, on the contrary, did not make people smile:

'We must give rise to repeated crises, and give a new and better value to the idea of death and martyrdom...If Iran disappears in the future, it is not important; what is important is to drown the whole world in a situation of crisis' [106].

'All the existing forms of corruption are the products of the nation and of nationalism' [107]. 'Those who think they are Iranian and who believe they must work for Iran are wrong' [108].

'Islam alone is to govern' [109]. 'We cannot grant some of the freedom we granted at the beginning. We cannot let political parties go on with their activities. We can only use violence against these wild beasts' [110].

The decree for the nomination of the first Islamic Head of Government already mentioned that 'according to the law of Islam, any opposition will be considered as a blasphemy' [111].

'Those who oppose us are like malignant tumours. They must be removed from society' [112].

'We deem that criminals must not be tried. They must be killed' [113]. 'The people who are in prison are criminals. Their identities must be checked, that is enough, and they must be killed. There is no need to try culprits. They must be killed' [114].

'Blood must be spilled, for the more Iran bleeds, the more the revolution will triumph' [115]. 'Blood must flow' [116].

---

* The official title given to the United States of America.

'A KIND OF SOCIAL-DEMOCRATIC SAINT'
'A miracle in Paris'

'The mother who reported her son so that he would be tried and hanged is an example for the people. It is a model of Islam. If your children, brothers and sisters do not follow the given advice [?], report them so that they can be chastised' [117]. 'Our dear pupils must keep a close watch on their teachers. The teachers must keep a close watch on themselves. The pupils, my dear children must keep a close watch on one another and report any deviation' [118].

'Israel must burn to ashes' [119]
Hundreds of other sentences could be quoted.

The regime that originated in the revolution applied ayatollah Khomeini's 'real discourse' with a frightening zeal. The people with a good conscience who had shown enthusiasm for the man looked away, kept quiet and let things happen, as had been the case long ago with so many other bloodthirsty dictators.

Khomeini was not 'a sort of social-democratic saint, a religious figure who was to be fundamentally admired', as the American ambassador to the UNO had said [120]. 'Imam Khomeini is a miracle in the whole history of human kind, there has never been a leader who could compare, and I do not think there will be another one', an eminent advisor from the White House had written, before adding that 'he had made the most beautiful moment in the history of Islam come true, the model of a peaceful revolution without a bloodshed, the example of a humanist government' [121].

Blindness, insincerity or simply hatred for a country were not solely germanopratine.

There was not the slightest regret shown on the other side of the Atlantic either.

'With Khomeini, Iran did not go back twenty years in time, but a century', a Franco-American analyst wrote recently [122].

Was it not the 'miracle' one expected?

'Even if it is recognized that Khomeini's character is very charismatic, it also incarnates one of the possible metamorphoses of pure Evil in people's minds, next to Hitler, Stalin and Pol Pot' [123]. How many famous Western intellectuals would still dare to show such clear-sightedness today?

*   *

*

The Shah having left Iran on January 16th 1979, the ayatollah hesitated on making his way home. He was openly negotiating with Western powers. The fear of a display of strength by the army paralyzed him. He postponed his departure several times although his supporters kept waiting for him at the international airport of Tehran [124], and the appointed Prime Minister, Chapour Bakhtiar, was only there to hand over the keys to him*.

On February 1st, he finally arrived with two hundred journalists in an Air France aeroplane which had been named Liberté ('Liberty') on the occasion**.

He granted an interview to the representatives of the Iranian national Radio and Television while he was on the aeroplane. The journalist asked him, among other things: 'What are Your Holiness's feelings on finding His way back home after so many years?'

'Hitshi' ('Zilch') 'His Holiness' answered. Everything had just been said, in substance and form. The future was to prove it.

---

* See chapter XVI: The fall of the monarchy and the triumph of the revolution – The handing-over of keys.
** The airline company was to ask for the payment of the rental of that aeroplane for years. Has it finally been paid? It was never said.

'A KIND OF SOCIAL-DEMOCRATIC SAINT'
A miracle in Paris

His life belongs to history between that day and June 5th 1989, the day he died.

On January 17th 1979, Ruhollah Khomeini was still the host of Neauphle-le-Château with the means, protection and facilities that are known, and Valéry Giscard d'Estaing was to declare to the Cabinet: 'The government is not to bear judgment or to intervene in events which are and must remain the responsibility of the Iranian people themselves' [125]. He was to have added in private: 'With Khomeini, we will finally have a stable situation in Iran' [126].

A few clashing opinions were soon to be buried under the clamour of the right-minded people.

Danièle Martin had written at the time: 'France has no political stand in this case, it lags behind and believes it is avant-garde, even if it is to deplore the blood flowing in Tehran tomorrow' [127].

*   *

*

A book of sometimes well written poems was published in Tehran soon after the imam's disappearance. It was officially attributed to Ruhollah Khomeini. Love, loyalty, exhilaration and beauty were celebrated in it – in a figurative and mystical sense, some people said.

The regime had a mausoleum built for him in 600,000 square metre landscaped gardens. It has a solid gold dome on its top. The funerary monument cost over 2 billion dollars [128] and is bigger than those dedicated to all the saints of Islam.

He had never stopped denouncing the personality cult he believed Mohammad Reza Pahlavi Shah to be the object of. It did not stop him conferring on himself the title of 'idol breaker' in the Constitution of the Islamic republic, among a dozen other titles.

Was it a last deception or the man's hypocrisy?

Chapter XII

IRAN AND THE WEST
Ambiguous relations

From the Second World War on, the tripartite treaty and especially the Azerbaijan crisis, Iran had been rightly taken for an ally of the West, especially of the United States. During the quarter of a century preceding the revolution, the country had a pivotal role in the defensive measures of the 'free world' when faced with Soviet expansionism.

There were privileged relations with the United States of America: It was the entry of Iran in the allied camp to face the Axis powers which rapidly created this situation.

When faced with the non-desired and awkward presence of Great Britain and of the Soviet Union who were allies, in theory, but who wished to interfere, Iran practised its traditional diplomacy and looked for alliances that could counterbalance the wishes.

All along the 19th century, this role was meant to be played by France, the Austro-Hungarian Empire and already the United States. Then, under Reza Shah, it was still played by France, but also by Germany. After the Second World War and the bipolarization of international affairs, the support of the United States had more clout and had become necessary when faced with a threatening USSR.

Without Washington and President Harry Truman's backing, Ahmad Ghavam would have found it difficult to defeat Joseph Stalin. It is true that this backing was an established privilege for other countries, but they had not had to resist. Iran had the historic chance of having a man who was as clever and sturdy as Ghavam at its head.

During the oil crisis, the American diplomatic attitude evolved considerably. It first supported Mossadegh's nationalist movement. It is true that it also favoured the interests of big American oil companies which were the rivals of British Petroleum. The latter had a monopoly of the exploitation of Iranian oil and shamelessly took great pleasure out of it.

When the Republicans came to power in the United States (1953), Washington favoured the downfall of the 'old lion' and the establishment of an authoritarian monarchy with London's backing, that time. They both worried about the deadlock situation the great nationalist leader's policy was in, and especially the swift rise to power of the communists, and thus of the Soviet Union in Iran.

This was how the country collapsed into the Western camp for a quarter of a century. The American influence became the determining factor. For eight years, from August 1953 until the return to power of the Democrats in 1961, Iran benefited from the full support of the United States, not only in its sometime clashing relations with the USSR, but also in the realization of its development projects. Some friction could not be avoided, as when Iran was given a negative answer concerning the realisation of its ambitious industrial projects by international authorities (IBRD and IMF) which the Shah knew were subjected to Washington.

A long parenthesis was opened with the Kennedy administration, with the scheme of a pro-American coup d'État against the Shah which was organized by the Head of the Savak, Bakhtiar, and that the host of the White House had given the impression of favouring, and the episode of Ali Amini's pro-American Cabinet.

Under Johnson's presidency and even more so under Richard Nixon's, Iran became again Washington's privileged and untouchable ally until 1974.

*   *

*

Some concern about the Iranian attitude nevertheless appeared from time to time in the high spheres of American diplomacy.

On August 6th 1966, the American ambassador to Iran, Armin H. Meyer, wrote the following to his department, worried about a change of political direction in the country: 'The September 1965 crisis between India and Pakistan has convinced the Shah that an excessive dependency of Iranian defence on the United States could have in store the same fate for Iran as for Pakistan. Iran wanted its freedom of movement' [1].

In another document which dates back to April 1974, there is concern over Iran's oil policy and its will to help developing countries – a policy which 'could divert from our objectives' [2]. In July of the same year, it was Iran's will to 'rely on its own military and industrial force' which was underlined [3]. Another 'analysis' was sent shortly afterwards and insisted on the 'growing complexity' [4] of Iranian-American relations.

On June 24th 1974, a long 'analysis' written in a worried tone revealed 'the increasing Iranian power' and concluded that 'It [Iran] should not be given a blank cheque' [5].

On May 1976, ambassador Richard Helms, the former Head of the CIA, was appointed to Tehran, and recalled 'the loss of trust the Shah and the Iranian government showed in the United States' capacity and relevance as Iran's main supplier of weapons' [6].

Despite the excellence of the relations between both countries, it could only be noted in the United States that the Shah had become more confident in the increasing power of his country, and did not hesitate any more to use hard or even threatening words when dealing with Washington.

Indeed, from the middle of the sixties and even before the beginning of the seventies, there was only talk of 'the policy of national independence' in official Iranian circles, and the example of De Gaulle's diplomacy was to be constantly and openly mentioned [7]. Washington found all this very irritating.

When alluding to the General, the Shah said later on: 'The Iranian people gave him an extraordinary welcome. Why? Because General De Gaulle represents everything that is most prestigious in our people's eyes. The people from our country love patriots, those who stand up against everything when it is in their country's interest, people who are courageous. Why wasn't the same enthusiasm shown to other visitors? Understanding this means discovering my people's mentality, and how everything which is patriotic has very deep roots in this country' [8].

*   *

*

From the beginning of the seventies, Iran progressively diversified its supply sources in weapons and military equipment. The United States of course remained its privileged partner, just like Iran remained its main strategic place in the region.

More and more weapons and military equipment were however bought in other Western countries: France, Italy, Great Britain, West Germany and Israel... Contracts for supplies were also signed with the Soviet Union, notably for the national gendarmerie. The balance of commercial exchanges with the USSR was vastly positive and made the position for negotiations with Moscow comfortable. Czechoslovakia was also interested in the matter and the contacts had gone far enough in 1978 to reach an agreement.

Iran had even gone further in launching the creation and rapid development of a sophisticated weapons industry. The obvious goal which was about to be reached was to get to the same level as Israel in that field.

From the middle of the seventies on, the United States did not have a monopoly in that field any more, far from it. It started annoying the Americans. They not only had to share an important market, but they risked to progressively lose an influential lever.

The country's financial means, especially after the oil 'boom', and the competence of Iranian engineers and technicians allowed for all ambitions to come true. Iran wished to reach an advanced level quickly, which, in itself, was not illegitimate at all. It corresponded to its capacity and role in history. The CIA saw in it a sign of 'the Shah's dangerous megalomania', an effect of the 'pawn role the Allies had given him because of he was of shameful common stock' [9]. Although the American Secretary of the Treasury, William Simon, was a Republican, he went so far as to publicly call Mohammad Reza Pahlavi a 'screwball' [10].

Would the leader of a Western country or of Israel have been called a 'dangerous megalomaniac' or a 'screwball' if he had shown such ambitions?

Despite the apparent and official excellence of the bilateral relations, the turning point in American and consequently in Western politics concerning Iran, dates back to the middle of the seventies, and not to President Carter's presidency. He sped up the new deal in Washington and made it become irreversible. It was perhaps written that 'the United States continued to back the Shah until the middle of December 1978... The Shah remained the best Western ally [for Carter]' [11]. It was less and less true, and it was already false in 1978, despite Carter's flattering speech in Tehran on New Year's Eve [12].

'[The Iranian revolution] was the revenge of the West after the Shah's escapades since 1974. Bani Sadr himself asserted that the United States' policy was to get rid of the Shah' [13].

*   *

*

'The Shah has to change his policy or he has to go' Henry Kissinger allegedly declared to the National Security Council in 1974 [14].

This stand seems to have been the outcome or the result of a long process the beginning of which should be found in the OPEC's decision to raise the price of oil, which was described in the West as 'the first oil crisis'. Mohammad Reza Pahlavi had long refused to admit that the Americans and the Western powers had not been his unconditional allies, but he ended up understanding it: 'Since 1974, the Americans have vowed to ruin me. From the middle of the sixties and the agreement Iran had concluded with Mattei*, they started losing trust in me, and in my will to break the shackles imposed on us by the big companies. It got worse and worse as I was getting successful, especially after the oil prices were readjusted at the beginning of the seventies. They are having their revenge now [15].

The Americans were in favour of a moderate increase in oil prices which would not really put them at a disadvantage. The moderate increase was a blow for the economy of their European and Japanese competitors, countries which imported oil and were dependent on it, but it spared the United States which was not dependent on the world market at the time.

Mohammad Reza Pahlavi had the support of King Faisal of Arabia who was to be assassinated as soon as in 1975. He took the initiative to go beyond what would have been agreed on. 'The Shah's and the Americans' interests had stopped being the same... He had the impression the Americans needed him as much as he needed them' [16]. 'The Americans did not want an ally but a vassal. Iran was not a banana republic but a great old country which had known its ups and downs... and retrieved its pride and political independence. There was a gulf between both points of view' [17].

More serious reservations were made on the Iranian attitude at the Head of the American Administration and within the think-tanks and lobbyist groups which gear its diplomacy, the latter giving the impression of being 'privatized,' to use Richard Labéviere's expression [18].

Some Ministers of the republican Administration,

---

* He was the President of AGIP, an Italian national oil company. His plane exploded during one of his trips. His policy annoyed that of the important oil companies.

William Simon, James Schlesinger, and then Donald Rumsfeld led a campaign to that effect. It was widely echoed in the American press.

Henry Kissinger's attitude when he tried to spare the Shah and not jeopardize the sale of American weapons to Iran showed a better awareness of the situation: 'When Mr Kissinger, who was Secretary of State at the time, spoke in front of the American National Security Council, in August 1974, he declared: 'If the Shah can maintain his present line of conduct in political and oil matters within the framework of the OPEC, he may logically believe that his regional influence will continue to grow...There will come a day when we will have to test him personally. There is no doubt that he is following a policy which will allow him one day to put such pressure on us that we will be led to consider him as non-productive or even counter-productive. He is dreaming of turning his country into a great power, not so much thanks to our help than through the help of some incentives his Russian neighbours might give him. Some of us here, think that the Shah must change his policy or that we must replace him' [20].

It was a cold and cynical analysis. The Shah was reproached for first taking into account Iranian interests and leading a national policy.

Iran's will to openly declare to be liberated from the American influence and to be an ally, a friend and a reliable partner for the West – not a 'pawn' – went directly against the objectives of Washington's diplomacy.

'The promotion of Islamic fanaticism that is inspired by Henry Kissinger and Zbigniew Brzezinski which aimed at promoting the creation of denominational States in the area could be of great use to American interests...The promotion of Koranic principles which would stop the development of any possible modernization in Muslim countries, would be of ideal benefit to American and Western capitalism. It would impart these under-developed countries with the status of a simple consumer's market for industrial products' [21]. This is what professor Nicolas Nasr, a Lebanese political scientist, wrote in 1983.

The ruin of the Iranian economy since 1979, the flight of capital, and even more so, the brain drain to the West, confirm that analysis.

The French political scientist, Alexandre Del Valle, goes in the same direction. A great part of his work, *Islamisme et États-Unis*, is on the Iranian revolution. He also places the beginning of the destabilization process of Iran in the middle of the seventies, because of the concern raised by Iranian ambitions:

'For Americans, the areas which are rich in raw material must remain, politically and economically speaking, weak, 'feeble' zones which are likely to harbour many potential consumers, without being able to become powerful States either, from a political, military and technological point of view. They must stay 'dependent' and thus remain 'soft-bellied'.

Although imperial Iran was anti-communist, its political, economic and military emancipation made it more and more difficult to manipulate for American secret services. That is why the latter decided to make sure that the revolution which was germinating in Iran – and which was due to the communists as well as to the Shiite clergy – should be taken over by the unknown octogenarian Ruhollah Khomeini. They were thus using their denominational lever, as usual.' [22]

*   *

*

A few options or suggestions made by Iranian diplomacy were to increase the discontent or tension towards the country, and thus reinforced the will to destabilize the imperial regime:

– the suggestion aiming at concluding a military security pact for the Persian Gulf and the Indian Ocean so as to 'bring them under control', thus eliminating the military forces of the non-neighbouring countries, meaning the American and Soviet forces first. Iran had the means to become the pivot of the pact. It had perfectly well demonstrated it in its military intervention for the pacification of the Oman sultanate, where the British had failed [23].

– The insistence of the Tehran diplomacy to see the denuclearizing of the Near and Middle-East. It was addressed to the Hebrew State, and irritated it.

– The acquisition of 10% of Eurodif's capital and the construction of four nuclear plants had made people fear that Iran might eventually, if it wished to, have nuclear weapons. The country had the necessary financial means, and especially the human resources. Its leaders kept repeating that they did not really mean to. It is known today that they were sincere, but the national and international ambitions shown by the Shah led people to believe the opposite, and inspired suspicion. 'In 1977, the United States decided to be done with the Shah... He managed to own some of Eurodif's capital. In five years' time, [Iran] was to become a nuclear power...He has to be overthrown...As usual, we are going to support an opponent to the current regime and secretly organize his rise to power...' [24]

Iran was trying to realign its diplomatic relations with the two great blocs and, in the middle of the sixties, it decided to officially proclaim that it would not authorize the setting-up of any foreign military base on its territory. It was reassuring news for its important Northern neighbour, but it obviously displeased its Western allies, and most particularly the United States.

Iran's attitude in the Arab-Israeli conflict was undoubtedly the last and main reason for the American discontent. Already in 1949, Iran had de facto recognized the Hebrew State. Iran was a country where the anti-Semitic feeling was completely non-existent and went against the cultural and national traditions – Had Cyrus the Great not been the 'liberator' of the Jewish people who had been deported to Mesopotamia? – The relations between the two countries which were bonded by numerous old links that were cultural and strategical, were excellent. The military, technical and scientific cooperation was constant. Iran had played a determining role in the evacuation of the Jewish community from Iraq after the first Arab-Israeli war. The Israelis were grateful for it.

These excellent relations had naturally not really prevented the support of Iran to the Palestinian cause, the right this people had to own a State, to find the honour and dignity of having a homeland. They existed despite the evident hostility of the Palestinian organizations towards Iran and their support to the Iranian radical opposition.

It was the episode of the Yom Kippur war in October 1973 which put a final end to the atmosphere of trust between Tehran, Washington and Tel-Aviv.

A few months before the beginning of the hostilities by the Egyptians and the Syrians – the only military half-success of the Arabs in their long confrontation with Israel – President Sadat had stopped in Tehran on his way back from Karachi to Cairo. Mohammad Reza Pahlavi was in the provinces. He interrupted his trip and went to the international airport of Mehrabad, in Tehran. Both men had a tête-à-tête conversation which lasted over three hours. There was no particular reason for the meeting and no reason was given. Did the Rais mention his intentions to the Shah then? It was considered to be the case later on and the Sovereign was reproached for not warning Washington.

During the months that preceded the Yom Kippur war, the Shah, Hoveyda, his Prime Minister, and Ardeshir Zahedi, his ambassador to Washington, were often heard insisting on the fact that 'a stable peace was necessary' between the Arabs and the Israelis, and that it should start between Egypt, the natural leader of the Arab camp, and the Hebrew State. The Shah used to tell whoever wanted to hear it that 'the Arabs would have to come out of their state of permanent losers, of humiliation, and find their honour back' to reach this state of stable peace.

On the eve of the Egyptian intervention, which took the Israelis and Americans by total surprise, and that is why it was successful at first, Anwar El Sadat went to Tehran to meet Mohammad Reza Pahlavi. His trip remained entirely secret. Were the American and Israeli intelligence services aware of it? It is most likely.

Both men then had a long conversation in the summer palace of the imperial family in Saad-Abad. Ambassador Amir Aslan Afshar, the future grand master of protocol, who had no official function in the capital at the time, was the one who went to fetch the Rais at the airport and then took him back there to catch his plane [25].

What did both heads of State say to each other? Nobody knows. Did they evoke the very next operation against Israel?

Did Sadat make sure he would get the support of Iran and of its Sovereign? It is a possibility.

As soon as the operation had been launched, and the Egyptian army had crossed the Suez Canal, the Shah authorized Soviet cargo planes to cross the Iranian air space to ship military equipment to Cairo, and he overlooked the protests from Washington and Tel-Aviv. Then, he had a billion dollar emergency aid granted to Egypt.

Iran was thus to play an important role in the half-success of the Egyptians. Arab opinion considered the operation to be a victory, the first over the Hebrew State and its American allies and protectors.

This was how the conditions for the negotiation of an honourable 'stable peace' were reached. They led to the Camp David agreements. Mohammad Reza Pahlavi and his emissaries played an active role in their preparatory phase.

Iran and its king's attitude were never to be forgiven however. It was thought that the Shah could have and should have warned his American and Israeli allies, and that he had failed in his duty. Iran should not have allowed the crossing of its air space by the Soviet cargo planes and granted Egypt an emergency aid.

It was to be another reason for American suspicion against the Shah. The Tehran-Tel-Aviv relations greatly suffered from it.

During the Iranian revolution, Iran was to lack Israeli support. Only General Rabin, the former and future Prime Minister, and a great visionary if there is to be one, rose against that attitude which he considered suicidal [26].

*   *

*

This was how reasons for discontent accumulated against the direction of Iranian politics during the early years of the seventies. Did the Tehran leaders, with the Shah in first position, feel apprehensive about this change of attitude and the use of the increase in domestic dissatisfaction by foreign powers?

'During the month of October 1977, Giscard took an official trip to Iran. He had, in all likelihood, been put in charge of warning the Shah that France and the United States would drop him unless he and his OPEC friends revised their position towards Westerners. The Shah might have overestimated his power. He did not yield' [27]. This is what Dominique Lorentz wrote.

The atmosphere during the trip, despite the apparent smiles, also seemed to be abysmal. The protocol was not always respected, even if there were only derisory incidents [28], but it should not be the only explanation. The Franco-Iranian relations, which had been excellent under De Gaulle – and this is only a euphemism, 'I do not think that Charles De Gaulle would have acted like that... But it was different then' [29], the Shah said later on – were good during Georges Pompidou's presidency despite a regretful incident during the Persepolis celebrations [30]. After having become normal, if not excellent, again, they deteriorated during the last year of the monarchy, especially from the moment the Giscard d'Estaing couple went to Iran. 'My brother never said the French president's name again', Prince Gholam Reza Pahlavi wrote [31].

*   *

*

There had been enough warnings though.

In 1977, two of the highest authorities from Turkey made the Iranian Sovereign know through a former ambassador to Ankara, that Washington was preparing 'a coup' involving certain religious authorities, and that he should beware of Americans [32].

Count Alexandre de Marenches' testimony is even more explicit, and of utmost importance because of his position, and also because of the esteem the Shah had for him: 'One day, I mentioned to the Shah the names of those who, in the United States, were in charge of envisaging his departure and his replacement. I had even taken part in a meeting where one of the questions was 'How do we get around making the Shah leave, and who do we replace him with?'

'The Shah did not want to believe me.' He said: 'I believe everything you said, except one thing.' 'Why does Your Majesty not believe me on that point as well?'I asked. 'Because it would be stupid to replace me! I am the best defender of the West in this part of the world... It would be so absurd that I cannot believe it.' He replied.

Count de Marenches concluded by saying: 'The Americans had indeed made up their minds' [33].

The Shah declared to the press: 'Can the United States, the non-communist nations allow to lose Iran? What will you do the day Iran is about to collapse? If you do not support your friends who spend their own money and are ready to give their own blood, you risk a military holocaust or other Vietnams' [34]. The future was to prove him right.

*   *

*

By counting on Ruhollah Khomeini to destabilize Iran, by 'building him up' already in Neauphle-le-Château to turn him into a 'charismatic leader' who was capable of subverting the country, the architects of the operation thought they could reach several objectives: stop the country's impetus, put an end to its ambitions and to the 'megalomania' of its leaders, get rid of the Shah whose regime was going through hard times – which was true but not really worse than in other countries, including those which like to teach the whole world lessons – and lead a team to power that could be easily manipulated but that would also be acceptable to public opinion thanks to its 'Islamic' denominational aspect.

The first phase of the operation was successful but the second failed. The wave of radical and violent Islamism that was launched by a few people who played at being God attests to it.

* *

*

The Shah of Iran who had so much wished and striven so that his country would be the 'oak', and would not bend like the reed, only seemed to have realized the international dimension of the Iranian crisis during the year of 1977. He only partially realized it and would not admit it. His State visit to the United States in November 1977 was a serious warning. The anti-Shah demonstrations were 'run like clockwork', according to his own words, and the obstacles on his supporters' demonstrations should have been an eye-opener fro him. He still thought he could master the situation. He was wrong and it was a serious mistake on his behalf. The domestic destabilization process had been launched.

He should have resisted the West when all his attempts at quietening the situation down had failed. He should have made reforms, lessened or eliminated the importance of vulnerable aspects of the system in the country so as to be better armed against outside machinations. King Hassan II and President Sadat strongly advised him to do so, and King Hussein of Jordan did the same. 'Sadat and Hussein [from Jordan] strongly advised me to stay and put an end to the mess. The Chinese did the same, in their own way and probably for other reasons' he said later [35]. 'Hussein [from Jordan] was right. In the early autumn [1978], he called me and said: 'What the Americans are doing in Iran is what they had tried to do with me in 1973 [the so-called Black September episode]. I held fast and quelled the subversion. They ended up negotiating with me; if you cannot give orders which will undoubtedly cause a-free-for-all, give me permission to come to Iran, spend three days in a little office next to yours, and tell the military commanders what they have to do in your name and on your behalf. You will see, everything will be settled, and the Americans will have to shut up' [36] He did not want to shed his people's blood however, like Louis XVI. He was wrong then, to trust his Western 'allies'. He was to bitterly regret it: 'It was a mistake to follow the advice of the Americans and of the British'. 'They [the Americans and the British] wanted me to leave the field open for those who were burning down public buildings, the terrorists and the looters...They were saying that they wanted the liberalization policy to go ahead...' [37].

*   *

*

The theoretical aspect of the explanation given for the American policy, the accusation for the non-respect of human rights meant, in fact, to justify the abandon of their former ally. It was an example of the traditional policy of selective indignation. The explanation was to be found elsewhere: '[Iran] was about to become the sixth military power in the world, thanks to an economic and social modernization that had never been seen on Islamic ground. Now, in American geopolitics, the ally must never be allowed to become too strong as far as his military or economic level is concerned' [38].

The communists, their bedfellows and all the right-minded leftists shared Washington's point of view on that matter. Even the Iranian communist leaders who greeted the Khomeini revolution in eulogistic terms admitted right then that the Americans were its architect and that they were at the origin of the 'neutralization' of the Iranian armed forces [39]. In that circle of influence 'it was absolutely necessary to prevent an imperial, monarchistic and fascistic Iran from achieving the unique, efficient economic take-off in the Third World. A take-off which, if successful, would have proved how inefficient the communist systems that had been adopted a little bit everywhere, were' [40].

The idea of suggesting, from then on, the possibility of the existence of a sort of 'tacit agreement', of a 'disparate coalition' against the Iran of the time, was a step forward which certain observers as the political scientist and journalist Danièle Martin did not hesitate to make. The evolution of events proved them right: 'In the last few years, the Shah wanted to industrialize his country too fast, while rearming it to protect the huge reservoir of oil it had become. The 2,500 kilometres of borders with the USSR, 300 with Afghanistan which was then a Soviet trust territory are enough for one to understand why one must be strong with such neighbours. The Sovereign believed that he would be untouchable in playing buddy-buddy with Moscow and with Washington at the same time. He was forgetting that multinationals, with the Rockefeller group (mainly oil) and American liberals want to be the leaders. Their programme is to control and rule over all the sources of raw material and their distribution all over the planet...This disparate but closely-linked coalition is ready to do anything to overthrow the regime and replace it. It totally disagrees, however, on the economic and political programme to follow...

[They want] to chase away a king who is embarrassing because he is strong and a nationalist, to then establish a compromise between themselves at the expense of Iranian interests' [41].

'Europe and America pretend to help [the Shah] and actually prepare his deposition and the annihilation of his work, for there was no question that a State like Iran could disrupt the established order and energy security of Westerners by getting industrialized. All the more so since the example could spread to neighbouring States'. This is what the political scientist Thierry P. Millemann wrote recently [42]. He, moreover, gives an interesting explanation for the way Khomeini was led to conclude a tactical alliance with the communists [43].

*   *

*

It is most interesting to revise over a quarter of a century later, the considerations, studies and standpoints made across the Atlantic so as to support the option of the Islamic revolution, especially in the eyes of public opinion.

Professor Richard Cottam from the University of Pittsburgh was a very popular advisor at the State Department and at the White House. He talked about the 'Islamic ideology' and believed he knew that 'ayatollah Khomeini was not at all interested in governing' [44].

Another very popular academic from the highest spheres of American power called Richard Falk presented the Islamic revolution like 'the most beautiful moment in the history of Islam, a model for a peaceful revolution without any blood shed, an example of humanistic government' [45].

Another one went even further: 'Imam Khomeini is a miracle in the whole history of human kind; there has been no leader that could compare, and I do not think that there will be another one' [46].

Ambassador Andrew Young, the one who saw 'a sort of saint' in Khomeini, thought that the movement launched by the ayatollah and the objectives of the Iranian revolution were inspired by the ideals of the Universal Declaration of Human Rights [47].

The way the situation was perceived sometimes bordered on the imaginative, if not on delusions: a professor from Rutgers University, called James D. Cockraft, who was highly respected by the Administration, published a 'very complete' presentation of ayatollah Khomeini's 'thoughts and programme' after meeting him and talking to him in Neauphle-le-Château:

– a redistribution of wealth in favour of the oppressed and a reinforcement of the control over the national economy.

– A modern industrialization, with the stress put on basic industries and not on assembly plants.

– A mechanization of agriculture with the exception of agro-business and the stress on ensuring the basic needs of the peasantry.

– A restoration of fundamental human and religious rights in Iran.

– The social protection of women's rights.
– The setting-up of a democratic system based on a multiparty system. The members of the clergy could be elected but they would not hold governmental posts.
– A total freedom for the religious minorities with a representation in Parliament, except for the Baha'is who had political links with the Shah [48].

'The machinery for a worldwide propaganda' if one is to repeat the expression used by Alexander Zinoviev [49], thus succeeded in the disinformation, diabolization and stigmatization that were necessary in that operation.

*   *

*

A few official declarations were of the same style: 'The Shah is one of the most brutal leaders in the history of human kind...The imperial power keeps people in a state of terror and violates human rights in the most cruel conditions' [50], Senator Edward Kennedy said.

A powerful group of the Upper Chamber of the United States that was led by Senator Church launched an open campaign against Iran. The very influential George Ball was sent to Tehran on a special mission. He was, indeed, received by the Shah and a few official personalities. Yet, the people who came rushing to his office which was, strangely enough, located in the building of the national radio and television, and not in his embassy or an embassy-related location, were especially the opponents to the regime who meant to back the fight against the Shah, the head of a State that was supposed to be a friend and an ally.

The military cooperation with Iran was virtually suspended. The big American companies including the ones from the Rockefeller group, started withdrawing from Iran and announced it publicly [51] so as to shake people's confidence.

The United States, Great Britain and Israel refused to sell to Iran the anti-riot equipment that its police forces badly needed [52]. They had not had to face domestic unrest for many years.

'This Administration is different. If the Shah thinks he will get what he wants as far as weaponry is concerned, he is going to have a surprise' [53], an influential member of the White House staff said.

The Voice of America, the Voice of Israel, and especially the BBC which was traditionally much listened to in Iran, became real instruments of propaganda against a regime and a country that were supposed to be their allies. The objectivity of information on the BBC more particularly gave way to disinformation, if not to a simple and pure propaganda – an attitude which goes fully against the British 'way' of doing things. The London radio even broadcasted the orders, hours and places for the demonstrations against the regime and in favour of ayatollah Khomeini, despite the timid protests made in Tehran. 'The BBC engaged in violent attacks against my regime in its programmes in Persian as soon as the beginning of 1978.It was as if a mysterious conductor had given the green light to take the offensive' Mohammad Reza Pahlavi wrote some time later [54].

In the West, 'it was the powerful confederation of Iranian students abroad which organized the first serious protest against the regime. It was encouraged by President Jimmy Carter's declarations on the universal aspect of human rights, but also by the financial largesse of several generous American donors' [55]. The activity of that organization which was a real minority, but which was particularly active had sometimes been denounced by the Iranian authorities. From the middle of the seventies onwards, and at the same time as the new deal on the oil market and the rise to power of Iran happened, it received a more and more obvious support form certain Western circles. It became an instrument for the destabilization of the country which was being manipulated by different people. The phenomenon did not escape certain analysts at the time [56]. It was that group which was at the origin of the organization of particularly violent demonstrations during the last State visit of the imperial couple in the United States in November 1977, 'where no order was given to ensure the personal safety of the Shah and of his spouse, even leaving them physically confronted by the Iranian opposition in Washington' [57].

*   *

*

A certain ignorance of realities was mixed with an angelic-like attitude, and insincerity, especially in official American circles.

Alexandre de Marenches had narrated to one of his close friends the conversation he had had with one of President Carter's advisors. 'He [Count de Marenches] wanted to convince him of what a dangerous new ingredient the Shiite religion was. The other person was taken aback. It could not be a mistake or a bad pronunciation. Alexandre de Marenches spoke perfect English. His interlocutor indeed ignored what the Shiite religion was, at the time when the revolution was starting in Tehran. He believed, the former head of the DGSE reported, that a new brand of whisky had just been created after Chivas, and that it was more or less in the wake of the traffic of new drugs' [58] It is an anecdote, of course, but it is a telltale sign and it would be hard to believe if one did not know how serious the former head of the French intelligence services and author of the testimony was.

There is something less anecdotic but nevertheless official: the American analysts did not have any copy of ayatollah Khomeini's work at their disposal. The State Department apparently did not have them, and neither did the CIA, which had asked the editors of the *Washington Post* if they could lend them a copy [59]. When certain American newspapers published a few extracts from his work, and depicted him as being anti-West, anti-American, anti-Zionist and anti-Semitic, the official authorities in Washington were most unhappy. Henry Precht, who was the person in charge of the Iranian sector at the State Department 'considered the texts, at best, as a collection of notes taken by students, and at worst, as forged' [60].

The *Washington Post* also expressed doubts: 'They were published without their context. The conferences were not held in Arabic. He was speaking to a Persian audience. Why would he have spoken Arabic? I have read the conferences in Persian and I do not find any ground to confirm these so-called anti-Semitic quotations' [61]. There was obviously a certain confusion in the minds of the experts on the great, and for all that, very serious American daily of note concerning the language spoken by ayatollah Khomeini. His writings, even they were often in a kind of gibberish, were in Persian. Arabic is as close to Persian as English is to Russian.

It was only during the winter of 1978-1979 and after a long exchange of correspondence between the United States embassy in Tehran and the Washington authorities, and after inquiries and counter-inquiries ordered by the White House that the existence and veracity of ayatollah Khomeini's books which were all in Persian, of course, were established...

*   *

*

On January 5th 1979, the Guadeloupe conference was opened. President Giscard d'Estaing had invited his 'three major partners' to it, to repeat the term he used himself [62]. The fate of Iran was definitely sealed there. It was written that the French president had been the most virulent head of State against the Shah during the talks, saying that '[if he] stayed on, Iran was on its way to a civil war and a huge blood bath. The communists would become more and more powerful. The American officers would enter the conflict, which would give a pretext to the Soviets to intervene...Washington had to accept the idea of a change' [63]. Valéry Giscard d'Estaing suggested a radically different version and was to have said that: 'At present, the Shah must be supported even if he is isolated and weakened, he has a realistic view of things and still holds the only existing force which is not religious, the army'. According to him, it was Jimmy Carter who first clearly stated that 'the Shah cannot stay on. The Iranian people do not want him any more... But we have no reason to worry' [64].

In fact, the United States gave contradictory messages for several months [65].

On the one hand, it seems that Zbigniew Brzezinski might have been the most suspicious of all at the idea of Ruhollah Khomeini and his supporters taking over power in Iran [66].

The policy followed by the State Department, President Carter's advisors and a great number of politicians, work groups and lobbyists on the other hand, was just the opposite for reasons which they had analysed, and it prevailed.

In Tehran, this attitude was systematically favourable to

the radical opposition movement, according to the documents seized from the United States Embassy. Even the preparations for Ruhollah Khomeini's arrival were supervised so that it could take place in good conditions [68].

The Huyser mission, which was the result of the conference of the four main Western countries where the change of regime was to be organized and finalized, seems in fact, to be the expression of a common decision of the participating countries to which Israel also gave its support because of the worry provoked by the rising power of Iran, and because of its attitude during the Yom Kippur war.

Just after the triumph of the revolution, Messrs Richard Holbrook, Leslie Gelb and Antony Lake, officials who had the power to do so, proclaimed in their report: 'We have become certain that the theocratic system of government adopted by Khomeini was auspicious for American interests in the area' [70].

Disillusionment was not long to occur and the Americans who were responsible for it accused one another of what Pierre Salinger called 'one of the biggest fiascos in history' [71]. President Carter first blamed it on the CIA. In August 1978, the agency had apparently assured him that 'the situation in Iran was neither revolutionary, nor even pre-revolutionary' [72]. As for his ambassador to Tehran, he thought 'he had lost his self-control' [73]. He accused Cyrus Vance, his Secretary of State, of 'having disobeyed him' [74].

Ambassador Sullivan made cutting remarks implicating 'certain civil servants from the State Department [who] allegedly wanted the Shah's downfall at any cost. American diplomacy has been completely wrong concerning Iran's future' [75].

*   *

*

This policy was strongly criticized, even before its consequences had become obvious, i.e. before the rise of radical Islam had taken the current dimensions – 'The West is also to blame in the development of the Islamic cancer' [76], and, of course, ever since.

Jane Kirkpatrick, the ambassador and academic, observed: 'The wrong ideas bring about the wrong consequences' [77].

Alexandre de Marenches wondered a few years back: 'Why did the American Administration of the time condemn and execute its best and most powerful ally in such a volatile and strategically essential area?' The answer, he suggested, was probably to be found in a mixture of short-sightedness, wrong information and historical naivety [78].

The eminent Yale Professor, Thomas Molnar wrote: 'Washington has no long-range objectives'

Robert McNamara had confessed the same failings during the Vietnam war. Was the destruction of Iran's power and ambition a tactical or strategic objective? In the first case, it would have been an error made by the powerful people who ran – and still run – American diplomacy through think-tanks, " 'College boys' who were as enthusiastic as they were ignorant" [80], thus ensuring the execution of their plans. In the second case, the possibility of a real international conspiracy, which so many authors favour, should prevail.

'Mohammad Reza Pahlavi had the grandiose dream of reviving the historical power of the old Persian Empire in a way that would have been even more spectacular than the splendour of the Persepolis celebrations: by restoring, and making of Iran – the fourth world producer in tons of crude oil in 1977 – a new world power whose wealth and might would be enhanced by a particularly favourable geographic situation, and which would arbitrate the opposed influences of America and the Soviet Union' [81] This is what was written in the weekly *L'Express*, in the midst of the revolutionary torment. It was a dream that was shattered by those he believed to be his allies and friends.

'Our erroneous policy concerning Iran provoked the downfall of the Shah. It is a black mark in the history of the United States. It is because of our policy that a fanatical lunatic was able to take over the power in Iran, and to send thousands of Iranians in front of the firing squads' Ronald Reagan said [82]. George Bush, the future president of the United States, also admitted and harshly criticized the American responsibility in the Iranian revolution, and the mistake General Huyser's mission to paralyze the Iranian armed forces was.

Richard Nixon, in an interview [84], Zbigniew Brzezinski in a fundamental work, and Henry Kissinger in an interview in London in *The Economist* go in the same direction. So did General Alexander Haig of course, who was the commander-in-chief of the integrated military forces of the North Atlantic Treaty Organization countries, Ronald Reagan's future Secretary of State, and who resigned from his position to protest against the mission given to his deputy, Huyser.

'What is striking, is the obstinacy shown by the Anglo-Saxon West to always repeat the same errors, that is, to favour Muslim fundamentalism to the detriment of the Islamic countries which accept, or try, to establish a certain secularism. The reason is simple. It is because this non-fundamentalist Islam is also nationalist and progressive' [87]. Jacques Duquesne wrote.

Does the Islamic regime not identify with the 'desire to destroy any Iranian value system which is inspired from nationalism, and is an expression of Western imperialism, and to take a decisive step forward on the way to Islamist globalism?'* [88].

The journalist and political analyst Thierry Desjardins wrote: 'Twenty years ago, all our well established thinkers were rejoicing over Khomeini's arrival in Tehran. When listening to them, the great country Iran is was finally to know democracy and progress...It was a beneficial return to authenticity. These gurus of our free world, who had just proclaimed themselves specialists in Iran, Persia and the Shiite religion, were asserting to us that the Iranian people had always been deeply religious, and since they were Shiites, they had been waiting for the announced return of the hidden Imam for centuries...It was the same thinkers who, four years earlier, had rejoiced over what they had called the liberation of Saigon, i.e. the invasion of South Vietnam by the communist troops of North Vietnam. As they wanted their monstrous errors to be forgotten – the world was starting to pay attention to the drama of the boat people – these caricatures of scholars had stopped talking about South-East Asia to talk about the Middle East.

It is true that, concerning Iran, our intelligentsia was in 'phase' with our greatest strategists in world geopolitics. Carter's United States had officially abandoned the Shah, James Callaghan's BBC broadcasted the ayatollah's tapes calling for insurrection in the Persian language for months' [91].

* * *

---

* 'All our tragedies come from nationalism. May nationalists go to hell! Shame on them!' [89].
'There is a fundamental contradiction between Islam and the notion of national homeland' [90].

481

'It was in the Near and Middle East that the American leaders showed their magnificent blindness with a maximum of perseverance.

[Neauphle-le-Château] is not the most glorious episode in French history. Is is difficult to understand why President Giscard d'Estaing was so benevolent and granted such means to this fake prophet [Khomeini].

The Pahlavis' Iran was certainly not perfect, but it was on its way to complete modernization and full expansion. Was it appropriate to encourage its replacement by a backward regime which is animated by blind fanaticism? The development of radical Islamism stems from there'.

These lines are taken from an article entitled 'Les stratèges aveugles' ('Blind Strategists'), signed by Maurice Druon [92].

Chapter XIII

MOSCOW AND TEHRAN
The Soviet Union's double game bear fruit

The policy of the Soviet Union in front of the events which shook Iran, was of a remarkable and genuinely Byzantine subtlety.

Moscow manoeuvred at different levels, being realistic as usual, and probably being unable to imagine that the Western powers were going to destabilize and abandon their most powerful ally in the region by following a policy 'worthy of the running of a kindergarten' [1].

The Soviets remained officially and strictly neutral as regards Iran until the departure of the Sovereign, on January 16th 1979. They just had to let Westerners do the work that they had failed to undertake and succeed in on several occasions, and then take over again thanks to their infiltrated agents. If Iran was to resist, and the Western undertaking to fail, Moscow would only have it easy as an irreproachable neighbour, thanks to the appearance of its official attitude. It was a double game that was worthy of appearing in diplomacy books.

*   *

*

Iran was the faithful and credible ally of the West. Its policy was to keep on neighbourly terms with the USSR because of geopolitical requirements which were only to get more specific and better asserted as time went by.

On September 15th 1962, Iran committed itself to the Soviet Union not to accept the setting-up of any foreign military base on its territory in a diplomatic note which was solemnised by its publication. This proclamation formed the starting point of a virtually discontinuous process of improvement of bilateral relations, and it even led to the end of the 'clandestine' propaganda programmes broadcasted for Iran.

During the months of riots in 1978, the Soviet radio channels abstained from directly criticizing the Shah, contrary to the Western media. The latter's Western friends were doing the work. Moscow remained prudent until the Shah had left Iran.

Since the beginning of the sixties, the economic relations and the technical cooperation had not stopped being developed to the benefit of both partners, and had taken a concrete shape through spectacular achievements.

Imperial Iran put firm obstacles to any ideological penetration and to subversion, unceremoniously fighting the Soviet-satellite espionage, while remaining extremely discreet about it. It maintained the permanent presence of a security zone in a sensitive region bordering the Soviet Union.

As long as the power which was constitutionally legitimate was in place, Moscow respected the appearance of diplomatic correctness between the two States while keeping the possibility to sacrifice, if necessary, the strategic preoccupation of an ideological expansion to the tactical imperative of cooperation with the existing power, which was beneficial to both parties.

In the spring of 1978, the Iranian Sovereign went on State visits to several countries of what was still then the solid Soviet bloc – Poland, Czechoslovakia, Hungary and Bulgaria. He received an exceptionally warm welcome everywhere*. He was made particularly interesting proposals concerning the reinforcement and the development of common projects.

Even during the last months of 1978, when the chances of survival of the imperial regime were seriously dwindling, and despite the more and more visible, and efficient, participation of the elements that were manipulated by Moscow to destabilize Iran, the official Soviet diplomacy was sending positive signals to the Sovereign. Moscow was playing a double game.

The ideological preoccupations, the desire to promote the 'anti-imperialist' revolution were there. Devious ways and means were used to reach them, as was usual with the Soviets.

The first example was the preparation of the Tudeh, the Iranian communist Party which had been fought by the imperial regime and temporarily put off by the Kremlin, to help it start resuming its activity on the Iranian political scene. It was to actually become operative as soon as 1977**.

---

* As I was among the half-dozen personalities who accompanied the imperial couple, I was actually the direct witness of this extremely warm welcome in the four countries.
** See chapter III: The Tudeh – Seventy years at the service of the Soviet Union.

Then there was the determining role played by the countries that had aligned themselves on the Soviet policy towards the Iranian revolution and the supervision provided by the Palestinian maximalist organizations.

All the available indications make it possible to assert that Libya sent considerable sums to the Iranian opposition. This is what many observers also noted. This help was increased during the months that preceded the triumph of the revolution. Pro-Soviet Syria also brought an active and permanent support to the revolutionaries by providing them with certain facilities, information and rearguard bases.

The most efficient backing undoubtedly came from the PLO, more particularly from its ultra-left branch.

As soon as the riots started, Yasser Arafat openly proclaimed that the Palestinian organizations would support ayatollah Khomeini and his followers [2]. 'Without our help, Khomeini would still have been in exile' [3] the latter said. The declaration was made once both men had fallen out, but it was still partly accurate. The help given by the extremist wing of the PLO to the rioters was true.

Massoud Radjavi, a Mudjahidin leader and an Islamic-Marxist from the most radical branch of Khomeini's supporters during the first stage of the revolution, admitted that from 1963 on, a few members of the organization had been trained in Egyptian camps, in Colonel Nasser's time [4.]

Numerous documents and studies attest the determining role played by the PLO and its extremist branches in the training of radical activists and Iranian terrorists [5].

Hundreds of Iranian men and women had thus been trained in urban guerrilla and terrorist techniques in Palestinian,

Cuban, East German or Czech camps... They were given heavy weaponry which was partially financed by Libya.

From 1976 onwards, owing to the liberalization of the Iranian regime, Palestinian activists and their followers could enter Iran in huge numbers, holding passports from a few Arab countries. Their presence was known, followed up and recorded by Iranian, Israeli and other intelligence services. They were kept under surveillance, but no concrete measure to put an end to their presence had been taken. The reason was that Iran did not want to lay itself open to the attacks of the detractors of the imperial regime in the West!

As soon as he had arrived in Neauphle-le-Château, Ruhollah Khomeini had had the visit of a Libyan emissary, major Salaheldin and that of the head of the political department of the PLO, Farugh Khaddumi. An agreement was concluded and it was accredited in an exchange of letters. The American-Iranian Ibrahim Yazdi [6] and Sadegh Ghotb-Zadeh acted as liaison agents.

Most of the technical help there was secured by the PDFLP (The Popular Democratic Front for the Liberation of Palestine) of Nayef Hawatmeh, and the PFLP (The Popular Front for the Liberation of Palestine) of George Habash – both Marxists and pro-Soviet. The contacts with the communists were made by a few Iranians who lived in Paris and by the Lebanese leader Mohsen Ibrahim.

It was a curious situation: 'An [in fact] Iranian government in exile was set up on the Paris doorstep with the authorization of the French government. It transformed the French capital into a centre of command for subversive action and a stabilization of riots [in Iran]' [7]. The BBC had become the voice of that rebellion. A permanent collaboration was established between rival, if not enemy, intelligence services to protect and help 'a fanatical lunatic'[8] overthrow the legitimate power of the main allied country of the West in the Near and Middle East, while kind souls praised the operation...

*   *

*

The integration of the Iranian Islamic revolution into International terrorism was thus firmly ensured and it was not to stop asserting itself until the fall of the Soviet Empire. It has actually not stopped since, but it has taken on a new form.

*   *

*

As soon as the revolutionaries took over power, there was a creeping Sovietization of the Iranian society and economy done under the cover of 'Islamisation', but also because the Marxists of different tendencies –communists from the Tudeh, Islamic-Marxists, Trotskyists, and Maoists...– had taken over many essential cogs in the country.

The economy was collectivized, the whole of the banking system was nationalized as well as the major part of industrial firms and big commercial and technical companies; the State controlled foreign trade and implemented a rationing system for the main common consumer goods.

The legal of de facto confiscation of a considerable part of real estate assets should be added to the list, not only to the benefit of the State, but also to that of the dignitaries of the regime, the mullahs, the leaders of the clans in power, the

Guardians of the Revolution etc... These confiscations were rapidly extended to the real estate assets and the personal properties of Iranians who lived abroad, even if they were in a legitimate situation as regards the regime*.

All the social classes and institutions that were likely to become an obstacle to the process were rapidly eliminated: the monarchy, of course, the army –twelve thousand officers were purged, over a thousand were executed in the months that followed Khomeini's rise to power -, the secular and nationalist parties, the University and the traditional religious hierarchy. An operation of the systematic destruction of the Iranian culture was launched at the same time, which aimed at annihilating the national identity. 'We do not know a country called Iran', Khomeini declared in a fatwa on the occasion of the seventh anniversary of the revolution [9].

*   *

*

In July 1981, two agreements of military cooperation on the supply of weapons and ammunition to Iran, and on the training of operatives and the setting-up of assistance were signed by Moscow and Tehran [10]. They were kept secret for several months.

Some time later, a protocol for a cooperation in matters of road transport was signed by both countries. It allowed

---

* These regulations have been relaxed in a partial and subjective way in the last few years. A few privatisations have been operated, almost always to the benefit of the caciques of the regime or of 'foundations' which today control 60% of the economic activity of the country without any control, even a formal one. They are not submitted to any tax contribution or custom duty. The clans of the regime share them. It is a unique and unprecedented situation.

Moscow to route its lorries across the national territory without the slightest form of control. Matching testimonies have been published showing that Soviet military reinforcements had been sent to Afghanistan using the Iranian road network. It happened at the very moment when the Islamic regime was proclaiming its support to the Afghan resistance movement. The official pretext for the cooperation in matters of transport had been to 'shelter Iran from a blockade in the Persian Gulf organized by the imperialists' [11]. Another agreement concerning technical assistance for getting the vast network of gas pipelines and oil pipelines into working order and maintaining it had been concluded soon after the first so as to complete it [12].

*   *

*

As for the war in Afghanistan, the Islamic republic has always wanted Muslim public opinion and the West to believe that it supported national resistance movements there. In fact, as was written in 1984, 'The Iranian authorities have paralyzed any action the Shiite resistance might have wanted to take in the West of the country for two years. After disarming those who had sometimes joined their refugee-families in Iran temporarily, they forced the Afghans to remain confined on camps or to go and fight on the Iraqi front. Several Soviet KGB officers supervised the neutralization of these resistance movements' [13].

At the time when the Tehran propaganda insisted on the help given to the Afghan resistance movements, one may wonder if that help was anything else than the supply of posters of Khomeini and copies of the Koran [14]. It was confirmed by some of the Afghan resistance leaders of the time, despite their carefulness so as not to worsen the situation of their compatriots who had found refuge in Iran.

'Neither Iran, nor the Arab countries give us any military aid' the future Afghan Head of State Borhanoldin Rabbani declared [15]. War chief Amin Wardak was to add: 'Far from helping us, Khomeini and his people only sowed the seeds of discord in our ranks. They even used other mudjahidins against us. Other refugees in Iran were forced under threat to go and fight against Iraqis' [16].

This was how slogans against Khomeini and the Islamic revolution were widely spread in Afghan resistance movements in 1984 and in the following years [17].

The reminder of these events can only be of a purely historic interest today. It nevertheless proves the mistake and the naivety of the forces in the West which favoured the triumph of the Islamic revolution in Iran. The attitude of the Islamic republic on the international scene finds its sources and explanations in its origin.

The big slogan 'Neither the East, not the West, but the Islamic republic' not only attracted crowds in Iran, but it also attracted many members of the Western intelligentsia. It has only been a huge deception since the beginning.

Two major events after the triumph of the revolution confirmed it.

*   *

*

On November 4th 1979, a group of 'Guardians of the Revolution', the Pasdaran, the political militia of the Islamic regime, proceeded with the first – and probably still officially the only – hostage-taking operation organized and carried out by a State in History.

The group was called Daneshdjouyaneh Khatteh Emam 'those who are studying' (or 'students in') the imam's line. The international press immediately called the hostage takers students. The general public was to mistake them for simple and real students. In fact, it was not the case for any of them. Several dozens of American diplomats were kidnapped, illegally confined, and then put in various prisons all over Iran.

A long crisis in the diplomatic history of the United States started. It was to last 444 days.

When a few days later, on New Year's Eve, the Red Army intervened en masse in Afghanistan, the United States, which was bogged down in the hostage crisis, only contented itself with a few gesticulations as a form of reaction, and Moscow was free to do what it wanted.

Already at that time, it should have made analysts think.

The authorities of the regime immediately launched an intense national and international propaganda on the operation: 'America has been colonizing us for two thousand years' Ruhollah Khomeini proclaimed to justify the hostage-taking [18]. It was presented as the 'founding action' of the diplomacy of the regime [19], 'a heroic action' [20], 'without precedent in the history of political and revolutionary movements in the world' [21], even as 'the greatest acquisition in the social history of human kind' [22]...

Some of the Western intelligentsia also gave their support to the operation; European leftist personalities even participated in an 'international seminar' in Tehran to give their support to the hostage takers.

That case has caused the flow of a lot of ink [23]. There are a few facts concerning it which are not well known and should be reminded now. The case is only of historic importance, at least in the way the West sees it.

The leader and chief of the team of hostage takers at the United States embassy in Tehran was a certain hodjatoleslam Mohammad Khoïniha who had been virtually unknown until then. His father had been the chief of the local 'militia' (police) of the town of Zanjan in Afghanistan, under the communist separatist regime of 1945-1946*. He was killed, or lynched according to some, during the people's anti-communist rebellion which preceded the arrival of the imperial army in the town. Very young Mohammad who was six or seven years old, apparently, was taken to the other side of the border by the Red Army, where his family probably came from. There, he received an appropriate education. At the beginning of the seventies, he ensured the liaison between the Eastern intelligence services and the clergy that was opposed to the imperial regime and which moved in the circles around Ruhollah Khomeini in Iraq [24].

His operational centre was apparently set up in Leipzig [25]. Was he trained to be a mullah in the training centre of the 'Shiite clergy' set up by the KGB in that city? [26] It is not impossible. The dangerous liaisons had already been revealed in the *Bulletin du Centre européen d'information* [27]. These are telltale signs [28].

Shortly before the crisis was to break out, Mehdi Bazargan and his Minister of Foreign Affairs, the American-Iranian Ibrahim Yazdi, had met President Carter's advisor for national security, Zbigniew Brzezinski, in Algiers. A progressive normalization of the relations between the two countries had been considered. According to the press and the declarations

---

* See chapter IV: The Azerbaijan crisis – The man who defeated Stalin.

made at the time, the Carter Administration was hoping to finally start reaping the fruit of the change of regime which it had contributed to orchestrate in Iran.

That was when the hostage-taking affair broke out – 'America was [its] captive for 444 days' [29]. An official document from the regime soon after revealed the objectives of that operation: '[The hostage-taking operation] was a revolutionary political action. Its goal was to prevent any rapprochement with America. The Shah's extradition and his fortune were only pretexts. One of our sacred objectives was to overthrow the provisional government [the Bazargan Cabinet]' [30], this is what Behzad Nabavi, the Senior Minister and main negotiator during the affair, declared to the army officers and to the Guardians of the Revolution in November 1982.

During that crisis, Mohamed H. Heykal, Colonel Nasser's minister, friend and confident, who was also close to Ruhollah Khomeini, and especially to his entourage, was asked by the Carter Administration to go to Tehran so as to try a mediation. Once there, besides the fact that there were official meetings, he tried to get in direct contact with the team of hostage takers. Having failed, he asked Mr Vinogradov for advice. He was the Soviet Union ambassador to Tehran and a long-time friend since he had been posted to Cairo. Ambassador Vinogradov immediately organized a meeting in his residence which was apparently frequented by Khoïniha and his team with no discretion at all [31]. It was a very significant detail which was not really in keeping with diplomatic etiquette as far as the Soviets were concerned. Was it not a 'message' addressed to the Americans? [32]

The hostage affair was to mark an irreversible turning-point in the Iranian regime's politics: in international affairs, there was to be a more and more active affiliation to the camp of the 'non-aligned', pro-Soviet countries like Syria and

Libya. It was to last until the end of the USSR. It meant a constant and unlimited support to international terrorism and a reinforcement of the cooperation with Marxist countries [33].

In domestic affairs, the hostage-taking affair was to speed up the radicalization of the regime and of its political discourse, the press-ganging of the population, the elimination of the 'moderates' and it provoked successive purges within the apparatus.

The most significant element was undoubtedly the explosion on June 28th 1981 of the headquarters of the Islamic Republic Party (IRP) which cost the lives of over seventy leaders, including the regime number 2, ayatollah Mohammad Beheshti. The latter had been the main partner of General Huyser, the one who had obtained the neutralization of the Iranian armed forces in front of the insurrection [34].

After the jolts of the first months of the revolution and the hostage affair, secret negotiations were held between ayatollah Beheshti and the American Administration to reach a normalization of the bilateral relations and a stabilization of the domestic situation. The Tehran authorities allegedly accepted a few concessions, in particular to obtain the release of the 11 billion dollars in Iranian assets that had been frozen in the United States after the hostage affair. These negotiations were disclosed thanks to some indiscretions [35]. The Soviet services, which were very present in Iran at the time, may have found out about them as well.

The explosion definitely put an end to the process by killing Beheshti as well as most of the leaders from his group.

The theory of a settling of scores that was organized by the pro-Soviet elements of the regime was sometimes evoked by Western observers [36], but it was only kept by one of them [37]. It is the most plausible theory though. The attack was attributed to the 'counter-revolution', vaguely claimed by Islamic-Marxists who had just become dissidents and who wanted to claim responsibility for everything so as to exist in the media. There was no follow-up though. There was probably a desire to cover up the origins of that settling of scores.

Rather disquieting facts were still fairly rapidly revealed, including in the Western press.

The attack could only have been prepared and carried out by people who had free access to the headquarters of the IRP which were in the best protected building in the capital. The explosives had been put in several carefully chosen places. Several important leaders who did not belong to the Beheshti group were absent from a meeting that they were normally supposed to attend [38], or had received a telephone call and had to leave the meeting just a few minutes before the explosion [39]. There was no explanation given to these strange facts later on, although they had been more or less related in the local press.

The military cooperation was extended to other countries of the Soviet camp after the attack, particularly to North Korea and East Germany, but also to Syria and Libya.

The presence of 300 North-Korean military experts was signalled in Iran [40] from the end of 1982 onwards. In 1983, Pyongyang actually supplied 40% of the weaponry bought by Iran [41]; soon after that, the bilateral military cooperation was to be extended to the nuclear field, and then developed. From that time on, young Iranians were to be sent to North Korea for various military training. There were at least a hundred of them in 1983 [42]. The same country participated at the time in the maintaining and improvement of Iranian port facilities in the Persian Gulf. It supplied instructors for the Guardians of the Revolution, the political militias of the regime, and trained the officers of that parallel air force with the help of East Germany.

A cooperation in matters of intelligence had been established between the USSR and the Islamic republic. Moscow was giving a technical assistance to the Savama, the political police of the regime [43]. The support given to the Iranian secret services by the KGB with about a hundred advisors, it seems [44], who mainly came from the USSR Muslim countries was, according to the *Revue de la Défense nationale*: 'an opportunity to show Soviet reality under an Islamic light' [45]. The USSR had also set up two listening and electronic espionage posts, one to cover the area of the Pakistani border and the Sea of Oman [46], and the other the Persian Gulf [47].

During the 1983, the number of experts from the USSR and from various Eastern or pro-Soviet countries had been assessed at 20,000 [48].

The measures taken against the Tudeh*, which were sometimes only a façade, did absolutely not affect the excellence of the relations with the USSR. Besides, the Tudeh spokesman declared right then: 'Even after the arrest of our leaders, our policy of support for the Islamic revolution has not changed' [49].

To confirm the excellence of those relations, the Soviet Union ambassador was received by Khomeini and later, by the Chairman of Parliament, a strong figure in the country, Ali Akbar Hashemi Rafsanjani. A maximum amount of publicity was made over the '[intensification] of the collaboration of two countries against world imperialism, the aggressions of the United States and the danger of nuclear weapons' [50].

---

* See chapter III: The Tudeh – Seventy years in the service of the Soviet Union.

The *Pravda* could thus attribute the measures taken against the Tudeh to 'the Iranian ultra-right' [51]. The campaign against the Tudeh was to stop from the middle of 1984 onwards.

*   *

*

The country of the Soviets had been able to realize all its strategic objectives which were a priority thanks to the Islamic revolution that had been promoted by the West, and more particularly by the United States, but towards which the Soviet Union meant to observe a façade of official neutrality. These objectives were: the elimination of the Western presence in Iran, the end of the role of 'gendarme of the Persian Gulf' played by imperial Iran, the alignment of Iranian diplomacy with the 'non-aligned' pro-Soviet countries, and a direct support to subversive and terrorist movements across the world, a support and aid given to the most radical Palestinian movements, and the transfer of several of their training centres to Iran.

Without the decline and collapse of the Soviet Empire, the Iranian Islamic republic would have been one of its major pawns on the world chessboard. The game led by the West at the time actually brought about the spectacular victory of the Soviet Union even if, in fact, the existence of a sort of agreement, at least a tacit one, to end the Iranian rise to power can certainly not be excluded.

Besides, the deep aspects of that influence are still visible in many ways: the regime that originated in the Islamic revolution continues to play a destabilizing role in the Near and Middle East. It is still strongly infiltrated and supervised by the former hostage takers of the United States embassy, and even threatens its close neighbours with the use of nuclear weapons.

Chapter XIV

THE IMPERIAL POWER HESITATES
'It's another Louis XVI'

1978 was indeed the year during which everything collapsed in Iran, even though everything could still have been saved within the order and the respect of the Constitution and the principles of the law.

It was a terrible year.

The process which led to the riots and then to the rebellion of some of the population, which an unwell Sovereign who had no strength left in him was to call 'revolution', started way before, probably in 1974.

'The Americans already wanted my ruin in 1974' the Sovereign said later. He was not wrong. It was however at about that period that the interior process of decline, a succession of errors, even of mistakes, of late decisions, useless demonstrations of strength and fatal weaknesses participated in creating and worsening the atmosphere which led to the real international conspiracy that triggered the revolution.

*   *

*

In 1973, Iran, 'the country of blue mosques and of an inflation-free growth' drew 3.5 billion dollars from the exploitation of its oil resources. The sum was to reach 18 billion dollars in 1974, and up to 30 billion in 1977. It was the time when the whole world wooed Iran and its leaders, the Shah, of course, coming first, and it came with a hypocrisy that was cruelly shown in later events.

The increase in State revenue went beyond the threshold of the absorption capacity of a dynamic economy with still precarious structures however, and was to provoke a series of economic and thus of social and, finally, political reactions.

Iran had known a period of remarkable price stability and thus of a real rise of the purchasing power from 1964 until the beginning of the seventies. There was a considerable development of the middle classes which are the backbone of any stable society.

From 1972, the tendencies changed. The annual rate of price increase was getting close to 10%. From 1974, a real inflationist pressure could be more and more felt.

Iran was not in a position to absorb the quadrupling of its oil revenues in such a short period of time, from 1973 to 1974.

A small part of the surplus was wisely affected to foreign investments. At the beginning of 1978, the market capitalization of Iranian State assets that were managed by a small cell within the leading members of the Council and by an office in the Grand Duchy of Luxemburg reached about twenty billion dollars. This was what the disinformation wanted people to take for the 'the Shah's fortune'.

Iran also generously engaged into a policy of aid to

THE IMPERIAL POWER HESITATES – '*It's another Louis XVI*'

developing countries. It was not done without any ulterior political motives, as is usually the case. Mohammad Reza Pahlavi was particularly fond of it since the fairest division of world riches was part of his constant and sincere preoccupations. He believed, and not without good reason, that the sharp increase in oil prices should not be detrimental to the development of poor countries. For him, the Iranian aid was compensation.

The aid for the development of third-world countries was nevertheless badly perceived in public opinion. Is it not often the same elsewhere? He thought that priority should be given to national needs. The authorities favoured discretion to a policy of straightforward communication. Nothing was hushed up but one did not insist too much either, except for the Sovereign, who made an asset out of this policy in order to flatter national pride, and who insisted on the fact that Iran, a country that had been aided until recently and despised in the past, would now be of aid to third-world nations. He was, however, probably the only one to have a clear line of communication in the matter.

The major part of oil revenues thus increased the money supply. A speeding-up of the realisation of on-going projects or projects that were to be prepared was technically impossible to achieve in the short-range. The outcome was an artificial growth of expenditures and income, an excess of the aggregate demand of products and services over supply, and the triggering of the infernal spiral of prices and salaries. To face it already from 1972-1973 on, there had been a progressive liberalization of imports. National production started suffering from it, but worse than that, the ports and communication routes were becoming saturated. It was difficult to make these bottlenecks situations disappear in the short-term. At the same time, dozens of thousands of foreign workers were allowed to come and work in Iran. It provoked an artificial increase in salaries, but, fortunately, no feelings of rejection and tension.

Prime Minister Hoveyda's and the Savak's first reactions were to cover the problem up. They both did not want to 'worry His Majesty'. The faking of clues was known all over Tehran. It had become the laughing stock of public opinion, and a justified motive for its discontent [1].

To face inflationist pressure – 25% in 1976, 34% in 1977 –, the government implemented a strict corporative structure which was inspired from the system Turgot had not succeeded in breaking before the French Revolution, and which was totally unsuited to a modern expansionist economy. This system was suggested and advocated by Amir Abbas Hoveyda. It was to be one of the main reasons for the exasperation of the lower middle and middle class which were traditionally supportive of the regime:

In a law that was hastily voted on and kept nearly secret, 'corporative chambers' which were not elected were set up all over the country. They had the authority to set work conditions and the sale prices of the retail trade without any control, and they were authorized to levy income taxes on the traders' incomes. Special 'courts' without any judicial guarantee, without the possibility of a recourse to an appeal court, and which were often made of henchmen imposed fines and the closure of trades, or condemned to exile traders who were deemed to be recalcitrant.

In a few months' time, a real network of rackets and harassment was organized throughout the country. Despite the unconditional support given by the Prime Minister and the Head of the Savak, who saw an instrument of control of the trading middle class in these corporative chambers, there were voices of protest and criticism. There was an attempt to stifle them.

In less than two years, that policy did not succeed in controlling inflation, the causes of which were to be found elsewhere, but in setting the lower middle and the middle class against the regime. It was this class which was to mainly support the revolution, seeing a way to break the yoke of the 'corporative chambers' which had become a proper social scourge.

From August 1977, the Amouzegar Cabinet officially recognized the existence of inflation and decided that its main task was to curb it. The austerity plan of the authorities included macro-economic measures of budget and credit restriction, the control of speculative transactions, the obligatory lowering of rents – which was not enforced – and the proclaimed intention – which could not be applied – to restrict the rights of the owners of rented accommodation, which only made the mounting tension and discontent worse. Inadequate measures succeeded an inadequate, if not frankly insincere policy.

The hesitations and errors probably form the most noticeable reason for the discontent of some of public opinion which was easily instrumentalised to destabilize the country.

The acts of violence and extortions made by those corporative chambers also contributed to giving rise to rumours of corruption which the propaganda of the radical opposition was to try to attribute to those in the high spheres of power.

*   *

*

It was a country where the great majority of the population was not illiterate any more thanks to the literacy programme, where the mass media were greatly taken into consideration and the international press was read by many people, where the middle class knew a full development, the universities flourished, towns were developed thanks to a rapid industrialization, and where the constant increase in the standard of living urged many people to travel. Was it possible, in these conditions, to continue to keep a sort of pseudo-Parliamentary government which was in fact, a government where personal power ruled and which relied on very often competent and honest technocrats, without a real participation of the citizens in the management of public affairs?

Dozens of thousands of Iranians were going to the West to study or continue their studies. When they were back home, and used to the freedom of speech, having the world press at their disposal without much restriction, and when they very often benefited from well paid jobs or could become richer in a situation of general economic prosperity, they rightly aspired to a 'Western style' political participation – even if it was sometimes only an illusion – to a democratic debate and to a less personalized management of State affairs. Now, the political system which offered them real possibilities for promotions was not able to efficiently organize the participation which the social transformation had made essential.

The two 'traditional' political parties – Iran-eh-novin which was presided by Amir Abbas Hoveyda and Mardom formerly created by Amir Assodollah Alam – did not have fundamentally different political opinions. They were more a sort of machinery used to mobilize citizens and practised of discreet form of populism. Under his guidance, the party of the Prime Minister had been progressively turned into a rather formidable network of influence which, towards the end, was dreaded by the Shah himself. He was becoming more and more suspicious of the increasing power of the Head of Government [2].

From the middle of the seventies, Mohammad Reza

THE IMPERIAL POWER HESITATES – '*It's another Louis XVI*'

Pahlavi gave the impression that he had become aware of the situation and of the necessity to find a solution.

*   *

*

In the winter of 1973, he suggested the idea of the creation of a 'Think-tank' made of intellectuals, technocrats, politicians who would work there when they had no party duties... and of 'all those who have something to say'. Their mission would be to observe and study the political, economic and social situation in the country, and 'give him their opinions, criticisms and suggestions of solutions to the existing problems, while proposing alternative options if necessary – all this, without the slightest restrictions, frankly, and freely'.

The constituent congress of the 'Think-Tank' was quickly invited to start its work on the initiative of the University of Tehran, the first and biggest in the country. Other universities and further education institutions lent their support and means.

The initiative knew immediate success. A thousand academics, top-ranking magistrates, notably the Public Prosecutor and some of the chairmen of Supreme Court chambers, lawyers, businessmen, and more or less famous writers and poets joined the tank. The Shah received the participants at the first constituent congress as well as those of the following years.

Numerous reflection and brainstorming committees were set up in Tehran as well as several provincial capitals. In just over four years, about a hundred reports were submitted to the Sovereign, the first* of which was to unfortunately be

---

* See further on.

premonitory. The ones that were handed in during the last months of the regime were to be many more and more worrying cries of alarm. The Sovereign often read them, especially the political reports, and sometimes showed a certain irritation to the point of wanting 'to make this intellectual gossip stop' [3]. He never did though, maybe so as not to unsay what he had said. All the documents were passed on to the government. Amir Abbas Hoveyda, who was even more intolerant when there were criticisms and who felt he was being got at, reacted violently. Djamshid Amouzegar was indifferent to them, even if, in private, he sometimes showed a certain irritation. The Think-Tank also published a quarterly magazine called *Djameh-eyeh-Novin* or New Society. Most of the reports which had been written in all sincerity, frankness and great expertise, were published in it.

It was, unfortunately to be useless work, even if the four years the Think-Tank was in activity were proof of a great freedom of expression and clairvoyance, and honoured its members who all came from different horizons and only worked for the national interest.

If people had listened to their work, the inner causes of the 1978 crisis and its instrumentalization by foreign interests could perhaps have been avoided.

Alluding to the Tank, the Shah's only surviving brother recently wrote: 'These men did a remarkable work of analysis. Their reports were read by the Shah without any concession. I am not sure he liked everything in them, but he, in no way, hampered their work, or made unpleasant comments against the signatories. He kept his respect for them and, in some cases, his friendship' [4]. He nevertheless added, without giving more precision that 'it is not fair to say that the Shah did not react to these reports [5]. The Shahbanoo seems to have shared the same opinion [6].

The Imperial Power Hesitates – 'It's another Louis XVI'

It was a somewhat belated homage...

*   *

*

On March 5th 1975, the Shah 'suggested' the creation of a 'rally' which would be called Rastakhiz – Revival or Resurrection – during a press conference which was broadcasted on line by the national Radio-Television. The system was to include all the legitimate political forces in the country and be, in fact, a 'one-party system'.

The importance of the Iran-eh-novin party machine which Prime Minister Hoveyda did not hide that he wanted to turn into a sort of sole, monolithic and disciplined group, in the way certain socialist countries do it – and the irritated reactions this project provoked in society, in the universities and intellectual circles – had eventually got the Sovereign worried. He was not hiding it any longer. He was not wrong, but was his reaction adapted to the situation?

'A sole party does not mean the suppression of particular opinions and opposed views', the Sovereign declared, before adding: 'The party would have no real influence on the development of the country in that case. On the contrary, it is precisely thanks to the differences and confrontations that the party proposed to lead the country to the highest level of progress and social evolution.

The evolution of ideas and the divergences of opinion must find their expression in several wings inside a whole which respects the three fundamental principles of the Iranian nation: the monarchical order, the Constitution and the White Revolution.

The Revival Party is thus not a traditional party, in the Western sense of the term, since all the political parties in the past are included in it, with their doctrines and particularities.

This party will be based on a constructive dialogue and will become a genuine school of political education at the widest national level... a place for dialogues and exchange of ideas' [7].

It was a strange, solitary decision – all the testimonies concur on that last point. The intentions were certainly laudable, but did not have the expected effects.

Only the communists and openly declared anti-monarchists were theoretically excluded from this 'rally' which did not have, and could not have, official membership holders. The various political parties nevertheless put paid to one another in order to integrate the new rally.

The Shah thought it was clever to choose – 'to suggest', as he said – his Prime Minister Hoveyda, the all-mighty president of Iran-eh-novin, as general secretary of the rally.

Two tendencies had been opposed since the early days over the organization of this strange party. Amir Abbas Hoveyda was in favour of a monolithic group with a hierarchy of the totalitarian style. Others suggested turning the experience into a progressive democratization of the country, an opening to pluralism in politics. The two tendencies were obviously incompatible. Strong tensions appeared which led, in fact, to a real liberalization of public debate, since everybody could express themselves with moderation if they declared they 'belonged' to a rally which had no members.

The Shah's disappointment was quick. He thought he had done well and was sincere about it. He was lost and decided to have Hoveyda replaced by Djamshid Amouzegar, who was Minister of the Interior and of the Civil Service at the time. The latter had thus become a senior Minister and was interdependent on the Head of Government. He was not really made to lead a political party. He did not like crowds, and only felt comfortable within technical offices and committees. After a few spectacular events and three changes of direction, the setting-up of two 'progressive' and 'constructive' 'wings, which bore no difference, the Rastakhiz only existed under the form of a group of buildings where often respectable bureaucrats worked. They were well paid but did not really know what they were supposed to do. This empty shell disappeared in September 1978. Did it ever really exist?

Abroad, the creation of that 'rally' without a specific ideology or members was used as a pretext to lead a vast campaign against the imperial regime. It was cruelly written that the Shah was thus starting 'a dialogue on equal terms with himself' [8]. Later, there was talk of the transition 'from dictatorship to totalitarianism' [9].

The consequence of the scuttling of political parties was that there was no intermediary between the power and public opinion on the eve of the revolution. Iran-eh-novin had relays in the working class and in primary and secondary school teachers' unions. The Mardom had some in the bazaar, in the local district associations and in some little circles of 'repentant' communists. A few young people who were nostalgic over the reconstruction of the Persian Empire expressed themselves within two groups, or rather two small ultranationalist groups.
On the eve of the fatal series of circumstances which were to lead to the collapse of the regime, the latter had lost all capacity to mobilize its followers.
'The experience was to unfortunately show that the

creation of the party was an error...The Revival Party did not manage to fulfil my objectives, and that was why it had been conceived: it did not convey ideas, needs and wishes between the nation and the executive power', Mohammad Reza Pahlavi was to admit later [10].

*   *

*

Mohammad Reza Pahlavi had not really forgotten, even if he never recalled it, that it was the fact that, in August 1953, he had not been able to retrieve his throne, that especially because of the intervention of the Shiite religious hierarchy in his favour and against Mossadegh, and that on the 19th of the same month, it was the authorization given by the great ayatollah Boroujerdi to the bazaaris to go down into the streets and demonstrate against the 'old lion' which had definitely made the capital city and the crowds go over to the movement led by General Zahedi.*

The Sovereign had from then on, never stopped keeping his reserve, even being suspicious of that power which he knew he could not control.

The sanctuary city of Najaf in Iraq, where Imam Ali's grave is, had been the centre of worldwide Shiism for at least two centuries. It was where the great guides (the sources of initiation or of reference) of that minority branch of Islam lived. It was to Najaf also, that the theology students used to go to complete their studies.

---

* See chapter VI: Iran's twist of fate – An exceptional general.

The Imperial power hesitates – 'It's another Louis XVI'

Iran had favoured a certain transfer of this centre of gravity to Qom for a few years, by using subtle manoeuvring. It was for reasons of prestige – Mohammad Reza Pahlavi's permanent worry – and also to stop the Iraqi government's influence on the religious hierarchy. There were regular tensions with that government.

This transfer had however not been used to establish cordial relations and a fruitful dialogue with the religious dignitaries, which was a permanent policy led by Iranian monarchs. His father, Reza Shah, used to settle the problem with sometimes the use of brutal force*, even if he had been pushed to the throne by the religious hierarchy. He followed Kemal Ataturk's way, his friend and role model.

Mohammad Reza Pahlavi could eventually have officially secularized institutions, and cut all organic links between the State and religion, which would have satisfied much of public opinion and thrown the foundations of saner relations with the clergy, all the more so since a quarter of the Iranian population was not, and still is not, Shiite**.

Mohammad Reza Pahlavi was a deep believer but he had had no religious education. It was the case of many Iranians of his generation who had been brought up in a 'secularized' atmosphere. In a long Moroccan document where Hassan II's declarations are reported, the latter considered this absence of religious culture to be one of the main inner causes of the

---

* See chapter I: I, Reza.
** The Kurdish provinces, Belushistan, the Turkman province in the North, some of the population of the coastal area of the Persian Gulf are Sunnis, in their great majority. Important Christian, Jewish, and Zoroastrian minorities equally belong to the national community, without forgetting the Baha'is who have never been officially recognized.

revolution [11]. The late King of Morocco probably ignored the fundamental difference between Shiism and Suniism in the matter, and even more so the historical and cultural traditions of Iran, where Islam has never played the same role as in Arab countries. He was, however, not totally wrong.

The last Shah of Iran 'always considered that one of his most imperious duties was to give and keep for [religion] the place it deserved' [12].

It was in that capacity that he personally supervised the restoration and embellishment of religious monuments. The grandiose renovation of the holy area in Meshed and of Imam Reza's tomb, which he often said he wanted to be comparable to the Vatican, was one example among others.

His relations with the clergy, which he sometimes despised,were never easy. Yet, he showed respect for religion as an instrument of the power of the State and a bond in the social structure of the nation.

The main heads of government from the 'technocratic period' of the power – Mansour, who stayed in power for less than a year, and was assassinated by an Islamic fanatic; Hoveyda, who was at the head of the executive for thirteen years, and Amouzegar, the last Prime Minister of the White Revolution or the first of the Islamic revolution process – had neither the training nor particularly the sufficient personal relations to establish and maintain the necessary dialogue with the religious hierarchy.

Their predecessors, Ala, Eghbal, Amini and Alam were not in the same situation. They had their contacts, intermediaries and manners which their successors were to lack. The Shah even showed a certain irritation and suspicion towards the few personalities of the regime who held cordial relations with the main religious dignitaries. From then on, the secret services and a few civil servants who particularly wished 'not to displease' took over, but without really convincing results.

The last Shah, in his constant wish for modernity and progress, was at the origin of many sometimes revolutionary measures towards a secularization of social institutions and of the State: the full and successful integration of minorities into social and political life, the man-woman equality in all fields, the laicization of education... He did not make the step for an official secularization because he probably believed that he would need the support of the clergy against the communist threat. He realized the 'damned alliance of the red and the black' [13] which was to organize the revolution too late.

When, from 1977 on, the popular discontent, for want of other means of expression – the 'Think-Tank', the only one which really expressed itself was, it must be admitted, too elitist –, could only be translated into religious manifestations and when some of the hierarchy was instrumentalized by foreign powers to destabilize the country, the Shah was either suspicious or hesitant, and he never managed to get on with good interlocutors on the subject, nor find religious forces that would support him.

*   *

*

Even before the 'year of the revolution', in 1978, there had been enough warnings on certain worrying aspects of the evolution of the domestic situation:

In July 1974, the 'Think-Tank on Iranian problems' had handed an ultra-secret report of several dozens of pages to the Sovereign in which there was a detailed and critical analysis of the strength and weaknesses of the regime.

It was not an indulgent inventory. It revealed the

corruption of a minority of political leaders or people who were close to the Court, the absence of a real political debate, the tense relations between the power and the clergy, the abuses committed by the Savak, the errors of governmental propaganda, certain dubious choices of public investments and the appearance of inflationist tendencies...

The spectacular successes of the country in all kinds of fields were not really hushed up, and neither was the central role of the political stability that the Sovereign was the pivot of...

The report specified that the nation and the State were capable of successfully dealing with problems. Corrective measures – within the framework of the Constitution and of the monarchy – were suggested. It was specified in the conclusion that if the measures were not taken quickly, a serious crisis was not to be excluded. It would jeopardize the political, economic and social balance in the country and could be exploited by its foreign enemies. The social and intellectual position of its authors* should already have been a warning. There was no question of 'opponents' gossip', but of a genuine signal of alarm given by devoted friends.

---

* The main signatories were Professor Abbas Safavian, the rector of the University of Melli and future GP of the Shah; Professor Farhad Riahi, the rector of the Franco-Iranian University of Avicenna; Professor Djamshid Behnam, the rector of the Farabi University; Professor Kazem Vadiï, a renowned academic, who was Vice-Minister of National Education at the time and the future Minister of Labour and Social Affairs; Professor Shahrokh Amir-Ardjomand, the Vice-Rector of the University of Tehran; Professor Mohammad Reza Djalili, the general secretary of the Centre of International Studies, as well as the author of this book who was then the rector of the University of Tehran and the chairman of the Tank who actually handed the report to the Shah.
Two persons who are in the country at the moment are not named for security reasons.

THE IMPERIAL POWER HESITATES – '*It's another Louis XVI*'

The document went against what the Shah heard everyday, against the reports of the secret services, and the discourse held by the Prime Minister. Does the very fact that its authors had all kept their social position and even had political promotions, that the Tank had been encouraged to go on with its activity even if it sometimes irritated people, not prove that the Shah was not the intolerant tyrant depicted by his enemies?

Mohammad Reza Pahlavi read the report during a whole afternoon in Nowshahr, on the Caspian Sea, where the imperial family was spending their summer holiday. He handed it over to Prime Minister Hoveyda, which was completely normal, who accused the authors of wanting to spoil the royal holiday, and who then launched a vivid campaign against universities.

The report was, alas, prophetic. During the summer of 1978, many civilian and military leaders, and even a few major embassies which knew of its existence without having ever seen it, tried to get it. The recommended remedies were not sufficient any more.

In November 1974, the armed forces in turn, decided to voice their opinion. The Commander-in-Chief of the General Staff of the imperial armed forces, General Gholam Reza Azhari, the president of the National Security Committee, had a long report sent to the Shah.

The imperial armed forces, it said, were among the best trained in the world. It was perfectly well disciplined, well organized, well equipped, had modern weaponry and was capable of efficiently resisting to any aggression, wherever it came from, and of preserving the independence and integrity of the nation. However, a country was not to only depend on its armed forces to be safe. Armed forces which are worthy of the name should be able to rely on a population who fully supports the fundamental principles which allow a nation to live and work in peace and harmony.

It is stated in the document that serious reasons for discontent had started appearing which could jeopardize national security in the short or long term.
The report was based, among other things, on the reports of hearings and on the minutes of the testimonies in military tribunals which had to know about the violations of international security and especially of national security.

Then there was a very straightforward and courageous analysis of the reasons for people's discontent, of young people in particular, and of the process which led some of the latter to joining radical movements.

The increase in prices was also noted in the report, as well as the errors made by the Savak, and the behaviour of certain people who were close to the Shah. The general actually showed great civilian and political courage in doing so. Of course, the document was classified 'top-secret'. It concurred in many ways with the report of the 'Think-Tank', even if the language used was very different.

The Shah had a copy sent to the chairman of the 'Tank' – the author of this book – and, through him, to the authors of the previous report. It was his particular way of telling them that he had 'understood' them, and that even 'his' armed forces shared their worries.
That was the end of it [14].
In the winter of 1977, shortly before President Carter arrived in Tehran, the three leaders of the National Front – Karim Sanjabi, Dariush Forouhar and Chapour Bakhtiar – had

a long letter handed to the Shah through the intermediary of the imperial cabinet. It more briefly contained the same remarks as in the two previous reports, in particular concerning the necessity of a transformation of politics.

There was no follow-up to that letter either.

Mohammad Reza Pahlavi's inertia and hesitations when faced with those warnings and the political immobilism of his governments seem distressing. He had known how to react in other times. He continued to flaunt a certain serenity and trust: 'Today, I do not really see what could make a Persian think that a change of regime would be favourable to him' [15].

The 'fatal' year of 1978 was to make him react, but often too late and in the wrong way.

*   *

*

From the middle of 1977, the religious hierarchy became more and more the voice of a disorientated public opinion because of the rise of discontent of a large part of the population which the lack of tonus of the executive power could not appease and because there had been a vast liberalization of the regime. There was a triumvirate at the head of the hierarchy, the great ayatollahs Shariat-Madari, Golpayehgani and Najafi. Ruhollah Khomeini, who was in Iraq, became more and more agitated*, but he had neither the influence nor the calibre to take the lead of the movement at the time; he was to be 'built-up' later. Three other great ayatollahs lived in Iran: in Tehran, Haj Agha Ahmad Khonsari, who was apolitical and a conservative; in Shiraz,

---

* See chapter XI: 'A sort of social-democratic saint' – 'A miracle in Paris'.

Mahallati, who was more of an opponent whose influence was nevertheless very limited; and the third was called Ghomi. He was said to be old and tired and really opposed to the regime, and theoretically lived under house arrest in a nice property in Karaj. In 1978, he was to go back to his native town of Meshed and launch a few vicious diatribes against the Shah before finally turning against Khomeini soon after the triumph of the revolution. He delivered a real ordinance (fatwa) condemning the revolution and nearly excommunicating the new master of Iran [16]. He was arrested, put under closely watched house arrest, humiliated, insulted and dispossessed.

Finally, great ayatollah Khoï, an Iranian and the real number one of the world Shiite hierarchy lived in Iraq. He generally kept outside politics as well. During the last days of the imperial regime, when the die was cast, he tried more or less discreetly to help the Shah. He could have been his saviour, as his predecessor great ayatollah Boroujerdi had been a quarter of a century before, during the events of August 1953. The Shah remained indifferent to him*.

In that context, great ayatollah Sayed Kazem Shariat-Madari quickly became the symbol of the movement of discontent, and the main interlocutor of the imperial power [17].

When Azerbaijan was being liberated, he was the architect of the people's uprising in Tabriz, his native town, against the separatist regime imposed by the Soviet Union**. He was an exceptionally intelligent man who was open to the outside world – he had the main articles on Iran in the international press translated – and who was a patriot before all.

As he had a very good understanding of State affairs, he had kept sending the Sovereign messages to express his

---

* See further on.
** See chapter IV: The Azerbaijan crisis – The man who defeated Stalin.

THE IMPERIAL POWER HESITATES – *'It's another Louis XVI'*

reservations concerning certain aspects of the policy followed by the authorities and the increasing danger in the country. He had not even been given a reply.

What he advocated did not go beyond the measures that had already been suggested to the Sovereign. He also wished to re-establish the traditional dialogue and consultation between the ones at the head of the religious hierarchy and those at the head of the State. He had suggested the choice of a Prime Minister that would be open to dialogue and closer to popular preoccupations as soon as 1977.

During the year of 1978, when things started going wrong, the Shah finally became aware of the necessity to have an exchange with the great ayatollah: emissaries were sent to him and his viewpoints were listened to, but it never went beyond that [18]. It was a useless dialogue. Once Ruhollah Khomeini had settled down in Neauphle-le-Château, ayatollah Shariat-Madari became more and more snowed under work and he ended up knowing a tragic fate [19] under the Islamic republic.

*   *

*

The article in the Tehran evening newspaper called *Ettela'at** 'which was neither the first, nor the last in a long series of blunders' [20] triggered the process of the riots – was it done deliberately, or was it a serious, involuntary mistake? – but also Ruhollah Khomeini's 'launching' operation.

On January 9th, the day after the article was published,

---

* See chapter XI: 'A sort of social-democratic saint' – 'A miracle in Paris'.

3,000 people demonstrated in Qom to protest, according to the official historiographer of the Islamic republic [21] – a figure one may consider to be exaggerated and which shows the weakness of Khomeini's public. One person died from his injuries.

On January 26th, the Rastakhiz called for demonstrations all over the country to celebrate the anniversary of the White Revolution. 500,000 people, one million according to the leaders of the party, walked down the streets of Tehran to acclaim the Shah. The regime still had a really great capacity to mobilize crowds. His supporters dared show their faces.

At the beginning of February, the 'Think-Tank' handed the Sovereign a report that had been written under the supervision of the sociologist Kazem Vadiï, in which was expressed his great concern for the situation, advocating 'a dialogue and understanding with the leaders of Qom'. The text was particularly well documented. The Shah got worried. An emergency committee was summoned on his order to study it. The chairman of the imperial cabinet, Nosratollah Moïnian, presided over it. The members were General Nassiri, the head of the Savak, and his close deputy in charge of national security, Parviz Sabehti; the chief of the national Police Forces; two serving Ministers; several political personalities, and ayatollah Sayed Hassan Emami, the religious leader of the capital who was also a close friend of the Shah. The author of this book and Kazem Vadiï represented the 'Tank'. The debates during the two long committee sessions were animated, and sometimes even stormy because of the radical position of the head of the Savak – whom his deputy did not seem to approve of – who asserted that the Iranian clergy had remained entirely 'loyal to His Majesty', and that the Tudeh, the 'clandestine' Iranian communist party, and a few people paid by foreign powers were solely to blame for the unrest!

THE IMPERIAL POWER HESITATES – '*It's another Louis XVI*'

A majority of the committee members adopted the head of the Savak's views. The two representatives of the Tank did not, and neither did the Tehran ayatollah [22]. That is how it all ended.

The whole of the Qom hierarchy progressively turned into an opposition which was not yet directed at the Shah himself, but which nevertheless called for changes in the constitutional framework. The Sovereign remained inert again, and the government was politically absent.

On February 18th, the 'forties' tactics' were inaugurated. On the occasion of the fortieth day of the death of the Qom demonstrator (January 9th) and because ayatollah Shariat-Madari had called for them, there were demonstrations in that town and also in Tabriz, the prelate's native town where they degenerated into riots. The 'war of the police forces' was at the origin of a bad handling of the problem. The headquarters of the Rastakhiz were set on fire. A few bank branches were stormed. The orders and counter-orders from Tehran gave the impression that the government had no clear strategy. There were victims.

'The demonstrations were organized by a few people who came from the other side of our borders', the Minister in charge of Relations with Parliament declared in front of the representatives. It is true that several young Iranians who had recently come back from the United States and who were known for their affiliation to small ultra-left groups, as well as people who had been trained in Palestinian camps, and even a few people who were not Iranian, had been arrested in Tabriz before being quickly released. The government actually was careful not to disclose it. The authorities had no communication strategy. The State media were doing nothing to 'fight against the continual intoxication' [23] which public opinion was the victim of. It was to be one of the major problems of the power during that fatal year*.

On March 1st, during the celebration ceremonies for the Day of Women's Emancipation, Mohammad Reza Pahlavi delivered a very firm speech in front of over 10,000 people: 'The caravan goes by and the dogs bark', he said, alluding to the mullahs who did not care for his remark at all. There was no reform or firm action taken afterwards.

Those in power remained hesitant.

During the days that followed, the 'Think-Tank' abandoned its usual habit of giving the Sovereign confidential reports, and published a long press release in a voluntary dramatic tone on the Tabriz events. The two main evening newspapers, the morning *Ayandehgan*, as well as the three dailies in foreign languages of the capital, *Kayhan International*, *Tehran Journal* and the *Journal de Téhéran* which were widely distributed and read by the foreign community, embassies and the journalists of the international press who were starting to come in great numbers, all published the unabridged version of the text. Only the Rastakhiz newspaper and the national Radio-Television ignored it.

The Tabriz events were presented and interpreted in those papers as the translation of popular discontent which had been skilfully exploited by radical opponents who were manipulated by foreign powers. The high increase in prices, corruption of a few people in charge, carelessness of the provincial administration – especially of municipalities- and the inappropriateness of certain industrial investments which were necessary as such because of the population's needs, were denounced in them. The 'Tank' firmly recalled the necessity of a political solution to the crisis. There was nothing exceptional

---

* See further on.

THE IMPERIAL POWER HESITATES – 'It's another Louis XVI'

about the text. It nevertheless constituted a bold warning for the time.

As soon as it was published, the government, the Savak and Hoveyda, the Minister of the Imperial Court, triggered a virulent campaign against the 'Tank'. The Tabriz town council was led to vote an official motion that qualified the 'Tank' of 'irresponsible political agitators'. Among these 'agitators' one could find the majority of the rectors in the country, the Director of Public Prosecutions and several chairmen of the Supreme Court chambers, the President of the Bar, writers, artists and famous researchers, a serving Minister and even one of the two notaries of the Imperial Court, and the personal GP of the Shah.

The people in power had got the wrong opponent.

The Shah observed the situation without reacting to it.

During the first two weeks of March, there were more and more demonstrations in support of ayatollah Shariat-Madari across the country. They did not yet mobilize crowds, but were of some importance. His portraits progressively started being seen all over the Tehran bazaar. The religious authorities expressed a growing hostility towards the power, without calling into question the regime or the Shah himself. The international press now widely covered the 'unrest' in Iran. Khomeini was not yet in the foreground of things. The radicalization was however soon to occur.

On April 2nd, the power tried to take up the challenge without doing anything on the political level. The Rastakhiz was supported by the workers' unions and the cooperatives – forces which were to remain loyal to the Shah for a long time – and organized a big demonstration of popular force [24] in Tabriz, the native town of ayatollah Shariat-Madari. Over 300,000 people took part in it. The Shah was vividly acclaimed. If Prime Minister Amouzegar, who had become the general secretary of the Party again, spoke there, he did not stay in town for very long and even refused to get out of his car and meet the inhabitants [25]. It is true that he did not like crowds.

This demonstration of popular force was not any better than the ones happening elsewhere. It was not only covered up by the international press, but the national Radio-Television even reduced it to a meagre level by specifying that it was mainly a ministerial trip [26], which allegedly horrified the Shah. The attitude of that organization was to cause more and more problems.

The government did not take advantage of the event either and did not encourage other demonstrations. That is the least one can say. It went on with its running of current affairs.

The Shah and the power still enjoyed a great support from public opinion which indeed expressed its claims, demanded reforms and the removal of a few profiteers from sensitive decision centres, and wished for a real participation, but did not really question the foundations of the regime and the monarchical institution. Ayatollah Shariat-Madari appeared as the main potential interlocutor of the people in power who remained atonic.

The Shah's attitude could not be understood.

On May 10th, in Qom, after a few skirmishes, the police forces went inside the residence of ayatollah Shariat-Madari as they were following demonstrators. There were two victims. Was it an error, or sheer provocation? It caused great emotion. The Prime Minister officially presented his 'regrets' to the prelate for the 'involuntary violation' of his home. The latter abstained from any excessive reaction and did not give the impression he wanted to make things worse.

The King and even the Prime Minister finally started to

The Imperial Power Hesitates – 'It's another Louis XVI'

want an exchange with him. Nothing concrete was to come out of these contacts which became more and more frequent until the collapse of the regime.

The power was hesitant and had no strategy.

On May 16th, the Sovereign declared that he wanted to start a liberalization policy. Many so-called political prisoners who had been mainly condemned for acts of violence such as attacks or bank robberies that had something to do with their political convictions, were released. The government had about 300 urban agitators arrested at the same time. These people were still unknown, politically speaking, and often belonged to the underworld, and thus, the arrests provoked no reactions on the political level or abroad. There was a definite lull across the country. The ones in power did not take advantage of it to try to find a political solution.

Frequent reports were sent to the government on the infiltration of Palestinians in the ranks of the radical opposition [27] on the links the latter had with Syria and Libya. International terrorist organizations were starting to take over the protest movement [28].

No particular measures for the surveillance of the borders or the control of foreigners were taken [29]. The people who had recently been incarcerated for being trouble-makers or having committed acts of violence were not brought before courts, they were progressively released. They resumed their activities. All these measures of good will were to be taken for signs of weakness.

On June 14th, the Shah received a thousand academics, writers, intellectuals, magistrates and business men, etc... in his Niavaran palace. They were gathered for the annual congress of the 'Think-Tank'. The congress gave a perfectly clear message, but of course also a respectful one, in which it demanded immediate political measures to face the crisis. Mohammad Reza Pahlavi was warmly and sincerely cheered by the audience. The immense majority of the Iranian intelligentsia, which was represented by the 'Tank', gave him their support. The Shah was obviously moved and delighted, and promised to take the required measures and make the necessary reforms. The Tank was not a real political party, but it was a coherent and influential force which the Sovereign could have used to the benefit of the nation in the difficult times it was going through. He always hesitated to do so. Perhaps he thought they were people who were too bold.

On that same day, General Nassiri was replaced at the head of the Savak by General Moghaddam, the chief of the 2nd Bureau of the armed forces*. It was a measure public opinion expected and wished for, and it was going in the right direction.

Contrary to his predecessor who was a limited man who had a very bad reputation although he was certainly loyal to the Shah, General Moghaddam was an honest professional who was known for his competence and his good relations with the intellectual world and the Shiite clergy. He always introduced himself as one of General Pakravan's disciples, and appeared to be well considered by Americans [29], contrary to his predecessor. At the beginning of the spring of 1978, General Moghaddam had given a 23-page report to the Shah on the crisis that the country was starting to go through and the importance of which his predecessor, the head of the intelligence services had, in all likelihood, tried to hide from the Sovereign. The document was written in a blunt straightforwardness. There was everything in it: the corruption of certain people who were close friends or relatives of the Sovereigns, names included, in particular those

---

* See chapter VII: The Savak. – A great misunderstanding.

The Imperial Power Hesitates – *'It's another Louis XVI'*

of three people related to the Shah, a cousin and two intimate friends of the Shahbanoo, the president of the biggest national company, two or three high-ranking civil servants of the Court, damning details on the racket organized by the corporative chambers when Hoveyda was in power – the general was not questioning the latter's personal integrity – the alleged abuses of the Savak, the true reasons for the increase in prices which caused popular discontent, and the catastrophic consequences of the growing conflict with the clergy. The document advocated spectacular and immediate measures so as to make the nation able to resist the subversion that was threatening it.

The general feared he would be placed under close arrest or demoted, but nothing of the sort happened. None of the advocated measures were enforced when they could have appeased public opinion and halted the rise of dissatisfaction in the country that was instrumentalized by foreign powers.

His nomination at the head of the intelligence services was a positive measure, but it came late and was insufficient.

A few days later, on June 26th, as he thought the tension had gone down, and as he had entered a dialogue with ayatollah Shariat-Madari and kept public opinion's bugbear away, the Shah took on a harder attitude and denounced 'the damned alliance of the red and the black as being contrary to nature'. He said that: 'Nobody can overthrow me. I benefit from the support of most of the Iranian people, of all the workers and of 700,000 soldiers' [31].

At the end of the month, the whole imperial family went on their annual holiday to the shore of the Caspian Sea. The calm still prevailed.

*   *

*

During that year of 1978, and well before, though less sharply, the attitude of the national Radio-Television was a permanent source of worry for the people in power, especially for the Shah. He wrote [32] the following: 'As for the propaganda tool which is perhaps the most powerful of all, that is the television, I must have had evidence that its Tehran staff had been infiltrated by mainly communists'.

That organization was run by Reza Ghotbi, a first cousin and almost a brother of the Shahbanoo who was of the same age. They had been brought up together in the home of the latter's uncle as she had lost her father. Reza Ghotbi was the holder of a degree from a French Grande École and he was known for his technical competence and integrity. His attitude during the last year of the regime nevertheless raised a few questions.

There were multiple incidents, and the Shah often reacted somewhat curtly, and even sometimes violently. Yet, he let people get away with it, probably out of respect for his wife. In the Iranian system of the time, the privileged relations between the 'two cousins' ensured a total autonomy to the Radio-Television, and even a certain immunity [33].

During the last eighteen months of the regime, the importance of most of the demonstrations which were in favour of the Sovereign was minimized, especially on the television. The example of the one in Tabriz has already been mentioned. On the other hand, there were more and more programmes with rather dubious sequences which made the Shah angry: more particularly a documentary on guerrilla training in India which was shown late in the evening. It was a street interview during which a person was interviewed and said: 'That country is rotten from head to foot'; the Shah had made the following comment at a meeting: 'I know who is at the head of the country, but when one talks about 'foot' here, is it the Iranian people that are being insulted?' and he added a few less than friendly remarks concerning the director of the National Iranian Radio-Television (INRT) in the presence of several dignitaries. During President Carter's visit to Iran, the INRT had not done what was necessary to provide the technical means so as to organize a televised interview with Barbara Walters. The Shah's words had been extremely violent, and then things had calmed down, probably thanks to the Shahbanoo's intervention, etc...

Parviz Adle, the Iranian ambassador to Brazil, was a specialist in press and communications issues. He had evoked the disastrous role played by the television in an audience at the beginning of the autumn of 1978. The Shah's reaction was stupefying: 'The Radio-Television is not at my disposal' [34].

Such was the reality of an authoritarian political system which was accused of being a dictatorship abroad.

The imperial power's hesitation in the matter was to cost it a high price.

*   *

*

After the 'harsh' declarations of June 26th, the Shah delivered a 'liberal' speech on August 5th. On the occasion of the proclamation of the Constitution of 1906, when a majority of opponents demanded a strict application of the text, he promised in his letter that the next elections which were planned for June 1979, would be '100% free' [35], and he also believed so himself. He added that the candidates who did not belong to the Rastakhiz would be able to run under the party ticket of their choice. It was the very end of the one-party system. On August 11th, the beginning of the Ramadan period of fasting gave rise to demonstrations of a limited magnitude in Esfahan but of an extreme violence. Only a few hundred people had taken part in them though. The main targets were cultural centres. It was the beginning of a radicalization of events, the inauguration of arson tactics. The government, with the approval of Parliament, declared that martial law was to prevail from then on: army vehicles full of soldiers, especially conscripts, were stationed outside a few public buildings and tourist centres. General Naji, the commander of the Esfahan garrison, went for regular strolls in town, shook hands and chatted with shopkeepers. That is all.

Three days later, on the 14th, the 'Tank' published a long press release which was taken over by the whole press and as usual, censored by the National Radio-Television, in which it condemned the violent acts that had taken place in Esfahan and recalled, once more, the need for urgent reforms to master the upsurge of radical extremism.

*   *

*

On August 19th, early in the afternoon, a terrible fire destroyed the Rex cinema of Abadan, the capital city of the Iranian oil industry. Documentaries on wild life were being shown to children and adolescents on the eve of the week-end. Many mothers had accompanied their children to the cinema.

All the exits of the building had been carefully locked before the fire broke out.

Four hundred and seventy-seven people, of whom a majority of women and children, choked to death or died in the flames. It was an atrocious and loathsome crime.

There was do doubt that it was a criminal act from the moment the investigation started.

The Imperial Power Hesitates – *'It's another Louis XVI'*

The authorities acted passively as if it had been a trivial event. The press was asked to go along with this theory, which it more or less did. Public opinion was astounded and scandalized. The explanation was to be given in the hours that followed the event.

* * *

*

On August 20th, there were the celebrations of the twenty-fifth anniversary of the Mossadegh's downfall and of the Shah's return to Tehran, in 1953.

Several thousand people, representatives and senators, local counsellors, ministers and civil servants, members of local associations and of sports clubs were invited to these celebrations by the Rastakhiz. It was to be its last sign of existence. The atmosphere that prevailed on that day, on square Mokhber-ol-Dowleh in the centre of the capital, was not quite cheerful, but the public was not sparse and the orators, including Prime Minister Amouzegar, who gave a lyrical speech as usual, were warmly applauded.

It is true that not much is known, even today, of the magnitude of the Abadan catastrophe.

On that evening, the big, traditional dinner party organized for the occasion by the Queen Mother, Taj Ol Molouk, gathered a thousand guests. The whole of the political and diplomatic Tehran of the time, old poets and artists, personalities from her husband's time and even from the Qajar dynasty were present.

Mohammad Reza Pahlavi could not hide his nervousness during a little private meeting with half a dozen guests, including me: 'But who could commit such a crime?' he wondered out loud, and kept repeating: 'This is horrible... this is horrible'. The number of victims was, however, as yet, not known.

Once among the crowd of guests, he looked contented as usual, and smiled at people, shook a few hands.

At the end of the meal, there were huge fireworks which the whole town could see from afar. Indeed, one did not know the extent of the Abadan tragedy at that time, but the consequences of such involuntary casualness were to be disastrous.

*   *

*

A serious mistake had just been made. Even if the high number of victims was not yet known, the first moves should have been made, the celebrations should have been cancelled as well as the ostentatious fireworks, and a day of national mourning should have been declared.

The Prime Minister did not even bother to go to Esfahan, neither did any of the other ministers.

The imperial family had always had for habit – and it was obviously their strict duty – to take part in such mourning, show their sympathy, and give help and comfort to those who needed it. The Shahbanoo who was always quick to act under such circumstances, asked her cabinet to help a few families who had asked for it, but she did it discreetly, and without dramatizing things. Therefore, her gestures of sympathy had no political impact. She later on wrote that the Prime Minister had dissuaded her from going to Abadan [36].

The Shah's brother went even further: 'It is true that the government had a surprisingly passive, even criminal attitude at the time' [37]. He put the blame on 'Djamshid Amouzegar, whose inability to reach a dialogue made him partly responsible for the problems that year' [38]

Why was there such negligence?

Only one explanation was given later in private: the idea was not to spoil the course of the celebrations which were to mark the twenty-fifth anniversary of Mossadegh's downfall and of the Shah's return to the throne. In those days of tension and protest, the authorities wanted the celebrations to display their strength and appear like a support to the Sovereign.

When the exact magnitude of the tragedy was known to all, the radical opponents exploited and denounced the sumptuous reception given by the Court and the other celebrations. When the whole town was in mourning, they were to say, people at the Court were having a feast, they danced and watched the firework displays. Appearances were unfortunately to prove them right. The political reaction of the government, and the way it dealt with the media on that occasion, were disastrous.

*   *

*

Who was at the origin of that heinous crime?

In the hours that followed the tragedy, Ruhollah Khomeini, whom no-one had accused of anything, published a press release: 'It is true that this inhuman act goes against the principles of Islam and cannot be blamed on the Shah's opponents. There are certain clues which show that the Islamic movement could be accused of that heinous crime' [39].

A few days later, the police investigation clearly showed that the responsibility of the crime rested on the members of ayatollah Khomeini's entourage. The perpetrators of the crime had fled to neighbouring Iraq. They were fairly swiftly arrested there [40]. Iran started their extradition procedure. The official authorities abstained from making the damning file public, out of a desire to 'calm' things down. The clergy should not be 'annoyed'. The only measure taken by Prime Minister Sharif-Emami who had succeeded Amouzegar, was to send emissaries to a few religious dignitaries so that they would know the content of the file and be able to know what their 'colleague' was capable of. They had apparently been really moved and ayatollah Shariat-Madari had allegedly cried his heart out.

Since the government had not reacted, they did not react either.

Three years later, Mohsen Rezaï, the commander-in-chief of the Guardians of the Revolution, who still is one of the leading dignitaries of the regime today, claimed responsibility in an official release for the acts of sabotage and arson committed during that period – there were about fifty cinemas destroyed by fire. He justified them by saying: 'A movement of an Islamic nature is fundamentally incompatible with the existence of places of corruption such as cabarets, dance halls, cinemas, banks, pornographic publication centres and all the manifestations of the stinking Western civilisation.

That is why many cinemas were burnt, and numerous bars attacked. During the period of the revolution, these acts were part of our main objectives' [41].

That revolutionary 'technique' was to be widely used in Algeria, Egypt and elsewhere by Islamists.

Faced with the inertia of the authorities, the international press almost unanimously insinuated that the crime could have been the work of the Savak, without ever explaining how it would have served the interest of a regime it was supposed to defend. Then, progressively, as events were narrated, this insinuation became an affirmation, a definite truth.

The Shah wrote in 1979 that: 'Despicable slander was immediately spread, and the government was made responsible for that monstrous attack...It had to be made responsible' [42].

The effect of the deliberate act of 'satanization' – 'to say the worst possible things about one's potential enemy, often in a purely free way, but by relying on disinformation media' [43] – was such that even the Sovereign who did know the truth could not write it, because he was absolutely certain he would not be believed.

When the truth was eventually established in revelations and, especially, in an official text that came from the revolutionary authorities, the West barely came back on it: 'In the light of the ten years of Islamic revolution, and when it is known that one of the targets of the Khomeini militants was indeed cinemas, as the symbol of depravity, it is not illegitimate to wonder if the fire which destroyed the Rex cinema was not the work of a few fanatics. It was not in the Shah's interest to commit that crime, which was not the case for the religious opponents. More than destroying a symbol of 'rottenness', they were mobilizing the population even more against the Shah's 'sanguinary' regime...In any case, the outcome was a greater isolation for the imperial power' [44]. Many precautions had been taken to make people understand what the revolutionary leaders had been claiming for years!

*   *

*

The Abadan tragedy marks a decisive turning-point. The

Shah deemed it necessary to go back to the capital city and to end his holiday which had been interrupted for a few hours so as to attend the Queen Mother's dinner party.

On August 23rd, Ruhollah Khomeini attacked the monarchical institution for the first time, and talked about an Islamic republic.

On the same day, his supporters burnt the vegetable market of Tehran. The government did not even react.

On the 27th, Djamshid Amouzegar was asked to resign, he stepped down from power.

*   *

*

During the last days of Mohammad Reza Pahlavi's reign, the Count de Marenches went to Tehran to meet with him and assess the situation. The next day, he wrote in his memoirs, he went to see the president of the French republic to give him the account of his mission: 'Valéry Giscard d'Estaing got up quickly to come towards me. So?' He said, and for once I did not follow the usual greeting traditions and said: 'This is another Louis XVI', to which he answered: 'Then, this is the end'.

Count de Marenches was to add: 'Having given much thought to the drama since then, I would like a talented historian to write a book to compare the ill-fated destinies of Louis XVI, Czar Nicholas II and of Mohammad Reza Pahlavi Shah. It is their weakness that caused their doom. If the monarchs had been well informed, they would have chosen a different solution, that of an enlightened firmness, which would have changed the course of History for each one of them' [45].

Chapter XV

PANIC AND DEATH THROES
The Shah 'hears' the voice of the revolution

It is not an exaggeration to say that 'the Amouzegar government fell after the attack on the Rex cinema' [1].

Its passive attitude had been blatant for a few months. The Shahbanoo wrote that she had noticed it [2]. An honest technocrat, he was obviously not the man of the situation.

Once Mohammad Reza Pahlavi was back in Tehran from his summer holiday on the Caspian Sea, he consulted his advisors to find a replacement for him.

After much hesitation between a government of enlightened firmness, of action and reforms, which would have required sacrifices for some, and a makeshift solution, he chose the second alternative [3].

The Shah's choice was Djafar Sharif-Emami, the seventy-year-old president of the Senate for fifteen years, who was also president of the Pahlavi Foundation, of the Bank for the Industrial and Mining Development, of a myriad various companies, and the S. Great Master of the Grand Lodge of Iran. The man had a dreadful reputation, whether this was true or not. General Moghaddam showed great courage and said that it was 'the most dangerous choice that could be made at the time... Insurrection would follow in the two months to come'[4]. 'It was a regrettable error on my behalf. I was wrong to let that unselfish man of good advice [Amouzegar] go'[5], the Sovereign later wrote. Public opinion wanted a spectacular gesture.

Keeping Amouzegar together with a political cabinet would probably have been a less bad choice. By wanting to save one knows not what, with a few measures as a sort of façade, Mohammad Reza Pahlavi lost everything. 'The Shah did not strike lucky', his brother later wrote [6].

The change was to be a turning-point. Faced with unrest which quickly turned into riots, subversion and then into a pre-revolutionary situation – it took a long time to understand that it was manipulated by foreign countries –, the people at the head of the State could never define and adopt a coherent policy. There was no policy of negotiation with those who represented the various levels of opinion, or with the religious hierarchy which succeeded the liberal positions that had been taken up. People still trusted the Sovereign and hardly questioned the constitutional legitimacy. Concrete political measures were announced on more than one occasion, but they were never implemented.

The declarations of firmness were never followed by the necessary acts of authority. Even when they were faced with organized subversion and the infiltration of foreign elements, the authorities remained completely inert, pretending to appear liberal and not wanting to displease the Carter Administration.
The opposition was faced with hesitant authorities which started having doubts over their own legitimacy. It was encouraged and financed by foreign elements and became radicalized. Its most responsible and sensible members were progressively snowed under.

Panic and death throes
The Shah 'hears' the voice of the revolution

This evolution led to a climate of violence and hatred which was conducive to ayatollah Khomeini's putting in orbit, the symbol of all extremes.

*   *

*

Certain people from the Shah's entourage believed that Sharif-Emami had good relations with the religious hierarchy [7] since he was the son of a little mullah, and that he had good contacts with Moscow, one does not really know why. He explained to me that: 'It was the unfortunate Hoveyda who twisted my arm...Sharif-Emami indeed had excellent relations with the Russians, which was essential under the circumstances. And besides, he benefited from a certain understanding from some high members of the clergy, so he really was the man for the situation. Poor Hoveyda gave me so many reasons to believe him that I did. Now, it was just when I had appointed Sharif-Emami Prime Minister that the oil workers, who were stirred by the communists, started going on strike and I quickly noticed that his relations with Qom were rather of an imaginary nature' [8].

It was a somewhat short explanation.

Sharif-Emami formed and presented a not very homogeneous Cabinet, three members of which, besides the Minister of War, were in fact imposed by the Sovereign, but, on the other hand, they had received full powers from the latter to make decisions. Sharif-Emami wanted to face a pre-revolutionary situation by taking artificial measures and favouring cheap political intrigues.

He first decided, without really announcing it, that there

would be a return to the use of the solar calendar, starting from Hegira (622, the departure of Prophet Mahomet from Mecca to Medina) which had been abolished a few years before and replaced by the imperial calendar. When he was president of the Senate, the new Prime Minister had been one of the most fiery defenders of this calendar which was not appreciated by public opinion. It was imposed by the Hoveyda government with the Shah's assent.

He also started closing down casinos and gambling places – there were less than a dozen of them in the country, but they almost all belonged to the Pahlavi Foundation which he was the president of.

These 'measures taken in public interest' were instantly mocked and forgotten.
A few days later, when a group of Free Masons led by the very influential senator Mostafa Tadjadod, the president and founder of the first private bank in the country, came to suggest him to organize a large-scale action against the rise of radical Islamism, with considerable financial means, so as to defend the regime, he opposed the idea and 'temporarily put off' the Iranian Freemasonry without even consulting its leading members. He did, however, inform the leaders of the radical opposition.

More blunders were to follow.

*   *

*

The new government wasted precious time by discussing small details in the measures to include in their programme with ministers and technicians. Consequently, twelve days after its

PANIC AND DEATH THROES
The Shah 'hears' the voice of the revolution

formation during the serious events of the 7th and especially of the 8th, the government had not yet been presented to the Chambers and had thus not got the vote of constitutional confidence.

On Thursday, September 7th 1978, on the occasion of the end of the Ramadan, 100 ,000 people participated in a public prayer and then, in a march on avenue Cyrus the Great in Tehran. For the first time, a few effigies of Ruhollah Khomeini appeared here and there, especially among the people at the back of the march where one could notice dozens of Palestinians and where slogans that were hostile to the monarchy could be heard. Yet, there was an uncountable number of portraits of ayatollah Shariat-Madari, and much dignity prevailed the whole time of the march.

On that same day, on the occasion of the National Day of Hospitals, the Shahbanoo made an unexpected visit to the Doctor Eghbal hospital of the University of Tehran, which is located in one of the densely populated areas of town.
She had multiplied that kind of unexpected visits in the previous months, and her protection was reduced to the minimum. Popular reaction had always been exceptionally warm, and showed how much the population still liked them.

Although it had not been announced, the presence of the Queen was soon known. A crowd of 5,000 to 10,000 people immediately gathered in the neighbouring streets. Cries of 'Long live the Shah!' burst out everywhere, and when the visit was over, the Shahbanoo walked to a cancerology centre a few hundred yards away in the midst of a real human tide. The welcome was unbelievable.
Strict orders of censorship were given by the Prime Minister on the radio and on the television – which had simply given

an account of the morning event – to hush up the spontaneous welcome the Shah's wife had witnessed so as 'not to annoy the opposition' [9].

This time, the initiative of the censorship of information that was favourable to the regime had not come from the television. The Shah later wrote that the latter 'had been infiltrated by communists' [10].

On that same Thursday the 7th, towards the end of the afternoon, the supporters of ayatollah Khomeini, that is from 3,000 to 5,000 people, gathered on square Jaleh, east of the capital. Their slogans were of an extreme violence. The Shah was openly shouted down for the first time. Another gathering was announced for the following day.

During the evening of that same Thursday, which was a crucial day in the destabilization process of the country, the National Security Council presided by the Prime Minister, met and decided to declare the enforcement of martial law in Tehran. The Cabinet was summoned in an extraordinary session and approved of the decision despite the Shah's reticence. The latter had been consulted over the telephone by the head of the government [11]. The martial law was extended to several major towns. General Gholam Ali Oveyssi, the commander-in-chief of the army, was appointed administrator of the martial law in the capital [12].

Once the deliberations of the Cabinet were over, General Gholam Reza Azhari, the Head of the General Staff of the armed forces who was exceptionally present at the meeting, insisted that the enforcement of martial law from the next morning on at 6 o'clock in Tehran, should immediately be made known to the population by the national Radio and by the Television, and repeated every half hour. The Prime Minister gave formal instructions to Manutshehr Azemoun, the Minister of State in charge of the Affairs of the presidency of the Cabinet to warn Reza Ghotbi, the director of the national Radio-Television, on the spot. The government's decision was only announced the next day at 6 o'clock, at the very moment when it came into force, while the crowd had already started gathering in some districts since the demonstration was planned for 8 o'clock.

Was the passing on of the Prime Minister's instructions by his services late, or was it a refusal to carry them out and a voluntary sabotage on behalf of the national Radio-Television?

Both theories were suggested. There is no doubt over a certain malfunctioning. It is highly likely that if the news had been made known to the public, there would have been fewer people in the streets, and the number of civilian and military victims would have been less important. What happened next would have been different.
However, from 7 o'clock on in the morning, there were police and army trucks and cars equipped with loud speakers at all the cross-roads. They were informed by observers who were in helicopters. The order to disperse was given to the demonstrators who wanted to go from square Jaleh to Parliament so as to occupy it and, according to reliable reports, proclaim the Islamic republic there.

The demonstrators were drawn together and urged to rebel by subversive elements. They set off. They were stopped in some places by the usual standard warnings. The policing of the area disintegrated. The soldiers first started shooting in the air. Then, when they saw their friends drop around them, wounded or shot by gunmen who were posted behind some windows overlooking the route or who were on the roofs of a few buildings, they shot at the rioters and the dreadful drama started. The opposition press called it 'Black Friday'. The break between the regime and some of public opinion had occurred.

It was another step in the dramatization of events after the Abadan tragedy.

How many victims were there exactly?

Chapour Bakhtiar, one of the spokesmen of the opposition, who already wanted to start a negotiation with the Shahbanoo at the time, as he admitted it in his memoirs later on [13], declared: 'Something irreversible has happened. There is no possible conciliation with the regime any more' [14]. Two French observers wrote: 'The day after Black Friday, Tehran was unanimous: there were at least 4,000 casualties' [15]. *Le Monde, Dossiers et documents* was more prudent in 1986: 'There were 180 official casualties, and 2,000 according to the opponents whose leaders were arrested' [16].

The exact number of victims was known two weeks later. The burial certificates for people who had died in unusual way were delivered by forensic experts and had to be registered at the Ministry of Justice. A detailed report was presented to the Cabinet shortly before the end of September and revealed the tragic assessment for that day: 121 casualties among the demonstrators, 70 among the police forces, all in all 191 victims, including the people who died from their wounds in hospitals. It was a bloody streetfight more than a unilateral repression.

The report also established that the rioters had not only opened fire on the police forces, but also on the demonstrators so as increase the number of victims and create irreparable harm. The outcome of the autopsy reports were incontestable on that point, since numerous victims had been killed by bullets which did not come from the police forces.

The investigation was to formally establish that Palestinians who had entered Iran with false papers had mixed with the demonstrators. When he later related the events of that day,

General Oveyssi declared: 'The Palestinian mercenaries were the ones who opened fire on the army' [17].

A few days later, a certain mullah who wanted to be called ayatollah Allameh Nouri was arrested. His real name was Nassirieh. Several passports from Arab countries were discovered in his home. It was established that he had received a sum of about 40 million tomans (just over 5.5 million dollars at the exchange rate of the time) from Najaf, and that he had put 18 million tomans on his children's savings accounts. The documents that were seized proved that the 'Black Friday' events had been carefully planned, organized and financed by foreigners [18]. Some of the seized documents were published in the press, and then, on order of the Prime Minister, the story was hushed up in a desire to 'calm things down', and the man was released. 'Public opinion was so moved that it would have not accepted any truth. Now, it understands that it has been deceived, and it should be told what actually happened' [19].

The political and psychological consequences of that day were catastrophic. The Shah was deeply affected. He kept repeating to his visitors: 'But what have I done to them?'

The ones in power were accused by the opposition and the whole of the world press of wanting to repress protest by using brutal force. 'But if he Shah wanted order, he had a fear of bloodshed, and he had his military leaders know that they had to restrain themselves... a martial law which would not be martial law' [20] He answered Alexandre de Marenches who was suggesting a certain enlightened firmness: 'Know, my dear Count, that I will never have my people shot at' [21].

In fact, the day right after the event, according to General Saneï, Minister Azemoun would sometimes call the administrators of martial law three times a day to make sure that it was not enforced!

Strict measures had officially been taken, but the

radical opponents were made to know that there would be no repression and that they could thus defy public order and the law with impunity. The military courts that were planned by the legislation were not set up, and the ban on gatherings was not really enforced, except for the supporters of the regime. Some of their associations, more particularly the feminist ones, were even dissolved!

By declaring martial law, then deciding not to enforce it and making their opponents know it, the authorities were condemning themselves.

Nevertheless, the most radical opponents had to maintain a 'an obsessive fear of bloodshed' [22], especially after Ruhollah Khomeini had settled down in France, and more particularly for the West: 'It was said later that many of the corpses that were exhibited were not the ones of people who had been shot dead, but corpses which had been brought from the morgue, smeared with blood and shown around the streets with cries of vengeance... There were, at the time, thousands of martyrs in Iranian people's minds' [23]... and for the Western media which were the main target of that operation of disinformation. It was meant to diabolize the Shah and promote the triumph of Islamism.

These remarks were made after the events by French or American observers and corroborated in Mohsen Rezaï's book. The latter theorized to resort to such methods, basing himself on the Iranian revolutionary experience: 'Fake funerals should be organized to have a repercussion in the media, and the coffins should contain weapons, especially knives which can be used at once in case the police forces intervene' [24]. 'There should be permanent professional men and women mourners in cemeteries used as political and religious weapons for the triumph of the revolution' [25]. 'Clothes with red stains should be

PANIC AND DEATH THROES
The Shah 'hears' the voice of the revolution

used as psychological, political and propaganda weapons so as to awaken and strike public opinion' [26].

The operation of manipulation relayed and completed the one which had started in Neauphle-le-Château with the complicity of we know who.

*   *

*

When, less than fifteen days after it was formed, the Sharif-Emami Cabinet presented itself to the Chambers, its chairman was already out of breath and had run out of ideas. The authorities were thrown into a panic and their death throes could be felt.

On September 10th, the 'Think-Tank' noted the open intentions of the revolutionaries to question the liberation of the Iranian woman, the social legislation and the agrarian reform which they deemed to be contrary to Islam, and warned the authorities against the dangers run by the nation: 'How could one let all the social, political and economic rights acquired by women, workers and peasants during the last fifteen years disappear?' the press release of the 'Tank' said.

There was to be no voice raised to bar the way into the abyss.

In mid-September, the country entered a state of anarchy.

*   *

*

The Sovereign nevertheless continued to appear in public, to look contented, to accomplish the duties of his position, but he showed no particular reaction to the events, except once.

On September 16th, an earthquake devastated the oasis town of Tabas, in the South of Khorasan. 70% of the town was destroyed. The number of victims was estimated at 3,000. The help from the State was supervised by the governor of the province, Hassan Saraj Hedjazi, and the help from the Red Lion and Sun (the Iranian Red Cross) arrived quickly and was correctly organized.

Two days later, Mohammad Reza Pahlavi went there. He had learnt a lesson from official indifference during the Abadan tragedy. Rumours had just been spread of a clandestine American nuclear experience in the desert which was supposed to be at the origin of the catastrophe! The Sovereign's long visit and the traditional welcome of the disaster victims quickly put an end to them. Taking advantage of the occasion, he went on a pilgrimage to the mausoleum of Imam Reza, in the town of Meshed, the main administrative centre of the region. Even though people had only been informed of the unexpected visit at the last minute, they warmly cheered him. He received a certain number of mullahs in the museum room next to the mausoleum. They expressed their respects and loyalty.

Mohammad Reza Pahlavi went back home comforted, and even surprised. He was still liked! The State media gave a brief but accurate account of the visit.

A few days later, the Shahbanoo also went to Tabas. The welcome was mitigated that time. The radio, and then the television felt free to magnify the negative reactions.

The Shah came out of his isolation on other occasions such as the inauguration of the parliamentary session where his speech was totally out of phase with the events; or the ceremony of the beginning of the academic year at the University of Tehran which he attended with the Shahbanoo. The welcome of the professors and the students was exceptional and the Sovereign was moved. There was also the traditional ceremony of the latest class of the Tehran Military Academy, where Mohammad Reza Pahlavi had actually done his military service and obtained the rank of second lieutenant. General Manutshehr Biglari, the commander of the Academy, went beyond the usual terms used on the occasion and declared: 'These young officers who make an oath of loyalty to you are today ready to defend their country and the King, whatever the circumstances and the enemy, whether he comes from inside or outside the country'. The Shah spent over three hours there and was visibly satisfied.

Did he understand that he still benefited from an immense capital of trust among his compatriots? He did not come out of his apathy, of an apparent indifference.

*   *

*

Right after the Shah's visit to Tabas, the government appointed a retired engineer and general who had been in charge of the Royal Engineers, and who was known for his integrity and devotion to the position of delegate to the reconstruction of the devastated region. The latter went there immediately and got the work under way.

The quick beginning of the reconstruction work and the quietening down of the population in Tabas were followed by the arrival there of small groups of mullahs who had come out of nowhere. They handed out sweets, a few clothes, and small sums of money to the disaster victims. Some representatives of the opposition then asked for an audience with the Prime Minister: since the clergy was taking care of the disaster victims, why not give it that possibility? These gentlemen would be so happy with such a proof of trust that it would improve the relations with the religious hierarchy, and be considered as a great political gesture.

The Prime Minister had an incredible attitude: the order was given to the general delegate to the reconstruction to pack his bags and come back to Tehran. The agents of the government practically deserted the area. The opponents immediately accused the authorities of being irresponsible and careless, and called its attitude criminal: all appearances were proving them right. Public opinion was shocked. All that had happened without the Shah being aware of it.

* *

*

While the situation in Tehran was getting worse and worse, the American and Western manoeuvring to destabilize the Iranian power went from subtle and diplomatic to direct and blatant.

Ardeshir Zahedi, the Iranian ambassador to Washington, commuted between both capital cities to give a psychological support to the Shah and to sort out a complex situation, but it was in vain.

Already, during the summer, the ambassador of the Federal Republic of Germany had organized 'poetry evenings' within the framework of his cultural department, the Goethe Institute. There, the opposition had made violent diatribes against the imperial regime, in the presence of a few scribblers who were looking for fame, and two or three second-rate poets. There was no diplomatic reaction from the ambassador.

Then, there was the episode of George Ball's visit to Tehran. He stayed in the building of the national Radio-Television and openly encouraged opponents to the monarch.

In October 1978, the American Department of State and Ambassador Sullivan opposed the delivery to Iran of anti-riot

PANIC AND DEATH THROES
The Shah 'hears' the voice of the revolution

equipment which the police forces badly needed, pretending that the deliveries would be an obstacle to the on-going national reconciliation process [27].

In November and December, the deputy head on the Human Rights commission at the State Department went to Tehran to ask that no brutal action should be taken against the opponents [28].

General Huyser's visit was to follow.

*   *

*

On October 7th, at 6 p.m. the Shah summoned an ad hoc meeting at the Palace, a sort of 'Crown Council' as his brother called it [29]. The Shah and the Shahbanoo both presided over it, which marked the official entry of the Empress in the management of State affairs, or in this case, what was left of them. She continued to play a determining role in them until the fall of the monarchy*.

'The situation is getting worse and worse everyday', the Shah said. 'That is why I wanted to gather a few ministers who have a political responsibility and the main military leaders. The question is how we must act. What must I do? I am asking each one of you to give a straightforward, frank, clear and even brutal point of view, without any ulterior motives.'

On the military side were Generals Azhari, Oveyssi, Gharabaghi, Moghaddam, and Samadianpour – the latter being the Chief of the National Police Forces.

---

* The people present were Prime Minister Sharif-Emami, the Minister of Justice Mohammad Bahehri, the Minister of Labour and social Affairs, Kazem Vadiï, the Minister without portfolio to P.M. Manutshehr Azemoun, and the author of this book, who was then Minister of Further Education and Sciences; Manutshehr Gangi, the Minister of Education, arrived late.

The meeting lasted until about 2 a.m. on Sunday, October 8th, and was interrupted by a dinner they quickly shared. The atmosphere was tense, and the discussions sometimes lively. There was a row between General Moghaddam, the head of the Savak, and Minister Azemoun, who was, indeed, a former civil servant from that organization.

Lines of conduct progressively appeared: the media had to be controlled again, particularly the radio and the television – the Prime Minister had dismissed Reza Ghotbi, but nothing had changed – a reinforcement of the measures for peace and order in the big cities, the arrest of trouble makers, the surveillance of certain districts so as to prevent confrontations, the organization of trials for some of the people responsible of particularly serious crimes...

The government would be reinforced and reshuffled to implement these measures and be, at last, able to enter talks with the religious hierarchy and the opposition, basing itself on clear and sound positions.

It was decided that these measures would come into force in the morning.

The next day, the day after and the following days, no decision was made. Was it due to the opposition of the American and British embassies which the Shah might have kept informed so as to have the support of their governments, or that of the Shahbanoo who had remained silent during the meeting?

The authorities were completely paralyzed. Several ministers left the cabinet to show their disagreement with this line of conduct. Did one really exist?

*   *

*

Panic and death throes
The Shah 'hears' the voice of the revolution

While the situation was getting worse and the government was being dismantled, and the strikes, particularly those of the banking and oil sectors progressively paralyzed the country, there was a stronger rumour everyday that the military had been called in to restore order. General Oveyssi's name was mentioned as that of the future Prime Minister, who, with the Shah's authorization, would be secretly getting ready, consulting and even choosing his potential ministers, who would mainly come from the military.

The people in command of the armed forces had prepared a securization plan for a return to peace and legality that was called 'Khach' from the name of a small town in Belushistan. The objective was to change the balance of power inside the country in a few hours, and put an end to the dismantling of the government so that the latter could negotiate with the opposition from a position of authority.

During the night which followed the general's nomination – which was to be made public shortly before the curfew hour was to come into force – units from the 'special forces' that were based in Lavizan and Mehran, from the guards of the National Police Forces based in Eshrat-Abad, and from the airborne brigade of Baghe-Shah, who were all elite professional soldiers and had been kept aside until then, were now to proceed with the arrest of about four hundred riot leaders and agitators. The majority of them were to be taken to the military area of the international airport of Mehr-Abad or to the air base of Doshan-Tapeh. In each one of these places, two C-130 air freighters would be ready to take off immediately so as to transport the people who had been arrested in Khach – thus the name of that operation. The army had quickly renovated and equipped the old barracks of that town which had been the headquarters of a brigade in previous years and were only used as warehouses for some disused equipment.

Foodstuffs and bedding as well as an emergency generator had been discreetly transported there.

As the strike of the oil industry and of the distribution of electricity started bothering the population, the two dozen people who were responsible for it had been spotted. Engineers and military technicians were to replace them as soon as they had been apprehended.

The Radio-Television was to be put under the control of the military.

The leaders of the opposition, the ones with whom there were to be negotiations later on to integrate them into the constitutional political system were not to be arrested, but put under house arrest ,or taken to the army officers' club, or to a residence for the foreign guests of the Savak, and treated with consideration.

According to the authors of that plan, there could not be a question of a coup d'État, of course, but it was a government which was to restore order and security in its country and ensure a return to legality. The intervention of the elite forces was to be short. The conscripts who were already present in the cities would be in charge of ensuring the static guard of sensitive areas, and also of keeping the residences of the people who had been apprehended under surveillance so that their families and possessions were sheltered from settlings of scores. It was hoped that once the decisive blow had been dealt, a normalization of the situation would rapidly occur.

The general and Prime Minister was expected to present himself to the Chambers and once approved of, to have full powers given to him for a limited period of time. Was he to dissolve Parliament or wait for the session to end normally?

Panic and death throes
The Shah 'hears' the voice of the revolution

The Shah had decided on the second possibility. In any case, an imperial ordinance was, in accordance with the Constitution, to decree when the next elections were to take place. They were normally due in June 1980.

The plan – a shock therapy to save the country – was highly likely to succeed. The military were reliable– and they proved it right through to the end – and perfectly operational. The elite forces had the ability to see the tasks they were given through. The people that were to be arrested were closely followed by the secret services and the police. The secret was really well kept. The essential effect of surprise was to play its part.

It was, for the country and the regime, the last chance to survive.

Indeed, the armed groups of a Marxist tendency had been brought together again for a few months, and fought on the side of the Islamists. Many Palestinian activists were also in Tehran now, but it was believed that the armed resistance would be quickly quelled, and that the Palestinians would try to leave in front of the firm attitude of the authorities, since they were not in an Arab country. They had come because they had been let in. They participated in the riots because they were sure of their impunity. It was not in their interest to stay and operate in a country where they were not liked, where they could not speak the language and were consequently easy to spot. They knew that no-one would cry over their fate.

That is how the number of civilian and military victims of the Khach operation had been estimated to a maximum of about fifty.

At the last minute, Mohammad Reza Pahlavi made a new fatal error, because he did not want, could not or did not dare to choose a firm attitude.

*   *

*

On November 5th, new riots broke out in Tehran. Banks, hotels, cultural centres, and schools were burnt by the supporters of ayatollah Khomeini. A film on the day's events was edited and shown on the national television that very evening. It showed scenes of repression, soldiers shooting at the crowds, and corpses. Only the rector of the University of Tehran, Abdollah Sheybani, who was filmed outside the campus begging his students to remain calm, gives an Iranian touch to the film.

They were, in fact, documents that came from foreign newsreels, especially Chilian ones, which had been skilfully edited in advance. One only needed to look at the uniforms and helmets of the police forces. The destructions and fires were, of course, covered up. Who was to pay attention to such details in the atmosphere of hysteria which prevailed at the time?

On that evening of November 5th, the electricity strike which was normally programmed for 8.30 p.m. so as to stop people from watching the news, had exceptionally stopped shortly before.

It was a remarkable frame-up.

In the evening, Prime Minister Sharif-Emami offered his resignation to the Sovereign who accepted it immediately. His government had only been fictive for a few days.

*   *

*

Mohammad Reza Pahlavi had followed the events of that day minute after minute. He seemed to have finally shaken himself up and gave the impression he wanted to react [30].

PANIC AND DEATH THROES
The Shah 'hears' the voice of the revolution

About ten military generals had gathered in the waiting rooms of the palace. They were all moved and scandalized, and had the King told that they were waiting for a firm and clear decision [31]. The latter summoned his Grand Master of the Protocol: 'Ask Oveyssi to stay in his office and to wait for my call'. 'I communicated the news to the high-ranking officers who were present in the waiting room of the palace.

They were full of joy', Amir Aslan Afshar wrote.
The preparations for the implementation of the Khach plan were triggered through a few quick telephone calls. Oveyssi was waiting.

The ambassadors of the United States and Great Britain were summoned to the palace and received. The Shah also had a long talk with the Shahbanoo.

After that, the Shah called the Chief of Protocol again and announced his decision to put General Gholam Reza Azhari, the Chief of General Staff of the armed forces, to form the new government. 'How about Oveyssi?' ambassador Afshar asked. 'Call him to tell him that he may leave', the Shah retorted. When the officers who were present in the palace heard the news 'which struck them like thunderbolt', they were filled with consternation [32].

'In Morocco [during the Shah's exile], His Majesty told me: the American and British ambassadors thought that Oveyssi would act firmly and make the situation worse, and that it would then be necessary to call in a moderate person so as to calm people down... I am sure that they [the Americans and the British] did not want his departure' [33].

The Shabanoo also admitted in her *Mémoires* that '[she] was not for the nomination of the general who was known for his severity' [34].

The Shah's brother later wrote too that: 'He believed them [the British and American ambassadors] to still be his friends. They gave him the worst possible advice, the one not to call for a firm man like General Oveyssi, but to appoint a moderate man as head of government so as to find peace' [35].

The Azhari Cabinet was thus formed overnight. The Chief of General Staff wanted to refuse the position he was offered. The Shah answered: 'It's an order'. The general obeyed.

Indeed, the Sovereign was right to think that 'he had no other choice but to re-establish military power' [36], but this military power only existed in appearance. The General and Prime Minister who was an excellent general staff officer, a former coordinator of the military forces of the CENTO – an extension of NATO –, was also a cultured man of a great integrity that was recognized by all, but he actually had a weakness: he did not have the reputation of an officer who ruled with a firm hand. 'He was everything but someone looking for power' [37].

If one is to believe Mohamed H. Heykal, who said he had questioned all the protagonists of those decisive days, the departure of the Shah and the implementation of a constitutional regency with the Shahbanoo were given serious consideration [38] in certain circles. The nomination of a general 'who represented the hard line of the military' [39] could have favoured the emergence of an Ayoub Khan or a Zia-ul-Haq who were, correctly or incorrectly, compared to Oveyssi, and make the plan fail [40]. It was a speculative hypothesis: general Oveyssi had the inflated reputation of a hard man. He was, however, fully loyal to the Shah, and the Iranian military was not the one of a coup d'État. These assumptions most likely came from the small circle of people in the Shahbanoo's entourage who were already doing what they could to push Bakhtiar to the head of the executive power and saw a real military government as an obstacle in their way. As for the Anglo-Saxons, they had already

PANIC AND DEATH THROES
The Shah 'hears' the voice of the revolution

made their choice, and a return to order would have prevented Mohammad Reza Pahlavi's departure and Ruhollah Khomeini's take-over of power, which they had planned.

At the end of the evening, as the Shah was leaving his office, he told his Chief of Protocol and the Chamberlains: 'Tomorrow, I will address the country', and he went away.

*   *

*

On Monday, November 6th, he arrived at his office at 10 o'clock sharp and summoned, Manutshehr Sanehi, the chamberlain who was on duty, a few minutes later: 'The team from the National Radio-Television should arrive any minute now', he said. When he heard that they were already there, he started nervously pacing his office. No-one from the Protocol knew who had drafted or was to bring the text of the message, it was Shoja Ol Din Shafa's responsibility, the Sovereign's cultural advisor who was absent from Tehran at the time.

A few minutes passed, and the wait continued. The chamberlain was summoned again: 'Reza Ghotbi [the former head of the Radio-Television, and first cousin of the Shahbanoo, who was like a brother to her] is to bring me the text of my broadcast. Where is he?' The chamberlain had no idea, but said that he would enquire. A few minutes later, the Shah was told that Reza Ghotbi was being received by the Shahbanoo with Hossein Nasr, her Cabinet chairman. The Sovereign got angry: 'Why are they with the Shabanoo? This is *my* message'. Aslan Afshar, the hierarchical superior of the chamberlain, called the Shahbanoo on the phone and conveyed the Shah's message.

A few minutes passed. The Shahbanoo, Ghotbi and Nasr finally arrived with the text and entered the imperial office.

559

Afshar was present as well, and he was to take notes of the meeting and publish his account of it later [41]. The Shabanoo and the other two presented the text to him. The Sovereign read it: 'Oh, no! I must not say such things', the latter said. 'No, Your Majesty, it is time You sided with the people and said things they like', Reza Ghotbi retorted. The Shahbanoo and Nasr approved of him.

'This message, which was supposed to be handed to my brother for a first reading (...), was only given to him a few minutes before he was due to intervene. He did not even have the time to think about what was written and what he should be saying. It may seem as strange to you as it seemed to us!' Prince Gholam Reza wrote [42] when he related the atmosphere in which the operation was carried out.

The Shah had the team of the Radio-Television come in. He sat at his desk and the message was recorded 'in a state of utter tiredness, a lump in his throat because of his sadness and emotion, and he did not change a word since he had been forced up against a wall', Amir Aslan Afshar noted.

'I have made a lot of errors (...) but I have heard the voice of your revolution (...) The course of events must be changed, I do know it. I have asked the head of general staff to form a really provisional government that will be in charge of re-establishing order so as to allow for the constitution of a civilian government and proceed with free elections (...) I commit myself to respect the Constitution from now on (...) I cannot but approve of the revolution of the Iranian people...'

It was beautiful, long prose, but an appalling speech with disastrous effects.

Public opinion was only to remember one passage: 'I have heard the voice of your revolution'. The word 'revolution' had never been uttered so far. It had now become official, with all

Panic and death throes
The Shah 'hears' the voice of the revolution

its connotations. The text included five instances of the Shah's confession that he had violated the Constitution that he had sworn to respect and that he was the guarantor of. He was made to publicly admit perjury. If he resisted by refusing to accept and do what he was asked, the Chamber could depose him with a single vote.

Sir Anthony Parsons, the ambassador of Great Britain particularly recollects the following about that day: 'Did the Shah really understand the consequences of what he had said? [43]

*   *

*

A few days before, on October 26th, the day of his birthday, the Shah had to cross a few main thoroughfares in Tehran to go to the Golestan Palace where the traditional ceremony in his honour was to be held. A huge, silent crowd had gathered on the pavements. There were no shouts of hostility and no usual cheers. He was being observed. People were waiting, trying to find the winner of the contest. The collapse had not yet occurred.

He had just surrendered on November 5th and 6th, by yielding in front of the American and British ambassadors and to the Shahbanoo's objections, and then by delivering that pusillanimous message which was a proper announcement of the end of the monarchy.

*   *

*

The formation of a military government still had a considerable impact on public opinion.

The presence of members of the military in the government made more than one person think. There was a return to calm. The super-ministers – each of the commanders-in-chief was at the head of several ministries, and other military people had been appointed to the head of a few departments – were welcomed in an atmosphere of peace and respect by the civil servants who had still been restless just two days before.

Life went on again. The strike of the oil industry stopped and the leaders of the strikers gave themselves up to the military governor of Khuzistan and asked for his protection of their families. The shops opened their doors again.

A few officers in uniform replaced the usual anchormen on the television. It was the only point of the Khach plan which was implemented.

Many leaders of the opposition got in touch with the personalities who were close to the authorities or the members of government to start a dialogue again.

In the afternoon of November 7th, Tehran gave the impression of a city where nothing had happened a few hours before. It was the same in the provinces.

In forty-eight hours, the opposition already felt beaten, and in a position of weakness.

The military were powerful and respected. The ones in power had finally done something positive.

*   *

*

Some of the decisions made by the 'military government' were welcomed, in particular the reform of the Pahlavi Foundation. Others were more controversial like the arrest of

Panic and death throes
The Shah 'hears' the voice of the revolution

former Prime Minister Hoveyda, with, indeed, the approval of the Shah and of the Shahbanoo. Was he going to be exposed to trial by the mob, as a scapegoat? It is true that the Shah reproached him with some of his recent errors: the regrettable article against Khomeini, and the nomination of Sharif-Emami. In the latter case, however, he was the one who was mainly responsible.

Illusion only lasts a short time. Instead of giving energetic messages, acting quickly and efficiently, stopping the rioters, arsonists, trouble makers and showing its determination and strength, the government appeared to be hesitant. When the general and Prime Minister presented his Cabinet to the Chamber, he made a speech in a tearful voice. He evoked at the same time the All-Mighty, religious problems and that ideal democracy the people must be able to attain. Then, he reshuffled his Cabinet to include civilians. The three commanders-in-chief who belonged to it as super-ministers were dismissed.

Heavy pressure was exerted on the Shah 'to dispel worries', not to annoy the opposition and seek 'peace'. He yielded.

The warnings given by ayatollah Shariat-Madari, many other religious dignitaries, local associations, the powerful association of officers and non-commissioned officers of the reserve, and numerous academics and personalities were ignored, sometimes even scorned at by some. Only opponents were listened to. Mohammad Reza Pahlavi, at least, remained courteous with his supporters, but he refrained them from taking action. He had no will to fight any more. He feared a civil war.

The opposition was free to act. Those who wanted to support the Sovereign, defended the Constitution and the respect of State laws were quelled.

'The military cabinet' had turned into a team of fearful politicians who had no imagination.

It was the death throes.

All that was left to do was to deliver the final killing blow.
'The revolution was over as soon as it broke out: it is wrong to believe that it overthrew the monarchy; all it did was to scatter its ruins' [44].

Chapter XVI

THE FALL OF THE MONARCHY AND THE TRIUMPH OF THE REVOLUTION
The handing over of keys

The illusion of a return to peace and order and the beginning of a process of normalization after the nomination of General Azhari only lasted for while, barely about ten days. 'Resorting to the use of the armed forces' was not one, and the whole thing was a masquerade. In fact, 'the Shah had played his last card' [1]. Another military man could have been called in, and benefited from a full delegation of power to take harsh political measures. Those at the top of power, the Shah and the Shahbanoo did not want it and the Western 'allies' even less. There was always the fear of the coming of an Iranian Zia-ul-Haq, even if he were secular.

Appealing to Ardeshir Zahedi had also appeared like another solution for weeks and was talked about in the political circles in the capital. The son of the man who had succeeded Mossadegh had become, for many, the symbol of another type of politics, and a return to order and new reforms. He held very good relations in the United States, especially in republican circles, and had an excellent list of international contacts which was to be of use to the imperial couple when they were in exile. Although he had been far away from Iran in the last few years, he had established excellent relations in many opposition circles and particularly with the religious hierarchy, and especially with the great ayatollah Khoï. He had many friends in all circles, notably in the bazaar, and was certainly the only politician who had such an influence over the military and could impose his opinions on it. He had so many considerable assets, but he also had fierce enemies at the Court, in particular a few members of the imperial family and certain people who were close to the Shahbanoo. His will to 'cut the rotten branches' was no mystery. Although he had serious chances of succeeding, he was put aside by the imperial couple whose entourage feared Zahedi's 'radical' attitude, and a 'negative reaction' from the American democratic circles. Was it only that? It was the same a few weeks later.

*　　　*

*

The State was now 'a boat adrift with nobody at the helm'. The authorities did nothing, had no strategy and were going adrift. Several businessmen and a few politicians who were criticized by public opinion were worried about the unrest and left the country. Most of the political, military and administrative leaders of the last two decades had nothing to reproach themselves with and stayed in Iran. Many of them were to be arrested, and most of them were assassinated afterwards.

It was in such a deleterious atmosphere that two lists of the names of personalities who were more or less well-known appeared in Tehran. These people belonged to political, medical or business circles and even included a few military leaders. Next to each name, there was a number which was meant to correspond with sums of money that had been transferred abroad through the banking system. Both lists came from a 'revolutionary committee of the Central Bank', which almost no-one obviously knew the existence of, or who belonged to. The list did not specify if the sums in question were in dollars or in other foreign currencies, in rials, the official currency, or in tomans – one toman = ten rials –-, the popular currency.

The psychological impact of these anonymous leaflets was disastrous, and that was the goal. The governor of the Central Bank, Youssef Khoshkish, contented himself with declaring that the flow of capital was free and that he would have his staff inquire into the matter, but they were on strike! The government nevertheless decided to forbid the accused to leave the country, including its own head, General Azhari! It was a decision which was not in accordance with the law since only the judicial power could make such a decision. Many claims were lodged for slanderous denunciations and for an abuse of power from the authorities.

Soon after the triumph of the revolution, the governor of the Central Bank who had been appointed by the Bazargan cabinet, an economist who was well-known for his competence and integrity, Mohammad Ali Molavi officially declared that those lists were totally erroneous and that he had not managed to find out who was responsible for them [2]. He published [3] the complete list of all the legal entities and natural persons who had made currency transfers for whatever reason during the years that preceded the revolution on November 3rd of the same year, and in 33 volumes. The deception was established [4]. The revolutionary regime still had Mohammad Ali Molavi's predecessor shot, as the one responsible for these transfers which had officially been recognized as shoddy fakes.

*   *

*

The final stage of the fall of the imperial regime started, one could say, on November 20th. The country was deeper and deeper plunged into anarchy.

The capital was partially paralyzed by the strike of public services. There was not enough petrol and there were often power cuts. The National Education system functioned rather well, but the banking system hardly did. The main factories in the suburbs were far away from the unrest. Business continued in the bazaars, but life became more and more difficult, and insecurity prevailed. Groups of so-called 'Palestinians' – was it still the case? – attacked many private residences at night and looted them in the name of the revolution. People lived in fear. The aeroplanes going abroad started being stormed. Many people took to the roads to cross the border with Turkey. Others tried to get on makeshift boats to sail to the South of the Persian Gulf.

The situation in the provinces varied. A sort of calm, almost indifference reigned over the Kurdish and Turkoman provinces, in Belushistan and in certain towns in the extreme Southern regions of the country. A majority of the population was Sunni, and the cameras were far away.

It was almost calm in the countryside. After the agrarian reform, the peasantry remained attached to the person of the Shah. Here and there, some peasants could be seen in a state of unrest. Their action was not directed against the regime, but against some of the big landowners who had been dispossessed by the reform. The latter were fighting on the side of the revolutionaries and trying to retrieve their lands with the help of henchmen who were paid handsome sums of money. These were counter-revolutionary jacqueries which were of not interest to the international press. In certain regions, however, the clashes that opposed the henchmen of the former landowners and the peasants were bloody.

THE FALL OF THE MONARCHY AND THE TRIUMPH OF THE REVOLUTION
The handing over of keys

There was far less unrest in Azerbaijan than in the rest of the country. Ayatollah Shariat-Madari still had a determining influence. The great prelate was getting more and more worried over the evolution of the situation and tried to put a halt to any excessive behaviour, and invited the population to calm down.

There was a lot of unrest in the urban centres of Mazandaran in the North of the country, in the province bordering the Caspian Sea, which were traditionally leftist and a former fief of the Tudeh. There existed everyday violence. In Guilan, where the influence of the clergy had always been insignificant, the situation was virtually calm everywhere, and life continued its normal course.

Esfahan, Shiraz, Yazd and Kerman, etc... saw the same scenes of violence as the capital city. In the latter, the confrontations between the workers and the anti-Khomeini peasants, and the bazaris and the civil servants who had become revolutionaries were particularly bloody.

From a sociological point of view, the population was less unanimous than what was reported in the Western press. The civil servants, workers of the public sector, and bazaris had taken to the streets. The workers of the private sector, especially from the big factories located in the West of the capital, many academics and the peasants from the close suburbs of Tehran were hostile to the revolution. Mohammad Reza Pahlavi discouraged demonstrations in his favour; he had left the game and was afraid of a civil war.

The police, the gendarmerie, and the armed forces remained loyal to the Sovereign and they were disciplined. All the attempts to provoke uprising within the ranks of the armed forces failed, with the exception of a collective movement of disobedience from a few dozen air force technicians, several of whom were actually immediately placed under arrest by the military police, and an attack that had no consequences in a mess on the Lavizan base.

The police and the secret services drew attention to a few thefts of uniforms here and there, from specialized tailors or private subcontracted workshops. It was also said that simple soldiers' uniforms which had not been ordered by the military, were being made in some workshops of the Sartsheshmeh area in Tehran. The Islamist were probably preparing the sudden appearance of fake policemen and soldiers to stir up trouble, like in Algeria later on, or during certain attacks in Egypt. The Western press could then have talked about military uprising. The speeding-up of events was to make these preparations useless.

As a whole, the military, the last bastion of order and legality, remained loyal and intact as long as the Sovereign was in his country. The situation was thus manageable, and a recovery was still possible without almost any bloodshed. It was a question of political will and of cohesion at the head of the State.

In fact, Iran had not been governed for months. All the attempts for a recovery had been quelled. The people were weary, disorientated and adopted a wait-and-see attitude. A vast majority of them were hoping for an end to the problems, for normal life to start again calmly, and to be able to breathe again.

* *

*

THE FALL OF THE MONARCHY AND THE TRIUMPH OF THE REVOLUTION
The handing over of keys

On November 18th, the Shahbanoo went on a pilgrimage to Kerbela and Najaf, sanctuary cities located in Iraq [5]. She received a very warm welcome from the pilgrims in the mausoleums who were almost all Iranian. The official reaction in Baghdad, where she stayed in a governmental palace, also showed the support of the Iraqi authorities to Iran. The president of the Republic was at death's door. The vice-president, Saddam Hussein, who was the president of the revolutionary council, and already the actual leader of the country, was received by the Shahbanoo upon his own request. Mohammad Taqi Sebt, the number two at the embassy who spoke perfect Arabic, acted as an interpreter. The fact that an audience was requested and the subject of the talks were both a form of support for Tehran.

The Shahbanoo was also received upon her request by the great ayatollah Abolgassem Khoï, the number one in the world Shiite hierarchy, in his spacious mansion in Najaf. The helicopter with the ambassador of Iran being late, the latter could not arrive on time. Mohammad Taqi Sebt was the one who accompanied the Shahbanoo and her suite. After the usual felicitations and cup of tea, the great ayatollah said to the assembly: 'Leave me alone with my cousin' (Farah Diba was a descendant of the Prophet Mahomet). Their tête-à-tête lasted thirty minutes. At the end of the meeting, the ayatollah's spokesman declared that the latter had conveyed a message of sympathy for the Shah in which he expressed 'his fervent prayers' for the Sovereign's health and success to the service of Iran and Islam. It was a message of support and a considerable success expressed in hardly diplomatic terms, which the utterly dismayed authorities were not able to exploit.

*   *

*

There were new demonstrations, sabotages and arsons in Tehran and in several provincial towns between November 20th 1978 and the first days of December. Some troops, especially conscripts, were still present in several areas of the capital, but the military had the order not to react and the opponents were almost officially informed. There were still fake corpses in hermetically closed coffins exhibited from time to time, and a few fake funerals organized for the Western television channels. The leaders of the revolutionary regime were to admit it later.

On December 2nd, on the first day of Moharram, the Shiite month of mourning, the Khomeini supporters inaugurated new tactics: as soon as the curfew came into force – it was fairly respected – many people would go to their terraces and balconies and shout 'Allah-O-Akbar', God is great. Loud speakers were installed on certain balconies and broadcasted the same message that had been recorded on tapes and repeated by many voices. The mixture of these real and fake demonstrations created a strange impression of anxiety in the nearly silent city under curfew.

The State was non-existent, and the Court was plunged into a state of anxiety. Many members of the imperial family actually went abroad. From the outside, there was the impression that the Shah and the Shahbanoo, who were closely associated to the running of affairs now, or what was left of them, did not follow the same line in politics. Could one say that the Shah had one?

The man who had appeared to be more and more haughty and distant with certain Anglo-Saxon politicians in the last few years, did not stop receiving the Washington and London ambassadors to consult them on the way he should run the country!

THE FALL OF THE MONARCHY AND THE TRIUMPH OF THE REVOLUTION
The handing over of keys

He also granted audiences to many intellectuals, politicians who had been kept aside or who had fallen into disfavour, retired generals and prelates who had come discreetly. He listened to them with great curtesy. They almost all advised him to hold fast, to react, to rely on the military who had remained loyal to him and could still put the country back on the rails, and to mobilize his numerous supporters.

The rumour of his departure started being spread, and those who came to see him asked him, even sometimes begged him not to abandon the country. Thus, over twenty odd mullahs, some of whom were important, came together on Ardeshir Zahedi's initiative, with representatives of certain corporations, local associations and sports clubs.

*   *

*

On December 3rd, Mohammad Reza Pahlavi was encouraged by the military to go to a training centre for army cadets and visited a high school nearby. He was very moved to receive the warm welcome of hundreds of his compatriots. He was always very much liked by a large part of the population. He had to appear in public, he had to show a will to redress the situation, but he had thrown in the sponge.

'If Louis XVI had appeared in public on horseback, he would have remained victorious', Bonaparte had written these words down in his notebook* on August 10th 1792.

The Shah did know History so well.

---

* On that 10th of August, the future emperor of France witnessed the storming of the Tuileries and the massacre of the Swiss guards by the mobs from the window of a neighbouring building. It was to mark him for ever. He was always to fear 'a town that has gone to the dogs'. He nevertheless took the risk of intervening and saving one the Swiss guards.

573

On December 11th and 12th, the days of Tassoua and Ashoura – days of mourning for the Shiites –, hundreds of thousands of people demonstrated in the streets of Tehran in support of ayatollah Khomeini. The military wanted to ban these demonstrations. The organisers were approached by generals Oveyssi, Rahimi and Khosrodad, and had been made aware of their responsibilities: the demonstrations were going to constitute a 'yellow line' that should not be crossed or the military would not back down even if it were to avoid a bloodbath could not be avoided. They had even been threatened of the intervention of the Shiraz para-commando brigade whose reputation was dreadful, even if they had never intervened anywhere. The opposition seriously feared a coup d'État – its leaders wrote something to that effect later on. The latter had ended up obeying and promising that they would be satisfied with a strong protest.

The deployment of a proper policing force in the city had just started. A unit of heavy tanks which was based 140 kilometres away from Tehran had started moving towards the capital, when the ban was lifted on order from the palace. The military did not dare disobey. Mohammad Reza Pahlavi had just stepped back again after the intervention of a few personalities who 'were wishing for the situation to calm down', and of the ambassadors of the United States and Great Britain, and that, it seems, of the Shahbanoo's entourage. His official biographer recently wrote the following, evoking the Shahbanoo's attitude during those decisive days: 'Farah always preached moderation' [6].
Even before the ban was lifted and the leaders of the opposition were informed of it, the BBC had already announced it.

The objective of the military leaders was political: they wanted to interrupt the momentum of revolutionary radicalism, score a point by making the opposition step back so as to be able to negotiate with it afterwards from a position of strength. They were about to succeed. The lifting of the ban was therefore a major, irreversible failure on the political level.

*   *

*

The failure of the Azhari Cabinet had become obvious, and the Shah and the Shahbanoo were consequently looking for a way out of the situation. Mohammad Reza Pahlavi then gave the impression he wanted to leave the country. There was pressure to that effect from Washington, London and Paris which actually supervised Khomeini's presence and action in Neauphle-le-Château. The cross-checking of all the testimonies and documents which are available today leaves no doubt about it – that impression was an obvious fact, he had decided to leave the scene and knew it would be forever. He was not trying to do it with dignity. He had no cards left, and the only possible solution would have been to involve the military, which the imperial couple did not really want. Louis XVI's, Nicholas II's, Faisal of Iraq's and the Negus's fates haunted him.

In fact, his first attempt was to form a coalition government, one to bring back calm, which was presided by a consensual personality. Abdollah Entezam, who was eighty years old, General Zahedi's former Minister of Foreign Affairs and then Managing Director of the National Iranian Oil Company often frequented the opposition circles now that he was retired and was full of cutting remarks on the regime in the more or less society meetings. He turned the offer down when it was made.

Mohammad Sorouri, who was said to be ninety, and a Minister during the forties, but more particularly a former president of the Supreme Court for over a decade, who had won unanimous respect, took his age as an excuse and apologized.

The same thing happened with Professor Mohammad Nassiri, the former dean of the Law School, governor of the National Bank under Mossadegh and then Senior Minister. He had the Sovereign told that he was honoured by his request, but that he was not the right man for the situation.

Mohammad Reza Pahlavi then turned towards a moderate from the opposition. Two emissaries [7] were sent to get in touch with the highly experienced sociology professor, Gholam Hossein Sadighi, and ask him if he would accept to be received in an audience, so as to have a tête-à-tête with the Shah. The latter was feeling so weak that he feared a refusal. Sadighi was naturally made aware of the purpose of that audience.

The seventy-year-old man, a former student of the École Normale Supérieure of Saint-Cloud, had a Phd in Litterature from the Sorbonne, and had been Mossadegh's Minister before becoming the number two of his government. He was considered as the spiritual heir of the 'old lion'. Since the latter's downfall, he had kept behind the scenes, abstaining from any political activity and refusing any favour or prebend. He had founded the Institute of Studies and Social Research of the University of Tehran which he ran with competence and authority. The Institute was to rapidly become a recognized international centre.

Mohammad Reza Pahlavi held a certain grudge against him because of his complete loyalty to Mossadegh, and of the distance he kept and showed towards the authorities. Gholam Hossein Sadighi felt the same about him, still remaining perfectly courteous with the Shah in both his public and private discussions.

Both men had somewhat forgotten that resentment during

the last years because of certain events at university. Messages of consideration and courtesy had been exchanged [8].

The answer the sociologist made to the Shah was marked with great nobleness: 'I no longer bear a grudge against the Sovereign for having kept me away from power for twenty-five years. I know that accepting to form a government today could cost me my reputation. What is the use of prestige if the nation is in danger, one cannot use it to try to save it?'

The appointment is immediately made, and the time for the audience is set. After having been received alone by the King, Professor Sadighi asked for a week to schedule the next moves and his list of ministers. He was also received alone by the Shahbanoo, and then by the Shah with Ali Amini and Abdollah Entezam. The Shah had assured him of the support of the military in a 'sincere and emotional' manner, according to Sadighi.

Several members or people close to the National Front accepted to follow him. Ayatollah Shariat-Madari's entourage whose influence was still determining, also assured him of their support. The bazaar and the intellectual circles were on his side. He thus had a serious chance of succeeding.

Sadighi only gave the Shah one condition: that he would accept to leave the capital, but not the country, and set up the regency council. That way, the unity of the military would be safeguarded and the Cabinet would have a free hand to face the crisis without the Shah being involved. He suggested to the Sovereign that he should settle down on a military base on the Persian Gulf for a few weeks, where the weather is mild and good to relax in, in the winter. That sole and only request was going against the American and British requests and the Shah's wishes, and so the latter refused, putting forward its unconstitutional aspect [9].

A new opportunity for the country had just been lost.

Four days before the Shah's final departure, Sadighi went to see the Sovereign to beg him not to leave the country. He knew it was useless. 'He told his entourage that 'it was his duty as a patriot'.

According to the testimony of a person close to him, he had tears in his eyes when he heard of the departure: 'Iran is lost with the Shah leaving' [10].

After the failure of that attempt, the Shah turned to another 'historical opponent' called Mozaffar Baghaï [11]. The philosopher, former student of the École Normale Supérieure of Ulm Street (Paris), and retired professor for years, was seventy now. He had been Mossadegh's closest friend for many years and had then moved away from him. He, indeed, did not have Sadighi's prestige or aura, but his integrity and quasi monastic life style inspired respect. He had numerous connections, 'networks' in the bazaar, and a few acquaintances in the intellectual circles.

After two long audiences with the Shah and a meeting with the Shahbanoo, his programme for order and reforms got more precise. He wanted to have full powers for a limited period of time and then dissolve the Chambers, quell the 'rebellion' by ordering mass arrests, even if it meant quickly releasing most of the people who had been apprehended.

He asked the Shah to please leave the capital city for a short while, to settle down on a military base, among his soldiers and officers, so as to leave a free hand to his minister. He did not even ask for a regency council.

Towards the end of December, the plan was ready, and the Shah did not seem to be opposed to it. Those who knew about the deal believed that the affair was settled. Baghaï, who was a formidable public speaker, prepared his nomination speech.

THE FALL OF THE MONARCHY AND THE TRIUMPH OF THE REVOLUTION
The handing over of keys

It was then that Chapour Bakhtiar's nomination as Prime Minister was made public, to everyone's surprise.

*   *

*

Chapour Bakhtiar's nomination at the head of the government seemed to result from a parallel effort with that of the Sovereign to find a political solution to the crisis. It was, in fact, made on the Shahbanoo and her entourage's initiative.

According to the person in question, who had never been contradicted until recently, the first encounter with the Shahbanoo had taken place 'three months before' [12] he was called to the government around mid-September. It occurred in the greatest discretion in the villa of the Shahbanoo's uncle, and thus also of her aunt through marriage, in Darrous, which is one of the residential areas to the North of Tehran.

The encounter had been organized by the Shahbanoo's aunt, Louise Samsam Bakhtiari – Mohammad Ali Ghotbi's wife – and especially by her son Reza, who was 'almost like a brother' to the Queen who often called him that way, and who was her close advisor as well. In fact, Louise Ghotbi was the sister of Chapour Bakhtiar's mother, thus his aunt, and Reza, his first cousin. The double cousinhood was therefore very useful.

That encounter was very long [13] and the two people immediately got on very well. They probably met yet another time. The Shahbanoo offered a volume of Eluard's work to Bakhtiar [14]. The latter did not hide his hatred for the Shah [15] but was full of praise for the Shahbanoo whose ideas he found 'very close' to his. Besides, Bakhtiar's radical position towards the Pahlavis was known to them: 'He did not hide his antipathy

579

for our family' [16]. During that same month of September 1978, his declarations about the regime were particularly vehement. He actually called the military a 'real occupation force which shoots at anybody and kills innocent people' [17].

Two decades later, after a lively debate on the circumstances of Bakhtiar's nomination, the Shahbanoo suggested that her first encounter with the latter had taken place after his nomination had been decided, thus in December [18]. Louise Samsam Bakhtiari wrote that it had taken place 'during a cold autumn day' [19], well before the nomination.

The crosschecking of these contradictory testimonies and the fact that the corrections came somewhat late lead one to think that Chapour Bakhtiar's version which was confirmed by Mohammad Ali Ghotbi, was the right one. This detail is not only anecdotal for the fact that Bakhtiar was called in was to have irreversible effects on further events and on the country's destiny.

At the time when the Sovereign was struggling to find a solution to the crisis by calling in Entezam, Sorouri, Sadighi and Baghaï to only name a few, Bakhtiar was getting ready, whereas he, in theory, had not been encouraged at all by him. On December 18th, during a luncheon with the ambassador of Great Britain, he virtually explained his programme to him [20].

Count Bertrand de Castelbajac wrote the following: 'The Shahbanoo had told Bakhtiar that his ideas were very close to hers. She really wanted the Shah to leave Iran for she had known for years that he had cancer and she could see him getting worse everyday. A transition had to be organized until the crown prince was old enough to reign. Bakhtiar also wanted the Shah to leave Iran for other reasons, and he knew that the Americans wanted the same ' [21].

The pressure on the Shah got worse during that month of December. Ghobad Zafar, a famous architect and an important personality for the Bakhtiaris wrote a letter to the Shah which he begged the Head of Imperial Protocol, Amir Aslan Afshar, to hand over to him. He suggested the nomination of Chapour Bakhtiar and vouched for his loyalty to the Sovereign and to the Constitution [22]. Other testimonies concur on the matter.

Thus, the die was cast. The Shahbanoo's clan had succeeded in putting the 'cousin' – as Chapour Bakhtiar was called in that small circle of people – into orbit [23].

During the second fortnight of December, the Sovereign received him twice in the palace. The first time, he was discreetly brought there by General Moghaddam, the Head of the Savak. On the 31st of the month, he was officially put in charge of forming the new government. It was to be the last of the monarchy.

From then on, the Shah, who did not care for him very much, only called him 'the last Prime Minister of the Empire'.

*   *

*

When he actually appeared in the political foreground, the new Prime Minister was sixty-five years old. His father, a clan chief from the Bakhtiari tribes who lived in the centre of Iran, had failed in an operation led against the regular army and had been brought before a court martial where he was sentenced to death. He was executed. It happened during the first years of Reza Shah's reign, when the latter was trying to stop the dismantling of the country and sought to put an end to all the separatist seditions.

The other chiefs of the Bakhtiaris who mostly supported the new Sovereign protected young Chapour, and made sure he would have the best possible education in Iran, in Lebanon and then in France where he passed his Phd in law, and became the first Bakhtiari to reach that level. He married a French woman and even did his military service in France, according to his official biographies.

When he was back in his country in 1945, he first tried but failed to get a teaching position at the Law School of the University of Tehran. He was then hired at the Ministry of Labour that had recently been founded by Ahmad Ghavam. At the time of the nationalization of oil, he had become a departmental director in the oil province of Khuzistan – an episode which caused a lot of controversy when he was nominated Prime Minister – before eventually getting a position of Under-Secretary of State at the Ministry of Labour during the last months of the Mossadegh government.

According to Hossein Makki, who was one of the politicians who was closest to Mossadegh, 'he was never a member of the National Front, or one of Mossadegh's close collaborators' [24], which seems to be true. He was nevertheless part of that camp. From 1953 to 1978, Chapour Bakhtiar went to jail on two occasions before he sat on various boards of administration of para-public companies or companies which entirely or partially belonged to the Pahlavi Foundation. That was the attitude of the Shah and of the imperial regime towards 'moderate' opponents. During the last years that preceded the revolution, he also presided over the very prestigious and posh French Circle of the Iranian capital city.

If, during that period, he did not often have the opportunity to publicly express his opposition to the Shah, which was indeed his right and nobody ignored it, he did not hesitate to do it in other circumstances, in particular with the American diplomats in Tehran. He showed them his analyses of the political situation so as to draw their attention to the role he pretended he could play.

THE FALL OF THE MONARCHY AND THE TRIUMPH OF THE REVOLUTION
The handing over of keys

Years later, as he was referring to that episode, he wrote: 'When the [American] embassy [in Tehran] was wrecked and some of the archives were taken, compromising documents were found about almost everybody, except me. How lucky Khomeini would have been if he had discovered the slightest relation with a diplomat that could support his accusations, but my name appeared nowhere, for a good reason' [25].

Nearly all of the 20th volume of these documents concern the relations held by Chapour Bakhtiar with the United States embassy in Tehran [26].

When Chapour Bakhtiar actually arrived at the head of the government, he was unknown to the general public and even in political circles [27]. He did not belong to the entourage of Mossadegh, the leader of the National Front, which he identified with. On the other hand, he was known to be extremely ambitious in the salons, and to show his hatred and rancour towards Mohammad Reza Pahlavi, complaining that he had been kept out of politics for a quarter of a century.

He seemed to be a bon vivant who liked and knew his French wines and fine cuisine. He was also known for his elegance of a purely British style and for his liking of Persian and French poetry. He had numerous volumes of it in the impressive library of his luxurious villa in an upmarket area to the North of Tehran. He was the President of the French Circle where all the famous people involved in politics in Tehran, as well as businessmen, writers, and the most famous architects gathered, and he often invited the famous people he wanted to be noticed with to his table for a meal or for a glass.

His sudden rise to the head of power seems to have resulted from a complex game between four forces:
– the Shah who was lost, ill, psychologically exhausted

was trying to find a man who accepted his departure from Iran to be at the head of the government. All the people he had considered – including Mossadegh's spiritual heir, Professor Gholam Hossein Sadighi, had shied away and demanded his presence on the national territory. History proved them right. So a Bakhtiar or another was of little importance to him, as long as he could leave in a minimum of dignity.

– the Shahbanoo, who worried about keeping the throne for her son – 'I am fighting for my son', she declared, 'and I hope that he will have the required qualities and strength to accomplish his duty' [28] – and was the only one who knew how serious her husband's illness was and how close to the edge of the abyss he physically was, would have liked to save the monarchy. She also wanted to make sure she could stay in power for a few years as constitutional regent. At least, that was the goal set by some of her close friends and relatives. It could have worked out with the backing of the military, so with even the Shah's implicit assent , but also with a man at the head of the executive who would show total self-denial and be able to inspire trust in public opinion and in, at least, some members of the clergy. In fact, that little circle around the Shahbanoo whom the Shah was suspicious of, despised and even hated, but who had an influence on her, actually wanted to take their revenge on the Sovereign. 'Cousin' Chapour Bakhtiar appeared to be the means or the instrument to reach that goal. He was known for his unlimited ambition, and thus for being easily swayed. Some people were dreaming of 'a social-democratic monarchy'. Had Bakhtiar not declared in his first message to the nation that he wanted to create a 'real social-democratic society?' [29]

– The West, Washington, London and Paris first, for reasons which have been analyzed many times since then, mobilized all their forces to force the Shah out of the country, openly betting on the takeover of power by Ruhollah Khomeini. The Westerners saw in him the instrument of a transitional phase, someone who would hand over the keys to the chosen successor, as for General Minh in Saigon in 1975.

– Finally,the man in question thought that the imbroglio was the chance of a lifetime. Like Herostratus, he did not want to be anonymous any more, and play an important role.

*   *

*

On January 6th, the new Prime Minister addressed the nation in a beautiful speech [30], which, because of its structure and some of its aspects, reminded one of the Shah's famous and ill-fated message: 'I have heard the voice of your revolution'.
He presented his ministers to the Shah. The latter could hardly wait until it was over and looked absent, distraught, but remained fully dignified.
The new Prime Minister wanted to look distant in front of the cameras, despite his reputation of courtesy and sense of decorum. Some of his ministers apparently did not want to have their pictures taken with the Shah, especially those who had been the dignitaries of a dying regime. Some were barely respectful. The most decent, allegedly were, the Minister of War, General Shafehgaht, and the Minister of the Post Office and Telecommunications, Lotf-Ali Samimi, the only obvious opponent who accepted to be part of the group [31].
One of the first measures taken by the Prime Ministe was to have the official portraits of the Shah removed from official offices and Iranian embassies abroad [32].
On January 10th, he presented his programme and his

ministers to Parliament. His speech was mostly devoted to a criticism of the regime he was the Prime Minister of, and included particularly severe judgments on the running of public affairs since Mossadegh's downfall [33]. As he was receiving several members of the offices of both Chambers, he actually told them about his intention to initiate a bill to bring all the Prime Ministers and Ministers of the last twenty-five years [34] before the courts and have them given 'very heavy sentences, including the death penalty' even by courts with a limited jurisdiction. He actually proposed such a bill to Parliament. The revolution was to carry out the task.

As soon as Chapour Bakhtiar was nominated, a long manifesto signed by Mozaffar Baghaï was published in Tehran. The new Prime Minister was accused in it of 'having been an agent of Great Britain for a long time' [35]. In fact, the manifesto reveals that at the time of the nationalization of oil and of the 'ousting' of the AIOC, the safe and the archives of the local Managing Director were impounded by a mission that had been appointed to that effect by Mossadegh, and which was presided over by Baghaï himself.

It revealed that Bakhtiar who was then the head of the Ministry of Labour in the oil region of Khuzistan, had been regularly paid out of British funds. According to other documents, there had been some fruitless pressure on the government so that it would become part of the Iranian delegation at the annual conference of the International Labour Organization, to possibly temper down the criticisms that Tehran's envoys might make there against the social management of the oil sector [36]. Had the information reached Mossadegh, or had he not been considered to be important enough to be kept away?

During Chapour Bakhtiar's nomination speech, the representative for Tehran, Dariush Shirvani, reiterated the same accusations and asked the Prime Minister to give an explanation. The latter refused.

*   *

*

A vote of confidence for the new government had been voted in both Chambers, and a regency council had been set up. Chapour Bakhtiar now incarnated legitimacy. He was automatically the commander-in-chief of the armed forces. 'Nobody has the right to make the slightest decision in the armed forces without my authorization' [37] he declared on the BBC. The local press echoed his virile proclamation.

The new Prime Minister was not wrong. The military was ready to follow him. It was actually the only real organized force in the country on which he could rely to reach a balanced political solution. He did not want it. The supporters of the monarchy, and especially of the Shah, still represented a considerable force in the country. They were to show it once the Sovereign had left. He did not want to have to rely on them. The Shah had prevented them from taking action because he feared a civil war [38]. Since he was voluntarily deprived of both elements, like when Kerensky was faced with the Bolshevik revolution in Russia, he did not represent anything anymore. He had already lost the game, if there had ever been one.

Washington and London were eager to make the Shah leave and expected Bakhtiar to make his departure easy. He did so by taking contradictory standpoints, and making declarations to take over power.

His whole attitude during the thirty-seven days he stayed in power reveal a great confusion.

On the one hand, he declared: 'Ayatollah [Khomeini] has run into a snag with me' [39]. He sent the latter a deferential letter in which he wrote: 'Your Holiness knows very well that the programme of this government, from beginning to end, in its general aspect as well as in its details, is everything which, during the long years of clandestinity, repression and oppression, constituted the objective of Your Holiness and of other militants who fought for what is right and for freedom' [40]. He then added: 'I courageously and sincerely enforce this programme and I hope I will benefit from Your Holiness's precious support' [41].

As he was presenting his programme to Parliament, he had declared that he would scrupulously respect 'the word and spirit of the Constitution' [42], even threatening Khomeini's supporters of arrest.

He nevertheless wrote to the same ayatollah that 'any change [should] occur peacefully, with serenity and calm, and according to democratic criteria' [43]. That is why he begged him to postpone his return to Iran. In fact, it seems that he would have liked 'to make Khomeini settle down in Qom if he were to come back, and try to obtain the Shah's abdication in favour of the crown prince on the first possible occasion' [44]. The prince foolishly declared to the AFP he was 'ready, if the people wanted it, to replace his father', adding that he had 'the necessary training to accomplish the task' [45]. He was forgetting or ignored that he could not do so according to the Constitution, since he was not over twenty years old yet.

There is an interesting document available about that period since it was published shortly after it: the political memoirs of Mr Lotf-Ali Samimi, the Minister of the Post Office and Telecommunications, the only personality of the National Front camp to have accepted to collaborate with Chapour Bakhtiar.

THE FALL OF THE MONARCHY AND THE TRIUMPH OF THE REVOLUTION
The handing over of keys

'Mister Bakhtiar had no suggestions to make concerning the running of State affairs' [46]. The former minister added, relating events of the days which were to lead to the collapse of the country: 'General Rahimi, the Chief of the police forces and Administrator of martial law in Tehran, told me that the military had enough of the Prime Minister's indecision and weakness which paralyzed the police forces...There was no Bakhtiar government any more... Those who, like me, thought he could be turned to, quickly realized their mistake' [47].

During those days, Chapour Bakhtiar nevertheless made decisions on paper, at least, which could have pleased such and such a group of opponents in a normal situation, but which had no effect under the circumstances, and were hardly related in the press which was actually in the hands of the revolutionaries; he declared in a Cabinet meeting that 'It was absolutely necessary to prevent even one casualty' [48]. Then, he gave order to the air force to bomb a whole district of Tehran. It was a foolish decision which was not carried out. He broke diplomatic relations with South Africa and Israel to satisfy the leftist intellectual opposition. He declared he wanted to dismantle the Savak. He took over in his own name a decision made by the Azhari Cabinet to reinforce State control over the Pahlavi Foundation, but he still did not have it enforced. He condemned previous governments, especially the last two, and proclaimed his will to bring before the courts the ministers of the past twenty-five years, and even to have them sentenced to capital punishment, but he let Djafar Sharif-Emami and General Azhari leave the country...

In fact, the country progressively sank into total anarchy.

*   *

*

After the Guadeloupe conference*, on January 5th 1979, the American Air Force General, Robert E. Huyser, who was Deputy Commander-in-Chief of NATO forces, was entrusted with an emergency mission to speed up the Shah's departure, neutralize the Iranian military and facilitate Ruhollah Khomeini's coming to power. 'The Carter Administration, in its stupid wish to change the political system in Iran, sent that general who, during a visit of the mess, warned the Iranian armed forces, which are the most professional and the best equipped in the region, and whose equipment is fully supplied by the Americans, that they would not have a single spare part should they react. That was how Khomeini was helped to power and how the revolution was triggered', Count Alexandre de Marenches, the head of the French secret services wrote [50].

The Shah who knew the American officer who was very familiar with Iran, was only informed of his presence after he had arrived.

The rumour spread in Tehran that he had come to take part in the preparation of a military intervention, even of a coup d'État, to stabilize the situation and put an end to unrest [51]. It was very quickly known that it was not the case. Huyser met up with the military leaders on several occasions and for a long time, and he took part in meetings with the revolutionary leaders, one of which lasted ten hours. After the Shah's departure, and before Khomeini's arrival, he even worried about a decent organization of the event. Huyser did not even deign to pay a visit to Prime Minister Bakhtiar. The latter was to say that he had never heard of him [52].

In the Shah's entourage, Ardeshir Zahedi suggested the

---

* See chapters XII, XIV and XV...

arrest of the American general for illegal entry on the national territory, and his expulsion [53]. The Shah refused.

The general who was accompanied by the United States ambassador to Tehran, was finally received by the Sovereign. The Shah wrote the following: ' What was on their minds was to know what day and at what time I would be leaving' [54].

It was even written, not without some reason, that 'the real master of Iran was General Huyser during that short period of time. He was organizing Khomeini's arrival' [55].

General Rabiï, the Commander-in-Chief of the Air Force on one of the bases where Huyser was staying, declared the following before he was executed by the revolutionaries: 'General Huyser threw the King out of the country like a dead mouse' [56].

*   *

*

Despite all the entreaties to dissuade him from going, the Shah left the country with the Shahbanoo on January 16th 1979 [57]. Even if the idea of his departure had been announced in Washington by Secretary of State Cyrus Vance on January 11th, the date given had been kept secret for security reasons and to avoid demonstrations from those who wanted to prevent the Sovereign from going away.

On the departure day, according to a trustworthy witness, the American ambassador called the palace every fifteen minutes to ask if the Shah had left Iran [58].

Contrary to what the Shah wrote [59], there were few personalities at the international airport of Mehrabad, no minister, except the Prime Minister, who had the indelicacy of arriving late and keeping the imperial couple waiting, and the president of the Senate did not come either. On the other hand,

591

many military leaders were present, those who wanted to once more show their loyalty to the Shah. The diplomatic corps was not represented. There were no military honours rendered to a King going into exile.

After Chapour Bakhtiar's late arrival, the Shah received him for a fairly long period of time in the private sitting-room of the imperial wing at Mehrabad. The Shah said later on that during their discussion: '[I asked] Chapour Bakhtiar to be in charge of the full security of the personalities of the regime, and, if necessary, to help them leave, which Bakhtiar had expressly promised he would do' [60]. The latter did not confirm that promise[61] when he related the Shah's wish. He apparently said the opposite to the imperial couple before adding that 'the Queen had intervened to tell him: 'Bakhtiar is making a sacrifice, he must be trusted' [62].

The imperial couple took leave of the personalities who were present and got on the aeroplane. The Shah, despite his extreme tiredness and as usual, at the controls of his aircraft, summoned his Prime Minister for a few last recommandations. He ended up by saying, with great emotion: 'I place Iran in your trust and leave you in the hands of God'. Bakhtiar kissed his hand before leaving.

Their destination was Aswan in Egypt. Mohammad Reza Pahlavi's exile with no return was starting.

*   *

*

The Shah's departure made the last element of an illusion of normality and of a slight hope of a return to calm and stability, disappear.

Things were to move really fast.

Chapour Bakhtiar continued to make declarations in which he especially criticized the Shah, his policy and the leaders of a regime which hardly existed anymore, evoking democracy and even warning against a return to dictatorship.

In order to be able to reassure a legitimist part of the population, he however contradicted himself a few times: 'We will die or we will defend the Constitution' [64].

On the other hand, he suggested to Khomeini, who actually refused, to take the lead of the first government of the Islamic republic which he would proclaim [65]. Later, Abol Hassan Bani Sadr, the first president of the new regime and close adviser to Khomeini in Neauphle-le-Château, was to confirm the existence of negotiations to that effect, but they failed; however, they were never denied [66].

* *

*

There were still demonstrations in the streets of the capital and in a few towns against the Shah and for Khomeini. There was hardly any repression. The Prime Minister and a few ministers continued to appear in their empty offices. A coffin was exhibited here and there from time to time, and journalists were invited to film these staged 'fake funerals' and give accounts of them to fuel the propaganda, maintain the pressure and prevent the demobilization of the crowds.

The main Western embassies, the head of government, two or three high-ranking military officers and delegates of ayatollah Khomeini negotiated to organize the latter's arrival. Bakhtiar decided to forbid it, without being able to enforce his decision, and then he lifted the ban.

The State did not exist anymore, society was at a virtual

standstill and there was a general state of insecurity. It was total chaos.

* *

*

Rumours of a coup d'État organized by certain elements of the army, airborne troops, 'special forces', the 'guard' of the national Police forces, and of the imperial guard – they were all powerful and extremely well disciplined – spread. They were not unfounded. A scheme for 'national safety' was set up. The idea was to severely hit the radical opposition, and set up a military government around General Badreï, the new commander-in-chief of the army. According to the same rumours, the new chief of the National Police Forces and Administrator of martial law in Tehran, General Rahimi, the High Command of the Navy and of the Air Force, the powerful army corps of Khuzistan that was under General Djafarian's orders, the airborne brigade based in Shiraz, whose commander, General Shafa'at, had said in public that he would have his men jump over the capital and had placed them in a state of alert, all supported the scheme.

In a declaration to the press, General Manutshehr Khosrodad, the commander of the airborne brigade based in Bagheshah, Tehran, implicitly confirmed these rumours in a solemn warning [67].

They were all waiting for an 'order' which never came.

The command structure of the imperial armed forces was decentralized, contrary to those, for example, of the Turkish. Everything had been conceived and organized to make a coup d'État impossible, so that the Shah, the constitutional commander-in-chief, would be the actual commander-in-chief and would be protected from any action taken by the military.

THE FALL OF THE MONARCHY AND THE TRIUMPH OF THE REVOLUTION
The handing over of keys

The 'political' high-ranking officers were kept away from strategic areas for decades, and were sometimes appointed ministers, or sent to embassies, to the Senate, to provincial governor's offices, or simply discreetly or not kept aside. The man of a coup, who, at that time, would not have happened without problems – as was the case later with the reaction of some of the Algerian military against Islamic subversion –, did not exist. A coup was politically and technically possible. It would have benefited from the support of a large part of public opinion. It had no leader and could not take place [68].

Later, American analysts who were not in favour of the policies followed by the Carter Administration, suggested that, among Iranian politicians, Ardeshir Zahedi was the only one to have the required authority on or in the ranks of the military command 'to solve the crisis in a positive way for his Sovereign and for his country' [69]. Only the Shah could give him that legal authority. He did not. 'Zahedi therefore believed that it was possible to organize a coup d'État...but only if, when he left Iran, the Shah let his friends fight in his name... He was the most likely to be able to save everything' [70]. The Sovereign did not entrust him with that mission, and he was not the kind of man to act against the Shah's wishes [71].

Mohammad Reza Pahlavi could have given the order to his loyal Badreï to take action. He was asked that question on numerous occasions between January 16th and February 11th. He never answered it.

The Prime Minister could have asked the armed forces to 'restore order'. He hated them and feared them even more than the revolutionaries whose ideals he pretended to share.

The Head of General Staff, General Gharabaghi, had the power, in theory, to trigger 'something'. He was negotiating with the revolutionaries and with General Huyser at how best to salvage something from the situation. He did not succeed, but he saved his life.

The Americans had a strong influence over the Air Force and the Navy, but not so much over the Army and even less so over the Police Forces and the gendarmerie, which would have made it easier to take action. They could, however, encourage them. They did everything in their power to neutralize the armed forces because they were totally obsessed with their hatred for the Shah, and thought they had found the man of the situation in Ruhollah Khomeini.

During the afternoon of February 11th, General Badreï made a desperate attempt. He was assassinated. All the high-ranking officers who were involved were executed during the night of February 11th to 12th, or shortly after the triumph of the revolution.

*   *

*

The Shah's departure released forces which he had managed to control and prevent from taking action for fear of a civil war or of bloody confrontations, those of the opponents to radical fundamentalism, to Ruhollah Khomeini and to the 'damned alliance' of the red and the black which was now openly flaunted.

The 'quality' newspapers of the capital were under the control of revolutionary committees. Small publications, which were quasi-confidential started appearing. Some of them openly campaigned against the theocracy and the revolution.

Only one important weekly, *Khândaniha*, which had been traditionally critical of the authorities for decades, and known for its mocking tone, however joined the trend. Its chief editor,

THE FALL OF THE MONARCHY AND THE TRIUMPH OF THE REVOLUTION
The handing over of keys

Ali Asghar Amirani, was to be assassinated after the revolution. The writer and lampoonist Mehdi Bahar published an opuscule against the theocratic threat which hovered over the country. Thousands of copies sold, were photocopied and secretly distributed. Small meetings were held to 'organize resistance', mobilize forces and create networks.

In the general atmosphere of anarchy that prevailed, a small committee took the control in Tehran of the Amdjadieh sports complex. The place was turned into the headquarters of the counter-revolution. Three public meetings were held there in the space of a few days [72].
The network – which had been well established for ages – of the 'local districts associations', a workers' union, a few agricultural cooperatives from the greater suburbs of the capital, two sports clubs and small ad hoc circles of academics gave their support to the movement. A committee of ten people who was presided by the young journalist and town councillor of Tehran, Mohammad Reza Taghizadeh was created, and decided to organize a popular demonstration for the loyalty to the Constitution in the streets. The date of February 25th was chosen. A delegation of the committee was sent to Chapour Bakhtiar who expressed serious reservations: 'You will not gather 2,000 people', 'You will make dissensions worse'. He could only yield in front of the organizers' will, and he did not have the demonstration banned. Until then, only the ones of radical opponents had been authorized. The Prime Minister asked for Mossadegh's portraits to be carried by demonstrators. The organizers then demanded that those of the Shah should be carried as well. He opposed his veto. It was decided that the national flag would be carried. The Prime Minister told them in the end that they should not be expecting any help or the slightest support from the authorities: 'I was asked to help with that demonstration, and I refused' [73].

On Friday, January 25th, columns of demonstrators left from twelve areas in the capital. The most important group came from the Amdjadieh complex. They were all going towards Baharestan square, in front of Parliament, a symbolical place which is full of history. Despite the repeated messages from the Radio-Television to dissuade the population from participating in the demonstrations, and the threats made by ayatollah Talehghani, a radical religious leader, there was a huge crowd: from 150,000 to 300,000 people according to the press which was in the hands of the revolutionary committees. If it had been a pro-Khomeini demonstration, their number would probably have been raised to half a million. It was barely referred to in the international press.

On Baharestan square, a famous preacher, hodjatoleslam Behbahani started speaking and urged the crowd to defend the nation: he was to be assassinated a few days later. Mohammad Reza Taghizadeh read the resolution. It was at that moment that a young man who could not be found afterwards, suddenly shouted 'Djavid Shah', Long Live the King! It was a familiar slogan which the huge crowd repeated with a lot of emotion. The demonstration was turned into a happening in favour of the exiled Sovereign.

The Prime Minister who had been told about the importance of the demonstration, had flown over it in a helicopter. Early in the afternoon, a cortege of about fifty thousand workers had come from the factories in the West of the capital and the police tried to stop them from joining square Baharestan. They managed to get near the presidential office of the Cabinet. After some hesitation, Chapour Bakhtiar received their representatives and voiced his surprised at the importance of the march and invited them to keep their calm and to break up.

THE FALL OF THE MONARCHY AND THE TRIUMPH OF THE REVOLUTION
The handing over of keys

The organization committee of the demonstration decided to organize another one two weeks later. Khomeini's return and the way events were turning out were to change the situation.

Other demonstrations of the people for the Shah followed in Kerman, Esfahan, Ahwaz, Kermanshah, and Rasht, and in minor towns.

On order of General Ali Neshat who was to be shot after the revolution, the imperial guard organized an impressive march in the streets of the capital, and showed its fire power, its armoured vehicles... The soldiers were warmly cheered in some neighbourhoods. In others, they had stones thrown at them.

Iran was really less unanimously against the Shah than the quality international press led people to believe.

Those who were taking those initiatives could not know that the die was cast and ignored the sordid transactions which were going on behind their backs. Some even think today that the national awakening of the last few weeks may have contributed to the speeding-up of the official collapse of the regime because of the fear that arose of a conjunction between the legitimist opinion and the military which had remained loyal to the Shah and to the Constitution.

*   *

*

On February 1st, Ruhollah Khomeini arrived in Tehran in an Air France plane called Liberty for the occasion. He was accompanied by about a hundred foreign journalists.
Even after the Shah's departure, he still prevaricated a

great deal. He was fearing an assassination attempt, a plane hijack, or being arrested by the military. His 'entourage' convinced him to leave Neauphle-le-Château. His movement might not have stood the test of time. He was welcomed to Tehran by a huge crowd.

As soon as he arrived, he set up a 'Council of the Islamic revolution', the formation of which still remains officially secret today [74].

On February 5th, while Chapour Bakhtiar was still granting a few interviews as Prime Minister and still going to his office, ayatollah Khomeini had settled down in the building of a private high school in Tehran. The latter made a decree to appoint Mehdi Bazargan Prime Minister of a republic which had not yet proclaimed itself, and had no Constitution. His nomination ordinance was already a sign of the direction taken by the regime that was to be set up: 'In accordance with the law of Islam, the opposition will be considered as a blasphemy' [75].

Bazargan was born in Tehran in 1905 into a family of shop-keepers, and he held a degree from the École Centrale of Paris thanks to a government grant that he had got under Reza Shah's reign. He was a professor of thermodynamics at the Technical College of the University of Tehran where he was dean for many years, and where he was remembered as an excellent manager. Bazargan joined Mossadegh's national movement at the time when a good deal of his colleagues belonged to the extreme-left wing of the political scene [76].

He was one of Mossadegh's close collaborators and advisers and the latter chose him to be the first managing director of the Iranian National Petroleum Company (INPC). After the 'old lion's' downfall, he took part in the work of various groups that came from the National Front, and then founded, in 1961, the Movement for the Liberation of Iran, trying to combine nationalism and religious precepts. Mehdi Bazargan was indeed deeply religious.

Even if he was incarcerated a few times for his opposition to the Shah between 1953 and 1978, he still remained a very prosperous public works contractor. He represented a famous American brand of air conditioning units in Iran. He created a distribution network, assembly workshops which employed many workers, technicians and engineers, and he became the main supplier of the State. He often went to national palaces and frequented the highest dignitaries of the government in the line of his work. His honesty and the good quality of the work done were recognized by all, even by his political opponents.

This scientist, who was deeply religious and benefited from a certain moral prestige, proved to have an extremely weak character when he was put to the test of the management of the State. As a member of the Council of the revolution, he played a part in all the crimes, covered up for them, and showed his inability in public, even taking the liberty of making moderate and useless criticisms.

While thousands of people are executed on order of the Council of the Revolution which he was a member of, his deputy, Vice-Prime Minister Abbas Amir Entezam declared: 'The government in general, and the Ministry of Justice in particular, can exert no control over the deliberations and decisions of revolutionary tribunals' [77]. He still managed to save the lives of a few people in prison and saved Persepolis from destruction, after the mullahs had ordered the latter. His government was reshuffled many times and soon fell into anarchy. He remained in Iran after he was dismissed soon after the hostage-taking affair of the United States embassy in Tehran, and played a more or less important role. He was transported to Switzerland when he was seriously ill and died there in January 1995.

*

Once the Shah was out of the country, and Khomeini was back in Iran, a Council of the Revolution, the supreme form of power, and a provisional government had been set up, and the only problem to solve was the one of the armed forces so as to end the operation.

*   *

*

As soon as February 6th, the ministries swore allegiance to Bazargan, the head of the provisional government, in press releases made by 'revolutionary committees'. Bazargan asked the Premier Vice-Ministers of each department to be in charge of them. Chapour Bakhtiar still chaired the Cabinet. 'That lonely man who sits at the back of his empty office, that chairman of the cabinet who presides over nothing' [78] nevertheless continued to make declarations which hardly appeared in the press, especially in the French press. When he was informed of Bazargan's nomination, he declared: 'If they want to make recommendations to me, or give me advice, I am ready to receive them. They can always proclaim what they want, it does not bother me. If they set themselves up in a government, and start giving orders, then I am telling you right now: I will have them arrested' [79]. 'If the government chosen by His Holiness ayatollah Khomeini is a Western-style 'shadow cabinet', 'I will not hinder its activity, but if it wants to take control of the ministries, we will react' [80].

THE FALL OF THE MONARCHY AND THE TRIUMPH OF THE REVOLUTION
The handing over of keys

*   *

*

On February 11th, he declared to the Senate that 'he would resist until the end', and then had a frugal breakfast in his office, 'a few leaves of lettuce', the press wrote [81]. Afterwards, he went to the Military Academy nearby, took a helicopter and disappeared 'to continue the fight', he was to declare later on [82].

Forty-eight hours later, there was a declaration of his arrest and transfer to Khomeini's residence where the most important personalities were detained [83]. Then, nothing was heard about his fate before he reappeared in Paris in July after having spent some time in Chambéry. He was savagely assassinated by agents of the Islamic republic in Suresnes, on August 6th 1991 [84].

On that same day of February 11th, the Senate, the House of Representatives and Regency Council put paid to one another.
That same day, General Rahimi, the administrator of martial law in the capital, decided to declare a curfew there from 4 p.m. onwards. The release was read on the radio at 11 a.m. Soon after, Ruhollah Khomeini asked the population on the same national radio to go down in the streets in masses and to bring their children so that the troops could not intervene.

*   *

*

Around midday, following the action taken by General Huyser, an ad hoc superior council of the military which had no legal existence or authorization from the Shah, who was still the Commander-in-Chief of the armed forces, or from the Regency Council, or from the Prime Minister, was summoned by General Hossein Fardoust, the head of the special intelligence bureau and General Gharabaghi, the Chief of General Staff of the armed forces.

Twenty-seven military leaders, including three generals, eighteen lieutenant generals, two admirals and four major generals came.

No minutes of the discussions are available. A 'proclamation' was drafted by General Fardoust, specifying that 'the council had unanimously decided its neutrality in the political quarrels which opposed factions, this because they wanted to avoid making the chaos worse as well as the prevailing anarchy, and also to avoid a bloodbath. Order had been given to the military units to go back to their barracks. The Iranian military would remain, as it had always been, the defender of the noble Iranian people. It fully supported the people's legitimate wishes [85].

Fardoust was undoubtedly the main architect of that operation with indeed, the backing of Gharabaghi. '[He] betrayed the Shah and, if that is the case, his story remains one of the most fascinating of that period' American analysts were to write later [86]. He indeed had a strange life and odd habits. He had been Mohammad Reza Pahlavi's school friend ever since primary school, then at the Rosey where he had been sent on the latter's special request. He had been the coordinator of all the security and intelligence services and even the Chief of the imperial Inspection service. He held the rank of general but was 'on a temporary assignment'. The doors of the imperial cabinet were virtually open for him. However, according to a trustworthy testimony, his visits had become sparse in the last few months, and then had stopped, without the Shah's slightest reaction being noticed at the court. The latter had become

The fall of the monarchy and the triumph of the revolution
The handing over of keys

indifferent to everything. The day after Mossadegh's downfall, it was already specified in a report from the 2nd Bureau that he was suspected of having dubious contacts with the Soviet services. The Shah had not taken it into account and his rise to power had continued. Western experts think that he was one of the KGB's 'sleeping agents', as there were several in the higher positions in the intelligence services of the 'free world' [87]. After the triumph of the revolution, he became the main founder of the Savama, which replaced the Savak. When Shahryar Shafigh, one of the Shah's nephews, and a courageous and brilliant officer of the imperial navy, was assassinated in Paris, the whole of the French press signalled his presence in France. He allegedly was the director of the crime. Later on, he appeared in television programmes that were particularly foul concerning the Shah, and perpetrated 'Memories' of the same style. In the middle of the eighties, his death was announced without any other comments made. Had he been exfiltrated to the Soviet Union as some thought? It is a possibility and has happened in other instances. The double or triple agent had no reason to be any more.

In the following hours, armed professionals, Islamic-Marxist mujahiddins, ultra-left-wing fedayins, who were Trostkyist and Maoist, and the Tudeh networks which had been reconstituted for a year, were reinforced by Palestinian combatants who had already arrived weeks before and by some who had arrived the night before in three airborne troop carriers (from Syria, and Libya?). They all took control of the main barracks of the capital [89]. The elite units had been given order to hand in their weapons, not to use them, and not to shoot at the people.

The slaughter that followed everywhere was terrifying. The exact number of victims of those last few hours will probably never be known – victims of the decision made by 'the superior council of the armed forces' under the pressure of General Huyser who had threatened to 'break the back' of the military if it resisted and especially if it used its weapons. There were undoubtedly several thousand victims. The Iranian military did not dismantle itself. It let itself be slaughtered because it had no leader. General Badreï, the commander-in-chief of the army who had shown the will to take up weapons and organize the resistance at the end of the council meeting, was to be shot shortly after his arrival at his command post, by a burst of automatic fire in the back. In Tehran itself, thirteen generals of the armed forces were shot within a few hours [90].

A chapter of the history of Iran had just been closed.

The imperial regime, like that of Louis XVI or of Nicholas II 'found itself deeply undermined before the final attack was launched' [91].

Those in power collapse, especially when they lose trust. Had the Shah not been driven to turn a riot into a 'revolution' by a pusillanimous speech?

EPILOGUE

EPILOGUE

THE SUFFERING AND TRAGEDY OF A LONE MAN

When he left his palace on January 16th 1979, Mohammad Reza Pahlavi knew that he was to never return. He said it later.

At the international airport of Tehran, although all the people present were struck by the fact that he carried himself proudly and showed great dignity, he still could not help the tears in his eyes when his loyal generals bade him moving farewells and begged him not to abandon the country and the military for the last time.

After take-off, and despite his extreme tiredness, he, as usual, took the controls of the plane. He said later that it was because he feared a hijack. Did he dread an action from his opponents, or rather his enemies, or from those in the military more particularly? The latter had opposed his departure and had carefully not been made aware of it, for fear of demonstrations at the airport or of a coup that would force him not to abandon his country [1].

*　　*

*

Aswan was the first stop-over of his exile on President Sadat's invitation. The Shah was still hoping to be able to go to the United States – a trip that Ardeshir Zahedi and Amir Aslan Afshar had prepared in all discretion during the first two weeks of January 1979.

Washington's reaction had not been negative: the stay would be private, but the Shah would meet President Carter and many American personalities. Mohammad Reza Pahlavi still believed he would be able to make the Americans turn against the Islamists. He was wrong. In fact, all Washington wanted was to speed up his departure and leave him hope.

Mohammad Reza Pahlavi was still the legal and legitimate Sovereign of his country. At the Aswan airport, the imperial couple were officially received by President and Mrs Sadat in all dignity: 'Be assured that this country is yours, and that we are your people's brothers' the Rais said. The Shah was moved to tears. Both men hugged warmly. Military honours were given. Thousands of people cheered the Shah and the Rais in the streets.

Sadat wished the Shah would stay in Egypt. He even suggested to have some of the Iranian navy and air force transferred to Egypt so as to use them as an asset or a springboard.

The Shah maintained his original idea of going to Washington. Two long conversations took place with Gerald Ford, the former President of the United States who was in Aswan to prepare his future meetings.

Washington's definite answer was late to come.

The Shah begged his Chief of Protocol to get it over

Epilogue – The suffering and tragedy of a lone man

with. Ambassador Afshar called the American representative in Cairo. Twenty-four hours later, the answer came: 'The government of the United States regrets not to be able to welcome the Shah on the American soil'.

There was no hope left there.

The Shah did not want to stay in Egypt. Sadat was about to go abroad. His presence in Aswan and the security measures it entailed could be a problem for the tourists who were numerous at that time of the year. He did not want to be in the way.

Where was he to go? Nothing was planned.

It was then that Ardeshir Zahedi, who had left Iran on the same day as the Sovereign, but on an airliner, called the King of Morocco and explained the situation to him at great length, and the difficult position the imperial couple were in. Hassan II immediately called the Shah and invited him to his country.

On January 22nd, the Pahlavis were accompanied to the Aswan airport by the Egyptian presidential couple, and after the official ceremony, they left for Marrakech.

* *

*

Once he had left Iran [2], the Shah had no trump card left. He did not want to, or could not, rely on all the armed forces and on a good part of public opinion which had remained loyal to him. His Western friends had betrayed him. He was unwell, but no-one knew it. When the Sovereign's Boeing landed on the Marrakech airport on January 22nd, King Hassan II was there to welcome him, but there were no military honours or cameras. The local press had been asked to remain discreet on a trip which was supposed to be private.

The imperial couple were put up in a palace on the outskirts of town that had a magnificent view, but was rather isolated.

Hassan II had accepted to receive the Shah out of friendship, and after he had been asked to. Both men appreciated each other and were on first-name terms. The hospitality was not to last long. The Shah's entourage was made aware of it as soon as the couple got off the plane.

Life became somewhat normal, even relaxed. After spending several days in Marrakech, the couple travelled to Rabat where they were housed in the Royal palace. The Shah took frequent walks in the garden, often in the company of his Chief of protocol, nearly always in a certain silence. The Iranian ambassador was also often present – this was to cost him dearly. The Shah took up golf and started the beginning of his memoirs which were later on to be published in French and Persian in Paris, and then also in English [3]. He gave a private audience to several journalists whom he trusted, and an interview to the *Daily Telegraph*.

He nearly always took his meals alone. He began a very discreet epistolary relationship with his second wife Soraya, refusing to accept the hundreds of demands for an audience from the Iranian Diaspora – there were hundreds of thousands Iranians fleeing the revolution. However, the Shahbanoo always had her close circle of friends, some of whom were little appreciated by her husband.

The military chiefs with the exception of the General Staff, continually sent messages asking for the "green light" to establish law and order. These messages were to be more and more alarming after the arrival of Khomeni in Tehran on the 1st of February. This met with no reaction or reply.

Epilogue – The suffering and tragedy of a lone man

* *

*

During the day of the 11th of February, the Imperial regime lived its final hours. The happenings in Tehran were followed by the imperial couple and their small entourage on several television sets. There was no longer any direct contact with Iran. The atmosphere was one of amazement, grief and already remorse. Bakhtiar's inconsistency plunged some of them into stupefaction and derision.

Mohammad Reza Pahlavi was more than ever distant, as in a state of limbo. He now knew that all was finished and that he was to be the last Shah of Iran.

The following day, the 12th, he came out of his stupor, and asked ambassador Amir Aslan Afshar to organise the return of 'Shahin' the imperial Boeing and to thank the crew. This was done. The curtain had now fallen on his reign. It was the end of his dreams.

* *

*

There were two sides to the medal.

The man who was, for several long years, one of the most important heads of State in the world, one of the arbitrators on the international scene, was exiled, a wanderer even undesirable.

The Moroccan courtesy was impeccable. The imperial couple and their small entourage were pampered by the Moroccan court. Those who came to visit them benefited from considerable advantages.

When the Shah arrived in Morocco, he was made to understand that it would be only for several days. Little by little he was to be shown the exit.

Where was he to go?

The imperial couple were to know the same misfortunes and cowardliness as Nicholas II and his family after the last Czar's abdication, who was even refused asylum by his British and Danish cousins and his closest allies, the French. The Shah, who had discreetly come to the aid of several exiled sovereigns, had nobody who would welcome him.

Mohammad Reza Pahalavi wished to prolong his stay in Morocco by several weeks, perhaps more, but King Hassan was more and more impatient to see him leave.

He begged a mutual friend, the Count of Marenches, to come and see Mohammad Reza Pahlavi, to explain the situation and the problems and threats that Morocco were facing through the presence of the Shah. 'This was to be one of the most tragic discussions of my existence. I had before me the man who was, up to recently, one of the most envied, the most adulated and most powerful on the planet' [5].

If one was to believe another document [6], Hassan II himself had explained to the Shah that with the forthcoming summit of the foreign ministers of the Islamic conference, his presence on Moroccan soil might cause problems and that such or such minister would use the pretext not to participate... 'I therefore preferred to ask him [the Shah] to leave Morocco, to choose another country of residence, even if it were to come back later on. He was uncomfortable and sad that I had asked'.

On top of this goings-on was enormous American pressure to distance him from Morocco, and to find another landing point. The American ambassador Richard Parker, an ex-under secretary of State, Don Agger, and some emissaries from the

EPILOGUE – THE SUFFERING AND TRAGEDY OF A LONE MAN

CIA were to succeed one another next to Mohammad Reza Pahlavi to reiterate the refusal of Washington to receive him, or more so, to welcome him. In fact, the United States had just recognised the Islamic republic and no longer considered him as head of state so their intention was to pressure him to leave the Maghreb and find another place of residence.

The Americans proposed Paraguay. The Shah refused point blank. Then they suggested South Africa, a friendly country for Iran and one ready to receive him with dignity. Mohammad Reza Pahlavi hesitated. He did not want to enter the country of Apartheid.

His enemies would not hesitate to use it against him. On top of that, South Africa brought back bad memories, his father, practically deported by the British, died there. Nevertheless, he did not say no.

The 21st of March, the Iranian new-year, a day of joy and festivity, was spent in worry and uncertainty.

Where to go?

The 24th, the American emissaries, informed of the decision of the Shah to leave Morocco, and determined to finish for once and for all, returned once more to the palace to inform him that Hassan II's aeroplane would be at his disposal on Friday the 30th. 'Your Majesty, I am only authorised to tell you that the aeroplane is ready for Friday', Don Agger said to him. It was hardly a polite expulsion order.

The flight-plan was set for South Africa. For several days, the Shah had expressed the wish to settle, perhaps permanently, in Mexico. During the past three or four days, the efforts of Ardeshir Zahedi, using once more his extraordinary address book, Princess Ashraf, David Rockefeller [7] and Henry Kissinger resulted in finding a new landing point, direction Mexico, the Bahamas. The agreement had been finalised.

On March 30th, Hassan II's aeroplane left the imperial couple at Nassau international airport. A man, called Robert Armao from the Rockefeller's entourage, awaited the couple on the Nassau tarmac. He would become responsible for the Shah's life. It was a rather bizarre situation. Who chose him? According to Princess Ashraf, it was David Rockefeller [8], who insisted that Armao, who had already 'retired from the Rockefeller Foundation' – he was only thirty years old! – make regular reports to his superiors on the Shah's day-to-day living and situation.

A small humid and uncomfortable villa belonging to a local businessman had been rented at an outrageous price on Paradise Island, one of seven hundred isles and islands that constitute the Bahamas archipelago. The imperial couple and a servant were housed there. The other companions from the small group were housed in local hotel rooms.

Despite a magnificent sea view and a warm welcome from those tourists who recognised the Shah, life was very hard. The couple were practically under house arrest, because "begged" not to leave the villa. The security was difficult to ensure. Above all, that month of April 1979, was to be one of the bloodiest throughout the repression that had descended on Iran .Every day, the radio told of the putting to death of ten to thirty people from the elite class of the imperial regime, people that the Shah had known and often appreciated and who had served him. In the one month more than a thousand people were assassinated in that fashion – 'bloody April', were to write the papers: ministers, such as Amir Abbas Hoveyda, generals, great intellectuals, academics, famous doctors, businessmen....

It was a nightmare.

Mohammad Reza Pahlavi was totally beside himself, he talked to nobody within his entourage, had taken up smoking again, and wanted, once again, to leave.

Epilogue – The suffering and tragedy of a lone man

To go where?

The Mexican government had been sounded out through the Rockefeller Foundation, the reply was not negative. However, there was nothing official. Ardeshir Zahedi, a personal friend of President Lopez Portillo, who had kept an excellent souvenir of his visit to Iran, visited the country and negotiated the settlement of the imperial couple and their entourage. He obtained the official agreement from the Mexican government and parliament that president Lopez Portillo gave him by letter during a dinner given in his honour [9]. The town of Cuernavaca is a beautiful pleasant residential city situated a hundred kilometres from Mexico, very much sought after and in fashion since the reign of Emperor Maximilian.

Three villas were rented by Ardeshir Zahedi, one, 'Villa of Roses', for the imperial couple, another nearby for visitors and guests, and a third for the personnel.

On June 10th 1979, the Shah, the Shahbanoo and their small entourage arrived in Mexico in a small hired private jet. "The most difficult part of the exile" [10] had come to an end, the Shah was to say in Mexico. He did not know what was awaiting him afterwards.

The first three months of the stay in Cuernavaca were peaceful. Mohammad Reza Pahlavi's general health improved. Above all, he got down to the drafting of two fully identical versions of *Answer to History* one in French, and the other in Persian. He started to read the international press again, as well as several historical works. He entertained, not only his children and some members of his family, but also personalities from international politics such as Richard Nixon, Henry Kissinger, David Rockefeller, Joseph Reed…….

Some rare Iranians were also to visit [11], such as Ardeshir

617

Zahedi, regularly and for long periods. The Shahbanoo's friends were however, very rare. Her elder sister Princess Shams, and her husband, Mehrdad Pahlbod, rented a villa not far from the residence of the imperial couple. Mehrdad Pahlbod became the favourite tennis partner of Mohammad Reza Pahlavi. The Queen Mother was also there, staying with Princess Shams and Pahlbod. Apparently, suffering from a serious illness, she understood little of what had happened and of what was happening around her.

*   *

*

The Shah had been suffering from his illness for a few years, and it was to become rapidly terminal. He had a terrible attack during the last week of September and it became public.

It was in April 1974, during an annual check-up by professor Fehlinger in Venice, that the first dangerous symptoms were discovered. From October 1974 onwards, a renowned medical team were sent for, and charged with the task of managing and treating the illness that Mohammad Reza Pahlavi [12] was suffering from. There was to be talk later on of Hodgkin's disease, then of a similar pathology, Waldenström's syndrome, which is confirmed in the Shahbanoo's *Mémoires* [13]. There were to be further complications, notably in the pancreas and the spleen.

Because of the Shah's deteriorating health, Robert Armao and his assistant, a certain Mark Morse, decided (by themselves?) that he should be treated by American doctors. After consulting the Rockefeller Foundation and probably the State Department, a New-York GP named Benjamin H. Kean, who was well-known in American high spheres, was called to the Shah's bedside. The conception of medical confidentiality being far less strict in the United States than in France meant that doctor Kean published in-depth explanations on his case and personality after his death [14]. Doctor Kean's point of view is somewhat different to doctor Flandrin's – that is the least one can say – which was certainly taken up and approved of by the Shahbanoo in her *Mémoires*.

To our understanding, the other GP's did not publish or reveal anything. It is thus difficult, from a strictly medical point of view, and without knowing every element of the file, to bear a judgment on his illness. From the historical point of view, it actually seems of secondary importance. On the other hand, the way the patient was followed and treated is worthy of attention, politically speaking.

Doctor Kean landed in Cuernavaca on September 29th. At first, his relations with the Shah were difficult. The latter apparently made him understand that he had not called him to his bedside. He refused the tests that the doctor had asked him to undergo, and did not have his medical file handed to him. The practitioner replied that he thought his case was serious, and that he would need much more sophisticated treatment than the one he had received so far, and he went back to New York*.

While the New York GP was going back to the United States, Doctor Flandrin arrived in Mexico on the Shahbanoo's request. The French man's conclusion was that the Shah should be quickly taken to hospital. Mohammad Reza Pahlavi accepted the idea, but refused to go to the United States, as was suggested. Ardeshir Zahedi and crown prince Reza shared the Sovereign's point of view. Princess Ashraf only trusted American doctors.

---

* Doctor Kean had a few reservations concerning the treatment prescribed to the Shah since 1974 after he had learnt more about his file. He actually placed the beginning of his illness in 1972.

At the beginning of October, the Shah enquired into the possibility of being hospitalized in Paris [15]. The answer was late in coming. The entourage and the doctors started quarrelling near the patient. Robert Armao arrived from New York and met doctor Flandrin for the first time. He informed Kean in New York. The latter did not really know the French physician. He found out about him that he was Jean Bernard's assistant, who enjoyed a worldwide reputation, and guessed the type of illness that Mohammad Reza Pahlavi might be affected with, and the 'reasons of State' which had motivated his refusal to have further tests.

A few days later, everyone in the United States was aware of the nature of the Shah's illness and the 'affair' remained in the headlines of the world press until he died.

The two GP's, Flandrin and Kean, only agreed on one point: it was urgent to take him to a well-equipped hospital, consequently, to a university hospital.

The American clan was opposed to the only possible choice: a Mexican university hospital where the appropriate department was headed by a professor of French training. Mohammad Reza Pahlavi was not in favour of the 'American option'. President Carter hesitated to authorize the transfer of the patient to the United States and consulted the Iranian government. However, apparently under Rockefeller's pressure and faced with the criticism of a major part of the political class, he ended up yielding. Over a quarter of a century later, a few questions remained unanswered: why was it decided to transfer the Shah to the United States? Who was at the origin of the final decision? Why was there a complete change of the medical team and why was the treatment started from scratch again? The departure for the United States represents the beginning of a real ordeal.

Epilogue – The suffering and tragedy of a lone man

In the night of October 22nd, as the Shah was at his worst, he left Cuernavaca and the peaceful Villa of Roses, the last place where he had been able to keep his illusions of hope. He could barely walk and suffered in silence. He was taken on board a rented plane.

The plane first landed in Fort Lauderdale in Florida, on Washington's orders, to proceed with the customs and immigration formalities. No-one had been officially told at the airport. The aeroplane was grounded. It was very hot inside, and the passengers were not allowed to disembark. An inspector came to make sure that the plane was not carrying plants and that no rubbish would littered on U.S. soil. It lasted almost two hours.

The Shah eventually arrived at La Guardia airport in New York in the early hours of October 23rd 1979. After the Florida heat, there was the cold and the humidity of New York.

The arrival was supposed to be kept secret. The travellers were disembarked with great discretion. There were cars awaiting them. It was preciously arranged that they should go to Princess Ashraf's residence in the East Side. A few hundred yards from destination, someone waved at them. A hundred photographers, television reporters and journalists from all over the world were waiting for them outside the Princess's residence.

The cars took another direction and went to the New York Hospital. The Shah was admitted under the name of David Newsome, a senior civil servant from the State Department.

In the minutes that followed the 'secret' arrival of the patient, the press was alerted and permanently squatted there.

Demonstrations against the Shah started outside the hospital as soon as on the 24th. They were authorized by the authorities. The patient's sympathizers tried to gather there as well, but they were not given permission to. Even the numerous bouquets of flowers that had been sent to the hospital were taken and then confiscated by the police.

Mohammad Reza Pahlavi was operated on, on that same day of October 24th.

Doctor Morton Coleman, a renowned specialist, was asked to perform the operation. He accepted. However, since the French team had been pushed to one side, he had to start from scratch again. The patient had stones and a swollen spleen which was three times the normal size, according to the press [16]. The surgeon wanted to have a precise answer whether or not the patient was suffering from Waldenström disease or from a similar pathology, and the extent of the damage. The press credited him with wanting to operate on the gall bladder and remove the spleen.

When Doctor Coleman arrived at the hospital, he was astounded to see that a 'second-rate' team was already at work!

Who called in that team? No answer has been given until today.

The removal of the spleen had been postponed. It was a fatal error, the specialists were to say later on. It might have sped up the progression of the illness, admitted Doctor Coleman, who had apparently nothing to do with the strange idea of calling in undesirable surgeons.

A week later, the follow-up X-ray showed that there was still a stone and that the bile duct was still blocked. The operation had therefore been a failure and it was barely conceivable to try a second attempt, considering the patient's condition.

It was thus decided to continue the treatment in a neighbouring centre, the Sloan-Kettering Memorial, which was linked to the hospital via a private tunnel. Years before, the Queen Mother had been treated there and the Shah had made a

EPILOGUE – THE SUFFERING AND TRAGEDY OF A LONE MAN

million-dollar donation to thank the doctors of the centre. When some doctors heard that Mohammad Reza Pahlavi was going to be treated there, they were against the idea. They ended up yielding when there were obvious threats of informing the press of their attitude. There was one condition however: it was that the irradiation treatment of the stones and the growth on his neck were to be made at night, at 5 a.m. at the latest. It was a humiliating and exhausting way of dealing with a patient who was already in agony and now also deprived of his sleep.

There were ten treatment sessions. On each occasion, the patient was woken up, put in a wheelchair and taken to the basement in the lift. Then they would speed him through the tunnel which was cluttered with all kinds of rubbish and things, with all his bodyguards around him. The atmosphere was one of terror and nightmare. The Shahbanoo ran behind her husband, trying in vain to protect him and comfort him.

On November 4th, while the patient's condition was stabilizing, Khomeini's henchmen stormed the United States embassy in Tehran and took the diplomatic staff hostage. The official pretext was to protest against the Shah's presence in the United States, to demand his extradition and the restitution of his 'fortune'.

It was made definitely clear afterwards that the operation had in fact been masterminded by Moscow so as to remove the pro-American elements from the head of the State in Tehran, and to make Washington focus on a serious crisis before the invasion of Afghanistan by the Red Army a few days later*. The Shah was only used as a pretext and the problem was elsewhere. The Americans had made the wrong analysis. The Shah had said so then to his GP [17].

---

* See chapter XIII: Moscow and Tehran – The USSR's double game bears fruit.

The affair provoked a new wave of hatred towards the Shah. He was particularly affected, all the more so, since it was physically and politically impossible for him to respond.

He nevertheless received thousands of letters and cards from his compatriots as well as from Americans who wanted to show him their sympathy and admiration for his work, and for the service he rendered to his country. Hundreds of bouquets of flowers also arrived at the hospital. There were so many that the police could not really filch them. A few personalities paid visits to the patient: David Rockefeller, Henry Kissinger, Giovanni Agnelli, the head of Fiat, Frank Sinatra who publicly denounced the Carter Administration's attitude towards the Shah and invited him to come and live in his house in Palm Springs during his convalescence. Ronald Reagan was running for president at the time and had been received in Tehran. He had a warm message delivered to the Shah.

Later on, during his electoral campaign, he did not find words that were hard enough to condemn Jimmy Carter's policy on Iran.

At the end of November, the patient's condition was such that a return trip to Cuernavaca could be envisaged. It was his wish. Order was given to get the Villa of Roses ready, but the Mexican authorities informed them that they were not welcome to Mexico any more.

The Americans were just as eager to see the Shah leave since they pretend to believe that it would help free the hostages.

The problem arose another time: where were they to go? The Shah expressed the wish to be able to spend a few days at his sister Ashraf's place in New York. The State Department officially told him that it was out of the question.

Epilogue – The suffering and tragedy of a lone man

One of Carter's advisers was sent to suggest to him to swiftly go to the Lackland airbase in Texas where he was told there was a decent hospital away from the demonstrators. He could then wait to be found a place to stay.

Mohammad Reza Pahlavi felt he had his back against the wall and resigned himself to that solution. He informed his wife. They were to leave at night.

On December 1st, shortly after midnight, the security staff put the Shah into a wheelchair and pushed him unceremoniously through the deserted hospital corridors, then across the basement where there were heaps of broken furniture and rubbish carts.

When they reached the garage, the wheelchair was hoisted into an ambulance with a dozen FBI agents around it who were armed to the teeth. It careered along to the airport, all sirens wailing and surrounded by many police vehicles.

The Shahbanoo was given the same treatment. She had been informed shortly before by the Shah that they had to go. Security agents came to fetch her at her sister-in-law's. There were even two of them in her car on either side of her, and security vehicles around them. Little Leïla, the couple's youngest child and apparently the Shah's favourite was woken up by the racket. She started screaming and looking for her mother all around the house. It was to mark her for ever [18]. The two convoys went to La Guardia. They were awaited by a military DC-9 and a crowd of men with machine guns, wearing bullet-proof jackets. The Shah was hoisted onto the plane and the Shahbanoo was pushed inside unceremoniously. It took off immediately for Texas.

Early in the morning, on Lackland airbase, there was an impressive deployment of security forces. The imperial couple were pushed into an old ambulance which looked like a Black

Maria and was very uncomfortable. It careered along to the psychiatric hospital of the base. Reza Pahlavi related his parents' trip and sufferings later: 'The King and the Queen were both sitting very uncomfortably, and badly shaken in the car by a driver who was going very fast on bad roads. Their heads were banged from side to side. How can a recently operated patient be transported in such a manner?' [19]

The couple were settled in a room with caged windows that were carefully closed. There were also shutters which had been tightly closed so as to stop outside light from penetrating into the room. There was no handle on the inside of the door. It was like a genuine prison cell.

Chains and straightjackets were ready in the next-door room in case the Pahlavis were to become loud and unruly.

The Couple had the impression they were being kidnapped and imprisoned to be handed over to Khomeini by Carter. Mohammad Reza Pahlavi remained dignified and silent, he was suffering physically and morally but not saying a word. The Shahbanoo's discontent exploded and she protested. She was told that it was the safest place on the base.

Hours later, the Shahbanoo was given permission to make a telephone call. She briefly informed American friends in New York of their living conditions. It was a guarantee of security. The couple's American friends quickly intervened. The next day, they were settled in a little three-room villa which was basically furnished. The main piece of furniture of the sitting-room was a vinyl settee. General Acker, the commander of the base, asked the couple not to go outside, but he invited the Shah and the Shahbanoo to dinner. He apologised on numerous occasions, also in his own name, for the conditions of their stay and the inconvenience imposed on them by order. He discreetly showed his disagreement with the official policy followed by the Administration. Life became somewhat normalized afterwards.

EPILOGUE – THE SUFFERING AND TRAGEDY OF A LONE MAN

Many Iranian pilots had been trained in Lackland and had made friends there. Several American officers had served in Iran and had kept good memories of their stay. As soon as they saw the Shah, they cheered him and showed their respect and sympathy. There were even talks about aviation and military issues. Mohammad Reza Pahlavi impressed them with his knowledge in the matter, and accepted to have his photograph taken. He also gave autographs. The Shahbanoo even played tennis once or twice. However, there was still tensions, even if things had improved.

Where were they to go?

On December 7th in Paris, Shahryar Shafigh, one of the Shah's nephews who was a brilliant and popular officer in the imperial navy was shot twice by terrorists armed with a revolver who were in the pay of the Tehran regime*. The Shah was crushed and fell deeply silent; he liked and respected his brave and honest nephew.

The White House was eager to sort out the Shah's case. American public opinion was deeply divided. Some criticized Carter for having hosted a controversial character, and thus provoked the American diplomats' hostage-taking. Others somewhat curtly denounced the weakness of the Administration, the fact that it had surrendered Iran to the ayatollahs and allowed, if not favoured, the setting-up in that country of an extremist regime which was obviously more and more manipulated by Moscow. The invasion of Afghanistan by the Red Army was to finally make the United States think about the main objective of the hostage-taking: get the United States involved in an endless crisis so as to prevent it from intervening on another scene.

---

*Tehran laid official claim to the crime. Months later, the commando leader was to be shot on the Iraqi front and there were State funerals. The French press overwhelmingly wrote that the crime had been planned and supervised by General Hossein Fardoust who was in Paris at the time. The French government did not follow up the case.

A few American editorial writers went so far, however, as to openly ask the Shah to give himself up to the Tehran regime in order to have the hostages released. The Shah's answer was not long to come: 'I have been called a lot of names, but I have never been called a fool'.

The idea of handing the Shah over to Tehran and exchange him for the American diplomats who had been imprisoned on Ruhollah Khomeini's orders seems to date back to that period. Anyway, he had to leave because he was getting in the way.

Egypt reiterated its invitation to the Pahlavis.

The Shah hesitated. He knew the problems the Rais had had since the Camp David agreements, and he did not want to cause new ones. He temporarily pushed the solution aside.

There was always South Africa. People close to him suggested Chile, or Taiwan. He pulled a face. These three countries had bad press in high circles. That was when an unexpected invitation arrived from Rumania. He thanked Ceausescu, but turned the invitation down. All the 'normal' countries had refused him access, as for Nicholas II and his family in the past, so there were only a few countries of Central America left.

Omar Torrijos, the strong man of Panama, and a friend of Fidel Castro, was also under an obligation to Carter because it was thanks to him that the treaty for the evacuation of the Canal area had been signed. So, he discreetly offered the State Department to welcome the exiled couple. Hamilton Jordan, the Chief of the Administration of the White House, was sent to see the Panamanian who confirmed the invitation.

After some hesitation, Mohammad Reza Pahlavi gave his provisional agreement.

The choice of 'that strange country' with limited hospital facilities was a sacrifice for the Shah, his GP, Doctor Kean, told

Epilogue – The suffering and tragedy of a lone man

him so [20]. He accepted however. It was to speed up his death.

Panama was the final choice and all the arrangements for the trip now needed to be made. Once more, Ardeshir Zahedi intervened. He knew Royo, the legal expert who was president of that country with no real power, very well indeed. He went there and brought with him Prince Reza, the imperial couple's eldest son. During a dinner party organized by President Royo for Zahedi and the Prince, General Torrijos stormed in and reiterated his agreement. He made the following remark: 'I do not understand how your King could abandon his country when he has a loyal military of 550,000 men, a powerful police force and so many people who are in his favour. Tell him, however, that we will welcome him here with open arms' [21].

Ardeshir Zahedi rented a villa in Contadora, a small island in the Pacific, less than fifty kilometres away from Panama City.

The villa belonged to one of Zahedi's friends, Ambassador Gabriel Lewis, who even offered to leave his small personal plane at the disposal of the imperial couple if they needed it.

As soon as the decision was made final, Colonel Djahanbini and Robert Armao went there to make the necessary arrangements.

On December 15th, the imperial couple and their little entourage landed on an American military base where they took a helicopter for the island of Contadora.

At first, the Shah's health condition somewhat improved. He went for walks, played tennis once, briefly, read a lot and pretended to do so in order not to be disturbed.

General Torrijos regularly came to see the Shah. He was apparently very obsequious, but addressed him using the expression Señor Shah, which greatly exasperated the latter. On the other hand, when President Royo came, as he was a cultured and well brought-up man, the visits took place in a courteous atmosphere and were appreciated.

Behind this façade of decorum, secret negotiations were organized between Washington and Tehran concerning the Shah's fate, but they did not remain secret for very long. In Washington, Jimmy Carter was ready to do anything to be re-elected. There were dealings going on to hand the Shah over to Tehran. Torrijos and his entourage and among other people, the famous General Noriega, who was a CIA agent and notorious drug dealer*, naturally heard about them. Their attitude towards the imperial couple changed.

Two hundred policemen and soldiers surrounded the Shah's villa. The telephone conversations were tapped. Their mail was intercepted, read and photocopied before it was handed to them. It was then simply confiscated and the telephone line was cut. The imperial couple were held prisoner once more.

Visits were not formally banned. The imperial couple's children came for a few days. The Shah and his wife had to look contented and less tense in their presence, and give them moral support. Ashraf, and Ardeshir Zahedi also came.

It was impossible to hand the Shah over to Tehran as long as he was on American soil; it would have damaged the reputation of the United States and caused a political scandal. From the minute they were in another country, even one which was fully under American influence, things were getting easier. That was what American diplomacy was actually working on.

---

* Noriega succeeded Torrijos and is now serving a prison sentence for life in an American penitentiary for his involvement in drug dealing.

Two emissaries from Tehran arrived in Panama on December 24th 1979: the French ultra-left lawyer Christian Bourguet, and the Argentine adventurer Hector Villalon. Their 'top-secret' mission was to negotiate the Shah's extradition did not remain secret for very long. Long dealings started between Washington and Tehran, and subsidiarily with Panama. Hamilton Jordan was to be the main American architect.

There was more pressure put on the Shah from the beginning of January onwards. He knew that Panama was negotiating his extradition, in other words, his handing-over for Washington [22]. The Shah consulted an eminent British legal expert called Lord Shawcross, a former Nuremberg judge, the president of The Iranian-British Friendship whom he thought to be a reliable friend. The Englishman reassured him that if any action were to be taken against him – which he thought was inconceivable – he would organize his defence and make it fail. A few days later, Shawcross called him and reiterated his legal point of view, but added with sincere regrets that he would be unable to defend his case 'for political reasons which are obvious to His Majesty' [23].

The Shah then believed that London was also was in league in the dealings and had dissuaded the eminent legal expert from intervening.

Hamilton Jordan did not stop harassing the Shah. It was suggested to officially ask for political asylum in Panama, undoubtedly aware that it would be rejected and would be a ground for expulsion, and thus a possibility to hand him over to Tehran. It was also suggested that he should abdicate, and renounce his claims to the throne. He violently refused. He never demeaned himself by asking for political asylum. He never abdicated.

Then, the suggestion was made to him that he should let the police arrest him and put him in jail to allow Washington to obtain the release of the hostages. He was formally assured that Washington would have him released afterwards!

He was also made aware of the possibility of an assassination attempt.

In Tehran, his arrest was even made public. A special cage was built for Mohammad Reza Pahlavi so that he could be paraded through the streets of the capital.

The dealings went on under Jordan's supervision. The couple were banned from leaving the villa. The Shah already knew in mid March that his arrest was imminent. He decided to leave at all costs.

His health condition suddenly deteriorated. It was the spleen problem again, which should have been solved in New York. Doctor Kean intervened. He suggested an immediate operation. There was hope that famous Doctor Coleman, who was supposed to be the man of the situation, would come. Washington sent – one does not know how or why – Professor Michael De Bakey, who was a world famous specialist in cardiovascular surgery! The removal of the spleen was deemed to be necessary. A Panamanian hospital was chosen. The local practitioners however demanded that they could perform the operation themselves, on Torrijos and Noriega's orders or with their support. Professor De Bakey could be their assistant, nothing else. The Shah was made aware of this and asked to make the final decision. He listened to the various points of view, got up and said: 'Have a good day, Sirs'.

They had to leave.

He told Benjamin Kean [24] it should be 'within the next half-hour', if possible. Their original tensions had disappeared and now they trusted each other.

Epilogue – The suffering and tragedy of a lone man

Aslan Afshar, a former ambassador to Washington, received a telephone call in Nice (France) from a very important American personality: 'Tell the King to leave Panama as soon as possible, otherwise he will be prevented from doing so' [25]. He conveyed the message.

On March 19th, Hamilton Jordan received the order to go to Contadora to dissuade the Shah from leaving. He first saw Doctor De Bakey who welcomed him drily, and told him about the White House's wishes. 'I doubt that anyone might be able to convince the Shah to have his operation here', the surgeon said. When Jordan insisted and mentioned the hostage crisis, he answered scathingly: 'This is your problem and the President's, mine is the Shah's health'.

There was no hope for him there and so he went to see Torrijos. He knew, thanks to the CIA, that the Shah was preparing to leave for Egypt, and told the dictator about it. He had to be dissuaded, but without using force because it might provoke reactions in the United States and be harmful to Jimmy Carter's campaign. No decision was made.

At the White House, Carter was adamant: 'There is no way he should be able to go to Egypt'. He called President Sadat and told him about his concern to see the Shah go back to Egypt: 'Don't worry about Egypt. Worry about the hostages. I want the Shah right now, and alive'.

There was only one possibility, it was to dissuade the Shah himself. Lloyd Cutler, Jimmy Carter's special envoy, arrived in Panama. He went to see the Shah with Hamilton Jordan and two other diplomats. The preparations for the departure were obvious at the villa. The Americans knew that all the bills of the imperial couple had just been paid and that the decision to go away was made. Lloyd Cutler recited arguments that had been prepared in advance; he talked about the existing friendship between the United States and the Shah – it should have made people burst out of laughter – and the question of the hostages. Mohammad Reza Pahlavi listened and remained serene. The suggestion was made that he should abdicate – it was to be the main worry of the American diplomacy until the Shah's death – so that he could go to the United States for his treatment. The Shah remained unmoved, and his reply was harsh: 'I will feel better among friends, I know that I am dying, but I want to die in dignity.' He ended the conversation and left the room.

In Panama City, there were negotiations to proceed with the Shah's arrest with a minimum of decorum. Everything was done to delay his departure while the agreement with the ayatollahs was being finalized.

A message arrived from Tehran: 'The hostages are gathered. If you stop the Shah from getting to Egypt, they will be immediately released'. The Carter camp had renewed hopes.

The President and Mrs Sadat had reiterated their invitation. They were waiting for the imperial couple. Their luggage was ready. A DC-8 was awaiting the Shah and his suite at the international airport of Panama City. They had to leave the island of Contadora. There were fifty kilometres that separated them from the liberty aeroplane that was ready to take off immediately.

Three small planes were successively rented, but never arrived. That was how the days of March 21st and 22nd were spent. The couple and their entourage had even forgotten that it was the Iranian New Year. At last, on Sunday the 23rd, an aeroplane that had been sent by Rockefeller arrived, and so they could fly to the international airport of Panama City. The imperial couple, Doctor Lucie Pirnia, their family doctor, Colonel Djahanbini and Nevissi, Amir Pour-Shodja, the

Epilogue – The suffering and tragedy of a lone man

Shah's loyal valet – the last faithful core – and Robert Armao and his assistant Mark Morse, stepped down from the aircraft positioned near to the DC-8, its engine ticking over.

Despite his suffering and extreme weakness, the Shah ran towards the other aircraft. The television cameras the world over immortalized the scene.

Between the instant that the Shah and his followers had landed at the airport, and the take-off of the DC-8 which already had its propellers turning, only a quarter of an hour had elapsed.

It was 2 p.m. Their stay in Panama had lasted three months.

Mohammad Reza Pahlavi was still worried, he feared a hijack. He gave the order to the army officer, Colonel Nevissi, to position himself in the cockpit. The Colonel, somewhat surprised, obeyed. He was told later that it was to give the impression that the crew was under surveillance [26]. It was a derisory precaution.

There was a stop-over in the Azores on an American military base. A group of officials were there at the arrival. Despite a high fever, and extreme tiredness, Mohammad Reza Pahlavi got dressed, welcomed and talked to each of them.

The aircraft had to refuel and leave immediately, but it was to remain grounded. The base refused to give permission to take off. It was to last two long hours. In fact, Hamilton Jordan and Omar Torrijos had intervened with the Defence Department in Washington to ground the aircraft. If, in Tehran the hostages were shown to be assembled in a safe place, a neutral embassy for example, then the King would have been arrested for crime of fleeing and subject to an extradition order from the Panamanian authorities.

In Tehran, night had fallen. Bani Sadr, the president of the republic was asleep, and apparently nobody had dared to waken him. The documents finalizing the operation were neither completely ready nor translated. One could no longer, in any decency, block the aircraft awaited by the Egyptian President. One was to later discover that the hostages had not been regrouped, that they had been dispersed in case of a possible attempt to free them by Washington. The authorities of the regime had once again been manipulating.

The aeroplane took off towards Cairo. There were to be no further obstacles. Mohammad Reza Pahlavi now knew that he would finish his days with dignity and on friendly soil.

The flight was without problems. He suffered atrociously but was appeased.

*   *

*

At Cairo international airport, the President and Mrs Sadat awaited the imperial couple. The Shah had not been warned and probably did not expect it after so much humiliation. When he was informed, he was noticeably deeply moved, he got up and without waiting for the others, was the first to leave the plane. The Rais gave him a long hug, Mohammad Reza Pahlavi had tears in his eyes.

The Rais's helicopter dropped the presidential couple and their guests off at Kubbeh Palace. By going there first, the Rais wished to show to the King that Egypt always received him with the honours that he deserved and not as a fugitive in exile. What imperial Iran had done for Egypt had not been forgotten.

After a break of a few minutes during which tea and coffee were served, the helicopter took off again and then dropped the two couples off at the Ma'âdi hospital in Cairo.

A complete medical team were awaiting the Shah: Professor De Bakey, Doctor Kean, Doctor Flandrin and a few others. Three eminent Egyptian practitioners including the Rais's own son-in-law also participated in the medical care and the operation.

On March 28th, his spleen was finally removed. The operation lasted an hour and twenty minutes. There were no problems. According to all the commentators, if the operation had taken place six months before in New York, it could have had positive effects in the long term and perhaps prolonged the Shah's life. Doctor Coleman had decided the operation should take place but he was virtually prevented from it.

The pancreas had stayed where it was.

After the success of the operation, the Rais, magnanimous as usual, gave decorations to all the members of the medico-surgical team.

The usual pathological tests that were made by the Egyptians soon revealed that the cancer had spread to his liver. It meant that the end was not far. Chemotherapy was prescribed.

Ten days later, the Shah left the hospital. His health condition was better. The return to a calm and dignified way of life had positive effects on him. He often met up with the Egyptian president and they talked geopolitics and diplomacy. He had the visits of close friends and relatives.

On April 25th, strange news arrived and perturbed the monotonous lives of the exiled: the American government, which had not succeeded in exchanging the Shah for the hostages, had decided on a spectacular military operation to free them. It was a total fiasco, and it would even be comical if people had not died. America was ridiculed and humiliated.

Towards the end of April, the patient's health condition suddenly deteriorated. He had violent stomach pains, nausea, vomited and had a high fever. Professor De Bakey and his team, Doctor Coleman, the renowned specialist who had been pushed aside in New York, was called by Princess Ashraf this time, Doctor Flandrin came on the Shahbanoo's request and a few others got together, consulted one another but agreed on nothing. Neither did the Shah's close friends and relatives. Ardeshir Zahedi hastily arrived and tried to settle the different opinions, to no avail.

It was decided to ask the patient. The whole medical team went to see the Shah. He was impeccably dressed, was smiling and joked with the practitioners. There was a remission. He was feeling better. He was auscultated, and the doses of some of the medication were altered, and then people left.

At the beginning of June, the patient's health condition deteriorated again. That time the end seemed to be near. The Shahbanoo sent for Doctor Flandrin who arrived with a team of surgeons under Doctor Pierre-Louis Fagniez's authority. Princess Ashraf apparently only trusted the Americans, and begged Doctor Coleman and his team to come to Cairo, which they did. There were sometimes bitter quarrels that opposed family members and also doctors. The Shahbanoo and President Sadat decided in favour of the medico-surgical French and Egyptian team. On June 30th, what was left of his pancreas was removed. The operation is successful but it should have occurred months before, according to some people.

Epilogue – The suffering and tragedy of a lone man

The patient's condition did not stop getting worse after a short interval. He was not to leave the hospital and was put in an intensive-care unit. Despite his suffering, he did not stop adding the last touches to the American version of *Answer to History* which is about ten pages longer than the French version. Knowing the end was near, he was less cautious and settled a few scores.

All the testimonies concur. He was in atrocious pain, he was bleeding a lot but he remained lucid and never complained.

During the last days of his life, he expressed several times the wish to be buried in his country, after the liberation of Iran, of course, and next to the officers and soldiers who had been tortured and executed by the revolutionaries.

According to certain information, the exact place he was thinking of and where he will probably be seen to rest when the day comes could even be guessed.

His detachment concerning what was happening around him was total. He only talked when he had the strength to do so, and in a less and less audible voice, and he talked about Iran. Three days before his death, he confided to his last Chief of Protocol, Amir Aslan Afshar, who had come to see him: 'I have done everything that was in my power for the grandeur of Iran and the happiness of Iranians. I wanted to lead my people to a great civilization. Now, they risk being annihilated...I am awaiting my fate, I do not stop praying for Iran, and for my people. I only think about their suffering' [27].

These were to be his last words.

On July 25th, after a strong and new infection and a high fever, he fell into a state of shock. It was only a question of hours now. The imperial couple's children were in Alexandria. They were called to Cairo in the night of the 25th to the 26th.

On the 26th, the medical team decided to let nature take its course and to stop any therapeutic treatment because it had become useless. The family gave their agreement. The 26th was the anniversary of his father's death.

The Shahbanoo, the couple's four children, Doctor Pirnia, Ardeshir Zahedi, Aslan Afshar, Mark Morse and Amir Pour-Shodja were permanently at the hospital. Some other Iranians followed the Shah's death throes from a hotel in Cairo. Colonels Djahanbini and Nevissi supervised the security in turn.

On Sunday 27th, very early in the morning, one could hear him breathe deeply several times, then there was a deep inspiration and it was the end [28].

All the tubes were removed from the corpse. Mrs Pirnia removed his wedding ring and gave it to his wife. An Egyptian nurse closed his eyes.

At 10 o'clock, his death was officially announced.

The funeral was to take place on the 29th. Mohammad Reza Pahlavi's mortal remains were placed in a big mosque of the Egyptian capital.

*   *

*

Mohammad Reza Pahlavi was thus the last of the Shahs of Iran who successively died far away from their country.

Epilogue – The suffering and tragedy of a lone man

Mohammad Ali Shah died in San Remo on April 4th 1924, after being deposed by Parliament after a two-year reign, in 1909.

His son, Ahmad Shah, the last of the Qajars, was also deposed by Parliament in 1925, and died on February 27th 1930 in Paris.

Reza Shah, the founder of the short-lived Pahlavi dynasty was forced to abdicate by the allies' invasion and died on July 26th 1944 in Johannesburg.

The last Shah was to die in Cairo.

Reza's mausoleum was destroyed by the revolutionaries. His ashes had been previously transferred to a safe place however. He is therefore the only one of the four to rest on his ancestor's land.

*   *

*

Mohammad Reza Pahlavi's fate reminds one of that of the other two Kings of Iran.

Mohammad Kharazm-shah who reigned at the beginning of the 13th century, was a great builder, a protector of the arts and sciences. He refused to confront the first hordes of Gengis Khan which he could have easily defeated. He was the leader of a great military.

He was forced to retreat from one province to another while his son, Djalal-Ol-Din fought bravely to his death. Mohammad Kharazm-shah's empire which was huge and had become rich in three years (1219-1222) was surrendered to the Mongols. He died in exile, disowned and abandoned by all.

Yazdgird III, the last emperor of the Sassanids, could not, despite his courage and efforts, reorganize and redress an empire in decline which was torn by internecine struggles.

He tried to resist when faced with the Arab invasion. Ctesiphone, the capital of the empire, fell in 635. Its palaces were devastated, and its fabulous treasures looted. Its immense library was set on fire.

Yazdgird tried to resist on Mount Zagros, but in vain. He lost the battle of Qadissia in 637, the one of Nahavand in 642 – a battle the Arabs called 'the victory of victories'. He then fled to Merv to seek help from the Eastern satraps and to gather an army to fight the invader. He found refuge in a mill and was assassinated in 652, the magnificence of his garments had betrayed him.

*　　　*

*

Mohammad Reza Pahlavi's record and reign as a modern and modernizing sovereign of the 20th century had nothing in common, of course, with that of the remote Shahs of Iran. Yet, his ambition and his dreams were shattered by a plague, the Islamic revolution, which, in many of its characteristics, resembles the Arab and Mongolian invasions, but which he could not master.

Iran has always survived, and overcome its invaders in the long term, and integrated them. It will come to life again. Four thousand years of history with so many ups and downs have taught this to Iranians.

THE PHOENIX IS ALWAYS REBORN FROM THE ASHES

ANNEX

A CHRONOLOGY OF THE **PRIME MINISTERS**
AND THEIR CABINETS

The end of the Qajar

25th Febuary 1921   **Sayyid Zia Ol-Din Tabataba'i**

25th April 1921   2nd gov. of Sayyid Zia Ol-Din Tabataba'i
Generalissimo Reza Khan, Minister of War

25th May 1921   Government of Ahmad Ghavam
Generalissimo Reza Khan keeps
the War portfolio
Mohammad Mossadegh, Minister of Finance

30th September   Second Ghavam Government
Reza Khan keeps the War portfolio
Mohammad Mossadegh to Foreign Affairs

8th October 1921   Ghavam reshuffles his cabinet
Reza Khan keeps the War portfolio
Mossadegh gets the Interior

22th January 1921   Hassan Pirnia (Moshir-Ol-Dowleh)
Generalissimo Reza Khan keeps
the War portfolio

17th June 1922   Ahmad Ghavam
Reza Khan keeps the War portfolio

14th Febuary 1923	Hassan Mostofi (Mostofi-Ol-Mamalek) Reza Khan keeps the War portfolio Mohammad Ali Foroughi to Foreign Affairs
14th June 1923	Hassan Pirnia (Moshir-Ol-Dowleh) Reza Khan keeps the War portfolio Mohammad Mossadegh to Foreign Affairs Mohammad Ali Foroughi to Finance
28th October 1923	First government of Generalissimo Reza Khan Mohammad Ali Foroughi to Foreign Affairs (Reshuffle 14th April)
29th August 1924	2nd Generalissimo Reza Khan government Mohammad Ali Foroughi to Finance
14th April 1925	The Parliament nominates Reza Khan as Military Commander-in-Chief
8th August	Third Generalissimo Reza Khan government Reza Khan gets the War portfolio Mohammad Mossadegh to Foreign Affairs Mohammad Ali Foroughi to Finance

The Decline of the Qajar dynasty

The Pahlavi Dynasty

19th December 1925	**Mohammad Ali Foroughi**
6th June 1926	**Hassan Mostofi** (Mostofi Ol Mamalek) Mohammad Ali Foroughi gets the War portfolio
18th September 1926	New Mostofi Ol Mamalek government Foroughi keeps the War portfolio

A CHRONOLOGY OF THE PRIME MINISTERS AND THEIR CABINETS

2nd June 1927	**Haj Mokhber-Ol-Saltaneh Hedayat**
20th November 1928	New Hedayat government
21st January 1931	Third Hedayat government Mohammad Ali Foroughi to Foreign Affairs
18th April 1933	Forth Hedayat government Mohammad Ali Foroughi to Foreign Affairs
17th December 1933	**Mohammad Ali Foroughi**
14th Juin 1935	Second Foroughi government
3rd December 1935	**Mahmoud Djam**
23rd December 1937	Second Mahmoud Djam government
1st September 1939	BEGINNING OF THE SECOND WORLD WAR IRAN PROCLAIMS IT'S NEUTRALITY
26th October 1939	**Ahmad Matin-Daftari** government
26th June 1940	**Ali Mansour** government
25th August 1941	INVASION OF IRAN BY THE ALLIED ARMIES
28th August 1941	**Mohammad Ali Foroughi** Ali Soheili to Foreign Affairs
16th September 1941	ABDICATION OF REZA SHAH

17th September 1941	MOHAMMAD REZA PAHLAVI TAKES THE OATH OF FIDELITY TO THE CONSTITUTION AND IS PROCLAIMED SHAH-IN-SHAH
21st September 1941	New Foroughi government Ali Soheili to Foreign Affairs
4th December 1941	Third Foroughi government Ali Soheili stays at Foreign Affairs
9th March 1942	**Ali Soheili**
9th August 1942	**Ahmad Ghavam** Mohammad Saed keeps the Foreign Affairs portfolio
17th Febuary 1943	**Ali Soheili** Mohammad Saed keeps the Foreign Affairs portfolio
15th December 1943	New Ali Soheili cabinet Mohammad Saed keeps the Foreign Affairs portfolio
26th March 1944	**Mohammad Saed** He keeps the Foreign Affairs portfolio
6th April 1944	Second Saed government
31st August 1944	Third Saed government
14th November 1944	**Mohammad Mossadegh** He steps down two days later

A Chronology of the Prime Ministers and their Cabinets

25th November 1944	**Morteza Gholi Bayat**
10 May 1945	**Ebrahim Hakimi**
12th June 1945	**Mohsen Sadre**
1st November 1945	**Ebrahim Hakimi**
14th Febuary 1945	**Ahmad Ghavam** Also Ministry of Foreign Affairs and Home Office
3rd August 1946	New Ghavam government Also keeps Foreign Affairs Three communist ministers enter the cabinet
20th October 1946	Third Ghavam government The communist ministers are ostracized
21st June 1947	Forth Ghavam government
11th September 1947	Fifth Ghavam government
28th December 1947	**Ebrahim Hakimi**
20th June 1948	**Abdolhossein Hagir**
16th November 1948	**Mohammad Saed**
14th January 1950	New Mohammad Saed government
26th Febuary 1950	Yet another Mohammad Saed government

28th March 1950	**Ali Mansour**
27th June 1950	**General Haj Ali Razmara**
7th March 1951	**Khalil Fahimi** He was to step down three days later
13th March 1951	**Hossein Ala**
2nd May 1951	**Mohammad Mossadegh** General Zahedi gets the Home Office
17th July 1952	**Ahmad Ghavam**
22nd July 1952	**Mohammad Mossadegh** called back to office
13th August 1953	The Shah nominates **General Zahedi** at the head of government. Mossadegh declares the decision unconstitutional and stays at his post. Riots cause his downfall
23rd August 1952	General Zahedi presents his government
22nd 1954	Second Zahedi government
9th April 1955	**Hossein Ala**
16th June 1956	New Ala government
4th April 1957	Professor **Manutshehr Eghbal**

A Chronology of the Prime Ministers and their Cabinets

31st August 1960	**Djafar Sharif-Emami**
11 mars 1961	Second **Sharif-Emami** government
9th May 1961	**Ali Amini**
19th July 1962	**Amir Assadollah Alam**
19th Febuary 1963	Second Alam government
21st October	Third Alam government
7th March 1964	**Hassan Ali Mansour** Amir Abbas Hoveyda to Finance Djamshid Amouzegar to Health
27th January 1965	**Amir Abbas Hoveyda** Djamshid Amouzegar minister of Health, then Finance, Home Office and Civil Service and finally Minister of State Amir Abbas Hoveyda remaining in position until the 6th august 1977, presenting during different elections and reshuffles successive cabinets.
6th August 1977	**Djamshid Amouzegar**
27th August 1978	**Djafar Sharif-Emami**
6th November 1978	Chief-of-Staff General **Gholam Reza Azhari**

31st December 1978   **Chapour Bakhtiar**

5th Febuary 1979,
Ayatollah Khomeini, having no official function, instructs
Mehdi Bazargan to form an Islamic government.

Between the 5th and 11th Febuary,
Bakhtiar and Bazargan coexist.

During the night of the 11th to 12th Febuary,
The Islamists take power.

— DOWNFALL OF THE IRANIAN MONARCHY —

NOTES

Notes

PROLOGUE

1 - Emineh Pakravan, *Agha Mohammad Ghadjar*, New Editions Debresse, Paris, 1963;
2 - Emineh Pakravan, *Téhéran de Jadis*, Nagel, Geneva, 1971.
3 - For the history of this dynasty see among many other works, Prince Ali Kadjar, *Les Rois oubliés, l'épopée de la dynastie Kadjare*, Editions N°1, Paris, 1992.
Also in Persian, the well-known classic *Tarikhé ..., Histoire de l'Iran sous la dynastie Qadjar* by Ali Asghar Chamim, 2nd edition, Elmi, Tehran, 1980, 666 pages.
4 – Emineh Pakravan, *Abbas Mirza*, Editions of the Franco-Iranian Institute, Tehran 1954.
5 – There is abundant literature on Amir Kabir. All the diplomats and foreign visitors who went to Iran during the 20th century talk about him a lot.
For a brilliant summary, see:
Fereydoun Adamyat, *Amir Kabir and Iran*, 3rd edition, Kharazani, Tehran, 1967, 776 pages. There have been many new editions since. Official Iranian documents and those of foreign chanceries on the period were checked and used by Mr Adamyat.
We would like to thank Professor Haj Hedayati for his contribution to our documentation on the Qajar period.
6 – A diplomatic report dated September 16th 1850, Adamyat, *op. cit.*, p. 285.
7 – Report dated back to December 19th 1850, Adamyat, *op.cit.*, p. 286.
8 – Answer dated back to February 11th 1851, same source, p. 287.
9 – The book in two volumes by Doctor Polak, published in Leipzig in 1863, translated into Persian by Keykavous Djahandari, Kharazmi, Tehran, 1990, under the title of *Iran and the Iranians*, is one of the best sources on Amir Kabir's reforms. *Vaghayeh-eh-etehfaghiegh*, a newspaper which was founded by the Chancellor, regularly related the advances of the plan (see more particularly n° 98 to 103).
10 – The account corresponds to all the testimonies, which were actually fairly similar, on the circumstances of the assassination.
11 – The gesture was reported by most chroniclers. We visited the place for the last time in 1977, on the occasion of the inauguration of Amir Kabir's statue in the Fin gardens. The stains can still be seen. This place was used for sacrifices and has become one of the popular destinations of pilgrims. Amir Kabir is a mythical person for Iranians.
12 – Two or three hours after the assassination, while the executioners were

already on their way back to the capital, the Princess, feeling that something dreadful had happened to her husband, left her apartment, and tried to leave the house. She noted that it was surrounded by soldiers who barred entrance. She saw that the exit doors were closed. She tried to open one, screamed, called her maids to her rescue. She managed to kick a door open with her fists and her feet. The guards obviously did not dare to intervene. A royal princess of her rank, the daughter and sister of the king, could not be touched. At last, the captain of the guards arrived and respectfully informed her that her husband had been 'executed' on 'the Shah's order'.

Ezat-Ol-Dowleh pulled herself together, and went to see Amir Kabir's remains. She ordered the necessary ritual ceremonies and had him temporarily buried. Then, she left for Tehran in the company of her two daughters and with the ladies of her entourage. According to chroniclers, the first encounter with her brother was apparently stormy.

Amir Kabir's remains were to be transferred to Kerbela some time later, which is in Iraq today. They were buried inside Imam Hussein's mausoleum. During the last years of the monarchy the room where the tomb was had been restored by the Iranian consulate in Kerbela which was in charge of its protection and supervision.

13 – Ali Kadjar, *Les Rois oubliés, op.cit.*, p. 284.

14 – H. Pakdaman (Nategh), *Djamal-ed-Din Assad Abadi, also called Afghani*, Maisonneuve, Paris, 1969.

15 – The Islamic republic celebrated the person in question and even had a poststamp published in his image, covers up that aspect of Assad-Abadi's life; Free-Masonry is actually forbidden in Iran today.

16 – Facsimiles in Nader Paymaï's *Reza Shah, from Alasht to Johannesburg*, 2nd edition, Los Angeles, pp. 23 and 24.

Part I

Resurrection and crises

Chapter I – I, Reza

1 – See in Persian:
Mostafa Alamouti, *The Pahlavis' Iran*, seven volumes, London, 1987, volume I, *Unusual aspects of Reza Shah's life*.
Ebrahim Safaï, *Reza Shah*, Tehran, 1977.

Notes chapter I

Reza Niazmand, *Reza Shah, from his birth to his coronation*, London Foundation for Iranian Studies, 1997.
Siavash Bashiri, *Sardar, Reza Shah's life in politics,* Parang, Levallois, 1991.
Nader Paymaï, *Reza Shah, from Alasht to Johannesburg,* 2nd edition, Los Angeles, 2002.
In English:
Amine Banani, *The Modernization of Iran,* 1921-1941, Standford University Press 1961.
Cyrus Ghani, *Iran and the Rise of Reza-Shah*, I.B. Tauris, London, 1998.

The political memoirs in Persian still, of many political actors and observers of the time are to be consulted with great care.
Former Prime Ministers Haj Mokhber-Ol-Saltaneh Hedayat, *Memories and dangers*, Zawar, Tehran, 1981; Mohsen Sadre, *Khaterate, Memoirs*, Vahid, Tehran, 1984.
And as well:
– *Notes and Documents*, by Pr Ghassem Ghani, 12 volumes, London, Ithaca Press, 1981-1984.
– Abolhassan Ebtehaj, *Memoirs*, two volumes, self-edition, London, 1991.
– Ali Akbar Siassi, *Memories of a Life-time*, self-edition, London.
– Soleyman Behboudi, *Memoirs*, Tarheh Now, Tehran 1992.
Behboudi was the Shah's steward and civilian aide-de-camp from 1921 until his death in South Africa. It is a particularly interesting document.

The quarterly magazine called *Talash* in Persian, which is published in Hamburg, devoted a special issue to Reza Shah in October 2004, n° 20, with thirty-one articles written by well-known specialists, 240 pages large format. Most of n° 23, July 2003, of that same magazine is devoted to cultural, education, publishing, and research work issues during Reza's reign.
Etc...
Other articles or books concerning certain aspects and events of the time are quoted in the various chapters of this book.
There are also two documents entitled *Journal* of Reza Shah's travels to Mazandaran, and to Khuzistan which were written by the chairman of his cabinet, Dabir Aazam Bahrami. Many editions.
2 – On the circumstances and episodes which led Reza Khan to the head of the Cossack division, see Nader Paymaï, *Reza Shah...*, *op. cit.*, pp.28-33; Siavash Bashiri, *op. cit.*, pp. 154 and 164.

3 – His son Gholam Reza, the only child of that brief marriage, narrates all its episodes in *Mon père, mon frère, les Shahs d'Iran*, Editions Normant, 2004.
4 – There is a full account in Ali Akhbar Siassi's *Gozaresheh…,The Memories of a Lifetime*, self-edition, London, pp. 74 to 78.
5 – Soleyman Behboudi, *op. cit.*, pp. 131 and cont'd.
6 - Thanks to Behboudi's memories, there is very detailed account of Reza Khan's activity. The steward took notes every day, even hour after hour.
7 – Nader Paymaï, *Reza Shah…, op.cit.,*pp. 60 to 81.
8 – Djalal Matini, *Négabi-bé…, A Glance at the political Career of Dr. Mohammad Mossadeq*, Ketab Corp., Los Angeles, 2005, pp. 59 to 61. Several documents are referred to.
Haj Mokhber-Ol-Saltaneh Hedayat, *Khaterate…, op. cit.,* p. 362. The author noticed : 'It was in fact the fall of the Qajars which had thus been decided on', *ibidem*, p. 363.
9 – Hélène Carrère d'Encausse, 'L'Iran en quête d'un équilibre, Remarques sur l'évolution de la politique iranienne depuis 1945', *Revue française de science politique*, Vol.XVII, n°2, April 1967, p. 217.
10 – Ceremony and details in S. Behboudi, *op. cit.*, pp. 277 and cont'd.
11 – The juridical and judicial reforms had been launched by the Moshir Ol Dowleh cabinets during the four years preceding Reza's reign. Since the latter ascended to the throne, the main architect of the real juridical and judicial revolution of Iran had been a legal expert trained in France and Switzerland called Ali Akbar Davar. See about this a long interview with the researcher Ali Asghar Haghdar, *Talash*, n° 20, October 2004, pp. 118, 129, and the reproduction of an article from Ali Akbar Davar himself, in which he exposes his ideas and insists on the central role of the State in those reforms, *Talash,* same issue, pp. 129-134.
Talash is a quarterly magazine in Persian that is published in Hamburg.
12 – See Djalal Matini, *Négahi-bé…, op. cit.*, pp. 368-405. Many documents have been published. According to British diplomatic reports that date back to that period, and which are available today and which are reproduced in the book, London was also hostile to the plan, fearing the opening of a fast road to its possessions in the Persian Gulf or in the Indian Empire.
13 – Nader Paymaï, *Reza Shah…, op. cit.*, pp. 101-104.
14 – Soleyman Behboudi, *op.cit.*
15 – See Dariush Ashouri on that subject in *Talash*, n° 20, October 2004, pp. 147 and cont'd.
16 - A tribute to the author from Amir Assadollah Alam.
17 – The accounts given in the publications of the *Société d'études*

iraniennes et de l'art persan by the various French participants, notably Professor Henri Massé, should be read with great attention, n° 12, 1934.

18 – Texts, same source.

19 – See Tshanguiz Pahlavan, Madresseh Oloumé Siassi, '*The institute of political science*', in Tehran, collective work, Ed. Rochangaran, Tehran, 1990, pp. 41-49.
Also see A. Mostofi, *Sharheh....The story of my life*, second volume, Zawar, Tehran, 1980, pp. 67-79. The author, a former student and holder of a degree from the first class of the school, gives a vivid description of the beginnings and of the functioning of the Institute, the former students of which were to constitute the structure of the Iranian diplomacy.

20 – Many works have been devoted to the history of the Iranian University. Among the latest ones, let us quote, A.A. Hekmat, 'How the University of Tehran was born?' *Talash*, n° 20, October 2004, pp. 150-156; Houchang Navahandi, 'The University of Tehran was a centre of the freedom of thought', *Talash*, n° 23, July 2005.

21 – Catherine and Jacques Legrand, *Le Chah d'Iran*, Chronique de l'histoire, 20, Bertelsmann, 1998, p. 41.

Chapter II – The Second World War

1 – Mohammad Reza Pahlavi, *Réponse à l'Histoire*, Albin Michel, Paris, 1979, p.48.

2 – Translation of the report from the British plenipotentiary minister to his government in Abdolhossein Meftah, Iran, pol'pirouzié djangué djananié dowom (Iran, The Victory Bridge…), London, Editions Marde Emrouz, 1987, p. 155. The 439-page book was written by one of the great figures in the Iranian diplomacy of the imperial period, and is exclusively based on the British official reports and documents that became accessible to researchers. It is of great interest.

3 – Winston Churchill, *Mémoires sur la Deuxième Guerre mondiale*, III, *La Grande alliance, l'Amérique en guerre*, Plon, Paris, 1950, p.105.

4 – Nasrollah Entezam, *Khaterate, Memoirs*, National Iranian Archives, Tehran, 1993, p. 9. N. Entezam was a senior civil servant in the Ministry of Foreign Affairs and was then the Chief of Protocol at the imperial court. He often acted as an interpreter for the Shah who only spoke Turkish and Russian. He then had a great career at the service of his country: ambassador to Washington and to Paris, Minister of Foreign Affairs…, and he presided over the General Assembly of the United Nations. He was arrested after the

revolution, even though he was retired and had not been at the government for a long time. He died in prison of the bad treatments he received there.

5 –Abdolhossein Meftah, *Iran...,op. cit.*, PP. 194 and cont'd.

6 – Mohammad Reza Pahlavi, *Réponse à l'Histoire, op. cit.*, p. 49.

7 – Nasrollah Entezam, *Khaterate, op. cit.*, p. 5.

8 – Text from *Carnameh pandjah sale shahinshahieh Pahlavi, Chronologie de l'histoire de la dynastie Pahlavi*, re-edition, Soheil, Paris, 1982, volume I, p. 173.

The chronology in 5 volumes and 2,243 pages relates all the events of the first fifty years of the Pahlavi dynasty which ended in January 1979, so two years later, a total of fifty-two years. The last three elements which are narrated are the inauguration of an oil complex on the island of Lavan (Persian Gulf) on March 14th 1977, that of an industrial town near Esfahan on March 15th, and of the Ministry of Foreign Affairs in Tehran on the 17th of the same month. The year 1356 of the Iranian calendar started on March 21st 1977.

9 – Winston S. Churchill, *Mémoires*, III, *op. cit.,* p. 112.

10 – Besides the works of A. Meftah and Nasrollah Entezam which have already been mentioned, see:

Mohammad Reza Pahlavi, *Réponse à l'Histoire,, op. cit.*

Mohammad Reza Pahlavi, *Mission for my Country*, Hutchinson, London, 1961.

Freidoun Sahebjam, *L'Iran des Pahlavi*, Berger-Levrault, Paris 1966.

Freidoun Sahebjam, *Mohammad Reza Pahlavi, Shah d'Iran, Sa vie, trente ans de règne*, Berger-Levrault, Paris 1971.

Freidoun Sahebjam, *L'Iran vers l'an 2000*, J-C. Lattès, Paris, 1977.

Amine Banani, *The Modernization of Iran*, 1921-1941, Standford University Press, 1961.

11 – Account given by Djavad Ameri to Nasrollah Entezam, written down by the latter, *op. cit.*, p. 17.

Entezam's Memoirs also constitute the most reliable account of the events at the Court during those decisive days. Thirty-seven years later, Ambassador Aslan Afshar the last Chief of Protocol was also to be the witness of the last jolts of Mohammad Reza Pahlavi's departure, and he narrated them with great honesty and precision. See *The Last Shah of Iran, op. cit.*

12 – Nasrollah Entezam, *Khaterate..., op. cit.*

13 – Same source.

14 – René Cagnat, 'L'URSS en Iran', *Revue de la Défense Nationale*, November 1982, p. 73.

Notes chapter II

15 – See Ahmad Kazemi Mousavi's article in *Ayandeh, Journal of Iranian Studies*, volume 19, n° 7-9, Tehran, 1993.
16 – A long account given by Mohsen Foroughi in *Ayandeh*, vol. 16, n° 9-12, 1990. All the memorialists of the time have confirmed the account, apart from a few details, for example, the right hour – was it 2 p.m. or a little later?
17 – One of Mohammad Reza Pahlavi's biographers, Count Bertrand de Castelbajac, wrote, probably according to other testimonies, that Foroughi had received the Shah in his dressing-gown in his library because he did not want to keep him waiting (*L'Homme qui voulait être Cyrus*, Albatros, Paris, 1987, p. 29). We have used Mohsen Foroughi's testimony that had been written and published before. The latter was present during the event and is fully credible.
18 – Bertrand de Castelbajac, *L'Homme qui voulait être Cyrus*, *op. cit.*, p. 29.
19 – This account repeats Ali Soheili's continued confidence in A. H. Meftah's *Iran...*, *op. cit.*, chapter 22, pp. 253 and cont'd. The British documents quoted by Ambassador Meftah concur.
20 – A. H. Meftah, *ibid.*, and many accounts and documents. Bertrand de Castelbajac, *L'Homme qui voulait être Cyrus*, *op. cit.*
21 – A note from Sir Oliver Harvey, Anthony Eden's private secretary, who was then Minister of Foreign Affairs, dated September 8th 1941. British Archives, appeared also in *Ayandeh*, volume 16, n° 9-12, 1990.
22 – This text can be found in N. Entezam's *Khaterate, op. cit.*, pp. 123 to 199.
23 – The main memorialists or witnesses to the events of those decisive days give the same account, with the exception of a few details. Our account is a summary, with supporting references.
See, more particularly:
Haj Mokhber-Ol-Saltaneh Hedayat (former Prime Minister), *Khaterate va Khaterate,* Memories and Dangers, Zavvar, Tehran, 1983.
Abolhassan Ebtehaj (former governor of the Central Bank), *Khaterate, Memoirs*, vol. I, London 1991.
Mohsen Sadre (former Prime Minister), *Khaterate, Memoirs*, Vahid, Tehran, 1984.
Ali Akhbar Siassi (former rector of the University of Tehran and former minister), *Gozareshe yek Zendegui, Memories of a Lifetime,* self-edition, London 1991.
Etc...
As for Mohammad Reza Pahlavi himself, he devoted a few pages to that

episode in his *Réponse à l'Histoire, op.cit*. He evokes a popular welcome as he was going to Parliament, which no other testimony confirms. His homage to Foroughi's role is limited to a minimum.

24 – Houchang Navahandi, *The Last Shah of Iran, op. cit.*, pp. 303 to 315. All the testimonies and references concerning that pitiful episode are to be found in it.

25 – Mohammad Reza Pahlavi, *Mission for my Country , op. cit.*, p. 75.

26 Mohsen Sadre, Khaterate, *op. cit.*, PP. 377-378. This former Minister of Justice and future Prime Minister was a member of the mission.

27 – Same source. 'Iran owes its independence to Foroughi', Sadre wrote on page 378.

28 – Documentation française, *Notes et études documentaires*, n° 2, 128, January 1956. Details and numerous documents and British reports on the dealings *in* Meftah, *Iran…, op. cit.*

29 – The last study that was published on the life and work of Mohammad Ali Foroughi: Davoudian, *Zendegui va Andisheh Mohammad Ali Foroughi*, Talash, 4th year, n° 20, October 2004.

Fernande Foroughi, the widow who is dead today, of ambassador Massoud Foroughi, the younger son of the philosopher and Prime Minister, wrote for her grand-children, her family and close friends very moving memories of her forty-two years spent in Iran. The roneotyped 152 pages, in large format, of these memories contain details and particularly interesting anecdotes on Mohammad Ali Foroughi, his descendants, the fate of his family after the revolution, even if there are a few minor historical errors. The notes end in Paris, Mrs Foroughi's native city, where she went to live again at the end of her life, on February 27th 1990. She died in the nineties. There is no printing date on the opus which was published thanks to Caline Chapot, a friend of the family. It constitutes an interesting reference for Foroughi's future biographers.

We would also like to thank Mrs Seda Aghassian for leaving a copy at our disposal.

Chapter III – The Tudeh

1- See *Iran va Djahan*, a weekly published in Paris, 6th year, n° 252 and n°253, September 9th 1985.

2- Concerning that episode, see the very detailed work of Babak Amir Khosravi (one of the last general secretaries of the Tudeh) and of Mohsen Heydarian, *Mohadjirate…, The socialist emigration and the Iranians' fate*,

Notes chapter III

Ed. Payam Emrouz, Tehran, 2001, pp. 2& to 85. On can find a very detailed biography in it, which is mainly due to former Iranian communists.
Also see Ehsan Tabari's memoirs, he was one of the 'historical' leaders of the Tudeh. They were published in Tehran after the Islamic revolution and reproduced in *Iran va Djahan*, n° 231, March 4th – 11th 1985, about that precise issue.
3 – Ehsan Tabari, *op. cit.*
4 – Heydar Amu-Oghli's life and action have been at the origin of abundant literature in Persian. Let us note the importance- for researchers especially - of the interesting biographies of E. Raïn and Reza Zadeh Malek which are both very apologetic. On the other hand, the studies made by Abbas Eghbal-Ashtiani and Abdolhossein Navaï are more impartial.
As for the role played by the character in the separatist movement of the Guilan province, the biographies of Mirza Kuchik Khan by Ahmad Ahrar and Ebrahim Fakhraï should be consulted.
The circumstances of the death of the last Iranian communist leader remain obscure and controversial. Some, like Édouard Sablier, (*Iran, la poudrière, les secrets de la revolution islamique*, Robert Laffont, Paris, 1980, p. 258) attribute it to an attempt that was organized by Mirza Kuchik's supporters, who worried about the Bolshevik influence on his movement which pretended to be Islamic and nationalist. Others do not exclude an internal settling of scores aiming at eliminating a leader who had become a problem as regards the Soviet efforts to create a rapprochement with Iran and a normalization of the situation with Great Britain. The latter was then involved in a policy of stabilization in the East.
5 –All the historical accounts on the communist movement in the USSR refer to that conference or deal with it. See, more particularly, A.Kiracofe Jr., 'Marxist-leninist theory and the Third World', *Journal of Social and Political Studies*, vol. 4, 1979, n°3, pp.211 to241.
6 – The father of the author of this book who was, at the time, a Russian teacher in a high school in Rasht, also worked as an interpreter on several occasions for Mirza Kuchik when he was to meet Russian personalities. He also knew and socialized with Heydar Amu-Oghli. He later depicted him as a cultured man who was courteous, a fine figure of a man who had relatively good manners, especially 'compared with his entourage', and who was sincere in his convictions, but 'more Bolshevik than Iranian'. He spoke fairly good Persian, it seems, but had a strong accent.
As for the circumstances of his death, my father thought he knew the leader of the group who had set up an ambush for him. Even though the latter was a man who could easily be 'bought' in Mirza Kuchik's direct entourage, it does not

mean that he was not manipulated by Heydar's own friends to eliminate him. It must be understood here that we cannot name the person in question out of respect for his family who still lives in Iran and abroad. Anyway, it was only a guess, even if there was supporting evidence.

7 – See Babak Amir Khosravi and Mohsen Heydarian, *op. cit.*

8 – Ehsan Tabari, *Memoirs, op. cit.*

9 – About that episode, and on top of an important literature in various languages, the cross-checking of the memoirs of several Iranian communist leaders that are available seems to be particularly informative. See, in particular: Anwar Khameï's memoirs, in seven volumes, Sazemaneh Entecharteh Hafteh, Tehran; the whole of the first volume (with no specific date), 280 pages, is devoted to the affair of 'the group of the 53' which the author belonged to.

Iradj Eskandari, *Mémoires politiques*, 3 volumes, Saint-Cloud, Rivero, 1987; the first volume is devoted to the affair.

Ehsan Tabari, *op. cit.*

Etc…

10 – Anwar Khameï, *op. cit.*, volume I, pp. 84 and 85.

11 – Anwar Khameï, Freidoun Keshavarz, Iradj Eskandari, Djahanshahlu…

12 – Iradj Eskandari tells that after he was arrested in the city, the officers of the Criminal Investigation Department were waiting for him outside his home to proceed with the statutory search in his presence (volume I, pp. 55 to 58). The same happened with Khameï whose mother invited the policemen to lunch. They only searched the place after the end of their meal. (volume I, p.119)!

13 – This was confirmed by Anwar Khameï all along his book, *op. cit.*, volume I.

14 – Iradj Eskandari, *Mémoires politiques, op. cit.*, volume I, p. 72. The author himself confirms the role played by Kambakhsh (p.36).

15 – JAMI, *Gozashteh…, the past throws light on the way to the future*, Ed. Samandar, Tehran, no specific date, p. 14.

16 – Dr. N. Djahanshahlu Afshar, *Mâ va Biganehgan, Sargozasht, Us and the foreigners*, narration, published in Germany, no specific date, p.77. The author now lives in Berlin, after thirty years spent in the Soviet Union.

17 – A. Khameï, *op. cit.*, volume I, p.224.

18 – ibid.

19 – Édouard Sablier, *Iran , la poudrière, les secrets de la révolution islamique,* Robert Laffont, Paris, 1980, p.265.

20 – Iradj Eskandari, *op. cit.*, volume II, pp. 37 to 51.

21 – Anwar Khameï, *op. cit.*, volume I, p. 238.

22 – Ehsan Tabari, *op. cit.*, n° 232, March 11th-18th 1985.

Notes chapter III

23 – Iradj Eskandari, *op. cit.*, volume II, p. 40.
24 – V. I. Lenin, *On the Foreign Policy of the Soviet State*, Progress Publishers, Moscow, 1968. Also see Dr Clifford A. Kiracofe Jr., The Kremlin, Iran and History, Manchester (New Hampshire), Union Leader, July 10th 1980.
25 – Iradj Eskandari, *op. cit.*, volume II, p. 40.
26 – Dr Freidoun Keshavarz, *Man Mottaham mikonam...I accuse the central committee of the Tudeh party*, a work of memories that was published in Tehran in December 1978, p. 30. The author was a member of the central committee, of the political bureau, a minister and representative of the party. He had to leave Iran shortly after the attempt against the Shah in 1949 that he was involved in. He lived in the Eastern bloc countries, in Algeria, and Iraq, before settling down in Switzerland. He is an admirer of the Khomeini revolution (according to the official party line) and still pretends to be 'an adept of scientific socialism, the only possible solution for the human kind', *ibid*, p.110. His book gives interesting information on that phase of the Tudeh's activity.
Also see Anwar Khameï's memoirs. He was another leader and ideologist of the party. *Op. cit.*, volume II, more particularly pp. 94 to 109, 127 to 148, 224 to 231.

In an interview with the author in Paris on November 7th 1985, General Hossein Azmoudeh, who was in charge of the military prosecution service, and had, because of his position, access to all the files about political attempts, confirmed to us that there was indeed a terror committee, but he said that he had no formal evidence that the orders were given by the central committee or the political bureau.
On the other hand, Khosrow Ruzbeh, who was sometimes called the 'Lenin of Iran', said, during his trial whose minutes were published in Tehran just after the Islamic revolution, that 'the order came from the higher authorities of the party'. Khosrow Rousbeh ended up being arrested and executed for his involvement in the assassinations.
27 – F. Keshavarz, *op. cit.*, PP. 110-115. A.Khameï, *op. cit.*, volume III, pp. 94 and cont'd.
The part played by the Tudeh in that attempt was also confirmed by N. Kianouri, another historical leader and general secretary of the party; Kayhan, n° 11951, August 28th 1983.
28 – F. Keshavarz, *op. cit.*, p.30.
29 – Khameï, *op.cit.*, volume III, pp.224-230. Keshavarz, *op. cit.*, pp.56-57.

30 – Lieutenant Ghobadi was later exfiltered to the Soviet Union by the secret services of that country and by the Tudeh networks. About his tragic career in that country and his end, see B. Amir Khosravi and M. Heydarian, *Immigration, op. cit.,* pp. 313-325. The testimonies given by both these authors are particularly interesting as regards life in the USSR.

31 – Declaration made by M. N. Kianouri, *Kayhan*, August 28th 1983. Keshavarz, *op. cit.*, p.30.

See, especially, the open letter addressed by Ahmad Lankarani, the deceased's brother, to the direction of the Tudeh, so as to have him rehabilitated, *Nameh Djebhe Nedjaleh* Iran, n°12, January 19th-26th 1983.

32 – A. Khameï, *op. cit.*, volume III, p.144.

33 – Many accounts of that attempt have been published. We can quote, among others, that of Ali Akbar Siassi, who was rector of the University at the time, and was beside the Shah, *Souvenirs d'une vie, op. cit.*, pp. 213 to 221; and that of Mohsen Sadre, who was the Minister of Justice at the time, and who was also present on the scene, *Memoirs, op. cit.*, pp.491-492.

34 – See the personal account given by the author of this book, who was in secondary school then, and happened to be the witness of a disquieting event related to this. H. Navahandi, *Iran, deux rêves brisés*, Albin Michel, Paris 1980, p. 30 to 32.

35 – F. Keshavarz, Djahanshahlu Afshar, Anwar Khameï, Noureddine Kianouri, the first three in books of memories which have already been referred to, and the last, in various declarations made after the revolution.

36 – Arthur Conte, *Paris Match*, September 23rd, 1983.

37 – F. Keshavarz, *op. cit.*, p.95.

38 – A. Bajano's memoirs; he was Stalin's private secretary, and his memoirs are quoted by Clifford A. Kiracofe Jr., in *The Kremlin, Iran and History, op. cit.*

39 – F. Kesharvarz, *op. cit.*, p.68, A. Khameï, *op. cit.*, volume III, pp.96 and cont'd.

40 – Conversation with General Hossein Azmoudeh, November 7th 1985.

41 – René Cagnat, *'L'URSS en Iran', op. cit.*, p.70.

42 – See Amir Khosravi and Heydarian, *op. cit.*

43 – Chahram Chubin, *The Leftist Forces in Iran, Problems of Communism*, 1980.

From the same specialist in the relations between the USSR and Iran, and the role played by the Tudeh, see 'The Soviet Union and Iran', *Foreign Affairs*, Spring 1983.

44 – John Ress, 'How Jimmy Carter balayed the Shah', *The Review of the News*, Feb.21st 1979.

45 – M. R. Pahlavi, *Réponse à l'Histoire, op. cit.*, p.272. Later, American analysts also realized the particularly important role played by the television that was controlled by the communists during the revolutionary process. See, among others, William Lewis and Michael Ledeen, *Débacle, Echec américain en Iran*, French translation, Albin Michel, Paris 1981, pp.135-136.
46 – Quoted by Édouard Sablier, *Iran, la poudrière..., op. cit.*, p.294.
47 – *L'Humanité*, November 27th 1978.
48 – Declaration made to the weekly *Omideh-Iran* on May 21st 1979.
49 – Édouard Sablier, *Iran, la poudrière..., op. cit.*, p.295.
50 – The Mujahiddins first rivaled with the Tudeh in their constant fawning of ayatollah Khomeini whom they called 'our spiritual father' (press release from the movement, dated April 5th 1979). Indeed, 'their methods have nothing to envy those of the hastiest mullahs (...) Their leader dreams of turning Iran into a sort of North Korea', this is what was written in *Le Monde*, on July 29th 1987 – a newspaper which has actually never been unfavourable to them.
It is a struggle for power which was at the origin of their elimination by another clan of the regime. By helping with the elimination, the Tudeh also believed it could get rid of a problematic rival. The episode recalls the bloody rivalries within the republican camp during the Spanish war. About the Mujahiddins, see, among others, a publication by *Iran libre (*4, rue Villaret-de-Joyeuse, 75017-Paris), no specific date is given; Mehdi Abrichamtshi, *Iran, Moudjahidine du people, la résistance aux ayatollahs*, preface by Yves Bounet, Jean Picollec, Paris, 2004 – written by historical leaders of the movement, this work virtually avoids mentioning the original ideological discourse of the Mujahiddins and their role at the beginning of the revolution; Alain Chevalérias, *Brûlé vif, au nom de Marx et de Mahomet, Enquête sur les Moudjahidine du people d'Iran*, Research centre on terrorism since September 11th 2001, Paris 2204 – a very detailed work on the recent phase of the activity of the movement.
51 – Éric Rouleau, 'La guerre bénie', *Le Monde*, from January 6th to 9th 1981.
52 – Declaration by the central committee of the Tudeh, September 6th 1981. *Information Bulletin*, twice monthly magazine, International Press, Prague, 1981, n°22, p.34.
53 – 'How to overcome difficulties in matters of defence, in the consolidation and development of our glorious revolution?' Declaration made by both the Tudeh and the Fedayaneh Khalgh (majority party, an ultra-left group that had remained loyal to Khomeini) November 1981, *Information Bulletin*, International Press, Prague 1982, n°5, p.50.
54 – N. Kianouri, interview, *Reuters, Express*, n° from September 8th to 24th, 1981.

55 – *Le Monde*, May 3rd 1983.
56 – *Le Monde*, May 6th 1983.
57 – *Le Quotidien de Paris*, May 6t 1983.
58 – *Le Figaro*, May 8th 1983.
59 – Philippe Rondot, 'L'Union soviétique et le monde arabe', *Défense nationale*, décembre 1983, p.63.
60 – Declaration by the spokesman of the party, *Le Monde*, April 22nd, 1983.
61 – New item from AFP, January 21st 1984.
62 – Pierre de Villemarest, *Lettre d'information* of the CEI, March 1983.
63 – *Kayhan*, the main evening daily in Tehran, August 13th 1983. About that episode, see H. Navahandi's 'Le procès de quelques membres du Toudeh', *Aspects de la France*, February 2nd 1984.
64 – *Le Quotidien de Paris*, May 2nd 1983.
65 – *Le Monde*, May 3rd, 1983.
66 – Jean Gueyras, *Le Monde*, May 3rd, 1983.
67 – *Le Quotidien de Paris*, August 30th, 1983.
68 – Erwin Veit, *Dans l'ombre de Gomulka*, Robert Laffont, Paris, 1971, pp.187-188. Erwin Veit was the Polish leader's secretary and interpreter.

Chapter IV – The Azerbaijan crisis

1 – These figures come from the book written by Ambassador Meftah, *Iran...*, *op. cit.*, chapter 35, P.424 and cont'd. The information given in the book is based on official British documents, which are thus less likely to be favourable to Iran.
2 – Same source, p.427.
3 – A chronology of the history of the Pahlavi dynasty' re-edition in Persian in 5 volumes, *op. cit.*, volume I, p.415.
4 – Freidoun Keshavarz, *Man mottaham mikonam comiteyeh markazieh hezbeh Toudeh-ra (I accuse the central committee of the Tudeh)*, *op. cit.*, Tehran, 1978, no name of publisher, pp. 40 and 41.
5 – Text from Siavash Bashiri's *Azareh Azarbaïdjan* (*Fire in Azerbaijan*), Levallois, Parang, 1984, p.59. Work with many documents and indications on the crisis.
6 – Same source pp. 60 and cont'd.
7 – *Bakhtar*, party publication, December 21 st, 1945.
8 – René Cagnat, *'L'URSS en Iran'*, *op. cit.*, p.75.
9 – Édouard Sablier, '*Iran, la poudrière...*, *op. cit.*, Paris 1980, p.276.

10 – *Iran-eh-ma*, March 15th 1946.
11 – Abolhassan Ebtehadj, *Memoirs, op. cit.*, volume I, p.227.
12 – Account given by Amir Khosrow Afshar to the author.
13 – We borrowed the account of that episode from the memoirs of Mr Anwar Khameï, the leader of the Tudeh, volume II, *Forsathayeh… (Great opportunities that were lost)*, pp. 301 and cont'd. The author's narration is written in a lyrical tone and the numbers were exaggerated, Ed. Hafteh, Tehran, 1983.
14 – *Rahbar*, May 2nd 1946.
15 – See E. Sutton, 'Political Parties in Iran', *Middle-East Journal*, January 1st, 3rd 1949, p. 45 to 62. Firouzeh Nahavandi, *Aux sources de la révolution iranienne, Étude socio-politique*, preface by Claude Javeau, L'Harmattan, Paris 1988, p.137 to 156. Firouzeh Nahavandi, 'L'évolution des partis politiques iraniens, 1941-1978', *Civilisations*, Volume XXXIV, 1984, n° 1 -2.
16 – Complete account of that episode and the text of the interview with journalist Édouard Sablier, *La Création du Monde*, Plon, Paris, p.194 to 199.
17 – André Fontaine, *Histoire de la guerre froide*, Fayard, Paris, 1965, volume I, p. 333.
18 – Bertrand de Castelbajac, *L'homme qui voulait être Cyrus, op. cit.*, p ;38.
19 – Chapour Bakhtiar, *Ma fidélité*, Albin Michel, Paris, 1982, p.44.
20 – Gholam Reza Pahlavi, *Mon père, mon frère, les Shahs d'Iran'*, Ed. Normant, 2004,, p.137.

Chapter V – The oil crisis

1 – Arthur Conte, 'Le Réveil de l'Islam', *Paris Match*, September 23rd, 1983.
2 – About General Razmara, see Mostafa Alamouti, *Bazigaran…, The actors of Iranian politics, from the constitutional revolution to the Islamic revolution,* 16 volumes, volumes 2 and 3, Paka, London, 1995, pp.120 to 165.
3 – Handwritten note by Mohammad Mossadegh, reproduced in Iradj Afshar's (ed.) *Mossadegh…, Mossadegh and legal and political problems*, Zamineh, Tehran, 1979, p.14.
4 – About Mossadegh, see:
Homayoun Katouzian, *Musaddig and the Struggle for Power in Iran*, I.B. Tauris, London 1999.
Mark Y. Gasiorowski, *Mohammad Mossadeg and the 1953 Coup in Iran*, Malcom Byrne Editors, Syracuse University Press, 2004.
Nour Mohammad Askari, *Shah, Mossadegh and General Zahedi*, Arash, Stockholm, 2000.

M. Alamouti, *The actors...*, *op. cit.*, pp. 166 to 261.

Fouad Rouhani, *Zendehgui...,Mossadegh's political biography*, Editions of the Iranian national resistance movement, London, 1983.

Abolmadjd Hodjati, *Mossadegh..., Mossadegh, the man of the year, of the century, of the millennium*, Simayeh Farhang, Tehran, 2005. This important, flattering biography contains chapters which are completely off subject, but also useful information.

According to the author, three great men have marked the history of Iran, Cyrus the Great, poet Ferdowsi, and Mohammad Mossadegh.

Djalal Matini, *Negahi beh...A look at the political achievements of Dr Mohammad Mossadegh*, Ketab Corp., Los Angeles, 2005, 538 pages. Rector Matini's work is of undeniable authority, and is today, the most complete and most unbiased work on the Iranian nationalist leader.

Ref. also to the already cited work which was published under the direction of Professor Iradj Afshar where there are many articles and notes from Mossadegh, some of his personal memories as well as original photographs.

5 – Extract from the Official Journal of the debates in the Iranian Parliament.

6 – Recently, Prince Gholam Reza, the only surviving brother of the last Shah, gives, in his memoirs, *Mon père, mon frère, les Shahs d'Iran, op. cit.*, pp. 151 to 172, a very nuanced opinion on Mossadegh, which is far from the official discourse of the propaganda from the imperial regime before the revolution.

7 – One of Mossadegh's notes gives an account of the conversation with Reza Shah, which was reproduced by M.Alamouti in *The actors..., op. cit.*, pp.179 to 183.

8 – He gives a personal account of three of these audiences in his notes. See Iradj Afshar, *op. cit.*, pp.113-115, 115-116, 137-138.

9 – Extract from the Official Journal of the debates in the Iranian Parliament, litteral translation. Mossadegh was then the leader of the opposition.

10 – Arthur Conte, 'Le Réveil de l'Islam', *op. cit.*

11 – *A chronology of the fifty years of the reign of the Pahlavi dynasty*, volumes 1 and 2, *op. cit.*

12 – See M. Alamouti about the encounters between the general and the leaders of the National Front, *op. cit.*, pp. 276 and cont'd.

13 – About the episodes of that trip, see Freydoun Zand-Fard, a future ambassador of Iran, who was a member of the permanent mission at the United Nations, *Khaterate...,Diplomatic memories, the face of the new Iranian diplomacy*, Abi, Tehran, 2005, pp.39 and cont'd.

NOTES CHAPTER V

14 – *New York Times*, October 16th 1951.
15 – M. Alamouti, *The actors...*, *op. cit.*, volume II, p.196.
16 – Same source, p;197.
17 – Abdolhossein Meftah, *La vérité...*, *op. cit.*, p.19.
18 – See the accounts of private talks given by professor Ebrahim Khalil Alami, Mossadegh's Minister of Labour,which we have given a long account of in *Iran, deux rêves brisés*, Albin Michel, Paris 1981, first part, chapter II. His words were confirmed later on by the governor of the National Bank (Issuing Institution), Mohammad Nassiri.
Also see the testimony of ambassador Abdolhossein Meftah, who represented Iran in Hamburg, and then at the Hague, when Mossadegh defended and won the cause of the country in front of the International Court of Justice, and then became vice-minister and temporary minister of Foreign Affairs, and the Prime Minister's confident: *Armaneh – Iran, The Iranian Ideal*, Ed. Houman, London, 1981, pp. 30-31, and *La Vérité...*, *op. cit.*
On Kazem Hassibi's role in the oil negotiations, also see Abolhassan Ebtehadj, *Memoirs, op. cit.* The author was then Iranian ambassador to France. Years later, – in 1976 – Mohammad Reza Pahlavi Shah told us: 'The stubborn old man [that was what he called Mossadegh in private] was in a better place than anybody else to solve the oil crisis. It had taken me fifteen years to get the results he could have got when he was in power', *Iran, Deux rêves brisés, op. cit.*
19 – The two letters from Ahmad Ghavam were reproduced and published in Tehran in March 1982 by his nephew, the former secretary of state to the presidency of the Council of the Amini Cabinet, Ali Vossough, in his memoirs entitled, *Tshahar Fasl, Four seasons*. He said he had texts in his possession that had been written by the former Prime Minister himself.
20 – The account of the events of those three days is taken from Hassan Arsanjani's memoirs that appeared in the weekly in Persian called *Iran-eh-Azad* published in Paris in the 1980's, from n° 116 to n°128, from September 11th to December 4th 1982. These memoirs were then published in paperbacks and regularly republished. The account tallies with many other testimonies on that period of time. The author of these memoirs was then Ahmad Ghavam's close collaborator and had been chosen to be part of his Cabinet as secretary of State to the presidency of the Council.
21 – Same source, n°124, December 4th 1982.
It is to be remembered that after the Islamist revolution, and despite the death threat that hovered over thousands of people, no Iranian tried to find refuge in a foreign embassy.

22 – Absolhossein Meftah, *Memoirs, op. cit.*, pp. 53 to 57. The diplomat here relates the accounts of that meeting in detail, and then of his intervention with the Prime Minister who said he was right.
23 – Same source, pp. 44-45.
24 – The memoirs of Empress Soraya, *Le palais des solitudes*, Ed. N° 1, Michel Lafon, Paris, 1991, p.142.
25 – *Ibid.*

Chapter VI – Iran's twist of fate

1 – See the article by M.A. Homayoun Katouzian, 'The measures taken by the British embassy for Mossadegh's downfall', *Ayandeh, Journal of Iranian Studies*, vol. 18, n° 1-6, 1992.
Fouhad Rouhani, *Mossadegh's political biography, op. cit.*, more particularly pp. 300 and cont'd, 359-368, 398-416, etc… This research work, like many others is based on official British reports and documents which are vastly quoted, and to which we will refer.
2 – About those dealings, see M.A. Homayoun Katouzian, *op. cit.*
3 – About General Zahedi, see:
- M. Alamouti, *The actors…, op. cit.*, pp. 261 to 325.
- Ebrahim Safaï, *Zendeguinameh…, General Zahedi's biography*, Elmi, Tehran, 1st ed., 1995.
The book was written by a respected historian and was published in Iran under the Islamic republic which is unfavourable to the general. It was consequently censored before it was printed and several passages were removed afterwards, from the edition we have. It still remains very precise and very impartial, and gives an amazing image of the life and political role of the character.
- Ezzatollah Homayounfar, *Az sepahigari…Du métier des armes à la vie de l'homme d'État, une biographie du général Fazlollah Zadédi*, Abnouss, Geneva, 1997. Big volume of 470 pages + 20 additional ones with numerous details, some interesting documents and a few original photographs.
- Nour Mohammad Askari, *Shah, Mossadegh and General Zahedi, op. cit.*, a volume with many accounts, documents and articles on the period as well as photographs, several of which are original.
4 – See chapter II, The Second World War – E. Safaï, *General Zahedi's biography, op. cit.*, chapter IV, pp. 78 to 85.
5 – A report from the ambassador of Great Britain in Iran, dated May 31st 1951, F.O./248/1518/May 31st 1951.
6 – On the relations of American diplomats with politicians in Iran, and

NOTES CHAPTER VI

the whole diplomatic game of these years of transition, see *Foreign Relations of the United States, 1952-1954*, volume X, *Iran 1951-1954*, Editor in Chief John P. Glennon, Department of State, Washington, 1989. All the books and articles devoted to that subject obviously deal with these relations. Preconceived ideas and guesses very often prevail over the precise study of reliable documents or direct testimonies.

7 – Entire text of the speech in E. Homayounfar, *Du métier des armes...*, *op. cit.*, pp. 206 to 211.

8 – Sheikh Zahed Guilani, a Sufi master, philosopher and ascetic,(who died in 1296). He had many children. Sheikh Safi (died in 1334), the ancestor of the Safavid dynasty which reigned over Iran from 1501 to 1736, was a disciple of Sheikh Zahed, and married his daughter. The Safavid dynasty descends from that marriage.

See H. Navahandi and Yves Bomati, *Shah Abbas, empereur de Perse*, Perrin, Paris, 1998 (work which was awarded a prize by the Académie française in 1999).

9 – That episode is related in detail, with citations from the reports of ambassador Bullard and other British envoys, by E. Homayounfar, *Du métier des armes..., op. cit.,* chapter VI, pp. 79 to 84, which also cites Iranian and German sources.

N.M. Askari in *Shah, Mossadegh and General Zahedi, op. cit.*, ch.XXI; pp.232-238, cites other sources, in particular the report from a British general who mentions Zahedi's sang-froid and great dignity when he was arrested, and a letter from the British ambassador to Tehran, after the general had been released, asking to meet up with him to 'clear the air'. Zahedi sent a haughty and rather dry reply, and refused to receive him (text and sources on page 237).

10 – M. Alamouti, *The actors..., op. cit.*, p.319.

Ahmad Maleki, a well-known journalist and a founding member of the National Front, gives interesting details on these encounters, including the menus of the dinner parties! His memoirs which are either out of print or have been banned from publication for decades have just been published again in Sweden: Ahmad Maleki,*The History of the National Front. Why it was created and how it was dissolved'* , with a (very interesting) introduction by Saïd Rahbar, Arash, Stockholm, 2005. Ahmad Maleki separated from Mossadegh afterwards.

11 – Various testimonies cited by M. Alamouti, *ibid.*

12 – Testimonies related by N.M. Askari, *op. cit.*, pp. 40 to 43.

13 – Testimonies made by Ardeshir Zahedi to the author of this book.

14 – Soraya Esfandiari Bakhtiari, *Le palais des solitudes, op. cit.*, p.148.

15 – After the triumph of the Islamic revolution, the private residence of the Zahedi family in Hessarak, on the hills to the North of the Iranian capital, was occupied and their belongings were confiscated – it was a fate reserved to thousands of other families. Among the archives and documents that were seized, there were letters written for years by the general to his son, letters which the latter kept scrupulously.
Recently, the Institute for Iranian Contemporary Historical Studies, of the Ministry of Foreign Affairs of the Islamic republic, published in its magazine *Tarikh-eh Mo'aser-eh Iran*, vol.2, n°7, Fall 1998, pp.122 to 180, about thirty letters from the time the son was a student in the United States until the last months of the general's life. One discovers a father who if full of attention but also authoritarian, who even went so far as to severely admonish his son for his private expenses, which he considered to be excessive, or giving him lessons in calligraphy! Financial problems are often evoked. On the political level, the general does hide his criticism, which can be harsh, against the Americans and the British. Later, after he had been pushed aside from power, he often expressed his sadness, or disapproval concerning such and such a decision made by the existing governments, particularly Ali Amini's, who had actually been his Minister of Finance.
About Ardeshir Zahedi, see N.M. Askari, *Gholehayeh..., The ones at the head of power during the last decade of the Pahlavi dynasty*, Beh-Afarin, Tehran, 2002, pp.153 to 549. See also, Mansoureh Pirnia, *Ardeshir Zahedi, Mehr-eh-Iran*, Los Angeles, 2005, 357 pages, many photographs.
16 – Confidential vs State Department Central Files, 78800/2355/ volume cited.
17 – That fact is vouched for in a correspondence between president Moazzami and general Zahedi, Ardeshir Zahedi's Archives. The latter will publish these documents in his Memoirs, which are now published in Persian (Ibex Publishers, 2006), and to be published in English in 2007 (by Aquilion). We would like to thank him for giving us the facsimiles.
18 – Soraya Esfandiari Bakhtiari, *Le palais des solitudes, op. cit.*, p.146.
19 – Crosschecking allows us to define his itinerary when he went underground and have the names of those who put him up: Mrs Zahedi, Bassir Homayoun's wife, Mrs Naraghi, both close relatives, Mr Amir Monazzam Hamzavi, Mr Mostafa Moghaddam – it was in the latter's house that he received the 'firman' appointing him Head of the Government -; and then Mr Hassan Kashanian, and Mrs Molouk Sadat Moshir Fatemi. He briefly stayed with Mr Seyf Afshar, an old friend. These people were all known and enjoyed a certain reputation – it was possible to check the information with their families.

Notes chapter VI

20 – See Kermit Roosevelt, *Countercoup*, McGraw Hill, New York, 1979, and Pierre de Villemarest's *Exploits et bavures de l'espionnage américain*, volume III, Ed. Famot, Geneva, 1978. Both books reflect the usual Western understanding of Mossadegh's downfall.

21 – Soraya Esfandiari Bakhtiari, *Le palais des solitudes, op. cit.*, p.147.

22 – With the exception of a few insignificant details, the account corresponds to all the testimonies that have since been published, as well as to the minutes of the examinations of the people concerned during the investigation and trial of Mohammad Mossadegh. These minutes were published after the revolution in Iran, by his lawyer, Colonel Djalil Bozorgmehr: *Mossadegh in front of the military tribunal*, Nashreh Tarikheh Iran, Tehran, 1980, 802 pages with many annexes, facsimiles of documents and original photographs. They form an undisputable document. Also see an analyst's recent comment, Elaheh Boghrat, 'Who organized the coup d'État?', *Kayhan*, (London edition) August 25th 2004.

23 – All the details on the travel between Kalardasht and Rome are related in the memoirs of former empress Soraya, *Le palais des solitudes, op. cit.* She was the only witness of that episode to mention it. All the studies and documents published since, in particular the news items and reports from the Iranian embassies in Baghdad and Rome, as well as other testimonies, concur with the deceased empress's testimony.

24 – Volume cited.

25 – Interview granted by A.A. Bashir-Fahramand to Ahmad Anwari, a journalist who was close to the National Front and chief editor of *Parkhash*, published in that newspaper in 1979 in Tehran, and reproduced by N.M.Askari, *Shah, Mossadegh and General Zahedi, op. cit.*,, p.106.

26 – Ibid.

27 – *Chahed*, September 12th 1953.

28 – The implementation of a 'United, anti-imperialist Front' is often evoked. See, in particular, the memoirs of Mr Anwar Khameï, a former leader of the Tudeh, *op. cit.*, volume III, end pages.

29 – See the text of an intervention in Parliament on May 25th 1950 in the *Official Journal of the debates in Parliament*. Also see the biography of that princess by Dr M. Sandjar, *Shahzadeh…, My favourite princess*, Alik, Los Angeles, 2002. About his relations with Mossadegh, see p.191.

30 – Ardeshir Zahedi was to relate the account of these decisive days to the Iranian monthly magazine *Ettela'ât mahyaneh* a few weeks later. His accounts were published in five successive issues during the autumn-winter of 1953. They are of interest because they show the unfolding of events, sometimes hour after hour, in one of the two protagonists' camps.

31 – *Ibid*. second one of the five deliveries.
32 – The whole account is taken from the memories of Professor Gholam Hossein Sadighi, *Ayandeh*, 14th year, n° 3 and n°5, 1988.
33 – Professor Sadighi gives no precise information on that point. End of his narration.
34 – Memories from Ardeshir Zahedi in *Ettela'ât mahyaneh, op. cit.*, third delivery.
35 – Volume already cited in American diplomatic documents.
36 – Texts in N.M. Askari's *Shah, Mossadegh and General Zahedi, op.cit.*, pp 172-173.
37 – *Le Monde*, August 21st 1953.
38 – Even General Azmoudeh, the military prosecutor, made a comment on the incredible aspect of his attitude when he was asked to testify in Mossadegh's trial. See the minutes published by his lawyer, Djalil Bozorgmehr, *op. cit.*
39 – K. Roosevelt, *Countercoup, op. cit.*
40 – Ardeshir Zahedi, 'The CIA and Iran, What really happened?' *New York Times*, May 22nd 2000.
41 – *Op. cit.*
42 – Testimonies given by Gholam Hossein Sadighi and Ardeshir Zahedi, *op. cit.*
43 – N.M. Askari, *Shah, Mossadegh and General Zahedi, op. cit.*, pp. 184-185 – E. Homayounfar, *Du métier des armes..., op. cit.*, pp.326-330.
44 – Summary of the enquiry led by N.M.Askari, *op.cit.*, pp.238 and cont'd. Ardeshir Zahedi confirmed the main lines of the discussions during that meeting to us.
45 – For the unfolding of the trial, see the minutes published by Mossadegh's lawyer, *op. cit.*, 2 volumes.
General Hossein Azmoudeh died in Paris in 1998. He published fragments of his memories in *Partow-Iran*, a monthly magazine published in Canada, n°68-69-70-71, years 1997 and 1998. What was said during the encounter at the prison of the prosecutor and Minister Sadighi was separately related by both.
The two volumes of the minutes of the trial are preceded by long introductions, 10+54 pages for the first, 23 for the second, behind the scenes of the trial, the conditions of the detention of the 'old lion', and his daily life when he was in prison. There are about a hundred photographs, including of the prisoner's 'cell'.
46 – Account of the episode on pages 17, 18, and 19 of the introduction to volume II of the minutes.

47 – N.M. Askari, *Shah, Mossadegh and General Zahedi, op. cit.*, pp.240-243.
48 – '...Could the Shah, who today owes his throne to the military, religious, even reactionary elements, more easily escape their demands?' this was written in *Le Monde* of August 21st 1953. It is probable that the pressure exerted by military leaders at the time for a more repressive policy was constant. By skilfully manoeuvring, Mohammad Reza Pahlavi progressively managed to take the full and effective control of the military, and to put generals who did not ask questions in the key positions. It was to cost the country a high price in 1978-1979. It can also be supposed that the Sovereign was looking for a counterweight to the influence – here, moderate – of his all-mighty Prime Minister. According to some, he feared him.
49 –Abdolhossein Meftah, *La vérité..., op.cit.*, pp.68-69.
50 – *Ibid.*
51 – E.Homayounfar has published a very interesting document on that subject, *Du métier des armes, op. cit.*, pp.373-376.
52 – Soraya Esfandiari Bakhtiari, *Le palais des solitudes, op. cit.*, p.199.
53 – *Ibid.*
54 – *Ibid*, p.200.
55 – That episode is narrated in detail in the biographies of the general, as well as various memories and chronicles of the time.
The words of many witnesses are naturally reported in the biographies.
See: Homayounfar, *op. cit.,* pp.390 to 426.
    Safaï, *op. cit.*, pp.207 to 216.
    N.M.Askari, *op. cit.*, pp.299 to 304.
    M. Alamouti, *op. cit.* Pp. 306 to 318.
    Etc...
56 – Ardeshir Zahedi managed to get the document which proves it. See his archives. He will publish it in his Memoirs that will come out in 2007 in English. A few other people have also been accused of getting 'sums' of money in 'reward' for their services from the CIA. There is no evidence and it has not been denied either.
57 – *Iranian Contemporary History*, vol.2, 1998, Tehran, pp. 122 to 179.

Chapter VII – The Savak

1 – Sazeman Amniat va Etéla'ât Keshvar, which means Security and Intelligence Organization of the country (or of the State as has often been the translation).

2 – Count Alexandres de Marenches, *Dans le secret des princes*, conversations with Christine Ockrent, Stock, Paris, 1986, p.249.
3 – To be consulted :
Christian Delannoy, *Savak*, Paris, Stock, 1990.
Siavash Bashiri, *Ghesseyeh Savak, Histoire de la Savak*, Parang, Levallois, 1987.
4 – *Newsweek*, October 14th 1974.
5 – *Le Monde*, December 27th 1978.
6 – Report published by Siavash Bashiri, *Ghesseyeh Savak, op. cit.*
7 – Édouard Sablier, *Iran, la poudrière, secrets de la revolution islamique, op. cit.*, pp.74-75.
8 – *Ibid.*, pp.73-74.
9 – Cited by William Shawcross, *Le Shah, exil et mort d'un personnage encombrant*, French translation, Stock, Paris,1989, p.222.
10 – Édouard Sablier, *Iran..., op. cit.*, p.73.
11 – On the Shah's exile and notably on the Mexican episode, see, among others, Houchang Navahandi, *The Last Shah of Iran*, Aquilion, 2005.
12 – Cited by William Shawcross, *Le Shah..., op.cit.* p.268.
13 – Mr Abdolkarim Lahidji, the general secretary of the Association (Khomeinist) for human rights, *Djonbech,* October 20th 1979. Mr Lahidji has since found refuge in Europe.
14 – Constitution of the Islamic Republic of Iran, preamble, paragraph 5.
15 – Christian Delannoy, *Savak, op. cit.*, p.132.
16 – *Ibid.*, p.183.
17 – Édouard Sablier, *Le Fil rouge, Histoire secrète du terrorisme international*, Plon, Paris, 1983. In the same line, among others, Charles Villeneuve and Jean-Pierre Péret, *Histoire secrète du terrorisme*, Plon, Paris, 1987.
18 - Jimmy Carter, *Keeping Faith, Memoirs of a President*, Bentam Books, Toronto, New York, London, Sydney, 1982, p.435.
19 – The complete text and analysis of this law-decree can be found in S. Bashiri's *Ghesseyeh..., op. cit.*, pp. 107 to 118.
20 – Article 1 of the law-decree on national security.
21 – Article 2.
22 – Article 5.
23 – Dariush Homayoun, minister of Information in the Amouzegar government. (1977-1978).
24 – Christian Delannoy, *Savak, op. cit.*, p.109.
25 – Alexandre de Marenches, *Dans le secret des princes, op. cit.*, p.250.

NOTES CHAPTER VII

26 – We owe this information to the crosschecking of several testimonies from former people in charge of the Savak or civil servants working for it who live in exile today.
27 – *Moarefieh gharibeh 8000 nafar az aazayeh khaer va djanieh savak beh pishgaheh melateh Iran*, Tehran, 1980.
28 – Christian Delannoy, *Savak..., op.cit.*, p.212. It was a clergyman called Mofattah who was killed shortly after the revolution in an attempt attributed to the counter-revolutionaries. 'A settling of scores is not to be excluded', the author of the book wrote.
29 – Alexandre de Marenches, *Dans le secret des princes, op. cit.*, p.249-250. The testimony of Mr Mohammad Hossein Moussavi, the senator for Tabriz, and number two of the Rastakhiz, a 'single' party created on the initiative of the Savak, is instructive: order was given to the secret services to transmit to the leaders of the Rastakhiz all the secret reports on the domestic political situation. In 1977-78, Djamshid Amouzegar, who was Prime Minister at the time, and leader of the party, thus automatically received all the reports.
Those concerning the domestic situation and which were destined to the party arrived by special courier on Senator Moussavi's desk.
In the heat of the 1978 riots, he only received 'top-secret' reports, on the power cut in some of the houses of a Northern town, or the strike in a minute company of cotton treatment...He gives numerous examples, day after day. There is nothing on the political situation. M.H. Moussavi, *Yadnameha..., Memories of a world which is no longer'* Mehregan, Köln, 2004.
30 – On the discussions and the report of that commission, see our *The Last Shah of Iran*, Aquilion, 2005. pp.85 to 87. See also our interview in the Iranian *Talash*, published in Hamburg, 4th year, n°21, January 2005.
31 – 'Tarikh va mahaleh dafneh ghorbanianeh regimeh Shah', *Ettela'ât*, Tuesday 29th, Esfand 1357, March 20th 1979.
32 – Ervan Abrahamian, *The Guerilla Movement in Iran*, 1963, 1977, Merip Report, Middle-East Research and Information Center, New York, March-April 1980, pp.14-15.
33 – *Madjmoueyeh Elamiyeha va mozehguirihayeh syassieh Moudjahidineh Khalgheh Iran,* Tehran, 27th Esfand, March 18th 1979.
About that movement, see two recent publications, the first is a flattering biography, and the second, a very detailed analytical enquiry:
- Mehdi Abrichamtshi, *Iran, Moudjahidine du peuple, la résistance aux ayatollahs*, preface by Yves Bonnet, ed. Jean Picollec, Paris, 2004.
- Alain Chevalérias, *Brûlé vif, Au nom de Marx et de Mahomet, Enquête sur les Moudjhidine du Peuple d'Iran,* Research Centre on Terrorism, Paris, 2004.

34 – Text of the press release and list of the victims in S. Bashiri's *Savak...*, *op. cit.*, pp.451 to 458.

35 – See Roger Mucchielli, *La subversion*, C.L.C., Paris, 1976. Vladimir Volkoff, *La désinformation, arme de guerre*, Julliard, Paris, *L'Âge d'Homme*, Lausanne, 1986, and *Petite histoire de la désinformation*, Ed. Du Rocher, Paris, Monaco, 1999.

36 – Declaration made by Mr Abol Hassan Bani Sadr, who was the main personality of the Islamic republic after ayatollah Khomeini, in *Le Monde*, of January 23rd 1981.

37 – Pierre Salinger, *Otages, les négociations secrètes de Téhéran*, French translation, Buchet-Castel, Paris, 1981, p. 119.

38 – Declaration made by Mr Bourguet, a lawyer of the Iranian government, to the enquiry commission of the United Nations sent to Tehran, quoted by Pierre Salinger, *ibid.*, p.168.

39 – Kurt Waldheim in *Weltpolitik in Glasspalast*, Düsseldorf, 1985. About that episode and the other disinformation operations against the imperial regime, please refer to the three volumes of the erudite, Sh. Shafa, *Djenâyat va Mokâfat, Crime et châtiment*, published in Paris, in 1991, in particular, volume I. The 2,070 pages of that very detailed work constitute an undisputable reference on the history of the Iranian revolution.

40 – There are few documents on the Iranian activists of the time and on their actions. Refer, out of interest, but with care, to Abbas Samakar's memories; he was one of the leading figures of the ultra-left extremism of the time – he does not regret or deny any of his actions, thus the interest one can have in his work - , *Man Yék Chouréchi hastam (I am a Rebel)* Ketab Corp., Los Angeles, 2001.

41 – Mohammad Reza Pahlavi, *Réponse à l'Histoire, op. cit.*, p.229.

42 – Massoud Radjavi, declaration to the *Matin*, August 3rd 1981.

PART II
The flight of Icarus

Chapter VIII – The authoritarian monarchy

1 – Quoted in *Le Monde*, August 4th 1985.

2 – Quoted by F. Sahebjam, *L'Iran vers l'an 2000, op. cit.*, P.68.

3 – Ardeshir Zahedi's archives.

4 – For a complete biography of Manutshehr Eghbal, see, M.Alamouti, *The actors...*, *op. cit.*, pp.326-354.

NOTES CHAPTER VIII

5 –The monthly magazine in Persian called *Golchin* published in Houston, Texas, gave a long list of these groups and of their activities, n° 153, March 2005.
Also see Éric Rouleau, 'L'Iran à l'heure de l'embourgeoisement', *Le Monde* of October 5th 1973. In that article, there is a long presentation of the rise to power of the private sector in Iran thanks to the white revolution and there are also interesting details on the Shahryar group (Rezaï brothers). According to Abdolmadjid Madjidi, who was formerly in charge of the organization of the Plan, after the revolution, 663 companies or private corporations were confiscated and appropriated by the Islamic republic or the para-state foundations which thus controlled over 80% of the Iranian GDP. The impetus of the private sector and of the spirit of enterprise was broken. *Talash,* 4th year, n°22, March 2005.
6 – Text in Ahmad Samiï, *Siva haft sale,* thirty-seven years, 4th ed., Chabaviz, Tehran, 1987, p.38.
7 – Many reports published in the 7th volume of the documents that were seized at the American embassy in Tehran after the hostage-taking of November 1979 certify it.
8 – For a long account of the change, from the point of view of the man himself, see Abolhassan Ebtehadj, *Memoirs..., op. cit.,* volume I, pp.430 to 452. Abolhassan Ebtehadj confirms the strong uneasiness caused in Washington by his replacement, and cites a report from the United States ambassador in Tehran dated February 21st 1959 to that effect (P.450). He adds, at the end of the chapter devoted to that episode, that he had allegedly been offered an important embassy, or to be co-opted into the Senate (pp.451-452) and that he turned the offer down.
9 – Account of an official encounter between the United States ambassador and Amir Khosrow Afshar who was number 2 of Iranian diplomacy at the time, in M. Alamouti, *The actors..., op.cit.,* p.342. Mostafa Alamouti was Secretary of State to the Prime Minister, who, according to him, had been made aware by the Shah and by the vice-minister.
10 – Diplomatic report classified 'secret and personal' dated February 25th 1961, 10118/61G, ref. F037/15799 which can be consulted today.
11 – William Shawcross, *Le Shah..., op. cit.,* p.174.
12 – For a rather subjective biography of Ali Amini, see Mostafa Alamouti, *The actors..., op. cit.,* pp.373 to 410.
13 – Mohammad Reza Pahlavi, *Réponse à l'Histoire,* Livre de Poche, 1980, p. 336. The pocket edition of the book has a second part (pp. 315 to 363) which is not found in the original edition (Albin Michel).
14 – Broadcasted speech, May 14th 1961.

15 – There is an English translation of that 'Journal' which was published in London, first in two, and then in five volumes, Amir Assadollah Alam, *The Shah and I, The Confidential Diary of Iran's Royal Court*, 1969-1977. I.B. Tauris Publishers, London, New York, 1991, in two volumes. The text in Persian is expurgated and modified, Tehran, 1992.
The authenticity of all of these texts which are sometimes contradictory has been questioned. To our knowledge, the person in question's descendants have made no public objections.
16 – Speech delivered during the inauguration of the National Congress of agricultural cooperatives, on January 9th 1963.
17 – Mohammad Reza Pahlavi, *Réponse à l'Histoire, op. cit.*, p.92.
18 – Allocution made on January 12th 1963 after a dinner party with the members of the agricultural cooperatives who participated in the Congress.
19 – The whole press at the time.
20 – There is abundant literature on the subject which mainly dates back to the 1960's and 1970's.
See, in particular:
M.R. Pahlavi, *Réponse à l'Histoire, op. cit.*
M.R. Pahlavi, *La révolution sociale de l'Iran*, translated from Persian by Fereidoun Hoveyda, Pahlavi Imperial Library, Tehran, 1977.
Amine Saïkal, *The Rise and Fall of the Shah*, Princeton University Press, 1979.
On the agrarian reform:
A.K.S. Lampton, *The Persian Land Reform*, Clarendon Press, Oxford, 1969.
A. Adjari, 'Les conditions de la réforme agraire en Iran' *Développement et Civilisation*, n°22, June 1965.
M. Eslami, 'Analyse des structures socio-économiques de l'agriculture de l'Iran' *Économie et Société*, the books of ISEA 5th GA 12. 1974.
Kh. Khosravi, *La réforme agraire et l'apparition d'une nouvelle classe en Iran*, Rural Studies, 34, April-June 1969.
F. Navahandi, *Iran, une expérience de réforme agraire*, Magazine from the Sociology Institute, ULB, 1980, n° 2.
If the socio-political impact of the agrarian reform, notably on what happened in the history of the country afterwards and the hostile reactions of a part of the clergy have often been tackled by analysts after the Islamic revolution of 1978-1979, its consequences on the evolution of the economy and on the growth rate have less been tackled. See, however, an excellent recent study in Persian: *Eghtessad-eh..., the Iranian Economy between 1963 and 1978* by Mehrdad Payandeh,

Talash, n°22, March 2005: the author shows in a remarkable way, with figures and analyses, that this reform is one of the main factors of the exceptional development of the Iranian economy before the Islamic revolution.

21 – Robert Dreyfus, *Hostages to Khomeyni*, New Benjamin Franklin House Publishing Company Inc., New York, 1980.

22 – Quoted by Édouard Sablier, *Iran, la poudrière, les secrets de la révolution islamique, op. cit.*, p.57.

23 – Mohammad Reza Pahlavi, *Réponse à l'Histoire, op. cit.*, p.208.

24 – Declaration made during a press conference of the Prime Minister, on August 16th 1962.

25 – See, about that party, Firouzeh Nahavandi, *Aux sources de la révolution iranienne*, L'Harmattan, Paris, 1988, chapter III.

26 – The whole press of the time.

27 – The researcher, Nour Mohammad Askari, *Gholehayeh Ghodrate..., The people at the head of the power during the last two decades of the Pahlavi dynasty, the Shah, Amir Abbas Hoveyda and Ardeshir Zahedi*, Arash, Stockholm, 3rd ed., 2004, pp.42-43 quoted testimonies that he neither confirms nor invalidates, and he also evokes the theory of a manipulation.

28 – Ali Akbar Hashemi Rafsanjani, an important figure of the Islamic republic for over a quarter of a century, openly claimed his participation to the murder conspiracy and said he had bought and supplied the assassination weapon. Document cited by Nour Mohammad Askari, The people at the head..., *op. cit.*, pp.18-19-20. The theory does not necessarily invalidate the one of a manipulation.

29 – A.A. Alam, *The Shah and I..., op. cit.*, pp.42,223,322.

30 – About Amir Abbas Hoveyda, see the work that has already been cited by Nour Mohammad Askari, and also Abbas Milani, *The Persian Sphinx, Amir Abbas Hoveyda and the Riddle of the Iranian Revolution*, I.B.Tauris, London, New York, 2000.

31 – Farah Pahlavi, *Mémoires*, Ed. XO, Paris, 2003, p.258.

32 – Édouard Sablier, France-Inter, April 9th 1979.

33 – Farah Pahlavi, *Mémoires, op. cit.*, p.277.

Chapter IX – A certain idea of Iran

1 – About the life and the end of Mohammad Reza Pahlavi, we can quote, among others, and in French :

- Freidoun Sahebjam, *Mohammad Reza Pahlavi, Shah d'Iran*, Berger-Levrault, Paris, 1971.
- Gérard de Villiers, *L'irrésistible ascension de Mohammad Reza, Shah d'Iran*, Plon, Paris, 1975.
- Bertrand de Castelbajac, *L'homme qui voulait être Cyrus*, Albatros, Paris, 1987.
- William Shawcross, *Le Shah, exil et mort d'un personnage encombrant*, translated from English by Françoise Adelstain, Stock, Paris, 1989.
- Catherine et Jacques Legrand, *Le Chah d'Iran*, preface by Boutros Boutros-Ghali, Ed. Chronique, Périgueux, 1998.
- Houchang Navahandi, *The Last Shah of Iran*, Aquilion, 2005.
We must not forget Gholam Reza Pahlavi's *Mon père, mon frère, les Shahs d'Iran, op. cit.*
And in Persian : Siavash Bashiri, *Shahinshah*, Ed. Parang, Levallois, 1990.
2 – About these episodes, see Soleyman Behboudi, *Biste sale..., Vingt ans avec Reza Shah, op. cit.*
3 – Mohammad Reza Pahlavi, interview, cited by S. Bashiri in *Shahinshah, op. cit.*, p.46.
4 – Mohammad Reza Pahlavi, interview realized in Morocco during the Shah's exile, by Freidoun Sahebjam, and published on the occasion of the fifteenth anniversary of his death, *Point de Vue*, August 1st 1995.
5 – Soleyman Behboudi, *Twenty years..., op. cit.*, p.275.
According to Soleyman Behboudi, who kept an eye on the crown prince's health to give accounts of it to the sovereign, he had allegedly said to him: 'I am going to get better. I have just dreamt of the Imam.' Same source, p.276. He sometimes evoked that dream in private without giving any details.
6 – Freidoun Sahebjam, *Mohammad Reza Pahlavi..., op. cit.*, p.39.
7 – Testimony given by Frederick Jacobi Jr. an American classmate of Mohammad Reza Pahlavi at the Rosey, *Newsweek*, February 20th 1949.
8 – Soleyman Behboudi, *Twenty years..., op. cit.*, p.352.
9 – *Ibid.*
10 – Anecdote narrated to the author of this book one day.
11 – Cited by Siavash Bashiri, *Shahinshah, op. cit.*, p.58.
In an article that was particularly venomous, the journalist (and future French ambassador) Éric Rouleau insinuated that he had been nominated colonel at the age of …twelve! *Le Monde*, July 29th 1980.
12 – There is a direct and reliable testimony on that episode, that of professor Ghassem Ghani, who was a representative at the time, and future minister and ambassador, and who belonged to that team. He

Notes chapter IX

later was a member of the mission that went to ask for the 'chosen one's' hand, Princess Fawzieh of Egypt: Ghassem Ghani, *Notes and Documents*, Ithaca Press, London, volume II, 1982, pp. 1 to 58.

13 – Judgment made in his memoirs by the former minister of Reza Shah, Mokhber-Ol-Saltaneh Hedayat, who participated in all the ceremonies and observed and took notes on everything, *Memories and Dangers, op. cit.*, pp.413 and cont'd.

14 – *Ibid.*

15 – Nasrollah Entezam, *Khaterate, Memoirs, op. cit.*, p. 16.

16 – Account of all the talks and texts from all the documents and reports, in Ghassem Ghani, *op. cit.*, volume VII, pp.57 to 215.

17 – See:
- Soraya, *Ma vie*, Plon, Paris, 1963.
- Soraya, *Le palais des solitudes, op. cit.*, Paris 1991.
- Henri de Stadelhofen, *Soraya, la malédiction des étoiles*, Ed. Pierre Marcel Favre, Paris, 1983.

18 – See :
- Jean-Michel Pedrazzani, *L'impératrice d'Iran, le mythe et la réalité,* Publimonde, Paris, 1977.
- Lesley Blanch, *Farah, Shahbanou of Iran*, Collins, London, 1978.
- Vincent Meylan, *La véritable Farah*, Pygmalion, Paris, 2000.

And there are two books signed by the Shahbanoo :
- Farah, Shahbanou d'Iran, *Mes mille et un jours*, Stock, Paris, 1978.
- Farah Pahlavi, *Mémoires, op. cit.*,

The publication of volume II of the *Mitrokhin Archives*, a master Soviet spy exfiltered to the West and taken in by the British secret services, allows us to have some information, which in theory cannot by verified, about the Shah's third marriage: a manipulating agent of the KGB, code name 'RION' was in the immediate entourage of young Farah Diba and allegedly continued to play a part in it later on , as well as another person from the same tendency. The patriotism and 'royalism' (Mitrokhin's expression) of the future empress were not put in question. However, a strange game that happened among her close friends is suggested. See Christopher Andrew and Vasili Mitrokhin, *The Mitrokhin Archive II, The KGB and the World*, Allen Lane, London, 2005,pp.171-173.

19 – This interview has already been cited, *Point de Vue*, August 1st 1995.

20 – At the time when this disposition was evoked in the Cabinet, the author of the book was Minister of Development and of Housing, and was present. The discussion was never about the principle, but it insisted on its details and on the formulation. Objections had been made on the

side. See the memoirs of Atâollah Khosravani, the general secretary of the governmental party *Iran-eh-Novin*, Minister of Labour and of Social Affairs, then to the Interior, in *Partow-Iran*, a monthly magazine in Persian published in Canada, more particularly n° 55 of March 1998.
21 – Conversation already cited, *Point de Vue*, August 1st 1995.
22 – A testimony from Ardeshir Zahedi to the author of this book.
23 – William Shawcross, *Le Shah…, op. cit.*, p.97.
24 – *Ibid.*, p.98.
25 – Refer to Marie Lebey, *Dix-sept ans, porte 57*, Baland, Paris, 1986. A moving and very tender account. The address of the house in question was fairly well known in some circles. The revolutionaries had located it. Abandoned by its keepers, it was taken and looted in the evening of the revolution, and the two watch dogs were killed.
26 – Christian Malar and Alain Rodier, *Reza Pahlavi, le fils du Shah, de l'exil à la reconquête*, Plon, Paris, 1986. p. 122.
27 – *Ibid.*
28 – There is a complete presentation of the various residences or holiday places of Mohammad Reza Pahlavi Shah and of the imperial family in *The Last Shah of Iran, op. cit.*
29 – Vladimir Volkoff, *La désinformation, arme de guerre, op. cit.*, and *Petite histoire de la désinformation, op. cit.*
30 – Freidoun Sahebjam, 'Il y a cinq ans la mort du Shah d'Iran. La "lumière des Aryens" s'éteint dans l'exil', *Le Monde* of Sunday 4th, Monday 5th 1985.
31 – Alexandre de Marenches, *Dans le secret des princes, op. cit.* p.242.
32 – Trial that was relate in particular in *France Soir* of November 12th 1967.
33 – Declaration made by Mr Behzad Nabavi, and published by *Saf*, the official press of the armed forces of the Islamic republic of Iran, n° 35, aban 1361 (October 21st-November 21st 1982), literal translation.
34 – *Ibid.*
35 – Cited by William Shawcross, *Le Shah…,op.cit.*, p.327.
36 – *New York Times, Washington Post, Le Monde, Le Figaro, London Times, L'Express, Newsweek, Time Magazine*…were read regularly. During the last few months, he was tired and somewhat had enough, he had stopped that habit. 'Some people' – Who? – made him only read *Libération*, which was further to the left and more radical than today and particularly not in his favour – this is what his personal GP Professor Safavian said, as he often saw him in the morning. Was it to demoralize him and break him even more?
While he was in exile, especially in Morocco and in Mexico, he took up reading the international press again.

37 – During the fifteen years while the author of this book had key positions, there was never a nomination imposed on him, even the least important one, or one even suggested by the sovereign. He never opposed his veto to any nomination suggested, even if in many cases, during the two rectorships of Shiraz and especially Tehran, the Savak and the Prime Minister had intervened to stop one.
38 – Gholam Reza Pahlavi, *Mon père, mon frère, Les Shahs d'Iran, op. cit.*, p.217.
39 – Words related by William Shawcross, *Le Shah..., op. cit.*, p.302.
40 – Alexandre de Marenches, *Dans le secret des princes, op. cit.*, pp.241-242.
41 – Ghassem Ghani, *Notes and Documents, op. cit.*, volume 3, 1980, pp. 157 to 162.
42 – Alexandre de Marenches, *Dans le secret..., op. cit.*, pp. 241-242.
43 – Charles de Gaulle, *Mémoires d'espoir*, Plon, Paris.
44 – John F. Kennedy, press conference, July 1962.
45 – Mohammad Reza Pahlavi, conversation with *Kayhan*, September 1976.
46 – Mohamed H. Heykal, *Khomeyni et sa revolution*, Ed. Jeune Afrique, Paris, 1983, p.108.
47 – Mohammad Reza Pahlavi, *Le lion et le soleil*, conversations with Olivier Warin, Stock, Paris, 1976, p.201.
48 – *Kayhan*, September 10th, 1976.
49 – Conversation with Jean-Marie Cavada of the French television, reproduced by *Kayhan*, January 10th, 1976.
51 – Alexandre Del Valle, *Islamisme et États-Unis, une alliance contre l'Europe*, L'Âge d'Homme, Lausanne, 1997, p.129.
52 – André Piettre, a member of the Institute; the remark dates back to 1974, I must say.
53 – William Shawcross, *Le Shah..., op.cit.*, p.191.
54 – Conversation with a journalist from *Associated Press*, reproduced by *Kayhan*, December 12th 1976.
55 – Two collections of various press interviews or political speeches delivered by Mohammad Reza Pahlavi Shah can be consulted with great interest: *Hochdarsha* (Warnings) ed. Zoroastre, Bonn, 1982, and *Dobareh Bèkhanim* (Let us read again), Parang, Levallois, 1988.
56 – Extract from the speech given by Pierre Pujo, the editor of the weekly AF 2000, and president of the steering committee of Action française, at the Crillon Hotel, during the ceremony to commemorate the twentieth anniversary of the Shah of Iran's death, in July 2000.

Chapter X – A policy of power and national independence

1 – Mohammad Reza Pahlavi, *Le lion et le soleil*, conversations with Olivier Warin, Stock, Paris, 1976, p.72.
2 – Éric Rouleau, 'Une politique de puissance', *Le Monde*, December 2nd, 1972.
3 – For all the information, beside the usual statistical directories, see: Jahanguir Amouzegar, *Iran, An Economic Profile*, Washington DC, 1977.
Freidoun Sahebjam, *L'Iran vers l'an 2000*, J.C. Lattès, Paris, 1977.
For a remarkable synthesis, see Mehrdad Payandeh, 'Iranian Economy, 1961-1978' *Talash*, n°22, March 2005.
4 – F. Sahebjam, *L'Iran vers l'An 2000*, op. cit. p.317.
5 – See an interview of Houchang Navahandi, *Talash*, n° 23, July 2005.
6 – Mohammad Reza Pahlavi, *Le lion et le soleil, op. cit.* p.201.
7 – See :
Houchang Navahandi and Yves Bomati, *Shah Abbas empereur de Perse*, work awarded a prize by the French Academy, Perrin, Paris, 1998, chapter 8, pp. 184 to 227.
A. Stierlin, *Ispahan*, ed. Princesse, Paris, 1980.
A. Stierlin, *Le monde de la Perse*, ed. Princesse, Paris, 1981.
M.R. Moghtader, *Paradise, Gardens of Persia*, Washington DC, Mage Publications, 1996.
E. Baudouin, *Ispahan sous les grands Shahs*, Urbanisme, Paris, 9133.
Etc.
8 – See Farokh Ghaffari, 'Vingt ans de cinéma en Iran' in *Regards sur l'Iran*, texts gathered and introduced by Firouzeh Navahandi, Civilisations, volume 38, Brussels, (ULB), 1990 ; pp.179 to 197.
9 – Extract from 'Address to Cyrus' delivered on October 12th 1971, at 11 a.m. by Mohammad Reza Pahlavi, outside the mausoleum of the first Shah-in-Shah of Iran.
10 – Speech given on October 13th 1971 at the International Congress on Iranology, at Pahlavi University, Shiraz. We would like to thank Mr Sh. Shafa for the documentation he was kind enough to leave at our disposal for that congress.
11 – *Kayhan*, September 10th 1976.
12 – Mohammad Reza Pahlavi, *Réponse à l'Histoire, op. cit.*, p.190.
13 – About the episodes that led to that agreement, see: John K. Cooley, *CIA et Jihad*, translated from American English by Laurent Bury, preface by Edward Saïd, ed. Autrement, Paris, 2002. The agreement in question was signed between General Moghaddam and his Chinese counterpart, Qiao-Shi. The author of the book describes in detail the efforts made by

the Iranian diplomacy to warn Washington against the dangerous rise of radical Islamism and the deterioration of the Afghan situation.
14 – Liesl Graz, *Les Omanis, nouveaux gardiens du Golfe*, Albin Michel, Paris 1981, pp. 73-74.
15 – Declaration made to the *Associated Press*, on December 8th, 1975.
16 – See Houchang Navahandi, 'Iran-Irak', *Revue universelle des faits et des idées*, n° 84, June 1982; M.R. Djalili, 'Le rapprochement irano-irakien et ses conséquences' *Politique étrangère*, n° 3, 1974 ; Paul Balta, *Iran-Iraq*, Anthropos, Paris, 1987; Siavash Bashiri, *The Iran-Iraq Treaty of 1975*, Shahiram, published in Germany, 1988, a book with the text of the treaty, the annals and proceedings and annexes with an English translation; Behrouz Soursrafil, *The Iran-Iraq War*, Caspian Communications, London, 1989, with a particularly well detailed bibliography of the relations between the two countries.
Also see: Pierre Péan, *La menace*, Fayard, Paris 1987; Walter Debock and Jean-Charles Deniau, *Des armes pour l'Iran*, Gallimard, Paris 1988.
17 – Nasser Amini, *Râheh Zendegui*, a weekly in Persian published in Los Angeles, n° 1059, July 29th 2005.
18 – Mohammad Reza Pahlavi, *Réponse à l'Histoire, op. cit.*, p.12.
19 – Same source, p .168.
20 – Jean Dutourd, *Le feld-maréchal von Bonaparte, considérations sur les causes de la grandeur des Français et de leur décadence*, Flammarion, Paris, 1996, pp.63-64.
21 – Alexandre Del Valle, *Islamisme et États-Unis, une alliance contre l'Europe, op. cit.*, p.129.
22 – Mohamed H. Heykal, *Khomeyni et sa révolution, op. cit.*, p.108.
23 – *Kayhan*, September 1976.
24 – William Shawcross, *Le Shah, exil et mort d'un personnage encombrant, op. cit.* p.191.
25 – Mohamed H. Heykal, *Khomeyni et sa révolution, op. cit.*, pp.107-108.
26 – *Kayhan,* September 10th 1976.
27 – Mohammad Reza Pahlavi, preface for *l'Iran vers l'an 2000, op. cit.*

PART III

The Islamic revolution

Chapter XI – 'A kind of social-democratic saint'

1 – Dominique Lorentz, *Une guerre*, ed. des Arènes, Paris, 1977, p.172.

2 – Thierry P. Millemann, *La face cachée du monde occidental*, Osmondes, Paris, 2005, p.162.
3 – Alexandre de Marenches, *Dans le secret des princes, op. cit.*, pp 248-249.
4 – Maurice Druon, 'Les stratèges aveugles', *Le Figaro,* November 18th 2004.
5 – Firouzeh Navahandi, *Aux sources de la révolution iranienne*, L'Harmattan, Paris, 1988, p.237.
6 – About Ruhollah Khomeini, see Amir Taheri, *Khomeyni*, Balland, Paris, 1985.
7 – Christian Delannoy and Jean-Pierre Pichard, *Khomeyni, la révolution trahie*, Carrière, Paris, 1988, p.67.
8 – Paul Balta, *Le Monde*, January 19th 1979.
9 – Pierre Accoce and Dr. Pierre Rentchnick, *Ces nouveaux malades qui nous gouvernent.,* Stock, Paris, 1988, p.282.
10 – Ruhollah Khomeini, declaration made to the Feyzieh school in Qom, on March 6th, 1979.
11 – About the emblem and its thousand-year-old history, see: Hamid Nayer Nouri, *Tarikhtsheh…, A History of the Iranian Flag and of the Lion and the Sun,* Tehran University, Institute of Studies ad Social Research, 1965. There are also a few explanations in our *Shah Abbas, empereur de Perse* (with Yves Bomati) Perrin, Paris, 1998, work awarded a prize by the French Academy.
12 – Cited by Gérard Beaufils, *Tous otages de Khomeyni,* Séguier, Paris, 1987, p.74.
13 – *Le Monde*, January 19th 1979.
14 – Minister and Prime Minister, then president of the Senate under the Pahlavi dynasty.
15 – Amir Taheri, *Khomeyni, op. cit.*, pp.29 to 68.
16 – Ruhollah Khomeini, cited by Christian Delannoy and Jean-Pierre Pichard, *Khomeyni, la révolution trahie, op. cit.*,p.76.
17 – Siavash Bashiri, *Toufandar…The storm of 57*, Parang, Levallois, 1982, p.58.
18 – Amir Taheri, *Khomeyni, op. cit.,* p.96. Gérard Beaufils, *Tous otages de Khomeyni, op.cit.*, P.76.
19 – Ruhollah Khomeini, *Kachfolasrar, The Key to Mysteries*, recent edition, Tehran, with no date and no publisher's name, pp. 186-187.
20 – Same source, p.234.
21 – Cited in the press of the time, and by Sh. Shafa, *Toziholmassaél, Explanations for the Problems*, Iranchahr, Paris, 1983, p.847
22 – The historian Homa Nategh, quoted by Christian Delannoy and Jean-Pierre Pichard, *Khomeyni, la révolution trahie, op. cit.* p.71.

Notes chapter XI

23 – See, among others, P. Guiraud, *Psychiatrie clinique*, M. François, Paris, 1956, pp.298-300, as well as P. Bernard and C. Brisset, *Manuel de psychiatrie*, 5th ed. Masser, Paris, 1978, pp.510-511.
24 – Oriana Fallaci, 'An interview with Khomeini', *New York Times Magazine,* of October 7th 1979.
25 – Declaration to *Le Monde*, May 6-7 1979.
26 – Ruhollah Khomeini, *Le Monde*, 6th-7th May 1979, text used again in *Pensées politiques, Présentation thématique au travers des écrits et discours depuis 1941*, translation and introduction by Y. A. Henry, Iranian Library, Ed. ADPF, Paris, 1980, p.41.
27 – Oriana Fallaci, source given before,
28 – Mohamed H. Heykal, *Khomeyni et sa révolution*, ed. Jeune Afrique, Paris, 1983, p.94.
29 – Constitution of the Iranian Islamic Republic, preamble, paragraph 2.
30 – *Le Figaro*, Saturday 18th – Sunday 19th June 2005. Article signed by Georges Malbrunot, who was himself the victim of a long hostage-taking by the Islamists, which shows how long falsehoods can last, even for people who are honest and supposedly informed.
31 – Quoted by Siavash Bashiri, *The storm of 57..., op. cit.*, pp.74 to 77.
32 – Same source, pp.82 to 86.
Anwar Khameï, the Tudeh leader, in his *Memoirs, op. cit.*, volume 2, describes the role of that character to be an influential agent and an infiltered Soviet agent into the Iranian political and religious circles;
33 – It was police lieutenant Seyf Assar, who belonged to a famous family of religious dignitaries, who made the arrest. He was, of course, sitting next to him in the car that were taking them back to Tehran. Discovering the policeman's identity, Ruhollah Khomeini relaxed, the policeman was to tell me later on. He apparently cried his heart out and said: 'This time, they are going to execute me!'.
After Khomeini had settled down in the state villa, the Prime Minister of the time, Hassan Ali Mansour, who was to be assassinated shortly after by a radical Islamist, (January 1965), asked State Minister Mohammad Nassiri to pay him a visit. The conversation was very courteous. A servant, probably a member of the security services, served tea. There were a plate of fruit and sweets on the sitting-room table. Khomeini begged his interlocutor to help himself and added: 'I hope that they are not poisoned' – he was afraid of everything, it seems. Both men nevertheless had cakes with their tea! The departure in exile of the man was then virtually negotiated. General Pakravan was also in its favour. Everything was done discreetly.
I was then a member of the government. Professor Nassiri had told me that 'little episode', it is therefore authentic.

34 – These details come from *Memories...*, by Freydoun Zand-Fard, the last ambassador of imperial Iran in Iraq, who stayed in his post for several months after the revolution, Nashré-Abi, Tehran, 2005, p.229.
35 – Alexandre de Marenches, *Dans le secret des princes...*, op. cit., p.245.
36 – Edouard Sablier, *Iran, la poudrière...*, op. cit., p.61.
37 – *Le Monde*, May 6th 1978.
38 – Mohamed H. Heykal, *The Return of the Ayatollah*, André Deutch, London, 1981, p.134.
39 – Gérard Beaufils, *Tous otages de Khomeyni...*, op. cit., p.81.
40 – *Bulletin from the European Centre of Information* (CEI in French) XXIXth year, n°3, March 15th 2000,,p.11. The director of the CEI, Pierre F. de Villemarest, had met and questioned Colonel Goleniewski himself.
The latter found refuge at the American consulate of West Berlin on December 25th 1960. When he arrived in Washington on January 13th 1961, the CIA housed him in McLean, in Virginia, not far from Langley where the Central had moved into new premises and he was first questioned by American experts, then by all of the major Western services until 1964. The exploitation of the information given by the defector made it possible to unmask several dozens Soviet spies who sometimes held key positions in the secret services and power circles of the West.
After a hearing on May 27th 1963 in front of the special sub-committee of the House of Representatives, the defector 'exceptionally' got American nationality for 'services rendered to the national security of the United States'. (resolution n° 5507). The affair, with its more or less incredible aspects caused a lot of controversy. It only presents a historical interest today. (archives of the CEI.)
41 – *Bulletin of the Centre of European Information* (CEI in French), January 5th 1971. In that study, all the names of all the groups which 'were to make' the revolution around Khomeini and who already found 'not only the money, but surprising facilities to coordinate their infiltration procedures while waiting for more', *ibid*.
42 – See, in particular, Michael Ledeen and William Lewis, *Rout, American* failure in Iran, op. cit., – probably the best – analysis today of the American policy regarding Iran. pp. 127 to 141.
43 – *Le Monde*, March 11th-12th, 1984.
44 – *Ibid*.
45 – *Ibid*. About the role played by that character, who was the team leader of the hostage takers at the United States embassy in Tehran, see Suzanne Labin, 'Pénétration soviétique en Iran', *Nouvelliste et feuille d'avis du Valais*, Switzerland, December 10th-11th 1983. About the

Notes chapter XI

relations between ayatollah Khomeini and the Soviet services, there are details in *L'Express* of July 6th-12th, 1984.
The reminder of these facts shows the trickery or naivety which prevailed during all the position takings in the West during the 1978 revolution.
46 – A complete account of that episode and of the dealings it involved can be found in our *The Last Shah of Iran*, Aquilion, 2005, pp.75 to 83.
47 – Dariush Homayoun, *Yesterday and Tomorrow*, work published in the United States in 1981, p.92.
48 – Freydoun Zand-Fard, who was then ambassador of Iran to Baghdad, gives an account of the diplomatic fluctuations, Iranian and Iraqi, on the subject in his *Memoirs...*, *op. cit.*, pp.220 to 224.
The book was published in Tehran (in 2005) and submitted to censorship, so it is obvious that everything could not be written freely. There are, however, a few interesting details.
49 – Pierre de Villemarest, *Bulletin from the European Centre of Information* (CEI in French), July 15th, 1984.
50 – Valéry Giscard d'Estaing, *Le pouvoir et la vie*, Compagnie 12, Paris, 1988, pp.95 to 117.
51 – Valéry Giscard d'Estaing, various declarations, notably quoted in *Le Vif, L'Express*, January 29th-February 4th 1999.
52 – Dominique Lorentz, *Une guerre...*, *op. cit.*, p.174.
53 – Édouard Sablier, *Iran, la poudrière...*, *op. cit.*, p.65.
54 – *Ibid.*, p. 62.
55 – Alexandre de Marenches, *Dans le secret des princes, op. cit.* p.247.
For a few years now, a rather voluminous text – 257 pages in the duplicated version which we got in Tehran – has been circulating in Iranian circles, and is attributed to a certain Sayed Djafar Sharif-Zadeh, a guardian of the revolution and head of the protection team for Ruhollah Khomeini. If the facts that are related on the episode of Neauphle-le-Château are often true or likely to be true, according to some crosscheckings, the authenticity of the accounts and the real identity of that person should be verified.
The text nevertheless contains interesting details on Khomeini's life in France, and on the relations his entourage had with the foreign intelligence services. The rivalries between the people who were in the first circle of Khomeini's Iranian entourage were known to all. Are the details given in that account, which are sometimes obscene, actually reliable? We cannot confirm it or invalidate it.
According to the rumour, after the clandestine publication of that text, Sharif-Zadeh allegedly disappeared.

56 – *Le Monde*, Janurary 31st, 1979.
57 – Interview granted to *Le Figaro Magazine*, on Saturday, October 4th 1980.
58 – *La Vie française*, March 26th-April 1st 184.
59 – Pierre de Villemarest, 'Quand Giscard aidait Khomeyni', *AF Hebdo*, January 21st-February 3rd, 1999.
60 – William H. Sullivan, *Mission to Iran*, Morton and Co., New York,1981, p.199.
61 – Thierry P. Millemann, *La face cachée du monde occidental, op. cit.* p.162.
62 – The President of the Tehran Bar, Hassan Nazih. *Le Figaro Magazine*, October 4th, 1980.
63 – M. A. Moezzi, *Le shi'isme doctrinal et le fait politique*, ISG, Paris, 1983, p. 61.
64 – Soudabeh Marin, *Une philosophie du droit en Islam ? Un exemple iranien*. French Society of philosophy and of legal and political theories (SFPJ in French), University of Paris X, Nanterre, 2004.
About that problem, also see H. Corbin, *En islam iranien, aspects spirituels et philosophiques,* vol. I, *Le shi'isme duodécimain*, Paris, Gallimard, 1971. Also, M.A. Moezzi and C. Jambet, *Qu'est-ce que le shi'isme*?, Fayard, Paris, 2004, pp. 127 -129.
65 – *Le Monde*, August 7th 1980.
66 – *Message to the Nation*, on the occasion of the Iranian New Year, March 21st, 1982.
67 – Figure given by Gérard Beaufils, *Tous otages de Khomeyni, op. cit.*, p.44.
68 – Dominique Lorentz, *Une guerre…, op. cit.*,p.174.
69 – Testimony given by Ibrahim Yazdi on the occasion of the twentieth anniversary of the revolution, *Iran-eh-Farda*, n°51, February-March 1999, p. 21. Mehdi Bazargan, Khomeini's Prime Minister, was to confirm these words later, in an interview to *Nehzat*, a weekly published in Paris, cited by Sh. Shafa in *Crime et châtiment*, volume II, *op. cit.*, p.963.
70 – *Le Figaro*, October 15th, 1978.
71 – Austrian television, November 1st, 1978.
72 – *Paris Match*, February 2nd, 1979.
73 – *Kayhan havaï*, newspaper for Iranians abroad, January 24th, 1979.
74 – 'Manifeste' or 'Discours de Paris' cited by A. H. Bani Sadr, the ayatollah's 'spiritual son' and first president of the Islamic republic, *L'Espérance trahie*, Papyrus, Paris, 1982.
75 – *The Guardian,* November 1st, 1978.
76 – *Le Monde*, January 25th, 1979.

Notes chapter XI

77 – *Ettela'ât*, May 20th 1979.
78 – *Réforme*, January 27th 1979.
79 – *Le Monde*, February 2nd, 1979.
80 – *Le Monde*, January 13th, 1979.
81 – *Le Monde*, January 13th, 1979.
82 – Press release from the steering committee of the SP, January 6th 1979, Documentation Centre of the French Socialist Party (CDPS in French).
83 – Press release from the executive bureau of the SP, Documentation Centre of the French Socialist Party (CDPS in French).
84 – *Kayhan*, n° 10621, January 30th 1979.
85 – *Kayhan*, n° 10642, February 21st, 1979.
86 – *Time*, July 16th 1979.
87 – *Le Monde*, January 19th 1979.
88 – See, in its French translation, *Ayatollah Khomeyni, Principes politiques, philosophiques, sociaux et religieux*, extracts from his major works, translated from Persian by Jean-Marie Xavière, with an introduction and explanatory notes, Éditions Libres Hallier, Paris, 1979.
Ayatollah Ruhollah Khomeyni, *Pensées politiques, op. cit.*,
Among his interviews with journalists from around the world, the one given to Oriana Fallaci does not seem to have been manipulated or rephrased and deserves attentive reading, *New York Times Magazine* of October 7th 1979.
89 – Ruhollah Khomeyni, *Principles…, op.cit.*, p.25.
90 – *Ibid.*, p.116.
91 – *Ibid.*, p. 39.
92 – Ruhollah Khomeini, speech to the civil servants of Radio Iran, June 22nd, 1979.
93 – Ruhollah Khomeini, *Principles…, op. cit.*, p.162.
94 – *Ibid.*, p. 22.
95 – *Ibid.*, p.94.
96 – *Ibid.*, p. 160.
97 – Ruhollah Khomeini, *Pensées politiques…, op. cit.*, p.32.
98 – Ruhollah Khomeini, declaration to the Feyzieh school of Qom, August 29th 1979.
99 – Ruhollah Khomeini, *Kachfolassar, The Key to Mysteries*, published in Tehran, with no publisher's name or date, p.292.
100 – For an exhaustive study, refer to erudite Shoja Ol Din Shafa's entire work. For a synthesis in French, see Houchang Navahandi, *Le grand mensonge, Dossier noir de l'intégrisme islamique*, Nouvelles Editions Debresse, Paris, 1984.

101 – Ruhollah Khomeini, *Principles…, op.cit.,* p.41.
102 – *Ibid.*
103 – *Ibid.*
104 – *Ibid,* p. 43.
105 – Ruhollah Khomeini, *message to the nation*, April 1st 1979.
106 – Ruhollah Khomeini, cited by A. H. Bani Sadr, *L'Epérance trahie, op. cit.* p. 350.
107 – Ruhollah Khomeini, speech to air force officers, February 8th, 1981.
108 – Ruhollah Khomeini, words spoken in front of Imam Moussa Sadr's family. August 28th 1979.
109 – Ruhollah Khomeini, *Pensées…, op. cit.,* p.32.
110 – Ruhollah Khomeini, message to the representatives of the assembly of experts (constituent) on August 18th 1979.
111 – Ruhollah Khomeini, decree for the nomination of Mr Mehdi Bazargan, on February 5th, 1979, text in *Le Figaro* of February 6th 1979.
112 – Ruhollah Khomeini, declaration to the representatives of the towns of Tabriz and Qom, September 19th, 1979.
113 – Ruhollah Khomeini, *Le Monde*, April 9th 1979, declaration used again in *Pensées…, op. cit.*, p. 40.
114 – Ruhollah Khomeini, declaration, April 2nd, 1979.
115 – Ruhollah Khomeini, *Le Monde*, May 6th-7th, 1979, text used again in *Pensées…, op. cit.*, p.41.
116 – Ruhollah Khomeini, *Libération*, March 7th 1979.
117 – Ruhollah Khomeini, message to police officers and non-commissioned officers, September 13th 1981.
118 – Ruhollah Khomeini, message on the occasion of the beginning of the Iranian school year, September 23rd, 1982.
119 – *Le Quotidien de Paris*, November 7th, 1983.
120 – Ambassador Andrew Young.
121 – Professor Richard Falk.
122 – Thierry Millemann, *La face cachée du monde occidental, op. cit.*, p.165.
123 – Claude Javeau, preface for *'Aux sources de la révolution iranienne'*, by Firouzeh Navahandi, L'Harmattan, Paris, 1988, p.14.
124 – *Le Monde*, January 26th 1979.
125 – *Le Monde,* January 18th, 1979.
126 – Testimony written and dated February 27th 1984, of François Charles-Roux, French ambassador, consulted by the Elysée.
127 – *Monde et vie*, November 1978.
128 – *Iranshahr*, n° 4, spring 1994.

Notes chapter XII

Chapter XII – Iran and the West

1 – Report to Department of State, documents from the embassy of the United States in Tehran, volume 8, p. 2.
2 – *Ibid.,* pp. 82, 83 and 84
3 – *Ibid.,* p. 103.
4 – *Ibid.,* p. 113.
5 – *Ibid.,* pp. 136 to 146
6 – *Ibid.,* p. 150, etc
This volume 8 contains a series of documents classified 'secret' on the evolution of Iranian politics which was more and more worrying for the Americans.
7 – Mehdi Mozaffari, 'Les nouvelles dimensions de la politique étrangère de l'Iran', *Politique étrangere*, 1975, n° 2.
8 – Mohammad Reza Pahlavi, *Le Lion et le Soleil, op.cit.*,p. 223. The citation of the Shah of Iran on a triumphal voyage as general of Iran in 1963. The welcome of the population was extraordinary, hundreds of thousands of people had come spontaneously to acclaim him in the streets, not only in Tehran but also in Shiraz and Ispahan. No other head of state had received up till then, or will ever receive such an overpowering welcome.
9 – Report from the CIA the contents of which were revealed in the American press in july 1975. See *Le Monde,* 29th July 1980
10 – Incident described in detail by William Shawcross, *Le Shah........, op. cit.*, pp. 197-198
11 – Paul-Marie de la Gorce, *Jeune Afrique*, n° 1987, 9th-15th Febuary 1999.
12 – 'Iran is an island of stability in one of the most troubled regions in the world. Iran owes this to the Shah's impressive leadership. Because of this, Your Highness, of your qualities as head of state, of the respect and admiration that the people have for you…..It means that we can benefit from the reliability of your judgements and sound advice. No other country in the world is even close to us concerning the professionalism of our armed forces. There is no other country with which we have such close talks on our respective regional problems and there is no other leader for whom I have such gratitude and great personal friendship'….
13 – *L'impact*, Geneva, March 1985.
14 – *Bulletin du Centre européen d'information* (CEI), 16th October 1980. This phrase was often reused in several other publications.
15 -Testimony of ambassador Amir Aslan Afshar, last Chief of protocol of the imperial court. These words were pronounced in Morocco in Febuary

695

1979. See our *The Last Shah of Iran, op. cit.,* chapter XIII, particularly pp. 418-420. Later on and until his death, the last Shah of Iran was to often use this theme, in private and in public.

16 – Mohamed H. Heykal, *Khomeyni et sa revolution, op. cit.*, p. 20.

17 – Gholam Reza Pahlavi, *Mon père, mon frère, les Shahs d'Iran, op. cit.,* pp. 255-256. It should be stressed that these remarks come from the only surviving brother of the Shah and could mirror what was to become his elder brother's inner conviction.

18 – Richard Labévière, *Les dollars de la terreur, Les États-Unis et les islamistes, Grasset,* Paris, 1999, pp. 205 and cont'd.

19 – Regarding the influence of certain circles of thinking and the pressure exerted by the CFR and the Trilateral Commission in the Iranian revolution see Siavash Bashiri, *Toufandar...The storm of 57, op. cit.*

20 – *Magazine de Beyrouth*, 2nd Febuary 1979.
The attitude and role of Henry Kissinger before, during and after the years that followed the Iranian revolution raised several comments.
See, among others, Alain Vernay, 'Giscard, Kissinger et le Chah', *Le Figaro,* 24th May 1975, *The Economist,* 17th February and 24th February 1979 (signed George Ball).
La Tribune de Genève, 27th November 1979, as well as Jean Lacouture, 'Un Kissinger rêveur', *Le Nouvel Observateur,* 3rd November 1980.
More recently, Henry Kissinger directed the publication of a report in the framework of the National Committee of American Foreign Policy suggesting the normalisation of relations between the United States and the Islamic republic, *Jeune Afrique,* n° 1913, 2nd -3rd September 1997.

21 – Nicolas Nasr, *Le suicide américain,* Dar-El-Amal, Beyrouth, 1983, p. 514.

22 – Alexandre Del Valle, *Islamisme et États-Unis, une alliance contre l'Europe,* preface by General Pierre-Marie Gallois, foreword by Jean-Pierre Peroncel-Hugoz, L'Âge d'Homme, Lausanne, 1988,p. 130.

23 – Mohammad Reza Pahlavi, *Réponse de l'Histoire, op. cit.*, pp. 175-179.

24 – Dominique Lorentz, *Une guerre, op. cit.*, p. 172

25 – Testimony of ambassador Aslan Afshar who has our enormous thanks.

26 – *Yedioth Ahronoth,* 12th January 1979.
See also the excellent article of Christian Pahlavan, 'De l'amour à la haine, Iran, Israel', *Politique Internationale,* n° 19, September 1983.

27 – Dominique Lorentz, Une guerre, *op. cit.*, p. 173.

28 – Several works mention them. For a full account see *The Last Shah* of Iran, *op. cit.*, pp. 240 to 246.

29 – *Le Monde,* Sunday 4th - Monday 5th August 1985.

Notes chapter XII

30 – President Pompidou had accepted to participate. Despite the exceptional relationship between the two countries and the crucial part played by French companies in the organisation of the festivities, he had to renounce at the last minute. He was represented by his Prime Minister Jacques Chaban-Delmas, whom, incidentally the Sovereign knew and appreciated. Georges Pompidou had in fact, yielded in front of the pressure of the cohort of 'germanopratine' petitioners, and of the campaign of a few leftist newspapers. The episode had provoked a cold atmosphere in the official French-Iranian relations for a few months.

31 – Gholam Reza Pahlavi, *Mon père, mon frère, les Shahs d'Iran, op. cit.* p.260. 'In October 1977, president Giscard d'Estaing made a state visit to Iran which left a slightly bitter taste…My brother did not care much for the haughty and disdainful attitude of the French president, who was very preoccupied with problems of etiquette. General De Gaulle and the whole of France behind him, had been sincere friends. Giscard d'Estaing was not made of the same wood.' *Ibid.*

32 – Testimony given by ambassador Djamshid Gharib, who is dead today, and who had briefly kept the author of this book as well as his son-in-law aware of the content of the message. 'Forget it, for ever. These are only salon talks' the Shah had retorted. Dariush Shirvani now lives in Germany.

33 – Alexandre de Marenches, *Dans le secret des princes, op. cit.,* pp.248-249.

34 – Declaration cited by William Shawcross, *Le Shah…, op. cit.,* p.199.

35 – See our *The Last Shah of Iran, op. cit.,* pp 486-487.

36 – *Ibid.* pp.228-229.

37 – Interview of the *Washington Post*, translation into Persian in the *Iran Times* (of Washington) on May 30th, 1980. This interview given in Cairo is probably the most severe arraignment Mohammad Reza Pahlavi ever made against Anglo-Saxon politics. It is true that the Shah knew his end was near, and did not follow his usual cautious diplomatic habits.

38 – Alexandre Del Valle, *Islamisme et États-Unis…, op. cit.* p.129.

39 – *Political Memoirs*, by Iradj Eskandari, one of the founders and historical leaders of the Iranian Communist Party (ICP) who is now the general secretary of the Tudeh., *op. cit.,* volume III, p.204.

40 – Alexandre Del Valle, *Islamisme et États-Unis…, op. cit.,* p.129.

41 – *Monde et vie*, November 17th, 1978.

42 – Thierry Millemann, *La face cachée du monde occidental, op. cit.,* p. 149.

43 – *Ibid* . p.152.

44 – Quoted by Michael Ledeen and William Lewis, *Débâcle,…, op. cit.,* p.199.

45 – Article for the *New York Times*, analyzed by Sh. Shafa, *Tavallodi digar…, Une renaissance…*, a 619 page-work on Islam in Iran, published

in 1999, with no precision of the place where it was published or a publisher's name, probably for security reasons, p. 487.
46 – *Ibid.*, p.488.
47 – *Ibid.*, p. 486.
48 – See the excellent work of the Indian political scientist, S. V. Vilanilam, *Reporting a Revolution*, Sage Publications, New Delhi, 1989, pp.122-123. The article of professor Cockraft was published in the *New York Times* on January 18th 1979.
49 – Quoted in the work of Vladimir Volkoff on disinformation.
50 – *Le Figaro Magazine*, July 24th 1999.
51 – Declaration on the San Francisco television on December 3rd, 1979.
52 – 'The orders hastily made to Great Britain were only delivered after the revolution', Christian Delannoy and Jean-Pierre Pichard, *Khomeyni, la révolution trahie...*, *op. cit.* p.129.
53 – Declaration made by Mr David Aaron, the adviser of vice-president Walter Mondale. See Richard Sale, 'Carter and Iran, From idealism to disaster', *Washington Quarterly*, Autumn 1980.
54 – Mohammad Reza Pahlavi, *Réponse à l'Histoire, op. cit.*, p.211.
55 – Richard Labévière, *Les dollars de la terreur, op. cit.* p.232.
56 – Pierre de Villemarest, 'L'ayatollah et la conspiration soviéto-américaine' *Monde et vie*, December 29th 1978.
57 – Thierry Millemann, *La face cachée du monde occidental, op. cit.*, p.149.
58 – 'Alexandre de Marenches, Un seigneur au service de l'Etat', article in homage of A. de Marenches by Pierre de Villemarest, *Monde et vie*, June 8th, 1995.
59 – Michael Ledeen and William Lewis, *Débâcle...*, *op. cit.*, p.154 and cont'd. The book contains a detailed account of the affair.
When ambassador William Sullivan paid me a visit in Tehran, in September 1978, (I was then Minister of Higher Education and of Sciences) a visit he alludes to in his memoirs, I evoked these writs. He knew nothing of them, and I did not have the impression he was pretending.
60 – Same source.
61 – *Washington Post*, January 28th 1979.
62 – Valéry Giscard d'Estaing, *Le pouvoir et la vie,* Compagnie 12, Paris, 1988, p.109.
63 – William Shawcross, *Le Shah..., op. cit.* p.140.
64 – Valéry Giscard d'Estaing, *Le pouvoir et la vie, op. cit.* pp .110-111.
65 – Michel Poniatowski who followed the Iranian file closely for the Elysée and had gone to Tehran on three occasions during the months which

Notes chapter XII

preceded the fall of the monarchy, spoke of 'five contradictory policies' in an interview to TF1, during the evening of Ronald Reagan's election to the presidency of the United States on November 6th, 1980.

66 – Pierre Salinger, *Otages, Les négociations secrètes de Téhéran,* French translation, Buchet/Chastel, Paris 1981, p. 43. Ardeshir Zahedi, Ambassador of Iran to Washington, was under the same impression. Testimony to the author. Dr Brzezinski's work follows the same line of ideas.

67 – Jane Kirkpatrick, *Dictatorships and Double Standards*, Simon and Schuster, New York, 1982, p.8.

68 – Volume 27, pp.100, 104, and 130-133.

69 – General Moshe Dayan, the Israeli Minister of Foreign Affairs, then declared that his country 'ha[d] no particular strategic interest' as regards the change of regime in Iran, *Paris Match*, February 21st, 1979.
See about that subject the article of the Israeli analyst Amnon Kapliouk in *Le Monde diplomatique* of March 1979; the interview of the Shah to Newsweek, on November 3rd 1977;the already cited article by Christian Pahlavan, *Politique internationale,* spring 1983; *Valeurs Actuelles*, July 19th 1982 etc...

70 – report cited by Michael Ledeen and William Lewis, *Débâcle..., op. cit.* p.241.

71 – Pierre Salinger, *Otages, op. cit.* p. 282.

72 – Jimmy Carter, *Keeping Faith, op . cit.* p. 438.

73 – *Ibid.*, p.446.

74 – *Ibid.*, p. 449.

75 – William Sullivan, *Le Monde*, September 9th 1980.

76 – Renaud Girard, *Le Figaro*, March 10th 1995.

77 – Jane Kirkpatrick, *Dictatorships..., op. cit.*, p.8.

78 – Alexandre de Marenches, *Dans le secret des princes, op. cit.* p.256.

79 – *Monde et vie*, May 13th 1999.

80 – *Ibid.*

81 – *L'Express*, 18th-24th of September 1978.

82 – Ronald Reagan, face-à-face on television with Walter Mondale, the democratic candidate during the presidential campaign, November 1984.

83 – *Washington Post*, January 26th 1979.

84 – *Politique internationale*, spring 1981.

85 – *Power and Principles*, New York, 1984.

86 – *The Economist*, February 10th 1979.

87 – *La Croix-L'Événement*, December 30th 1998.

88 – *Sorouch,* a publication from the ministry of Islamic Orientation in Tehran, n° 10, 1983, p.39.

89 – Ruhollah Khomeini, message to the congress of the liberation of

Qods (Jerusalem) August 9th 1980.
90 – Hodjatoleslam Khoïniha, Kayhan, August 12th 1982.
91 – *Le Figaro*, February 1st, 1999.
92 – *Le Figaro*, November 18th 2004.

Chapter XIII – Moscow and Tehran

1 – The expression is from Z. Brzezinski in his work *Powers...,op. cit.,*
2 – See, in particular, the messages dated August 21st and September 27th 1978. People in Tehran thought they knew that Yasser Arafat had been secretly received by the Shah in 1977. It is to be noted that, before the revolution, no Iranair aircraft which had regular flights across the world, and whose level of protection sometimes left to be desired, had ever been subjected to a hijack, and the latter were frequent at the time. The rumour also was that the secret services – the Savak espionage and counter-espionage branches for external security had done the necessary through financial compensations to 'ensure' this security. It is likely to be true but cannot be proved. It was also said or written about a few other major airliners.
Air Field Marshal (Reserve Component) Ali Mohammad Khademi, the managing director of Iranair, was assassinated, according to some, or committed suicide, according to others, during his arrest. He might have known about the arrangements.
3 – Interview granted to *Kayhan*, (London) in April 1985. It is also cited by Sh. Shafa in *Djenâyat..., Crime et Châtiment, op. cit.,* volume I, p.126.
4 – Interview for *Afrique-Asie*, July 4th 1982.
5 – For an exhaustive recension, see Sh. Shafa, *Crime et Châtiments, op. cit.,* volume II, pp. 970 to 1030.
6 – Khomeini's real mentor, who is often alleged to have been, or is even presented as, a CIA agent (Documents from the American embassy, volume 10, in particular, document 8779 dated August 10th 1979, p.110; volume 18, p.158, ibid, p.180.) The *New York Times* (September 30th 1979) noted that an American citizen was not legally allowed to work for a foreign government without the authorization of the Minister of Justice or, at least, the preliminary agreement of the CIA. Now, the paper added, Yazdi held the position of Minister of Foreign Affairs in another country (Iranian Islamic republic) without the slightest reaction from the United States. The famous American paper omitted to mention the role Ibrahim Yazdi had had in the bloody repression in Iran and the fact that he belonged to the Islamic revolution Council, the supreme state apparatus.

Notes chapter XIII

7 – Richard Nixon, *The Real War*, Warner Books, New York, 1980, p.274.
8 – Ronald Reagan, face-à-face on the television with Walter Mondale, the democratic candidate, November 1984.
9 – Proclamation on the occasion of the seventh anniversary of the revolution, February 11th, 1986.
10 – *L'Express*, November 26th-December 2nd 1982, for the text: Houchang Navahandi, 'A propos des accords militaires irano-soviétiques', *Le Quotidien de Paris*, December 7th 1982; *Le Point*, January 17th 1983, etc..
11 – Radio Moscow, programme in Persian, November 19th 1983, information partially used again by *Présent*, November 23rd 1983.
12 – *Présent*, June 29th 1984; *Le Figaro Magazine*, July 7th 1984.
13 – *La Vie française*, 14th-20th May 1984.
14 – Patrice Claude, 'L'an V de la djéhad afghane', *Le Monde*, December 30th 1983.
15 – *Monde et vie*, June 8th 1984.
16 – *Ibid.*
17 – *Présent,* June 27th 1984; *Iran-eh-Azad* of July 7th 1984.
18 – As he was receiving 'his dear children', the representatives of the hostage takers.
19 – *Iran, une première république*, under the direction of Morteza Kotobi, Paris, p.240. The events that were to follow showed that the apologetic sentence was not said without reason.
20 – Eslam Kazemich (one of the 'ideologists' and people who praised the first phase of the revolution, and who later found refuge in Paris). *Djonbech*, January 27th 1980.
21 – Eslam Kazemich, *Djonbech*, March 9th 1980.
22 – Abol Hassan Bani Sadr, who was then president of the Islamic republic, *Le Monde*, January 3rd 1981.
23 – See more particularly, Pierre Salinger, *Otages, op. cit;*
24 – 'La longue marched du KGB en Iran', *Le Monde*, March 11th-12th 1984.
25 – *Ibid.*
26 – Robert Lacontre, 'La machine Andropov', *Le Spectacle du Monde,* February 1983.
27 – From January 5th 1971.
28 – Shortly before the revolution, that very special hodjatoleslam was to be found at the head (imam) of a nice little mosque on the northern heights of the Iranian capital city, just a stone-throwing away from the Niavaran palace, an imperial residence. It had, apparently, not caused any reaction from the security services.
29 – Expression used in the *New York Times*.
30 – *Saf*, official publication of the armed forces of the Islamic

republic of Iran, n° 35 of October 21st-November 21st 1982.
31 – Mohamed H. Heykal, *Khomeyni et sa révolution, op.cit.*, p.18.
32 – To our knowledge at the time, only one analyst paid attention to this fact, Suzanne Labin, 'Pénétration soviétique en Iran', *Nouvelliste et feuille d'avis du Valais*, December 10th-11th- 1983.
33 – Refer to René Cagnat in particular, 'L'URSS en Iran, vers la percée', *National Defence*, November 1982 ; Thierry Wolton, 'Comment l'URSS infiltre l'Iran', *Le Point*, January 17th 1983 ; John J. Metzlere, 'Soviets ready to take Iran', *Washington Inquirer*, December 10th 10982; Chahram Chubin, 'The Soviet Union and Iran', *Foreign Affairs*, Spring 1983; Houchang Navahandi, 'Iran, vers le modèle libyen' *La Revue des Deux Mondes*, July 1983, etc..
34 – Among many others, the Israeli expert Schmuel Seges analyses that role in *The Iranian Triangle*, work summed up in *The Morning Call Allen Town* (PA) on June 24th 1981.
35 – *New York Times*, June 23rd 1981.
36 – Robert Lacontre, *Le Figaro Magazine*, July 4th, 1981.
37 – Pierre de Villemarest, *Valeurs Actuelles*, July 6th 1981.
38 – MM Farsi, Ayat, Behzad Nabavi and Bâhonar, the latter having immediately been nominated the successor of ayatollah Beheshti.
39 – MM Rafsandjani, Ahmad Khomeini.
40 – *New York Times*, December 19th 1982.
41 – *Wall Street Journal*, September 26th 1983.
42 – *VSD*, November 3rd 1983; *Le Figaro Magazine*, February 4th 1984.
43 – Refer to Chahram Chubin, *The Soviet Union and Iran, op.cit.*,
44 – *VSD*, November 1983
45 – René Cagnat, 'L'URSS en Iran', *op. cit.*
46 – *Défense Nationale*, November 1982.
47 – *Présent*, July 15th 1983, Suzanne Labin, '*Pénétration soviétique en Iran*', *op.cit.*
48 – *Der Spiegel*, February 14th 1983.
The number of those who had come straight from the USSR was estimated to be from 2,000 (*International Herald Tribune* of March 9th 1982 ; *New York Times* of October 31st 1982 ; Pierre de Villemarest, *Lettre d'Information du CEI,* March 1982) to 3,000 (*VSD* of November 1983).
49 – *Le Monde*, April 2nd, 1983.
50 – News item, January 17th 1984.
51 – *Pravda*, December 10th 1983.

NOTES CHAPTER XIV

Chapter XIV – The imperial power's hesitation

1 – At the end of 1976, the Think-Tank on Iranian problems which has already been mentioned, decided to write a report which would formally establish the falsification and thus denounce the economic and social consequences of the inflation that had been hidden from the head of state. Two young and brilliant economists and academics, Farhad Rad-Serecht and Mohammad Reza Etminan were put in charge of drafting it. Their investigations, more particularly an enquiry into the bazaar, were discovered by the Savak and the Prime Minister. As Rector of Tehran and president of the Tank, I was then put under a lot of pressure, there were even threats made, so that I would stop the enquiry. The report was drafted and typed outside the secretary's office of the Tank which we thought, was under surveillance. I was even told that it would be intercepted so that it would not reach the imperial cabinet! It was then the deputy director of my cabinet, Nader Malek, whom I asked to take the document to the commander of the 'Immortals', General Ali Neshat, so that he could hand it over to the Shah himself. It was an exceptional way of proceeding. Mohammad Reza Pahlavi read it, got angry, and had me told that I was, 'like all intellectuals, a symbol of pessimism'.
The report was however transmitted to the government. Hoveyda and the Savak reacted somewhat curtly, but the King had a parallel enquiry led by independent experts. The reality of the situation was eventually admitted. A few months later, during the presentation of the Amouzegar government which succeeded the Hoveyda, the Sovereign took up the conclusions of the report nearly word for word when he was addressing his new Prime Minister whose fight against inflation was the real priority. Maybe it is an isolated fact, but it speaks for itself, and the other protagonists still remember it.
2 – We often happened to hear discreet allusions made by the Shah concerning that issue, from 1974 onwards. Several passages of Amir Assadollah Alam's 'diary', *The Shah and I', op. cit.*, explicitly confirm it. The Sovereign was also very uhappy, even irritated, by the interference and manoeuvres of that party in the universities.
3 – Testimony of Amir Assadollah Alam that appears several times in his 'diary', *op. cit*. In the English translation, *op. cit.*, pp.415,435,436.
4 – Gholam Reza Pahlavi, *Mon père, mon frère, les Shahs d'Iran, op. cit.* p.248.
5 – *Ibid.*
6 – Farah Pahlavi, *Memoirs, op. cit.* p.257.
7 – Extracts from the Shah's declarations.

703

8 – *Le Monde*, March 5th 1975.
9 – Christian Delannoy, *La Savak, op. cit..* p.135.
10 – Mohammad Reza Pahlavi, *Réponse à l'Histoire, op.cit.*, p.202.
11 – A 190-page document from the Moroccan Court. Chapter 8 is fully devoted to the relations between the Shah and the Malek, and to the latter's positions concerning the Iranian rebellion in its domestic aspects as well as on its external causes, which the King of Morocco actually recognized. Facsimile and translation from Arabic into Persian, Ardeshir Zahedi's archives.
12 – Mohammad Reza Pahlavi, *Réponse à l'Histoire, op. cit.* p.46.
13 – *Ibid.*, p.207.
14 – A few days after having had that report, I was received by the Shah, as rector of the University of Tehran. The Azhari report was evoked. 'Your Majesty, if a report of that sort were submitted to the head of State of a parliamentary democracy like France, for instance, there would be only two solutions: either the Chief of General Staff would be placed under close arrest, and nothing of the kind has happened here, or the Prime Minister would resign. Your Majesty can see His Prime Minister and his Chief of General Staff throw each other into each other's arms from further away than they can actually see each other'. After laughing at my remark, the Sovereig retorted: ' You are too occidentalized'.
I must say today that I had a certain illusion on the moral and political rigour in certain Western democracies which are quick to give lessons to the whole world!
15 – Mohammad Reza Pahlavi, *Le lion et le soleil, op. cit.*
16 – *Le Monde*, April 11th 1981. ; *Iran-eh-Azad*, n° 198, June 9th 1984 ; *Aspects de la France*, June 28th 1984 ; *Présen*t, June 28th 1984.
Great ayatollah Ghomi declared : 'Everything that is done here, goes against Islam and Shi'ism : the massacres, spoliations, looting, characterized violations of human rights…These people [the leaders of the revolution] follow neither the Koran nor holy commandments. They have invented their own Islam, which is not God's nor the Prophet's, nor the Koran's… I have told Khomeini all that. I have warned him. It was of no use… I wonder if he is not a foreign agent.' One is to remember that great ayatollah Ghomi was a member of the group of 'imitation sources' who gave the 'édjtéhad' to Khomeini, and the title of ayatollah.
About all the positions of the Shiite authorities concerning the Khomeini movement, and radical Islamism, see Houchang Navahandi's *Le grand mensonge, le dossier noir de l'intégrisme islamique'* Nouvelles Editions Debresse, Paris, 1984, chapter X, pp.112 to 123.

Notes chapter XIV

Contrary to what the West has often been made to believe, Islamism has often been condemned by the greatest authorities of Islam, especially the Shiite's. These condemnations went against the general belief, which has always considered fundamentalist radicalism to be revolutionary, thus intrinsically 'progressive', and were not much echoed in the quality international press. They do exist, nevertheless.

17 – About the life and death of ayatollah Shariat-Madari, see, among others, *Aspects de la France*, April 10th 1986.

18 – The author of this book was, from the spring to the beginning of winter 1978, the main intermediary between the Shah and the great ayatollah. The episodes of their useless dialogue are narrated in detail in *The Last Shah of Iran*, Aquilion, 2005.
The senator for Azerbaijan, Mr Hossein Moussavi, the number 2 of the hierarchy of the Rastakhiz, originated from the same town as the ayatollah, Tabriz, and he knew him well. He also met him during that period and conveyed his remarks to Prime Minister Amouzegar, and tried to warn the Shah, who had then heard the same things we had had told him, and which the Savak had also repeated since Nassiri's replacement. It was useless! See the memoirs of senator Moussavi, *Yadnaméha..., Memories of a World that is no longer*, Köln, 2004.

19 – He tried all he could to oppose the abuses and the crimes committed by the revolutionaries whom he condemned in several 'fatwas' on February 24th, July30th and October 18th 1979. He was then progressively reduced to silence, put under house arrest in 1982 already, then imprisoned, tortured and exhibited on television. He was even denied the right to have the doctors of his choice look after him. His death was announced in April 1986. He was paying the price for his patriotism, his moderation and especially his anti-communism. The Soviets and their agents were very influential in Iran at the time, and they had not forgotten his role during the collapse of the separatist regime of Azerbaijan. His ordeal resembles a lot that of Hungarian cardinal Mindszenty during the communist regime in his country.

20 – Dariush Homayoun, Minister of Information at the time, *Yesterday and Tomorrow*, published in the United States, 1981, p.92.

21 – Ali Davani, *Nehzaté...The movement of the Iranian clergy*, Bonyad, Farhangui Emam Reza, volume VII, Tehran, p.24.

22 – After the revolution, several people who were close to general Nassiri were to invoke the necessity of 'not worrying His Majesty', of not 'demoralizing' him, to justify that official position of the Savak which, apparently, did not ignore anything about the unrest that was rising in the country!

23 – Mohammad Reza Pahlavi, *Réponse à l'Histoire, op. cit.* p.223.
24 – For all the details and episodes concerning that event, see *Memories, op.cit.*, by Mr Mohammad Hossein Moussavi, the senator for Azerbaijan, who was in charge of its organization, pp.426-434.
We would like to thank M. Hossein Sepehri who was under-secretary of State to Agriculture for his precisions on that event.
25 – M.H. Moussavi, *Memories, op. cit.*, p.427.
26 – *Ibid.*
27 – Dariush Homayoun *Yesterday and Tomorrow, op.cit.*, p.63. The author was Minister of Information at the time;
28 – In Tabriz, for example, the presence of people who spoke only Arabic was noticed in a few hotels. There was no checking. They participated to the riot, often armed with knives. M. H. Moussavi, *Memories, op. cit.* p.419.
29 – William H. Sullivan, *Mission to Iran, op. cit.*, p.99. Barry Rubin, *Paved with Good Intentions, The American Experience in Iran*, Oxford University Press, New York, 1980, p.207.
30 – As he wanted to 'have witnesses,' or to avoid having to hand it over personally to his commander-in-chief, the colonel begged me to read the report, before he gave it to the Shahbanoo – to beg her to be kind enough to hand it to the Shah. I did so, not without congratulating the author for his courage and his patriotism, and reminding him that for three or four months, the 'Tank' had said the same thing, although phrased differently, to the Shah.
31 – *US News and World Report*, June 26th 1978.
32 – Mohammad Reza Pahlavi, *Réponse à l'Histoire, op. cit.*, p.272.
33 – Abbas Samakar, one of the activists of the ultra-left terrorist networks who was also working for the television, says in his memoirs – an interesting document – that it was even possible to hide weapons in the buildings of the INTR. *Man..., I am a Rebel, A Memoir about the Prison*, Ketab Corp., Los Angeles, 2001, pp.18-21. It doesn't mean, of course, that it was done with the agreement of the director of the organization.
34 – Parviz Adle, *Khaney'ma..., Our House in Fisher-Abad, Souvenirs*, Ketab Corp., Los Angeles 2004, p.172. The book contains a very detailed analysis of the subject, to which one should refer.
The situation recalls in a way that of the French audiovisual media during the 'events' of May 1968, relatively speaking. It was only on France Inter that a small group of journalists gathered around Édouard Sablier had been able to ensure a minimum service of information that were 'not revolutionary'.
35 – Radiotelevised message to the nation.

Notes chapter XIV

36 – Farah Pahlavi, *Memoirs, op. cit;*
37 – Gholam Reza Pahlavi, *Mon père, mon frère, les Shahs d'Iran, op.cit.*, p.264.
38 – *Ibid.* p. 268.
39 – Press release entirely quoted in Ali Davani's *The movement of the Iranian clergy, op. cit.* p.225.
40 – Parviz Adle gives a documented analysis of that enquiry in *Our House in Fisher-Abad, op, cit.*, pp.43-48, which we have summed up.
It was about a certain Achour and his three accomplices. The plan for the attempt had been prepared in the very residence of the ayatollah. The four criminals had received 5,000 Iraqi dinars and 11,000 US dollars. The explosives had been given to them in Abadan by Fouad Karimi. The ayatollah's son, Ahmad, and two other future personalities of the Islamic regime, Hadi Ghaffari, (the man who had boasted he had killed Amir Abbas Hoveyda in his prison corridor) and Modaressi, had supervised the operation.
A printing-house in Khorramshahr, a harbour town near Abadan, had even printed the hand-outs which accused the imperial regime of ordering the fire. Hassiri, the owner of that small company, was to admit it later, he said he had done it for 70,000 tomans, about 10,000 dollars at the time – a week before the fire.
Mohammad Reza Ameli, the Minister of Information of the Sharif-Emami cabinet, had a copy of all the elements of the investigation and of the file in order to be able to have them published in case the Prime Minister decided so.
During the riots in the capital, his office was stormed and set on fire. One could think that it was done to destroy the elements in question.
As for Minister Ameli himself, he was arrested after the triumph of the revolution and atrociously tortured, and sentenced to ten years in prison. After the trial, the president of that court ayatollah Khalkhali shot him. It was then declared that he had been given the death penalty and had been executed.
41 – Mohsen Rezaï, *Tactics and techniques of the revolution*, official publication of the guardians of the revolution, February 6th 1982, Tehran, p.51.
42 – Mohammad Reza Pahlavi, *Réponse à l'Histoire, op. cit.*, P.225.
43 – Vladimir Volkoff, *Petite histoire de la désinformation, Du cheval de Troie à l'Internet*, Editions du Rocher, Paris, Monaco, 1999, p.150.
44 – Christian Delannoy and Jean-Pierre Richard, *Khomeyni, la révolution trahie, op.cit.*, pp.123-124.
45 – Alexandre de Marenches, *Dans le secret des princes, op. cit.*, p.255.

Chapter XV – Panic and death throes

1 – Gholam Reza Pahlavi, *Mon père, mon frère, Les Shahs d'Iran, op.cit.*, p.268.
2 – Farah Pahlavi, *Memoirs, op.cit.*, p.277.
3 – Detailed account in our *The Last Shah of Iran, op.cit.,* pp.154-160.
4 – See our *The Last Shah of Iran, op.cit.*, p.162-163.
5 – Mohammad Reza Pahlavi, *Réponse à l'Histoire, op.cit.*,p.233.
6 – Gholam Reza Pahlavi, *Mon père, mon frère, les Shahs d'Iran, op.cit.*,p.268.
7 – Fereidoun Hoveyda, *La chute du Shah, op. cit.,* pp.48 to 51 ; Édouard Sablier, *Iran, la poudrière…, op. cit.* p.49.
8 – Conversation held in Cairo, on May 9th 1980, at Kubbeh Palace, *Iran, deux rêves brisés, op. cit.* pp.262-263.
9 – As chairman of the board of administrators of the University of Tehran, and as Minister of Sciences and of Higher Education, I had been asked by the Shahbanoo to accompany her. It was normal, and it was my duty. We took a helicopter near the summer palace and went to the heliport of the hospital. In the afternoon, I had an extremely unpleasant phone call from the Prime Minister who reproached me with letting that visit happen, and especially with having accompanied the Shahbanoo. A vivid exchange of words followed. It is true that the Prime Minister knew that the Shahbanoo did not hold him in high esteem.
10 – Mohammad Reza Pahlavi, *Réponse à l'Histoire, op. cit.*, p.272.
11 – Testimony of Ardeshir Zahedi who was spending the evening with the imperial couple, in *Untold Secrets…*, a collection of articles and interviews in English and in Persian, Pari Abasalti, Los Angeles, 2002, p.6.
12 – About that episode, and the events that happened under martial law and until the fall of the monarchy, we have a unique document, the *Notes et souvenirs* of lieutenant general Djafar Saneï, second in command after the commander-in-chief of the army. He held the same position with the the administrator of martial law. We would like to thank general Saneï for leaving a copy of the manuscript at our disposal ; he now lives in Canada. Many thanks also to our friend and former collaborator, Nader Malek for his contribution to this book.
13 – Chapour Bakhtiar, *Ma fidélité*, Albin Michel, Paris, 1982, p.97.
14 – Chapour Bakhtiar, declaration in *Le Monde*, September 10th-11th 1978.
15 – Claire Brière, *Iran, la révolution au nom de Dieu*, Seuil, Paris, 1979, p.61.
16 – *Le Monde, Dossiers et documents*, Histoire au jour le jour, 1974,1985, October 1986, p.134.
17 – Interview published in *Jasha* (Bulletin of a group of former officers

of the imperial military), Paris, n°1, August 22nd 1982.
On the role of these Palestinians or pseudo Palestinians, (people speaking Arabic) also see *Memories...*, of Senator Moussavi, *op. cit.,* pp.489 and cont'd.
18 – Allameh Nouri-Nassirieh admitted his role in that riot and boasted about it on the occasion of the twentieth anniversary of the Islamic revolution. *Iran-eh-Farda*, n°51, February-March 1999.
19 – Interview of general Oveyssi, *Jasha, op. cit.*
20 – Michael Ledeen and William Lewis, *Débâcle, op. cit.*p.164.
21 – Alexandre de Marenches, *Dans le secret des princes, op. cit.* p.255.
22 – The word comes from Mohsen Rezaï, *Tactics and techniques of the revolution, op. cit.,* p.40.
23 – Christian Delannoy and Jean-Pierre Pichard, *Khomeyni, la révolution trahie, op. cit.*, p.135.
24 – Mohsen Rezaï, *Tactics...*, *op.cit.*,p.51.
25 – *Ibid.*, p.38.
26 – *Ibid.*, p.40.
27 – Zbigniew Brzezinski, *Power and...*, *op.cit.*,p.355.
28 – 'Disastrous years' in *Encounter*, November 1984.
29 – Gholam Reza Pahlavi, *Mon père...*, *op. cit.*, p.280.
30 – There are testimonies of ambassador Amir Aslan Afshar, the last great Chief of Imperial Protocol on these decisive hours for the country and for the regime, among other documents: 'Fragments of memories' *Partow-Iran*, monthly in Persian published in Canada, n°65, February 1998/Interview given to *Ara*, September 11th 1987. Ambassador Afshar was kind enough to give us many points on that day and the following ones in writing. He is the only perfectly credible, reliable and honest witness who was with the Shah. We deeply thank him for his precious contribution to this book and to History.
31 – Testimony given by Amir Aslan Afshar.
32 – *Ibid.*
33 – *Ibid.*
34 – Farah Pahlavi, *Memoirs, op. cit.*, p. 283.
35 – Gholam Reza Pahlavi, *Mon père....*, *op.cit.*,p.282.
36 – Private conversation quoted by William H. Sullivan, in *Mission to Iran, op. cit.*, p.178.
37 – *Ibid.* p.180
38 – Mohamed H. Heykal, *The Return of the Ayatollah, op. cit.,* p.150.
39 – Barry Rubin, *Paved with....*, *op.cit.*,p.227.
40 – Mohamed H. Heykal, *The Return of...*,*op.cit.*, p.151.

41 – *Ara*, September 11th 1987; *Partow-Iran*, n°65, February 1998; handwritten note for the author of this book.
42 – Gholam Reza Pahlavi, *Mon père..., op.cit., p*.282.
43 – Sir Anthony Parsons, *The Pride and the Fall, Iran 1974-1979*, translation into Persian, pp.154-155. The politician and historian Mostafa Alamouti also gives a long account of that episode: *Rahâvard* n°74,2006. His account is the same as ours and as that of Prince Gholam Reza.
44 – François-René de Chateaubriand.

Chapter XVI – The fall of the monarchy and the triumph of the revolution

1– *Washington Post*, November 7th, 1978.
2 – *Ayandegan*, July 30th 1979.
3 – *Ayandegan,* November 3rd,1979.
4 – About that affair, also see, Sh. Shafa, *Crime et Châtiment, op.cit.*, volume I, pp.271 to 279. The episode reminds one of 'the affair of the Queen's necklace' in France before the Revolution.
5 – About that trip, see F. Zand-Fard, *Memories..., op.cit.,* pp.219-226. We were able to consult a very detailed written report on that trip which was for Ardeshir Zahedi, part of the latter's archives.
F. Zand-Fard was ambassador in Baghdad at the time and he kept his position after the revolution. His Memories were published in Tehran and were censured. It is not the case for the report that was written for private use by a diplomat from the embassy.
The Shahbanoo gives a brief account of the encounter with the ayatollah in her *Memoirs, op. cit.,p.* 285.
6 – Vincent Meylan, *La véritable Farah, op. cit.*, p.248.
7 – Mohiodine Nabavi Nouri, professor of international law, a close friend of Sadighi and Houchang Navahandi, the author of this book.
8 – About this, see our *The Last Shah of Iran, op. cit.*, p.335 to 341.
9 – Mohammad Reza Pahlavi, *Réponse à l'Histoire, op. cit*., p.240.
10 – Testimonies of Mrs Minou Meftah, *Kayhan,* (London) n° 1072, September 8th-14th, 2005.
11 – Testimony given to the author by Dr Dariush Shirvani, representative for Tehran and in charge of the first contact. He followed all the negotiations with Baghaï. This testimony is confirmed by Ardeshir

Notes chapter XVI

Zahedi who had backed the attempt and made Mozaffar Baghaï's contacts with the leaders of the military easier.

12 – Chapour Bakhtiar, *Ma fidélité, op.cit.*,p.97.

13 – The house was available for six hours. The Shahbanoo and Bakhtiar had a tête-à-tête that lasted about two hours. Bakhtiar then had a long conversation with his aunt. Testimony of Mohammad Ali Ghotbi given to the author.

14 – Chapour Bakhtiar, *Ma fidélité, op. cit.*,p.97.

15 – The reading of Bakhtiar's memoirs, *Ma fidélité*, shows the irrational nature of that hatred.

16 – Gholam Reza Pahlavi, *Mon père....., op.cit.*, p.284.

17 – Declarations made to Jean Gueyras, *Le Monde*, September 10th-11th 1978.

18 – Farah Pahlavi, *Memoirs, op. cit.,*p.288.

19 – *Kayhan*, (London), n° 1062, June 30th-July 6th 2005.

20 – Sir Anthony Parsons, *The Pride and the Fall of Iran, 1974-1975*, translation into Persian, op. cit., p.175.

21 – Bertrand de Castelbajac, *L'Homme qui voulait être Cyrus, op. cit.* p.159.

22 – Testimony given by Amir Aslan Afshar to the author, cited in *The Last Shah of Iran, op. cit.*, pp.352-353. The same account was given by the same person to *Kayhan* (London) n°1063, July 7th-13th, 2005.

23 – Following a vivid polemic on the subject, Mohammad Moshiri, the secretary of state to the presidency of the Council under Bakhtiar, and his very close collaborator, wrote in *Kayhan* (London): 'Even if this is true, what is the problem?' n° 1061, June 23rd-29th 2005.

24 – *Kayhan*, January 7th 1979.

Many newspapers and documents of the time, which are sometimes referred to in this book, were sent to us by Senator Ali Rezaï, who lives in Costa Rica today. We express our thanks.

25 – Chapour Bakhtiar, *Ma fidélité, op. cit.*,p.157.

26 – *Assnadé...The documents from the nest of spies*, volume 20, Tehran, 198 pages + 98 pages of facsimiles.

At the time of the fall of Saigon, the Americans had left behind them many documents which allowed the communists to identify and eliminate thousands of people who were considered to be close to the United States. It was the same after the first Gulf war and the Kurdish rebellion which was encouraged, even organized, by the CIA against the Baghdad regime. When, faced with the Iraqi reaction, the American Central had to quickly evacuate the area, it abandoned a major part of its local collaborators as well as documents allowing to identify others. They were all treated with extreme brutality by the Iraqi authorities and armed forces.

As for the documents from the American embassy in Tehran, they rather prove that those who 'collaborated' with the Americans were almost never the ones the revolution was accusing, but almost always opponents to the Shah. Chapour Bakhtiar's example is an example among many.

27 – Shortly before the nomination of Chapour Bakhtiar was made public, so during the last days of December 1978, the Shah summoned the bureau members of both Chambers. The meeting was held in the conference room near the imperial cabinet and people were sitting at a big table. The Sovereign presided over the meeting. To his right, there was the eighty-year-old president of the Senate, Mohammad Sajadi, and the members of the High Chamber, to his left, those of the Majlis, Dr Djavad Saïd, and his colleagues. The Sovereign explained the reasons for his choice to them and asked for both chambers to support the Minister who had been chosen.

The next day, the Majlis met in a private session. Dr Saïd and the members of the bureau gave a report to the representatives. 'Most of the representatives say they do not even know Bakhtiar!' Extract from the long article by Mostafa Alamouti, then vice-president of the Majlis, the house of representatives, based on his notes and on the proceedings, *Rahâvard*, n°53, autumn 2000, pp.256 and cont'd.

28 – Exclusive interview in *Paris Match*, September 22nd 1978.

29 – *Kayhan*, January 6th 1979.

30 – *Ibid.*

31 – Cyrus Amouzegar, the Minister of Information of the new cabinet, gives his own version of that ceremony in *Kayhan* (London) n° 1059, June 9th-15th 2005, a version that is invalidated concerning several points by the Chief of Imperial Protocol, Amir Aslan Afshar, who was present during the presentation of the ministers, *Kayhan* (London), n°1062, June 30th-July 6th 2005.

32 – Testimony given by ambassador Reza Ghassemi who received the order from the Minister of Foreign Affairs with the mission to convey it to all the diplomatic missions of Iran abroad. *Kayhan* (London) n°1062, June 30th- July 6th 2005.

Testimony given by Mrs Minou Meftah, a diplomat, who was the witness of the removal of the portraits at the ministry of Foreign Affairs and who relates the emotion and protest of some of her colleagues, *Kayhan*, (London) n°1072, September 8th-14th 2005.

33 – *Kayhan*, January 11th 1979.

34 – Testimony of Mostafa Alamouti, the vice-president of the House of Representatives, art. cit.

35 – Mozaffar Baghaï, *Manifesto*, Tehran, January 1979, pp. 3 and 4.

Notes chapter XVI

36 – All these documents were published in Tehran in 1979 by Bongahé Tardjomeh va Nachré Kétab in 401 pages.
The accusations also appear in a clandestine book that was published in Tehran in 1980, Mozaffar Baghaï, *Chénakhté naghighat, The knowledge of truth,* Mozaffar Baghaï spent a few years in Iran after the revolution. He manifested his opposition to the regime and was arrested. He died under torture. About the man's life: see *L'Express* of November 11th 1987.
37 – *Kayhan,* January 17th.
38 – During the meeting of the bureaux of both chambers in the presence of the Sovereign, Mrs Chokate-Malek Djahanbani, a senator, and Mr Djalal Taghavi, a representative, had vividly protested against the obstacles put by the authorities to the activities of the supporters of the regime, which went so far as to ban certain legitimist organizations and associations. Mrs Djahanbani said: 'Women's associations have been dismantled, our meetings are banned, and we are invited to remain calm. The opponents do what they want, and benefit from all the means'. The Sovereign gave a vague answer and invoked foreign intrigues. Account given by Mostafa Alamouti, *op. cit.*
39 – Interview in *Paris Match,* January 1979.
40 – Letter to ayatollah Khomeini, January 24th 1979.
41 – *Ibid.*
42 – Declaration to Parliament, *Ettela'ât,* January 12th 1979.
43 – Letter to ayatollah Khomeini, *op.cit.*
44 – Testimony cited by Amir Aslan Afshar, *Kayhan,* (London), n° 1062, June 30th-July 6th 2005.
Bakhtiar had indeed declared in Tehran that he would allow Ruhollah Khomeini to 'create a small Vatican in Qom', *Ettela'ât,* February 5th 1979.
45 – *Ettela'ât,* January 18th 1979.
46 – Political memoirs of Lotf-Ali Samimi, *in Ahangué Siassi,* published in Paris, n°3, December 9th 1981.
47 – *Ibid.*
48 – *Ibid.*
49 – Chapour Bakhtiar, *Ma fidélité, op.cit.* p.180.
50 – Alexandre de Marenches, *Dans le secret des princes, op. cit.,*
51 – The whole of the Tehran press ; see, in particular, *Ettela'ât* of January 17th and 18th 1979. The same newspaper had accused Ardeshir Zahedi on February 3rd, of preparing that coup, even though the latter had already left Iran for over two weeks.
52 – Declaration made to AFP and reproduced in *Ettela'ât* and *Kayhan* of January 11th 1979.

53 – Ardeshir Zahedi, *Untold secrets, op. cit.*, p.9.
54 – Mohammad Reza Pahlavi, *Réponse à l'Histoire, op.cit.*, p.246.
55 – Gholam Reza Pahlavi, *Mon père,...*, *op.cit.*, p.290.
56 – Declaration made to the Islamic revolutionary tribunal of Tehran, which the Shah sadly recalls in his *Réponse à l'Histoire, op., cit.*, p.247. Most of General Huyser's interlocutors were assassinated after the revolution. The witnesses of the 'original sin' had to disappear. Only General Gharabaghi was spared by Prime Minister Bazargan, according to the Shah. (*ibid*).
57 – For all the details on that episode, see our *The Last Shah of Iran, op.cit.*, chapter XII, pp. 377 to 394.
Also see Janine Dowlatshahi, the palace librarian, *La Reine et moi*, Éditions JMD, Geneva, 1980, pp.165 and cont'd. ; Houchang Navahandi, Les six jours qui ébranlèrent l'Iran, *AF Hebdo*, n° of January 21st to February 3rd 1999. We would like to thank Colonel Cyrus Khiltach, the head of the intelligence services of the imperial guard for the information on the last days of the imperial couple in Iran.
58 – Gholam Reza Pahlavi, *Mon père, mon frère...*, *op. cit.*, p.284.
59 – Mohammad Reza Pahlavi, *Réponse à l'Histoire, op. cit.*, p.249.
60 – Conversation of the author with the Shah in Cuernavaca, Mexico, on September 20th 1979. See Houchang Navahandi, *Iran, deux rêves brisés*, Paris, Albin Michel, 1981, p.251.
61 – Chapour Bakhtiar, *Ma fidélité, op.cit.*, p.151.
62 – *Ibid.*
63 – Testimony of ambassador Amir Aslan Afshar, chief of imperial Protocol, given to the author. He gives a brief account in *Kayhan* (London) n° 1062, June 30th-July 6th 2005.
64 – *Ayandehgan*, January 25th 1979.
65 – Ibrahim Yazdi's *Memoirs, Akharine..., Last efforts during the last days*, Ghalam Tehran, 1983, pp.137 to 172.
Mehdi Bazargan, *Enghéhbab...,The Iranian revolution in two movements*, self-edition, Tehran, 1982, pp.74 and cont'd.
66 – *Le Quotidien de Paris*, May 3rd 1984.
67 – *Ettela'ât*, January 9th 1979.
68 – We would like to thank brigadier general Manutshehr Biglari, the last commander of the military Academy of Tehran, for the memorandum he was kind enough to write for us on the structures of command, the vertical and horizontal hierarchies and the decision-making process within the imperial army.
69 – Michael Ledeen and William Lewis, *Débâcle...op.cit.*, p.204.
70 – *Ibid.*

Notes Chapter XVI

71 – The analysis given by another American personality who was in Iran during those decisive months is of the same nature, Gene E. Bradley, *The Story of One Man's Journey in Faith*, Xulon Press, USA, 2003, pp.63 to 69.
At about the same time, the *Sunday Times*, in an article sent from Tehran, alluded to Ardeshir Zahedi, and ran over four headlines, 'One man who might rescue the Shah'.
72 – We would like to thank Mohammad Reza Taghizadeh, who is a professor in a British university today, for the file he was kind enough to give us on that episode.
Also see the precisions and memories of Mrs Minou Meftah, a diplomat, who belonged to the team which organized the event, *Kayhan* (London) n°1072, September 8th-14th 2005.
73 – Chapour Bakhtiar, *Si va..., Trente-sept jours après trente-sept ans*, Entécharaté Radio Iran, Paris (17 bd Raspail), editions which disappeared after the former prime minister's assassination, p.71.
74 – As soon as in 1981, we were able to establish the composition of that council thanks to reliable information. Beside Ruhollah Khomeini himself, it was formed of: ayatollah Mahmoud Talehghani, the doctor in theology and mullah Mohammad Beheshti, the doctor in theology and mullah Hossein Ali Montazeri, the retired brigadier general Ali Massoudi, the science professor Yadollah Sahabi, the Iranian-American Mostafa Tshamran, a member of the Amal militia in Lebanon, mullah Djavad Bâhonar, mullah Ali Khamenii, mullah Ali Akbar Rafsanjani, mullah Mohammad Reza Mahdavi Kani, Mehdi Bazargan, Abol Hassan Bani Sadr, the Iranian-American Ibrahim Yazdi, Sadegh Ghotb-Zadeh, and mullah Abdol Karim Moussavi Ardabili.
On July 19th 1979, a 'mixed commission', a revolution-government Council was set up so as to ensure the coordination between the two apparatus of the supreme power. Mehdi Bazargan was to reveal a few names in 1983, (*Portrait of the provisional government from birth to death*, Tehran, 1983, p.25).
His list was to be refuted by the quasi official newspaper of the regime, *Djomhouri Eslam*, dated February 13th 1983. On the occasion of the twentieth anniversary of the regime, several personalities gave contradictory lists of the members (private information from MM Yazdi, Sabbaghian, Sahabi, Minatshi, etc..) *Iran-eh-Farda*, monthly magazine, published in Tehran in February 1999.
The secret was kept voluntarily and the contradictions could come from the fear of reprisals or of a trial for crime against humanity, which are

theoretically imprescriptible in front of an international court.
75 – *Le Figaro*, February 6th 1979.
76 – For a very eulogistic biography of Mehdi Bazargan, see *Le Monde*, February 7th 1979.
77 – Declaration to the press, March 11th 1979.
78 – Georges Menant, *Paris Match*, February 16th, 1979.
79 – *Ibid*. As fate would have it, the interview was published after his downfall and his flight.
80 – Declaration to *Ettela'ât*, February 10th 1979.
81 – *Ettela'ât*, February 13th 1979.
82 – *Le Quotidien de Paris*, October 22nd, 1980.
83 – Chapour Bakhtiar's arrest was first announced by the official agency called Pars, then it was confirmed by Khomeini's bureau (*Ettela'ât*, February 13th 1979). The government spokesman confirmed it officially the next day (*Ettela'ât*, February 14th 1979), *Le Monde,* whose special envoys were well introduced in the leading circles of the revolution states that it 'had the information on good authority that the former head of the government was in a safe place, and was in contact with M. Mehdi Bazargan.' (February 13th 1979). When he reappeared in Paris, there were various comments and a vivid polemic in Tehran. He wrote himself that he left the international airport of the Iranian capital with 'a slightly changed physiognomy thanks to a small beard and black glasses, and a foreign passport' (*Ma fidélité, op. cit.*, P.192).
It was written in Paris that 'his life was spared only because he entertained a long friendship with his successor Mehdi Bazargan' (Freidoun Sahebjam, *Au nom de Dieu clément et miséricordieux*, Mercure de France, Paris, 1983, p.9) . Bertrand de Castelbajac's conclusion is fairly similar: 'Some say that he was incarcerated for a week and then released on Bazargan's intervention and he stayed hidden for some time' (*L'homme qui voulait être Cyrus,op.cit.*,p.165).
In Tehran, the radical wing of the regime accused MM. Bazargan, Beheshti and Sandjabi who was Khomeini's Minister of Foreign Affairs at the time, of having organized his departure for another country. (weekly *Djavanan*, n°650, July 15th 1979; *Kayhan,* February 17th 1980, etc..) The man himself never denied it. Recently, his daughter France Mokhâtab-Rafii asserted the opposite – her father had not been arrested – and she added that she would go to see him everyday in Tehran, for six months, *Kayhan* (London) n° 1065, July 21st-27th 2005. This would mean that the visits were at the same time as her father was in France where he had actually been for a few weeks, and had publicly reappeared in Paris.

Notes chapter XVI - Epilogue

84 – About his assassination, see Yves Chaperon and Jean-Noël Tournier, *Enquête sur l'assassinat de Chapour Bakhtiar*, Editions n°I, Paris 1992.

85 – The facsimile of the proclamation with the signatures of the officers who were present was published in *Ara*, the newspaper of 'the liberation army of Iran', 2nd year, N°7 and N°8 of August 7th 1980. The text also appeared in the local press, notably in *Ettela'ât*, of February 12th 1979. There have been doubts over the authenticity of the signatures.

86 – Michael Ledeen and William Lewis, *Débâcle,...op. cit.*, p.210.

87 – For a particularly striking portrait of Hossein Fardoust, see the memories of M. Mohammad Hossein Moussavi, the senator for Azerbaijan, *Yadnaméha..., Memories of a world that is no longer*, Méhrégan, Köln, 2004, 500 pages, chapter24, pp.412 and cont'd. The book is an important document on the last months of the imperial regime, particularly because certain facts are related in which the author was involved, or which he was the eye witness of.

88 – As soon as Khomeini arrived, activists supervised and controlled the riots.
The Islamists, properly speaking, had no weapons yet, and only intervened later. About the supervision of the first days of rioting, see the documentary in *Kayhan,* February 2nd, 1979. The settling of scores between the factions were to become bloody afterwards, 'the children' of the revolution were fighting one another to death.

89 – Michael Ledeen and William Lewis, *Débâcle...,op.cit.*p.211.

90 - *Ettela'ât* of February 12th 1979.

91 – Thomas Molnar, *La contre-révolution*, translated from American English by Olivier Postel-Vinay, La Table Ronde, Paris, 1982, p;41.

Epilogue – The suffering and tragedy of a lone man

1 – The account was given by ambassador Amir Aslan Afshar to the author and in various declarations which have already been mentioned. He was constantly near the Shah during the last weeks of the reign and at the beginning of the exile. He is the only witness who is fully trustworthy concerning that short but tragic period.

2 – We would like to thank colonels Kioumars Djahanbini and Yazdan Nevissi for the details given on the Shah's travels and experiences during his exile. They ensured his safety as soon as he left Tehran until his death in Cairo and now live in the United States.

3 – *Réponse à l'Histoire*, Albin Michel, *op.cit.* Although the two

original texts were written in French and in Persian – the Shah had signed each page of the manuscripts of both versions to authenticate them – the Tehran regime recently had a translation published of the English version, which is totally falsified and accompanied by disagreeable comments.

4 – Édouard Sablier, Freidoun Sahebjam and, very briefly, Pierre Salinger.

5 – Alexandre de Marenches, *Dans le secret des princes, op. cit.*, p .258.

6 – Interview granted by Hassan II to a foreign journalist, apparently Éric Rouleau, a document from the Court of Morocco, in Ardeshir Zahedi's archives, *op.cit.*

7 – David Rockefeller devotes a long chapter of his memoirs to his relations with the Shah, and tried to minimize them – translated into Persian, *Rahâvard*, n°66, 2004, pp. 220 to 232.

8 – *Ibid.*

The role of the Rockefeller APPARATUS in the Shah's life until the last stop-over in Cairo, when he actually was not fully aware of it any more, is rather controversial. According to Pierre de Villemarest, the question was to 'keep the Shah in control, for he could still be dangerous' AF 2000, January 21st-Februart 3rd 1999. There is no doubt however, that during the Shah's ordeal, the help provided by that APPARATUS for very positive for the exiles, whatever the reason for it was.

9 – Ardeshir Zahedi's archives. The letter will be published in the second volume of Zahedi's memoirs which should come out in English in 2007.

10 – Mohammad Reza Pahlavi, *Réponse à l'Histoire, op. cit.*, p.250.

11 – We had a long meetings between September 18th and 23rd 1979. See our *The Last Shah of Iran, op. cit.*, chapter XIV, pp.427 and cont'd.

12 – Professors Jean Bernard and Paul Milliez, doctor Georges Flandrin, who was then Jean Bernard's assistant, and professor Abbas Safavian, trained in France.

13 – Farah Pahlavi, *Memoirs, op.cit.*

In that book, the Shahbanoo published various medical reports from Dr Flandrin.

14 – *American Medical News*, August 7th 1981.

15 – We were the intermediaries for that request which was given to the Elysée by Alain Peyrefitte, who was Minister of Justice at the time, 'Garde Des Sceaux'. The written refusal was sent to us and we received it on November 15th. It was pointless then. See our *The Last Shah of Iran*, op. cit.

16 – Seven times, according to Dr Kean, *op.cit.*, but he does not give the precise date. It was apparently some time later.

Notes Epilogue

We would like to thank our friend and former collaborator, H. B. who lives between the United States and Iran for giving a file of articles from the American press concerning the affair.

17 – Dr Benjamin Kean, *op. cit.*

18 – Episode narrated in the press and in many books. Also see the account given by the Shahbanoo in her *Memoirs, op. cit.*, pp.340-341.

19 – Testimony given by the Shah's eldest son, Christian Malar, Alain Rodier, *Reza Pahlavi, le fils du Shah de l'exil à la reconquête*, Plon, Paris, 1986, p.89.

20 – Dr Benjamin Kean, *op.cit.*

21 – Testimony given by Ardeshir Zahedi.

22 – Many books relate those transactions in a similar way. Hamilton Jordan also wrote his memories in *Crisis* which was translated into Persian. The reading is not very gratifying for the American diplomacy. Our brief account is a synthesis. It also corresponds to the perception the Shah had of the transactions.

23 – Testimony of the Shah given to the author of this book.

24 – *Op.cit.*

25 – Testimony given to the author of this book.

26 – Testimony given by Colonel Nevissi to the author of the book.

27 – Testimony given by Ambassador Amir Aslan Afshar.

28 – 'During his life, he had to face many assassination attempts: military, religious and political ones, but the attempts of medical assassination finally caused his end' the Franco-American analyst Thierry Millemann wrote, after a long account of the Shah's illness (*La face cachée du monde...,op.cit.*, p.164.) The author alludes to the care and operations on the Shah, and especially the operations he did not undergo in the United States and in Panama. After the Shah's death, the hodjtoleslam Hashemi Rafsandjani, who was already a leading figure in Iran, declared: 'The Carter Administration has killed the Shah to put an end to our requests of extradition'(!) *Le Monde*, January 23rd 1981.

Index

NOTE : Some names put in brackets are the patronymics used before the creation of a registry office in Iran in the twenties.

The last Shah of Iran, Mohammad Reza Pahlavi, does not appear in this index for his name and actions are present on nearly every page.

INDEX

25 Shahrivar Theatre (in Tehran), 395
9/11, September 11th 2001, 665

A

'Affair of the Queen's necklace' (in France before the Revolution), 710
'Auspicious for American interests in the area', 478
'Authentic nonalignment', slogan of the islamic revolution, 153
Aaron, David, adviser of vice-president Walter Mondale, 698
Abadan tragedy (see also Rex cinema), 531, 532, 533, 535, 544, 548
Abbassi, Abolhassan, captain, clandestine communist, assassin of the journalist and writer Mohammad Massoud, 146, 147
Abbas II, Safavid king, 93
Abbas Mirza, son of Fath Ali Shah, 2, 19, 20, 21, 22, 23, 25, 28, 32, 33
Abrahamian, Ervan, professor at New York University, leftist American academic, 292, 293, 677
Abrichamtshi, Mehdi, 665, 677
Abu Musa, key island of the strait of Ormuz, 404
Académie française, 4
Academy of Arts (of the University of Tehran), 395
Accoce, Pierre, 688
Achaemenids, dynasty, 68
Achour, criminal, 707
Acker, General, commander of Lackland airbase, 626
Action française, 685
Adamiyat (mankind), Masonic lodge, 195
Adamyat, Fereydoun, 653
Address to Cyrus, 686
Adelstain, Françoise, 682
Adjari, A., 680
Adle, Parviz, Iranian ambassador to Brazil, 529, 706, 707
Adle, Yahya, professor, famous surgeon, 143
Afghanistan, 23, 33, 201, 344, 403, 405, 490, 492, 623, 687
Afghan hordes, 412
Afghan Mujaheddin, 490, 491
Africa, 121, 341, 373
Afrique-Asie, 700
Afshar, Amir Aslan, Ambassador, Grand Master of Protocol, 464, 557, 559, 560, 581, 610, 611, 613, 633, 639, 640, 658, 695, 696, 709, 711, 712, 713, 714, 717, 719
Afshar, Amir Khosrow, diplomat, 174, 667, 679
Afshar, Heydar Khan (also called Amu-Oghli), first leader of Iranian communism in history, 130, 132, 133, 134, 661, 662
Afshar, Iradj, Prof., 667, 668
Afshar, Seyf, 256, 672
Afshars, dynasty, 68
AF 2000, French weekly, 685, 692, 714, 718
Agahi, intelligence service of the Iranian national Police force, 289
Agence France Presse (AFP), 588, 666, 713
Agger, Don, ex-under secretary of State, 614, 615
Aghassi, Hadji Mirza, Mohammad Shah's private tutor, 22, 23
Aghassian, Seda, Mrs, 660
Aghayan, Mr, top Tehran barrister, member of the Chamber, 136
AGIP, Italian national oil company, 459
Agitators, 523, 525, 553, 563
Agnelli, Giovanni, head of Fiat, 624
Ahmad Shah, the last of the Qajars, 37, 50, 58, 60, 63, 64, 65, 69, 132, 343, 641
Ahrar, Ahmad, 661
Air France, 450, 599
Akhtar, Iranian journal founded in Istanbul in 1875, 34
Ala, Hossein, PM, 164, 194, 233, 271, 272, 303, 308, 378, 512, 648
Alaï, Amir, Minister of Justice, 199
Alam, Amir Assadollah, close friend to the Shah, PM, 271, 272, 316, 317, 318, 323, 324, 325, 326, 329, 330, 332, 377, 504, 512, 649, 656, 680, 681, 703
Alami, Ebrahim Khalil, Mossadegh's Minister of Labour, 245, 669
Alamouti, Mostafa, 256, 654, 667, 668, 669, 670, 671, 675, 679, 710, 712, 713
Alexander I, 19
Algeria, 534, 570
Algiers agreements, 433
Ali, Imam, 57, 510
Aliev, Geïdar, head of the KGB in Soviet Azerbaijan before being appointed incumbent of the Politburo of the CPSU and

later number 2 in the Soviet hierarchy under Gorbachev, before he finally became President of Azerbaijan after the collapse of the USSR, 430
Allies, 100, 104, 113, 114, 118, 120, 121, 122, 124, 125, 126, 127, 137, 140, 151, 158, 159, 160, 232, 272, 302, 306, 326, 453, 457, 458, 463, 465, 469, 473, 474, 480, 488, 565, 641, 645
Amal militia in Lebanon, 715
Amdjadieh, sports complex turned into the headquarters of the counter-revolution, 597, 598
Ameli, Mohammad Reza, Minister of Information of the Sharif-Emami cabinet, 707
Ameri, Djavad, Minister of Foreign Affairs, 105, 110, 658
American Congress, 400
American Medical News, 718
American satellites, 448
American secret services, 278, 461, 464
Amini, Ali, PM, 267, 268, 314, 315, 316, 317, 318, 455, 512, 577, 649, 669, 672, 679
Amini, Nasser, 687
Amir-Ardjomand, Shahrokh, Professor, Vice-Rector of the University of Tehran, 514
Amirani, Ali Asghar, Khândaniha's chief editor, assassinated after the Islamic revolution, 597
Amir Ahmadi (Ahmad Agha Khan), general, Cossack division chief, later to be Minister, 39, 53, 54, 112, 118
Amir Kabir, the 'Great Chancellor', 2, 24, 25, 26, 27, 28, 29, 30, 31, 32, 33, 34, 89, 90, 91, 93, 96, 653, 654
Amnesty International, 276
Amouzegar, Cyrus, Minister of Information, 712
Amouzegar, Djamshid, PM, Hoveyda's successor, 333, 334, 389, 432, 433, 503, 506, 509, 512, 523, 531, 532, 536, 537, 538, 649, 676, 677, 703, 705
Amouzegar, Jahanguir, 686
Amouzegar, Parviz, Rector, 12
Amu-Oghli, Heydar (see also Heydar Khan Afshar), 661, 662
Anarchists, 151
Anarchy/chaos, 17, 52, 58, 109, 129, 141, 223, 303, 547, 568, 589, 594, 597, 604
Andjomane Assar Melli (Association for the Conservation of the National Heritage), 74
Andjomane Iran Djavan (Young Iran Association), think tank, 62
Andrew, Christopher, 683
Andropov, 701
Anglo-Iranian Oil Company (AIOC), 113, 138, 145, 190, 200, 213, 226, 266, 267, 586
Anglo-Persian Oil Company (APOC later to be AIOC), 79, 81
Answer to History ('*Réponse à l'Histoire*'), by Mohammad Reza Pahlavi, 612, 617, 639, 657, 658, 660, 665, 678, 679, 680, 681, 686, 687, 698, 704, 706, 707, 708, 710, 714, 717, 718
Anti-Khomeini peasants, 569
Anti-riot equipment, 474, 550
Anwari, Ahmad, journalist close to the National Front and chief editor of Parkhash, 673
Apartheid, 615
Ara, newspaper of 'the liberation army of Iran', 709, 710, 717
Arab-Israeli conflict, 463
Arab-Muslim world, 156
Arabs' voice, 321
Arab countries, 304, 305, 373, 404, 440, 464, 487, 491, 512, 545
Arab invasion, 68, 89, 108, 385, 400, 412, 642
Arab League, 304
Arab liberation movement, 156
Arab masses, 156
Arab occupation, 68, 412
Arafat, Yasser, 486, 700
Araï, Nasser Fakhr, member of the Tudeh, attempted to assassinate the Shah Mohammad Reza Pahlavi, 143
Aramech, Ahmad, minister in charge of the Plan, 313
Ardabili, Abdol Karim Moussavi, mullah, 715
Arfa, Madam, French governess of Moahammad Reza Pahlavi, 336, 337
Ariana, Bahram, General, 321
Aristotle, 447
Armani, Youssef, ex-convict, 64
Armao, Robert, man from the Rockefeller's entourage, 616, 618, 620, 629, 635
Armenia, 19, 21, 130
Arsacids, dynasty, 68, 400
Arsanjani, Hassan, Minister of Agriculture, 318, 325, 669

INDEX

Artillery school of Fontainebleau, 57, 284
Asfia, Safi, brilliant ex-student from the École Polytechnique, in charge of the Plan, 324
Ashouri, Dariush, 656
Ashrafi, Colonel, administrator of martial law, 248
Ashtiani-Zadeh, member of Parliament close to the extreme left, 200
Askari, Nour Mohammad, 268, 667, 670, 671, 672, 673, 674, 675, 681
Aslani, Nassrollah Kamran, delegate from the Comintern, 135
Aspects de la France, 666, 704, 705
Assad Abadi, Seyed Jamal ed Din, dignitary and religious reformer, one of the forerunners of Free Masonry in Iran, 34, 35
Assar, Seyf, police lieutenant, 689
Associated Press, 685, 687
Association for the Defence of Peace (Stockholm Appeal), 145
Association for the Safeguard of the National Heritage, 108
Association of Iranian Women, 145
Astane Ghodose, museum of religious art, 94
Aswan, dam, 402
Atabaï, Abolfath, 'Master of the Royal Hunt' of the imperial Court, 262
Ataturk, Mustafa Kemal, 67, 85, 86, 344, 511
Austria, 20, 27, 29, 410
Austro-Hungarian Empire, 453
Automobiles (production), 389
Avicenna, Persian philosopher, 379, 392, 395, 447, 514
Avicenna University in Hamadan (see also University of Hamadan), was to be Franco-Persian, 392, 514
Axis (powers, countries), 85, 99, 100, 101, 103, 105, 122, 123, 140, 453
Ayadi, general and doctor, 182
Ayandeh, Journal of Iranian Studies, 144, 659, 670, 674
Ayandehgan, morning newspaper, 522, 710, 714
Ayat, 702
Ayatollah Khomeini's Support committees, 441
Azam, Sepahdar, PM, 39
Azemoun, Manutshehr, Minister of State in charge of the Affairs of the presidency of the Cabinet, 543, 545, 551, 552
Azerbaijan, 9, 19, 20, 21, 23, 54, 77, 125, 129, 131, 132, 133, 137, 141, 157, 160, 162, 163, 164, 165, 166, 167, 168, 171, 172, 177, 178, 179, 181, 182, 183, 184, 187, 196, 209, 210, 233, 269, 283, 305, 308, 355, 369, 370, 392, 430, 453, 493, 518, 569, 666, 705, 706, 717
Azerbaijan crisis, 132, 141, 157, 187, 209, 233, 269, 283, 305, 369, 666
Azhari, Gholam Reza, General, PM, 286, 515, 542, 551, 557, 558, 565, 567, 575, 589, 649, 704
Azmoudeh, Hossein, General, military prosecutor, 260, 663, 664, 674

B

'Baghdad' pact, 305
'Black Friday', 544, 545
'Bloody April', 616
Babayan, Ali, Shah's body guard assassinated, 365
Babre, destroyer, 142
Bachir-Farahmand, Ali Asghar, general manager of the State radio station, 244
Badreï, General, commander-in-chief of the army, assassinated, 594, 595, 596, 606
Baghaï, Hassan, General, Chief of the National Police, 233, 234
Baghaï, Mozaffar, 215, 252, 427, 578, 580, 586, 711, 712, 713
Baha'is, 28, 30, 417, 473, 511
Baha'ism, 28, 34
Baha' Ullah, 28
Bahamas, 615, 616
Bahar, Malek-Ol-Shoara, great poet of the 20th century, 95
Bahar, Mehdi, writer and lampoonist, 597
Bahehri, Mohammad, Minister of Justice, 551
Bâhonar, Djavad, successor of ayatollah Beheshti, 702, 715
Bahrain Islands, 34, 404
Bahrami, Dabir Aazam, Reza Shah's chairman of cabinet, 655
Bahrami, Hossein, grandson of Bahram Khan, 136, 420
Bajano, A., Stalin's private secretary, 664
Bakhtar, Iran Party publication, 666
Bakhtiar, Chapour, the Shah's last Prime Minister, 'the last Prime Minister of the

725

Empire', 187, 237, 450, 516, 544, 558, 579, 580, 581, 582, 583, 584, 585, 586, 587, 588, 589, 590, 591, 592, 593, 595, 597, 598, 600, 602, 613, 650, 667, 708, 711, 712, 713, 714, 715, 716, 717
Bakhtiar, Teymour, General (formed at Saint-Cyr), first Head of the Savak, 253, 281, 282, 283, 313, 316, 430, 431, 455
Bakhtiari, Louise Samsam, spouse of Mohammad Ali Ghotbi, aunt of Farah Diba and of Chapour Bakhtiar, 579, 580, 711
Bakhtiaris (tribes), 69, 70, 174, 581, 582
Ball, George, CFR, Bilderberg and Trilateral Commission member, 473, 550, 696
Balta, Paul, 687, 688
Banani, Amine, 655, 658
Bandara, small English steamer (during Reza Shah's exile), 120
Bani-Ahmad, Ahmad, pro-Khomeini representative, 292
Bani Sadr, Abol Hassan, first president of the Islamic republic, 277, 458, 593, 636, 678, 692, 694, 701, 715
Bank for the Industrial and Mining Development, 537
Bank Kechavavzi, 75
Bank of Industrial and Mining Development, 183
Bank Rahni, 75
Barley (production), 387
Bashir-Fahramand, Ali Asghar, 673
Bashiri, Siavash, 655, 666, 676, 678, 682, 687, 689, 696
Bastien-Thiry, 366
Batmanghehlitch, Nader, head of General Staff, 253, 256
Baudouin, É, 686
Bayandor, Gholam Ali, Commander-in-Chief of the navy, 57, 80, 93, 107
Bayar, Djelal, President of Turkey, 304
Bayat, Morteza Gholi, PM, 125, 162, 164, 647
Bazargan, Mehdi, PM, 368, 428, 493, 494, 567, 600, 601, 602, 650, 694, 714, 715, 716
Bazaris, 43, 177, 217, 252, 423, 509, 523, 566, 569, 577, 578, 703
BBC, 474, 481, 487, 574, 587
Beaufils, Gérard, 688, 690, 692
Beetroot (production), 387
Behbahani, Sayed Mohammad, ayatollah, son of one of the founding fathers of the liberal Constitution of 1906, assassinated, 193, 217, 251, 253, 598
Behboudi, Soleyman, Reza Shah's steward and civilian aide-de-camp from 1921 until his death in South Africa, 655, 656, 682
Beheshti, Mohammad, ayatollah, main partner of General Huyser, 495, 496, 702, 715, 716
Behnam, Djamshid, Professor, the rector of the Farabi University, 514
Behrouz, Zabih, erudite, 231
Belgian kingdom, 35, 270
Belgium, 195, 310, 311, 390
Belushistan, 34, 69, 82, 392, 568
Beneš, Edvard, 82, 173
Bernard, Jean, Prof. famous French physician, 620, 718
Bernard, P., 689
Bessouye-Ayandeh, famous morning newspaper subservient to the Tudeh, 144
Beyzaï, Bahram, film-director and dramatist, 395
Biglari, Manutshehr, General, commander of the Tehran Military Academy, 549, 714
Bismarck, 186, 269
Black Africa, 373
Black September, 469
Blanch, Lesley, 683
Blasé societies, 382, 410
Blast furnaces, 310, 402
Bloodshed/bloodbath, 449, 545, 546, 570, 574, 604, 717
Boghrat, Elaheh, 673
Bokharaï, Mohammad, young terrorist member of a sub-group of the Muslim Brothers, assassin of Hassan Ali Mansour (PM), 329
Bolshevik gaols (see also Gulag), 156, 296
Bolshevik party, 130
Bolshevism, 38, 49, 95, 661
Bomati, Yves, 4, 12, 671, 686, 688
Bonnard, Abel, member of the French Academy, 89
Bonnet, Yves, 677
Book of Kings by Ferdowsi, 89
Boroujerdi, great ayatollah of Qom, 252, 253, 510, 518
Bounet, Yves, 665
Bourguet, Christian, French ultra-left lawyer, 631, 678
Boustan, Saadi's work, 109

INDEX

Boutros-Ghali, Boutros, 682
Bouzardjomehri, Karim, colonel later to be general, real 'Baron Haussmann-style' Iranian, 65, 77
Bozorgmehr, Djalil, retired Colonel, laywer of Mossadegh, 262, 673, 674
Bradley, Gene E., 715
Brest-Litovsk, treaty (March 3rd 1918), 36
Brezhnev, Leonid, 156, 442
Brière, Claire, 708
Brisset, C., 689
British Empire, 30, 83, 102, 124, 404
British Museum, 400
British Petroleum (BP), 69, 226, 267, 454
Brzezinski, Zbigniew, 460, 477, 480, 493, 699, 700, 709
Bulgaria, 485
Bullard, Great Britain's ambassador, 232, 671
Burma, boat (during Reza Shah's exile), 121
Bury, Laurent, 686
Bush, George Herbert Walker, US President, 367, 480
Bushehr, harbour, 33, 80, 175
Business Institute of Moscow, 130

C

'College boys', 479
'Cossack', military division, 37, 38, 39, 44, 47, 48, 49, 55, 230, 655
'Coup' operation, 39, 54, 55, 58, 92, 226, 230
'Crown Council', 551
'Cut the rotten branches', 566
Cabanier, Admiral, head of general staff of the French navy, 364
Cagnat, René, 658, 664, 666, 702
Cairo radio channel, 321
Callaghan, James, 481
Calligraphy, 46, 115, 229, 336, 339, 341, 394
Camp David agreements, 465, 628
Canada, 674, 684, 708, 709
Carlos, terrorist, 333
Carnal, Henri, Director and son of the founder of the Rosey school, 340
Carnal, Madam, spouse of Henri Carnal, 340
Carnal, Mr, founder Blegian of the Rosey School in 1880, 340

Carrère d'Encausse, Hélène, 73, 656
Carter, Jimmy, US President, 148, 278, 312, 313, 458, 474, 475, 477, 478, 481, 493, 494, 516, 529, 538, 590, 595, 610, 620, 624, 625, 626, 627, 630, 633, 634, 664, 676, 698, 699, 719
Carthage, 383
Castro, Fidel, 318, 628
Cavada, Jean-Marie, 685
Ceausescu, 628
Cement (production), 389
CENTO (Central Treaty Organization), 305, 558
Central Bank, 205, 567, 659
Centre of International Studies, 514
Centre Européen d'Information (CEI, see also Faillant de Villemarest), 12, 435, 493, 666, 690, 691, 695, 702
CFR (Council on Foreign Relations), 696
Chaban-Delmas, Jacques, French PM, 697
Chafagh, professor, specialist in Persian history and literature, 378
Chahandeh, General, Chief of the Police Forces, 248
Chahed, Persian journal, 673
Chaperon, Yves, 717
Chapot, Caline, friend of the Foroughi family, 660
Charles-Roux, François, French ambassador, 694
Cheka, 132
Chevalérias, Alain, 665, 677
Chile, 628
China, 203, 379, 402
Chirac, Jacques, French President, 367
Chivas (whisky), 475
Christians, 28, 71, 511
Chubin, Chahram, 664, 702
Churchill, Winston S., 105, 126, 218, 657, 658
CHU (university hospital) of Paris, 325
CHU (university hospital) of Tehran, 91
CIA, 239, 253, 254, 278, 282, 304, 313, 359, 416, 429, 434, 435, 456, 457, 476, 478, 615, 630, 633, 674, 675, 686, 690, 695, 700, 711
City Theatre (in Tehran), 395
Clandestine American nuclear experience (rumours), 548
Claude, Patrice, 701
Clemenceau, Georges, 186
Clergy, 27, 29, 35, 67, 71, 75, 87, 150, 151,

727

155, 178, 193, 229, 237, 254, 272, 279, 291, 300, 338, 358, 420, 422, 423, 429, 461, 473, 493, 511, 512, 513, 514, 517, 520, 526, 527, 534, 539, 549, 552, 569, 584, 680, 705, 707
Clinton, Bill, US President, 367
Cockraft, James D., professor from Rutgers University, highly respected by the US Administration, 472
Colbert, 78
Cold war, 158, 218, 282, 295, 430
Coleman, Morton, Dr, renowned specialist, 622, 632, 637, 638
Comintern (Communist International), 130, 134, 135
Committee for anti-terrorist activity, 289
Communist Party of the Soviet Union (CPSU), 155, 163, 430
Communist propaganda, 132, 137, 142, 153, 321
Compagnie Française de Pétrole, 267
Company for the protection of the national heritage, 395
Confederation of Iranian students abroad, which organized the first serious protest against the regime, 474
Conference of the Peoples from the Orient, 133
Confucius, 13
Congress (international) on Iranology, 399, 400, 686
Conspiracy of Silence, 376
Constantinople, 86
Constitution of the Islamic republic, 294, 419, 438, 452
Contadora, 629, 633, 634
Conte, Arthur, historian, 145, 191, 664, 667, 668
Cooley, John K., 686
Corbin, H., 692
Corporative chambers, 502, 503, 527
Costa Rica, 711
Cottam, Richard, Professor from the University of Pittsburgh, very popular advisor at the State Department and at the White House, 471
Cotton (production), 387
Council of the Islamic revolution, 290, 600, 601, 602
Council of the revolution (in Iraq), 433
Countercoup, 239, 673, 674
Counterespionage, 281, 282, 287, 295

Crédit Foncier, 75
Crescent of the Sultan of Constantinople, 86
Crimean War, 33
Crime against humanity, 715
Crude oil exports, 389
Ctesiphone, 400, 642
Cuban camps (urban guerrilla and terrorist techniques), 487
Cuernavaca, 277, 617, 619, 621, 624, 714
Cultural Iran-Soviet Association, 145
Cutler, Lloyd, Jimmy Carter's special envoy, 633
Cyrus the Great, 86, 88, 397, 429, 463, 541, 659, 668, 682, 686, 711, 716
Czechoslovakia, 99, 106, 173, 187, 339, 402, 457, 485
Czech camps (urban guerrilla and terrorist techniques training), 487

D

d'Arcy, William Knox, 79, 80
d'Arcy concession, 81
Dabestaneh nehzam, military primary school of Mohammad Reza Pahlavi, 336
Dadsehtan, General, administrator of the martial law, 251, 256
Daftar-eh-vigeh, 'special bureau', 289
Daftari, General, Mossadegh's nephew, cousin of Ahmad Matin-Daftari, 248, 253, 256
Daily Telegraph, 612
Danechvar, Simine, woman of letters, 443
Daneshdjouyaneh Khatteh Emam ('those who are studying'), hostage takers from the United States embassy in Tehran, 492
Dangerous liaisons (between the Eastern intelligence services and the clergy), 493, 497
Darius I, 390
Dar ol-Fonun, first modern western-type university founded in Iran, 28, 29, 32, 89, 90
Dashti, Ali, great eminent writer of the 20th century, 95
Davani, Ali, 705, 707
Davar, Ali Akbar, Minister of Justice, 82, 656
David, founder of Jerusalem and King of Israel, 446
David Newsome, Shah's entrance pseu-

INDEX

donym to the New York Hospital, 621
Dayan, Moshe, General, Israeli Minister of Foreign Affairs, 699
Day of Women's Emancipation, 522
Debock, Walter, 687
Dehghan, Ahmad, anti-communist journalist assassinated by the Tudeh, 142
Dehkhoda, Ali Akhbar, the 'Iranian Littré', initiator of the Iranian encyclopedia which was to bear his name, 246, 378
Delannoy, Christian, 676, 677, 688, 698, 704, 707, 709
Del Valle, Alexandre, French political scientist, 461, 685, 687, 696, 697
Democratic Party of Iran, Ahmad Ghavam's own political group, 177, 184
Democrats (in the USA), 333, 454, 566
Deniau, Jean-Charles, 687
Denikin, Anton Ivanovich, General commanding the White Army, 132
Derakhchani, brigadier general, Tabriz garrison commander, involved in a spy network for the benefit of the Soviet Union, 164, 165
Der Spiegel, 702
Descartes, René, 109, 447
Desjardins, Thierry, journalist and political analyst, 481
De Bakey, Michael, Prof., world famous specialist in cardiovascular surgery, 632, 633, 637, 638
de Balkany, Robert, spouse of Princess Maria Gabrielle de Savoie, 354
de Beauvoir, Simone, leader of ayatollah Khomeini's Support committees, 441
de Castelbajac, Bertrand, Count, 580, 659, 667, 682, 711, 716
de Chateaubriand, François-René, 710
De Gaulle, Charles, General, French President, 126, 186, 303, 366, 380, 405, 456, 466, 685, 697
de la Gorce, Paul-Marie, 695
de Marenches, Alexandre, Count, the most famous head of the French Secret Services, 276, 286, 290, 291, 364, 375, 380, 416, 427, 435, 467, 475, 479, 536, 545, 590, 614, 676, 677, 684, 685, 688, 690, 691, 697, 698, 699, 707, 709, 713, 718
de Stadelhofen, Henri, 683
de Villiers, Gérard, 682
DGSE (Direction générale de la sécurité extérieure), French international intelligence agency, 288, 475
Dhimmitude, 28
Diba, Farah, Shahbanoo, spouse of Mohammad Reza Pahlavi, 216, 217, 223, 238, 243, 332, 333, 334, 355, 356, 357, 359, 360, 365, 372, 393, 402, 475, 485, 506, 527, 528, 529, 532, 537, 541, 544, 548, 551, 552, 557, 558, 559, 560, 561, 563, 565, 566, 571, 572, 574, 575, 577, 578, 579, 580, 581, 584, 591, 592, 610, 611, 612, 613, 614, 616, 617, 618, 619, 623, 625, 626, 627, 628, 629, 630, 633, 634, 636, 638, 640, 681, 683, 703, 706, 707, 708, 709, 710, 711, 718, 719
Diba, Sohrab, Father of Farah, 355
Diba (née Ghotbi), Taji (also called Farideh), mother of Farah Diba, 355
Discours de la Méthode (by René Descartes), 109
Divan, Fath Ali Shah's collection of poems, 21
Djafarian, General, commander of the army corps of Khuzistan, 594
Djaffari, Hassan, member of the Tudeh, murderer of journalist Ahmad Dehghan, 142
Djahanbani, Amanollah, Qajar prince, Brigadier General, 56, 57, 347
Djahanbani, Chokate-Malek, senator, 713
Djahanbini, Kioumars, Colonel, Shah's personal body-guard, 629, 634, 640, 717
Djahandari, Keykavous, 653
Djahanshahlu, Afshar Nosratollah, Dr, communist, 137, 662, 664
Djalal-Ol-Din, son of Mohammad Kharazmshah, 641
Djalili, Mohammad Reza, Professor, general secretary of the Centre of International Studies, 514
Djam, Mahmoud, PM, 345, 645
Djameh-eyeh-Novin ('New Society'), quarterly magazine of the Study Group of Iranian problems, 506
Djavadof, Sayed Djafar (under the name of Pichevari), communist commissioner in the Department of the Interior, 132, 134, 135, 139, 164, 178, 181, 182
Djavanan, weekly, 716
Djomhouri Eslam, quasi official newspaper of the Islamic regime, 715
Djonbech, weekly, 443, 676, 701

Doctor Eghbal hospital of the University of Tehran, 541
Donya, monthly journal published - not a clandestine one - of the 'Group of the 53', 135, 137
Don Juan, 236
Dowlatshahi, Esmat, Qajar princess, spouse of Reza Shah, 61
Dowlatshahi, Janine, palace librarian, 714
Drama companies, 395
Dreyfus, Robert, 681
Druon Maurice, Perpetual Secretary of the French Academy, 416, 482, 688
DST (Direction de la surveillance du territoire), French internal state security department, 288
Dubreux, Louis, 2
Dulles, John Foster, 218, 304
Duquesne, Jacques, 480
Dutourd, Jean, 687

E
'Ensheab', scission within the Tudeh, 141
East-West entente, 433, 436, 470, 487
East German camps (urban guerrilla and terrorist techniques training), 487
Ebrahim-Khan, Mirza, 2
Ebtehaj, Abolhassan, Governor of the National Bank, 174, 271, 307, 311, 655, 659, 667, 669, 679
École Centrale of Paris, 600
École libre des sciences politiques in Paris (Free School of Political Science), 195
École Normale Supérieure (Iranian), 90
École Normale Supérieure of Saint-Cloud (France), 576
École Normale Supérieure of Ulm Street (Paris), 578
École Polytechnique, 206, 324
École spéciale d'architecture (in Paris), 355
Eden, Anthony, 659
Eghbal, Manutshehr, PM, 143, 308, 312, 317, 325, 327, 328, 512, 648
Eghbal-Ashtiani, Abbas, 661
Egypt, 204, 237, 238, 323, 344, 348, 349, 373, 402, 405, 465, 534, 570, 592, 610, 611, 633, 634, 636, 683
Egyptian camps (urban guerrilla and terrorist techniques training), 486
Egyptian communists, 156
Eisenhower, US President, 218, 227, 266

El-Bakr, Iraqi President, 433
Eluard (Eugène Grindel), Paul, French poet, 579
Élysée, French presidential palace, 362, 694, 698, 718
Emami, Sayed Hassan, ayatollah, 208
Emamzadeh Hachem, mausoleum, 46
Empedocles, Greek philosopher, physician and legislator of the 5th century BC, 446
Encounter, 709
Entezam, Abdollah, former General Zahedi's Minister of Foreign Affairs, then chairman of the NIOC, 303, 575, 577, 580
Entezam, Amir Abbas, Mehdi Bazargan's Vice-Prime Minister, 601
Entezam, Nasrollah, Reza Shah's head of protocol, 106, 110, 657, 658, 659, 683
Erani, Taqi, Dr, communist, main leader of the 'Group of the 53', 85, 135, 136, 137, 143
Erhardt, Ludwig, Professor, Vice-Chancellor and Minister for the Economy of the FRG, 310
Erieh, Morad, eminent figure of the Jewish community, 243
Esfahani, Sayed Abolhassan, Supreme Leader of the world Shiite community, 179
Esfandiari, Haj Mohtachem ol Saltaneh, President of the Chamber, 118, 378
Esfandiary Bakhtiari, Eva, mother of Princess Soraya, 350, 351
Esfandiary Bakhtiari, Khalil, father of Princess Soraya, 350, 351
Esfandiary Bakhtiari, Soraya, Empress, spouse of Mohammad Reza Pahlavi, 198, 216, 217, 235, 239, 242, 258, 259, 272, 274, 283, 350, 351, 352, 353, 356, 359, 612, 670, 671, 672, 673, 675, 683
Eskandari's memoirs, 138, 662
Eskandari, Iradj, Soleyman Mirza Eskandari's nephew, Qajar prince, general-secretary of the Tudeh, 136, 137, 138, 140, 147, 149, 150, 662, 663, 697
Eskandari, Soleyman Mirza, Qajar prince, future president of the Iranian communist party, 60, 138, 147
Eslami, 680
Espionage, 269, 275, 282, 287, 484, 497
Etminan, Mohammad Reza, economist and academic, 703
Ettehadiehs, family, 235

INDEX

Ettela'ât, Tehran evening newspaper, 419, 431, 432, 443, 519, 522, 677, 693, 713, 714, 716, 717
Ettela'ât mahyaneh, Iranian monthly magazine, 673, 674
Eurodif, 367, 415, 462
Evine, prison, 288
Ezat ol Dowleh, princess, sister of Naser ol-Din, spouse of Amir Kabir, 30, 31, 654

F

'Field of Cloth of Gold', 397
'First oil crisis', 458
'Free world', 386, 403, 453, 481, 605
F14, jet fighter, 406
Façade of official neutrality, 498
Faculty of Arts, 90
Faculty of Medecine, 90
Faculty of Science, 90, 379
Fagniez, Pierre-Louis, Doctor, 638
Fahimi, Khalil, PM, 194, 648
Faillant de Villemarest, Pierre, 12, 435, 666, 673, 690, 698, 702, 718
Faisal, King of Arabia, 459
Faisal I, King of Iraq, 88, 575
Faisal II, King of Iraq, 243, 305
Fake funerals, 546, 572, 593
Fake prophet, 482
Fakhraï, Ebrahim, 661
Falk, Richard, very popular academic from the highest spheres of American power, 472, 694
Fallaci, Oriana, journalist, 424, 689, 693
FAO (Food and Agriculture Organization), 243
Farabi University, 514
Fardoust, Hossein, friend and fellow student of the Shah, manager of 'special bureau' Daftar-eh-vigeh, was a double or triple agent or mainly worked for the Soviet KGB, openly betrayed the Shah in the end, 269, 289, 338, 604, 627, 717
Farmanfarmaian, Abdol Aziz, Qajar Prince, architect, 361, 399
Farsi, 702
Faruk, King of Egypt, 344, 346, 348, 349
Fateh, Mostafa, Iranian employee of the British Secret Services, 138
Fatemi, Hossein, 215, 216, 218, 245, 246, 249, 264, 270
Fatemi, Molouk Sadat Moshir, Mrs, 672

Fath Ali Shah (see also Khan Baba Khan), 18, 19, 21, 22
Fatima, 438
Fatwa, religious ordinance, 211, 425, 426, 489, 518, 705
Fawzieh of Egypt, Princess, eldest daughter of Fouad I of Egypt and sister of King Farouk, 237, 344, 346, 347, 348, 350, 352, 683
FBI, 625
Fedayeen of Islam ('Fedayane Islam'), Iranian branch of the Muslim Brothers, 171, 194, 605
Fehlinger, Professor, GP, 618
Femina prize, 284
Ferdowsi (or Fidousi), greatest Persian poet, 44, 74, 86, 89, 94, 108, 392, 395, 396, 668
Ferdowsi University in Meshed, 392, 396
Festivities, 194, 346, 347, 373, 382
Feyzieh school of Qom, 688, 693
Fiat, 624
Fin gardens, 30, 653
Firouz, Maryam (also called 'the red princess'), wife of Nourreddine Kianouri, 152
Firouzcouhi, primary school in Tehran, 11
Flandrin, Georges, Dr, French physician, 619, 620, 637, 638, 718
Fontaine, André, ayatollah Khomeini flatterer, 186, 385, 441, 667
Ford, Gerald, US President, 610
Foreign Affairs, 664, 702
Foroughi, Fernande, widow of Ambassador Massoud Foroughi, 660
Foroughi, Massoud, younger son of the philosopher and Prime Minister, 660
Foroughi, Mohammad Ali, PM, 2, 37, 60, 70, 72, 74, 81, 82, 87, 90, 95, 107, 108, 109, 110, 112, 114, 115, 117, 118, 119, 120, 121, 122, 123, 124, 126, 187, 197, 232, 269, 300, 369, 383, 644, 645, 646, 659, 660
Foroughi, Mohsen, architect, son of Mohammad Ali Foroughi, 115, 659
Forouhar, Dariush, one of the leaders of the National Front, later to be Khomeini's Minister of Labour, 516
Forouhar A., General Razmara's Minister of Finance, 193
Fort, Paul, poet, 89
Fortune, American magazine, 390
Fort Lauderdale, 621
Foucault, Michel, leader of ayatollah

731

Khomeini's Support committees, 441
Fouladvand, General, 250
France, 19, 20, 27, 36, 56, 57, 58, 62, 65, 74, 86, 92, 102, 117, 126, 153, 203, 209, 288, 305, 308, 314, 336, 347, 380, 415, 419, 428, 436, 450, 451, 453, 457, 466, 546, 573, 582, 619, 669, 691, 704, 716, 718
France Inter, French radio, 706
France Soir, French evening newspaper, 684
François, M., 689
Fraser, William, Sir, president of the AIOC, 266
Free Masons/Free Masonry, 123, 195, 200, 211, 279, 540, 654
Free services, 387
French Academy ('Académie française'), 4, 89, 671, 686
French Circle (of Tehran), 582, 583
French history, 416, 482
French intelligence services, 435, 476, 590
French lycée of Tehran, 355
French National Defence, 12
French National Library, 400
French Revolution, 384, 502
FRG (Federal Republic of Germany), Western Germany, 182, 310, 366, 457, 550
Fuad I, king of Egypt, 344, 347

G
'Great civilization', 383, 411, 639
'Great Satan', the official title given to the United States of America., 448
'Group of the 53', communist network, 135, 136, 137, 138, 139, 662
Galerie des Glaces in Versailles, 361
Gallois, Pierre-Marie, General, 696
Gangi, Manutshehr, Minister of Education, 551
Gasiorowski, Mark Y., 667
GDR (German Democratic Republic), East Germany, 365, 430, 431, 496, 497
Gelb, Leslie, 478
Gengis Khan, 641
Georgia, 18, 19, 45
Germanopratine, related to Saint-Germain-des-Près (in Paris), 449, 697
Germany, 58, 62, 85, 92, 99, 102, 122, 126, 135, 157, 167, 339, 453, 496, 697
Gestapo, 276
Gha'em-Magham-é-Farahani, Mirza Abolghasem, murdered Chancellor, 22, 23, 24, 25, 27
Ghaffari, Farokh, 686
Ghaffari, Hadi, the man who had boasted he had killed Amir Abbas Hoveyda in his prison corridor, 707
Ghani, Cyrus, author, 655
Ghani, Ghassem, 345, 348, 378, 379, 655, 682, 683, 685
Ghanoon, Iranian journal founded in London by Mirza Malkhom Khan, 34
Gharabaghi, General, Head of General Staff, 551, 595, 604
Gharib, Abol Azim, a famous grammarian and an authority in Persian literature, one of the school masters of Mohammad Reza Pahlavi, 336
Gharib, Djamshid, Ambassador, 697
Ghasghais (tribes), 70
Ghashghai, Nasser, chief of the eponymous tribe, 174
Ghassemi, Reza, ambassador, 712
Ghavam, Ahmad (Ghavam Saltaneh), PM, 2, 51, 54, 58, 59, 64, 124, 125, 167, 168, 169, 170, 171, 172, 173, 174, 176, 177, 178, 179, 180, 183, 184, 185, 186, 187, 190, 192, 198, 209, 210, 211, 212, 217, 226, 227, 233, 245, 252, 267, 269, 270, 300, 307, 308, 314, 331, 369, 370, 371, 383, 396, 454, 582, 643, 646, 647, 648, 669
Ghazi (brothers), 164, 181
Ghazvini, Mohammad, erudite, 378
Ghobadi, lieutenant, put into the police force by the Tudeh's network, 142, 664
Ghomi, great ayatollah, 518, 704
Ghotb-Zadeh, Sadegh, Minister of Foreign Affairs, 295, 436, 487, 715
Ghotbi, Mohammad Ali, uncle of Farah Diba (Shabanoo), 355, 528, 579, 580, 711
Ghotbi, Reza, first cousin of Shabanoo Farah, director of Iranian National Television and Radio, 355, 528, 529, 543, 552, 559, 560, 579
GI, 125, 415
Gilda (see also Talâ), serious loving affair of Mohammad Reza Pahlavi, 359
Giscard d'Estaing, Valéry, French President, 416, 434, 451, 466, 477, 482, 536, 691, 692, 696, 697, 698
Glennon, John P., 671
Godard, André, 90, 94

INDEX

Goethe Institute, 550
Golchin, monthly magazine in Persian published in Houston, Texas, 679
Goleniewski, Michel, Colonel, number 2 in the Soviet-Polish counter-espionage who defected to the West, 429, 690
Golestan, Saadi's work, 109
Golestan, Treaty (ratified in 1813), 19, 20, 72, 73, 361
Golestan Palace, 72, 73, 398, 561
Golpayehgani, great ayatollah, 517
Gomulka, 156, 666
Gorbachev, Mikhail, 430
Grady, Dr, US ambassador to Tehran, 226
Grand Lodge of Iran, 537
Graz, Liesl, 687
Greater and Lesser Tunb, key islands of the strait of Ormuz, 404
Great Britain, 6, 20, 25, 26, 36, 37, 40, 50, 55, 81, 100, 104, 105, 106, 117, 139, 158, 159, 160, 166, 168, 198, 202, 214, 223, 232, 240, 271, 304, 312, 344, 346, 382, 410, 453, 457, 474, 586, 661, 670
Great Depression, 103
Greece, 166
Greek conqueror, 412
Greenwich (time), 445
Guadeloupe conference (in January 1979), 477, 478, 590
Guardians of the Revolution, 489, 491, 494, 496, 534, 707
Gueyras, Jean, 666, 711
Guilani, Freidun, poet, 443
Guilani, Sheikh Zahed, Sufi master, philosopher and ascetic, ancestor of Zahedis, 230, 671
Guiraud, P., 689
Gulag (see also Bolshevic goals), 147, 156, 296
Gulf war (first one), 711

H

'Honourable correspondents', 290
'Humanistic government', 472
Habash, George, Marxist and pro-Soviet, leader of the PFLP, 487
Habl el Matin, Iranian journal founded in Calcutta in 1893, 35
Haeri Yazdi Haj, Agha Abdolkarim, master of Ruhollah Khomeini, 420
Hafiz, poet, 108, 109, 379, 395
Hagh-Chenass, Djahanguir, Minister of Transports, 245
Haghdar, Ali Asghar, researcher, 656
Haghighat, newspaper published in Tehran, 134
Hagir, Abdolhossein, PM, 647
Haig, Alexander, General, commander-in-chief of the integrated military forces of the North Atlantic Treaty, 480
Haj Rezaï Tayeb, ex-convict with a long record, 322, 425
Haj Sayed Djavadi, Ali Asghar, journalist, 443
Hakimi, Ebrahim, PM, 125, 163, 167, 210, 647
Hamid, Mirza, Qajar prince, 117
Hamzavi, Amir Monazzam, 672
Haristchi, businessman, 250
Harriman, Averell, 207, 233, 314
Harvey, Oliver, Sir, Anthony Eden's private secretary, 659
Hassanli, Djamil, 182
Hassan II, King of Morocco, 283, 469, 511, 512, 611, 612, 614, 615, 616, 704, 718
Hassibi, Kazem, oil advisor of Mohammad Mossadegh, 206, 207, 218
Hassiri, owner of a small printing-house in Khorramshahr, 707
Haussmann, baron, 78
Hawatmeh, Nayef, Marxist and pro-Soviet, leader of the PDFLP, 487
Hedayat, Abdollah, General, 259
Hedayat, Haj Mokhber-Ol-Saltaneh, PM, 645, 655, 656, 659, 683
Hedayat, Khosrow, 178, 311
Hedayat, Mirza, father of Mohammad Mossadegh, 194
Hedayat, Sadegh, great eminent writer of the 20th century, 95
Hedayati, Hadi, 12
Hedjab, 88
Hedjazi, Hassan Saraj, governor of Khorasan, 548
Hedjazi, Mohammad, great eminent writer of the 20th century, 95
Hedjazi, Taha, 443
Hegira, 540
Hekmat, Ali Asghar, Minister of Education, 91, 657
Henderson, Ambassador, 244, 266
Hendi, small coach line created by the three

733

Khomeini brothers, 422
Hendi-Zadeh ('of Indian ancestry'), 420
Hendi ('Indian'), 420, 422
Henri IV, French King, 337
Henry, Y. A., 689
Hermitage museum in St Petersburg, 21
Herostratus, 585
Heshmat-Ol-Dowleh, feudal lord from Khomein region, 418
Hessam ol-Saltaneh, Orad Mirza, 'Conqueror of Herat', 'The last great man of the dynasty', son of Abbas Mirza, 33
Heyat, Ali, Minister of Justice, 259
Heydari, Amir A., 11
Heydarian, M., 660, 662, 664
Heykal, Mohamed H., Egyptian politician and journalist, 380, 409, 425, 428, 494, 558, 685, 687, 689, 696, 702, 709
Hidden Imam, 481
High School of Political Science (in Iran), 195
History of Old Iran, 235
Hitler, Adolf, 450
Hodgkin's disease, 618
Hodjati, Abolmadjd, 668
Hodjatieh, ideological lobbyist group, 154
Holbrook, Richard, 478
Holy War, 20
Homayoun, Bassir, uncle of Fazlollah Zahedi, 672
Homayoun, Dariush, Amouzegar's Minister of the Information, 432, 676, 691, 705, 706
Homayounfar, Ezzatollah, 670, 671, 674, 675
Hoover, Herbert J., 266
Hostage-taking by the terrorist Carlos, 333
Hostage-taking from the United States embassy in Tehran (masterminded by Moscow), 291, 294, 368, 492, 493, 494, 495, 498, 601, 623, 624, 627, 632, 633, 634, 635, 638, 679, 681, 690, 699, 701, 712
House of Savoy, 354
Hoveyda, Amir Abbas, PM, 237, 282, 286, 328, 330, 331, 332, 333, 356, 376, 377, 389, 402, 432, 464, 502, 504, 506, 507, 508, 509, 512, 515, 523, 527, 539, 540, 563, 616, 649, 681, 703, 707
Hoveyda, Fereidoun, 680, 708
Hua, Guofeng, Chinese president, 402, 403
Hull, Cordell, Secretary of State, 104
Human Rights commission, 551

Hungary, 99, 106, 134, 187, 339, 402, 485
Hussein, Imam, 654
Hussein, King of Jordan, 469
Hussein, Saddam, Iraqi President, 404, 433, 571
Huyser, Robert E., General, Deputy Commander-in-Chief of NATO forces, 478, 480, 495, 551, 590, 591, 595, 603, 606, 714
Huyser mission, 478
Hygiene corps, 320

I

'International seminar' in Tehran (with European leftists personalities participants to give their support to the hostage takers), 492
'I have heard the voice of your revolution', 560, 585
Ibrahim, Mohsen, Lebanese leader, 487
IBRD (International Bank for Reconstruction and Development), 454
Icarus, 297, 678
IMF (International Monetary Fund), 312, 315, 324, 328, 390, 454
Immortals, replica of Darius' 'Immortals', 703
Imperial calendar, 540
Imperial library of Ctesiphone (capital of Arsacids and Sasanids), 400
India, 19, 33, 69, 367, 405, 419, 455
Indian Empire, 34, 86, 133, 656
Indian hordes, 412
Indian Ocean, 93, 406, 462
Indian sub-continent, 411
Information Bulletin, twice monthly magazine in Prague, 665
Institute of Studies and Social Research (of the University of Tehran), 576
Institut Pasteur of Tehran, 59
International conspiracy, 385, 479, 499, 538, 550
International Court of Justice in The Hague, 2, 81, 202, 203, 205, 213, 669
International Herald Tribune, 702
International Labour Organization (ILO), 586
International press, 104, 182, 261, 294, 344, 350, 351, 353, 362, 372, 375, 399, 410, 428, 432, 433, 492, 503, 504, 518, 522, 523, 524, 534, 545, 568, 599, 617, 620, 621, 684
International terrorism, 152, 153, 154, 282,

INDEX

288, 295, 486, 488, 495, 498, 525, 665, 676
Iran, political party, 166, 173, 178
Iran-eh-Azad, weekly in Persian published in Paris in the 1980's, 669, 701, 704
Iran-eh-Farda, 692, 709, 715
Iran-eh-ma, Persian journal, 667
Iran-eh-novin ('New Iran'), political party (formerly 'Progressive Circle'), 327, 332, 504, 507, 508, 509, 684
Iranair, national civil aviation company, 390, 700
Iranian-British Friendship, 631
Iranian 2nd Bureau, 147, 284, 286, 289, 365, 377, 526, 605
Iranian Academy, 86, 87, 108, 378
Iranian Archaeological Service, 102
Iranian Azerbaijan Democratic Party (IADP), 163, 182, 430
Iranian Constitution/Revolution of 1906, 79, 111, 131, 193, 213, 235, 310, 317, 321
Iranian culture, 397, 400, 401
Iranian diaspora, 156, 612
Iranian film industry, 394
Iranian nationalism and patriotism, 51, 86, 89, 108, 161, 169, 231, 237, 254, 269, 270, 310, 337, 369, 399, 407, 448, 454, 471, 480, 481, 705, 706
Iranian National Petroleum Company (INPC), 600
Iranian National Television and Radio (INTR), 101, 144, 149, 154, 233, 249, 251, 285, 355, 366, 394, 450, 473, 507, 521, 522, 524, 528, 529, 530, 541, 542, 543, 548, 550, 552, 554, 556, 559, 560, 598, 706
Iranian New Year, 52, 634, 692
Iranian tourists, 386
Iranian tradition (of the 7th century), 399
Iranology, 399, 686
Iranshahr, 694
Iran libre, 665
Iran Times (of Washington), 697
Iraq, 51, 82, 88, 104, 152, 166, 179, 207, 216, 217, 243, 284, 304, 305, 344, 345, 404, 408, 415, 421, 427, 428, 430, 431, 433, 463, 493, 510, 517, 534, 571, 654, 687
Iraqi invasion (of September 1980) and Iran-Iraq War, 151, 152, 490, 491, 627
Ironside, General, leader of a British task force, 39
Irvanlu, Abol Qasem Khan, uncle of Reza Shah, 46

Islam, 34, 68, 92, 135, 148, 171, 194, 195, 323, 338, 347, 353, 423, 424, 425, 426, 438, 440, 445, 446, 448, 449, 451, 472, 479, 480, 481, 510, 533, 547, 571, 667, 704, 705
Islamic-Marxists, 487, 488, 496, 555
Islamic belt, 150
Islamic cancer, 479
Islamic conference, 614
Islamic Republic Party (IRP), 495, 496
Islamic Revolutionary Council, 290, 700
Islamic Revolution Party, official governmental group, 151
Islamist globalism, 481
Islamization, 357
Israel, 309, 392, 407, 440, 446, 449, 457, 458, 462, 463, 464, 465, 474, 478, 589
IS (Intelligence Service), 434
Italy, 80, 93, 102, 353, 390, 457

J

Jacobi, Frederick, Jr., American classmate of Mohammad Reza Pahlavi at the Rosey, 682
Jambet, C., 692
JAMI, Iranian communist organization, 662
Japan, 29, 104, 126, 157, 383, 390, 411
Japanese Empire, 157
Jasha, Bulletin of a group of former officers of the imperial military, 708, 709
Javeau, Claude, 667, 694
Jeanne-d'Arc, French school, 355
Jebb, Gladwyn, Sir, 203
Jeune Afrique, 695, 696
Jewish community from Iraq, 463
Jews, 28, 71, 243, 417, 429, 445, 446, 463, 511
Jihad, 686
John-Paul II, Pope, 277, 441
Johnson, US President, 455
John XXIII, Pope, 353, 354
Jordan, 405
Jordan, Hamilton, Chief of the Administration of the White House, 628, 631, 632, 633, 635, 719
Journal de Téhéran, 522
July 14th 1789, 408

K

'Khach', securization plan for a return to peace and legality, 553, 554, 555, 557, 562
Kadjar, Ali, Prince, 653, 654

Kaftaradze, Serguei, Soviet Deputy Minister of Foreign Affairs, 140
Kalali, Amir Teymour, 199
Kamal, General, head of the 2nd Bureau, 365
Kambakhsh, Abdolssamad (also called Kambakhsh Qajar), communist, air force officer and Qajar Prince, 136, 137, 147, 662
Kamran, Mirza, son of Shah Naser ol-Din, 46
Kapliouk, Amnon, Israeli analyst, 699
Karbalaee, Ghorban, Amir Kabir's father's name, Mirza Bozorg Khan's cook, 24
Karehgah, theatre in Tehran, 395
Karimi, Fouad, 707
Kashani, Sayed Abolghassem, ayatollah, 193, 194, 211, 212, 213, 215, 218, 221, 222, 251, 423
Kashanian, Hassan, 672
Kashmiri, origin of the Khomeinis, 419
Kasrani, Ahmad, Mr, top Tehran barrister, one of the most famous Iranian historians of the last century, 136, 171
Katouzian, Homayoun, 667, 670
Katyn (massacre), 164
Kayhan (of London), 447, 673, 700, 710, 711, 712, 713, 714, 715, 716
Kayhan (of Tehran), 182, 444, 663, 664, 666, 685, 686, 687, 693, 711, 712, 713, 716, 717
Kayhan havaï, newspaper for Iranians abroad, 692
Kayhan International, 522
Kazemi, Bagher, 85, 199, 214, 215, 216, 218, 280
Kazemi, Hossein, 2
Kazemich, Eslam, one of the 'ideologists' and people who praised the first phase of the revolution, and who later found refuge in Paris, 701
Kean, Benjamin H., New-York GP, 618, 619, 620, 623, 628, 632, 637, 718, 719
Kechvar, small transitional political group, 222
Kennedy, Edward, US Senator, 473
Kennedy, Jacqueline, 314
Kennedy, John Fitzgerald, US President, 283, 284, 312, 313, 314, 315, 330, 380, 455, 685
Kennedy brothers, 315

Kerbela, sanctuary city, 65, 71, 571, 654
Kerensky, 587
Kesharvarz, F., 664
Keshavarz, Freidoun, 662, 663, 664, 666
KGB, 172, 255, 276, 289, 430, 434, 490, 493, 497, 605, 683, 691, 701
Khaddumi, Farugh, head of the political department of the PLO, 487
Khademi, Ali Mohammad, Air Field Marsha (Reserve Component)l, 700
Khadjenouri, Nezam, Iranian ambassador to Rome, 243
Khalatbari, Abbas, Ardeshir Zahedi's successor at the Ministry of Foreign Affairs, assassinated by the revolutionaries, 405
Khalkhali, Sadegh, ayatollah, 707
Khameï, Anwar, communist, Tudeh leader, 137, 139, 255, 662, 663, 664, 667, 673, 689
Khamenii, Ali, mullah, 715
Khan, Abbas Ali, father of Reza Shah, 45
Khan, Agha Mohammad, founder of the Qajar dynasty, 18
Khan, Ahmad Agha (Amir Ahmadi), Qajar dynasty's founder, 39, 53
Khan, Ayoub, President of Pakistan, 558
Khan, Baba Khan, crown prince, nephew of Agha Mohammad Khan (see also Fath Ali Shah), 18
Khan, Bahram, small local landowner, assassin (out of revenge) of Ruhollah Khomeini's father, 418, 419, 420, 437
Khan, Ehsanollah, communist leader, 53
Khan, Hakim Ali, doctor and captain under Kamran Mirza's orders, 46
Khan, Kazem (Sayah), colonel, Cossack division, 39
Khan, Massoud (Keyhan), sergeant major, Cossack division, 39
Khan, Mirza Bozorg, father of Gha'em-Magham, 24
Khan, Mirza Malkhom, ambassador fallen into disfavour, 34
Khan, Morteza (Yazdan Panah), Cossack division chief, 39
Khan, Nimtaj Khanoum (later to be Taj ol Molouk, mother of Mohammad Reza Pahlavi), 48
Khan, Reza (later to be Reza Pahlavi, see also Reza Shah), 38, 39, 40, 43, 44, 46, 47, 49, 50, 51, 54, 55, 56, 57, 58, 60, 61, 63, 64, 66, 67, 68, 69, 70, 71, 72, 83, 89, 92, 133,

INDEX

168, 196, 230, 262, 643, 644, 656
Khan, Reza Gholi (Amir Koshravi), Cossack division chief, 39
Khan, Tehshragh-Ali (titled Amir Akram), uncle and pishkar (steward and private tutor) of young Mohammad Reza Pahlavi, 336
Khan, Teimour, father of Nimtaj Khanoum (later to be Taj ol Molouk), 48
Khândaniha, important weekly, 596
Kharazm-shah, Mohammad, shah of the beginning of the 13th century, 641
Kharg island, biggest oil port in the world, 33, 389
Khatam, Commander, military pilot, 243
Khayyam, Omar, poet and mathematician, 108, 109, 395
Khazaal, Abdollah Djasseb, sheikh, son of sheikh Khazaal, 166
Khazaal, sheikh, Khuzistan potentate, official protégé of the British, 67, 69, 70, 71, 73, 83, 166, 230
Khiltach, Cyrus, Colonel, head of the intelligence services of the imperial guard, 714
Khofieh-nevisses, intelligence service, 27
Khoï, great ayatollah, number one of the world Shiite hierarchy, 518, 566, 571
Khoïniha, Mohammad, hodjatoleslam, leader and chief of the team of hostage takers at the United States embassy in Tehran, 493, 494, 700
Khomeini's books, 476
Khomeini's tapes (sent in diplomatic bags, calling for insurrection), 416, 431, 435, 481
Khomeini, Agha Morteza Passandideh, eldest brother of Ruhollah Khomeini, 418, 419, 421
Khomeini, Ahmad, grand-father of Ruhollah Khomeini, 417, 419, 420
Khomeini, Ahmad, son of Ruhollah Khomeini, 421, 702, 707
Khomeini, Mostafa, eldest son of Ruhollah Khomeini, 421, 428, 429, 437
Khomeini, Mostafa, father of Ruhollah Khomeini, 417, 418, 419, 420, 437
Khomeini, Nurollah (also called Agha Nur), second brother of Ruhollah Khomeini, 418
Khomeini, Ruhollah, ayatollah, 148, 149, 150, 154, 193, 277, 285, 290, 292, 296, 322, 323, 324, 415, 416, 417, 418, 419, 420, 421, 422, 423, 424, 425, 426, 427, 428, 429, 430, 431, 432, 433, 434, 435, 436, 437, 438, 439, 440, 441, 442, 443, 444, 446, 447, 449, 450, 451, 452, 461, 468, 470, 471, 476, 481, 482, 486, 487, 490, 491, 492, 493, 494, 497, 518, 519, 520, 523, 533, 535, 536, 539, 541, 546, 556, 559, 563, 572, 574, 575, 583, 585, 588, 590, 591, 593, 596, 598, 599, 600, 602, 603, 612, 623, 626, 628, 650, 663, 665, 681, 685, 687, 688, 689, 690, 691, 692, 693, 694, 696, 698, 699, 700, 704, 713, 715, 716, 717
Khomeyni's mausoleum, 451
Khonsari, Haj Agha Ahmad, ayatollah, 427, 517
Khoshkish, Youssef, governor of the Central Bank, 567
Khosravani, Atâollah, general secretary of the governmental party Iran-eh-Novin, 684
Khosravi, Babak Amir, one of the last general secretaries of the Tudeh, 660, 662, 664
Khosravi, Kh., 680
Khosrodad, Manutshehr, General, commander of the airborne brigade based in Bagheshah, 574, 594
Khun, Bela, 134
Khuzistan, 67, 69, 77, 82, 107, 113, 138, 220, 230
Kianouri, Nourreddine, Dr, general-secretary of the Tudeh, 149, 150, 151, 152, 154, 663, 664, 665
Kiracofe, Cliford A., Jr., 661, 663, 664
Kirkpatrick, Jane, ambassador and academic, 479, 699
Kirov, Bolshevik leader, 133
Kish (island), 278
Kissinger, Henry, 458, 460, 480, 615, 617, 624, 696
Komiteyeterror ('terror committee') within the Tudeh, 141
Koran, 119, 400, 445, 490, 704
Koranic principles, 460
Korea, 166
Kotobi, Morteza, 701
Kremlin, 83, 153, 170, 485
Krupp, 367
Kurdish rebellion, 711
Kurdistan, 53, 133, 162, 163, 169, 178
Kurdistan Democratic Party, 163
Kurds, 161
Kuwait, 207, 433

L

"Les Immortels" (of the French Academy), 89

'Lenin of Iran', 663
'Liberation army of Iran', 717
L'Express, French weekly, 480, 665, 684, 691, 699, 713
L'Humanité, 665
L'impact, 695
Labévière, Richard, 459, 696, 698
Labin, Suzanne, 690, 702
Lackland, airbase in Texas, 625
Lacontre, Robert, 701, 702
Lacouture, Jean, 696
Lahidji, Abdolkarim, Mr, general secretary of the Association (Khomeinist) for human rights, 676
Lake, Antony, 478
Lampton, A.K.S., 680
Lankarani, Ahmad, brother of Hessam and Hossein, 664
Lankarani, Hessam, leader of the Tudeh, eliminated by the latter, 142
Lankarani, Hossein, sheikh, pro-Soviet mullah, 427
Lashkari, Ayat, Shah's body guard assassinated, 365
Lavrentiev, Anatoli, said to be from the secret services and a 'specialist' in the brutal changes of regimes, 219, 264, 265
Law and Political Science Faculty, 379
Law Faculty, 245, 576, 582
La Croix-L'Événement, 699
La Fontaine (Jean de), 385
La Guardia airport in New York, 621, 625
La Revue des Deux Mondes, 702
La Tribune de Genève, 696
La Vie française, 692, 701
League of Nations, 81, 82, 108
Lebanon, 104, 284, 331, 345, 581, 715
Lebey, Marie, 684
Ledeen, Michael, 665, 690, 697, 698, 699, 709, 714, 717
Legrand, Catherine & Jacques, 657, 682
Lenin, V. I., 140, 663
Leninist principles, 156
Les Roseaux, institute in Lausanne (Switzerland), 351
Lewis, Gabriel, ambassador, friend of Ardeshir Zahedi, 629
Lewis, William, 665, 690, 697, 698, 699, 709, 714, 717
Le Figaro, 666, 684, 688, 689, 692, 694, 696, 699, 700, 716

Le Figaro Magazine, 692, 698, 701, 702
Le Matin, newspaper, 678
Le Monde, 185, 253, 276, 428, 430, 435, 441, 544, 665, 666, 674, 675, 676, 678, 679, 682, 684, 686, 688, 689, 690, 692, 693, 694, 695, 696, 699, 701, 702, 704, 708, 711, 716, 719
Le Monde diplomatique, 699
Le Nouvel Observateur, 696
Le Point, 701, 702
Le Quotidien de Paris, 666, 694, 701, 714, 716
Le Spectacle du Monde, 701
Le Vif, 691
Libération, French newspaper, 415, 684, 694
Liberté ('Liberty'), Air France's plane that brought ayatolah Khomeini to Iran on February 1st 1979, 450, 599
Libya, 486, 487, 495, 496, 525, 605
Lion the sun, iranian national emblem since ages, 86, 419, 688
Literacy corps, 319, 320
Littré, 246
London Foundation for Iranian Studies, 655
London Times, 684
Lorentz, Dominique, 415, 439, 466, 687, 691, 692, 696
Louis XI, French King, 18, 337
Louis XIV, French King, 337
Louis XVI, 606
Louis XVI, French King guillotined by the revolutionaries, 337, 376, 384, 408, 469, 499, 501, 503, 505, 507, 509, 511, 513, 515, 517, 519, 521, 523, 525, 527, 529, 531, 533, 535, 536, 573, 575
Luxemburg, 367, 500

M
M.R.M., friend of author, 11
Ma'âdi hospital in Cairo, 637
Madaule, Jacques, journalist at Le Monde, ayatollah flatterer, 441
Madhe Olya, Queen Mother of Naser ol-Din, 23
Madjd Ol Dowleh, prince, Chief of one of the important branches of the Qajars, 60
Madjidi, Abdolmadjid, formerly in charge of the organization of the Plan, 679
Magazine de Beyrouth, 696

Index

Maghreb, 344, 615
Mahallati, Bahaoldin, sheikh, ayatollah, 427, 518
Mahdavi Kani, Mohammad Reza, mullah, 715
Mahomet, Prophet (of Islam), 331, 418, 419, 438, 445, 540, 571, 665, 704
Majlis, Parliament, 135, 185, 431, 668, 673, 712
Makki, Hossein, 215, 582
Malar, Christian, 684, 719
Malbrunot, Georges, who was himself the victim of a long hostage-taking by the Islamists, 689
Malek, Nader, deputy director of Houchang Nahavandi's cabinet, 703, 708
Malek, Reza Zadeh, 661
Malek, Saïd, medicine general, head of iranian armed forces health service, 57
Maleki, Ahmad, well-known journalist and a founding member of the National Front, 671
Maleki, Khalil, leader and later dissident of the Tudeh, 141
Man-woman equality, 320, 321
Mansour, Ali, PM, father of Hassan Ali Mansour (assassinated), 101, 105, 107, 648
Mansour, Hassan Ali, PM, assassinated, 285, 326, 327, 328, 329, 330, 331, 332, 394, 512, 649, 689
Maoism, 151, 379, 488
Maoists, 293, 605
Marble Palace, 398
Marco Polo, Italian liner, 345
Mardom, political party created by Amir Assodollah Alam, 504, 509
Maria Gabrielle de Savoie, Princess, 353, 354
Marin, Soudabeh, 692
Martial law, 43, 220, 244, 248, 251, 253, 256, 280, 281, 282, 283, 530, 542, 545, 546, 603, 708
Martin, Danièle, political scientist and journalist, 451, 470
Marx, Karl, 665
Massé, Henri, Prof., 657
Massoud, Mohammad, journalist and writer assassinated by the Tudeh, 142, 147
Massoudi, Ali, retired brigadier general, 715
Matin-Daftari, Ahmad, PM, Mossadegh's nephew, cousin of General Daftari, 99, 100, 255, 645
Matini, Djalal, 656, 668
Mattei, President of AGIP (Italian national oil company) whose plane exploded during one of his trips, 459
Matzneff, Gabriel, writer, 442
Mauritius, 121
Maximilian, Emperor, 617
McNamara, Robert, 479
Mecca, 540
Medes, people, 68, 229
Medical confidentiality, 619
Medical school of Lyon, 57
Meftah, Abdolhossein, Ambassador, 215, 216, 218, 264, 265, 657, 658, 659, 660, 666, 669, 670, 675
Meftah, Minou, Mrs, 710, 712, 715
Mehemet Ali, royal Egyptian yatch, 346
Mehemet Ali (1769-1849), 345
Meiji, era in Japan, 29
Melli University in Tehran, 392, 396, 514
Menant, Georges, 716
Menderes, Adnan, Turkish Prime Minister, 304
Mercedes, 367
Merciers, Swiss family who accomodated Mohammad Reza Pahlavi from 1931 to 1932, 339
Mesopotamia, 463
Metzlere, John J., 702
Mexico, 2, 238, 277, 353, 615, 617, 619, 624, 684, 714
Meyer, Armin Henry, American ambassador to Iran, 455
Meylan, Vincent, 683, 710
Middle-East Journal, 667
Middle East, 239, 304, 380, 392, 411, 462, 481, 482, 488, 498
Mikaelian, Avetis (known under the name of Soltan-Zadeh), 130, 135
Milani, Abbas, 681
Milani, Hadi, sayed ayatollah, 427
Military Academy of Tehran, 56, 57, 92, 102, 104, 284, 286, 342, 343, 549, 603, 714
Military holocaust, 467
Millemann, Thierry P., political scientist, 449, 471, 688, 692, 694, 697, 698, 719
Milliez, Paul, Professor, 718
Minatshi, 715
Mindszenty, Hungarian cardinal, 705

Minh, General (in Saigon), 585
Mint (Zarrabkhaneh Shahinshahi), 75
Mirza, Kuchik Khan, visionary, truly patriotic figure, 53, 132, 133, 231, 661
Mirza, Taqi Khan, Vice-Governor, 23, 24, 31
Mitrokhin, Vasili, master Soviet spy, 683
Mitrokhin Archives, 683
Mitterand, François, French President, 362, 367, 442
Moazzami, Abdollah, President of the Chamber, 209, 218, 221, 222, 227, 239, 280, 672
Moazzami, Seyfollah, Minister of Mohammad Mossadegh, 251, 255, 256
Modabber, General, Chief of the Police Forces, 248
Modaress, Sayyid Hassan, religious dignitary, 66, 67
Modernization in Muslim countries, 461
Moezzi, M. A., 692
Mofattah, Mohammad, mullah, 677
Moghaddam, Doctor and Colonel, 257
Moghaddam, Mostafa, 241, 672
Moghaddam, Nasser, General, head of the Savak, 286, 526, 537, 551, 552, 581, 686
Moghtader, Mohammad Reza, architect, 398, 400, 686
Mohammad Ali, King Faruk (of Egypt)'s uncle, 344
Mohammad Ali Shah, son of Mozaffar Ol Din and grand-son of Naser Ol Din Shah, 36, 641
Mohammad Hassan Mirza, crown prince, brother of Ahmad Shah, 63, 64, 66, 67, 72
Mohammad Shah, 22, 23, 25
Moïnian, Nosratollah, chairman of the imperial cabinet, 520
Mojahed, Sayyid Mohammad, fanatical and violently anti-Russian religious leader, Russia's 'agent provocateur', 20, 21
Mokhâtab-Rafii, France, Daughter of Chapour Bakhtiar, 716
Molavi, Mohammad Ali, governor of the Central Bank after the Islamic revolution, 567
Molière, 90
Molnar, Thomas, eminent Yale Professor, 479, 717
Molotov, Soviet Minister of Foreign Affairs, 170

Momtaz, Colonel, Guards' Commander of Mohammad Mossadegh, 241, 242
Mondale, Walter, US Vice-President, 698, 699, 701
Monde et vie, 694, 697, 698, 699, 701
Mongol invasion, 385, 412, 641, 642
Montaigne, 109, 352
Montazeri, Hossein Ali, mullah, 715
Morocco, 238, 283, 512, 557, 611, 614, 615, 682, 684, 695, 718
Morse, Mark, Robert Armao's assistant, 618, 635, 640
Moscow trials, 168
Moshar, Youssef, Minister of Mossadegh, 199, 262
Moshiri, Mohammad, secretary of state to the presidency of the Council under Bakhtiar, 711
Mossad, 278, 282, 295, 304, 464, 487
Mossadegh, Ahmad, qualified at the Ponts et Chaussées, eldest son of Mohammad Mossadegh, 195
Mossadegh, Gholam Hossein, doctor, second son of Mohammad Mossadegh, 195, 197, 257
Mossadegh, Mohammad (Mossadegh ol Saltaneh), the 'old lion', PM, 2, 67, 69, 71, 76, 139, 140, 141, 145, 146, 148, 166, 190-209, 211-222, 225, 226, 227, 228, 229, 233, 234, 236, 237, 239, 240, 241, 242, 244-270, 273, 279-285, 300, 301, 303, 306, 314, 315, 317, 327, 331, 347, 351, 353, 369, 370, 371, 401, 423, 427, 443, 454, 510, 531, 533, 565, 576, 578, 582, 583, 584, 586, 597, 600, 605, 643, 644, 646, 648, 656, 667-671, 673, 674, 675
Mostashar, Mr, was to bring to perfection Mohammad Reza Pahlavi's knowledge of the Persian language and literature, the history of his country, and was to pay attention to his mastery of calligraphy, 339, 340
Mostofi, A., 657
Mostofi, Hassan (Mostofi Ol Mamalek), PM, 59, 65, 66, 644
Mostofis, group of experts, 26
Mousavi, Ahmad Kazemi, 659
Moussavi, Mohammad Hossein, Mr, senator for Tabriz, and number two of the Rastakhiz, 677, 705, 706, 709, 717
Movement for the Liberation of Iran, 600
Mozaffari, Mehdi, 695

INDEX

Mozaffar Ol Din, son and crown prince of Naser Ol Din, 35, 36, 79
Mucchielli, Roger, 678
Mujaheddin Khalgh Organization (the People's Fedayeens), ultra-left group that has remained loyal to Khomeini, 293, 665
Museum of contemporary Art, 395
Museum of Tehran, 94, 102
Muslim Brothers, 171, 194, 308, 329
Mussolini, 102

N

'Neither the East, not the West, but the Islamic republic', 491
'Neutralization' of the Iranian armed forces, 470, 490, 495
Nabavi, Behzad, one of the main leaders of the Islamic revolution, 368, 494, 684, 702
Nader, 'the last Asian conqueror', 2, 17, 18, 73, 86, 93, 395
Nadjmabadi, Mehdi, Sheikh, Reza Khan's notary, 65
Nafissi, Moadab, pishkar (steward and private tutor) of Mohammad Reza Pahlavi, 336, 339, 340, 345
Nafissi, Saïd, great writer of the 20th century, 95
Nahas Pasha, Mostafa, 204, 344
Nahavandi, Firouzeh, 667, 680, 681, 686, 688, 694
Nahavandi, Houchang, 330, 349, 364, 379, 514, 516, 520, 532, 551, 657, 660, 661, 664, 666, 667, 671, 676, 682, 683, 684, 685, 686, 687, 693, 697, 698, 701, 702, 703, 704, 705, 708, 710, 711, 714, 719
Najaf, sanctuary city, 68, 179, 193, 421, 427, 430, 431, 436, 510, 545, 571
Najafi, great ayatollah, 517
Naji, General, commander of the Esfahan garrison, 530
Nakhdjavan, Ahmad, air vice-marshal, 111
Napoleonic campaigns, 337
Napoleon Bonaparte, French Emperor, 17, 19, 27, 121, 573, 687
Naraghi, Mrs., Fazlollah Zahedi's close relative, 672
Nariman, Mahmoud, 280
Naser Ol Din, Mohammad Shah's crown prince then his successor, 23, 24, 25, 30, 31, 32, 33, 34, 35, 38, 46, 195
Nasr, Hossein, Shahbanoo's Cabinet chairman, 559, 560
Nasr, Nicolas, Lebanese political scientist, 461, 696
Nasser, Gamal Abdel, 143, 156, 304, 321, 323, 348, 349, 373, 402, 425, 426, 429, 486, 494
Nassiri, Mohammad, Professor, Governor of the issuing Bank, 205, 219, 280, 327, 576, 669, 689
Nassiri, Nematollah, Colonel then General, commander of the imperial guard, head of the Savak from 1965 to 1978, 241, 242, 244, 254, 285, 286, 290, 291, 329, 377, 520, 526, 705
Nategh, Homa, historian, 688
Nationalization of oil, 193, 194, 200, 206, 207, 208, 211, 213, 225, 226, 259, 267, 319, 423, 582, 586
National Association of Academics, 148
National Bank of Iran, 75, 174, 216, 218, 271, 273, 280, 327, 576, 669
National Carpet Museum, 395
National Committee of American Foreign Policy, 696
National Day of Hospitals, 541
National Front (Mossadegh's Party), 141, 148, 199, 209, 222, 228, 233, 239, 245, 247, 252, 262, 314, 443, 516, 577, 582, 583, 588, 600, 668, 671
National Institute of Agronomics, 90
National Institute of Pharmacology, 90
National Institute of Political Science, 90
National Institute of Trade, 90
National Insurance Company, 327
National Iranian Oil Company (NIOC), 267, 325, 329, 331, 390, 575
National Law Institute, 90
National Library, 94, 102
National Museum of Earthenware and Ceramics, 395
National Security Council (US), 458, 460
National War Institute, 92
NATO (North Atlantic Treaty Organization), 304, 406, 480, 558
Navaï, Abdolhossein, 661
Navid, Tudeh's newspaper, 148
Nazih, Hassan, President of the Tehran Bar, 435, 692
Nazi goals, 296
Nazli, Queen of Egypt, spouse of Fuad, mother of Faruk, 346, 347

741

Near East, 392, 462, 482, 488, 498
Neauphle-le-Château (France), 416, 417, 425, 426, 434, 435, 439, 440, 441, 442, 447, 451, 468, 482, 487, 519, 547, 575, 593, 600, 691
Negus (Haile Selassie), Emperor of Ethiopia, 575
Nehzat, weekly published in Paris, 692
Neshat, Ali, General, Commander of the 'Immortals' (replica of Darius' 'Immortals'), 599, 703
Netherlands, 390
Nevissi, Yazdan, Colonel, 634, 635, 640, 717
Newsweek, 276, 676, 682, 684
New York Hospital, 621
New York Times, 669, 674, 684, 697, 698, 700, 701, 702
New York Times Magazine, 689, 693
New York University, 292
Ngo, Dinh Diem, President of the Republic of South Vietnam, 313
Niavaran palace, imperial residence, 361, 362, 365, 525, 701
Niazmand, Reza, 655
Nic-Khah, Parviz, leader of group of assassins, death sentenced but pardoned and commuted by the Shah, then finally arrested and executed after the revolution for having benefited from the Shah's mercy, 365, 366
Nicholas II, Czar of Russia, 330, 384, 536, 575, 606, 614, 628
Nik, Mohammad, also called ayatollah Reycharri, who was well known to Western anti-terrorism services, 154
Nikomachos from Stagira, 447
Nixon, Richard, US President, 455, 480, 617, 701
Noriega, General, CIA agent and notorious drug dealer, 630, 632
North Korea, 496, 665
North Vietnam, 481
Nouri, Fazlollah, Sheikh, ultra-reactionary prelate, grand-father of Nourreddine Kianouri, 150
Nouri, Mohiodine Nabavi, professor of international law, 710
Nouri, Nategh, Minister of the Interior, 154
Nouri, Saïd, Prime Minister in Baghdad, 304, 305
Nouri (his real name was Nassirieh), Allameh, ayatollah, involved in 'Black Friday', 545, 709
Noush Afarin, mother of Reza Shah, 45, 46
Nouvelliste et feuille d'avis du Valais, 690, 702
Nuclear (plants, industry, weapons), 381, 388, 390, 406, 415, 462, 496, 497, 498
Nuri, Mirza Agha Khan, openly corrupted by the British Embassy, 30, 31

O

'One of the biggest fiascos in history', 478
'Original sin', 714
Oasis of peace and stability, 375
October Revolution (Bolshevik revolution), 21, 36, 50, 130, 131, 230, 330, 587
OECD (Organisation for Economic Co-operation and Development), 390
Olympic Games (7th) of Asia (in 1974), 399
Oman (sultanate), 403, 462
Omar, caliph, 400
Omideh-Iran, weekly, 665
OPEC (Organization of Petroleum-Exporting Countries), 333, 415, 458, 460, 466
Organisation of the Plan, 183, 190, 307, 311, 328, 679
Ormuz (strait), 404, 406
Ottoman Empire, 23, 412
Ottoman invaders, 17
Oufkir, General, 283
Oveyssi, Gholam Ali, General, commander-in-chief of the army, 542, 545, 551, 553, 557, 558, 574, 709

P

'Promotion of Islamic fanaticism' (inspired by Henry Kissinger and Zbigniew Brzezinski), 460
Pahlavan, Christian, 696, 699
Pahlavan, Tshanguiz, 657
Pahlavi, Abdol Reza, prince, son of Reza Shah, 61
Pahlavi, Ahmad Reza, prince, son of Reza Shah, 61
Pahlavi, Ali Patrick, son of Ali Reza Pahlavi and Christiane Cholewski, 352
Pahlavi, Ali Reza, prince, son of Reza Shah (Khan), young brother of Mohammad Reza Pahlavi, 48, 338, 352
Pahlavi, Ashraf, princess, daughter of Reza

INDEX

Shah (Khan), 48, 87, 142, 173, 216, 615, 616, 619, 621, 624, 625, 630, 638
Pahlavi, Fatemeh, princess, daughter of Reza Shah (Khan) and Esmat Dowlatshani, 61
Pahlavi, Fatemeh (later to be called Hamdam ol Saltaneh), daughter of Reza Shah (Khan), 47
Pahlavi, Gholam Reza, Prince, son of Reza Shah (Khan) and half-brother of Mohammad Reza, 60, 187, 246, 374, 466, 532, 538, 551, 560, 656, 667, 668, 682, 685, 697, 708, 709, 710, 714
Pahlavi, Hamid Reza, prince, son of Reza Shah, 61
Pahlavi, Leïla, youngest child of Mohammad Reza Pahlavi and Farah Diba, 625
Pahlavi, Mahmoud Reza, prince, son of Reza Shah, 61
Pahlavi, Reza, crown prince, son of Mohammad Reza Pahlavi and Farah Diba, 356, 360, 580, 584, 588, 619, 626, 719
Pahlavi, Shahnaz, Princess, 237, 274, 347, 348, 355
Pahlavi, Shams, princess, daughter of Reza Shah (Khan), 48, 87, 246, 350, 352, 579, 618
Pahlavis (dynasty, family, imperial couple), 63, 68, 83, 196, 216, 217, 218, 223, 230, 243, 348, 359, 360, 365, 475, 482, 485, 566, 575, 591, 592, 612, 613, 614, 616, 617, 626, 628, 630, 633, 634, 636, 641, 644, 658, 666, 672, 681, 688
Pahlavi Foundation, 316, 368, 396, 400, 537, 540, 562, 582, 589
Pahlavi National Library in Shiraz, 399, 401
Pahlavi University (formerly University of Shiraz), 326, 330, 391, 392, 396, 686
Pahlbod, Mehrdad, 2, 11, 618
Pakdaman (Nategh), H., 654
Pakistan, 285, 286, 304, 403, 405, 455
Pakravan, Emineh, 653
Pakravan, Hassan, Major General, second head of the Savak, 284, 285, 329, 330, 427, 689
Palestine, 51, 226, 232
Palestinians (infiltrated in the ranks of the radical opposition), 525, 541, 544, 545, 555, 568, 605, 709
Palestinian camps (urban guerrilla and terrorist techniques training), 486, 521
Palestinian cause, 463
Palmerston, Lord, Great Britain's minister, 25, 26
Panahian, General, IADP officer, 430
Panama, 353, 628, 629, 631, 633, 634, 635, 719
Paradise Island, 616
Paraguay, 615
Paris, Treaty (signed on March 4th 1857), 33
Paris Match, 664, 667, 692, 699, 712, 713, 716
Parker, Richard, American ambassador, 614
Parkhash, journal, 673
Pars, official agency, 716
Parsons, Anthony, Sir, ambassador of Great Britain, 561, 574, 580, 710, 711
Partow-Iran, monthly review in Farsi published in Canada, 68, 674, 684, 709, 710
Party for Justice, 130
Pasdaran, a group of 'Guardians of the Revolution', political militia of the Islamic regime, 491
Patronymic names, 87, 721
Payandeh, Mehrdad, 680, 686
Paymaï, Nader, 654, 655, 656
PDFLP (Popular Democratic Front for the Liberation of Palestine), 487, 498
Péan, Pierre, 687
Pedrazzani, Jean-Michel, 683
Pentagon, 416
People's Mujaheddins, 151, 293, 296, 486, 605, 665
Péret, Jean-Pierre, 676
Peron, Ernest, 340
Peroncel-Hugoz, Jean-Pierre, 696
Perse, 4
Persepolis, 95, 326, 349, 363, 382, 392, 399, 466, 479, 601
Persia, 86, 101, 105, 343, 345, 481
Persian Empire, 17, 397, 399, 479, 509, 641, 642
Persian Gulf, 23, 25, 33, 54, 76, 80, 81, 93, 120, 175, 201, 278, 321, 346, 388, 389, 390, 403, 404, 406, 462, 490, 496, 497, 498, 511, 568, 577, 656, 658
Pessian, Mohammad Taqi Khan, colonel, 54
Peter the Great, 140
Petrochemical industry, 309, 390

743

Peyrefitte, Alain, French Minister of Justice, 718
PFLP (Popular Front for the Liberation of Palestine), 487, 498
Phantoms (jet fighters), 406
Phoenix missiles, 406
Pichard, Jean-Pierre, 688, 698, 709
Pichevari, Dariush (or Kaveh, according to other sources), son of Djafar (Djavadof) Pichevari, 182
Pichevari, Djafar (see also Sayed Djafar Djavadof), 164
Piettre, André, 685
Pirnia, Hassan (Moshir Ol Dowleh), PM, 58, 59, 66, 67, 90, 235, 643, 644, 656
Pirnia, Hossein (Motamen Ol Molk), Hassan Pirnia's brother, President of the Chamber, 66, 69, 90, 235
Pirnia, Lucie, Doctor, Pahlavis's family doctor, 634
Pirnia, Mansoureh, 672
PLO (Palestine Liberation Organization), 486, 487, 498
Point de Vue, 682, 683, 684
Point IV (of the Truman doctrine to manage technical, social and humanitarian aid to developing countries), 236, 266
Polak, Doctor, 29, 653
Poland, 99, 106, 187, 339, 402
Policy of the oak, 385, 468
Policy of the reed, 385, 468
Polish refugees, 125
Political asylum, 434
Politique étrangère, 687, 695
Politique internationale, 696, 699
Pol Pot, 151, 450
Pompidou, Georges, French President, 466, 697
Poniatowski, Michel, 698
Ponts et Chaussées, 195
Portillo, Lopez, President of Mexico, 617
Postel-Vinay, Olivier, 717
Pour-Shodja, Amir, Shah's loyal valet, 634, 640
Power and Principles, 699
Pravda, 498, 702
Precht, Henry, in charge of the Iranian sector at the State Department, 476
Présent, 701, 702, 704
Pro-American coup d'État, 455
Pro-Soviet countries, 345, 486, 487, 494,

495, 496, 497, 498, 525
Pro-Soviet military coup d'État in Baghdad (on July 14th 1958), 305
Professional (men and women) mourners, 546
Progressive Circle (see also Iran-eh-novin), 327
Prussia, 20, 27
Pujo, Pierre, editor of the weekly *AF 2000*, and president of the steering committee of Action française, 685
Pythagoras, Greek mathematician and philosopher, lived in the 6th century BC, 446

Q

Qadhafi, Mu'ammar al, 435
Qajar, era, dynasty, tribu, princes, princesses, 18, 20, 23, 37, 45, 46, 56, 60, 61, 64, 68, 71, 73, 79, 95, 97, 117, 132, 135, 136, 147, 152, 168, 194, 195, 196, 230, 246, 262, 314, 335, 336, 343, 350, 352, 361, 395, 398, 531, 643, 644, 656
Qajar era Art Museum, 395
Qiao-Shi, Chinese counterpart of General Moghaddam, 686
Qom, 68, 87, 193, 252, 322, 323, 329, 420, 422, 425, 427, 431, 511, 520, 521, 524, 539, 588, 688, 693, 694, 713

R

'Revolutionary committee of the Central Bank', 567
'RION', manipulating agent of the KGB, 683
Rabbani, Borhanoldin, Afghan Head of State, 491
Rabiï, General, Commander-in-Chief of the Air Force, 591
Rabin, General, Israeli PM, 465
Racism, 410
Rad-Serecht, Farhad, economist and academic, 703
Radek, Bolshevik leader, 133
Radio Iran, 693, 715
Radio Moscow, 701
Radjavi, Massoud, historic leader of the people's Mujaheddins, Islamic-Marxist from the most radical branch of Khomeini's supporters during the first stage of the revolution, 296, 486
Radmanesh, Reza, exiled Tudeh's general-secretary, 147

INDEX

Rafsanjani, Ali Akbar Hashemi, 497, 681, 715, 719
Rahâvard, Persian publication published in the USA, 710, 712, 718
Rahbar, Saïd, 671
Rahbar, Tudeh's banned paper, 145, 667
Râheh Zendegui, weekly in Persian published in Los Angeles, CA, 687
Rahimi, General, Chief of the Police and administrator of the martial law in Tehran, 574, 589, 594, 603
Rahimi, Mostafa, leftist writer, 443
Raïn, E., 661
Raskolnikov, political commissar commanding the red troops, 132
Rastakhiz ('Revival' or 'Resurrection'), one-party system, 507, 508, 509, 510, 520, 521, 522, 523, 529, 531, 677, 705
Rastakhiz newspaper, 522
Razavi, Ahmad, 246, 249, 250, 261
Razi University in Kermanshah, 392
Razmara, Haj Ali, General (trained in Saint-Cyr), PM, 57, 144, 176, 192, 193, 194, 233, 648, 667
Reagan, Ronald, US President, 480, 624, 699, 701
Red Army, 105, 123, 124, 129, 132, 138, 139, 140, 160, 161, 162, 163, 164, 168, 170, 171, 172, 181, 182, 370, 412, 492, 493, 623, 627
Red Lion and Sun, the Iranian Red Cross, 59, 548
Reed, Joseph, 617
Réforme, 693
Regency council, 246, 247, 357, 577, 578, 603, 604
Rentchnick, Pierre, Dr, 688
Republicans (in the USA), 454, 565
Republic of Ecuador, 203
Research centre on terrorism since September 11th 2001, 665, 677
Ress, John, 664
Reuters, 665
Revue de la Défense nationale, 497, 658, 666, 702
Revue universelle des faits et des idées, 687
Rex (see also Abadan tragedy), cinema of Abadan destroyed by fire by members of ayatollah Khomeini's entourage, 530, 535, 537
Reycharri, 'ayatollah' (see also Mohammad Nik), 154

Reza, eighth Shiite Imam, 94
Reza, Imam, 76, 512, 548
Rezaï, Ali, Senator, who lives in Costa Rica today, 711
Rezaï, Mohsen, commander-in-chief of the Guardians of the Revolution, 534, 546, 707, 709
Reza Abassi Museum, particularly dedicated to Safavid art, 395
Reza Shah, 2, 37, 71, 72, 73, 76, 80, 82, 83, 85, 86, 87, 88, 89, 96, 97, 98, 109, 110, 111, 112, 113, 114, 115, 116, 118, 119, 120, 121, 138, 146, 149, 161, 176, 187, 197, 231, 257, 335, 340, 341, 343, 345, 346, 347, 348, 349, 392, 393, 395, 398, 418, 419, 437, 511, 581, 600, 640, 641, 645, 654, 655, 656, 668
RG (Renseignements Généraux), French special branch, 288
Riahi, Esmaïl, General, Minister of Agriculture, 325
Riahi, Farhad, Professor, rector of the Franco-Iranian University of Avicenna, 514
Riahi, Taqi, General, Chief of General Staff, 248, 250, 261
Rice (production), 387, 388
Richelieu, 86, 269, 337
Rockefeller, David, 615, 616, 617, 620, 624, 634, 718
Rockefeller Foundation, 616, 617, 618
Rockefeller group, 471, 474
Rodier, Alain, 684, 719
Rollin, Henri, Professor, eminent Belgian legal expert, 205
Romania, 402
Roman army, 412
Rondot, Philippe, 666
Roosevelt, Kermit, head of the CIA's Middle East, 239, 255, 673, 674
Roosevelt F.D., 106, 123, 126
Rosey school, Francophone school in Switzerland, 338, 340, 341, 378, 604, 682
Rouhani, Fouad, 668, 670
Rouleau, Éric, 665, 679, 682, 686, 718
Rousta, Reza, union leader of Shoraye Mottahedeh Markazi, 138, 139
Royal Dutch Shell, 267
Royo, President of Panama, 629
Rubin, Barry, 706, 709
Rumania, 628
Rumsfeld, Donald, 460
Rusk, Dean, American Secretary of State, 375

Russia, 19, 23, 30, 33, 36, 37, 38, 56, 101, 102, 104, 131, 133, 167, 587
Russian Empire, 34
Rutgers University, 472
Ruzbeh, Khosrow (also called the 'Lenin of Iran'), captain, member of the Tudeh, murderer of journalist Mohammad Massoud, 142, 663

S

'Shah's fortune', 368, 500, 623
'Shah's New York skycraper', 368
'Stinking Western civilisation", 534
Saadi, poet, 108, 109, 395
Saad Abad pact, 88
Sabbaghian, A., 715
Sabehti, Parviz, General Nassiri's close deputy in charge of national security, 520
Sablier, Édouard, 138, 150, 167, 185, 277, 428, 661, 662, 665, 666, 667, 676, 681, 691, 706, 708, 718
Sadat, Anwar El, President of Egypt, 349, 463, 464, 465, 469, 610, 611, 633, 634, 636, 637, 638
Sadat, Jihan, spouse of President Sadat, 610, 634, 636
Sadegh, Hossein, Iranian civil servant from the FAO, 243
Sadighi, Gholam Hossein, highly experienced sociology professor, 216, 247, 248, 249, 251, 255, 256, 261, 280, 576, 577, 578, 580, 584, 674, 710
Sadjadi, Mehdi, 2
Sadr, Moussa, Imam, 694
Sadre, Mohsen, PM, 125, 420, 647, 655, 659, 660, 664
Sadtchicov, Soviet ambassador to Tehran, 171, 172, 180, 181, 219
Saeb, great Persian poet, 395
Saed, Mohammad, PM, 117, 124, 140, 369, 646, 647
Saedi, Gholam Hossein, leftist writer, 443
Saf, official press of the armed forces of the Islamic republic of Iran, 684, 701
Safaï, Ebrahim, 654, 670, 675
Safavian, Abbas, Professor, rector of the University of Melli and personal GP of the Shah, 514, 523, 684, 718
Safavid, art, dynasty, era, 31, 73, 93, 386, 393, 395, 671
Saffari, Mohammad Ali, general, chief of police, 143
Safi, Sheikh, 21, 671
Sahabi, Yadollah, science professor, 715
Sahebjam, Freidoun, 658, 678, 682, 684, 686, 716, 718
Saïd, Djavad, Dr, 712
Saïd, Edward, 686
Saigon, 481, 585, 711
Saïkal, Amine, 680
Saint-Cyr, French military school, 57, 92, 102, 176, 192, 281, 284, 355
Saint-Germain-des-Prés, used to be the stronghold of 'intellectuals' (leftists) in Paris (see also Germanopratine), 441
Saint Graal, 434
Sajadi, Mohammad, Secretary of State, 259, 712
Salaheldin, major, Libyan emissary, 487
Salamine, military defeat, 93
Saleh, Allahyar, communist, Minister of Justice, 173, 202, 209, 215, 218, 227, 280
Salinger, Pierre, 294, 478, 678, 699, 701, 718
Samadianpour, General, Chief of the National Police Forces, 551
Samakar, Abbas, one of the activists of the ultra-left terrorist networks who was also working for the television, 678, 706
Samiï, Ahmad, 679
Samii, Hossein, great master of imperial protocol, famous poet, 85, 87, 378
Samimi, Loft-Ali, Minister of the Post Office and Telecommunications, 585, 588, 713
San'atis, family, 396
Sandjar, M., Dr, 673
Saneï, Djafar, General, who today lives in Canada, 545, 708
Saneï, Manutshehr, chamberlain, 559
Sanjabi, Karim, one of the leaders of the National Front, later to be Khomeini's Minister of Foreign Affairs, 199, 218, 516, 716
Sarfaraz, Djalal, poet, 443
Sartre, Jean-Paul, leader of ayatollah Khomeini's Support committees, 441
Sassanid, period, dynasty, 30, 68, 400, 642
Saudi Arabia, 191, 207
SAVAK, 9, 146, 237, 268, 269, 275, 276, 277, 278, 279, 281, 282, 283, 284, 285, 286, 287, 288, 289, 290, 291, 293, 294, 295, 296, 304, 313, 327, 329, 331, 332, 354, 356, 362,

INDEX

373, 375, 377, 411, 427, 428, 430, 440, 455, 487, 497, 502, 514, 516, 520, 521, 523, 526, 527, 534, 552, 554, 555, 570, 589, 605, 675, 677, 678, 685, 700, 703, 704, 705
SAVAMA, political police of the Islamic regime, successor of the SAVAK, 497, 605
Schlesinger, James, 460
School of Fine Arts, 95
Scientific socialism, 156
SDECE (Service de documentation extérieure et de contre-espionnage), French Intelligence and Counter-Intelligence Services), 434
SEATO (Southeast Asia Treaty Organization), 304
Sea of Oman, 497
Sebt, Mohammad Taqi, number two at the Iranian embassy in Iraq, 571
Security Council, 163, 168, 171, 202, 203, 207, 213
Senegal, 405
Sepahbodi, Anoushivaran, Minister of Foreign Affairs, 157
Sepah Bank, first wholly Iranian bank, 75
Sepehri, Hossein, under-secretary of State to Agriculture, 706
Shafa'at, General, commander of the airborne brigade based in Shiraz, 594
Shafa, Shoja Ol Din, Shah's cultural advisor, architect, 68, 400, 559, 678, 686, 688, 692, 693, 697, 700, 710
Shafehgaht, General, Minister of War, 585
Shafigh, Shahryar, one of the Shah's nephews, a courageous and brilliant officer of the imperial navy, assassinated, 605, 627
Shah-Abadi Mohammad Ali, master of Ruhollah Khomeini, 420
Shahbakhti, colonel and later general, 53, 257
Shahbaz, aeroplane manufacturing plant, 92
Shahin, aeroplane manufacturing plant, 92
Shahin, Imperial Boeing, 611, 613
Shahryar, metallurgical group, 389
Shahyad, kings' memorial, work of young architect Hossein Amanat, 399
Shah Abbas the Great, 4, 18, 20, 30, 74, 86, 95, 96, 405, 671, 686, 688
Shah Esmail, founder of the Safavid dynasty, 73
Shah Nameh, legendary history of the kings of Iran from the very beginning, 108
Shari'a, 28

Shariat-Madari, Sayed Kazem, ayatollah, 181, 427, 517, 518, 519, 521, 523, 524, 527, 534, 541, 563, 569, 577, 705
Sharif-Emami, Djafar, PM, 251, 311, 314, 433, 534, 537, 539, 547, 551, 556, 563, 589, 649
Sharif-Zadeh, Sayed Djafar, guardian of the revolution, 691
Sharoudi, ayatollah, 427
Shawcross, Hartley, Lord, former Nuremberg judge, 631
Shawcross, William, 313, 409, 676, 679, 682, 684, 685, 687, 695, 697, 698
Shayegan, Ali, influential lawyer, 218, 245, 246, 247, 249, 261
Sheybani, Abbas, Dr, 'the highest scientific authority in the country', rector of the University of Tehran during Khomeini's rule, president of the Order of Physicians, former Minister, 447
Sheybani, Abdollah, rector of the University of Tehran, 556
Shiism, 193, 438, 475, 481, 510, 512, 572, 692, 704
Shiite (community, hierarchy), 17, 67, 179, 252, 300, 353, 421, 423, 437, 438, 461, 481, 490, 510, 511, 518, 526, 571, 574, 704, 705
Shiite (indisputable) point of view, 438
Shiraz festival, 359
Shirvani, Dariush, representative for Tehran, 586, 697, 710
Shoraye Mottahedeh Markazi, trade union confederation created by the Tudeh, 138
Siassi, Ali Akbar, rector, 63, 143, 655, 656, 657, 659, 664
Simon, John, Sir, Foreign Office Secretary, 81
Simon, William, American Secretary of the Treasury, 457, 460
Sinatra, Frank, 624
Skrine, Clermont, Sir, Governor of Bombay, 121
Sloan-Kettering Memorial, hospital, 622
Socialist Party (French), 442, 693
Société d'études iraniennes et de l'art persan, 656
Socrates, 446
Soheili, Ali, PM, 110, 114, 116, 117, 121, 124, 168, 226, 645, 646, 659
Solar calendar, 109, 540
Solomon, David's son and successor,

747

reigned from 970 to 931 BC, 446
Sorbonne, 89, 576
Sorouch, publication from the ministry of Islamic Orientation in Tehran, 699
Sorouri, Mohammad, Minister during the forties, former president of the Supreme Court, 575, 580
South Africa, 121, 367, 390, 589, 615, 628
South Vietnam, 481
Soviet-satellite (espionage, subversion, camp, bloc), 275, 295, 309, 405, 484, 485, 495, 497, 498, 663
Sovietization (done under the cover of 'Islamisation'), 153, 488
Soviets agents, 165, 689, 690, 705
Soviet (expansionism, Empire), 129, 134, 150, 156, 453, 488, 498, 690, 702
Soviet hospital in Tehran, 265
Soviet radio channels, 484
Spain, 6, 387, 390
Spanish civil war, 151, 665
Spartacists, 134
Special forces, 403, 407, 553, 554, 555, 594, 605
Stalin, Joseph, 9, 126, 130, 132, 146, 157, 159, 161, 163, 165, 167, 169, 170, 171, 173, 175, 177, 179, 181, 182, 183, 185, 186, 187, 209, 219, 233, 269, 283, 369, 450, 454, 493, 518, 664
Stalinist purges, 130, 134
Steel (production), 389, 390, 402
Stierlin, A., 686
Stockholm Appeal, 145
Stocks, Richard, 207
Stolypin, Russian Chancellor, assassinated, 330
Strike of the oil industry, 554, 562
Study Group of Iranian problems ('Think-Tank'), 377, 505, 506, 513, 514, 515, 516, 520, 521, 522, 523, 525, 526, 530, 547, 703, 706
Subversion, 105, 153, 275, 280, 295, 304, 384, 468, 469, 484, 487, 498, 521, 527, 528, 543, 546, 547, 595, 623, 678
Suez Canal, 204, 344, 346, 465
Sullivan, William H., American Ambassador to Tehran, 478, 550, 574, 591, 692, 698, 706, 709
Sultan of Oman, 403
Sunday Times, 715
Suniism, 512

Sunnites, 438, 511, 568
Sutton, E., 667
Swiss guards, 573
Switzerland, 2, 62, 195, 273, 284, 338, 339, 340, 341, 347, 348, 353, 601, 663, 690
Symphonic Orchestra of Tehran, 94
Syria, 345, 486, 494, 496, 525, 605

T
'The machinery for a worldwide propaganda', 473
'The most beautiful moment in the history of Islam', 449, 472
'The only effective economic take-off of the Third World', 381, 409
'The Seven Sisters', informal oil cartel which was powerful, 226, 329
'The Shah must change his policy or that we must replace him', 460
'The way to urinate and to defecate', 445
Tabari, Ehsan, number two of the Tudeh, 154, 661, 662
Tabas, oasis town devastated by an earthquake, 548, 549
Tabataba'i, Sayyid Zia Ol-Din, journalist and talented polemicist, then after PM, 37, 39, 40, 50, 51, 58, 226, 230, 643
Tadjadod, Mostafa, president and founder of the first private bank in the country, 540
Tadzhikistan, 34
Taghavi, Djalal, representative, 713
Taghavi, Nasrollah, former president of the Iranian Academy, 378
Taghizadeh, Hassan, Finance Minister, Ambassador, 79, 81, 82, 164, 168
Taghizadeh, Mohammad Reza, young journalist and town councillor of Tehran, leader of the counter-revolution, 597, 598, 715
Taher, Baba, Kurdish poet, 395
Taheri, Amir, 688
Taiwan, 628
Taj Ol Molouk, spouse of Reza Shah (Khan), Queen Mother, 48, 61, 87, 339, 531, 536, 618, 622
Talash, quarterly magazine, 655, 656, 657, 660, 677, 679, 681, 686
Talâ (or Gilda), serious loving affair of Mohammad Reza Pahlavi, 359
Taleghani, Mahmoud, ayatollah, radical religious leader, 598, 715
Tarikh-eh Mo'aser-eh Iran, magazine of the

Index

Institute for Iranian Contemporary Historical Studies, of the Ministry of Foreign Affairs of the Islamic republic, 672
Tea (production), 387
Tehran Journal, 522
Tehran Opera, 394
Television channels, 394
Teymourtach, the all-mighty Minister of the Imperial Court, 84, 338
Teymourtach affair, 84
TF1 (French TV channel), 699
The cursed alliance of red and black, 323, 513, 527, 596
The Divine Comedy, 108
The Economist, 480, 696, 699
The Guardian, 692
The Last Shah of Iran, 4, 658, 660, 677, 682, 691, 696, 705, 708, 710, 711, 714, 718
The Little Red Book, 379
The most likely to be able to save everything, 595
The National Association of Writers, 148
Third World, 147, 190, 202, 369, 381, 382, 403, 404, 405, 409, 410, 470, 501
Time (New York magazine), 213, 684, 693
Torrijos, Omar, General, strong man of Panama, friend of Fidel Castro, 628, 629, 630, 632, 633, 635
Tournier, Jean-Noël, 717
Transiranian, 76, 77, 159, 342, 402
Trilateral Commission, 696
Tripartite treaty, 158, 168, 453
Trotskyists, 151, 488, 605
Truman, Harry, US President, 179, 203, 236, 454
Tshamran, Mostafa, Iranian-American, member of the Amal militia in Lebanon, 715
Tudeh ('the masses'), Iranian communist party, 60, 83, 85, 127, 129, 130, 133, 135, 136, 137, 138, 139, 140, 141, 142, 143, 144, 145, 147, 148, 149, 150, 151, 153, 154, 155, 160, 161, 163, 166, 167, 170, 173, 177, 178, 179, 185, 192, 204, 212, 213, 218, 219, 220, 221, 233, 247, 253, 254, 255, 264, 265, 268, 270, 279, 283, 284, 291, 306, 315, 323, 363, 426, 485, 497, 520, 569, 605, 660, 661, 663, 664, 665, 666, 667, 673, 697
Tuileries (France), 573
Turgot, 502
Turkey, 65, 67, 77, 85, 86, 87, 88, 104, 304, 344, 467, 568
Turkish-Iraqi alliance pact, 304
Turkmanchay, treaty, 21
Typhoid, 338, 351

U

'Universal Jewish government', 446
Ulbricht, Walter, founding member of the Communist Party of Germany, General Secretary of the Socialist Unity Party of Germany, 156
Ultra-left, 148, 151, 153, 254, 278, 289, 293, 365, 366, 521, 600, 605, 665, 678
Umberto, last King of Italy, 353
United Council of Unions (belonging to the Tudeh), 178
United Nations, 163, 164, 168, 171, 202, 205, 213, 274, 277, 294, 353, 449, 657, 668, 678
United States, 27, 56, 57, 59, 79, 104, 106, 113, 123, 126, 147, 150, 159, 160, 161, 170, 171, 184, 203, 218, 223, 233, 236, 237, 240, 253, 266, 271, 283, 285, 294, 299, 302, 304, 311, 312, 313, 314, 315, 317, 329, 331, 333, 347, 368, 384, 386, 387, 390, 392, 402, 415, 416, 435, 436, 448, 453, 454, 455, 456, 457, 458, 459, 461, 462, 463, 466, 467, 468, 471, 473, 474, 475, 476, 477, 478, 480, 481, 492, 493, 495, 497, 498, 521, 565, 583, 591, 601, 611, 615, 619, 620, 623, 627, 630, 633, 634, 672, 679, 685, 687, 690, 691, 696, 697, 700, 705, 711, 719
Universal Declaration of Human Rights, 472, 474
Université libre de Bruxelles (ULB), 680, 686
University of Belushistan in Zabedan, 392
University of Esfahan, 396
University of Hamadan (see also Avicenna University), was to be Franco-Persian, 392
University of Kent (linked to the Pahlavi University), 392
University of Kerman, 392
University of Liege (Belgium), 195
University of Mazandaran, called 'Reza Shah' (the name of a child from these parts), 392
University of Neufchâtel (Switzerland), 195
University of Paris X, 692
University of Pennsylvania (linked to the Pahlavi University), 392

University of Rasht, was to be dedicated to the practise of Persian and German, 392
University of Shiraz, 326, 398
University of Tehran, biggest and oldest university in the country since it was created in the middle of the 19th century, 90, 91, 101, 102, 135, 143, 208, 209, 261, 308, 310, 342, 379, 391, 392, 395, 398, 514, 541, 548, 556, 576, 582, 600, 657, 659, 688, 704, 708
University Press of Tehran, 396
Urban guerrilla, 486, 525
USSR, 9, 37, 50, 77, 83, 85, 100, 101, 103, 105, 127, 129, 130, 131, 133, 134, 135, 137, 138, 139, 141, 142, 143, 144, 145, 147, 149, 150, 151, 153, 155, 156, 158, 159, 160, 162, 165, 167, 168, 171, 173, 181, 182, 186, 189, 190, 192, 193, 203, 207, 218, 264, 265, 268, 278, 305, 306, 309, 317, 339, 389, 401, 402, 430, 453, 454, 457, 470, 480, 483, 484, 485, 487, 489, 491, 493, 494, 495, 497, 498, 518, 605, 623, 661, 664, 666, 702
USSR Muslim countries, 497
US News and World Report, 706

V

'Vietnams', 467, 479
Vadiï, Kazem, Professor, renowned academic, Minister, 514, 520, 551
Vaghayeh-eh-etehfaghiegh, newspaper, 653
Valeurs Actuelles, 435, 699, 702
Vance, Cyrus, Secretary of State, 478, 591
Vaqaye Etefaqieh, first newspaper founded in Iran, 27
Vatican, 512, 713
Vegetable market of Tehran (burnt by Khomeini's supporters), 536
Veil, 87
Veit, Erwin, Polish leader's secretary and interpreter, 666
Versailles, 361
Vichinsky, Andreï, the notorious prosecutor from the Moscow trials then Minister of Stalin, 168
Victor Emmanuel de Savoie (Vittorio Emanuele di Savoia), brother of Princess Maria Gabrielle de Savoie, 354
Vietnam, 166, 285, 313
Vietnam war, 479
Vilanilam, S. V., Indian political scientist, 698
Villalon, Hector, Argentine adventurer, 631

Villa of Roses, 617, 621, 624
Villemarest (see also Faillant de Villemarest), 12, 435, 666, 673, 690, 691, 692, 698, 702, 718
Villeneuve, Charles, 676
Vinogradov, Soviet Ambassador to Tehran, 494
Voice of America, 474
Voice of Israel, 474
Volkoff, Vladimir, 363, 678, 684, 698, 707
Vossough, Ali, secretary of state to the presidency of the Council of the Amini Cabinet, 669
Vossough, General, close relative of Mossadegh and Ahmad Ghavam, 212
Vossough (Vossough ol-Dowleh) Hassan, elder brother of Ahmad Ghavam, poet, former PM, 37, 87, 168, 174
VSD, French magazine, 702

W

'Women and their periods', 445
'Worldwide lie', 363
Wafd, Egyptian political party, 344
Waldenström's syndrome, 618, 622
Waldheim, Kurt, general secretary of the United Nations, 277, 294, 295, 678
Wall of Berlin, 182
Wall Street Journal, 702
Walters, Barbara, 368, 529
Wardak, Amin, War chief, 491
Warin, Olivier, 685, 686
War in Afghanistan, 490, 492, 623, 627
Washington Inquirer, 702
Washington Post, 476, 684, 697, 698, 699, 710
Washington Quarterly, 698
Weizmann Institute in Israel, 392
Wheat (production), 387
White House, 314, 449, 455, 471, 474, 476, 627, 628, 633
White Revolution, 299, 301, 303, 305, 307, 309, 311, 313, 315, 317, 318, 319, 321, 323, 325, 327, 328, 329, 331, 333, 334, 371, 424, 507, 512, 520
White Russian army, 38, 49, 132
Wilhelm II, 186
Wolton, Thierry, 702
Women (political, social rights, recognition, emancipation, etc), 86, 87, 88, 261, 319, 320, 322, 325, 350, 358, 359, 400, 423, 424,

INDEX

425, 440, 473, 513, 522, 547
World Bank, 79, 204, 207, 267, 310, 402
World War I, 36, 131, 186, 191
World War II, 9, 78, 85, 91, 96, 99, 101, 102, 103, 105, 107, 109, 111, 113, 115, 117, 119, 121, 123, 125, 127, 132, 268, 307, 369, 378, 418, 453, 645, 670
WTO (World Trade Organization), 355

X

Xavière, Jean-Marie, 693

Y

Yahya, Gholam, Soviet citizen and KGB officer, 172
Yale University, 479
Yassami, Rachid, 345
Yazdan-Panah, Morteza, general, 378
Yazdgird III, the last emperor of the Sasanids, 642
Yazdi, Ibrahim, American citizen of Iranian origin, ayatollah Khomeini's real mentor, 420, 433, 439, 440, 487, 493, 692, 700, 714, 715
Yom Kippur war (in October 1973), 463, 464, 478
Young, Andrew, American ambassador to the UNO, 449, 472, 694
Yugoslavia, 203, 355

Z

'Zilch', 450
Zadeh, Assadolah Ghaffar, 130
Zadeh, Heaeri, 215
Zafar, Ghobad, famous architect and an important personality for the Bakhtiaris, 580
Zahedi, Ardeshir, son of General Fazlollah Zahedi, Iranian Ambassdor to Washington, Minister of Foreign Affairs, 11, 234, 235, 236, 237, 238, 240, 246, 252, 256, 259, 260, 274, 317, 347, 354, 355, 373, 377, 404, 464, 550, 565, 566, 573, 590, 595, 610, 611, 615, 617, 619, 629, 630, 638, 671, 672, 673, 674, 675, 678, 681, 684, 699, 704, 708, 710, 711, 713, 714, 715, 718, 719
Zahedi, Fazlollah, General, PM, 2, 39, 53, 57, 71, 126, 134, 174, 175, 176, 192, 199, 213, 220, 223, 227, 229, 230, 232, 233, 234, 235, 236, 238, 239, 240, 241, 244, 246, 247, 248, 251, 252, 254, 256, 259, 264, 265, 267, 268, 270, 271, 272, 273, 274, 299, 300, 301, 303, 305, 307, 353, 401, 510, 575, 648, 667, 670, 671, 672, 674, 675
Zahedi, Homa, sister of Ardeshir Zahedi, 235
Zahedi, Mahnaz, daughter of Ardeshir Zahedi and Princess Shahnaz, 347
Zahedi, Mrs, aunt of Fazlollah Zahedi, 672
Zahedi, Reza, General, cousin of Fazlollah Zahedi, 257
Zahedis (family), 230, 355, 672
Zahmatkehchan, dissident parties of the National Front, 252
Zand, Karim Khan, "Vakil-Ol-Roâyâ", 18
Zand-Fard, Freydoun, the last ambassador of imperial Iran in Iraq, 668, 690, 691, 710
Zands, dynasty, 68
Zia-Ashraf (titled Zia-ol-Saltaneh), daughter of King Naser Ol Din, spouse of Mohammad Mossadegh, 195
Zia-ul-Haq, Mohammad, General, President of Pakistan, 558, 565
Zinoviev, Alexander, 473
Zinoviev, Grigory Evsyevitch, Bolshevik leader, 133
Zirak-Zadeh, Ahmad, Under-Secretary of State in the Industry Department, 245, 249
Zolfaghar, military order, name of the sword carried by Imam Ali, 57
Zolfaghari (brothers), guerrilla fighters leaders, 167, 169
Zoroastrians, 28, 71, 511